# Being Viking

## Contemporary and Historical Paganism

*Series Editors*

Nikki Bado†, Iowa State University,
Chas S. Clifton, Colorado State University-Pueblo
Scott Simpson, Institute of European Studies, Jagiellonian University

This series seeks original work on contemporary and revived Pagan religious traditions around the world, as well as re-examinations of ancient polytheistic religion from new perspectives. Contributions are invited from diverse disciplines, including religious studies, popular culture, musicology, anthropology, sociology, ethnography, and feminist philosophy of religion.

# Being Viking
## Heathenism in Contemporary America

Jefferson F. Calico

SHEFFIELD UK   BRISTOL CT

Published by Equinox Publishing Ltd.
UK: Office 415, The Workstation, 15 Paternoster Row, Sheffield,
South Yorkshire S1 2BX
USA: ISD, 70 Enterprise Drive, Bristol, CT 06010

www.equinoxpub.com

First published 2018

© Jefferson F. Calico 2018

All rights reserved. No part of this publication may be reproduced or transmitted in any form or by any means, electronic or mechanical, including photocopying, recording or any information storage or retrieval system, without prior permission in writing from the publishers.

British Library Cataloguing-in-Publication Data

A catalogue record for this book is available from the British Library.

ISBN-13   978 1 78179 222 3   (hardback)
          978 1 78179 223 0   (paperback)
          978 1 78179 757 0   (ePDF)

Library of Congress Cataloging-in-Publication Data

Names: Calico, Jefferson F., author.
Title: Being Viking : heathenism in contemporary America / Jefferson F. Calico.
Description: Bristol : Equinox Publishing Ltd., 2018. |
Series: Contemporary and historical paganism | Includes bibliographical references and index. |
Identifiers: LCCN 2018009693 (print) | LCCN 2018026599 (ebook) | ISBN 9781781797570 (ePDF) | ISBN 9781781792223 (hb) | ISBN 9781781792230 (pb)
Subjects: LCSH: Paganism—United States. | Vikings—Religion.
Classification: LCC BL432 (ebook) | LCC BL432 . C35 2018 (print) |
DDC 299/.940973—dc23
LC record available at https://lccn.loc.gov/2018009693

Typeset by Swales & Willis, Exeter, Devon, UK
Printed and bound by Lightning Source Inc. (La Vergne, TN), Lightning Source UK Ltd. (Milton Keynes), Lightning Source AU Pty. (Scoresby, Victoria)

# Contents

| | | |
|---|---|---|
| | *List of Illustrations* | vii |
| | *Acknowledgments* | xi |
| | *Preface: Regarding Words* | xiii |
| | Introduction | 1 |
| 1 | A Brief History of American Asatru | 50 |
| 2 | Tributaries of the Heathen Movement | 110 |
| 3 | Metagenetics | 173 |
| 4 | Spears and Shieldwalls: The Self and the Struggle of Life | 216 |
| 5 | Hard Polytheism in a Soft World | 264 |
| 6 | Animal Sacrifice and the Blót | 307 |
| 7 | Kith and Kin: Asatru as Family Religion | 334 |
| 8 | Asatru as a Magical Religion | 371 |
| 9 | The Windswept Tree: Nature Religion in Asatru | 428 |
| | *Conclusion* | 480 |
| | *Bibliography* | 487 |
| | *Index* | 503 |

## List of Illustrations

| | | |
|---|---|---|
| 1 | The Odin Fish. | 34 |
| 2 | Statue of a Monk from the Canoe Race at East Coast Thing. | 36 |
| 3 | Tyr's Vé at East Coast Thing. | 41 |
| 4 | Odin Altar, Lexington, KY. | 86 |
| 5 | Kickstarter Package from Tauring's Crowdfunded Project. | 108 |
| 6 | Kaplan's Spectrum of Racial Attitudes. | 126 |
| 7 | Gardell's Triangle of Racial Positions. | 128 |
| 8 | Tributaries of Racist Heathenry. | 135 |
| 9 | Tributaries of Progressive Heathenry. | 147 |
| 10 | Tributaries of the Wolves of Vinland. | 167 |
| 11 | Preparing for Ritual at Lightning Across the Plains. | 227 |
| 12 | Heathen Soul Complex and Its Connections to the Past. | 239 |
| 13 | Eiwaz Rune. | 249 |
| 14 | Ancestor Altar at Lightning Across the Plains, 2012. | 258 |
| 15 | Odin and Thor Vé at East Coast Thing. | 266 |

| | | |
|---|---|---|
| 16 | Thor Statue Carried in a Wain at East Coast Thing. | 268 |
| 17 | The Mobile Freyja Shrine at East Coast Thing. | 273 |
| 18 | Communing with the Goddess at Frigg's Vé, East Coast Thing. | 282 |
| 19 | Altar for Freyja Blót at East Coast Thing. | 295 |
| 20 | Godpole at East Coast Thing. | 301 |
| 21 | Gothi Addressing Worshipers at Lightning Across the Plains. | 314 |
| 22 | Creation of Meaning in the Blót. | 331 |
| 23 | Families Launching Rockets at East Coast Thing. | 342 |
| 24 | Author and Son Prepared for Sumbel. | 349 |
| 25 | Order of the Sumbel Ritual. | 357 |
| 26 | The Inner/Outer Dyad of the Sumbel. | 360 |
| 27 | The Longitudinal Dyad of the Sumbel. | 361 |
| 28 | The Community Gathered for Sumbel at Lightning Across the Plains. | 362 |
| 29 | The Asatru Superfamily. | 365 |
| 30 | The Vertical Dyad of the Sumbel. | 367 |
| 31 | Friedenhof Kindred Banner Written in Runes. | 392 |
| 32 | Kari Tauring with Author, Trothmoot, 2011. | 423 |
| 33 | Ivakhiv's Four Constructions of Nature. | 434 |
| 34 | Four Constructions of Nature with Heathen Exemplars. | 439 |

*List of Illustrations*

35  Hailing the Land-Vaettir at Lightning Across the Plains.   442

36  A Page from the Trothmoot Nature Walk Booklet.   454

37  The Sun Wheel.   462

38  Harvest Garland at East Coast Thing.   463

# Acknowledgments

This work represents a life-changing experience in my life. It could not have happened without the influence and support of many others. I would like to recognize James D. Chancellor, a fabulous ethnographer and researcher who served as my PhD supervisor and mentor. At a crucial moment, he steered me toward the study of contemporary Paganism, a choice I had not considered but that proved to be exactly right. I want to thank the Contemporary Pagan Studies Group of the American Academy of Religion and the scholars involved for including me in a supportive learning environment. The group warmly received my presentation on the sumbel. The feedback and encouragement given by other scholars was important throughout the process. My family has also played an important role in this work. My parents, Forrest and Patricia Calico, provided constant support. My father would have been proud to see the end result. My wife, Cari, shared my enthusiasm, tolerated my absences, and encouraged me every day. During the years of research and writing, my children have grown up with Vikings and Norse mythology as a significant part of their lives. Carson and Quincy traveled and attended Heathen events with me, sharing experiences we will never forget. My gratitude and appreciation go to Equinox Publishing, the team at Swales & Willis, and the amazing group of editors with whom I had the opportunity to work: Chas S. Clifton, Scott Simpson, and Nikki Bado. You were immensely gracious and wonderfully rigorous. I have learned so much from your help and felt at times like I was receiving another graduate education. Your questions and suggestions have made this book so much better. I would finally like to thank the many Heathen people who took a chance on a researcher, who included me in your events and shared your lives and experiences. I am so proud to know you and thank you for your contributions to my life.

**Preface**

Regarding Words

One of the great pleasures of a study such as this is the necessity of delving into new areas of learning. One of these areas was language, particularly the Germanic family of languages. This is a field in which I had little familiarity and can make no claims of expertise. The Heathen movement makes frequent use of words from Old Norse, Old Icelandic, Old English, and other Germanic languages, often creating new anglicized forms of these words as part of the vocabulary of the movement. The use of these words inspired by Germanic languages carries great symbolic weight among adherents, representing the reconnection to the Pagan past. Heathens take language seriously and from the early years of the religion have regarded the Germanic origin of these words as spiritually important. However, there has been little consistency in the treatment of these words. One encounters a variety of approaches among Heathen writers, as well as a variety of spellings as authors transliterate words in different ways. As linguistic knowledge and expertise has increased among adherents through the years, more care and rigor is evident. For these reasons, I have chosen to italicize the first instance of these specialized words and preserve their spellings and diacritical marks when they are used as transliterated Old Norse and Old English words. In cases in which words have become common anglicized additions to the parlance of American Heathens, I adopt a standardized spelling. For instance, the Old Norse (ON) word *sumbl* would be italicized and the common anglicized form, sumbel, used thereafter. In cases in which an author uses a particular linguistic variant, such as the Old English *symbel*, I preserve the author's spelling. Some words represent particularly complex cases, such as the ON words *seiðr* (masculine) and *seið* (feminine and neuter) referring to a type of

Norse Pagan magic. Heathen writers have variously transliterated the word as seid, seidh, seidhr, seidr, even seidth, and in other instances have retained the ON word itself. There are two competing values at work in American Heathenry concerning these linguistic issues. One common approach is to create a comfortable English terminology for the movement that maintains a loose connection to a primary source language, leading to a transliteration such as "seidh." Another approach values the retention of the original languages and demands a degree of expertise in its use, thus favoring the use of the ON masculine nominative, *seiðr*. My own approach is to reference the term in the original language but to use an English transliteration throughout the book. I do this to indicate that a difference exists between contemporary Heathen practice and that of the Norse. Whatever terms such as *seiðr* or *sumbl* referred to in their original context, American Heathen practice presents us with interpretations and a contemporary range of meanings, not an exact correspondence. These transliterations should be both recognizable to adherents within Heathenry and suitably distinct for readers who are less familiar with the movement.

## On Rune Names

Runes are the letters of the writing systems, or scripts, developed in Pagan Northwestern Europe prior to the adoption of the Latin script, and collected in an alphabetic-like list known as the *fuþark* (futhark). Each rune represented a sound, but also carried important conceptual and magico-religious significance.[1] The runes are an important piece of contemporary Heathenry, used extensively for aesthetic, symbolic, divinatory, and magical purposes. Although runes were part of American Heathenry since its earliest period, they received their first systematic treatment in Edred Thorsson's 1984 book *Futhark: A Handbook of Runic Magic*.[2] Thorsson introduced the elder or older futhark, a prehistoric set of twenty-four runes. As a result, the elder futhark became established in American Heathenry as the most widely adopted set of runes. Heathens commonly

---

1. Ralph W. V. Elliott, *Runes: An Introduction* (Manchester: Manchester University Press, 1959), 2–3, 47.
2. Edred Thorsson, *Futhark: A Handbook of Runic Magic* (San Francisco: Weiser Books, 1984).

and unproblematically refer to these runes using proto-Germanic names that scholars have reconstructed from historical sources, such as the Icelandic, Old Norse, and Old English rune poems. Among scholars, the names and sounds are a matter of debate, and reconstructions are usually indicated by an asterisk, e.g. *fehu, *ūruz, *þurisaz, *ansuz, *raiðō, and *kēnaz.[3] Only rarely would a Heathen practitioner asterisk or italicize rune names. Generally, Heathens have adopted a standard set of anglicized names, though some variations among practitioners result from reliance on different sources. For instance, one of the more complex reconstructions is of the fifteenth rune, ᛉ, the z rune. Two prominent Heathens call the rune by different names: Diana Paxson prefers Elhaz, while Patricia Lafayllve uses Algiz, yet both quote the rune poem that refers to elk-grass without referring to the corresponding Old English rune name *eolh*. Instead of distinguishing among variations (for instance, drawing exclusively on Old English rune names and meanings), American Heathens tend to syncretize and draw comprehensively on the range of meanings available from the sources. For this book I have used common anglicized names for runes and noted further information in footnotes.

---

3. These reconstructed names are from Elliott, *Runes*, 48. For further discussion of reconstructed rune names, see Elliott, *Runes*, 45–61; Raymond Ian Page, *Runes* (Berkeley: University of California Press, 1987), 14–22.

# Introduction

We were standing on a hilltop ringed by trees under a brilliant starry sky in the American heartland just on the edge of the Great Plains. From where I stood, the circle of people curved around to either side into the dark night, two hundred shadowy faces only dimly visible in the flickering orange light of the bonfire. Despite the large number of people, the gathering was quiet enough for the crackling and popping of the fire to be heard. Everyone stood, waiting, and I waited not knowing what to expect. Then, over sounds of the night, I heard a low guttural growl that slowly grew in intensity and power. The sound was disorienting at first, rolling out of the darkness, and seemed to come from everywhere at once, eerie and intense. The rumbling enunciation, called *galdr* by these Heathen religionists, was the work of a large man standing near the central fire who was leading this ritual honoring the Norse deity Odin.[4] This was Magni, a *goði*, an Asatru priest.[5] His embroidered tunic and long blonde braid were barely visible, but the spear that he held glinted in the

---

4. Patricia M. Lafayllve, *A Practical Heathen's Guide to Asatru* (St. Paul, MN: Llewellyn Publications, 2013), 229. Heathen author Patricia Lafayllve explains galdr as "a harsh, atonal chant or 'singing' of the runes for magical effects." This definition reflects common usage of the term among American Heathens. See chapter 2 for further discussion.

5. Geir T. Zoëga, s.v. "goði," *A Concise Dictionary of Old Icelandic* (Mineola, NY: Dover Publications, 2004). Goði or gothi refers to a Heathen priest and is derived from the Old Norse word for a god, goð. A Heathen priestess or female religious leader is called by the related word gythja, from the Norse *gyðja*. In Icelandic history, the goði was a chieftain, a local leader who exercised social and political power and acted as a decision maker at the althing. See *A Dictionary of Old Norse Prose*, s.v. "goði." University of Copenhagen, http://onp.ku.dk/english/. The title Alsherjargothi or Allsherjargothi derives from the historical Allsherjargoði position in Pagan Iceland, where it signified the chief priest or religious leader of the island. The leader of the Icelandic *Ásatrúarfélagið*, the main state-recognized Asatru religious organization in Iceland, now goes by the title.

firelight. His vocalization now rose to a low roar reminiscent of chanting Tibetan monks, polyphonic and multilayered, "Aaahnn-suuuz!" filling the air with palpable tension of this rune, a sacred syllable chanted under the moonlight to invoke the power of an ancient god. The circle of people seemed collectively to hold its breath in rapt attention as Magni held out the vibrations in a long drawl and then released them into the night.

What had brought me to be standing on this remote hill on this crisp autumn night? It was the culmination of a scholarly pilgrimage begun months before when I had read a short list of ethical values, known as the Nine Noble Virtues.[6] The Noble Nine are significant values drawn from the ancient Norse myths, legends, and epics that outline a moral code of life significant to the adherents of Asatru, a movement reconstructing the religion of the ancient Norse, the religion of Odin and Thor.[7] When I first encountered Asatru, it had been presented to me as a radical, violent, and racist fringe movement, a savage religion of modern Vikings bent on rampage and ruin. Yet this list of values seemed to tell a different story. The ideals of courage, honesty, honor, loyalty, strength, hospitality, industriousness, self-reliance, and perseverance seemed respectable, even admirable. I recognized these values as part of the collective mythology of the pioneering spirit so important to the American character. I had grown up with these ideals, as had many others, in the stories of George Washington, Ben Franklin, Daniel Boone, Davy Crockett, and Abraham Lincoln. Here were people talking about family, pulling together as a community, the importance of hard work, the value of a person's word, doing honorable deeds, and taking responsibility for one's actions. While I had often heard the loss of these values lamented by mainstream Americans, these Midwestern Asatruars were attempting to instill these values back

---

6. The Odinic Rite, a Heathen group originating in Britain, first codified the Nine Noble Virtues in the 1970s. The list itself has been adapted, changed, and explicated by different individuals and groups since then. These foundational, guiding virtues have become an acknowledged part of Heathen culture, even if they are not always well accepted.

7. *Dictionary of Old Norse Prose*, s.v. "áss," and "trú." Usually pronounced OUW-sa-tru or AH-sa-tru, "Asatru" is a neologism formed from two Old Norse words: *áss* referring to the gods, the Aesir, and *trú*, meaning "loyalty" or "faithfulness." Diacritical marks that would be standard in Icelandic, *Ásatrú*, are only occasionally included in American sources.

into their lives, to learn to live by them once again and to create a community bound together in that pursuit.[8]

Yet Asatru is more complex than simply a revival of old-fashioned values. These were people who were calling on Norse gods as real beings, who carried out ceremonies that were unfamiliar and different, but also compelling, and who were debating Old Icelandic texts with which I was unfamiliar. And then there was the spectre of racial Odinism, a watering hole for a virulent strain of white supremacy. Who were these people? The diversity and the deeply compelling contradictions contained within this small religious movement seemed to stretch its identity and meaning to the breaking point. How could these people and this religion be so familiar on one hand, yet so strange and difficult on the other?

Asatru, also called Heathenry, is a new religious movement that seeks to construct a contemporary religious culture inspired by pre-Christian Norse and Germanic societies. Contemporary Norse Paganism has become a worldwide phenomenon. Many researchers and scholars are accomplishing significant work in describing the history, thought, and practice of Heathens in Europe and elsewhere. Although it looks to ancient Europe for its inspiration, the Asatru movement I write about is an American religion, part of the thriving contemporary Pagan scene in the United States. Just how a Viking-flavored religion came to be part of the religious landscape of America is a good question that will be explored more thoroughly in the next few chapters. But to begin answering the question, we should consider several important factors. First, the Asatru movement in America began to take form in the early 1970s, a period in American history in which many people were experimenting with new ideas, developing new forms of identity, and asserting those identities through political activism and religious exploration. Consider that 1973, the year the first official Asatru group formed in the United States, also saw the occupation of Wounded Knee by militant activists from the American Indian Movement. The same year saw the passage of the Americans with Disabilities Act, after years of vigorous social protest that brought together disabled Americans as an identity group for the first time

---

8. The term "Asatruar" signifies more than one Asatru adherent. The "-ar" suffix represents an Old Norse plural form. It is commonly used in the movement and appears synonymously with "Asatru adherents" in this study.

and visibly leveraged their political influence. The late 1960s and early 1970s also saw the burgeoning of the Black Power movement taking revolutionary action in the streets. The United Farm Workers and the Salad Bowl strikers were chanting "*Si, se puede!*" in the streets as Cesar Chavez went on hunger strikes. The Stonewall Uprising in the summer of 1969 catalyzed the Gay Rights movement. The prominence of these identity conscious movements challenged the ethnic, racial, and social categories that had structured American society.

Along with these identity movements, a religious revival was occurring in the United States during the decades of the 1960s and 1970s, which saw new religions and revitalized sects transforming the religious landscape.[9] Among them were the conservative Christian evangelicals, who began organizing and growing as an identifiable religio-political movement through groups such as the Moral Majority led by Jerry Falwell. But the American counter-culture also proved to be fertile ground for new religious ideas that challenged the values and assumptions of mainstream society. Often denigrated as cults, these movements were both numerous and diverse, spanning the religious spectrum from Jesus Freaks to Hindu Hare Krishnas and Pagan witches. The Asatru movement participated fully in this cultural search for religious solutions to troubled times, forming a small and little known addition to the Pagan explosion. We should note that the emergence of contemporary Paganism and other new religions did not happen in the United States alone. Many of the new religions that have flourished in the United States have their origin or their roots elsewhere. Wicca and Druidry, two prominent forms of contemporary Paganism, began in in the United Kingdom, flowered in the United States, and continued to spread throughout Europe and other parts of the world. Others, such as the Native Faith movements that grew or re-emerged in Eastern Europe following the fall of the Communist regimes had little or no presence in the United States.

In addition to the religious awakening that swept across the country, a third factor precipitating the development of Asatru was simply the presence of Northern European ancestry and culture in the American population. English, Germanic, and Scandinavian cultures and traditions had long been a part of multicultural

---

9. Philip Jenkins, *Mystics and Messiahs: Cults and New Religions in American History* (Oxford: Oxford University Press, 2000), 165–86.

America. Immigration into America in the mid-1800s originated predominantly from Western Europe with Germanic/Scandinavian cultures second only to the Irish. These Northern European immigrant groups often retained their language and culture, forming cultural enclaves throughout the northern states. These ethnic identities were prominent enough that during the period of World War I, the US government considered German-speaking Americans a national security threat. Despite that, German and Scandinavian culture has been an important part of American culture. A testament to this cultural receptivity was the Norse god Thor, who became an icon of American pop culture in the early 1960s as a character in the Marvel comic book series. Thus through direct and indirect contact, many Americans had experienced Germanic and Scandinavian culture, heard its stories and myths of the Norse gods, and developed an affinity for the culture. Given this cultural continuity, it is not surprising that some would gravitate towards northern European heritage in their search for identity and meaning.

These three factors—the rise of identity politics and ethnic consciousness, the growth of alternative religious practices, and the affinity for aspects of Germanic and Norse culture—created a cultural space in which Asatru began to develop as a new religious practice. Of course, the full story is considerably more complex as we shall see. While it initially may seem surprising and incongruous to find Odin and Thor being worshiped in the American heartland, Asatru found fertile ground among a type of alternative religionists in the United States. In contrast to the universalistic, optimistic, future-looking, and mystical new religions that became popular during the 1960s and 1970s, Asatru was culturally specific, even nativist, past-glorifying, and action-oriented. It offered a set of fierce gods who called their followers to a way of life different from gentler Goddess-oriented ways of Wicca. Asatru was antagonistic toward mainstream American culture, but it also extolled the American ideals of rugged individualism, self-reliance, courage, and boldness—ideals for which many Americans are nostalgic. Being Viking had an allure that continues to grab the attention of people seeking a different way of life.

Readers will note that throughout the book, I use "Asatru" and "Heathenry" as interchangeable terms, using both to refer in a general way to contemporary Norse Paganism as it occurs in America. "Asatru" more appropriately refers to more distinctly

Icelandic-oriented practice to which only a portion of the followers of Heathenry adhere. Heathen is another word that is widely used within the movement itself and is perhaps the best term to designate the family of practices included in the revival of Norse and Germanic Paganism. There are a number of other terms meaningful to Heathens: Odinism, Vanatru, Forn Sidr, Irminist, Theodist, Rokkatru, and more, each of which designates a particular orientation within the context of American Norse/Germanic Paganism. Throughout this book, I call Asatru or Heathenry a "movement." It is driven by ideas about meaning and identity, and has a highly fluid nature without the degree of coordination, structure, and integration that characterize a church-like religious institution.[10] Like other forms of Paganism, Heathenry is best understood as a loose grassroots leaderless movement, drawing on a shared milieu of religious ideas, that are shared through a network of relationships mediated through face to face, online, and print contexts. Within this movement, a number of charismatic individuals have developed formal organizations with more consistent social, belief, and ritual structures. These organizations have maintained loose and often oppositional relationships within the Heathen world. Michael York describes these qualities of the Heathen movement with the term Segmented Polycentric Integrated Network, characterized by small groups or segments integrated in informal and fluid ways, through shared literature, concepts, and relational networks rather than formal and authoritative structures.[11] This structure allows for a great deal of freedom to evolve and social space for adherents to exercise creativity and innovation in the formation of religious culture. At the same time, the absence of definitive leadership and the nebulous nature of the movement makes it difficult to define. The boundaries of the movement are under constant negotiation.

## *Researching Asatru*

I first discovered Asatru during a student discussion on radical religion in a doctoral seminar on new religious movements. In that

---

10. Ron Eyerman, "Social Movements," in *The Cambridge Dictionary of Sociology*, ed. Bryan S. Turner (Cambridge, UK: Cambridge University Press, 2006), http://search.credoreference.com/content/entry/cupsoc/social_movements/0?institutionId=4309.

11. Michael York, *The Emerging Network: A Sociology of the New Age and Neo-Pagan Movements* (Lanham, MD: Rowman & Littlefield, 1995), 325.

context, Asatru was presented as a fringe religion characterized by millennial fervor and racist attitudes. Yet that portrayal seemed insufficient. Other elements of Asatru did not comfortably fit within that pattern. In particular, the Nine Noble Virtues of Asatru, the widely accepted table of virtue ethics for Heathens, lauded the ideals of loyalty, truth, industry, and steadfastness, among others.[12] A fellow student asked the question, "What do we find objectionable about these values?" His comment prevented an all-too-quick dismissal of the religion by suggesting that these virtues, which seemed quite consistent with many American ideals, deserved more consideration. This first exposure to Asatru raised in my mind a note of discordance between its presentation as a radical racist religion and the compelling, even commendable, virtues espoused by its adherents. I wondered if there was more to Asatru than may have been initially apparent. Could further research resolve this tension and round out a more robust picture of the nature of the Asatru movement? Could I find out more about this movement that was growing in the American heartland?

What follows is my initial attempt to present a fuller and deeper picture of Asatru, its people, worldview, and religious expression. My account is rooted in extensive participant observation in the movement, numerous interviews with practitioners, and deep reading of both insider and scholarly materials. However, there is always more to be said. As my mentor and friend mentioned at one point in the research process, an ethnographic researcher is never really done. Despite the goal of naturalistic inquiry to arrive at a point of saturation or "informational redundancy," that goal can be difficult to achieve in a movement as fluid and disparate as Asatru.[13] Despite its relatively small size and its shared orientation toward Norse and Germanic culture, opinion and practice among Heathens diverge fairly widely. Heathenry seems to have moved beyond its initial founding into a phase of creativity and expansion, in which innovative and divergent subsets of beliefs and practices are multiplying.

The book has grown out of five years of research done within the Asatru movement from 2010 to 2016 carried out along three lines of

---

12. For a discussion of all nine noble virtues, see Kveldúlf Gundarsson, *History and Lore*, Vol. 1 of *Our Troth* (Charleston, SC: Booksurge, 2006), 525–42.

13. Yvonne S. Lincoln and Egon G. Guba, *Naturalistic Inquiry* (Beverly Hills, CA: Sage, 1985), 219.

inquiry. The primary component involved participant observation in Asatru life, including large and small religious gatherings. I was involved in regular participation in a local "kindred," in Kentucky for over two years and had the privilege of experiencing with them the real dynamics of Asatru life.[14] Running an Asatru kindred in a conservative southern town is a difficult undertaking, yet the key members of this group, Michael and Jordsvin, were not only welcoming to me, but dogged and creative in their determination to provide an educational and social expression of Asatru in their context. For this they have my thanks and admiration. Many times, when I would have given up, they reinvented the group to maintain a continuous Heathen religious presence because it was deeply important to them. In this way, they exemplified the Asatru ethos of striving and persevering against the odds. I additionally attended each of the major Heathen events in the country at least one time during that five-year period, including Trothmoot, East Coast Thing, Northern Folk Gathering, Pantheacon, and Lightning Across the Plains. Several of these I attended on multiple occasions. Attending these events allowed for observation of a broad spectrum of Heathen life and its regional diversity. These focused weekend gatherings function as important social and religious events through which the Asatru community enacts its most important values. Participant observation was supplemented by nearly fifty interviews with adherents, most of which were recorded, transcribed, and analyzed. Interviews were sought based on two primary criteria. First, I focused on opinion leaders in Asatru; and second, on adherents who had expertise in certain areas such as theology, leadership, ritual, or magic. Choosing to speak with people who are extensively engaged in the production of Heathen religious meaning had significant benefits for understanding the religion and culture. These were important learning experiences for me, and I am deeply grateful for those individuals who took the time to talk and email with me and carefully discuss their experience of Asatru. These interviews demonstrated to me the seriousness, sophistication, and depth that Asatruar often bring to their faith and

---

14. "Kindred" is a Heathen term that refers specifically to a group of Asatru adherents who regularly practice their religion together. Unlike colloquial usage, in which "kindred" usually refers to a network of biological family relationships, a Heathen can be a member of a kindred without implying any familial or biological connections to the group.

religious practice. They added complexity and depth of insight in certain areas and, more importantly, brought the voices of Heathen practitioners into the study.

The third component involved textual research in the religious literature of the movement as well as previous scholarly work on the movement. Heathens have been prolific writers, who have produced a growing body of material in a variety of forms including books, journals, websites, video, and podcasts over the past forty years of the movement's history. A significant amount of religious construction has been achieved through the development of this material. Much of this material reflects the Heathen interaction with the "canon" of Icelandic and Old Norse texts known as the Lore: the *Poetic Edda* and *Prose Edda*, and the numerous Icelandic sagas composed at the end of the Viking Age. In addition, I am grateful for the work of other scholars who have devoted time and effort to make many important contributions to understanding the movement. Jeffrey Kaplan's work provided careful documentation of the early years of Asatru's development as well as groundbreaking insights into the topography of the movement. Mattias Gardell further explored the issue of racial attitudes in the movement, uncovering and analyzing the connections between white supremacist ideology and Heathenry. Michael Strmiska's writing helpfully expanded research into the religious culture of Asatru and the personal religious experience of its adherents. While working in the field, I met several other researchers. Jennifer Snook was a dogged researcher with thoroughgoing insight into both insider and outsider perspectives. Her book, *American Heathens*, is a sophisticated sociological examination of the Heathen movement. Thad Horrell was a valued friend and thoughtful observer of Asatru, who pushed me to think more deeply about the phenomena I was experiencing. Kristen Horton had a familiarity with Hinduism that added an interesting dimension to her analysis.

As a researcher, I attempted to experience the movement as much from the inside as possible, in some sense to become Viking with thousands of others who make Asatru or Heathenry their religious home. I attempted to approach Heathenry first as a religious movement. If there are important political and social implications, these arise from the primary attempt to construct religious value. I felt that an ethnographic approach was important. Religion happens within the context of history and theology, but is ultimately a lived experience. It occurs at the level of the human life and its meaning is personal. Wilfred Cantwell Smith has written that "the study of religion is the study of persons . . . and indeed human lives at their most intimate, most profound, most primary, most transcendent."[15] As Smith indicates, religion is always about people and their experience; it continues to be an important way in which people construct their own identities and mediate their interaction with the wider world. The great scope of history, the ancient creeds and doctrines, the rituals of the religious traditions, our place in the "cumulative tradition," provide the backdrop and the stage upon which people enact this living quality of religious experience. This focus on the personal dimension has shaped both my understanding of religion and my approach towards the study of religion. Studying religion requires grappling with the nexus of belief and action in human experience since, "the primary locus of religiousness is persons."[16] In order to encounter and understand Asatru on the level of human experience, this study has made the people of Asatru its focus and has taken an ethnographic approach in its methodology. It is may be inevitable that misunderstandings arise between religious communities and those who research them, as each has different goals. As a researcher starting from an outsider position, I have been influenced by Jone Salomonsen's method of compassion.[17] She describes a balance of honesty, subjective experience, embodied critical thinking, and respect that became fundamental to my own praxis and engagement with Heathenry.

At an earlier time in my life, I dismissed new religions as fairly unimportant and ephemeral phenomena. In this sense I began my study of religion with a certain bias against new religions. I discounted them as groups lacking not only the pedigree but also the substance and seriousness found in the grand traditions of the major world religions. Admittedly, I shared in the fairly widespread "popular dismissal of these movements as fraudulent [and]

---

15. Wilfred Cantwell Smith, *Towards a World Theology: Faith and the Comparative History of Religion* (London: Macmillan, 1981), 48.

16. Ibid., 87.

17. Jone Salomonsen, "Methods of Compassion or Pretension? Conducting Anthropological Fieldwork in Modern Magical Communities," *The Pomegranate: The International Journal of Pagan Studies* 8, May (1999): 4–13.

shallow," poor imitations of real religions.[18] New religious groups have often been portrayed as aberrant, bizarre, or dangerous.[19] Over time it became clear to me that new religions represent a type of creative religious innovation that may be characteristic of pluralistic and free societies.[20] As Philip Jenkins demonstrates in his book *Mystics and Messiahs*, fringe movements and unconventional ideas have long been a part of the American religious experience.[21] In coming close to Heathenry and sharing in the experiences it has to offer, a more nuanced reality has emerged for me. Heathenry is a complex religious culture with growing depth and sophistication. From their marginal social vantage point, Heathenry and other new religions have opportunities to offer dissenting positions on cultural issues. They present alternative religious solutions to social tensions found within modern American life and left unresolved by mainstream religious groups. They may serve both as creative sources of new worlds of meaning as well as sites of social and personal experimentation with both positive and negative results. Those who participate, and I speak specifically of the many Heathen adherents with whom I interacted, often find positive spiritual, personal, and social resources within untraditional religious forms. Indeed, many of the great religions of the world began as small movements with new religious ideas and were often regarded as cults by their host societies. Understanding their world is an essential element in preventing the violence that has too often characterized the relationship of American society with minority religions and for building a multicultural society in which religious expression is a genuine right safe-guarded for all.

As Lorne Dawson writes, new religions offer "a good opportunity to study many of the essential elements of religious life in smaller and more manageable forms" as well as serving as "barometers of the larger social transformations occurring around us."[22] By

18. Carole M. Cusack, *Invented Religions: Imagination, Fiction and Faith* (Burlington, VT: Ashgate, 2010), viii, 2.
19. Jenkins, *Mystics and Messiahs*, 5.
20. Rodney Stark and William Sims Bainbridge, *A Theory of Religion* (New Brunswick, NJ: Rutgers University Press, 1996), 187, 312. See also Gordon J. Melton, "Perspective New New Religions: Revisiting a Concept," *Nova Religio* 10, no. 4 (2007): 109.
21. Jenkins, *Mystics and Messiahs*, 5, 16.
22. Lorne Dawson, *Comprehending Cults: The Sociology of New Religious Movements* (Ontario: Oxford University Press, 2006), 179–80.

taking new religions seriously, we gain insight into the structures and processes of religious life such as conversion, ways of knowing, the development of religious organizations, religious conflict, and the varieties of religious expression. They break up dominant paradigms, restructure social roles, introduce new religious ideas. Listening to these religious voices helps us to understand more thoroughly our own history and cultural trends, but also deepens our understanding of the religious impulse in human life and ourselves as religious beings. By learning about new religions, we come to know ourselves better.

### The Growth of Heathenry

The segment of new religions identified as contemporary Paganism is a growing demographic of the American religious milieu. As one scholar suggests, "primal religion, what you might call Paganism, is making a remarkable comeback in the West . . . even here in North America you see the growth of new Paganisms . . . all of which are drawing back on the old religions that pre-dated Christian faith."[23] While we live in a time when religions such as Islam garner much interest and awareness, contemporary Pagan religious expressions continue to grow and to influence the religious culture of America. This trend in the American religious context caught my attention and became a motivating insight that shaped my work on Asatru. I had been taught that the rise of Christianity represented enlightenment and freedom, a release from the ancient Pagan conditions of fear, ignorance, and barbarism. Why would anyone want to "go back" to the superstition and futility of Pagan religion?[24] Yet the growing numbers of people who are seeking out pre-Christian religious worldviews and experiences confounded such a perspective and motivated deeper exploration.

Although pinpointing the number of Pagan religionists in the United States poses some real problems, several studies indicate

---

23. James D. Chancellor, personal communication with author, 2010. As my PhD supervisor, Chancellor encouraged me in the study of contemporary Paganism.

24. Michael F. Strmiska, "Comparative Perspectives," in *Modern Paganism in World Cultures: Comparative Perspectives*, ed. Michael F. Strmiska (Santa Barbara: ABC-Clio, 2005), 42. Strmiska raises the point that Christianity, from a theological perspective, and modern science, from a perspective of rationalism and empiricism, both evaluate Paganism as an inferior belief system.

that the number of contemporary Pagan adherents has grown significantly in the past two decades.[25] In 2007, James R. Lewis presented data indicating a thirty-eight-fold increase in the number of contemporary Pagans in the United States from 1990 to 2001. This phenomenal rate of growth was not limited to the American context. Lewis discovered similarly dramatic rates of growth in the United Kingdom, Canada, New Zealand, and Australia, stating that "the data ... clearly indicates that the Pagan movement has been growing explosively in recent years."[26] Estimates for the number of Pagans in the United States range from Lewis' conservative estimate made in 2007 of slightly more than 300,000, to Margo Adler's estimate of 400,000 Pagan adherents made in 2006.[27] The American Religious Identification Survey (ARIS) is a nationwide scientific poll that has tracked religious trends in the United States since 1990. In 2008, the ARIS survey indicated even more significant growth than Lewis and Adler had previously estimated. The ARIS report notes a "marked increase in preferences for personalized and idiosyncratic responses as well as increases in the Neopagan groups." Using hard numbers of self-identifying adherents, the report shows growth from 300,700 participants in 2001 to 711,000 contemporary Pagans in 2008 showing that the movement roughly doubled within that seven-year period.[28] Michael Cooper, writing in 2010, confirms this trend and states not only that "contemporary Paganism is a viable movement in Western society," but that "the growth rate

---

25. Michael York, *Pagan Theology: Paganism as a World Religion* (New York: New York University Press, 2003), 60–61. In keeping with current practice, this study adopts the term contemporary Paganism to refer to the practice of Pagan spirituality in the modern world. "Neopagan" is an older term still occasionally used to describe the movement.

26. James R. Lewis, "The Pagan Explosion: An Overview of Select Census and Survey Data," in *The New Generation of Witches: Teenage Witchcraft in Contemporary Culture*, ed. Hannah E. Johnston and Peg Aloi (Burlington, VT: Ashgate, 2007), 13–23.

27. Margot Adler, *Drawing Down the Moon: Witches, Druids, Goddess-Worshippers, and Other Pagans in America* (New York: Penguin Books, 2006), 104.

28. Barry A. Kosmin and Ariela Keysar, "American Religious Identification Survey 2008 Summary Report," *ARIS*, March 2009, http://commons.trincoll.edu/aris/publications/2008-2/aris-2008-summary-report/, 7. Detailed statistics on contemporary Paganism that do not appear in the main report were provided for me upon request. The total number of Pagan adherents depends on which survey categories are included. I obtained the figure of 711,000 by combining the following survey categories: Wiccan, 342,000; Druid, 29,000; and Pagan, 340,000.

seems to be nothing less than phenomenal."[29] The contemporary Pagan community itself recognizes the growing prominence of Pagan forms of religion within the American context. Some Pagans suggest that the movement will become the third largest religious movement in America in the near future.[30] Scholars have attributed this growth to several factors, such as the positive presentation of Witchcraft and occult themes within the popular culture and the accessibility of contemporary Paganism on the Internet.[31] Like Wicca and Witchcraft, Heathen-related images have also appeared in an increasingly positive light in American popular culture, a trend that I will examine in more detail in chapter 2.

More recent scholarship suggests that the explosive growth experienced in the late 1990s and early 2000s has been slowing, with some scholars suggesting that Paganism is shifting toward a period of stabilization and consolidation.[32] Lewis himself anticipated that the growth of Paganism would slow considerably, a trend he associated with the tapering off of the "Teen Witch" phenomenon.[33] Because the 2011 Canadian census data was not yet available at the time of his first article on the Pagan explosion, Lewis suggested that Canadian statistics could act as a test case. He predicted a slowing of the phenomenal, explosive growth that Canadian Paganism witnessed in the decade 1991–2001, during which Pagan adherence grew by 282 percent, a rate of growth significantly higher than any other category of religion during that decade.[34] His prediction of slower growth seems justified by the data. From 2001 to 2011, census

---

29. Michael Cooper, *Contemporary Druidry: A Historical and Ethnographic Study* (Salt Lake City: Sacred Tribes, 2010), Kindle e-book.

30. Ed Hubbard, "Christians and Pagans Agree, Wicca Emerging as America's Third Religion," *Witch School*, www.prweb.com/releases/2005/4/prweb231351.htm.

31. Peg Aloi and Hannah E. Johnston, *The New Generation Witches: Teenage Witchcraft in Contemporary Culture* (Burlington, VT: Ashgate, 2007); Helen A. Berger and Douglas Ezzy, *Teenage Witches: Magical Youth and the Search for the Self* (New Brunswick: Rutgers University Press, 2007).

32. Douglas Ezzy and Helen Berger, "Witchcraft: Changing Patterns of Participation in the Early Twenty-First Century," *The Pomegranate: The International Journal of Pagan Studies* 11, no. 2 (2009): 165–80.

33. James R. Lewis, "The Pagan Explosion Revisited: A Statistical Postmortem on the Teen Witch Fad," *The Pomegranate: The International Journal of Pagan Studies* 14, no. 1 (2012): 131–32.

34. Statistics Canada, "Religion," 2001 Census, www12.statcan.ca/english/census01/products/highlight/religion/PR_Menu1.cfm?Lang=E.

data indicates that Canadian Pagan adherence grew from 21,080 to 25,495.[35] This represents significant growth at a fast pace — 20 percent growth over the ten-year period — but considerably slower than the previous decade. The 2011 Canadian census further subdivided the Pagan category into two subcategories: "Wiccan" and "Pagan n.i.e" (not included elsewhere). Wiccans numbered 10,225 while other Pagans, a category that would presumably include any Canadian adherents of Asatru/Heathenry, numbered 15,265.

Lewis notes census data from New Zealand indicating that Druids experienced a slow but steady incremental growth from 1996 to 2006, missing out entirely on the explosive Teen Witch factor. He suggests that the young, predominantly female demographic represented by the Teen Witch trend was not interested in male-oriented Druidry.[36] For similar reasons, it seems that the Teen Witch trend discussed by scholars had a negligible impact on Heathenry. The androcentric nature of Asatru was only one of several high boundaries that new adherents would have to negotiate. These factors may have insulated American Heathenry from those explosive gains as well as their slow decline. It is possible that the Teen Witch phenomenon impacted Heathenry indirectly, as Wicca and Witchcraft are common entry points for those who later settle into a Heathen religious identity. A common narrative of Heathen adherence involves people first entering the Wiccan scene and gradually drifting into Heathenry as part of their conversion career. However, no numbers exist regarding adherents who first entered Paganism through Wicca and Witchcraft and drifted into Heathenry. We can also attribute a good deal of Heathenry's incremental growth to its heavy presence on the Internet since the mid-1990s.[37]

The percentage of Asatru adherents within the larger Pagan movement is a matter of speculation. Anecdotal evidence from adherents who have been in the movement for years, and from observing the number of Heathen events across the United States, suggests that Heathenry has partaken of slow but steady growth since the 1970s. Though casual estimates of 10,000 adherents are sometimes heard among Asatru leaders, a reasonable estimate of the

35. Statistics Canada, *2011 National Household Survey*, Statistics Canada Catalogue no. 99-010-X2011032.2011, www12.statcan.gc.ca/nhs-enm/2011/dp-pd/dt-td/index-eng.cfm.
36. Lewis, "Explosion Revisited," 134–35.
37. Ibid., 139. See also, Ezzy and Berger, "Witchcraft," 167.

number of American Heathens is difficult to determine.[38] An online survey of Heathens conducted by Karl E. H. Seigfried reported 7,878 self-identified Heathens in America.[39] He also reported 6,087 in Europe (1,000 of those in Iceland) and 16,700 total worldwide.[40] In his own analysis of the Worldwide Heathen Census, Seigfried notes a discrepancy between the number of his respondents and the actual number of practicing Heathens.[41] He suggests that the Worldwide Heathen Census underreports the numbers of Heathens and estimates the population of Asatru adherents in the United States in 2013 at over 17,000.[42] Although this number is speculative, his intuition is likely accurate that a discrepancy of some magnitude exists. We might conservatively place the number between 8,000 and 20,000 making the anecdotal 10,000 not a baseless figure. If there are roughly 700,000 Pagans in the United States, numbers like these put the Heathen movement at 1–3 percent of contemporary American Pagans.[43] The growing number of kindreds and Heathen

38. I have heard estimates from Asatru adherents ranging from several thousand to ten thousand practitioners. Field notes by author, Minnesota, 2012.

39. Karl E. H. Seigfried, "Worldwide Heathen Census 2013: Results and Analysis," The Norse Mythology Blog, January 6, 2014, www.norsemyth.org/2014/01/worldwide-heathen-census-2013-results.html.

40. Some of these may have been American and European military personnel stationed abroad, as there seems to be no other explanation for the six Heathens in Afghanistan in 2013.

41. For instance, there were one thousand respondents to the Worldwide Heathen Census from Iceland. Because Ásatrú is a state-recognized religion, information is available on the number of registered adherents. At the time of the Worldwide Heathen Census, government records show 2,173 Icelanders officially registered with Ásatrú religious organizations. This figure is based on the number of people registered with the National Register of Persons in Iceland as members of The Ásatrú Association, 2,148, and Reykjavik Chieftainship, 25, another Norse religious group in 2013. This number has since grown to 2,696 in 2015, an overall growth rate of about 25 percent over those years. Government records report the number of registered Ásatrúar at 879 in 2005, indicating that the number of Icelandic adherents has grown approximately 300 percent as a result of very steady incremental annual growth of 20–25 percent. See *Statistics Iceland*, "Religious Organizations," www.statice.is/statistics/society/culture/religious-organisations/.

42. Seigfried, "Worldwide Heathen Census." Seigfried suggests multiplying the results of the survey by 2.173, based on the number of nonrespondents in Iceland, in order to obtain a more accurate number that compensates for nonrespondents.

43. Helen A. Berger, Evan A. Leach, and Leigh S. Shaffer, *Voices from the Pagan Census: A National Survey of Witches and Neo-Pagans in the United States* (Columbia: University of South Carolina Press, 2003). In the Pagan Census, Helen Berger identified Heathens as comprising approximately 3 percent of her respondents. In keeping with these findings, I set the high end of my range at 3 percent.

events indicates that growth is occurring and Asatru organizations speak optimistically of a "reawakening" to Nordic Paganism that has been intensifying since the 1970s.

The cultural influence of contemporary Heathens may be greater than their numerical presence. Despite the common assumption that contemporary Pagans do not proselytize, some Asatruar speak optimistically both of growing numerically and of influencing the culture of America. Stephen McNallen, founder of the Asatru Folk Assembly, is a capable promoter quite comfortable with the goal of growing the Asatru movement by using social media to communicate the positive aspects of the religion. McNallen is convinced that Asatru has the potential to increase its numbers substantially if the religion can be marketed in the right way to the American public, a focus that sounds peculiarly like proselytizing. Perhaps more tellingly, he hopes to "spread certain ideas to the larger culture," and writes that "we want to have an impact that is out of proportion to our modest numbers."[44] His organization, the Asatru Folk Assembly, takes as its mission both "calling back" those of European descent to their native religion and popularizing Heathen ideas within the cultural mainstream, indicating that changing minds and influencing lives is an important goal.

### *Religion and Class in American Heathenry*

While determining the size of the Heathen movement is difficult, efforts to identify the socioeconomic location of American Heathenry also have their complexities. Social class has often been defined and measured by a consideration of income, occupation, and education. A couple of data sets exist that give some insight into how the Heathen movement relates to these categories. The work of Helen Berger, Evan Leach, and Leigh Schaffer in *Voices from the Pagan Census*, compiles data from their large comprehensive survey of the American Pagan community and looks briefly at Heathens, whom the authors call Odinists.[45] Of the 2,089 completed surveys included in the

44. Steve McNallen, "The AFA's Mission in 2011," *Asatru Rising* podcast, January 16, 2011, http://asatrurising.podbean.com/e/the-afas-mission-in-2011/.
45. Berger, Leach, and Shaffer, *Voices from the Pagan Census*. The Pagan Census conducted by Berger, Leach, and Shaffer represented a groundbreaking collection of demographic data and analysis of contemporary Paganism in America. The term "Odinist" used in the study is now obsolete for the Heathen movement as a whole,

study, sixty of these respondents identified as Odinists, representing approximately 3 percent of the total respondents. The authors report that a majority of their Odinist respondents are college-educated, although less likely than other contemporary Pagans to be attending or to having completed graduate school. They report that the median income for Odinist respondents is between $20,000 and $30,000–$10,000 less than other categories of contemporary Pagans. This data places Heathens within a category of socioeconomic vulnerability that has recently emerged in contemporary America. The respondents fall among those Americans who are educated but for various reasons have fallen short of a fully middle-class lifestyle. It was once the case that a college education served as a reliable bridge from the working to the middle class. While college continues to be regularly touted as a ticket into a white-collar job and a middle-class lifestyle, this result is no longer a guarantee in contemporary America. Education does not represent the reliable road to class mobility that it once was, resulting in a class of the educated but under-employed. *Voices from the Pagan Census* seems to indicate that Heathens are among the Americans who have faced this harsher reality.

More recent survey research done by Josh Cargle also touches on the socioeconomic location of Heathenry.[46] Although income ranges were not included in this survey, questions about education and occupation were asked. The data on education seems to reinforce Berger, Leach, and Schaffer's findings from fifteen years earlier. American Heathens are substantially represented among the college-educated: 73 percent of American respondents to his survey reported either "some college" (33 percent), a "two-year degree" (20 percent) or a "four-year degree" (20 percent). Regarding occupation, the highest percentages fall into four categories consistent with the middle class: "business" (17 percent), "health care" (9 percent), "arts/design and entertainment" (8 percent), and "education" (8 percent). Cargle draws attention to a higher than average participation in military and police (6 percent of respondents), which he attributes

referring instead to a particular subset of Heathens with their own political and religious perspective. Most American Heathens would not choose "Odinist" as the most appropriate descriptor for the movement.

46. Josh Marcus Cargle, "Contemporary Germanic/Norse Paganism and Recent Survey Data," *The Pomegranate: The International Journal of Pagan Studies* 19, no. 1 (2017): 77–116.

to the warrior ethic of Heathenry.[47] Considering these numbers from the perspective of class provides another interesting interpretation. Working-class people often use careers in the military and police forces as bridges into the middle class. While the benefits of a college education have proven to be rather unreliable or slow to materialize, these occupations continue to provide social mobility to working-class Americans. Without denying the possibility of Heathen ethical affinity with these jobs, a class analysis also suggests that social mobility may be another reason for the over-representation of Heathens in these occupations. This analysis is congruent with the data from *Voices of the Pagan Census* that places Heathenry in a transitional socioeconomic location spanning the American working and middle classes.

Much of the ethnographic research on religion and class in America has consisted of studies focused on particular communities and the class-stratified religious options available within them. For instance, Liston Pope's classic study, *Millhands and Preachers*, examines class-inflected religion within the community of Gastonia, North Carolina. More recent examples include Matthew Pehl's historical look at working-class religion in Detroit, and Richard Callahan, Jr.'s forays into the mountain religion of Eastern Kentucky, as well as others.[48] By examining the religious options available within a community, these studies have shown a strong relationship between class and religious practice, particularly Christian denominations and churches that are stratified by class. Religious groups appeal to, accommodate, or arise from specific socioeconomic classes. Longitudinal analysis of the General Social Survey has demonstrated that these denominational class distinctions hold across geographical and temporal differences.[49] However, beyond the conclusion that class influences religion, these results do not seem particularly applicable to Heathenry or other alternative religions. Heathenry in America is not one of the class-

47. Ibid.
48. Liston Pope, *Millhands and Preachers: A Study of Gastonia* (New Haven, CT: Yale University Press, 1965); Matthew Pehl, *The Making of Working-Class Religion* (Urbana: University of Illinois Press, 2016); Richard J. Callahan, Jr., *Work and Faith in the Kentucky Coal Fields: Subject to Dust* (Bloomington: University of Indiana Press, 2008).
49. Christian Smith and Robert Faris, "Socioeconomic Inequality in the American Religious System: An Update and Assessment," in *Religion and Class in America: Culture, History, and Politics*, eds. Sean McCloud and William A. Mirola (Leiden: Brill, 2009), 27–43.

stratified religious options within any given community and does not represent a readily available class option. Rather, as a dissenting religion that occurs among solitary practitioners and small kindreds dispersed throughout the American continent, adherents discover and choose Heathenry for reasons other than their socioeconomic location, motivated by a variety of affinities not readily explainable by class.

Recent approaches to religion and class have begun to look beyond the socioeconomic conditions that shape class—income, education, and occupation—to how class informs culture. Class shapes one's approach to the world as a set of socially conditioned internal dispositions and attitudes anchored within socioeconomic locations. Several concepts have been used to support these observations of class and its influence. One approach, drawing on the work of Pierre Bourdieu, understands class as "habitus," a set of socialized norms or tendencies that influence behavior and thinking.[50] Habitus is the socioeconomically inflected world inhabited by groups and individuals, which instills in them certain dispositions or "tastes." Social classes distinguish themselves around these tastes—predispositions to express themselves through distinct aesthetics, forms of organization, and styles of discourse, as well as to evaluate the world around them. Timothy Nelson suggests that habitus can be a productive concept in describing the social location of a religious group.[51] He examines the aesthetics, linguistic style, and physical expression of religious practice among Christian congregations of different social locations to demonstrate how class and religion interact. Similarly, Sean McCloud suggests that class culture (a concept similar to Bourdieu's habitus) shapes lived religion, lending certain forms, styles, and linguistic patterns to religious practice. Class culture, he writes, informs the "strategies of religious actions, the structures of group worship, and the extent to which religious symbols, beliefs, and languages are comparatively elaborated or constricted."[52] Matthew Pehl's study of Christian

---

50. Timothy J. Nelson, "At Ease with Our Own Kind: Worship Practices and Class Segregation in American Religion," in *Religion and Class in America: Culture, History, and Politics*, 45–68. For a list of similar studies, see Nelson, "At Ease with Our Own Kind," 56.

51. Nelson, "At Ease with Our Own Kind," 53.

52. Sean McCloud, "The Ghost of Marx and the Stench of Deprivation," in *Religion and Class in America: Culture, History, and Politics*, 102. McCloud defines

churches in Detroit draws on ethnographic data to demonstrate the influence of class-determined tastes on the practice of religion. Writing about the diaspora of Southern working-class African Americans to Detroit in the early twentieth century, Pehl suggests that these tastes had a definitive impact on religious choice:

> Northern churches had long internalized the importance of "respectability" in the public performance of religions, and many ministers were embarrassed by the exuberant worship style of the southerners. A deacon in one storefront church, for example, explained to a researcher that his "long, loud prayer" seemed displaced in the larger and more affluent congregations, so he left to organize his own storefront. Indeed, the spread of church storefronts was evidence of ruptures within the African American community, and the refusal of southern migrants to accommodate a religious style they read as unwelcoming from both a theological and a class perspective.[53]

Here, we see religious choices not only stratified by economic distinctions but also expressing distinct cultures or styles mediated by taste. The discomfort felt by the poor southern deacon reflects both his own taste for a certain style of prayer as well as the distaste of the northern affluent congregation. While class is not determinative of religious choice or religious style, it does shape and influence people's approach to religion. The ways in which religion is performed may seem quite natural and appealing among a certain class culture, while those socialized into other socioeconomically situated tastes must overcome higher social boundaries in order to participate satisfactorily in that religious culture. The boundaries of taste are often strongly internalized, thus discouraging or preventing religious participation across classes. Those shaped by divergent class cultures may reject certain forms of lived religion as unsuitable if they are unwilling to undergo the extent of cultural adaptation necessary for full participation. However, if individuals are highly motivated, they may choose to do the internal work necessary to alter their class tastes. Individuals

---

"class culture" as the "range of cultural repertoires (styles, objects, tools, and strategies) found among a particular group of people who are related by similar social locations and material conditions." He suggests that upper-class religion may be more expansive, while working-class forms of religion would be more limited in their range.

53. Pehl, *The Making of Working-Class Religion*, 24.

with significant reasons to participate in a dissenting religion may find ways to adapt to class differences, such as by learning to appreciate practices anchored in a lower or higher class location, or broadening the religious culture by importing and incorporating their own religious styles and tastes.

I suggest that something like this cross-class adaptation has been occurring in American Heathenry. Again, as an alternative and dispersed religion, Heathenry does not exist as part of the class spectrum of religious choices within a locality. However, it may be the case that class culture and tastes influence the style and practice of Heathenry. As a first step in considering class in relation to Heathenry, I suggest that ethnographic observations corroborate the conclusions drawn from the demographic data discussed above that place Heathenry at a transition between the working and middle classes. While American Heathenry has a good deal of aesthetic variety, American Heathen tastes are generally amenable to a working-class social location. This is the predominant class context at the present and may provide an important outlet for working-class Paganism in America. However, there are other Heathen practices anchored in middle-class culture, forming a dynamic class interaction. I will look briefly at aspects of dress, music, and drinking that speak to class-inflected tastes and practices within the Heathen movement.[54] Taken by themselves, any one of these practices is not sufficient to situate Heathenry in the working class. Rather it is in the cumulative bricolage of these phenomena that a predominant class culture is defined.

## Dress

A visitor to a Heathen gathering will notice several things about the clothing worn by adherents. Perhaps first is simply its diversity. Everyday Heathen dress ranges from bohemian to biker, from jeans and t-shirts, to the occasional suit. One type of dress that stands out is "garb," the Viking-styled clothing that some, though not all, Heathens

---

54. Nelson, "At Ease with Our Own Kind," 55–66. Nelson analyzes the class culture of worship practices among Christian congregations by looking at three categories: aesthetics, such as the architecture and décor of worship space, and styles of dress; linguistic styles, relating to the vocabulary and eloquence of prayers and sermons; and physical expressions, such as use of the body and patterns of behavior.

wear.⁵⁵ Garb is worn primarily at Heathen gatherings and especially during ritual occasions. The origins of the practice of donning cultural and period-like dress can be linked to the Renaissance Fairs that began in California during the early 1960s. Garb was further developed over time, becoming a major element of the Society for Creative Anachronism as well as the reenactor community, both of which were influenced by the Renaissance Fair subculture.⁵⁶ The Heathen practice of wearing garb has been influenced by these sources, representing one way that popular culture, or a subset of pop culture, has contributed to Heathenry. Another noticeable aspect of dress is the taste for the biker aesthetic, particularly black leather biker vests, patches, and related gear. Biker-like clothing is a prominent tendency observable in Heathen culture, though not a requirement or even a dominant trend. However, a noticeable percentage of Heathens adopt some aspects of biker aesthetic as part of their everyday attire. This look originated in the working-class biker clubs of the 1960s, epitomized by the outlaw rebel culture of the Hells Angels. Contemporary mainstream American culture has co-opted the biker look, commercializing and gentrifying it. Middle-class Americans can spend a good deal of money being outfitted at the Harley Davidson stores found in most cities. But the Heathen version of this aesthetic retains the gritty authenticity and distressed look of the outlaw biker gangs. Whatever the reasons behind the popularity of this aesthetic among Heathens, it is clearly anchored in a working-class cultural context. It is a taste that makes the middle class uncomfortable, because of its implications of the outlaw life: hard, hostile, and potentially violent. The aesthetic speaks of being untamed, disdainful of material attainment and social status, defiant, and in tension with the values of most middle-class Americans.

## Music

The music associated with Heathenry has a hard edge, a distinctive taste for heavy metal. The Pagan-influenced lyrics and imagery of the

---

55. *Oxford English Dictionary Online*, s.v. "garb," www.oed.com. The term "garb" is derived from the French *garbe* and Italian *garbo*, words that refer to elegance, or a graceful or fancy style. The OED also suggests origins in Old High German *garawî*, referring to adornment. The term is now used in a variety of contexts, generally for any sort of distinctive dress or costuming.

56. Rachel Lee Rubin, *Well Met: Renaissance Faires and the American Counterculture* (New York: New York University Press, 2012), 45.

Scandinavian heavy metal scene have found a receptive audience in American Heathenry. The label "Viking metal" might not be used by adherents but is descriptive of the music shaped by Norse themes whose heavy driving rhythms evoke the pounding of Thor's hammer and the apocalyptic death songs of the mythic valkyries. While the Swedish bands *Bathory, Unleashed,* and *Amon Amarth* may be some of the most well-known examples, there are numerous other bands representing this genre and Heathen culture supports a variety of local heavy metal garage bands. The music is best described as death or black metal—harder, more intense forms of music that evolved from the speed and thrash metal of the 1980s. The class origins of heavy metal are well attested. As metal became more commodified and mainstream, these heavier forms emerged. Their lyrical content, vocal distortion, and aesthetic elements pushed the boundaries of the genre in order to maintain tension with the Western societies and values the music protested.[57] Even if death metal is not representative of the working class in general, it emerged from and gave voice to the discontent of white working-class youth. And even if the audience for the music has broadened in the ensuing years, the style and lyrics continue to exude working-class anger, perhaps one of the only musical genres left to do so. It remains anchored in sensibilities outside of the middle class and almost instantly disliked and rejected by these sorts of Americans, who hear it as offensive noise. Black metal and death metal are simply not representative of middle-class America: the imagery, rhythms, sonic qualities, and the scene in which the music lives are in high tension with the American middle class. Of course, black metal is not the only sort of Heathen music. Neofolk, a genre exemplified by bands such as Norway's *Wardruna*, is another important genre that expresses Heathen religious themes and is widely listened to by Heathens. However, death metal continues to represent a prominent segment of Heathen music that anchors Heathenry in a working-class location.

## *Drinking*

Drinking is, of course, a social activity found cross-culturally and among all social classes. But the ways in which social drinking is

---

57. For a more detailed discussion of the relationship between death metal and Heathenry, see Michael Moynihan and Didrik Søderlind, *Lords of Chaos: The Bloody Rise of the Satanic Metal Underground* (Los Angeles: Feral House, 2003).

performed may be influenced by class. A story from the very first national large-scale Heathen gathering I attended might illustrate how this occurs in Heathenry. During the afternoon of the first day, I found myself sitting with a small group of four or five men. The event was being held at a state park and a few men were assigned to watch and mediate with any curious public. A couple of these guys had bottles with them of home-brewed beer they had brought to the gathering. As we talked, I noticed that the two bottles began to circulate among the group. These were single 12- or 16-ounce bottles meant for individual consumption, but were being shared, passed from man to man around the circle. I was at first taken aback, that is, I felt a "taste" arise internally that made me uncomfortable at the thought of drinking from the same bottle as several strangers. However, when the bottles came around to me, I took a swig, hopefully without too noticeable a hesitation.[58]

In hindsight, the initial reaction I experienced was based partly in a socialized middle-class aversion to this sort of sharing. While middle-class persons might tolerate it among children in limited occurrences, sharing each other's drinks is generally avoided and socially sanctioned. That these concerns are often couched in the discourse of hygiene and health does not mean that they are not also anchored within a class culture. I did encounter other forms of social drinking at Heathen events, such as a mead tasting that was modeled on the decorum and sophistication of a wine tasting. This event was refined, included fairly complex discourse about mead, and did not involve drink sharing. However, drink sharing among Heathens is quite common, especially in ritual and social settings. It was something that I encountered many times: always in the *blót* and *sumbel* rituals, but very commonly in the social gatherings at Heathen events.[59] Only rarely did I hear grumbling about this, such as a comment that "We'd be the first ones to go," if there was an outbreak of communicable disease. The primary way that drinking is practiced involves mead or another beverage in a horn *passed around and shared* by a group of people. Again, class alone does not fully explain this phenomenon: there are also religious

---

58. Field notes by author, 2012.
59. The terms *blót* and *sumbel* designate the two primary rituals of Heathenry. They are referenced frequently in the book. The blót, pronounced "bloat", is a sacrificial rite discussed in more detail in chapter 6, while the sumbel is a communal drinking ritual discussed in chapter 7.

and ideological reasons behind it. However, the practice does form a type of social boundary that instantly raises the concerns of middle- and upper-class tastes. I found, however, that by adapting my tastes, participating in the passing of the mead horn became a meaningful practice. I came to experience it as a concrete physical activity that drew participants into the experience of important religious principles. Drink sharing enacts Heathen kinship so that it does not remain an idea or sentiment but takes on a shape in the world — the ideology of belonging is embodied in the circuit of the horn.

These examples represent three class-inflected practices that I interpret as anchoring Heathenry in the working class. However, within the habitus of American Heathenry, other values also occur that reflect tastes more commonly associated with an affluent, college-educated social location. I am referring to the prominence of scholarship and its attendant disciplines of reading and writing, and practices such as poetry, theology, and storytelling that involve elaborative and sophisticated discourse. These are not anomalies or marginal practices. Heathens place significant value on reading, writing, scholarly pursuits, and Lore-mastering. The ability to speak well, to communicate high-level ideas, to give a speech, a scholarly talk, or to recite poetry are important and recognized skills. Every Heathen gathering includes workshops discussing aspects of Heathen theology, and semi-scholarly articles are published in Heathen journals. There is a recognizable degree of respect given to those Heathens who excel in these areas, unlike the disdain or suspicion frequently directed at intellectual life in some working-class contexts. The value placed on reading is a case in point. As I found throughout my fieldwork, reading is highly encouraged among Heathens. Reading lists abound and books are often the subject of or feature prominently in conversation. Reading and discourse about reading are simply not characteristic of the modern American working class. So the extent that writing and reading books remains a significant dimension of the culture shows that American Heathenry cannot be defined solely as a working-class religion.

These examples seem to indicate that Heathenry has developed as a context in which elements of differing class cultures converge in complementary ways. Contemporary America has seen the rise of a new class configuration, that of the educated but not financially advantaged. It is this transitional group, whose jobs and income may not match their level of education, which is predominantly represented in Heathenry. Earlier research by R. George Kirkpatrick, Rich Rainey, and Kathryn Rubi, identified a similar trend of "status inconsistency" among contemporary Pagans in the 1980s, suggesting that this is something of a chronic issue.[60] They also note a corresponding low "status concern" among their respondents, who tend to value their religious practice as more important than social, career, and economic status.[61] This is another characteristic that contemporary Heathens seem to share with other Pagans and may contribute to the mix of social classes found in American Heathenry. As a dissenting religion, Heathenry appeals to people across the class spectrum. My observations in the field indicate that this interaction of class in the Heathen social context has been creative and productive for the most part. Both working- and middle-class individuals find elements within Heathenry that are appealing to them, while at the same time being introduced to new tastes. Those adherents who remain in Heathenry show the sort of motivation necessary to stretch the class socialization they received. They also have some degree of flexibility in adapting to new types of culture: receiving new forms of music or learning to place more value on reading. Of course, this convergence could easily prove to be unstable in the future, resulting in a clash of class interests or widening divisions in the movement occurring around class tastes. Future work might examine the role of class in the fracturing of American Heathenry into distinct groups and organizations. While class was not a primary category of my research, I have come to see class analysis as an important consideration for future work on Heathenry. These observations will hopefully serve as the beginning of an analysis that other researchers might both draw upon and push against.

## *Being Viking?*

While its leaders and adherents may talk about a reawakening to the ancient Norse gods, the Asatru movement is still a small segment of

60. R. George Kirkpatrick, Rich Rainey, and Kathryn Rubi, "Pagan Renaissance and Wiccan Witchcraft in Industrial Society: A Study of Parasociology and the Sociology of Enchantment," *Iron Mountain: A Journal of Magical Religion* Summer (1984): 33.
61. Ibid., 34.

American Paganism, less numerous and less well known than Paganisms such as Wicca or Druidry. What Asatru lacks in size, it makes up for in the intensity and genuineness of feeling found among the Asatru adherents. The religiosity of the movement might come as a surprise to the secular minded. Many Asatruar feel called into the movement through supernatural experiences with gods and ancestral beings, and many early leaders of the movement have stories of extremely powerful theophanic conversion experiences. Jorvik's story of finding Asatru through dreams is representative of this sort of calling into the religion.[62] Jorvik was a rough and ready young man from the streets of Fort Collins, Colorado who described himself as "fairly lost spiritually" prior to finding Asatru. He said that he began having dreams filled with strange images that did not make sense to him. After sharing some of those dreams online, he was contacted by a person who asked if Jorvik had ever heard of Asatru, "because those dreams are Odin speaking to you." Jorvik followed that advice and began looking into Asatru, eventually coming to see in his dreams the power of the Heathen gods awakening something deep inside him. What began with a confusing dream has become a deep and life-changing involvement with Asatru in which Jorvik has found meaning, purpose, and strength, which has inspired and fueled his family commitments, entrepreneurship, and other pursuits. Jorvik is not alone in awakening to a religious world in which ancient European gods speak and interact with their human kin, in which numinous power courses through the cosmos through runes and other symbols, and where human beings strive to create brave and noble lives from the chaos and flurry of modern existence. Many Asatru adherents share similar stories and backgrounds.

One of the vivid images used by some Heathens to describe their experience comes from Carl Jung's essay "Wotan," in which he describes the god as an archetype of the Germanic psyche.[63] Jung compares the human psyche to a desert landscape, carved and

---

62. Jorvik, telephone interview with author, October 22, 2011.

63. The Norse god known as "Odin" is often presented as the principal deity of the Germanic/Norse pantheon. In his regional variations, he is known by related names. *Wotan*, the name used by Jung, derives from Old High German. Similarly, he is known as *Woden* in Old English, and *Oðinn* in Old Norse. While most American Heathens use the standard English version, Odin, the linguistic variants are also sometimes found as Heathens strive for more linguistic accuracy in their terminology.

grooved by old waterways. Like dry streambeds where powerful rivers once flowed, the experiences and cultural lifeways developed by ancient cultures leave traces etched into the minds of their descendants. The experiences and memories of the old gods of the distant past are etched in the subconscious minds of contemporary people, little used but still present. Although patterns of thought and action may have been diverted in new directions by modernity, the old archetypes are still capable of carrying powerful mental and emotional currents should the right circumstances arise. Jung writes:

> It was not in Wotan's nature to linger on and show signs of old age. He simply disappeared when the times turned against him, and remained invisible for more than a thousand years, working anonymously and indirectly. Archetypes are like riverbeds which dry up when the water deserts them, but which it can find again at any time. An archetype is like an old watercourse along which the water of life has flowed for centuries, digging a deep channel for itself. The longer it has flowed in this channel the more likely it is that sooner or later the water will return to its old bed.[64]

Jung used this idea in 1936 to explain the seemingly sudden rise of the Nazi party in pre-World War II Germany, describing it as an atavistic recurrence of the ancient Germanic Pagan psyche. His treatment of the subject stands as an extremely deficient and ahistorical explanation for the horrors of Nazism. Jung's treatment of the Wotan archetype raises troublesome assumptions about race and culture, particularly the essentialist and racialist idea that culture is a product of biological ancestry. While most Asatruar would reject such extreme conclusions, assumptions similar to Jung's have taken root and persisted among some Heathens, such as the racial Odinist wing of the movement. Many Asatruars would simply deny the connection between a modern person's racial or ethnic background and their religious proclivities, while others would maintain that ancestry, though not race, is the primary factor in relating to the ancient gods. However, Jung's statement resonates in the movement. Many adherents feel that they are discovering within themselves an identity both ancient and ancestral. For these

---

64. C. G. Jung, *Civilization in Transition, The Collected Works of C. G. Jung*, Vol. 10 (London: Routledge & Kegan-Paul, 1964), 189.

adherents, being Viking is not simply the mercurial choice of a consumer in the religious marketplace choosing from the available options a religious brand that suits him or her. It is a discovery or awakening to something much deeper and more primal. The theme of "coming home" is a common narrative of contemporary Pagan identity construction, but it is not characteristic of the Heathen conversion path.[65] More frequently American Heathens describe a journey of discovery, an awakening to something that had been dormant, or a process of learning and mentorship. In almost all cases, Heathen narratives of belonging revolve around the religious imperative to become informed and shaped by the past, a style of religion-making often called "reconstructionist" Paganism.

At Heathen gatherings, I have often heard the rhetorical question "What would we have been like if we had been able to evolve for another thousand years?"[66] The question is something that Heathens often muse upon. It signifies a rift in the heart of Heathen experience, a sense of interruption that is felt personally and viscerally. If Northern Europe had not been converted, if the religious practice of the ancient northern cultures had not been systematically dismantled, what would Heathenry have looked like in the twenty-first century? This sense of the violent and unnatural end of ancient Heathenry imparts to the contemporary movement a careful determination to recover and rebuild a religious culture that authentically resembles that ancient spirituality. Heathens search for a way to reconnect to that flow, like a river that has been lost underground. To a great extent, Heathens lay the blame for this rift at the feet of Christianity, whose history of colonial domination and religious intolerance changed the face of Europe and much of the globe. McNallen describes the conversion of Northern Europe as a thousand-year war against the Germanic people during which the Vatican plotted, financed, and carried out a campaign

---

65. Berger and Ezzy, *Teen Witch*, 56–59. The "coming home" narrative provides an alternative path to religious belonging distinct from the path of conversion. "Conversion" generally indicates turning away from one's previous lifestyle and ideas to adopt a new identity, while "coming home" involves finding a name and a community reflective of one's long-held spiritual beliefs.

66. I have often heard statements similar to this at Heathen gatherings. Heathen authors also occasionally raise the question. See, for instance, Galina Krasskova, *Exploring the Northern Tradition: A Guide to the Gods, Lore, Rites, and Celebrations from the Norse, German, and Anglo-Saxon Traditions* (Franklin Lakes, NJ: New Page Books, 2005), 22, 25.

of manipulation, murder, and desecration.⁶⁷ As indicated by the frequently used qualifier "pre-Christian," Heathens seek to practice a religion free from Christian influence, to discover "the way of life that our ancestors followed prior to Christianity being moved northward into Northern Europe by Rome."⁶⁸ Asatru adherents, who might disagree on many other things, find common ground in the perception that Christianity interfered with, corrupted, or hijacked the ancestral religions of Europe, an interpretation that turns the Christian-influenced story of Western civilization on its head. Far from "saving" the West, Christianity colonized Europe and engaged in several hundred years of systematic and deeply damaging cultural re-programming. During this militant campaign of conversion, Christians regarded the wisdom and lifeways of Heathen peoples with disdain and foisted upon them a "malignant desert philosophy" and a "life-denying paradigm."⁶⁹ Similarly, many Heathens would attribute problems of the modern world to the influence of these imperialistic monotheistic cultures.⁷⁰ Christian-fueled modernity has left contemporary people alienated and disaffected, lost in a disenchanted world, shorn of their roots to a rich and life-giving past, distanced from their relationship with nature, disrupted in their social roles, and adrift without meaningful spiritual knowledge.

Almost all contemporary Pagan religions reject Christianity to one degree or another. As Michael Strmiska indicates, "in the popular discourse of modern Paganism . . . Christianity is frequently denounced as an anti-natural, anti-female, sexually and culturally repressive, guilt-ridden, and authoritarian religion that has fostered intolerance, hypocrisy, and persecution throughout the world."⁷¹ Heathens particularly criticize Christianity as a life-denying religious culture, which uses concepts of sin and guilt to dwell on what is wrong with people. In contrast, Heathens describe their religion

---

67. Stephen A. McNallen, *Asatru: A Native European Spirituality* (Nevada City, CA: Runestone Press), 55–60.

68. Mark L. Stinson, *Heathen Gods: A Collection of Essays Concerning the Folkway of Our People* (Kansas City, MO: Jotun's Bane Kindred, 2010), 6.

69. Eowyn, "Midgarth 911 (US) and 999 (UK)" *Odinic Rite Guardians* blog, www.odinic-rite.org/Guardians/midgarth-911-us-and-999-uk/. As this language suggests, the discourse of the early twentieth-century völkisch paradigm has significantly influenced Heathen views of Christianity.

70. McNallen, *Asatru*, 13–15.

71. Strmiska, *Modern Paganism in World Cultures*, 29.

as a world-affirming culture that emphasizes the goodness of the world and the strength, ability, and beauty of human life.[72] Reconstruction is one way to pick up where the last Heathens left off in 1,000 CE, a conscious attempt to draw on the pre-Christian past in order to create a post-Christian religion and culture.

The deep antipathy toward Christianity is quite close to the surface for many American Heathens, expressed in ways that range from anger and outright dismissal to a general disdain, mistrust, and suspicion. Even more so than in other forms of contemporary Paganism, the rejection of Christianity, a consciously anti-Christian stance, has formed an important dynamic with the Heathen movement. Early in the development of Heathenry, rituals were written to wash off or reverse a Christian baptism, to allow adherents to break from a Christian legacy that was perhaps forced onto their ancestors.[73] Many Heathens have personal narratives in which they weave together the historical and contemporary offenses of Christians. For instance, during an email exchange with a Heathen woman, I commented that my cousin was an Anglican Christian. This generated an intense and immediate response: "Aren't they the ones who oppressed our people?"[74] During a conversation with a long-time Heathen about my Christian background, he related that his suspicion of Christians originated from being treated with hostility by conservative Christian students on a university campus.[75] A Heathen leader mentioned to me that his car was egged because of his faith while others talk about discrimination at work or school.[76] I personally witnessed an incident of harassment at the first national Heathen moot I attended in the Midwest. After a ritual, two women dressed in Heathen garb encountered some local citizens who shouted "Demon worshipers" and cursed them.[77] During a conversation in another kindred meeting, the members stated that if someone was a Christian they would not be welcome in

---

72. Jarl, telephone interview with author, February 2015.
73. Kveldúlf Gundarsson, *Living the Troth*, Vol. 2 of *Our Troth* (North Charleston, SC: BookSurge, 2007), 241–42, 466–71.
74. Hilde, email to author, April 4, 2011.
75. Field notes taken by author, Oklahoma, June, 2011.
76. Mark Stinson, email to author, July 26, 2011. See also Mark Stinson, *Heathen Tribes: A Collection of Essays Concerning the Tribes of Our Folk* (Kansas City, MO: Jotun's Bane Kindred Temple of Our Heathen Gods, 2011), 229–31.
77. Field notes by author, Oklahoma, June, 2011.

the kindred, as dual allegiance of this sort would not be tolerated.[78] Almost universally, Asatru kindreds would reject any attempt to mix Heathen and Christian affiliation as unthinkable. These sentiments are more pronounced among Heathens of a folkish persuasion, who might also discourage or reject affiliations with Wiccan and other Pagan orientations.

Experiences such as these confirm in Heathen experience the salient narrative about Christianity. As we have discussed, Heathens connect emotionally to the stories of historical Christian aggression and oppression and use these stories to re-imagine their own experience with Christianity. Some Heathens also argue that Christianity is a declining faith on the wrong side of history. The slump in the number of Christian adherents in America is given as an indication of this gradual decline. Mark Stinson states, "I think Christianity is losing its grip on our people. After centuries of religious domination by these foreign beliefs, people are finally starting to break free. It could very well be that they are able to break free because the Christian culture is failing."[79] For many Heathens, especially those with a folkish orientation, the decline of Christianity in the West is inevitable. Despite more than a thousand years of Christian history in Europe and America, Asatru was only suppressed, not replaced.[80] As Stephen McNallen has memorably stated, "We have been Europeans for about forty thousand years. We have been Christians for considerably less than two thousand years."[81] Heathens are confident that the ideological hold of Christianity over culture, thought, and ways of life is unraveling. American and European societies are moving swiftly and decisively toward becoming post-Christian cultures. Asatru is poised to meet the growing post-Christian religious need. For these Heathens,

78. Field notes taken by author, Lexington, KY, 2011.
79. Stinson, email.
80. Stinson, *Heathen Tribes*, 229. See also Stephen A. McNallen, *What Is Asatru?* (Nevada City, CA: Asastru Folk Assembly, 1985). While the Troth does not speak about Christianity as an "alien faith"—language used primarily within folkish Asatru circles—the organization sees Asatru as the traditional indigenous religion of Europe and Christianity as a non-European religion. See the Troth, "Heathens and Heathen Faith" (pamphlet).
81. Stephen McNallen, "Asatru—A Native European Religion," YouTube video, 5:45, posted by Stephen McNallen, October 17, 2008, www.youtube.com/watch?v=cDvPdWBeEFc&list=UUuWPZGha53HHRFox Fd7-7eQ&index=18. Quote appears 1:16–1:32 into the video.

Figure 1. The Odin Fish. (Image used with permission.)

"post-Christian" means a return to pre-Christian religion and an opportunity for the emergence of older ways of being. The commitment of Heathen reconstruction is to recover a pre-Christian way of life in the Northern European mode.

While "Christian-bashing" is often evident, Heathens frequently exhibit these attitudes in light-hearted ways. As with other marginalized groups, humor functions among Heathens as a means to communicate countercultural attitudes while mitigating the level of social tension and the potential for hostile backlash. "The value of humour seems to reside in constructing alternative meaning systems that do not promote binary oppositions," but allow marginalized groups "alternative ways to impinge on hegemonic traditions."[82] Satire, parody, and other such uses of humor and playfulness are subversive, couching serious and contentious social critique within a mischievous or prankish gesture. The Odin Fish mocks the popular Christian ichthus image by playfully re-imagining it as a fish with eight legs, wearing a horned Viking helmet and carrying a spear (see figure 1). The image references Odin's eight-legged steed Sleipnir and his spear Gungnir from Norse myth and often pictures a wriggling Jesus fish impaled on the spear shaft. The image is meant to be goading, especially to Christians. It makes a visceral point about Heathenry's oppositional stance against the religious mainstream and imagines a revaluation of current social norms. Yet it couches those meanings within a common cultural reference,

---

82. Ivette Cardeña, "On Humour and Pathology: The Role of Paradox and Absurdity for Ideological Survival," *Anthropology & Medicine* 10, no. 1 (2003): 120, 122.

a playful contribution to the cultural struggle for social currency enacted across the American highways on the bumpers of cars. Many Heathen gatherings feature an afternoon of Viking games in which participants compete in events such as archery, hammer toss, ax throwing, and other athletic events. One such event at East Coast Thing featured a canoe race in which the racers go "a-viking." The race involved rowing the canoes to a beach representing the Lindisfarne monastery where participants hopped from the canoe and use a foam sword to chop off the "head" (a baseball with a face drawn on with a Sharpie) of a monk statue (see figure 2) before continuing to the finish line.[83] Participants clearly understood this as a light-hearted game and not as training or preparation for violence. Yet at the same time, the game imagines and rehearses a particular Heathen reading of history in which the growth and dominance of Christianity is interpreted in a decidedly negative light. James Scott writes about the carnival as a means of social resistance, a "ritual of reversal" in which dominant social paradigms are turned upside down through play, mockery, and parody.[84] This sense of carnival infuses the Viking canoe race: chopping the head off the monk statue is subversive game play. We play at "what if" — what if Pagan Vikings had subjugated Christianity? What if Heathen culture had become the norm? Enacting the raid as a game builds a social zone where this alternative reality might be experienced as the norm, a vision of a subversive countercultural reality. Heathens in general are not content to exist quietly within a Christian cultural context. The game allows Heathens to exist as participants in the American context while at the same time envisioning Christianity is a dying cultural force and the Heathen community as engaged in a struggle to bring about a post-Christian period.

One last subversive note on the use of humor and carnival techniques in the Heathen community. If Heathens can play with Christian meaning through parody and mockery, then dominant Heathen values can also be subverted in similar ways as well. The

83. Field notes taken by author, Pennsylvania, June, 2012. The statue itself was a cement garden figure and its head was a baseball adorned with a face drawn in black marker. The leader of East Coast Thing had found the discarded broken statue while browsing at a garden center and thought it would make a humorous addition to the Viking games.

84. James C. Scott, *Domination and the Arts of Resistance: Hidden Transcripts* (New Haven, CT: Yale University Press, 1990), 172–73.

Figure 2. Statue of a Monk from the Canoe Race at East Coast Thing. (Photo by author.)

god Loki represents a considerable point of tension in Heathenry, provoking strong feelings ranging from suspicion to aversion among many.[85] As Jennifer Snook states, honoring Loki is "one of the most contentious debates among Heathens."[86] As recounted in Norse myth, Loki's actions are often ambiguous and create problems with complex ramifications, most problematic being his role in Ragnarok. In the minds of most Heathens, Loki's choice to fight against the gods shows him to be a traitor and enemy to the gods and all those who follow them. The narrative of Loki's betrayal overwhelmingly counts against other mythic narratives in which

85. Lafayllve, *A Practical Heathen's Guide*, 219–23.
86. Jennifer Snook, *American Heathens: The Politics of Identity in a Pagan Religious Movement* (Philadelphia: Temple University Press, 2015), 73.

Loki acts to protect and cooperate with the Aesir. There is, however, a small demographic of Lokean Heathens who have a more complex interpretation of Loki as a trickster god, some of whom approach him as a patron god. Loki-centric spirituality has been rejected by most Heathens, vigorously suppressed in some cases and consistently marginalized with Lokeans seen as troublemakers, religiously eclectic, and potentially socially and sexually deviant. The small community of Lokean Heathens has existed primarily online, networking, and developing its own theology and ritual practice.[87] Attempts to interpose Loki into Heathen social spaces can be seen as a carnival technique turning Heathen norms on their heads. By calling the name of Loki in blót or sumbel, raising a Lokean *vé* on the outskirts of a Heathen event, wearing Lokean t-shirts, or by staging alternative rituals for Loki, widely recognized cultural norms against the inclusion of Loki in Heathen practice are contested and problematized.[88]

In addition to the rejection of Christianity, the Heathen movement is known to express a great deal of ambivalence regarding other forms of Paganism. While Christianity is rejected for the reasons described above, attitudes towards contemporary Paganism are influenced by a Heathen critique of Pagan eclecticism. While Wicca is often the target of such critiques, all forms of Paganism are potential recipients of Heathen disdain. Heathens, who seek to reconstruct Norse religion with an eye towards historical accuracy, contrast their approach to religion with that of "fluffy" Pagan spirituality characterized or stereotyped as shallow, confused, and even silly. "Pagans," by which Heathens mean those who are influenced

---

87. Ibid., 72–79.
88. Richard Cleasby and Gudbrand Vigfusson, s.v: "Vé," *An Icelandic-English Dictionary* (Oxford: Clarendon, 1957). Vé is an Icelandic word referring to a house or home, used to indicate the home or space devoted to a god or spirit. It is used for a type of outdoor and unroofed sacred space, designated and enclosed with a cord, rope, or fence. It was devoted to a god or other spiritual entity and considered a sacred and protected precinct. The boundaries marked the sacred space into which humans should not transgress. Offerings for gods and nature spirits could be left. For further discussion see Jordsvin, "Hofs and Harrows: Then and Now," *Jordsvin's Norse Heathen Pages* website, http://home.earthlink.net/~jordsvin/Jordsvins%20 Writing/Hofs%20and%20Harrows.htm, also found in Idunna, no. 55 (2003); Nigel Pennick, "Heathen Holy Places in Northern Europe: A Cultural Overview," in *Tyr: Myth – Culture – Tradition, Vol. 2*, eds. Joshua Buckley and Michael Moynihan (Atlanta: Ultra, 2003–2004), 139–49.

by Wicca, are seen as flirting with romantic notions of the past, and borrowing excessively from a diverse mix of ancient cultures and other eclectic sources.[89] Thus for many Heathens, contemporary Paganisms are simply "made-up" syncretic religions suffering from many of the failures of modern identity, having a closer resemblance to New Age spiritualities than the actual polytheist religions of the ancient world.[90] These attitudes create in the Heathen movement a dynamic of identity construction based on the rejection of Christianity and the maintenance of high boundaries and considerable tension with the greater American Pagan community.

## *What Is Reconstruction?*

The common thread running through the disparate elements of the Heathen movement is the commitment to building a way of life drawn substantially from the pre-Christian tradition. This shared religious goal involves reconstructing the pre-Christian religion of northern Europe, although what this means is not always clear. For Asatruar, reconstruction does not require replicating life in pre-modern society, "going back" to live as the ancestors did. For instance, Josh Rood, a Heathen practitioner from the East Coast who studied at the University of Iceland, acknowledges the impracticality as well as undesirability of somehow returning to a past way of life. "Some things are outdated," he says, "and some things are no longer possible."[91] While it may not mean re-establishing an ancient Viking society, reconstruction involves an orientation toward the past as a vital source of information for the present. The wisdom expressed within the culture and religion of the ancestors guided people and their societies into situations of productive human thriving. The past provides a pattern, a template for a *hálig* (Old English) or *heilag* (Old Norse) life, one that is whole, healthy,

---

89. Sarah M. Pike, *Earthly Bodies, Magical Selves: Contemporary Pagans and the Search for Community* (Berkeley: University of California Press, 2001). See Pike's chapter on Pagan borrowing. Issues of borrowing and cultural appropriation also arise within Heathenry, as adherents draw on a historical culture not obviously their own. Both reconstruction and metagenetics can be seen as different ideological strategies that lend a type of legitimacy to cultural appropriation.

90. Devyn Gillette and Lewis Stead, "The Pentagram and the Hammer," *Raven Online*, www.ravenkindred.com/wicatru.html.

91. Josh Rood,"Interview," *Eternal Haunted Summer* Autumn (2011), http://eternalhauntedsummer.com/issues/autumn-equinox-2011/josh-rood/.

and holy. This ancient pattern can be uncovered or discovered through the study of Old Norse words and literature, archaeology, comparative religion, and immersion in ancient cultural practices. Bil Linzie, a Heathen in the Southwest who has written a great deal on the process of reconstruction, uses the example of a violinist to explain the reconstructionist goal. While a classically trained violinist can learn to play a folk tune, he writes, the violinist lacks any real understanding of the culture that produced that folksong, lending a degree of inauthenticity to the playing of the song. Rather than just learning the song, a reconstructionist aims to inhabit the folk culture itself, "the heart within which the melody conceived, developed and was fostered."[92]

The Asatru movement has a number of sources from which to draw in this process of reconstructing a lost religious culture of the past. First and most important are the number of textual sources that concern pre-Christian Norse society. These include sources of mythology such as the *Poetic Edda*, a collection of poems telling the stories of the Norse deities and heroes. The oldest known manuscript of the *Edda*, known as the *Codex Regius*, was written in the twelfth century.[93] Another important source is the *Prose Edda*, written by Snorri Sturluson, an Icelandic politician and folklorist. He was a Christian whose interest in Icelandic culture and history caused him to compile and synthesize Scandinavian legends in the thirteenth century. Heathen practitioners also obtain cultural and religious information from the Icelandic sagas, epic stories of families, heroes, and gods written from the eleventh century onwards. The fact that these textual sources are products of the Christian age complicates their usage, requiring modern Heathens to engage in a process of textual criticism to separate the Pagan core from the distortions caused by Christian ideology.[94] In addition, Asatru adherents make regular use of contemporary scholarship concerning northern European cultures, such as archeology, linguistics, and anthropology. Heathens also undertake their own study of historical texts and sources when scholarly resources fall short. These Heathen scholars are generally well read in the source

92. Bil Linzie, "Reconstructionism's Role in Modern Heathenry," *The Seidhman Rants*, July 12, 2008, www.angelfire.com/nm/seidhman/reconstruction-c.pdf.
93. Heather O'Donoghue, *From Asgard to Valhalla: The Remarkable Story of the Norse Myths* (New York: I. B. Tauris, 2008), 12.
94. Strmiska, *Modern Paganism in World Culture*, 19.

materials and may have some knowledge of source languages such as Icelandic, Old Norse, and German. They receive a great deal of respect in the movement, writing books and articles of considerable depth.[95] Heathen gatherings and several Heathen journals provide a forum for these scholars to publish and discuss their research in lectures and workshops. A final, albeit controversial, source for reconstruction is the religious experience of contemporary Asatru practitioners themselves, sometimes referred to as unverified personal gnosis or "UPG." UPG is a type of knowledge obtained in the course of a person's own experiential religious practice of working with gods and other spiritual beings, trying magical practices, or engaging in ritual.

Reconstruction is more than an attempt to gloss over a new religious paradigm with references to the past to make it seem ancient.[96] It has been suggested that early Christian practice in northern Europe incorporated aspects of Paganism, producing a folk Christianity that retained significant Pagan elements. This is a significant and influential thesis found in James Frazer's *Golden Bough*, for instance.[97] Diana Paxson draws on this theory of survivals when she writes that even as Christianity came to dominate Scandinavia, the "old beliefs lingered long in the countryside, and as in Iceland, the land spirits were honored even when the old gods were denied."[98] A similar theory of continuity accepts that Pagan religious practice was extirpated from Europe, but suggests that practices and concepts were retained in the subconscious. While the religion fell from practice and conscious memory, its elements were retained in cultural memory. Again Paxson states, "[a]lthough the religion had been suppressed, the lore remained, and buried in the collective unconscious of the Germanic peoples, the old gods waited for men and women to call on them once more."[99] For others, these long-forgotten symbols, words, and customs are windows

---

95. Ibid., 137.

96. Cooper, *Contemporary Druidry*, chapter 2. Cooper discusses "ancientization," which he describes as applying a historical veneer to an otherwise new religion in order to legitimize its practice.

97. James G. Frazer, *The Golden Bough: A Study in Magic and Religion* (New York: Macmillan, 1951), 358–59.

98. Diana Paxson, *Essential Ásatrú: Walking the Path of Norse Paganism* (New York: Citadel Press, 2006), 43.

99. Ibid., 44.

and doors into the past. Placing oneself in the context of these surviving vestiges of Heathen spirituality, by making use of runes, words, images, and ritual forms, makes possible the recovery of this ancient Norse religious experience in the modern world. The old ways can be revived or re-awakened from a subconscious state of dormancy. Michael Strmiska writes that, "Nordic Pagans, like other Reconstructionist Pagans, are involved in a dialogue with the past, seeking not so much to imitate the past as to learn from it, for the purposes of the present and the future."[100]

This dialogue with the past has two important effects for Heathenry: it constructs a past with authoritative implications and functions as a strategy of identity creation. First, Asatru adherents look to the past as authoritative: the more a practice resembles the past, the more authentic and "right" it is deemed. This reconstructionist imperative has a profoundly formative effect on the movement, influencing everything from what Heathens drink to how they worship. They want to drink what the ancestors

Figure 3. Tyr's Vé at East Coast Thing. (Photo by the author.)

---

100. Strmiska, *Modern Paganism in World Cultures*, 142.

drank, thus the movement-wide obsession for imbibing homebrewed mead from drinking horns, although it is anyone's guess whether this practice is more a result of cinematic imagination or the historical record. They want to compose and recite poetry in ancient Scandinavian meters because this is how the arch-Heathens addressed the gods, whose ears turn quickly towards these ancient sounds.[101] Heathens seek to build holy spaces like the Norse Pagans did—the *vé* and *hof* rather than a church (see figure 3).[102] They practice ancient arts such as spinning, weaving, and blacksmithing. Heathen artists incorporate ancient Scandinavian designs and symbols, even when their meanings and functions are unclear, as part of constructing a Heathen aesthetic. Some Heathen leaders urge practitioners to emulate the ancient Norse by not having their sons circumcised.[103] All these are examples of the ubiquitous influence of the past on reconstructing a religion for modern life.[104] The approach suggests that by re-inhabiting ancient patterns of life, the old channels of thought, worship, and interaction with the sacred world will also emerge. Graham Harvey notes the selective nature of much contemporary religious reconstruction. While the shaman has become a potent symbol for many people, substantially fewer seek to reconstruct the life and religion of northern English shepherds. This is despite the fact that shepherds "live as 'close to nature' as shamans do," represent a culturally authentic way of interacting closely with animals, and were undoubtedly more representative of Pagan communities of the past.[105] Heathenry also falls prey to this overspiritualizing tendency and may have its over-representation of rune casters and seið workers. Yet at the same time, there are sizeable numbers of Heathens whose religious goals include mastering the art of blacksmithing. Heathen reconstruction seeks

---

101. Field notes taken by author, Pennsylvania, August, 2012.

102. Cleasby and Vigfusson, s.v. "hof," *An Icelandic Dictionary*; Ron Landreth, email to author, July 11, 2012. Hof refers to a hall, often used to designate a temple or a building used for Heathen worship. A hof specifically refers to a roofed temple, an inside space, as opposed to sacred spaces located outside such as a hörg or a vé.

103. Mark Stinson, "Reasons Heathens Should Reject Circumcision," in *Heathen Families: Fables and Essays* (Kansas City, MO: Jotun's Bane Kindred Temple of Our Heathen Gods, 2011), 28–31.

104. Strmiska, *Modern Paganism in World Cultures*, 129–30.

105. Graham Harvey, *Contemporary Paganism: Religions of the Earth from Druids and Witches to Heathens and Ecofeminists* (New York: New York University Press, 2011), 105–6.

to reclaim some of the more mundane aspects of the Pagan past: brewers, poets, and a few who practice their Heathen spirituality through farming.

But religious reconstruction is not re-enactment. It involves more than modern people living with and among ancient things and practices. It also involves renovating identity according to ancient ways of looking at the world. The most important aspects of Pagan reconstruction involve reshaping the self. Reconstructionists want to build *new* people based upon an *old* model. The Heathen thinker Josh Rood puts it succinctly: "Recon is about shifting our worldview, shifting our way of thinking."[106] For Heathens, this involves dismantling a way of seeing the world shaped by oppressive Christianity and materialistic modernity. As Rood states, "over time you start to set aside the Christian worldview, and replace it with a Heathen one. I think this is a lifelong process for us, but our kids will have it easier."[107] One strategy commonly utilized in the pursuit of reconstruction involves tracing the etymology of contemporary words back to their linguistic roots. For instance, in her work on the god Frey, Ann Sheffield discusses the meaning of "Frey" in light of its roots in Proto-Germanic and Proto-Indo-European, as well as a cognate form, *frôno*, in Old High German.[108] She uses a similar approach to understand Frey's characteristic of fertility as described in the Old Norse word *ár*, building its linguistic domain from the Proto-Indo-European and Proto-Germanic, the Old Icelandic and the Old English cognate *gēar*.[109] The appeal of these Germanic and pre-Germanic languages is not simply practical, nor nostalgic. The primary sources for Heathenry are written in Old Norse and Old Icelandic and there may be a romantic thrill to offering a prayer or blessing in Old Norse. The real appeal for Heathens lies precisely in the antiquity of these languages. The etymology locates the meaning of the word in pre-Christian culture, an origin entirely Pagan in nature. Thus the etymology of the word uncovers or opens the contemporary practitioner to the conceptual world of the arch-Heathen. By thinking and re-imagining the world through these root words, Heathen reconstructionists seek to deconstruct

---

106. Field notes taken by author, Pennsylvania, June, 2012.
107. Josh Rood, "Interview."
108. Ann Gróa Sheffield, *Frey: God of the World* (Raleigh, NC: Lulu.com, 2007), 8.
109. Ibid., 19–21.

the Christian-influenced aspects of their own worldviews and view the world more like their pre-Christian ancestors. For Rood and other Heathens, the real work of reconstruction is internal: a re-Paganization of the mind. By restructuring the mind according to Heathen categories and concepts, authentic Heathen practices may emerge organically from that recovered worldview. The myth of a golden age is evident in this reconstructionist approach, even if the historical location of old Europe's golden age in time and space may be disputed. Actually, many Heathens do not see the Viking Age as an ideal goal for the contemporary reconstructionist movement. They are quite willing to critique the Viking Age as a period of cultural turmoil and to find self-destructive tendencies in those people and events. Yet source material and evidence for pre-Viking time periods is slim, complicating the reconstructionist approach. Both the longing to discover a pure Pagan past and the difficulty in doing so are implicit in the reconstructionist agenda that to one degree or another underlies the entire Heathen movement.

If Heathens are engaged in a dialogue with the past, they are just as significantly engaged in a dialogue with the present. Heathen reconstruction is a type of social critique that responds to modernity and incorporates aspects of modernity within itself. In its dialogue with the present, Heathenry should be seen as a dissenting religious community.[110] The Heathen critique of modern American life ranges across issues, some of which we will address in this book, such as a perceived weakening of family life and the disenchantment characterizing the modern experience of nature. Unlike new religions that orient toward a vision of future harmony, the Heathen critique of modern life particularly looks to the past for solutions. Despite the longing for a pure understanding of the past, Heathen perspectives of the past are shaped by important contemporary intellectual tributaries. Heathens are actively engaged in a process of negotiating with these contemporary social and intellectual forces. Some, such as Christianity, they seek to root out or eliminate from their thinking. Other tributaries are embraced and allowed to have a profound shaping effect on the way the past is received.

---

110. Stephen J. Stein, *Communities of Dissent: A History of Alternative Religions in America* (New York: Oxford University Press, 2003).

## *The Road Forward*

To better understand the context in which American Heathenry has developed, I will begin with two chapters that provide an overview of the movement. In the first chapter, I discuss the history of the movement, how Norse culture came to become a religious practice in America. Putting together this history is complicated process to which many scholars have contributed. What I present here is by no means a comprehensive account, although I do attempt to fill in some of the gaps and advance the narrative into the near present. In any short overview, much will be left out and what is included reflects my own judgment about the personalities and events that have indelibly shaped the trajectory of the movement. The second chapter provides a more conceptual overview of Heathenry. In dialogue with other scholars and observers, I use the descriptive metaphor of a watershed to better understand the dynamics of the movement and make sense of its convolutions and diversities. Some critical observers have discovered an overriding consistency in Heathenry: consistently racist, consistently conservative, or consistently presenting an aggressive masculinity. What I found in my own journey through Heathenry was an important degree of diversity amidst those trends. From my perspective, any useful metaphor, any acceptable metacognitive framework for the movement must account for both the norms and the divergences from those norms. Framing the movement in this way risks abstraction, yet it is worthwhile in helping us to appreciate the movement's complexity and in serving as a descriptive as well as a potentially predictive device.

The following chapters explore more specific topics related to Heathenry. In chapter 3, I discuss the significant personality of Stephen McNallen, who is often identified as the founder of American Asatru. I address his theory of metagenetics, which frames Asatru as a religion rooted in race and ancestry. Tensions over racial attitudes have figured prominently in the movement, as adherents have struggled over how to think about their connection to Norse religion. Throughout it all, McNallen and metagenetics have been at the heart of the struggle. In fact, the tensions over racial attitudes have been so pronounced that the majority of previous scholarship on Heathenry, conducted during a period of national concern over right-wing terrorism, focused primarily on the influence of white supremacist ideology in the movement. Through the focus on McNallen, I attempt to discern the motivations and ideas that have given shape to the debate, the confluence of völkisch and contemporary Pagan ideologies that continue to foment acrimony within Heathenry.

This book attempts to develop a holistic assessment of Heathenry that examines many aspects of the movement. In that regard, it moves beyond the discussion of racial attitudes to engage more deeply with important elements of Heathen religious practice. chapter 4 begins this process, where I look more closely at the role of cosmological and anthropological ideas current in Heathenry. In particular, I seek to understand how the idea of struggle in Norse cosmology functions as an ideological resource in Heathenry in the construction of a dissenting vision of the human self. In contrast to the atomistic conceptions of individuality arising from the Enlightenment, Heathens are working on a more ecological understanding of the self, of an individual connected to sublime powers, the living past, ancestors, and other divine beings. This robust Heathen individuality is suited to a cosmological environment in which one must struggle to survive.

At the core of Heathen religious experience are the incredibly potent figures of the gods. Heathens interact with the gods in a variety of ways, although the movement has earned a reputation for its hard polytheism. Hard polytheism, the topic of chapter 5, is a religious approach that takes the gods to be real individual beings. Although the priapic god Frey illustrates one sense of hard polytheism, the term refers more appropriately to the substantive nature that pertains to the Heathen gods. Heathen hard polytheism is often contrasted with soft polytheism associated with Wicca and Witchcraft. These traditions approach the various divine beings as personifications of greater cosmic forces represented by but not constrained within specific personalities. As polytheistic new religions such as Heathenry emerge in societies once dominated by monotheism, it has become increasingly important to better understand the dynamics of polytheistic systems. In that context, I examine Heathenry as a developing polytheist culture.

In chapter 6, I focus on the core ritual practice of Heathenry, the blót.[111] The blót is a Norse sacrificial ritual directed toward venerating

---

111. Amanda Wolfe, "The Blót: A Heathen Ritual Practice," *Council of Societies for the Study of Religion Bulletin* 37, no. 3 (2008). See also *A Dictionary of Old Norse Prose*, s.v. "blót." The word blót refers to an offering, sacrifice, or worship.

divine beings. The chapter primarily focuses on the growing practice of live blót, the sacrifice of live animals to the gods. I am interested in how the development of animal sacrifice is working in the Heathen movement both ethically and sociologically. The Heathen approach to animal sacrifice has generated some reflection among Heathens concerning the ethics of eating. We will look at a Heathen development of a critique of the modern food industry, which loses sight of animal well-being and the sanctity of life in its rush to reduce animals to meat products. Sociologically, the live blót has the potential to give rise to urban/rural networks in Heathenry that might sustain a more ethical and ecological approach to eating and community.

Chapter 7 addresses the important dynamic of family in Asatru. This value has proven enormously important as a source of dissent and ideological development. While American Asatru initially idealized the image of the heroic warrior, the integrity and stability of family and community life has taken on greater importance. In the Heathen communities of the Midwest, for instance, the role of chieftain has developed beyond its warlike connotations to signify a community leader who guarantees the health of the social unit. Here, as in chapter 6, the interaction between ideology and ritual becomes important. We will examine how the sumbel, a socially oriented drinking ceremony derived from Norse culture, is interpreted as a religious solution to the issues of modern rootlessness and the breakdown of family life.[112]

The most well-known contemporary Pagan movements in the United States, Wicca and Witchcraft, have been predominantly magical religions. So in the minds of many Americans, magic is synonymous with Paganism. However, Asatru is one form of Paganism that breaks this mold and takes a more skeptical approach to magic. In chapter 8, I will examine how the interplay of its intellectual tributaries gives rise to the contested environment of magical practice within Asatru. Despite its contested nature, magic is a pervasive element of Heathenry that draws on a long magical tradition in Norse and Germanic culture. Magical roles

---

112. Sumbel is one common spelling of this word among American Heathens, but other spellings are frequently encountered. Sumbel, as well as the alternative English spelling "sumble," reflect the Old Norse word *sumbl*, which refers to a banquet. Another common spelling is "symbel," reflecting the Old English word, *symbel*. I have also seen "sumbal," which is derived from Old High German.

like the völva, and magical forms such as seið, have been utilized particularly by Asatru women to create an intensively female social space in the movement.

The natural world runs as an important theme through the experience of Heathens. While a few scholars have characterized Asatru as a nature religion, the details of that have yet to be discussed in any significant way. In chapter 9 I begin the process of more thoroughly examining the place of nature within Heathen religious thought and practice. While nature acts as an important mythic and symbolic resource for the movement, nature religion is a growing reality as Heathens incorporate animism, strands of Green religion, and sacred experiences of nature. I will also consider the potential for a bio-regional ecological ethic to emerge from within Heathen culture.

Several factors make this a fortuitous time to be learning about Asatru. By all indications, the movement seems to be gaining rather than losing momentum and is now transitioning from a small, nebulous, and fractious network into a more viable movement, or as Graham Harvey puts it, "growing numerically and in coherence."[113] At this point, the movement is able to support four national organizations that represent a spectrum of religious and ideological viewpoints.[114] There is real diversity within the movement that is expressed organizationally as well as in ritual and theology. In addition to a well-developed exoteric side based in textual study and ritual, Asatru also has a fully esoteric component and is thus situated to engage a variety of participants with different spiritual interests. There are also aspects of the religion, such as its emphasis on family, which seem to reflect a degree of continuity with the values of the broader American context. Thus in many ways the movement seems poised for further growth.

This project will attempt to take stock of the Asatru movement, assess various aspects of its development, and consider its prospects for the future. But most importantly, it is about people, their search for meaning, and for a place in the world. Back in the American heartland at the hilltop ritual, the goði, Magni, placed his hand over

---

113. Harvey, *Contemporary Paganism*, 53.

114. The four national Asatru organizations currently active in the United States are the Odinic Rite, the Ásatrú Alliance, the Asatru Folk Assembly, and the Troth. In additional there are many regional organizations and kindreds that make up the various levels of the Heathen community.

a bowl filled with mead and intoned the blessings of Odin. As he began walking around the circle of worshipers, people huddled together in groups of families, friends, and kindreds, removing their hats and moving smaller children to the front. Magni greeted each cluster of people and stood in front of them. He dipped a leafy branch in the bowl and flicked the contents over them, drops of holy mead falling on faces and raised hands. "May the blessings of the Gods be with you," he said. People smiled and nodded or hugged each other. Kids flinched and laughed as the cold drops landed their faces. I stood there watching as he continued around the circle and groups began drifting off into the dark night. Under that starry sky were people seeking to stand in a sacred cosmos of meaning and purpose, to live in community with the company of gods and kindred, to learn a way of life in which personal wholeness and significance could be realized, and to build a lasting religious legacy. "So this is Asatru," I thought. Whatever else it might entail, being Viking means looking for blessing in a complex world.

# Chapter 1

## A Brief History of American Asatru

The dark waters of the Rhine River flow through Asatru imaginations with an almost legendary mystique as a symbol of Heathen strength, the bulwark upon which the seemingly invincible expansion of the Roman Empire ground to a halt. Pushing inexorably northward eight hundred miles from the Alps to the North Sea, the Rhine effectively divided the Romans on its southwest from the Heathen tribes who inhabited the forests of Germania to its northeast, a border marked by blood as much as by water. Although the armies of Caesar Augustus had pushed across the Rhine as far east as the river Elbe, the Battle of the Teutoburg Forest in 9 CE altered the balance of power and delivered a devastating blow to Roman morale. The Cherusci, a Germanic tribe led by the chieftain known as Arminius or Hermann, together with an alliance of other tribes ambushed and annihilated three Roman legions led by the unfortunate Roman general Varus.[115] Tacitus, the first-century CE Roman historian, remembers Teutoburg Forest as the culmination of successive waves of Roman military might that broke upon the Rhine, "the Germans routed or captured Carbo, Cassius, Aurelius

---

115. Arminius, the leader of the victorious alliance, was identified in this way by Tacitus in his Annals. See Cornelius Tacitus, *The Annals: The Reigns of Tiberius, Claudius, and Nero*, trans. and eds. John Yardley and Anthony Barrett (Oxford: Oxford University Press, 2008). Tacitus' graphic description of the aftermath of the Battle of Teutoburg, as witnessed by the forces of the Roman general Germanicus in 15 CE can be found in Taciticus, *The Annals*, I. 60–61. The translators of the Oxford edition give Martin Luther credit for renaming Tactitus' Arminius with the Germanic Hermann, both names meaning "army man," an important part of the process through which Hermann became recognized and celebrated as a German hero. See Tacitus, *The Annals*, xxviii. Similarly, Herbert W. Benario suggests that Luther's commentary on Psalm 82 may have been the source of the linguistic transformation of Arminius to Hermann, "It was Martin Luther himself who may have been the first to equate the name Arminius with the German Hermann, thereby expanding his popular appeal." See Herbert W. Benario, "Arminius into Hermann: History into Legend," *Greece & Rome* 51, no. 1 (2004), 87.

Scaurus, Servilius Caepio, and Mallius Maximus, and robbed the Republic, almost at one stroke, of five consular armies. Even from Augustus they took Varus and his three legions."[116] With such a statement, Tacitus contributed to the elevation of Hermann as a symbol of German, and Heathen, strength that withstood the seemingly invincible Roman military machine.

The story is recounted among contemporary Heathens with panache and passion, taking on important elements of folkloric truth.[117] Within the heroic image of Hermann and the devastating defeat delivered to the Roman forces, Heathens sense and celebrate their own movement as a dissenting and oppositional force in contemporary culture. At a Heathen gathering in Minnesota, the legendary account of Hermann was the subject of an afternoon workshop. As Snook recalls the event, it was part historical lecture and part pep rally. "Hermann the German" continued to be hailed throughout the weekend.[118] In actuality Varus' defeat in the Teutoburg Forest precipitated the retaliatory campaigns of the Roman consul Germanicus. During the years 14–16 CE, Germanicus and his eight legions crossed the Rhine several times, inflicting serious defeats on several tribes and even capturing Thusnelda, the pregnant wife of Arminius, and parading her in triumph in Rome. As a result, Germanicus became a well-loved Roman hero.[119] While it is not the case that the defeat of Varus eliminated the Roman

---

116. Tacitus, *The Agricola and the Germania*, trans. H. Mattingly and S. A. Handford (New York: Penguin Books, 1970), 132.

117. Matthias Egeler, "A Retrospective Methodology for Using Landnámabók as a Source for the Religious History of Iceland? Some Questions," *The Retrospective Methods Network Newsletter* 10 (Summer 2015): 79–80. Folkloric truth reflects the contemporary understandings of those recounting a historical event, a telling from a perspective currently held to be true by the redactor. I use the term to indicate that the Heathen telling of the Teutoburg Forest battle makes use of the event to indicate not only the strength of the ancient Germanic tribes, but as a way of reflecting upon the contemporary Heathen sense of opposition to contemporary culture. It serves a rhetorical function of calling Heathens to this sort of high-tension stance.

118. Jennifer Snook, *American Heathens*, 48–49. Snook recounts how the story of Hermann was told with passion and panache at the event. I missed the workshop in which the story of Hermann's victory in the Teutoburg forest was told because I arrived at the event the next morning. However, in my field notes, I record the repeated references to "Hermann the German" during the rest of the weekend. This set of circumstances brought home for me the complexities of fieldwork and how timing affects our perception events.

119. William Smith, *The History of Rome: From Earliest Times to the Establishment of the Empire* (Luton: Andrews UK, 2010), 450.

threat to the north, it is significant that despite over two hundred years of military pressure, Rome failed to colonize Germania and never managed to cross the Rhine with any permanent settlement. The German success at Teutoburg did contribute considerably to a state of affairs that ultimately afforded the Heathenry of Northern Europe another thousand years of life.

The boundary marked by the Rhine was more than political and military; it was also cultural and religious. As Christianity gradually spread through the Roman Empire, the Germanic tribes behind the Rhine retained their polytheism. Christianity came to the tribes only as the Roman Empire crumbled and the Germanic tribes spilled over the Rhine and Danube rivers during the Migration Age.[120] Even then, as the Germanic invaders established new kingdoms and gradually adopted Christianity, the tribes who remained north of the Rhine resisted that transformation. Charlemagne's brutal campaigns among the Saxons eventually completed the Christian conversion of the continental Heathens of northwest Europe. Not until the 780s CE, after years of war, massacres, and forced deportations, was Charlemagne able to impose his law code, the *De Partibus Saxoniae*, upon the Saxons that mandated the death penalty for those who persisted in their rejection of the Christian faith.[121] Still, many northmen of Scandinavia, bulwarked beyond Charlemagne's reach by the Dannevirke and the North Sea, held onto a fierce Pagan religiosity during much of the Viking Age, for another two hundred years.

Still, the world was changing and the pressure to Christianize, with the political and economic advantages it afforded, proved unavoidable. With the conversion of Iceland in 1000 CE, the pre-Christian Pagan religions of these northern Germanic areas ceased to be overtly practiced.[122] The Heathen age had come to an end.

---

120. The Migration Age, approximately 300 to 600 CE, involved large-scale population changes in Europe. While much of the migration occurred outside of the Roman Empire, the Germanic tribes also took advantage of the Empire's weakening boundaries to leave their traditional homelands. These tribes reshaped the population and political boundaries of Europe by migrating throughout Western Europe, repeatedly sacking Rome and establishing the kingdoms that would characterize post-Roman Europe.

121. Robert Ferguson, *The Vikings: A History* (New York: Penguin Books, 2009), 50–51.

122. The tribes in the western Baltic, the last remaining remnant of native European Paganism, retained their religion for several centuries after the conversion of the Norse. From the thirteenth to the fifteenth centuries CE, continual pressure and

Few practitioners of contemporary Heathenry seriously contend otherwise. Asatru reconstructionists employ other strategies to legitimize contemporary Asatru in light of this thousand-year cessation of northern European Paganism. However, it is worth noting that no serious or broadly supported revision of history emerged within Asatru arguing for the continuity of Heathen practice from the Viking Age to the contemporary period. This broad acknowledgment that the religious culture of the ancient Norse polytheists or "arch-Heathens" passed out of practice distinguishes the Asatru approach to its origins from that of the early contemporary Pagan movement. As Ronald Hutton documents in his work *The Triumph of the Moon*, the beginnings of the Wicca in England and America were marked by intellectual efforts to interpret and frame the new religion as the authentic survival of old Pagan Europe, an ancient religious and magical practice that had existed into the modern age.[123] Margaret Murray, an Egyptologist by training, became convinced of these ideas and wrote important books such as, *The Witchcult in Western Europe* and *The God of the Witches*, which gave scholarly support for existence of the "Old Religion."[124] According to her claims, an ancient Pagan fertility religion venerating a Pan-like horned God had been ubiquitously practiced in pre-Christian Europe.[125] Others suggested that the old religions of Europe were primarily oriented toward the divine feminine. Particularly influential was Robert Graves, whose wide-ranging work on mythology, *The White Goddess*, traces appearances of the Goddess from the poetry of the Greeks to that of William Shakespeare.[126] Graves identifies her as the Triple Goddess, who

warfare by crusader forces resulted in the subjugation and conversion of these Baltic peoples. The Duchy of Lithuania was the last to convert officially in 1387, although western Lithuania successfully resisted Christianization until the early 1400s.

123. Ronald Hutton, *The Triumph of the Moon: A History of Modern Pagan Witchcraft* (Oxford: Oxford University Press, 1999), 194–99, 206. See also Chas Clifton, *Her Hidden Children: The Rise of Wicca and Paganism in America* (Lanham, MD: AltaMira Press, 2006), 74–75.

124. Margaret Alice Murray, *The Witch-Cult in Western Europe: A Study in Anthropology* (New York: Barnes & Noble Books, 1996 [1921]); Margaret Alice Murray, *The God of the Witches* (London: Oxford University Press, 1970 [1931]).

125. Hutton, *The Triumph of the Moon*, 194–201.

126. Robert Graves, *The White Goddess: A Historical Grammar of Poetic Myth* (New York: Faffar, Straus, & Giroux, 1978). Originally published in 1948, the book went through several subsequent editions in the 1970s, no doubt due to its role in stimulating the development of Wicca and Goddess religion.

appears ubiquitously in the mythological stories of the ancient world often accompanied by a male figure whether her son or lover, and linked to the sky, earth, and underworld:

> As Goddess of the Underwold she was concerned with Birth, Procreation and Death. As Goddess of the Earth she was concerned with the three seasons of Spring, Summer, and Winter: she animated trees and plants and ruled all living creatures. As Goddess of the Sky she was the Moon, in her three phases of New Moon, Full Moon, and Waning Moon.[127]

These natural phases are in turn connected to or more aptly embodied in the female lifecycle: the girl, the woman, and the crone, the life stage of mature feminine insight and wisdom.[128] Already in Graves, we find many of the themes and images coming together that will be so influential in the development of contemporary Pagan thought and experience, not only in the emerging identity of the Goddess but also in the meme of a primal Goddess religion. Others, researchers as well as Pagan practitioners, have put forward the idea of an ancient, matriarchal or matrilineal, Goddess-revering culture. Merlin Stone finds tantalizing signs of this culture preserved in the law codes of the Ancient Near East, and observes in the lines of the Hebrew scriptures the suppression of Middle Eastern Goddess religion.[129] She calls out the Hebrew prophet Isaiah for waging his own cultural war against the primal Goddess religion, heaping "derisive accusations" on the Goddess, identified as Ishtar, and deprecating "Her self-assurance and Her sexuality, as well as Her magical powers and spells."[130] The prophet, she writes, "looked forward to the day of male glory, when all independent women would choose to be the property of a man." Maria Gimbutas' illustrative and groundbreaking books unearth evidence for Goddess religion in the archaeological finds of Paleo- and Neolithic Europe. Her *Language of the Goddess* is a heavy coffee-table-sized tome filled with encyclopedic pictorial evidence that symbols of the divine feminine

---

127. Ibid., 386.
128. Harvey, *Contemporary Paganism*, 38–39.
129. Merlin Stone, *When God Was a Woman* (San Diego: Harcourt Brace, 1978). See chapter 3, "Women—Where Woman Was Deified," for her discussion of remnants of matrilineal, matriarchal, and Goddess worship in the law codes of the Ancient Near East.
130. Ibid., 186.

abounded in the iconography of ancient European societies.[131] Similarly, Max Dashu, whose presentation on the iconography of female shamans I attended at Pantheacon in 2011, has compiled thousands of images in her Suppressed Histories Archives and argues extensively for recognition of the magico-religious agency of women in ancient societies.[132] These and other works expand on the motif of the suppression of ancient Goddess religion and matricentric cultures. They describe how migration by war-like Indo-European societies and later by the ascendancy of Abrahamic religions oppressed indigenous Goddess-worshiping cultures. The motif also figures prominently in significant works of fiction, such as *The Mists of Avalon*, a novel by Marion Zimmer Bradley.[133] Based on the Arthurian legends, Bradley's story involves a developing tension between the Goddess religion of the Druids and priestesses of Avalon and the growing power of Christianity. The book has enjoyed a formative influence among contemporary Pagans. Other work develops this thesis in regard to the witch-hunts in Europe during the fifteenth through the seventeenth centuries CE, known as the Burning Times by many contemporary Pagans. The religious persecution of women and other traditional healers, it is suggested, stamped out the remaining influence of those who had continued to practice the old ways. Like Hermann the German for Heathens, the idea of the Burning Times has taken on an element of a folkloric truth suggesting that the Witchcraft of ancient Europe was driven underground, hidden but not forgotten.[134] According to

---

131. Marija Gimbutas, *The Language of the Goddess: Unearthing the Hidden Symbols of Western Civilization* (San Francisco: Harper & Row, 1989).

132. Max Daschu, *Suppressed Histories Archives*, www.suppressedhistories.net/.

133. Marion Zimmer Bradley, *The Mists of Avalon* (New York: Random House, 1982).

134. Anne Llewellyn Barstow, *Witchcraze: A New History of the European Witch Hunts* (San Francisco: Pandora, 1994). The Burning Times, so-called by contemporary Pagans, refers to the period of Witchcraft trials and executions in Europe and America during the fifteenth through the eighteenth centuries. Although only a part of a much wider phenomenon, the most well-known example for Americans is the Salem witch trial, part of the New England witch-hunts in the late 1600s. Rather than being taken as literal history, the Burning Times motif has primarily taken on metaphoric value for Wiccans and practitioners of the Craft. For more discussion of the use of the Burning Times motif, see Laurel Zwissler, "In Memorium Maleficarum: Feminist and Pagan Mobilizations of the Burning Times," in *Emotions in the History of Witchcraft*, eds. Laura Kounine and Michael Ostling (London: Palgrave, 2017), 249–68.

this reading of history, they continued to be practiced under the veneer of Christianity, carried on secretly by clandestine covens and family traditions passed on through the folk practices of Europe, in kitchens and on farmsteads. This ancient religious tradition resurfaced, in the modern period, as contemporary Wicca. Following the example of Gerald Gardner, early covens found a type of social legitimacy in claiming an unbroken connection of heritage and practice back to pre-Christian Europe.[135] Chas S. Clifton points out that, for a time, claims of continuity with the Old Religion were important for the revival of modern Witchcraft whose adherents "positioned themselves as heirs of—and often as directly connected to—ancient Pagan coreligionists."[136] Yet this approach was never seriously pursued by Heathen adherents. Instead, the beginnings of contemporary Heathenry are marked as a new start, a new birth, for a religion that had effectively died out under relentless suppression by the religious and political power wielded by European Christendom. The contemporary Heathen movement is acknowledged as a revival, or more accurately, a reconstruction of a religion that had ceased to be practiced for close to a thousand years.

## The New Awakening

Despite the abandonment of Heathen practice in the early second millennium CE, contemporary Heathen movements can now be found throughout the world in the United Kingdom, Scandinavia, continental Europe, even Australia and South America, but most significantly in Iceland where Ásatrú is recognized as a state religion. These new religious populations, which may be geographically and culturally linked to ancient Pagan practice, often lay claim to it as an ethnic religion. However, a significant part of this contemporary growth has occurred in the United States, which seems both culturally and geographically distant from the old gods Odin, Thor, and Frey. How did it happen? How did a religious practice seemingly lost beyond the gulf of a thousand years and a continent away, only vaguely described in the small corpus of Old Norse and Icelandic

---

135. Hutton, *Triumph of the Moon*, 342, 348. The discourse of Wicca as an ancient religion of woman was also taken up by American Pagans such as Starhawk and others in the 1970s and 1980s.

136. Clifton, *Her Hidden Children*, 49.

texts, come to inspire a growing contemporary American religious movement? In many ways, American Asatru is a result of the globalization of religion as ideas, symbols, and practices originating in Europe gradually spread abroad. The work of nineteenth-century German folklorists such as the brothers Grimm, the outright revival of Germanic polytheist spirituality in the work of German völkisch activists of the early twentieth century, and the integration of Norse and Germanic content in the work of scholars such as Dumezil and Jung made their way into the American context and became seeds for the incipient Asatru movement. As well, American adherents look to a European past for their religious inspiration and maintain an enthusiastic awareness of the movement's transcontinental presence. Americans are curious about the practices of Heathens elsewhere and have had long-running interests in international connections. However it seems that many contemporary American Asatruar, like many Americans, are more enamored with the idealized past of Europe than with looking to contemporary Europe for direction and leadership. American Asatru has, to a large degree, appropriated a European past and made use of it on its own terms. As far as I am aware, only the Odinic Rite maintains an intentionally international leadership at the highest levels of the organization, the Court of the Gothar. The Rune-Gild, an esoteric initiatory society devoted to rune lore, has had an international membership and focus from its beginning in 1980. Founded by Stephen Flowers, better known by his Heathen name Edred Thorsson, the Rune-Gild's impact has mainly been among a select set of individuals and Heathen leaders. Stefanie von Schnurbein observes that the exchange of ideas among an international network of Heathens most often occurs at an individual level. She writes that "day-to-day, Asatru groups are primarily involved in their own affairs; most contacts and controversies between groups remain limited to their respective national context."[137] Efforts to build substantial contemporary ties among American and European co-religionists are ongoing. However, working across these contexts with their differences in language, culture, and history has resulted at times in misfires

---

137. Stefanie von Schnurbein, *Norse Revival: Transformations of Germanic Neopaganism* (Leiden: Brill, 2016), 77. See Schnurbein's discussion in chapter 2 for more on international Heathen crosscurrents.

and misunderstandings that hamper cooperative engagement.[138] Much of American Heathenry has developed with limited influence and cross-pollination from outside the United States, particularly shaped by its own events and personalities.[139]

The origin of contemporary Asatru is often referred to as the New Awakening or Rebirth by those within the movement and has taken on something of a mythic quality. In the early 1970s, almost simultaneously and without knowledge of each other, individuals throughout North America and Europe were drawn to the Norse religious heritage and began to pursue it as a viable religious practice. Among these individuals were Stephen McNallen who formed the Viking Brotherhood in 1972 in the United States, Sveinbjörn Beinteinsson who formed the Ásatrúarfélagið in Iceland also in 1972, and John Yeowell who formed the Committee for the Restoration of the Odinic Rite (now the Odinic Rite) in Britain in 1973. As well, Garman Lord developed a movement called Theodism, a reconstruction of Anglo-Saxon Paganism, in 1971.[140] Theodism is often considered a distinct movement because of its strict hierarchical structure and its emphasis on ritual polarity of the sexes, derived from its Wiccan origins. However, the practice fits within the broader Heathen movement, however uncomfortably, and Theodish writers, who tend to be reconstructionist in their

---

138. For example, see "The Icelandic Pagan Association Receives Hate-mail from Reactionary Pagans Abroad," *Iceland Magazine*, July 14, 2015, http://icelandmag.visir.is/article/icelandic-pagan-association-receives-hate-mail-reactionary-pagans-abroad. In the wake of its announcement regarding plans to build a Heathen temple, the *Ásatrúarfélagið* received hostile comments from Heathens outside of Iceland regarding its support for same-sex marriage. These comments originated from a few extreme voices. See Karl E. H. Seigfried, "Heathenry in Iceland, America and Germany: The mainstream and the fringe," *Iceland Magazine*, August 14, 2015, http://icelandmag.visir.is/article/heathenry-iceland-america-and-germany-mainstream-and-fringe. However, the event provoked tensions among Heathen groups and demonstrates the difficulties of sustained cooperation.

139. See the following sources for early history of the American Asatru movement: Jeffrey Kaplan, *Radical Religion in America: Millenarian Movements from the Far Right to the Children of Noah* (Syracuse, NY: Syracuse University Press, 1997); Mattias Gardell, *Gods of the Blood: The Pagan Revival and White Separatism* (Durham, NC: Duke University Press, 2003); Adler, *Drawing Down the Moon*; and Gundarsson, *History and Lore*, Vol. 1 of *Our Troth*.

140. A series of articles on the history of Theodism, written by Garman Lord and published in *Theod* magazine in the mid-1990s, are available online. See Garman Lord, "Theodish History Online," *Gerod Theod: The Official Website of Theodish Belief*, http://gamall-steinn.org/Gering/.

approach, have been quite influential as a source of scholarship for the Heathen movement.

From the perspective of many Asatru adherents, this remarkable and sudden religious awakening is clear evidence of divine activity. In their eyes, the old gods have stirred, becoming active again after their long dormancy and are calling their people back to the old ways. Amid the slow decay of Western Christendom, cracks have opened in the social, intellectual, moral, and religious framework of modernity, openings through which the old gods have reemerged. These early converts or creators of this new faith often experienced powerful theophanic events, in which the gods, often Odin himself, forged new bonds between themselves and their chosen human kin. For these early adherents, the religious entrepreneurs of Asatru, the Norse heritage, history, customs, and stories suddenly and powerfully took on more than historical and cultural significance. They awakened to a new lifeway, a paradigm that could transform life, a road map for the creation of a new culture. The Christian age was over. The time had come for the old gods to reassert themselves among their human kin in the reconstruction of an ancient religio-cultural community.

Whatever one makes of these early Heathen experiences, the emergence of contemporary Asatru shares many features with other new religions. With even a cursory look at the history of new religions in America, of which Heathenry is one, it becomes stunningly clear that new religions are nothing new. For numerous reasons, America has been and continues to be a fertile context for the prolific development of new religious movements, a context in which religious innovation occurs continually and with intensity. American history, from its colonial beginnings to the contemporary period of the twenty-first century, is filled with the stories of minority religious movements: Brownists (better known as the Pilgrims), Shakers, Latter-Day Saints (Mormons), Scientologists, the International Society for Krishna Consciousness (Hare Krishnas), Branch Davidians, and Wiccans to mention just a few of the better known. One scholar writes that new and alternative religious movements are "so commonplace in American history that it is difficult to speak of them as fringe at all."[141] While it can be meaningfully argued that several distinct periods of American

---

141. Jenkins, *Mystics and Messiahs*, 5.

history have yielded a notable degree of religious creativity and florescence, it is also the case that the formation of new religious movements has been a rather continuous process. While tension, and even violent conflict, between state, society, and alternative religions is not uncommon in the United States, religious innovators continue to find space within the religious milieu to construct new forms of religious practice. As a new American religion that began to formally organize in the mid-1970s, Heathenry benefited from this American context in which a fairly wide degree of latitude and tolerance was available for starting religions, building religious organizations, publishing and disseminating religious material, and organizing religious gatherings.

In addition to the fertile American religious context, a second notable feature is the turbulent life cycles that characterize new religions, which frequently experience periods of difficulty, struggle, and conflict during their birth, development, and often their decline. These difficulties take many forms: external pressure, internal tension, and personal misbehavior being a few. Because of their generally small size and marginality, new religions often lack the resources or the will to absorb or resolve tensions in ways that seem acceptable to the mainstream. As Catherine Wessinger and others have shown, the pressure placed upon marginal religions by their external critics, particularly official law enforcement groups operating within a perceived role as guardians of mainstream values, have in several notable examples escalated tensions in dangerous and unmanageable ways.[142] Additionally, non-state entities may organize forms of reaction and resistance to new religions, such as private groups in the United States that came to be known as the anti-cult movement. New religious movements have also faced various unorganized expressions of opposition, waves of popular fear regarding the public welfare and the protection of social and religious orthodoxy. Internal tensions have also marked the history of new religions, including theological shifts, political rivalries among leaders, and changing demographics that grow or shrink movements set off periods of change. Another source that often receives significant public attention includes personal problems and misbehavior on the part of leaders and members. All introduce

---

142. Catherine Wessinger, *How the Millennium Comes Violently: From Jonestown to Heaven's Gate* (New York: Seven Bridges Press, 2000).

change into the life cycles of new religions that may hasten the decline and disintegration of a movement, or result in its reform, realignment, or schism. Heathenry is no stranger to these sorts of pressures, tensions, and controversies. As might be expected, the common difficulties experienced by new religions have taken a particular shape due to the cultural context of American Heathenry. Conflicts with external critics have been an episodic source of tension, particularly with authorities such as the Federal Bureau of Investigation and the Bureau of Alcohol, Tobacco, and Firearms. Heathens have seen leaders caught up in scandal, turf wars between Heathen groups, conflicts over identity, a ubiquitous and perennial lack of resources, and occasional incidents of suspicion and antipathy from the mainstream public. Many of these are documented in the work of earlier observers of Heathenry, such as Jeffrey Kaplan and Mattias Gardell.[143]

While for the most part Heathenry has avoided sexual scandal, its bête noire has been a persistent association with racism and violence. In the 1980s and 1990s, public concerns began to grow about domestic terrorism originating from armed groups of radical-right white supremacists. Incidents such as the 1992 gunfight between US marshals and the Weaver family at Ruby Ridge, Idaho; the 1993 federal siege of the Branch Davidian property in Waco, Texas; and Timothy McVeigh's 1995 bombing of the Oklahoma City federal courthouse fueled these rising fears. At the same time, these events heightened suspicions of the federal government among many on the Right—conservatives, libertarians, preppers, militia movements, and white nationalists—who would come to be called the alt-right. In this political climate, Asatru became a target of suspicion and increased surveillance, drawing the attention of federal authorities and watchdog groups like the Southern Poverty Law Center. The violent racist rhetoric that emanated from some Heathen groups, ties to white supremacist organizations, and prison-related racial violence perpetrated by Heathen inmates cast a shadow over the entire movement. These fears regarding Asatru's racist ideology resulted in the first wave of scholarship that

---

143. Jeffrey Kaplan, "The Reconstruction of the Ásatrú and Odinist traditions," in *Magical Religion and Modern Witchcraft*, ed. James R. Lewis (Albany: State University of New York Press, 1996), 220–22; Gardell, *Gods of the Blood*, 193–99. Kaplan has a detailed discussion of problems within the Ring of Troth, while Gardell looks at the Brüder Schweigen, also known as The Order.

explored racial attitudes within the movement. As a result of these seasons of controversy, the prominence and existence of specific groups and personalities have both risen and declined within the larger Heathen movement, an aspect to which we will soon turn in our discussion of the Heathen cultic milieu.

A third feature is that many new religions function as communities of dissent. These movements serve as social spaces in which alternative ideas and practices are pursued, contexts in which individuals who dissent from mainstream religious beliefs and lifestyles find a place for themselves. These dissenting religions challenge the dominant ideas and practices within a society, bring to light tensions and inconsistencies that are ignored by the social and religious mainstream, and propose different visions for what constitutes wholeness. New religious movements often reflect tensions within their host or majority societies, the dominant social orthodoxy, and develop alternative solutions to religious, social, and personal problems such as the anti-slavery activism of the Christian abolitionists, alternative theologies, and structures of family in movements like the early Church of the Latter-Day Saints, or expanded accessibility of religious expression and leadership for women in the contemporary Pagan movement. Because of their contentious stance, religious dissenters have often been misunderstood, stereotyped, and persecuted by mainstream society. Heathenry also serves as a context in which social tensions and majority opinions are questioned and challenged. For instance, Heathens like other contemporary Pagans are profoundly at odds with the general American acceptance of monotheism as the dominant and culturally approved form of religious belief. As we will discuss in later chapters, new modes of social organization, new concepts of human nature, use of magical arts as new modes of being, and new experiences of nature are all part of the dissenting tendency of American Heathenry. Given the intensely and emotively held positions regarding religion, this sort of dissent often places practitioners of alternative religions in socially marginalized positions, facing the ire of society. Yet we should remember that religious dissenters and minority religions are robustly exercising the constitutionally protected freedoms of Americans citizens and have often been at the center of efforts to protect and expand those freedoms in ways that have benefited all Americans. From this perspective, the story of new religions in America, including

Heathenry, is one of "bold men and women who affirmed their deepest religious values, often in the face of physical hardship and overt hostility."[144] If it had not been for religious dissenters, the scope of religious freedom might well have been curtailed in America.

In these general ways, Heathenry is not unique but is situated within a long history of new religious movements in America, comprised of many different groups with varying lifespans and levels of influence. We might think about this history of new American religions as a sort of variety show, a stage performance in which a dizzying diversity of acts appear in succession. In this show, a series of actors, scenes, and performances come and go on stage, seemingly unrelated but originating from and supported by a "backstage." The backstage of a variety show theatre is a seemingly chaotic riot of color and energy, a creative collection of actors, skills, scripts, costumes, from which the acts themselves are built, a history of bits and pieces, props and personalities, stagecraft and styles that inform and shape the acts that appear on stage. A similar apparatus is at work in the history of new religious movements. While alternative religious groups may appear on this "stage" of American history, emerging into and then disappearing from the spotlight, they are supported by a "backstage," a creative repository of beliefs and practices, stigmatized knowledge, methods and ritual forms upon which various groups, movements, and individuals draw.[145] It is examining this "backstage" that serves as our larger issue in looking at the history of the Heathen movement: we want to examine the forces or tributaries that flow into and make up the Heathen milieu.

---

144. Stein, *Communities of Dissent*, xii.
145. Michael Barkun, "Conspiracy Theories as Stigmatized Knowledge: The Basis for a New Age Racism?" in *Nation and Race: The Developing Euro-American Racist Subculture*, eds. Jeffrey Kaplan and Tore Bjørgo (Boston: Northeastern University Press, 1998), 61–62. Barkun develops Colin Campbell's term "rejected knowledge" into the broader category of "stigmatized knowledge." Stigmatized knowledge involves "claims to truth that the claimants regard as empirically verified despite the marginalization of those claims by the institutions that conventionally distinguish between knowledge and falsehood—universities, communities of scientific researchers, and the like." He identifies five types of stigmatized knowledge, one of which is "rejected knowledge" defined as "knowledge claims that are specifically rejected as false from the outset." Other types of stigmatized knowledge include forgotten, superseded, ignored, and suppressed knowledge.

## Precursors to the New Awakening

The idea of the New Awakening remains a pervasive meme in Heathenry. Hilmar Örn Hilmarsson, the current *allsherjargoði* of the *Ásatrúarfélagið* in Iceland, shares in the notion that the contemporary movement represents a re-awakening of the ancient divine powers from a long period of cultural dormancy. He notes that after centuries of repression by the rationalism and technicalism of modernity, the gods are returning: "The gods had to come back ... We had some years of rationalism — the Industrial Revolution, people losing their ties with nature and repressing religion and focusing on science and knowledge ... In an atmosphere like this, the gods need to come back, because they've been repressing them so long."[146] Yet there is more to the story than this, for the Norse gods and the mystique of the North had never really disappeared from history. Centuries of ongoing tradition have served as inspiration for the contemporary movement.

Foundational to the development of contemporary Heathenry are the Old Norse and Old Icelandic texts written in the early second millennium and often referred to within the movement as the Lore. These old texts serve as the primary sources for the movement, representing the closest link to the actual living Heathen societies of Northern Europe. One of the oldest and most well known is Snorri Sturluson's compilation of Norse myth, known as the *Prose Edda*.[147] Sturluson, a historian and politician in thirteenth-century Iceland who served twice as the Lawspeaker for the nation prior to its annexation by Norway, was concerned for the loss of his national poetic tradition. He collected, edited, and synthesized Norse myth, creating what was at the time the only surviving record of the Norse gods and mythological stories. Sturluson was also the author of the *Heimskringla*, a history of the kings of Norway, another respected source in contemporary Heathenry. It was evident that Sturluson must have relied on some sources to compile his *Prose Edda*. This was confirmed in the mid-1600s, when an Icelandic bishop acquired

---

146. Karl E. H. Seigfried, "Interview with Hilmar Örn Hilmarsson of the Ásatrúarfélagið, Part Three," The Norse Mythology Blog, July 12, 2011, www.norsemyth.org/2011/07/interview-with-hilmar-orn-hilmarsson-of.html.

147. Snorri Sturluson, *The Prose Edda: Norse Mythology*, trans. Jesse L. Byock (London: Penguin, 2005).

a manuscript, now known as the *Codex Regius*, containing twenty-nine Old Norse poems of a mythological nature. These works including the *Völuspá*, meaning the vision of the *völva*, in which a seeress describes to Odin the creation of the cosmos and its eventual destruction in the battle of Ragnarok, and the *Hávamál*, a collection of Norse wisdom aphorisms. Delivered to the king of Denmark in 1662, the manuscript remained housed in the Danish Royal Library until it was returned to Iceland in the 1970s as a national treasure. Written in the thirteenth century, the vellum pages of the *Poetic Edda* contain the oldest collection of Old Norse sacred poetry, some of which is directly quoted within the *Prose Edda*, and the most direct link to the Pagan past. Here at last was one of Sturluson's sources. Another important Old Norse source are the sagas, written from the twelfth through the fifteenth centuries, comprising a literary genre with a variety of content including stories of legendary heroes, known as *fornaldarsögur*; the histories of Icelandic families, known as *Íslendingasögur* or sagas of the Icelanders; and accounts of the Norse kings, the *konungasögur*.

The discovery of Tacitus' *Germania* in the 1420s also represents an important event in the creation of Heathen Lore. Tacitus was a Roman official and perhaps the greatest Roman historian, whose works include the *Germania*, written at the close of the first century CE, the *Histories*, and the *Annals*, which document the first one hundred years of the Roman Empire. A manuscript containing his *Germania* was discovered in a German monastery in the 1420s CE, brought to Rome in 1455, and first published in 1470. The work is an ancient ethnography in which Tacitus describes the people and cultures of Germania by drawing on the considerable first-hand interaction of the Romans with the Germanic tribes. The *Germania* remains the oldest written account of the Germanic tribes in their Pagan context and for that reason it is treasured by contemporary Heathens as a window into the living religion and culture of the ancestors, often called "arch" or "elder" Heathens within the movement. Heathens refer as well to Saxo Grammaticus' *History of the Danes*, written in the thirteenth century, as a source grounded in history. While colored by the perspectives of their authors, as all histories are, these texts remain important sources of authentic insights into pre-Christian Northern Europe. Various other sources are also of considerable importance, not least of which is *Beowulf*, an epic poem in Old English preserved from at least the eleventh century. Three poems known as the Old English, Icelandic, and Norwegian rune poems also constitute important sources for the interpretation of runes and their magical uses by contemporary Heathens.[148]

## *The Lore: A Brief Interpolation*

These sources make up many of the important texts referred to as Lore. The term "Lore" has become a ubiquitous reference within Heathenry, used as shorthand to designate the core texts of Heathenry, and seems to have entered the movement's vocabulary by the early to mid-1980s. When asked about the origins of the term, even long-time practitioners cannot pinpoint a time when it came into use and seem to simply have inherited the term.[149] Related to the German *Lehre* meaning teaching or doctrine, the term indicates the special, somewhat canonical, status attributed to these texts within the movement. Heathens often describe their faith as a "religion with homework," referring to the heavy emphasis on reading and studying the body of material known as the Lore. Lore is a somewhat loose category, making it difficult to adequately list all the texts that might be regarded with this sort of status. "When one of us speaks of 'lore,'" writes Galina Krasskova, "we're referring to written texts. That includes the Prose and Poetic Eddas, the Icelandic Sagas, Old English texts, and contemporary historical, archaeological, linguistic, as well as any other relevant scholarly work."[150] While Krasskova's perspective may diverge at times from that of many Asatruar, she is a thoughtful participant and scholar and her statement communicates a concise and accurate view of the Lore's extent.

At its most essential level, the Lore involves a core group of sources considered primary texts, most importantly the *Poetic Edda* and the *Prose Edda*, but also including the sagas and a number of other

---

148. R. I. Page, "The Icelandic Rune-Poem," *Viking Society for Northern Research* (University College of London, 1999), http://vsnrweb-publications.org.uk/The%20 Icelandic%20Rune-Poem.pdf. The three extant rune poems consist of stanzas describing runes and their magical effects. These include an Old English poem preserved in a tenth-century manuscript now destroyed by fire, an Icelandic rune poem preserved in two manuscripts from the sixteenth century, and an Old Norse rune poem.

149. Field notes taken by author. I asked a several long-term practitioners well known for their scholarship about the origins of the term "Lore." All of them suggested that the term pre-dated their involvement in the movement.

150. Galina Krasskova, "Lectio Divina Heathen Style," *Wyrd Ways* blog, February 15, 2015, http://polytheist.com/wyrd-ways/2015/02/15/lectio-divina-heathen-style/.

historical texts. There are quite a few sagas, which range in popularity from the very familiar and oft quoted to the lesser-known and later sagas given less authority in the movement. Important ones include *Völsunga Saga* whose story of the Volsungs, particularly the hero Sigurd, was known throughout the pre-Christian North. The story is well attested, appearing in numerous pictorial references on ancient standing stones, in poems of the *Poetic Edda*, the *Prose Edda*, and in the Middle High German epic *Nibelungenlied* that Wagner used for the basis of his Ring Cycle. Other significant sagas include *Egil's Saga* with its well-known references to runic magic, *Eyrbyggja's Saga* with its interest in religious aspects of the Norse tradition such as an early settler of Iceland who threw his high seat pillars into the sea and established his family dwelling and temple to Thor where they came ashore; *Njal's Saga*, which contains a vivid image of the valkyrie's weaving the fates of men; and *Eirik the Red Saga*, famous for its account of a magic worker, a *seiðkona*, who holds a divination session in a Greenland farmhouse.[151] There are many more examples: any of the sagas could potentially be considered and used as Lore. As a second tier of texts, the historical works mentioned above such as *Germania*, *Heimskringla*, and the *History of the Danes*, are also read, studied, and referenced by Heathens. A third layer of Lore would consist of scholarly works by more contemporary authors whose focus on issues of archaeology, culture, and history have had a significant impact on Heathen thinking and that serve as indispensable sources of information and inspiration. Vilhelm Grönbech's *The Culture of the Teutons* is a nineteenth-century work that Heathens draw on for historical and cultural information. Books by H. R. Ellis Davidson, who is occasionally and wryly referred to as Saint Hilda, might also be in this category. For instance, her work on Norse conceptions of the afterlife, *Road to Hel*, is highly regarded as essential reading by Heathens.[152] *The Well and the Tree*, written early in the career of English professor

---

151. "High seat pillars" were timbers placed on either side of a Norse chieftain's seat of honor. In the *Eyrbyggja* saga, chapter 4, one of Thorolf's high seat pillars was carved with an image of Thor, and also embedded with god nails, the function or meaning of which are unknown. "Seidkona" is the common Heathen anglicization of the Old Norse *seiðkona*, a magical woman. It is sometimes translated as witch or sorceress, referring to a female practitioner of seið magic, commonly understood by Heathens as a Norse shamanic tradition.

152. Hilda Roderick Ellis Davidson, *The Road to Hel: A Study of the Conception of the Dead in Old Norse Literature* (Cambridge: Cambridge University Press, 2013).

Paul C. Bauschatz, is another source that has been widely embraced by Heathens for its exploration of time and cosmology in ancient Germanic culture.[153] Stephen Pollington, whose work has focused on Anglo-Saxon culture, is also regarded as a scholar friendly to Heathen reconstruction. His books, such as *The Meadhall: The Feasting Tradition in Anglo-Saxon England*, are used by Heathens to peer into the world of pre-Christian Northern Europe and as sources that provide historical models for contemporary practices.[154] There are also classic books by Heathen authors that have been formative to the way people think about the religion, one of the best examples being Eric Wódening's *We Are Our Deeds*, the title of which has become a frequently quoted catchphrase summing up Heathenry's most basic theological and ethical suppositions.[155] The unifying feature of all these works is their connection to the past. All of them, whether through the myths and legends, archaeology or etymological studies, in one way or another link contemporary Heathens to the historical past of the arch-Heathens. Magni Torsen, a long-time influential Heathen leader of Mjolnir Kindred in Colorado, affirms the important of this historical orientation: "What I consider to be Lore . . . are all these things that go back to the historical, the archaeological aspects of what was found . . . that are more factually based."[156] His phrase "what was found" is significant. For many practitioners, Heathenry is not a religion of revelation or imagination, but a religion based upon what has been found. This found quality is carefully guarded, reassuring Heathens that their religion is anchored in historical reality, in a continuity with the actual practice of historical Paganism. While Heathens are willing to consider a wide variety of historical evidence, the Lore is almost universally held as a reliable and essential guide to the religious culture of the arch-Heathens, a more or less direct window into how they thought, worshiped, and lived.

It is still the case in Heathenry that knowledge of the Lore is seen as appropriate for all practitioners, not merely for an elite group of clergy or scholars. Clergy training programs in the Heathen

---

153. Paul C. Bauschatz, *The Well and the Tree: World and Time in Early Germanic Culture* (Amherst: University of Massachusetts Press, 1982).

154. Stephen Pollington, *The Meadhall: The Feasting Tradition in Anglo-Saxon England* (Ely: Anglo-Saxon Books, 2010 [2003]).

155. Eric Wódening, *We Are Our Deeds: The Elder Heathenry, Its Ethic and Thew* (Baltimore: White Marsh Press, 2011).

156. Magni Torsen, phone interview with author, August 12, 2015.

national groups—the Troth, the Asatru Folk Assembly, and the Odinic Rite—all include significant reading lists and focus heavily on mastery of texts. Yet at the same time, Heathens go to great efforts to make texts accessible to all and encourage each other to study them. As one young Heathen put it, "I wholeheartedly believe that there are only really two ways to approach Heathenry: Either through a LOT of difficult and diligent scholarship to learn as best as possible the thoughts and actions of our ancestors, or by learning from someone who has put this effort in. Or a combination of those two things."[157] To be an authentic Heathen requires this foundation in the historical tradition. Many kindreds maintain libraries and circulate books for their members to read. This practice has been facilitated by online access to books. Many kindreds have made online libraries or "book hoards" available on websites. Heathens had been putting copies of old, out-of-print, and hard-to-find books online in digital form long before Google Books was launched. Every kindred I am aware of across the country regularly includes Lore study as part of its meeting schedule, and Heathen gatherings are notorious for the detailed discussions of these texts. The Well of Wisdom and Elkhorn kindreds in central Kentucky, both of which I participated in, read and discussed the *Völuspá*, the *Hávamál*, *Njáls Saga*, as well as an ongoing discussion of the runes during the time I was involved. The implication is simply that Heathenry is founded upon or intimately connected with these texts and that practitioners should be familiar with them. Heathen scholar Patricia Lafayllve provides insight into this connection when she states, "My scholarship informs my spirituality. It is worth spending the time to do the work, and a number of things can be learned by studying primary and secondary source materials, archeology, and history."[158] At its root, Heathens see their religion as informed by and building upon the actual religious beliefs and practices of their ancestors in the faith. What makes for authentic Heathenry is the demonstrable connection to factual history. That authenticating foundation of historical knowledge is acquired primarily through study: "My scholarship informs my spirituality."

157. Thorin, "A Response to Criticism," *Heathen Talk* blog, December 23, 2015, http://heathentalk.com/2015/12/23/a-response-to-criticism/.
158. Patricia Lafayllve, "Pagan Interviews: Patricia Lafayllve," *Through the Grapevine* blog, November 11, 2015, interviewed by Sean Harbaugh, www.patheos.com/blogs/throughthegrapevine/2015/11/pagan-interviews-patricia-lafayllve/.

This connection to the past legitimates these texts as Lore; they could not be considered Lore without it. The Lore carries its authority through its direct connection or insight into the past—because these texts are artifacts of and witnesses to the Heathen age—not through any sense of divine revelation, or because they originate with an authoritative individual. In this way, the Lore functions as an authenticating body of material that provides a context for the development of the religion, as well as a limiting boundary around it. Religious innovation without regard for the Lore is deemed inauthentic. This approach is occasionally criticized as excessive, a sort of Heathen fundamentalism.[159] Yet for all the weight it carries, the Lore is not necessarily sacrosanct or beyond critique. Heathens have a fairly sophisticated understanding of the historical limitations of their texts, from the effects of *interpretatio Romana* in Tacitus to the complications involved in the processes of textual preservation and translation. Recognizing that most of the core primary texts were products of the post-conversion period, the influence of Christianity on the texts is of particular interest. Most Heathens would not go so far as to say that the texts are corrupted, while others take a more critical stance, stating outright that "the Lore is Christian."[160] But all would acknowledge that to one degree or another a Christian reading has been overlaid on a purportedly autochthonous oral text, resulting in Christian re-interpretations or interpolations in material that was either unintelligible to or deemed unsuitable by the Christians who recorded or translated the texts. *The Prose Edda* is a case in point. Sturluson recorded and collected a significant quantity of Norse material, without which our understanding of Norse myth and culture would be significantly reduced. At the same time, he was a thirteenth-century Icelandic Christian who shaped and altered the material for his own context and purposes, intertwining his Christianity and the old Pagan material in ways that are difficult to identify and almost impossible to disentangle. That is enough to earn him disrepute and a harsh critique among some Heathens. Still, Heathens are dependent on Sturluson and other sources that have a Christian provenance, necessitating a critical approach to their own literature. Heathen readers might ask how the story of Balder has been altered by

---

159. Krasskova, "Lectio Divina Heathen Style."
160. Field notes by author, Georgia, June, 2017.

Christian comparisons to Christ or how to uncover a more Pagan account of Ragnarok beneath any influence of Christian eschatology. Heathens have developed something of an in-house religious studies effort for discerning and untangling this original Heathen material from the Christian overlayment, applying numerous solutions from exegetical techniques, to comparative work, to UPG-inspired insights to their reading of the Lore.

At the same time, not all Heathens are scholars. The range of textual expertise varies widely: from the few Lore-hounds who know the sources thoroughly, to those who can stumble through one of the most widely quoted passages of Lore:

> Cattle die, and kinsmen die,
> the self must also die;
> but the glory of reputation never dies,
> for the man who can get himself a good one.[161]

There are other Heathens who emphasize the organic nature of the religion and downplay the role of Lore precisely to avoid what they see as the trap of a textual religion, the tyranny of the book. However, I have yet to meet a Heathen who denies the importance of Lore altogether, familiarity of and reverence for which are deeply embedded in Heathen culture. Heathens negotiate this balance between the experiential and textual dimensions of religion in different ways. Paul Waggoner of the Wolves of Vinland writes,

> Heathen lifestyle allows for much interpretation, our freedom is found in a general lack of set guidelines. The various aspects of our lifestyle manifest uniquely in each individual. However, there comes a point when personal expression expands far beyond the breadth of our belief's foundation. Without a solid base any structure will crumble. Absent the strict nature of today's popular theologies, Asatru still follows certain "dogmas" set forth in the teachings of Havamal, the cosmic wisdom of Voluspa and the sociology of the sagas.[162]

One's skill in handling those texts imparts legitimacy upon the Heathen practitioner. Authors are analyzed frequently in this way, derided for playing fast and loose with history or esteemed for

---

161. Carolyne Larrington, "Sayings of the High One (Havamal)," stanza 76, in *The Poetic Edda* (New York: Oxford, 2014), 22.
162. Paul Waggener, *Neo-Tribes* 2, no. 10.

their solid grounding in the Lore. Within the text-oriented culture, a variety of approaches to the Lore are evident. Even those with facility in the Lore will still reference it as a way to lend authority to their statements, "as it says in the Lore . . ." Consider two different Heathen events that drew upon Lore: the first was a workshop given by Ristandi on the East Coast concerning the contemporary uses of runes, the second a talk by Hege in the Midwest about her experiences with land-vaettir in her backyard. Ristandi's presentation began with a deeply scholarly appraisal of references to rune-work in the ancient sources, with a six-page handout and numerous quotes from the Lore.[163] He drew from familiar, widely used sources such as the *Havamal* and the *Germania*, as well as several lesser-known sources such as *Yngvars saga viðförla* (The saga of Ingvar the far-traveled). Ristandi's strategy involved establishing his discussion of contemporary rune magic on a detailed study and knowledge of the Lore and its careful and thoughtful application to a contemporary problem. On the other hand, Hege's discussion of the land-vaettir was much more grounded in personal experience, "unverified personal gnosis" or UPG.[164] She filled her presentation with personal stories and insights of an entertaining and practical nature, such as how her house wights, spirits who dwell in and look after the house, preferred Irish whiskey. Hege described an incident in which she ran out of Irish whiskey and substituted vodka in a small glass as an offering to her house wights. There it sat untouched for a week. Finally buying and setting out a small glass of Irish whiskey, she found it gone almost immediately. Reflecting on that story, she warned her audience to avoid complacency when interacting with the spirits of nature: "There are many stories in our Lore about people going into the woods and not coming back."[165] Hege seasoned her talk with statements such as this. She did not quote from the Lore but used generalized references that provided a sense of legitimacy to her otherwise eclectic and idiosyncratic

---

163. Field notes taken by author, Pennsylvania, 2012.
164. Zoëga, *A Concise Dictionary of Old Icelandic*, s.v. "vættr." The word vaettir signifies a spirit being inhabiting the land, a nature spirit. This anglicized word derives from the Old Norse *vættr*, plural *vættir*, referring to a living being of some sort, but especially a supernatural being. The word seems to be cognate to the Old English *wiht*, commonly written as "wight." Both terms, vaettir and wights, are often used interchangeably in American Heathenry to indicate spirit beings.
165. Field notes taken by author, Kansas, 2012.

talk. Both of these examples represent very common but divergent Heathen approaches to the Lore.

While not every Heathen can quote the Lore, a widely held respect for this loosely defined body of texts can be found throughout the movement. Heathens recognize degrees of significance among these texts, emphasizing some more than others. For instance, I have met Heathens with particular interests in the *Germania*, or those who consult and refer to the *Volsunga Saga* particularly. These are books with a recognized status, an authority, and a weight, treated differently than other books. Although not seen as sacred writings in the way Christians might consider the Bible or Muslims the Qur'an, they are also not merely reference books. They define and limit what it means to be a contemporary Heathen. Reliance on the Lore frames Heathenry as a reconstructive religion, reflecting the desire that what contemporary Heathens do will have a basis in the past. This is a boundary that Heathens work hard to maintain, as Thorin explains:

> There is no right way to be a Heathen, but there are a lot of wrong ways. These are identified when the praxis falls outside of the Heathen worldview . . . My ancestors thought in certain ways, and I strive to understand that and to build on it something appropriate for the modern world and modern Heathenry, without losing the soul of what is Heathenry in the process.[166]

The Lore is first of all regarded as an authenticating touchstone with a specific cultural past. Heathenry, adherents insist, is not made up, not a flight of fancy, not LARPing in an imaginary world.[167] And second, the Lore is seen as the primary source of ancient cultural wisdom. The pre-Christian arch-Heathens understood life holistically and lived it in a more full and integrated manner. They understood life in a way that we are missing now. This ancient worldview has been lost or at least subverted by Christianity and some aspects of modernity (although Asatru generally is not antimodern). By pushing into these sources in a scholarly way, Heathens seek to uncover aspects of this ancient lifeway and to transform their own thinking and way of living.

166. Thorin, "A Response to Criticism."
167. "LARPing" is live action role-playing, a type of game play in which players dress in garb and enact the roles of their characters, usually in a fantasy setting.

## The English Literary Connection

This ancient lore went through a significant journey to be transmitted and made available as a source for the contemporary Heathen movement. During the period of the 1600s, several Scandinavian scholars began to translate and comment on this material, such as Peder Resen who translated the *Prose Edda* and significant passages of the *Poetic Edda* into Latin, and Olaus Wormius (Ole Worm), who wrote what may be the first treatise on runes in Latin.[168] The work of these scholars had the effect of broadening the influence of the Norse material by making it accessible to the intelligentsia of Europe for the first time. Literary circles were particularly taken by the material with its strong themes, powerful stories, and its graphic and often gruesome imagery. English scholars and poets of the eighteenth century retold these Norse stories and made use of the gods and heroes in their own creative ways.[169] The poet Thomas Gray, best known for his poem "Elegy Written in a Country Churchyard," was one of the European writers drawn to this revival of ancient literature. He made use of Latin translations of Norse material by the Icelandic historian Torfaeus (Þormóðr Torfason) and Danish scholar Thomas Bartholin as inspiration for his own work. His poem *The Fatal Sisters* relied heavily on their rendering of *Darraðarljóð*, a poetic section of *Njal's Saga* in which a man witnesses the valkyries singing a battle dirge on the eve of the battle of Clontarf. In Gray's adaptation, the mythic sisters foretell the doom that the warriors face, the glittering heroics of the battle as well as its gore and death:

> Ere the ruddy sun be set,
> Pikes must shiver, javeline sing,
> Blade with clattering buckler meet,
> Hauberks crash, and helmet ring.
>
> (Weave the crimson web of war!)
> Let us go, and let us fly

---

168. O'Donoghue, *From Asgard to Valhalla*, 108–9.

169. Erik Ingvar Thurin, *The American Discovery of the Norse: An Episode in Nineteenth-Century American Literature* (Lewisburg, PA: Bucknell University Press, 1999), 21–26. See Thurin for a more complete discussion of the use of Norse material in English literature in the 1700s–1800s.

> Where our friends the conflict share,
> Where they triumph, where they die.[170]

Gray also finds inspiration in the figure of Odin, god of wisdom, war, and magic. Odin travels into the Norse underworld seeking answers from the ancient *völva*, a seeress who lies there.[171] Gray's work, *The Descent of Odin*, appropriates a scene recounted in the opening passages of the *Völuspá*. These lines from his poem eerily recount the mysterious moment when the völva is called forth by Odin's rune magic:

> Thrice he traced the runic rhyme;
> Thrice pronounced, in accents dread,
> The thrilling verse that wakes the dead;
> Till from the hollow ground
> Slowly breathed a sullen sound.[172]

Writing in the 1760s, Gray employed the emerging template of Gothic literature for Odin's conjuring. Odin's mount, Sleipnir, races into "Hela's drear abode" past the bloody jaws of Garm, a mythological canine associated with the underworld. In Gray's poetic imagination, Garm becomes the "dog of darkness," a gothic horror reminiscent of Stephen King's Cujo:

> His shaggy throat he open'd wide,
> While from his jaws, with carnage filled,
> Foam and human gore distilled;
> Hoarse he bays with hideous din,
> Eyes that glow and fangs that grin[173]

Thundering past the gruesome beast, Odin rides to the portals of hell. Dismounting, Odin seats himself on the "moss-grown pile,"

---

170. Thomas Gray, "The Fatal Sisters," in *Eighteenth-Century Poetry and Prose*, 2nd edition, eds. Louis I. Bredvold, Alan D. McKillop, and Lois Whitney (New York: Ronald Press, 1956), 602.

171. *Völva* is a Norse term for a female magic-worker, a seeress, prophetess, or sibyl. The word is related to the Old Norse *völr*, meaning a stick or staff. The völur, the sibyls of the Norse world, carried a staff as the symbol of their role.

172. Thomas Gray, "The Descent of Odin," in *Eighteenth-Century Poetry and Prose*, 603.

173. Ibid.

the burial mound of the völva. This invokes the practice of *útiseta*, widely known in the Norse world, in which a person in need of guidance sat out on a burial mound, communing with the dead within and seeking their wisdom.[174] While in Mary Shelley's later work, *Frankenstein*, electricity is the power that brings forth life from the grave, Gray introduces runic magic, writing, and chanting a rune poem as the source of Odin's powerful act. In this way, the poem preserves these practices and makes them accessible to the English-speaking tradition.

We should not get the impression that Gray or any of these other writers were consumed by Norse religious themes, representing as it does only a small fraction of their literary attention. While recognizing the literary and cultural value of Norse tradition, they in no way anticipated its religious significance beyond a romantic attachment to the antiquated religious beliefs of a lost people. They appropriated it in their own search for a revival of the national and individual spirit. Yet, this literary lineage is not tangential to the contemporary phenomena of Norse/Germanic Paganism. The Norse themes contained in the works of important English writers such as Thomas Percy, Thomas Gray, and William Blake lead directly to the early twentieth-century literary work of C. S. Lewis and J. R. R. Tolkien. For both these authors, the Norse material became a source of inspiration. Lewis, strangely enough, awoke to the power of Norse myth by reading Henry Wadsworth Longfellow, the American writer who had also imbibed deeply of the Norse tributary in English literature. Lewis writes about his encounters with Longfellow's poem "Tegner's Drapa," and later with Arthur Rackham's illustration of "Siegfried and the Twilight of the Gods," as a life-changing moment in which he was engulfed by a feeling of "pure 'Northernness.'" In language reminiscent of a religious experience, he describes how "instantly, I was uplifted into huge regions of northern sky, I desired with almost sickening intensity something never to be described (except that it is cold, spacious, severe, pale, and remote)."[175] For Lewis, this experience of transcendence associated with Norse myth, this yearning for

---

174. H. R. Ellis Davidson, *Gods and Myths of Northern Europe* (New York: Penguin, 1990 [1964]), 157.

175. C. S. Lewis, *Surprised by Joy/The Four Loves* (Boston: Houghton Mifflin Harcourt, 2011), 69, 23.

"Northernness," remained a feeling that was eventually resolved in his acceptance of Christianity.[176] Tolkien went further—loving Northernness in its specifics and incorporating many details from the Norse material into the fictive world of Middle Earth. The names of many characters, the runes, the aesthetics, the stories, and plots are all directly influenced by the Norse material. In doing so, he created a fully immersive world, a "Secondary World" as he describes it, that his readers could inhabit in their imaginations and that they came to share as a community.

By the late nineteenth centuries, the predominant culture of the West, Britain and the United States particularly, had become transformed by the industrialization, technicalism, efficiency, and rationality of modernity. Yearning for a deeper, more soulful experience and unable to find that in religion, modern people began turning to fiction as an inner space where enchantment could be found. As Michael Saler discusses it, this period in the late nineteenth and early twentieth centuries saw the development of a new type of fiction: the imaginary world.[177] These literary creations were well developed and coherent, alternative worlds combined with a degree of realism that could be embraced by modern readers, integrating it with the magic, mystery, spirituality and myth lacking in the mundane world of disenchanted modernity. They transcended the novel, creating series of works often with their own imagined histories, languages, and geographies. In conjunction with these literary developments, Saler suggests the emergence of a new type of modern mentality: the "ironic imagination," a posture of doublemindedness that allowed readers to deeply invest in imaginary worlds without compromising their hold on the real one.[178] Tolkien's imaginary world continues to enchant readers and now viewers, even as new ones multiply in the contemporary context. For all its realism, Middle Earth remained a fictive world for Tolkien. For all his love of the Norse material and his own ability to inhabit it imaginatively, he could not or would not take it farther. As Diana Paxson mentioned to me, despite their own deep and creative immersion in these worlds of myth, it in no way crossed their minds that they could actually do these things.[179]

176. Ibid., 76.
177. Michael Saler, *As If: Modern Enchantment and the Literary Prehistory of Virtual Reality* (Oxford: Oxford University Press, 2012), 25-30.
178. Ibid., 30-31.
179. Diana Paxson, interview by author, Oklahoma, June, 2011.

It would take the next generation, stirred by their time in imaginary enchanted worlds to see the Norse material in a new way, as a real religious world.

Tolkien himself understood that participation or playing in these Secondary Worlds could influence participants' interaction with the real or Primary World, allowing them to "apprehend the Primary World with the same open and flexible perspective" that they brought to the imaginary world.[180] The imaginary worlds created by these authors, particularly Tolkien's Middle Earth, proved a crucial link in making the Norse mythology and tradition accessible to religious seekers in the English-speaking world.[181] Many practitioners were steeped in these imaginary worlds before taking the step into Heathen belief and practice. I am not by any means suggesting that Heathenry is a type of imaginary world or that its adherents demonstrate a type of ironic consciousness. Nor am I suggesting that the imaginary world of Middle Earth has suddenly become real, as if Heathens have lost the sophisticated psychology of the ironic consciousness. (It is interesting in this light to hear C. S. Lewis reassure his readers that for all his engagement with imaginary worlds, he never lost his grasp on reality, "Remember that it never involved the least grain of belief; I never mistook imagination for reality," he writes.)[182] Heathens in fact participate in imaginary worlds, such as Middle Earth, Howard's Cimmeria, Lovecraft's Cthulhu mythos, Marvel superheroes, *Star Wars*, and *Harry Potter*, like many other Americans—with the ironic consciousness fully intact. Rather, I suggest that these imaginary worlds were part of a cultural shift, a temporary stopover, towards the Pagan revival. And for many individuals who came to take part in contemporary Paganism, participation in imaginary worlds is part of that spiritual journey towards Paganism. Participation in the imaginary world serves as a step in transcending or reimagining the world, from seeing one's disenchanted, monotonous, routinized

---

180. Saler, *As If*, 188.

181. Tolkien retold important Germanic material including the Old English *Beowulf* and the story of Sigurd, found in the *The Prose Edda* as well as the *Völsunga Saga*. See Christopher Tolkien and J.R.R. Tolkien, *Beowulf: A Translation and Commentary Together with Sellic Spell* (London: Harper Collins, 2014); J. R. R. Tolkien and Christopher Tolkien, *The Legend of Sigurd and Gudrún* (Boston: Houghton Mifflin Harcourt, 2009). The latter work contains Tolkien's own thoughts about the transmission of Norse material into the English literary tradition. See pages 16–32.

182. Lewis, *Surprised by Joy*, 76.

existence as the only possibility. It is a sort of liminal experience, from which some people come back choosing to inhabit a Primary World that no longer adheres totally to those rules of disenchantment. They are able to see around the socialized veil of disenchantment into a Primary World invested with the magic, drama, and vitality of an alternative religious interpretation, to see a new Primary World in which the gods are real.

How might this happen? First, "play" or "practice" in imaginary worlds introduces participants to ideas, material, and resources to which they might not be exposed in their mundane lives. Like many of the Heathens I encountered, my own introduction to Norse myth, gods, and runes, came through time spent in Tolkien's as well as other imaginary worlds like that of the game Dungeons & Dragons. Second, as the quote above indicates, the mind that engages with Secondary Worlds is no longer so tightly subject to the dominant narrative of the disenchanted Primary World. It raises the possibility that there may be more than one way to look at the world, that things learned in the Secondary World expand the possibilities of the Primary World. Conservative cultural critics have noted this tendency, sometimes castigating it as a negative influence, or even devilry. Perhaps, from the perspective of modernist practicality or religious orthodoxy, there are dangers of Secondary Worlds, such as escapism, redolence, detachment, or corruption. Yet, from my perspective, engagement with Secondary Worlds can also transcend amusement to inspire a refreshing, revitalizing, and creative response to the world. A person's mental and emotional space, re-enchanted through experience with literary or other sorts of imaginary worlds, can grow and seek a deeper more meaningful engagement with the Primary World.

In several ways, then, it was literature that served as an important precursor to contemporary Heathenry by preserving the Norse material, bringing it into the contemporary world in accessible ways. Of course, we should note that outside of the British literary tradition, Norse and Germanic material was also being compiled and developed on the European continent, most notably by the Brothers Grimm in the mid-nineteenth century in their collections of fairy tales and myths.[183] The British tradition was particularly

---

183. Thurin, *American Discovery of the Norse*, 13–21. Thurin discusses how literary revivals of the Norse material in Scandinavia and Germany contributed to those nationalistic movements.

important for American Heathenry because it was in English most obviously, but also because it was the latest of the Norse revivals directly impacting twentieth-century literature at a crucial time and became part of popular culture. It also evolved a new type of literary form, the imaginary world, dramatically changing the way people interacted with literature and becoming part of the cultural shift that made contemporary Paganism possible.

A final point about the literary use of the Norse: it did not leave the material static. In addition to its guardianship and preservation of the material, literature also shaped and developed the way the Norse legacy was perceived and understood. The image of the tragic Northern hero willing to suffer and die before abandoning his warrior ethic, the sense of Teutonic virtue and character, the idea of the strength and even superiority of Norse culture and ethnicity, as well as the important theme of English freedom, democracy, and individualism as the legacy of the Northern Heathenry, were all ideas that developed in this literary tradition. All came into focus by the nineteenth century, just in time for the furor of nationalism sweeping across Europe.[184]

## The Völkisch Movement

While the Norse material was primarily a source of literary inspiration for the British writers, and decades prior to the widely recognized birth of British Wicca in the middle of the twentieth century, on the Continent, a full-blown Pagan religiosity was emerging in Germany as part of the late nineteenth- and early twentieth-century völkisch movement. The völkisch movement developed as part of the larger search for a German identity, which had not been fully satisfied by the unification of Germany in 1871 by Wilhelm I and Chancellor Otto von Bismarck. While the nationalism of this German Reich was pronounced, as seen in such acts as the erection of the *Hermannsdenkmal* in 1875, it fell short of the ambitions of some German nationalists. For instance, the fact that some German-speaking populations lay outside of the new Reich's borders became an issue, giving rise to a push for a Greater Germany as well as lingering questions about "Germanness" that transcended notions of citizenship and state boundaries. Bismarck's

---

184. O'Donoghue, *From Asgard to Valhalla*, 107, 125.

drive to create a modern nation-state fell short of capturing more romantic or idealist understandings of an essential German spirit, a *Volkgeist*, within the German people, the *Volk*, which came to be increasingly defined in terms of race.[185] Fundamental to the völkisch movement was the desire to both discover and express this spiritual essence of Germanness. In doing so, the movement became quite multifaceted and völkisch pursuits were not only political, but also included music, art and aesthetics, ecology, farming and rurality, healthy lifestyles, eugenics, and esotericism.

Unfortunately, racism became integral to the völkisch agenda. While anti-Semitism was endemic throughout Europe, it had taken on the air of modernity through notions of Social Darwinism and racial science prevalent and widely accepted during this period even among the mainstream. This toxic combination played into the völkisch search for authentic Germanness. The pure German spirit became defined in contrast to other polluting influences, against Jewish people for sure, but as representatives of a postulated Jewish spirit and cultural influence. The social renewal envisioned within the völkisch milieu came to involve the cleansing of social elements seen as diluting or polluting the pure folk soul, a philosophy further radicalized and taken in horrific reality by the National Socialist regime of the 1930s and 1940s.[186] For most Germans, this involved the Germanization of Protestant Christianity and the rejection and suppression of Catholicism and Judaism. Yet as the movement developed, some völkisch thinkers began to seek this pure German spirit in a golden age of the deep past, "The *Volk* was increasingly to be seen to have existed in its ideal form in a lost, innocent, pre-industrial past."[187] For a few, this meant a turn away modern forms of religion altogether and toward the revival of the Pagan spirituality of the ancient pre-Christian Teutons. Germanness was linked to the ancient gods of the folk soul, to Wotan and Thor.

The *Germanische Glaubens Gemeinschaft* (Germanic Faith Community or GGG) was one such group that sought to unlock the German

---

185. Bernard Mees, *The Science of the Swastika* (New York: Central European University Press, 2008), 20

186. Eric Kurlander, "Völkisch-Nationalism and Universalism on the Margins of the Reich: A Comparison of Majority and Minority Liberalism in Germany, 1898–1933," in *German History from the Margins*, eds. Neil Gregor, Nils H. Roemer, and Mark Roseman (Bloomington: Indiana University Press, 2006), 86.

187. Ibid., 20.

spirit through the renewal of Paganism. Led by the völkisch artist Ludwig Fahrenkrog, the GGG emerged in 1912 and quickly developed a ten-point statement of faith and an annual religious gathering called the Althing, which attracted members from across Europe. The GGG also developed religious rituals and iconography, such as the use of Thor's hammer for ritual blessings as well as a symbol of the movement, a ritual calendar and sacred spaces that venerated the German landscape, including plans for a Heathen temple. Already at this early stage the movement saw tension emerge between proponents of text-based religion rooted in the Eddas versus a more imaginative, organic-based practice rooted in personal experience, foreshadowing the contemporary debates between reconstructionist Heathens and those practitioners more willing to consider and integrate UPG into religious practice. In many ways, this early movement can be seen as a notable precursor to contemporary Heathenry:

> The GGG can be regarded as one of the first Germanic religious societies that resurrected and put into practice elements that today have become widespread among the Ásatrú community and other Germanic neo-heathens. It was definitely among the first groups that regularly practiced religious rites which at least partially (in accordance with the still-limited historical knowledge of the time) were based on old Germanic pagan rituals. The GGG held annual Althings and used a special bronze Mjölnir, or Thor's hammer, in its rites.[188]

Esotericism also formed an important aspect of the völkisch movement. These German esotericists did not see their interests as opposed to modernity, but as integrally related to modern scientific pursuits, as an alternative interpretation of modernity. The problem they identified was the strict materialism of modern science: by failing to account for spirit and will, science was distorted by a materialist ideology. "This provided a prime opportunity for occult thinkers to stake their claim as proponents of an improved and revived science freed of its materialist distortions."[189] This völkisch esotericism, best exemplified by writer and runologist, Guido List, quickly found a

---

188. Markus Wolff, "Ludwig Fahrenkrog and the Germanic Faith Community: Wodan Triumphant," in *Tyr: Myth – Culture – Tradition* 2, 239–40.

189. Peter Staudenmaier, "Esoteric Alternatives in Imperial Germany: Science, Spirit, and the Modern Occult Revival," in *Revisiting the "Nazi Occult": Histories, Realities, Legacies*, eds. Monica Black and Eric Kurlander (Rochester, NY: Camden House 2015), 26.

basis in the runes, ancient symbols that List claimed to contain the lost wisdom of a uniquely Germanic spirituality, unlocking a race-based spirituality. In his book, *The Secret of the Runes*, List hints at obtaining mystical insight into the runes while recovering from cataract surgery and describes in detail his system of Armanen runes, derived from the eighteen rune charms found in the *Hávamál*.[190] Through his occult group founded in 1908, the Guido von List Society, List also developed a system of runic rituals and practices that purported to lead the practitioner toward higher states of spiritual evolution. The work of List, popularized through the activities of the society, were influential among occultists, engendering a fascination with the runes and their magical potential.[191] Experimentation with rune magic among völkisch occultists included the development of runic postures or runic yoga by Friedrich Marby and Siegfried Kummer in the early 1930s, and runic mudras or hand gestures by both Kummer and later adapted by Karl Spiesberger in the 1950s.[192] As we will see, Edred Thorsson's engagement with List and his successors essentially created the basis for much of contemporary Heathen rune magic.

Völkisch occultism was surprisingly eclectic and was influenced particularly by the burgeoning Theosophy movement, which may account for the interest in a Norse/Hindu connection among later völkisch thinkers. According to Staudenmaier, völkisch esotericism was "a remarkable convergence of disparate occult ideas" and displayed a fascination with "the exotic traditions of Egypt, India, and other reaches of the ostensibly mystical East."[193] Connections between astrology, alternative science, ariosophy, and runology can be found in such rituals as the Ritual of the Ninth Night, a ritual of empowerment created by völkisch occultist Peyrt Shou.[194] His ritual seeks to "transform the body of the magician into an antenna for certain cosmic streams of power."[195] By assuming certain runic

---

190. Guido List, *The Secret of the Runes*, trans. Stephen E. Flowers (Rochester, VT: Inner Traditions, 1988), 41–46.

191. Schnurbein, *Norse Revival*, 42. Schnurbein includes a detailed discussion of the völkisch precedents of Heathenry in chapter 1 of her book.

192. Thorsson, *Futhark*, 15. See also Edred Thorsson, *Rune-Might: History and Practices of the Early 20th-Century German Rune Magicians* (Smithville, TX: Runa-Raven Press, 2004), 37, 76.

193. Staudenmaier, "Esoterica Alternatives in Imperial Germany," 29–30.

194. Thorsson, *Rune-Might*, 96–101.

195. Ibid., 96.

postures in combination with the intoning runes and meditation, the occult practitioner esoterically aligns himself with the constellation Cygnus and draws down radio waves to achieve heightened states of awareness.

While German nationalism, race-consciousness, and other völkisch ideas were widespread among German speakers in the early twentieth century, the religious and magical aspects of the völkisch movement remained relatively marginal. As Mees points out, "There were still many notable examples of those who classed themselves German nationals who did not subscribe to the full-blown form of the new völkisch ideal—and it is evident that many German nationals thought their rune-fancying and race-obsessed radical right-wing brethren ridiculous."[196] The movement was not well regarded by the Nazis and several important völkisch leaders were actively persecuted by the regime. A similar dynamic seemed to be at work in the United States where völkisch, pro-Nazi political and racial sentiments were circulating in some circles. The German-American Bund was an influential and active pro-Nazi organization in the United States, holding public speeches, marches, and summer camps and estimated to have had over twenty thousand members. The Guido von List Society had connections to the Theosophical Society as well as the Ordo Templi Orientis, and it is clear that the ideas and works of List and other völkisch esotericists were available to some American occultists. Yet despite this, völkisch ideology seems to have had little lasting effect on the religious milieu in America. There does not seem to be a direct relationship between the German-American Bund, völkisch groups, secret rune societies, and contemporary American Heathenry, and no evidence that the earliest founders of American Heathenry, like McNallen, knew or were inspired by these groups. Much of the indirect influence came later through the scholarship of Stephen Flowers, whose intellectual and academic work mined the völkisch resources on runes and magic. As a Heathen innovator writing under the pen name Edred Thorsson, he introduced the völkisch magical milieu into Heathenry in its second decade, shorn of its most obvious racist connotations. The political and racial elements were actually introduced earlier through one particular individual, Else Christensen. Known to some as the "Folk Mother" for seeding the völkisch worldview into

---

196. Mees, *The Science of the Swastika*, 24.

the new movement, Christensen brought a political, racially based Heathenry, which she called Odinism, to the United States. Her work and influence touched many of the first generation of leaders who built a truly American Heathen movement and, as we will see, she is the connection through whom the Odinist/völkisch tributary begins.

## The Pagan Explosion of the 1970s

All these precedents in one way or another served as tributaries that began to flow together in American in the late 1960s, flowing and churning potently within the atmosphere of social and religious upheaval, the esotericism of alternative religion, and the identity politics of the civil rights movement, in which Black, Hispanic, Native Americans, and others were all asserting their presence in American society. In these turbulent years, many Americans began to call themselves by different names: new identities began to emerge and many of these were distinctly religious in nature. Wicca was one of these new religious identities that would come to have a profound impact on the American religious scene. Wicca had emerged in Britain in the 1950s primarily through the work of Gerald Gardner, a religious entrepreneur whom some observers refer to as the father of modern Witchcraft. Once established in the United States, Wicca grew rapidly, becoming an incredibly vibrant movement conducive to many of the cultural identity movements of the time. Expressions of feminism, environmentalism, the LGBTQ movement, alternative lifestyles, as well as minority ethnic identities found Wicca with its magical and polytheistic structure to be a resonant and friendly context. It is through Wicca's engagement with these movements and identities that contemporary Paganism in all its delicious diversity and vitality emerged as an American religious movement. The introduction of Wicca into the American context at the right time served as a starter, a catalyst for a Pagan explosion that continues to evince a great deal of religious creativity and freedom. While Wicca still remains the largest and most influential segment of American contemporary Paganism, it is now only one part of a large and diffuse movement. For all its distinctiveness, American Heathenry arose within the broad creative milieu of contemporary Paganism inspired in many ways by Wicca. While Heathens have often considered their identity and community as distinct

Figure 4. Odin Altar, Lexington, KY. (Photo by the author.)

from Paganism, they are indebted to this movement not only for creating the social context in which Heathenry could flourish, not only for the creation of a religious paradigm and practices that were quite influential in early Heathenry, but also for a group of people whose religious sentiments and ideas were first stirred by the Pagan contribution before developing a new religious identity as Asatru practitioners. Stephen McNallen and Garman Lord are notable early leaders within the Heathen movement who came from Wiccan backgrounds and numerous Asatru adherents since those early years have trace their religious search from a journey that began with Wicca.

## *A Brief History*

### *Beginnings: The 1970s*

American Heathenry entered its fifth decade during the period in which I have been studying the movement. I mentioned earlier in this chapter that Heathenry emerged as a visible movement in America during the early 1970s. During this time, several individuals including Stephen McNallen and Garman Lord came to self-consciousness as religious devotees of the Norse gods and began to form religious organizations focused on Norse religion and culture. In his description of the period, Lord alludes to the retrospective sense of supernatural activity, as well as the tentativeness and experimental nature of the movement's beginnings:

> There were obviously eldritch gods whom no one had thought serious religious thoughts about in centuries, suddenly at large in the world again, and obviously with something to say; something so strange and uncanny that it would be awhile before even the most questing minds and ears would begin to hear and understand it all that clearly. Like several "mad scientists" each independently simultaneously discovering something that just seems to be "in the air," none of these men was aware of the work or even the existence of the others, none really understood at the time the potential significance of what he was doing, and all proceeded along in it by fits and starts.[197]

These beginnings were fueled mostly by enthusiasm and a sense of spiritual calling, with these founders drawing on the bits of Norse mythology, language, and history that they knew or learned. McNallen's first organizational effort, the Viking Brotherhood, was organized by 1972 and achieved tax-exempt status as a federally recognized religious organization. As he willingly admits, Asatru at this point was long on Viking bravado and short on religious knowledge and practice. But at the same time, McNallen cut his teeth as a religious leader with the Viking Brotherhood and began creating awareness about this new religion. In the 1970s, it would be hard to call Asatru a movement: the primary activity of the Viking Brotherhood was the circulation of McNallen's Asatru journal, *The Runestone*, which he produced on "a rickety typewriter and a mimeograph machine, and the first run was of eleven copies."[198]

---

197. Garman Lord, "The Evolution of Theodish Belief: Part II The Witan Theod," *Gerod Theod: The Official Website of Theodish Belief*, http://gamall-steinn.org/Gering/Evol-pt2.htm.

198. Stephen McNallen, "Three Decades of the Ásatrú Revival," in *Tyr: Myth – Culture – Tradition* 2, 206. The article has been republished in a revised form. See McNallen, "How the Gods Came to North America," in *Asatru: A Native European Spirituality*, 61–69.

Margot Adler's landmark book, *Drawing Down the Moon*, was an investigative report on Paganism with successive editions that spanned almost thirty years. Adler's book was the first of its kind, remarkable for its comprehensive scope examining the breadth of Paganism and its unsensational, respectful approach to the controversial subject matter. However, it was Adler's style that made the book particularly different, melding Adler's sensitivities to Pagan experience as an insider, a practitioner, with her training as a journalist. Adler approached Paganism with empathy and insight missed by most academic researchers of the time. (The study of Paganism has improved much since the 1970s and 1980s, although the complications of the outsider/insider dilemma of ethnography are still apparent and endemic to the discipline.) At the same time, she applied a reporter's methodology. She knew how to investigate a lead, search out and talk with relevant sources, and write up a good story. Her excellence as a journalist shines through in *Drawing Down the Moon*. All these factors make it one of the most widely read books on Paganism.

In light of this, *Drawing Down the Moon* makes an excellent template against which to gauge the growth and development of Asatru. Looking at Heathenry through the different editions provides interesting insights into how the Pagan community perceived the movement. Notably, Asatru is nowhere to be found in the first edition of *Drawing Down the Moon*, published in 1979. Adler left it out completely. Her decision is not entirely surprising and confirms what we know of the movement at the time: it was small, consisting of perhaps no more than a few hundred people loosely organized around Stephen McNallen. For the most part, Asatru in the late 1970s was not well connected to the broader Pagan movement; for instance, it did not publish or advertise in *Green Egg*.[199] Instead, McNallen had been advertising his Viking Brotherhood in *Soldier of Fortune* magazine and publishing his own newsletter, *The Runestone*, through his own mailing list. These two facts alone brilliantly indicate the distance between the Pagan and emerging Heathen movements. There was very little crossover with the Pagan

---

199. *Green Egg* is the journal of the Church of All Worlds, the influential Pagan religious group founded by Tim Zell. First published in 1968, *Green Egg* was arguably the most important Pagan publication in the United States throughout the 1970s when it functioned as a central point of communication and expression for the burgeoning Pagan movement.

movement and what there was occurred circumstantially on the individual level rather than purposefully on the organizational. Yet Adler was too good of a journalist to simply overlook Asatru. While it was a small and new movement, that could also be said for other groups that Adler did include. In the second edition, published in 1986, Adler gives what amounts to an amazing confession: "When *Drawing Down the Moon* appeared in 1979, one of its most glaring oversights was the omission of Norse Paganism."[200] She continued by describing the movement as so entangled with "right-wing and Nazi activities" that it seemed impossible to discern the sincere religious adherents from those using Norse Paganism as a cover for racist political and social agendas. As an illustration, Adler shared the example of a neighbor who had Nazi paraphernalia on one wall of his apartment and Pagan paraphernalia on the other wall. It seemed to be "a can of worms that I just didn't want to open," she writes.[201] This seems to be the real reason that she did not include Asatru in the first edition.

Nor was Adler alone in her feelings about Asatru. She noted that "the common notion within the Pagan movement was that Norse Paganism was filled with such people."[202] In fact, I take her book as something of a bellwether expressing a sentiment broadly shared by Pagans at the time. Even though American Paganism was already quite pluralistic by the end of the 1970s, Asatru and its practitioners were perceived as different than other sorts of Pagans. *Drawing Down the Moon* demonstrates that even in its infancy Asatru was tainted by associations with racism and the political far right and that the lines of distrust had been drawn. Adler's discomfort with Asatru was in part a result of her own perspective: in all due respect, it fell outside of her parameters of acceptable Paganism in her considered opinion. Any time an onlooker examines a religious movement in a sustained way, he or she must eventually decide what it includes and what it does not. Adler was uncomfortable with some ideas and associations that did not seem to express Paganism as she understood it. It seemed too concerned with race, blood, and ancestry, too patriarchal, too violent and aggressive in its rhetoric to fit comfortably within Adler's Pagan paradigm. Yet

---

200. Margot Adler, *Drawing Down the Moon* (New York: Penguin, 1986), 273.
201. Ibid., 274.
202. Ibid.

Adler also accurately perceived something about Heathenry that did set it apart from the rest of contemporary Paganism, if by that we mean Wicca and Witchcraft. As we will see in the next chapter, the headwaters of the Heathen worldview did not originate solely, or even primarily, within the same context as Wicca. Many of the values and attitudes she identifies flowed in to Asatru from sources and tributaries not shared by other contemporary Pagans.

The Viking Brotherhood was short-lived and soon took on a more robust form. McNallen's organizational reboot, the Asatru Free Assembly, coincided with his release from active military duty in 1976. Now the pace of development picked up and Asatru began to take on the shape of a religious movement. Over the next few years the Asatru Free Assembly, and other adherents outside of this organizational body, developed the basic religious structure that continues to give shape to the Heathen movement. Familiarity with the Lore brought increasing depth to Asatru beliefs, cosmology, and experience with the Norse deities. They formalized the basic ritual of the blót in McNallen's three-part *Rituals of Asatru*.[203] The sumbel was developed sometime after this as a ritual of communal fellowship.[204] The AFA also introduced the first systematic seasonal calendar for religious practice.[205] The Nine Noble Virtues, credited in their original form to the Odinic Rite, came to summarize and express values that were to distinctively characterize Heathen religious life including courage, truth, honor, fidelity, discipline, hospitality, industriousness, self-reliance, and perseverance. McNallen offered his own revision that contrasted the noble values of Asatru with the distorted values of Christian culture. Later, Theodish leader Eric Wódening presented twelve thews or ethical customs including values such as community, individuality, moderation, and wisdom. While the "Noble Nine" have fallen out of style for most American Heathens, the idea of distinctively Heathen values drawn from the Eddas and sagas remains a notable aspect of Heathen culture. The Asatru Free Assembly continued to publish *The Runestone*, while other Asatru-specific journals such as *Yggdrasil*, *The Raven Banner*, *Mountain Thunder*, and *Idunna* served as forums in which

---

203. Stephen A. McNallen, *The Rituals of Asatru* (Payson, AZ: World Tree Publications, 1991).

204. For a further discussion of the sumbel as a ritual of communal fellowship, see chapter 7.

205. See chapter 9 for more discussion of Heathen calendars.

contributors shaped these foundations over the ensuing decades. Several important personalities who would leave lasting impacts on the movement became influential during this period, such as Edred Thorsson and Valgard Murray. Until 1986, the Asatru Free Assembly served as the most significant institutional face for Asatru. Yet as tensions began to emerge in McNallen's loosely held together organization, it became quite clear that Asatru would not develop as a centrally organized group. Instead, the religion would take a diffuse, more amorphous form. The mix of tributaries would give rise to numerous confluences of idea configurations, disparate groups, leaders, and practitioners. The primary commonalities would be a core of texts, rituals, and concepts, as well as the adherence to a Northern European context.

### Conflict and National Organizations: The 1980s

Despite its absence from the first edition of Adler's compendium of American Paganism, the first ten years of Asatru—from the mid-1970s to the mid-1980s—were actually quite significant. Quite a lot occurred to lay the foundations for the movement. Adler included a section on Norse Paganism in the 1986 edition of *Drawing Down the Moon*, wryly noting that "Pagans interested in Norse mythology just won't go away," as if other Pagans were wishing that they would. Adler's apprehension about Asatru was far from settled in 1986, so while she includes Asatru, she does so circumspectly. Allotted approximately eight of the book's 450 pages (without including the appendices), her treatment of Asatru is an extended conversation on whether a religion that is conservative, probably racist, and definitely patriarchal can be included within the family of contemporary Paganism. Asatru remained an outlier from the mainstream Pagan world, the strange distant cousin with whom no one was quite comfortable. Adler's concerns included the ethical orientation of Asatru, which seemed unduly focused on duty to kin to the neglect of the universal good. She comments that "an AFA member would score low on Kohlberg's morality test, where morality is rated by how far you put the good of all people above the good of those you are personally tied to."[206] What she was observing was the emergence of a tribal form of moral reasoning that has come to

---

206. Adler, *Drawing Down the Moon*, 278.

characterize the ethical thinking within contemporary Heathenry. Heathens certainly understand and appreciate the common good, yet they prioritize responsibility to one's closest relational ties, often referred to by the term "innangarð."[207] The relationships signified by innangarð include family and kin, yet also encompass the voluntary relationships of tribe and kindred. Some Heathens might also include neighbors and co-workers whose lives and well-being are intertwined with one's own on a close and regular basis.[208] Another of Adler's concerns was the masculine and patriarchal dynamic of Asatru in the mid-1980s. Again, she was observing a quickly evolving movement that began as a Viking boys club but would continue to attract and involve more women over the years.

By and large, the major concerns expressed in this edition focus on attitudes about race and ancestry, and with good reason: in the mid-1980s the divergent views on race and ancestry were coming to a head in Asatru. In the wake of the Brüder Schweigen affair of counterfeiting, conspiracy, bombings, and murder in pursuit of a revolutionary racist agenda, the dangers of white supremacy were obvious. Several members of that group, including David Lane and Richard Scutari, had or would have ties to Norse Paganism. Although McNallen explains that the dissolution of the Asatru Free Assembly was not primarily about race, the issue clearly played a significant role.[209] By that time, distinct philosophies had emerged about the nature of Asatru and the Asatru Free Assembly was caught up in the clash. Some saw it as primarily an ethnic religion, the manifestation of an ethnic "folk soul." For others, Asatru was *about* a specific culture but could be authentically practiced by any sincere seeker. Stephen McNallen attempted to hold these increasingly divergent perspectives together for several years, eventually enunciating a theory called metagenetics to support his position of "folkish" Heathenry. Since I will discuss metagenetics in more detail in chapter 3, suffice it to say that folkish Heathenry advocates Asatru as a religion for people of Northern European ancestry while eschewing racial supremacy and hatred. On one hand, the hard-core

207. Innangarð is derived from the Old Norse *innangarða* meaning "within the fence," or "within the yard." See Cleasby and Vigfusson, *An Icelandic Dictionary*, s.v. "innan." It is often used in Heathenry to refer to one's most significant relationships.
208. Josh Heath, telephone interview with author, December 26, 2015.
209. McNallen, *Asatru*, 63–64.

racialist Norse Pagans, with their deep ties to the American white supremacist movement, railed against McNallen for his alleged cowardice in not embracing a fully racist position. This position is often, though perhaps not accurately, referred to as Odinism in contrast to the more inclusive Asatru position. Else Christensen, Wyatt Kaldenberg, Peter Georgacarakos, the White Order of Thule, and eventually David Lane, who founded Wotansvolk to propagate an extreme racist interpretation of Norse Paganism, all exemplify this racial approach. Lane, who would eventually go to prison for racially inspired murder, was profoundly influential in the world of American white supremacy and crafted a form of Norse Paganism to suit those purposes.[210] On the other hand, a number of other Norse Pagans represented by Edred Thorsson, James Chisholm, Dianne Ross, Prudence Priest, William Bainbridge, and others strongly advocated an inclusive form of religion that welcomed anyone who felt called by the Norse gods to devote themselves to the Norse/Germanic path of Asatru, a position that has been termed "universalist." These competing expressions produced tensions that eventually grew beyond the ability of McNallen and the Asatru Free Assembly to hold together. The group dissolved in 1987 and McNallen, exhausted from years of difficult leadership and stung by religious politics, went into a hiatus, withdrawing from active participation in the movement.

In McNallen's absence new leaders and groups had the opportunity to emerge and fill this gap. Two new groups took shape: the Ásatrú Alliance and the Ring of Troth. Jeffrey Kaplan, whose work provides a detailed picture of the movement at this time, describes these two groups as embodying the ideologies of the two predominant branches of Heathenry:

> These groups, the Ásatrú Alliance and the Ring of Troth, came to represent the contentions surrounding the central dichotomy of the AFA: the more politicized, racialist majority of the AFA, and those for whom the magical and scholarly potential of the movement were at the forefront of the reconstruction of the Norse/Germanic religion, and for whom race was either of little interest or for whom racialist thought was anathema.[211]

---

210. Gardell, *Gods of the Blood*.
211. Kaplan, "The Reconstruction of Ásatrú and Odinist Traditions," 205.

The Ásatrú Alliance (AA), led by Valgard Murray, most obviously carried the banner of McNallen's defunct group and its folkish perspective. In the AA, the organizational focus was on creating ties among independent kindreds through the annual Althing. Begun by the AFA, the Althing was maintained by the AA as an annual gathering of diverse kindreds and tribes inspired by the Icelandic Althing, which provided a form of self-government in Iceland prior to encroaching Danish hegemony after 1000 CE. The AA developed its own publishing and merchandising arm, World Tree Publications, and magazine, Vor Trú, which published writings with a folkish bent. The leader of the AA, Valgard Murray, was also a dynamic figure. Known for his earlier involvement in white supremacist movements, Murray also controversially testified for the state of Ohio in a religious liberty hearing regarding a Heathen inmate's request for religious accommodation.[212] The other important group to emerge at this time was the Ring of Troth, from the vision of Edred Thorsson, James Chisholm, and others who saw it as an alternative to the folkish AA. The Ring of Troth was more clearly a national organization, accepting individual members rather than kindreds. Its objectives were to encourage scholarship and develop clergy. While firmly committed to maintaining focus on the Norse paradigm, this group was much more open to the influence of the Wiccan and Witchcraft tributary in its more ready acceptance of inclusive membership, magical practice, and female leadership.

These two organizations represented different approaches to Asatru. The divide was about more than racial attitudes, and really involved two different visions about what it meant to be Heathen. As these two sides became more entrenched over the years, the distance and dissonance would increase. However, we should be careful about making too much of the divide. On the ground and in the lives of Heathen practitioners the division was not so evident. Not only did Heathens participate in both groups, but there was significant commonality. Jeffrey Kaplan was the first scholar to identify the differences between the Odinist and Asatru persuasions, yet he writes, "[i]t cannot be overemphasized, however, that the

---

212. Casey Sanchez, "Correctional Officials Around the Country Struggle with a Court Ruling Accommodating Odinism, a Sometimes Racist Religion," *Intelligence Report*, August 21, 2009, www.splcenter.org/fighting-hate/intelligence-report/2009/supreme-court-requires-prisons-give-special-consideration-racist-pagans.

Odinist/Ásatrú break offers no clear lines of differentiation."[213] We should just note briefly that in these early years, each group struggled with its own internal politics to establish a clear identity, and against the ongoing marginalization as a racist and potentially dangerous religious gang. There was significant pressure on these nascent organizations. Yet in the long run, the diversification of the movement in this way, the development of new ideologies, and new leadership opportunities was quite important for the continued growth and success of the movement. Despite its own tendency toward infighting, the scope of the movement increased in the late 1980s and early 1990s and began to include a wider variety of participants, especially those who began drifting from Wicca into involvement with Asatru. This changing demographic led to the sort of experimentation that would result in a new level of dynamic growth during the 1990s.

## Proliferation of Heathenry: The 1990s

The 1990s became a time of growth for Asatru. Before describing the contour of that growth, let us briefly consider two factors that contributed to it: the integration of the Internet into Heathen culture, and the publication of Heathen books. Contemporary Pagans in general were early adopters of the Internet and Heathens were no exception. The national organizations quickly had an Internet presence, while kindreds and individuals began publishing copious amounts of information about Asatru religion and practice online. This activity made the religion widely accessible for the first time, especially for a younger generation of religious seekers who had not experienced the New Awakening of the 1970s. Most importantly, Heathens could easily communicate with each other across the United States and the world, exponentially increasing the transfer of ideas, religious knowledge and experience, the development and nurturing of relationships and connections, and the validation of Heathen religious identity. Of course, with that ability to easily communicate came added tensions and conflicts. The fierce debates about metagenetics, for instance, tore through Heathen chat rooms and email lists like a maelstrom throughout the 1990s. While Facebook has tended to replace chat rooms, waves of controversy

---

213. Kaplan, "The Reconstruction of Ásatrú and Odinist Traditions," 200.

continue to wash across its posts and in the blogs and websites of Heathens with the viral quality made possible by these new platforms. Heathens have embraced the Internet so completely that the movement has seen some kickback against online armchair Heathenry, with many Heathen leaders insisting that authentic Heathenry demands action and face-to-face relationships in the real world.

Even with the adoption of the Internet, books have served an incredibly important role in the Heathen movement and continue to be an important part of Heathen identity. So we should note that the 1990s saw the publication of numerous books by Heathen authors that became highly influential in the movement. Particularly important were Kveldúlf Gundarsson's book on magic, Diana Paxson's and Freya Aswynn's books on the runes, and Eric Wódening's book on Heathen ethics and theology, to name a few.[214] These books accomplished a couple of important things. First, they exemplified a "scholarly" approach that came to mark Heathen books in that they paid close attention to the Lore and grounded their discussions in a thorough knowledge of these sources. In this way, these books really set the standard for future Heathen authors. Second, these books were practical, serving as guides in the hands of adherents for living out a Heathen lifestyle in the contemporary period. They explored Heathen worldview and practice in a new degree of depth and practical application that had not been available before. The authors had read and digested the Lore and now gave that back to their readers in ways that could be put into practice, taking what had been done in the past and specifically reformulating it for the contemporary movement. These expert voices, who are now considered to be elders of the Heathen movement, were bringing Heathenry to life for a mass audience. This period marks the beginning of a renaissance of Heathen creative production and shows the Heathen movement moving beyond the turmoil about racial attitudes and into the real work of building a positive religious culture.

---

214. Freya Aswynn, *Leaves of Yggdrasil: A Synthesis of Runes, Gods, Magic, Feminine Mysteries, and Folklore* (St. Paul, MN: Llewellyn Publications, 1990); Kveldulf Gundarsson, *Teutonic Magic: The Magical and Spiritual Practices of the Germanic People* (St. Paul, MN: Llewellyn Publications, 1990); Diana Paxson, *Taking Up the Runes: A Complete Guide to Using Runes in Spells, Rituals, Divination, and Magic* (Boston: Redwheel/Weiser, 2005); Wódening, *We Are Our Deeds*.

The big event of the 1990s was the return of Stephen McNallen to active leadership. By the mid-1990s clear partisan sides were emerging, formalized by McNallen's founding of the Asatru Folk Assembly in 1994 with a clear and robust commitment to the folkish ideology. As McNallen describes it, "I saw signs that a corrupt faction was making inroads into the Germanic religious movement in the United States. Individuals and groups had emerged which denied the innate connection of Germanic religions and Germanic people."[215] He was responding to the success of the Troth, which had become a social location for much of the new development in Asatru. "This error," he states, "could not be allowed to become dominant. I decided to reenter the fray."[216] Unfortunately, the tension and conflict between these two organizations and a hardening of their respective positions has often overshadowed the other developments of this period. The near-constant bickering and sniping about who is a racist has not been particularly good for Asatru nor productive in evolving more sophisticated approaches.

One development since the 1990s has been the emergence of the tribalist perspective, which is often put forward as an alternative to both the folkish "Asatru is for white folks" banner and inclusive "Asatru is for all folks" umbrella. Jennifer Snook, Thad Horrell, and Kristen Horton describe tribalism along these lines, "Those wanting a middle way between the extremes have turned to 'tribalism' in an attempt to reconcile the desire to be inclusive and avoid accusations of racism, while maintaining a degree of exclusivity through an 'authentic' historical social structure."[217] Tribal Asatru seeks to avoid blanket statements about the faith as a whole and suggests that the local group is the locus of value. The tribe autonomously forms its own set of tightly knit and long-term relationships, bound together by its own standards and customs (*thew*) and judging for itself who is worthy of inclusion or exclusion. Hence, the dynamics of a tribe are not based on overarching categories such as race but on the consideration of individuals themselves and how they fit within the values of a tribe and its network of trusting relationships.

215. McNallen, *Asatru*, 65.
216. Ibid., 66.
217. Jennifer Snook, Thad Horrell, and Kristin Horton, "Heathens in the United States: The Return to 'Tribes' in the Construction of a Peoplehood," in *Cosmopolitanism, Nationalism, and Modern Paganism*, ed. Kathryn Rountree (New York: Palgrave Macmillan, 2017), 53.

In addition to the Asatru Folk Assembly, other national organizations came onto the scene during the 1990s offering new options for belief and practice. A small but influential example is the Odinic Rite. The Odinic Rite (OR) remained a primarily British group until the late 1990s when it expanded into North America under the leadership of Jeff "Heimgest" Holley, who became the leader of the organization in 1989. The OR fought its own battles over the racial issue in the early 1990s, which led to a split of the organization. Heimgest successfully steered the group toward a more cultural and esoteric focus. However, the OR retains much of the distinctiveness of Odinism, including a racial outlook influenced by völkisch ideas. Like other Odinist groups, the OR maintains a fairly closed structure and tight leadership network, preferring a quiet behind the scenes focus on internal development. Holley has felt that involvement in the "Heathen scene" has often been non-productive. For instance, the OR attempted to cooperate with the AFA and the AA in the formation of an international umbrella group, the International Asatru/Odinist Alliance. This effort led to a cataclysmic conflict of organizational and personal interests, which eventually led the OR to withdraw from almost all interaction with the broader Heathen community as well as a realignment of their own leadership and values.[218] The OR maintains a strong esoteric emphasis, which focuses on spiritual evolution toward a higher state of awareness called Odinic Consciousness as well as a very idiosyncratic reading of Norse myth. The group's rhetoric has a revolutionary flair with decidedly political and apocalyptic overtones and is highly critical of mainstream American culture. Additionally, the OR views most of contemporary Asatru as not serious and religiously shallow, too concerned with play-acting a Viking fantasy rather than pursuing the sort of consciousness-raising and community building that the OR values: the rediscovery of folk consciousness and culture. For instance, the OR was the first Heathen group to give organizational priority to the development of Odinist education for members' children. A branch of the OR known as Acorn Hollow established a home school in the Pacific Northwest region of the United States and worked to develop curriculum for other Odinist home schools. Much like the homeschooling efforts of other religious groups, the idea was to create an educational environment conducive to Odinist

---

218. Jeff Heimgest Holley, interview with author, May 19, 2011.

ideology and free from the negative influences of American society, or as the OR might put it, "resisting the Wolf Age" and the "cultural darkness devouring Mother Jorth."[219] This approach arises from the idea that religion is an all-inclusive system, linking human beings with their past, their ethnic community, their land, and their gods. Additionally, the OR has been very active in prison ministry, establishing kindreds within the federal prison system throughout the United States, particularly in California, Washington, Texas, and a number of southern states. This work, done by the OR's Prison Affairs Bureau, garnered significant attention from federal agencies as well as the Southern Poverty Law Center in the 2000s, putting significant pressure on the group for several years.

Wotansvolk also emerged in the 1990s as the overt face of racist Norse Paganism, a confluence in which the ideological streams of American white supremacy became systematically merged with Norse mythology and religion.[220] The face of Wotansvolk was the notorious white supremacist David Lane, whose involvement with the revolutionary racist group Brüder Schweigen and his subsequent life imprisonment for murder afforded him a great deal of credibility among white supremacists and their organizations in the federal prison system. He and his wife, Katja Lane, who published their material under the name 14 Words Press, merged their efforts with another racist Heathen, Ron McVan and his Temple of Wotan. Wotansvolk was more of a publication endeavor and an ideology than a kindred, never really functioning as a group of local adherents who gather for community and religious practice. Instead, Wotansvolk has served primarily as the publisher and promoter of David Lane's and Ron McVan's racist writings. Together they have enunciated a form of Heathenry in which militant ideology is marshaled in pursuit of a racial holy war for the survival of the Aryan race and the building of a white nationalist state.[221] Mattias Gardell reports that a "meteoric rise" in the group's popularity in the late 1990s resulted in the dissemination of its ideology and

---

219. Redwald, "Resisting the Wolf Age," *The Odinic Rite*, June 9, 2015, www.odinic-rite.org/main/resisting-the-wolf-age/.

220. Gardell, *Gods of the Blood*, 191. Gardell includes a detailed discussion of Wotansvolk in his examination of racist Heathenry. David Lane died in 2007.

221. Mattias Gardell, "Black and White Unite in Fight?" in *The Cultic Milieu: Oppositional Subcultures in an Age of Globalization*, eds. Jeffrey S. Kaplan and Heléne Lööw (Walnut Creek, CA: AltaMira Press, 2002), 170.

material across the world.[222] As a registered vendor for the US federal prison system, Wotansvolk was influential in propagating the virulent racially charged culture that characterizes many of the white supremacist Norse Pagan groups in prison.

The growth of independent Asatru kindreds throughout the United States formed another important aspect of these years. From my perspective, this trend has proved as important as McNallen's return and the founding of the new AFA for the development of Heathenry. These new kindreds were often started by people who may not have been active participants in the national Heathen organizations, but who were inspired by the broader Pagan revival and other cultural elements that preconditioned their interests toward Heathenry. In their religious seeking, they became disillusioned by mainstream Christianity, drifted into the Wiccan scene only to be unsatisfied by its "fluffy bunny" and eclectic approach. Often, these new adherents became aware of Asatru through the Internet and by the publications or activities of the national organizations and began to build their own practice. Many of these new kindreds were a flash in the pan, surviving for only a short time, while their members drifted into other kindreds or out of the movement altogether. The short-lived nature of most kindreds is typical of new religious movements: the huge investment of time and energy necessary to organize and maintain a small group of disparate individuals, the difficulties involved in leadership, lack of funding, issues of personality and emotional maturity, and more, all conspire to make most organizational forms quite ephemeral.

However, what is notable about Asatru in the 1990s was the emergence of many gifted leaders and the formation of several long-term kindreds that continue to operate now twenty or more years later. The impact of these kindreds is inestimable in the overall growth of the movement. Some of these include Raven Kindred in the northeastern United States, Murray's Arizona Kindred in the southwest, Diana Paxson's Hrafnar Kindred in the San Francisco Bay area on the West coast, and Mjolnir Kindred in the Mountain West. While numerous kindreds now exist in the southeastern United States, the development has been somewhat slower given the conservative cultural and religious nature of this region that made Pagan expression difficult. Note the wide geographical area

---

222. Ibid., 341, 225–26.

of these kindreds. They were instrumental in growing Asatru into a movement spread through the United States by providing long-term local leadership, introducing new people to the faith and practice, spawning new kindreds, and creating regional Asatru identities and communities. For example, Raven Kindred was formed in the early 1990s by Lewis Stead. Since that time, it has directly participated in the development of several other kindreds, such as Raven Kindred North and Raven Kindred South. While these kindreds have fluctuated in size and activity, they have nourished people who have gone on to become regional leaders and form other groups throughout the northeast.

Gladsheim Kindred, started and led by a long-time Asatru gothi and leader Joe Marek, is an example of this trend. In addition to his twenty years of leadership of Gladsheim Kindred, Marek's major impact on Asatru comes from starting and running East Coast Thing (ECT), the most important regional Asatru gathering on the East Coast that has met annually since 1998.[223] What happened at ECT was not like an althing, in that there were no obvious decision-making or adjudications meant to be binding on all in attendance. Rather it was organized around having fun, building informal relationships, educational workshops, and opportunities for religious practice. ECT has been influential in forming a truly regional identity on the northeastern coast with its own history, personalities, and customs, and has offered opportunities for numerous leaders such as writers and teachers, poet and musicians, farmers, and others. In addition, the event has been part of developing a second generation of young Heathen leaders on the East Coast. These include the leadership of the Open Halls Project, a non-profit organization advocating for Heathens in the military; young Heathens who are pursuing higher education in the study of Old Norse and Icelandic language, history and culture; and others who are developing innovative subsets of practice such as Manx-oriented Heathenry.

Another example is Mjolnir Kindred, founded in 1995 in Colorado and led by Torsen, who appeared earlier in the book's Introduction leading an Odin blót at a gathering in Kansas. It was his leadership of this ritual that first caught my attention. In some ways, Torsen is characteristic of the leaders that emerged in the 1990s. He has a big and vibrant personality with plenty of charisma. He is both

---

223. Joe Marek, phone interview with author, February 23, 2015.

an inspiring visionary and someone who has dedicated himself to learning and studying, becoming knowledgeable of the Lore. One of the centerpieces of his religious life is his bookshelf filled with both new and classic works. He is also a gifted gothi, skilled with the runes and with leading ritual. Born in eastern Kentucky and raised by a Danish grandfather who encouraged his religious curiosity, Torsen claims to have never identified as a Christian.[224] As his name indicates, he came into religious maturity as a follower of Thor. Only later did he feel called to become a devotee of Odin. Torsen describes this as a shift in his approach to religion in which new Odinic characteristics emerged in his life. He began to explore this new side to himself as a scholar and teacher. Over the twenty years of Mjolnir's existence, many new Heathens have been nurtured by Torsen's leadership. While kindreds tend to be somewhat fluid in membership and participation, Torsen was able to grow Mjolnir to a significant size, so much so that it earned the nickname "The Empire." But one of the most significant contributions was Torsen's cooperation and collaboration with other kindreds to create a tangible Midwestern Heathen identity and community. Eventually a chain of inter-connected kindreds arose through the American Midwest from Minnesota to Texas. As this occurred, the cultural center of gravity shifted from the national organizations, both the AFA in California and the AA's Althing in the Southwest, to independent gatherings in the Midwest.

This network attained a good deal of attention in the Heathen community with the emergence of the Midwest Tribes as a regional identity and Lightning Across the Plains (LATP) as the largest American Heathen gathering in the late 2000s. The movement was inspired by the charismatic and gifted leadership of Mark Stinson, leader of Jotun's Bane, another independent kindred located in Kansas City. Stinson made a splash by leaving or, depending on your source, being expelled from the AFA. He enunciated a very strong and coherent form of tribal and regional Heathenry in several books, which seemed to fit well with the culture and ethos of the Midwest. In his writings he also documented the growth of Jotun's Bane from his first hopeful search for other Heathens in his area, to its development as a strong and disciplined tribe. With the help of his Jotun's Bane kindred, he established Lightning Across the Plains

---

224. Torsen, interview.

as a regional event that provided opportunities for other leaders, called chieftains in this Midwestern Heathen culture, to participate and share power in cooperative ways. As one of the experienced and influential chieftains in the Midwest, Thorsson and Mjolnir Kindred were at the heart of this movement, demonstrating once again that the presence of long-term leaders holding together kindreds with organizational viability contributed significantly to a context for the rapid expansion of the movement.

The development of magic as a significant Heathen practice can also be traced to the 1990s. Runes had been a significant part of the movement for some time, particularly as a result of Flowers/Thorsson's involvement in the movement. But it was the introduction of seið practice, an ancient Norse shamanic practice by Diana Paxson and Hrafnar Kindred, which began to shift the movement towards the wider prominence of magical practice. We will hear more from Diana Paxson and examine seið magic in greater detail in later chapters. However, she is an example of another charismatic leader around whom a long-term kindred took shape, resulting in a subset of Heathen practice that substantially changed the movement as a whole. Paxson discovered Paganism as a religious seeker in college, where she also honed her skills as a writer.[225] She later married into the family of Marion Zimmer Bradley, who was also the author of the best-selling novel *The Mists of Avalon* and other fantasy books. The book, which retells the story of King Arthur and includes the prominent theme of an ancient Goddess religion clashing with the advent of Christianity in the British Isles, has nourished the religious yearnings and imaginations of countless contemporary Pagan practitioners. Paxson worked closely with Bradley and went on to author a well-received series of fantasy novels that carried on the story begun in the *Mists of Avalon* series. Paxson's spiritual journey took her deep into Wicca and the Goddess movement, where she developed as a writer and leader of ritual. While she had explored some Norse myths, it was her interest in shamanic practice that brought her to Asatru. While learning the art of shamanic journeying, she encountered the god Odin in a vision that would eventually alter the direction of her life. She began researching the Lore for information about the Norse practice of seið and with the help of her kindred formulated a workable practice that brought

---

225. Paxson, interview.

this ancient magical practice into the contemporary age. Since that time, Paxson has published several books and trained hundreds of Heathen practitioners in her Hrafnar method of seið. But perhaps even more importantly, her introduction of the practice contributed to a context in which many Heathens, both men and women, began exploring magical practice in a Heathen context.

## A Vibrant Multi-Faceted Religious Culture: The 2000s

All this growth and change in the Heathen movement were not lost on Margot Adler. By the 2006 edition of *Drawing Down the Moon*, there are clear changes in how she portrays Heathenism, as she calls it, reflecting the broader religious context that had emerged over the last decade.[226] While the concerns over racism and far right politics are still apparent, the most critical comments have been removed from this ultimate edition. For instance, her comment in 1986 that "I might not share these values but the movement needs to be represented fairly," was absent from the 2006 edition, as well as the indictment of Heathens for scoring low on Kohlberg's morality assessment. Several other aspects of Adler's 2006 edition demonstrate her reassessment of the quality and place of Heathenry. She was able to draw on and quote from a broader spectrum of Heathen groups and adherents, including members of the Troth, which as we have seen represents a version of Heathenry closer to the normative values of many contemporary Pagans. Gone was the dichotomy between racist Odinism and the slightly less racist version of folkish Asatru. Instead she recognizes the growing diversity of approaches to Heathen religion, such as universalist and tribalist forms. She includes a discussion on the variety of folkish interpretations that exist within Heathenry, indicating that the term is wider than McNallen's metagenetics theory alone.[227] Perhaps the most important aspect of growth from Adler's perspective is the emergence of seið as a magical practice in Heathenry, a development that brought Heathenry significantly closer to Wicca and Witchcraft.[228] Diana Paxson receives a great deal of attention, discussing her own discovery of the practice in the Lore and the Hrafnar method of inducing trance, shamanic journeying,

---

226. Adler, *Drawing Down the Moon* (2006), 284–99.
227. Ibid., 293–94.
228. Ibid., 295–97.

and oracular visioning. Adler also touches on other approaches to seið, calling it "one of the most exciting developments in the last decade" within Heathenry.

All told, Adler paints a picture of Asatru as quickly evolving into a form more compatible with the larger world of contemporary Paganism, a movement that is increasingly reaching out to network with others. Casting most of her original hesitancy aside, she concludes her examination with a very positive assessment: "There is no question," she writes, "that Heathenism is one of the most important and creative parts of contemporary Paganism today."[229] I have to agree that my assessment was much the same, several years after Adler's last revision. As I traveled across the country, I found a degree of diversity, a sense of creativity, and a growing religious culture. Adler definitely sensed the important and positive trajectory of this religion. At the same time, other directions and trajectories are evident. As we will explore further in chapter 3, the tensions and high boundaries surrounding folkish Heathenry continue to strain relationships with inclusive Heathens and the broader Pagan community. And as we will discover throughout the book, the variety of Heathen identities continues to multiply.

We have seen how an association with racist ideology has shadowed Heathenry since the late 1970s. Adler describes this perception within the Pagan community. But an additional dynamic was the level of increased scrutiny received by Asatru and Odinist groups by anti-racist watchdog groups and federal authorities. In the wake of the Oklahoma City bombing by white supremacist Timothy McVey, the late 1990s and the first decade of the 2000s became interesting times for Asatru and Odinist groups. The federal security agencies had a heightened awareness of domestic terrorism associated with white supremacist groups. Beginning in the late 1990s the Southern Poverty Law Center began releasing reports on the potential dangers of Odinism and Asatru as propagators of racial hatred and potential violence. The surveillance and negative press coverage did not affect most practitioners in any direct way. Kindreds were not being raided by the ATF or taken for questioning by the FBI, yet there was a general perception by many in the movement of increased social pressure and a shadow that categorized all Asatru adherents as racists and neo-Nazis.

---

229. Ibid., 299.

Kindred leaders found themselves having to differentiate Asatru from racist Norse Pagans and explain away the presumption of guilt to inquirers. Jeffrey Kaplan's research looked at this dynamic and clearly distinguished the violent potential in the millennialism and rhetoric of racialist Odinism from the non-violent ideology and culture of Asatru. However, despite his work and that of others since, associations and accusations of racism continue to occasionally cast a shadow over the movement.

While independent kindreds and regional identities seem to predominate Heathenry in the second decade of the 2000s, national organizations remain important. The AFA and the Troth continue to thrive and play substantial roles in the movement and seem to have stabilized for the time being as representatives of two differing Heathen ideologies. After a long career as the major personality and visionary leader of the AFA since its founding in 1994, McNallen announced in 2016 that he was stepping down from his executive role and turning over the daily leadership to the AFA's board of directors. McNallen initially stated that he would pursue new directions as a writer and spiritual leader, a trajectory indicated by the publication of his first book, *Asatru: A Native European Spirituality*. However, he seems to have chosen a more political and controversial path instead, siding openly with the racist right.

Since its inception, the Troth has had a more democratic leadership structure than the AFA, with a board of directors called the High Rede led by a Steersman, all of whom are elected by the membership of the Troth. After some rocky years and leadership struggles in the 1990s, this democratic rotation of leadership seems to be working well with several capable and creative Steersman: the scholar and ritualist Victoria Clare, and the writer and wit Steven Abell. The current steer, assuming the role in 2016, is Robert L. Schreiwer, an avid gardener and herbalist who developed and practices Urglaawe, a type of Heathenry drawn from his Pennsylvania German heritage. As with so many other volunteer leaders who populate the Pagan landscape, they exercise their gifts of creativity and leadership because of their commitment to building the religion and culture of Heathenry. Under their leadership the Troth has become the strongest organizational representative of diversity and inclusivity in the Heathen movement.

Since 2010, a significant development has occurred in the use of the Internet, affecting the entire Heathen movement. Financial scarcity has challenged Heathenry, and all of contemporary Paganism for that matter, since its earliest days. Not only are adherents widely dispersed and often facing personal economic challenges as a result of class disparities in America, but an ethos of individualism has prevented the accumulation of capital and wealth in the movement. For the most part, kindreds have not "passed the plate" as many Christian churches do, nor do they make demands on their members for money. Nor have I met a goði or gyðja or any other Heathen leader who was being compensated for their religious work. Stephen McNallen shares a story about how the demise of the Asatru Free Assembly was hastened by this attitude, relating that in addition to their full-time jobs, he and his wife were working a hundred hours a week on AFA related matters. "We could not continue putting out this effort without financial compensation," he writes. "When we approached the membership, the general reaction was negative. Some accused us of trying to 'establish a priesthood' or of being 'money hungry.'"[230] These sorts of economic challenges have taken their toll on the development of the movement, which generally speaking lacks any sort of infrastructure. Organizations have limped along with minimal members' dues and most kindreds lack any sort of budget, reducing their ability to complete sizeable projects or maintain property. In the face of this situation, Heathens have increasingly been turning to online crowdsourcing websites such as GoFundMe and Kickstarter to raise money and generate capital (see figure 5). Crowdsourcing has the benefit of being voluntary— Heathens can choose to support the projects of their choice without feeling the pressure or expectation of mandatory giving. Heathen innovators and entrepreneurs can reach out directly to an international Heathen audience and make a case for their project. As one might expect, the level of a Heathen's reputation and the extent of their network in the community will have much to do with the success of these campaigns. In addition, it spreads out the financial base so one small group is not continually being mined for funds. The beauty of crowdsourcing is that small voluntary donations by a large group of people can raise significant amounts of money.

Heathens seem to be well disposed toward this crowd-sourcing method and adopting it on a wide scale. The projects that Heathens post are not always religious in nature, some having to do with

230. McNallen, *Asatru*, 64.

Figure 5. Kickstarter Package from Tauring's Crowdfunded Project. (Photo by author.)

supporting the needs of other Heathen people. For instance, a GoFundMe campaign was started and completed to support a Heathen who ran into legal trouble. Another campaign sought to raise money to help with medical bills for a Heathen who fell ill. These sorts of fundraising efforts are opportunities for Heathens to network, build and maintain friendships, and practice the value of generosity. Other campaigns have sought to fund religiously oriented projects. A Heathen campground, Thor's Hollow, has been supported in part by donations received through a crowdsourcing site. Kari Tauring, a musician and völva who also appears throughout this book, has funded two album projects through Kickstarter, successfully raising enough money to afford studio time and cover production costs. Her albums are the results of her study of Norse culture and traditions, including trips reconnecting to her ancestry, and magical and musical explorations of Norse and Heathen-related themes. The Wolves of Vinland have also used a crowdfunding campaign to raise approximately five thousand dollars towards the construction of a hall on their land in Virginia. McNallen and the Asatru Folk Assembly achieved a stunning success in Heathen crowdfunding in 2015. They raised over fifty thousand dollars through the donations of close to three hundred backers for the purpose of buying property and renovating a building for a religious site. The property consists of three acres and a large community building, which the AFA has converted into a hof, which will be used for AFA events. What this means for the future of the AFA and its profile in the Heathen movement remains to be seen, although it definitely gave a boost to McNallen's status and vision. With successful campaigns such as these, we should expect to see increasing numbers of Heathens turning to crowdfunding.

## Chapter 2

## Tributaries of the Heathen Movement

Early one summer morning in 2012 in a state park in rural northern Minnesota, about fifteen of us fled the voracious clouds of mosquitoes and gathered together in the small meeting room of a rustic cabin. At the group leader's suggestion, we moved an arm's length apart and stood in loose lines in what looked at first like the beginning of a yoga or a Zumba class. Then following the direction of the leader, we began to move our bodies into the runic poses called "stadhagaldr."[231] The term was coined by Edred Thorsson as part of his project to domesticate völkisch sources for use within American Asatru. As contributors to the runic revival inspired by List in the early twentieth century, Friedrich Marby and Siegfried Kummer developed systems called *Runengymnastick* or *Runenyoga* as part of an Ariosophic regime of physical and spiritual health.[232] Thorsson adapted the practice for his own runic system, renaming it in Old Norse to legitimate its place in Heathenry, and introducing it to an American, and eventually an international audience, in his book *Futhark: A Handbook of Rune Magic*.[233] Thorsson's stadhagaldr involves taking on bodily postures, which Thorsson refers to as

---

231. The word "stadhagaldr" is a neologism created by Edred Thorsson and derived from two Old Norse words: *staða*, referring to a standing place or position in this case understood as a bodily posture; and *galdr*, which means a magical song, spell, an incantation. See Cleasby and Vigfusson, *An Icelandic Dictionary*, s.v. "staða" and "galdr." For Thorsson, the activity of taking on the physical shape of the rune stave is a type of incantation, or magic working in which the energies of the rune move through the body.

232. Schnurbein, *Norse Revival*, 115–16. Schnurbein notes that runic yoga as fashioned by Marby and Kummer was tied to their racial views. See also Thorsson, *Futhark*, 124.

233. Thorsson's *Futhark* has been so formative to rune magic in American Heathenry that it might be considered as part of the modern Lore. Schnurbein indicates the global reach of the Thorsson's work when she mentions that many of her European respondents had his books as part of their personal libraries. See Schnurbein, *Norse Revival*, 118, n. 124.

*stödhur* (singular *stadha*) in a way similar to the asanas of hatha yoga. Each stadha is meant to resemble or imitate the staves or physical shapes of the runic letters. Our morning routine in Minnesota closely followed the basic practice outlined by Thorsson. Following our teacher, we slowly moved our limbs from one runic pose to the next until we had shaped the entire elder futhark with our bodies. Pausing between movements, we held each stadha for a few seconds while intoning the rune name in a quiet humming chant. Thorsson refers to this vocal practice of chanting rune names as "galdr." In the Old Norse tradition, the term galdr seems to have referred broadly to a range of songs, vocal incantations, formulas, and spells, as well as a poetic meter known as *galdralag* associated with magical uses.[234] While Thorsson acknowledges these traditions, he tends to use the term more narrowly to refer to the incantation of individual rune names and sounds. While representing a possible reconstruction of galdr, this specific practice does not seem to be attested in the medieval Norse sources.[235] Instead, Thorsson has derived the practice from his völkisch sources, the use of mantras in Hinduism, as well as Theosophy and ceremonial magic. Thorsson's practice is related to his idea of "rune streams," in which the runes are understood as cosmic energies, vibrations that flow through the world. Just as the stödhur act to shape practitioners' bodies into antennae for these energies, so galdr allows the body to vibrate with the runic power. This has the effect of shaping the practitioner's body into a runic talisman through which these natural energies move into the phenomenal world, "so that he or she *becomes a walking rune tine!*"[236]

Like yoga or t'ai chi, the movements and postures of stadhagaldr are practiced in conjunction with controlled breathing and

---

234. Britt-Mari Näsström, "Healing Hands and Magical Spells," in *Old Norse Myths, Literature and Society: Proceedings of the 11th International Saga Conference*, eds. Geraldine Barnes and Margaret Clunies Ross (Sydney: Centre for Medieval Studies, University of Sydney, 2000), 357–59; Mircea Eliade, "The Yearning for Paradise in Primitive Tradition," *Daedalus* 88, no. 2 (1959): 258. Both Näsström and Eliade suggest that "singing" galdr may be associated with the shamanic imitation of birdsong.

235. Thorsson, *Futhark*, 20, 134–35. Thorsson states that the practice of chanting rune names, which he refers to as galdr, represents the "root form of incantation, or if you will mantra, which is the vibratory embodiment of the rune." He briefly mentions the Norse meanings of galdr and suggests that his readers engage in further study.

236. Ibid., 125.

meditative states of mind. All this resonates with the idea that the runes are magical letters, whose sounds and shapes carry esoteric meaning and power. By forming the runic stave with one's body, enunciating the sound, the tonal vibration of the rune, and by mentally concentrating on the rune, one draws the specific power of the rune, allowing it to flow through oneself. Adherents suggest that the practice can be used for healing, emotional control, magical manipulation of energy, and the development of higher states of awareness.[237] Stadhagaldr is thus a type of health and wellness practice situated within the context of Germanic völkisch ideology. Here we were, a group of middle-class Americans from the Midwest heartland, many of whom had a long personal history of contemporary Pagan practice, all engaging in a German völkisch natural health ritual from the 1920s. How did such an interesting and unexpected event occur? This is no accident of history, but the drawing together of varied intellectual tributaries into a new form of religious practice. In the following pages, we will explore the ways that ideas and practices have flowed together to create the diverse forms of Heathenry we find in the movement today.

## *Rivers and Living Religions*

In the process of researching the Heathen movement and writing this book, my family and I moved to a new location quite near Cumberland Falls in southeastern Kentucky in the heart of the Cumberland River watershed. Living so close to the river has been an interesting experience. My commute to the university takes me across the river each day, bringing it continually to my attention. My children and I participated in the Cumberland River clean-up day, held annually now for nearly forty years, in which volunteers work to remove some of the vast quantity of trash that washes down the river and collects around the Cumberland Falls in the spring floods. My son and I have clambered over the boulders along the riverbank bagging up large trash bags full of plastic, glass, and Styrofoam debris. We have hiked the trails in the hills along its length, and taken time to sit quietly on its bank listening to its voice and meditating on its slow but inexorable and infinite motion. We have observed the deer, fish, and birds who make the watershed their home. We

---

237. Thorsson, *Rune-Might*, 38–39.

have been caught up in its amazing power and energy while rafting a section of its length. We have traced its length on a map with our fingers and followed its meandering path on Google Earth. The river has come to inhabit a part of my consciousness.

But what is the river? I speak as if it is one thing, one entity, but that is only an abstraction, not really the case at all. Its headwaters are three small streams that flow together in the Appalachian Mountains near Harlan in eastern Kentucky. As it moves through Kentucky and Tennessee toward its ultimate conjunction with the Ohio River, the Cumberland River becomes itself only as other tributaries contribute to it. The Laurel and Rockcastle rivers in Kentucky, Stones River in Nashville, Tennessee, and west of it, the Harpeth River, and many other tributaries flow together to form what we call the Cumberland. At each confluence, the river changes somewhat as the tributary adds something new and alters the character of the river. Each tributary carries with it the history of its own unique watershed, mixing it into the Cumberland. Depending on how the streams combine, the confluence might be smooth and clear or muddy and turbulent, slow and easy or driven by a fast current. Each tributary creates new and distinct sorts of flows and currents, eddies and ecosystems, contours and water qualities. It is important to note that these tributaries are not simply one-time additions to the river, but are continually acting upon and shaping the river. As those tributaries ebb and flow, so does their effect on the river system. The river is not one static entity but a dynamic system that changes with the confluence of each tributary.

In a way, the river system has become a metaphor through which I think about religions. Religions, like rivers, are not static entities but dynamic systems with their own tributaries and confluences that add to and alter the character of the religion, that create subsets, change its shape, and account for its contours. These tributaries of religion are distinct memes: ideas and practices, intellectual histories and traditions that contribute to and shape the religion. As they mix in different confluences, they create new and different forms of religious life within the tradition. Buddhism, flowing into China, takes on the tributary of ancestor veneration. Hinduism flowing into the American context converges with the important cultural meme of women's empowerment to produce yoga classes predominantly female in composition. As American Christianity flows through the cultural turn towards environmentalism, enough surface tension is broken to produce small currents of green Christianity. For such a relatively new and small religious movement, Heathenry is marked by a surprising diversity of practice: from strict scholarly reconstructionists, to nature-loving animists, to black leather bikers with a Viking warrior ethic. What accounts for this diversity are the tributaries that flow together to create what we call Asatru or Heathenry. The labels and boundaries themselves are fluid and contested. The contours of the religion can only begin to make sense if we think about Heathenry as a river system and begin to explore and understand the tributaries that are flowing into it and the confluences they create. This river system insight has brought a great deal of clarity to my understanding of this complex movement. This chapter will attempt to begin that exploration, charting some of the most apparent tributaries and noticing the distinct subsets of belief and practice that result from their confluences. My analysis is much in debt to the scholars and observers of Heathenry who have shared their own perspectives on the movement. Each has been a valuable contribution to our understanding and comprehension of the movement.

## *The Heathen Watershed*

A watershed is a term designating the geographical region draining into any particular waterway. I briefly described the watershed of the Cumberland River above, the region consisting of all the streams that flow into the Cumberland. Applying this hydraulic term to Heathenry, we can think of a range of ideas, practices, and movements that flow into and contribute to the formation and diversity of Heathenry. I have adopted this term by thinking about Colin Campbell's important idea of the cultic milieu, introduced in his 1972 essay "The Cult, the Cultic Milieu and Secularization."[238] In the essay, Campbell noted two salient characteristics of alternative religions: on one hand, their ephemeral nature, with many groups having a fairly short lifespan; but on the other hand, the continual presence of alternative religions in society, caused by the frequent and ongoing innovation of new religious groups and movements.

---

238. Colin Campbell, "The Cult, the Cultic Milieu and Secularization," in *The Cultic Milieu: Oppositional Subcultures in an Age of Globalization*, eds. Jeffrey Kaplan and Heléne Mööw (Walnut Creek, CA: AltaMira Press, 2002), 12–25.

Campbell proposed that beneath the rise and fall of these groups a more persistent source must exist to support the production of new forms of alternative religion. He called this the "cultic milieu," and envisioned a cultural repository of alternative knowledge, beliefs, and practices that had been rejected by the orthodoxy of mainstream society, but continually used and reused by alternative religionists. The milieu functions in the intellectual margins of society, consisting of "all deviant belief systems and their associated practices," collecting and recirculating them into the culture. Imagine a disparate group of religious innovators all reading the same books and journals, sharing ideas in articles, and repackaging old ideas in new forms. The cultic milieu, he wrote, "is continually giving birth to new cults, absorbing the debris of the dead ones and creating new generations of cult-prone individuals."[239] Updating his language, we might say that this rich repository of ideas and practices serves as the intellectual aquifer of alternative religion in America, supporting the development of alternative religious groups and shaping new generations of individuals receptive to alternative religion.

Despite the diversity and range of ideas found within the cultic milieu, everything from quasi-scientific beliefs to ancient mythology, Campbell observed a remarkable unity among those who draw upon it as a source of ideas and practices. One source of unity is what we might call the "camaraderie of the marginalized," which may be found among those who are pushed to the social margins and exist outside of the ideas, lifestyle patterns, and social structures approved by the mainstream, who may receive ridicule and even hostility from the agents of mainstream society. Campbell also found that these diverse groups and movements shared a high degree of receptivity towards each other's ideas: that ideas tend to flow among these movements, in a fluid way without clear boundaries, generating a degree of syncretism. As we will see, there is no doubt that Heathenry, like other new religions, is a bricolage, an "amalgamation of many bits and pieces of diverse cultural systems," as Bron Taylor puts it.[240] The sharing of ideas was facilitated through "overlapping

---

239. Ibid., 14.
240. Bron Taylor, "Diggers, Wolves, Ents, Elves and Expanding Universes: Bricolage, Religion, and Violence from EarthFirst! and the Earth Liberation Front to the Antiglobalization Resistance," in *The Cultic Milieu: Oppositional Subcultures in an Age of Globalization*, eds. Jeffrey Kaplan and Heléne Mööw (Walnut Creek, CA: AltaMira Press, 2002), 28.

communication structures" within the milieu. For Campbell, writing in 1972, these communication structures consisted primarily of literature produced by various groups: magazines and pamphlets in which ideas, articles, and advertisements drove a process of cross-fertilization among specific groups and movements. This process has been shifted into overdrive since the appearance of Campbell's article, driven now by the massive online participation of alternative religious groups through websites, discussion forums, and online publication of religious material. The factor of the Internet helps to explain the dramatic growth in alternative religious adherence in contemporary American society because it serves as an important interface between alternative religions and more mainstream or orthodox members of society. Online, the traditional boundaries between mainstream and alternative or heterodox ideas become blurred. Small alternative groups and once-marginalized religions become easier to find and take on a greater appearance of parity, appearing side by side with socially accepted mainstream ideas. The online context has facilitated a quicker flow of alternative ideas into the mainstream, as well as contributing to a flatter religious world in which alternative ideas, shorn from an association with stigmatized publications, can compete with more orthodox ideologies. These communication structures facilitate not only the flow of ideas, but also linkages among groups that review one another's literature, and advertise each other's meetings. Campbell described a process that has grown immensely in importance, helping to explain the movement of people through the alternative religion scene. Why, for instance, many Asatru adherents begin their religious search in other places, such as in the practice of ceremonial magic, or neo-shamanism, or tarot card reading, or Wicca, or as we will see racial movements or underground black metal music. By both haphazard religious exploration and by intentional religious choice-making, seekers make their way toward Heathenry, drifting along the tributaries and confluences of the watershed through a series of linkages formed through books, journals, websites, meetings, and conversations.

*The Boundaries of the Watershed*

The study of Heathenry demonstrates the continued relevance of Campbell's theory in that Heathenry also draws from the tributaries of alternative knowledge. One notable feature of Heathen culture is the resistance to and outright rejection of certain ideas. Rather than share, include, and syncretize, there are many elements of the cultic milieu, many alternative ideas, which a great many Heathens vociferously resist. Indeed, observing the tendency toward syncretism by many alternative religious groups, Heathens have tended to set themselves apart and to be vigilant in identifying and weeding out ideas and practices that seem "un-Heathen" or not Germanic or Norse in their origin. Heathens recognize the tendency for a sharing or blurring of ideological boundaries, and do not wish to resemble other Pagans and New Agers, who are perceived as eager to embrace and accept everything coming. That is, Heathens tend to reject a shared identity with other alternative religions, a position they enact by rigorously vetting ideas and practices to avoid syncretism. Thus, Campbell's theory of the cultic milieu proves an incredibly powerful tool in understanding the history of Heathenry, both in how it fits and how it does not.

Campbell's description of the cultic milieu as consisting of all deviant beliefs and associated practices gives the impression of an inchoate mass of alternative, marginal, and dangerous ideas. But is this the case? A study of Heathenry suggests that in contrast, the cultic milieu is structured and organized in two ways: by intellectual traditions or lineages, which I shall call tributaries; as well as by the preferences of distinct movements themselves in approving certain types or sources of knowledge and disapproving others. Rather than drawing indiscriminately on the repository of alternative ideas, groups may create criteria for selecting from the variety of streams of alternative knowledge available to them. Through the use of criteria, movements define and give shape to distinct sets or intersections of approved ideas, a confluence of intellectual tributaries that inform their own distinct sub-milieus, a watershed of ideas that flow into the movement. This bounded set of tributaries is formed and maintained through any group's ideological process: the internal dialogue and politics of the movements themselves that give shape to the watershed by approving some intellectual streams and disapproving others.

The nebulous quality of the cultic milieu, as well as the syncretism and blurring of ideas that arises from it, are substantiated and challenged by the Heathen movement. While all marginal ideas might exist within the cultic milieu, de facto boundaries are established, negotiated, and contested in the living practice of groups and movements, through real time connections, modes of communication, ideological and theological positions and other factors. These boundaries may be more or less ephemeral and are imposed upon it by various interpreters and practitioners, yet they are no less real for that. The most intense sorts of political and personal wars may be waged upon these battlements. Syncretism may be the natural result of the indeterminate nature of the cultic milieu; ideas flow among groups and are appropriated in innovative ways. But that does not mean that such borrowing or stealing is uncontested at all times. The boundaries established by groups are policed or maintained in many different ways, including censorship, social isolation, the personal authority of a guru or charismatic leader, or through a community process in which ideas are vetted, approved, or disapproved. A sub-milieu, an ideological watershed, is almost a curated event: defined, shaped, and presented according to the gatekeepers of a movement or group. This is not merely an accident of history, but also a result of an ideological process. In the Heathen world, in which syncretism is a dirty word and considered almost moral failure, such borrowing passes through an informal community process of critique. Heathens are continually contesting the value of ideas and resources and subjecting them to a rhetorical process that puts into effect this bounding of the Heathen milieu. Every idea must show itself worthy by undergoing a social struggle through which it is accepted or rejected.

### The Heathen Milieu and the Blank Rune

The discourse around runes illustrates how ideas are bounded, approved and disapproved, and understood within the Heathen movement. Speaking anecdotally, there is a fair degree of interest in runes in the contemporary Pagan community. This interest arises, I think, from the broader interest and usage of systems of divination by Pagans. Runes, in addition to being an ancient writing system of Northern Europe, have a pedigree of magical use. In the modern period, runes are closely associated with divination and many techniques have been developed for casting and interpreting runes as a magical means of acquiring occult knowledge. In addition to the stream of scholarly books on runes, numerous books on the magical uses of runes, particularly as divination tools, have been published representing a diverse range of approaches and philosophies. But not all of these runic streams flow into Heathenry. Heathens tend to understand runes as more or less particular to the Germanic/Norse cultures, a magical system closely, even inextricably, associated with Heathen religious worldviews. For this reason, Heathens approach rune books with caution and have been aggressive in rejecting those that stray too far from approved ideas and sources. Through this ideological process, certain streams of thought, represented by books, have been accepted or rejected to produce a bounded watershed of Heathen discourse on runes.

The so-called Blank Rune is an example of how this process occurs. In 1982, Ralph Blum released a book entitled *The Book of Runes*, perhaps the first of its kind aimed at the popular market of modern alternative religious practitioners to achieve wide recognition and sales.[241] In it, Blum discusses the runes, their Norse origins, and techniques for divinatory practice. Even though a significant number of rune books have been published since, *The Book of Runes* remains in print and a twenty-fifth anniversary edition was released in 2008, indicating the success of the book.[242] Despite its popularity and its focus on one of the most important aspects of Heathen spirituality, Blum's book has been subjected to a great deal of negative critique from Heathens with the Blank Rune at the epicenter. In the book, Blum introduces a blank or empty tile meant to represent, as he puts it, the Unknown, the Divine element of possibility in every situation.[243] This Blank Rune, which does not appear in any Norse sources, has been received with derision by Heathens who see it as a sort of New Age innovation that disregards the integrity of the runes. Blum is summarily dismissed by Heathens as someone who lacks serious research and fails to fully appreciate the Norse context

---

241. Ralph H. Blum, *The Book of Runes: A Handbook for the Use of an Ancient & Contemporary Oracle* (Los Angeles: Oracle Books, 1982).

242. Ralph H. Blum, *The Book of Runes Twenty-Fifth Anniversary Edition* (New York: St. Martin's Press, 2008).

243. Blum, *The Book of Runes*, 1982 edition, 118. The Blank Rune was not in fact Blum's invention, though he was responsible for introducing it to a widespread audience. He attributes it to the "woman who lived on Trindles Road, in the Surrey town of Redhill." See *The Book of Runes*, 1982 edition, 29. This woman was later identified as British occultist Murry Hope. Hope herself took credit for the Blank Rune, "After several years of experimenting, I settled for the 24 basic runes and added one blank to represent fate or karma, making a total of 25 . . . My magical workings are based on this system." See Murry Hope, "Practical Rune Magic," *Fate* 38, no. 3 (March 1985): 88.

of the runes.[244] A typical Heathen response to the Blank Rune is well represented by this statement:

> You may have picked up a book about runes or purchased a rune set that includes a "blank rune," "Odin Rune" or "Wyrd Rune." This is a very strong clue that the author is not an authority on runes . . . use of his [Blum's] flawed interpretations reveal the user as a novice and lacking in knowledge of true runelore. If you've bought one of his books or another of similar ilk . . . toss the book in the trash.[245]

The writer first questions the authority of Blum's book itself, "the author is not an authority on runes," by which she means that Blum lacks sufficient knowledge and appropriate use of the Lore. By doing so, she writes the source as out of bounds. But next, she castigates those who make use of the book. Such a person could only be "a novice and lacking . . . in true runelore." She cannot consider users of Blum's book to be real Heathens. Now the book is doubly written off as an appropriate source: using it would not only lead to bad information but it would also clearly identify the user a non-Heathen. These sorts of comments draw effective boundaries and are found throughout the continuum of Heathen life. When I was new to the Well of Wisdom kindred and getting to know its members, I was given almost identical advice about rune books. Similarly, a popular Heathen radio show, Raven Radio, dedicated an entire broadcast to critiquing Asatru books, assessing their value and usefulness to the movement, with comments such as "These books are crap. They're not even worthwhile to start a campfire with . . . Here's how bad I dislike those books . . . I will eat lutefisk before I read another one."[246] In 2017, I attended a rune workshop at the Mystic South Pagan conference, during which a non-Heathen attendee asked, "So what about the Blank Rune?" It was an honest question that brought immediate and raucous laughter from the Heathens in the room. The name "Ralph Blum" was sarcastically mentioned and the Blank Rune was quickly dismissed as a practice

---

244. See, for instance, Luther Kovac, "The Rune that Never Was," *Irminfolk* blog, July 1, 2013, http://irminfolk.com/tag/ralph-blum/.

245. Ingrid Halvorsen, "The Blank Rune," *Runes, Alphabet of Mystery* blog, www.sunnyway.com/runes/blank_rune.html.

246. Raven Radio, "Episode 61, Best and Worst Books on Asatru," podcast, August 7, 2011, www.ravenradio.info/download/raven61.mp3. Quote appears at 22:00.

insufficiently based in the Lore. In these ways, the approbation reserved for the Blank Rune and books that espouse it has achieved a level of disapproval as close to dogma as is possible in Heathenry. However, it is not just any sort of innovation that draws the ire of these Heathen critiques. Significantly, the Blank Rune represents the sort of innovation associated with "fluffy bunny" neo-religion, a hopelessly syncretistic religious muddle, indiscriminately drawing on a mix of ideas and carelessly adapting those ideas in ways that sever them from any sort of historically accurate context. Blum's book is one of many that are rejected as representatives of this sort of careless religious practice.

Blum's book has remained "popular among Neopagan and eclectic magic-users," who incorporate runic divination into their practice in innovative ways and may regard runes as an alternative to other divination systems such as the Tarot deck, I Ching, or another of many tools to be appropriated for divination and "fortune-telling" practices.[247] Yet the failure to anchor the use of the runes in their historical and cultural context is anathema from a Heathen perspective. No self-respecting Heathen would walk around with a Tarot deck (at least not in Heathen social spaces). Not because the Tarot itself is "fluffy," but because it does not arise from one of the approved tributaries of Norse/Germanic Paganism. It lacks the sort of pedigree necessary for inclusion in most Heathen circles. Some Heathens would use the Tarot deck for divination, but only in contexts that do not demand practices to be legitimized in this way. From the context of the Heathen milieu, the runes are not simply a less colorful equivalent to the Tarot. To misunderstand them as such is to disembowel the runes of their specific historical, cultural, and magical character and therefore show oneself as not really Heathen. Blum's book makes a similar ideological mistake and as a result has become disapproved and virtually removed from the Heathen milieu.

Interestingly enough, Blum's *A Book of Runes* was published in 1982, just a few years before the publication of Edred Thorsson's book on rune magic, *Futhark*. Unlike Blum's book, Thorsson's text remains a prominent resource for Heathen rune magic. This is

---

247. Association of Independent Readers and Rootworkers, "Runic Divination," *Readers and Rootworkers* website, http://readersandrootworkers.org/wiki/Category:Runic_Divination.

so even though Thorsson relies heavily on rune magician Guido List and other völkisch occultists, who introduced many more innovations to the runes than Ralph Blum, essentially creating their own idiosyncratic runic systems. List himself claimed personal revelation as a source, something that contemporary Heathens would label UPG. Thorsson negotiates problems of legitimacy in several ways. Unlike Blum, Thorsson had established himself as a Heathen, well known in the community and respected for his thorough credentials. He also avoids or tones down the types of innovation that could be considered eclectic and neo-religious from a Heathen perspective by grounding his work in the Norse tradition. He uses the elder futhark, for instance, and having earned a PhD with a dissertation on runes and magic, his approach is scholarly and thorough.[248] Occasionally, it is spectacularly spurious, such as when he uses Old Norse "word garb" like the neologism "stadhagaldr" to dress up innovations in Heathen clothing. He also legitimizes List and the other völkisch sources by downplaying their connections to racist Aryan ideology and presenting them as critical links connecting the runes of the past with the emergence of contemporary runic magic of the Heathen awakening.[249] Thorsson's approach was effective in legitimating *Futhark* as an authentic book of runic magic to a Heathen audience. The Heathen watershed is carefully bounded and its tributaries maintained through an informal process of community critique, negotiation, and evaluation, even though it is sometimes difficult to trace the processes, criteria, and politics by which something gets situated on one side or the other of the boundary.

The strong reconstructionist emphasis within Heathenry places a premium on reviving the religion of the arch-Heathens, demanding a degree of connection to the historical practice of Germanic/Norse Paganism. This influences and limits the types of sources and tributaries that have been available to contemporary Heathens. The received interpretations of some, perhaps many, of those sources

---

248. Stephen Edred Flowers, "Runes and Magic: Magical Formulaic Elements in The Elder Tradition" (PhD diss., University of Texas, 1984).

249. Thorsson, *Futhark*, 15. Thorsson separates List's aims, "which were political in nature" from his system of Armanen runes, which "was based solely on the textual authority of the 'Rune-Song' in the Eddic lay 'Havamal.'" However, he also states that the völkisch ideas "were not very traditional as far as the runes were concerned."

have been influenced by historically recent racial paradigms, such as those that arose during the period of nineteenth-century European nationalism as well as the twentieth-century völkisch material. This means that many of the sources available to Heathens contain some element of, or potential for, racialism. Given this situation, Heathens have faced a choice: to receive non-racial but also less Heathen sources, or to receive the more Heathen even when they are entangled to some degree with racial attitudes. Some Heathens doing this sort of work reject those sources altogether, assiduously avoiding völkisch and Traditionalist authors.[250] More often, the tendency has been to accept those sources, but to do some ideological work around them. Heathens sort through those sources in order to separate out the currents of historical and religious validity from the racial attitudes entangled with them. This approach argues that while racial attitudes may have characterized the völkisch esotericists, those attitudes were not vital to their magical systems. The Nazis, who were the real racists, rejected and even persecuted many of the völkisch Pagans of the time. There is a trade-off with this approach. It adds to the storehouse of religious and cultural data that can be used for reconstruction. However, it also has serious methodological, ethical, and social problems. Promoting völkisch sources has meant that racial concepts have continued to circulate within the movement. When the social context or cultural moment lends itself to these radical themes, they can emerge from Heathenry more vocally and forcefully.

Heathens root their religious identity in a sense of Germanic/Norse authenticity, variously defined. This value has influenced the inclusion of intellectual tributaries. Additionally, it has led to attempts to define boundaries between Heathenry and other varieties of American Paganism. To many outside observers Heathenry may seem indistinguishable from other forms of Paganism. However, many Heathens resist that association and seek to differentiate their religious culture as distinct from Paganism. "Heathen" serves as a marker of that boundary. The Heathen movement is influenced by a range of ideas that are different in specific and often oppositional

---

250. Schnurbein, *Norse Revival*, 80n105. Schnurbein quotes Hilmar Örn Hilmarsson, *Allsherjargoði* of the Icelandic *Ásatrúarfélagið*, saying, "When I hear a mention of Julius Evola I head for the hills." Of course, as an Icelander, Hilmarsson's relationship with the texts is substantially different than that of American adherents.

ways to the tributaries of the broader American Pagan movement. This is not merely an accident of history. It arises from the fact that Heathenry has been shaped by a different set of historical circumstances, giving rise to different sources of thought and a different set of approved ideas. The cultic milieu is not a flat world or an inchoate well of ideas, but is actually constructed and curated in distinct ways by different movements. The Heathen watershed is that dynamic set of symbols and ideas that flow from the approved intellectual tributaries. These represent the boundaries of accepted knowledge: the ideas that Heathens regard as more or less vital to their religious endeavors.

*Religions and River Systems*

By applying the hydraulic terminology of rivers and river systems, I want to convey the dynamism that characterizes religious systems, especially new religious movements. Rivers are formed as tributaries combine, move with incredible power, meander slowly and calmly, carve new channels, pour over high waterfalls or trickle through deep caverns, even stagnate and turn brackish, so religions are shaped in comparable ways. I envision ideas and practices, intellectual lineages, and streams of thought as tributaries that flow, move, separate, and combine. The tributaries represent the historical streams of thought and practice that flow into any religious movement as resources for religious production. Groups are shaped by the tributaries that flow into them. They also interact with those tributaries, utilizing them in new ways. Some tributaries are large and powerful, others small trickling streams. At the junction of these tributaries arises a confluence, the water pattern resulting from two or more streams flowing together. Heathenry and other religious movements take shape as distinct movements by the array of tributaries flowing together to create these confluences: particular, distinct religious and cultural patterns. As disparate tributaries flow together creating new patterns, distinct religious communities arise. These confluences are often highly dynamic as tributaries are brought in or diverted from the confluence to create shifting patterns of practice and theology. All religious systems can be thought of in these terms. A world religion may simply be that confluence whose primary tributaries have remained intact for long periods of time, carving channels in the riverbed, a "main stream" that has accumulated a depth of cultural hegemony. This mainstream responds slowly and more gradually to the influence of other tributaries, more likely to incorporate them than be disrupted by them, remaining more or less undisturbed by the play of tributaries forming eddies around its edges. New religious movements, on the other hand, represent confluences that remain dynamic, highly fluid, and changeable, very responsive to the inflow of new tributaries.

So what are the "main streams" of Heathenry, the primary tributaries without which there is no Heathen movement? Campbell states that the content of the cultic milieu may be difficult to describe until a "detailed cultural map" can be drawn.[251] His comment gives rise to the question: Can we map out to some extent the main intellectual tributaries that give shape to the cultural confluence called the contemporary Heathen movement? Heathenry includes a bewildering diversity—vegetarian environmentalists alongside of Odinist berserkers, bookish scholars, and leather-clad bikers. While these are radically different persuasions of Heathenry and while there may be great animosity between such groups, there are compelling similarities that are hard to ignore. These patterns of difference and similarity, enmity and friendship, only begin to make sense when we look at Heathenry as a number of disparate tributaries forming confluences. By examining and tracing the intellectual tributaries that flow into the American Heathen movement, we begin to make out the relationship among these diverse religionists.

## Two Denominations?

Significant research on Heathenry began in the mid-1990s when Jeffrey Kaplan pointed out what seemed to be two distinct ideologies, or "paths" as he called them, within Heathenry. One, which he called Odinist, was hard-edged, with millennial, racial, and potentially violent tendencies with ideological links to the far right. The other, which he termed Ásatrú, expressed itself in more universalist and non-racial tendencies with links to the magical, occult community of Wicca and Witchcraft.[252] Within the Ásatrú path, Kaplan identified two differing approaches to the issue of ancestry and religion

---

251. Campbell, *Cultic Milieu*, 16.
252. Kaplan, *Radical Religion in America*, 16.

(see figure 6). The first was modernist ideology that *distinguished* religion from ancestry, accepted any who expressed an interest in the gods of Northern Europe as authentic adherents, and represented a type of contemporary Pagan religion. The second was a "geneticist theory" that *derived* religion from ancestry and saw Ásatrú as the native religion of Northern European people.[253] He specifically noted that Odinism had a separate and distinct ideological history that brought it into closer proximity with the political far right. He observed that a key component or characteristic of the Odinist path involved the knowledge of Alexander Rudd Mills, pointing to an intellectual lineage or tributary that was influential among those he described as Odinist.[254] He identified the millenarian approach and race-centered ideology as important cleavages that separated Odinism from Ásatrú. While clearly describing the differences, Kaplan also acknowledged that significant overlap existed between Ásatrú and Odinist ideologies. These two paths may share a good deal of their ritual, iconography or terminology, making it "no easy task to demonstrate a definite point of demarcation between the adherents of Odinism and Ásatrú communities."[255]

Kaplan's insightful and nuanced observation of the Heathen movement in the early and mid-1990s is important for a couple of reasons. He drew attention to this ideological cleavage in American Norse Paganism and did the investigative work to demonstrate that, in contrast to the prevailing opinion, the majority of Norse Pagans

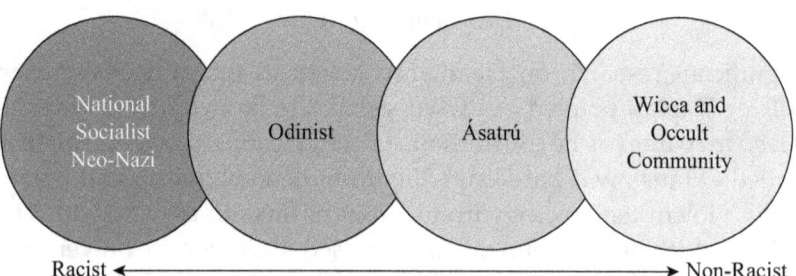

Figure 6. Kaplan's Spectrum of Racial Attitudes.

253. Ibid., 73–84.
254. Kaplan, "Reconstruction of the Ásatrú and Odinist Traditions," 195.
255. Kaplan, *Radical Religion in America*, 72.

were not violent neo-Nazis. More importantly, he began to identify the key ideological resources that distinguished the two sides of the cleavage.

A later phase of research undertaken by Mattias Gardell focused on tracing the connections between Norse Paganism and the racist world of white separatism.[256] Gardell tended to downplay Kaplan's two divisions, often lumping the two terms together as Asatrú/Odinism, and suggesting that the world of Asatrú (Gardell's preferred spelling) is more diverse, complex, and ambiguous.[257] However, like Kaplan, he identified "three distinct positions" comprising an "Asatrú triangle," each of which differently defined the nature of Asatrú and who could properly be involved in it (see figure 7). Like Kaplan's modernist ideology, Gardell associated the anti-racist position with the Ring of Troth (later the Troth), two competing scholars (Edred Thorsson and Kveldúlf Gundarsson), and "a strictly antiracist and antisexist ideology."[258] The radical racist position, to which Gardell also referred as Odinism, defined Asatrú as a racial religion, a religion of the blood, for white people. The race consciousness, millenarian apocalypticism, and violent tendencies of this position were represented by the white supremacist Paganism of Wotansvolk and what Gardell terms Darkside Asatrú, Norse Paganism mixed with "Satanism and occult fascism."[259] Ethnic Asatrú, Gardell's third position, has a more religious and cultural focus than the radical racist Heathens, concerned less with politics and more with rebuilding ancestral, Heathen tribes. Gardell identifies four proponents of this position: McNallen and the AFA, Valgard Murray and the AA, Robert Taylor and his artistic kindred the Tribe of Wulfings, and Max Hyatt, the mystic gothi in the Pacific Northwest and his Wotan's Kindred.[260] At the same time, the ethnic position retains race as a fundamental dimension of the religion.

The efforts of these two scholars have been extremely helpful and influential in laying the groundwork for understanding the landscape of American Heathenry. Gardell's research was primarily

---

256. Gardell, *Gods of the Blood*. See also Gardell, "Black and White Unite in Fight?" 168–69.
257. Gardell, *Gods of the Blood*, 152–53.
258. Ibid., 162–64. Gardell spells Gundarsson's name "KveldúlfR."
259. Ibid., 284.
260. Ibid., 258–66.

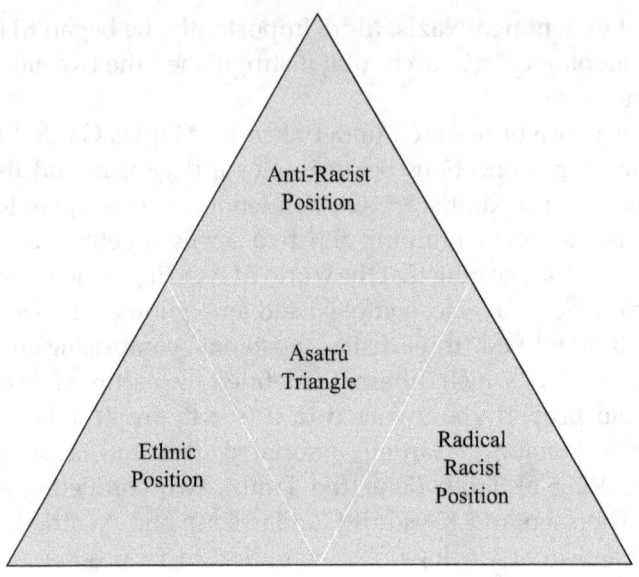

Figure 7. Gardell's Triangle of Racial Positions.

focused on the radical racist camp, and he thoroughly traces the intellectual lineage of Odinist thought, not only identifying the tributaries of racist Heathenry but also describing its content in depth. Gardell further develops a model for categorizing the ideological positions of racialist Heathens (and other extreme and revolutionary movements) along three parameters: a political/economic left–right spectrum, a social authority axis from centralized to decentralized, and a cultural axis from monocultural to multicultural.[261] This valuable work adds to our ability to understand the complexity of the movement. Although Gardell makes it clear that Norse Paganism is quite diverse, his work has left the impression among some readers that Norse Paganism is dominated by a white supremacist agenda, an inaccurate perspective that has unfortunately shadowed Heathens of all sorts. Snook, for instance, writes "My research has led me to believe . . . that although the

---

261. Ibid., 334–39. See also Kaarina Aitamurto and Scott Simpson, "The Study of Paganism and Wicca: A Review Essay," in *The Oxford Handbook of New Religious Movements*, vol. 2, eds. James R. Lewis and Inga Bårdsen Tøllefsen (New York: Oxford University Press, 2016), 490.

vocal white supremacy that Gardell discusses is loudly present, it is not representative of the majority."[262]

Out of this work, a sort of common wisdom developed that Heathens were characterized by two or three well-delineated camps resembling denominations with the defining characteristic being that of race and racial attitudes. Each path, the Asatru and the Odinist, were thought to represent a clear, distinct, and independent intellectual lineage.[263] However, this reification of Heathenry into clear ideological positions over-characterizes the real nature of what is occurring in Heathenry and over-simplifies the work of these two scholars, both of whom acknowledge that the ideological terrain of the movement is more complicated. For instance, Gardell points out that,

> The differences between the two schools of thought are sometimes said to be of such a magnitude that Odinism and Asatrú are better described as two separate religious movements, with Odinism revolving around the primacy of race and Asatrú serving as its nonracist counterpart, positioned squarely in the wider milieu of neopaganism and the occult. In reality, however, there seems to be no such neat division, but a much more complex picture, with self-defined Asatrúers centered on race and active Odinists heavily involved in occult pagan practices.[264]

A nuanced approach that more closely approximates the complex picture of Asatru is suggested by Kaarina Aitamurto and Scott Simpson. They describe contemporary Paganism as "a broad spectrum of overlapping sets of ideologies, practices, and communities that share a family resemblance."[265] In this description Aitamurto and Simpson attempt to hold together the continuity of the Pagan movement with the complex influences at work within it. They indicate that Paganisms of all stripes, Odinists and Wiccans, share from among a set of common characteristics, perhaps including an emphasis on polytheism, animism, and earth-based ideology.

---

262. Jennifer Snook, *American Heathens*, 155.
263. Egil Asprem, "Heathens Up North: Politics, Polemics, and Contemporary Norse Paganism in Norway," *The Pomegranate: The International Journal of Pagan Studies* 10, no. 1 (2008): 45–48.
264. Gardell, *Gods of the Blood*, 152.
265. Kaarina Aitamurto and Scott Simpson, *Modern Pagan and Native Faith Movements in Central and Eastern Europe* (Durham: Acumen, 2013), 3.

At the same time, there are significant and often discordant distinctions among them. Aitamurto and Simpson note that these distinctions fall into recognizable peaks of emphasis, characterizing Paganism as a "polymodal continuum . . . in which there is more than one point at which we find peaks of frequency."[266] While leaving room for a variety of combinations and permutations of Paganism expressed at the regional, local, and organizational levels, they find that two peaks are particularly significant: a left-leaning Paganism characterized by the individualism and Romanticism of the nineteenth-century English poets, and a right-leaning Paganism characterized by the nationalism and traditionalism of early twentieth-century political movements. While Aitamurto and Simpson are looking at Paganism in Central and Eastern Europe, these two peaks are also descriptive of the context of America Paganism. At one level, they are indicative of the tensions observed by Margot Adler between Wiccan-influenced Pagan practice and the Norse Pagan paradigm of Heathenry. At another level, these peaks are remarkably congruent with the two positions or poles identified by Kaplan and Gardell in American Heathenry: left-leaning Asatru and right-leaning Odinism. *Both peaks* are found within the one movement, among groups closely linked by their participation in an American Heathen milieu. At the surface, there may seem to be little difference between the two. There is a family resemblance between the two positions: *both* share the runes as sacred symbols while diverging in their interpretations and uses of those symbols. This creates a contentious situation and an ongoing struggle over identity. When a left-leaning Heathen sees a neo-Nazi carrying a rune-emblazoned flag at the Unite the Right demonstration in Charlottesville, VA, as happened in 2017, there is something personal at stake. While recognizing that these two peaks form an important contour in the movement, it is Aitamurto and Simpson's insight into the polymodal nature of the Pagan milieu that is especially helpful. American Heathenry gives evidence of more than two peaks of frequency and some of these are not easily characterized by distinctions of left and right.[267]

266. Ibid.
267. Aitamurto and Simpson's analysis takes into account this complexity, noting that while this left–right spectrum exists in Central and Eastern European Paganism, the scene is more fully described by the polymodal aspect of their model.

Jennifer Snook also observes that American Heathenry presents a more complex picture than the two or three positions that have often been ascribed to it. While the folkish and universalist categories exist and function within the movement, most Heathens live "between racial exclusivity and complete inclusivity in a historical and cultural context that demands that race be taken into account."[268] Snook attempts to help complicate the contours of Heathenry by identifying four peaks of frequency around which varieties of Heathens may cluster. The first is to identify Heathenry as an indigenous tradition, a northern European religion tied exclusively to northern European culture and ethnicity.[269] Her discussion of this position seems to line up with a hardline racist form of Heathenry that naively draws a direct line between white Americans and a Norse folk soul. A second peak of frequency would see Heathenry as an ancestral faith or family folkway, reminiscent of Gardell's ethnic position, which she describes as "a complex folkway struggling to be ethnic while resisting racist labels."[270] While this position might acknowledge the more complicated ethnic identity of most Americans, Snook points out that "the ancestral focus ... is a slippery slope, where ancestral reverence often translates into prowhite sentiment."[271] Her third peak of frequency represents Heathens who approach the religion as solely a spiritual system focused on spiritual experience and a "mystical experiences of the gods" for which ancestry is irrelevant."[272] This peak resembles Kaplan's modernist path, which seeks to create a religious path reconstructed from the Norse material, a Norse/Germanic Paganism available to anyone who would feel drawn towards it. While the term "tribalism" has been part of Heathen thought since Else Christensen, it represents Snook's fourth and emerging peak of frequency. She writes that "the tribalist's goal is to re-create a solid familial socioreligious community based on fictive kinship."[273] This fictive kinship is based on tribal *thew*, a term used in Heathenry to indicate the shared ethos of a small group of Heathens tightly bound together by oaths of commitment. Ideally, the tribal bond is maintained by friendships, personal commitments

---

268. Jennifer Snook, *American Heathens*, 143
269. Ibid., 145.
270. Ibid., 143.
271. Ibid., 152.
272. Ibid., 156.
273. Ibid., 158.

to the group, and the *thew*, the shared history, ritual, and cultural norms that act as social glue and guide members' behaviors, and need not consider ethnicity at all. However, in reality ancestry often becomes a decisive factor as "many tribalists identify as folkish and believe that Heathenry is based on ancestry."[274] This is not surprising, since tribalism comes into Heathenry through the völkisch tributary. Non-racial forms of tribalism, such as that described by Troth member John T. Mainer, are newer emerging confluences in Heathenry forming as this völkisch idea is absorbed and transformed into non-racial forms of Heathenry.[275]

The "more complex picture" noted by all these observers of American Heathenry is made clearer by the idea of a Heathen watershed with many confluences formed by a variety of important tributaries that flow into the Heathen movement. Distinct manifestations of Heathenry, an organization, kindred, or individual, may draw on the diverse tributaries to form specific confluences. Within the Heathen watershed tributaries spill over and are shared among otherwise oppositional groups. A particular Heathen group or individual is likely to manifest ideas from *many* tributaries in different patterns and formulations. Heathens draw on a bounded but contested set of ideas into which specific intellectual tributaries flow in order to curate their own specific topography of Heathen identity.

### The Tributaries and Implications of the Valknut

A powerful example of this occurred even as I was writing this chapter. I was skimming a magazine one evening while the local news played on the television. A report came on describing a fugitive who had been involved in a home invasion and the assault of several persons. Looking for his wayward girlfriend, the suspect had gone to her family's home. When her family members refused to divulge her location, the assailant lost his temper and proceeded to beat several of them with a baseball bat. While the story aired on the TV in the background, it barely registered with me, being only a slightly more egregious version of the typical evening news fare. Another local news story about a violent family incident seemed all

---

274. Ibid., 159.
275. John T. Manier, "Diversity in Heathenry," in "Perspectives on Racial Issues in the United States," *The Troth* blog, January 12, 2015, http://thetroth.blogspot.com/2015/01/perspectives-on-racial-issues-in-united.html.

too common. However, at the end of the report, the news anchor made a comment that suddenly grabbed my attention: "The suspect has several tattoos including three triangles on his throat."[276] While this statement might seem to be a rather meaningless piece of trivia to someone unfamiliar with Heathenry, to me it was both startling and provocative. I must have had a bewildered expression on my face as I immediately looked up at the TV with wide eyes and exclaimed, "That's got to be the valknut!"

The valknut is a symbol from the early Viking period composed of three interlocking triangles. It appears on several ancient rune stones, such as the Stora Hammars 1 stone located in Gotland Sweden. The term "valknut" or "death knot" signifies a later interpretation of the symbol and originates from the Norwegian *valknuter*, which translates as "knots of those fallen in battle."[277] While its exact meaning and usage is unclear, contextual evidence suggests that during the Viking Age it was associated with Odin and may have marked something devoted or set apart for Odin such as a person or a sacrifice. Within the contemporary Heathen movement, it is a prominent and potent symbol, worn on clothing, as a pendant or on the body as a tattoo, and taken by followers of Odin to indicate the special relationship between themselves and the deity. While the television news report didn't elaborate or provide context beyond the "three triangles" reference, a little searching on my part eventually located a mug shot of the suspect with his throat clearly visible and indeed, a valknut was crudely tattooed on his throat. Clearly, the authorities were intrigued by this symbol.

Later coverage of the story went beyond merely identifying the fugitive by this tattoo. The next day, further reporting stated that the suspect was covered in hate group tattoos and that the state police were "extremely worried" about these tattoos and what they might suggest about the fugitive.[278] The media coverage

---

276. WTVQ-TV, "Grant Co. Deputies: Man Used Club To Beat Victims With Special Needs," *ABC 36 Lexington* website, www.wtvq.com/2014/12/17/grant-co-deputies-man-used-club-to-beat-victims-with-special-needs/.

277. Rudolf Simek, "Hrungnir's Heart," *Dictionary of Northern Mythology* (Cambridge: D. S. Brewer, 1993), 163.

278. Brian Mains, Jason Law, and Ally Kraemer, "Boone Co. Deputies Arrest Man Accused of Beating 6 People in Dry Ridge, KY," *WCPO 9 Cincinnati* website, December 17, 2014, www.wcpo.com/news/region-northern-kentucky/home-invasion-report-puts-dry-ridge-ky-elementary-on-lockdown. Authorities also suggested that the suspect had Mexican gang tattoos, indicating the level of confusion experienced by both the authorities and the media.

made a clear association between the "three triangles" and hate symbols, interpreting the valknut as one of the hate group tattoos worn by the suspect and therefore indicative of violent criminal tendencies. This implication would come as quite a shock to my many Heathen friends who have valknut tattoos yet who are not part of any hate group. Compare this suspect's valknut with that of my friend Perchta who wears *two* valknut tattoos. Perchta is a lower-middle-class woman, a mother of three, an artist who makes beautiful jewelry, who posts frequent and politically liberal comments on Facebook, and who is outspoken in her opposition to racism, sexism, fascism, and homophobia. The valknut represents her deep affection for Odin, her personal commitment to the deity through the ups and downs of life, a god who is often difficult, yet who rewards his followers with hard-won wisdom. In Perchta's experience the valknut is a deeply spiritual symbol, not a racist symbol, and even with her two valknuts she is as far from a white supremacist as one can be. The blanket attribution of "hate group" or "racist" to the valknut is clearly both misleading and misguided, misconstruing the attitudes of many Heathen adherents who include the valknut as part of their devotion or practice, and who use the symbol without appropriating racist ideology along with it. One cannot conclude that because someone wears a valknut, he or she is therefore a dangerous racist or has a proclivity for random violence. It is this sort of misguided stigmatism that perpetuates misinformed and unhelpful stereotypes of Heathen practitioners. In the particular incident described above, which turned out to be an incident of partner abuse, racism, and racially motivated violence played absolutely no part in the incident, nor did any religious ideology. That being the case, the whole "hate group" issue was a red herring, raised by the authorities and disseminated by the media outlets simply to further discredit the suspect.

The rather loose way in which such attributions are often made by culturally authoritative entities has been a perennial problem for NRMs. For most viewers of the local news, the presentation of the "three triangles" as a hate group symbol reinforced the idea that the valknut is a predictable indication of the wearer's violent and racist character. However, that characterization arises from and perpetuates a misunderstanding of the realities of Heathen religious life. Unlike the swastika, whose appropriation by the Nazi party indelibly skewed its domain of meaning in the West, the valknut flows into the Heathen iconography as a culturally neutral symbol from the tributary of Norse mythology and culture. The symbol may be joined together with a contemporary Pagan a-racial tributary constituting primarily a spiritual connection to Odin in the bearer's life; or it might be connected with a völkisch or white power tributary in which Odinic identity and racial power might be intertwined. It is not the symbol itself, but its association with additional tributaries of the Heathen milieu, its place in the bricolage of Heathen identity, which determines its contextual meaning. The entire incident shows the multivalent nature of Heathen iconography. The valknut is a potent symbol utilized by a variety of Heathen practitioners who also draw upon other ideological resources and tributaries within the Heathen watershed. The valknut itself is not a "hate group" symbol

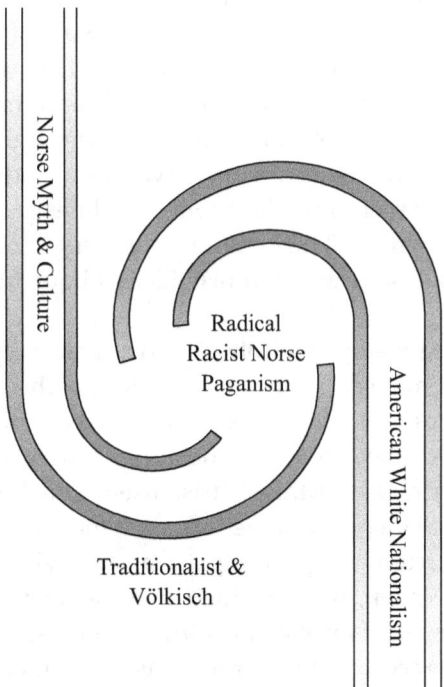

Figure 8. Tributaries of Racist Heathenry.

and cannot be simply understood as a symbol of racial Odinism. Instead it appears within any practitioner's life in confluence with other tributaries and can only be successfully interpreted in light of these additional associations.

As the example indicates, there are not two distinct camps within Heathenry, one racist and the other non-racist, which can be identified simply through their symbols and ideas. Instead, Heathens appropriate elements from several tributaries to form distinct expressions and identities: symbols and ideas flow among groups and individuals of different sorts and are used in a diversity of approaches to Heathen identity. Another example is illustrated in the notion of the folk soul. The folk soul is an idea most strongly associated with the German völkisch movement, which advanced the notion of a Germanic or Aryan soul, a type of soul specific to the Germanic people group. More generally, the folk soul expresses the idea that a particular way of life, philosophy, spirituality, morality, and world-outlook are organic to a particular people, or "folk," products of a particular culture. In this way of understanding ethnicity, every folk group has its own particular folk soul that represents the spiritual essence of the people and their culture. This idea passed into contemporary Heathenry through the lineage of the Odinist Else Christensen, who served as a bridge between the American Odinist scene and the intellectual lineage of the Germanic völkisch movement.[279] Thus, there is a very strong connection between the folk soul and Odinist ideas about blood, race, and religion.

Over time, the idea of the folk soul has gradually disseminated throughout the movement and is now found throughout diverse Heathen communities. As it has flowed, it has mixed with other tributaries to produce different meanings and uses. While some Heathens may draw on Mills, Christensen, and Jung to create an essentialist, racial ideology of the folk soul, the idea is not simply an idea that arises from and promulgates a racist vision of the world. Others like McNallen, with his theory of metagenetics, attempt to shed the harder racist implications from the idea. For these folkish Heathens, each race or ethnic group has its own cultural wisdom, its own gods and lifeways to which its members are most naturally attuned and to which they should return, without suggesting that

---

279. Gardell, *Gods of the Blood*, 171.

one ideology is superior or should dominate the others. The folk soul idea is also appropriated and even further adapted by Pagan-influenced Heathens who describe the folk soul as the accumulated folk wisdom of ancient people, deep insights for survival and thriving that are latent within us. If we learn how to listen to it, we can now draw on this folk knowledge to create a more holistic and integrated lifeway in the modern world and to produce a more healthy post-Christian society. For instance, Kari Tauring, a practitioner of the arts of the völva, a type of ancient Norse healer and magic-worker, connects the folk soul to the cultural wisdom and identity that mothers passed along to their children through songs, seasonal traditions, and stories.[280]

As Colin Campbell described in his theory of the cultic milieu, ideas do not stay fixed in one ideological point, but have a tendency to be shared or stolen, appropriated and utilized by groups for their own purposes. In this river system model, tributaries that originate in one place might flow through many different confluences as religious innovators draw on streams of thought and practice, bringing them into new patterns of flow. The valknut is one such Heathen example that flows through and pokes holes in the common wisdom of two Heathen denominations. Is a valknut wearer either Odinist or Asatru? And what about a Heathen who draws inspiration from the thought of sharing in an ancestral folk soul? Rather, a more useful exercise is to identity tributaries of the Heathen milieu and attempt to trace out how those tributaries are arranged or connected in any particular manifestation of Heathenry. It is at the point of confluence where these tributaries meet that we see specific forms of Heathenry expressed, and different types of Heathen spirituality developing. And each of these tributaries is further linked to other possible connections into the cultic milieu. For instance, the tributary of Wicca contributes an important intellectual influence in the Heathen watershed while at the same time being in touch with further branches and tributaries, such as the environmentalist milieu. In this way a type of confluence develops drawing together Norse Myth, contemporary Pagan, and Environmentalism that gives rise to a green, vegan, valknut-tattooed Heathen. On the other hand, the Norse Myth tributary joined to the Germanic völkisch tributary and then flowing together with an Anarcho-primitivist tributary

---

280. Kari Tauring, interview with author, June 4, 2011.

produces a grungy, ecstatic, will-to-power, runic magician. The confluence of Norse Myth, völkisch Odinism, with the tributary of American white supremacy and its further links to paramilitarism, creates a racist skinhead Heathen who listens to White Noise/Viking metal on his smartphone (see figure 8). Through the confluence of these various tributaries, and their linkages into various other corners of the cultic milieu, certain distinct confluences come into being, accounting for the diversity that characterizes the broader Heathen movement, as well as the animosity and alliances that simultaneously fracture and hold together the landscape of the movement. Once we see how this works, we can begin to trace or outline a cultural map of the tributaries that are major contributors to the Heathen milieu. We will look at several: the tributary of Norse Myth and Culture, which flows into Heathenry through scholarly sources; the folkish/Traditionalist tributary, which is most strongly influenced by völkisch tradition; the Wicca and Witchcraft tributary, through which come the ideas, the culture and values of the English Wiccan tradition; and the tributary of Popular Culture. Finally, we will briefly discuss a newer group that seems to be growing and asserting itself in Heathenry, the Wolves of Vinland, which incorporates an anarchist/primitivist tributary into the milieu.

## Tributaries of the Heathen Watershed

### Norse Myth and Culture Tributary

Of course, the tributary of central importance is that of Norse culture and religion. If knowledge of Norse culture had died out after the conversion of Northern Europe to Christianity, attempts to revive or reconstruct a Norse Pagan religion would look very different. As it is, there has been an ongoing stream of Norse culture, history, and religion that has flowed into contemporary American society. For instance, many Heathens were exposed to Norse myths as children. Not because they read the Eddas at a young age, but because they read a collection of Norse myths retold by a contemporary author. The mythology, the stories of Northern gods and heroes flows into the Heathen watershed in the form of collections of mythology such as those by Ingri and Edgar Parin d'Aulaire, Kevin Crossley-Holland, or Neil Gaiman. Beyond that, as we have seen, Heathens are receptive to the work of scholars and much of this cultural information has been made accessible in scholarship that has been received and incorporated by Heathen practitioners. For instance, Josh Rood, who is part of the Heathen community on the East Coast begins by introducing new Heathens to this scholarly material: "Someone would tell us that they are new to Heathenism, and ask what they should read, and we would point them to Terry Gunnell or Simek's *Dictionary of Norse Mythology*."[281] Scholarly work in all sorts of Norse related material contributes to this tributary: archaeology, textual criticism, linguistics and translations, interpretations of Norse history and culture. Discussion of the merits of the various English translations of the *Poetic Edda* often become lively and interesting conversations among Heathens. As Rood suggests, the scholarly works that make up the Norse myth and culture tributary are often recommended before specifically "Heathen" books. When I was first meeting Heathens and becoming introduced to the movement, James Russell's *Germanization of Early Medieval Christianity* was recommended to me several times, especially by friends who were aware of my own Christian background. The presence of this tributary represents an important aspect of Heathenry as a reconstructionist religion, the insistence that contemporary Heathens have a strong grounding in actual history. Rood emphasizes this value as vital to the religion. "It really simply boils down to the fact that we strive to develop and grow as Heathens in a manner that is consistent with historical Heathenism, and some of us have done a lot of research in that field, and we feel it's only appropriate to fact check, and fact check again, and to cite all of our sources, and compare and contrast our research," says Rood. Heathens not only vet these various scholarly sources but also become interpreters of this material to the broader Heathen community. "I'll be the first to admit, scholarly works can make a person's eyes glaze over, and a lot of people don't have the time to essentially earn a Master's degree in their free time in order to be a heathen."[282] Noting the growing importance of this role among Heathen clergy and scholars, Lorrie Wood, a Heathen leader from California discusses the changing composition of the community:

281. Josh Rood, "Interview," *Eternal Haunted Summer*, Autumn Equinox (2011) https://eternalhauntedsummer.com/issues/autumn-equinox-2011/josh-rood/. Rood mentions Terry Gunnell, a professor of folkloristics at the University of Iceland, under whom Rood studied.
282. Ibid.

> We now have a laity and this is kind of hard to get our heads around because Paganism in general and Heathenry in particular in their early formative years were both marked by a base competency almost equivalent to a bachelor's degree in the relevant material. As we grow in popularity, they want to know the stories and they want to feel part of this cultural context and swept up in it. But then I say "And here's a reading list!" And they sort of give me the blink, you can almost hear the "blink, blink" sound effect when they blink. We're having to do a lot of things that deal with that, which is why we now have Heathenry 101 meetings.[283]

Her observation of a "laity" emerging in Heathenry fits the long recognized process of routinization in which patterns of leadership and adherency take on forms sustainable over the long term. Ezzy and Berger describe the process as "a tendency for groups to move from a small group of virtuosi to a larger but less committed group of participants."[284] As Rood and Wood point out, the new Heathen adherents are not "less committed," but differently committed. Many are intensely interested in the practice and culture of Heathenry but do not have time or interest in the more scholarly pursuits. For this reason, various points of entry for this scholarly tributary are important. One such point of entry is obviously the books themselves. Heathens recommend books, make book lists, and encourage others to study. Another point of entry is academics and scholars who, while not Heathens themselves, are seen as friendly to the movement. A good example is Stephen Pollington, an independent British scholar whose research on Anglo-Saxon culture has been widely read by American Heathens and incorporated into religious practice. As we will see in chapter 7, his work on the historical Anglo-Saxon sumbel has been widely embraced, directly influencing the understanding of the sumbel ritual among Heathens.[285] In addition, Pollington also serves as a consultant for *Óðrœrir*, a Heathen journal whose self-stated purpose is "bridge the gap between academic knowledge of ancient heathen religion and the implementation and reconstruction of traditions today."[286] But Heathens have also seen the importance

283. Lorrie Wood, interview with author, November 21, 2011.
284. Ezzy and Berger, "Witchcraft," 178.
285. Pollington, *The Meadhall*; Stephen Pollington, "The Mead-Hall Community," *Journal of Medieval History* 37 (2011): 19–33. He substantially develops his ideas about the symbel ritual in these two sources.
286. "About Odroerir," *Óðrœrir: The Heathen Journal* website, http://odroerirjournal.com/about-odroerir/.

of taking on this role themselves, positioning insiders as interpreters of the scholarly material, who take academic work and put it into a form useful to the Heathen community. The term "Heathen scholar" designates such a person in the movement. While these Heathen scholars have been part of the movement for years as amateur experts in the Lore, there is growing interest among Heathens in obtaining academic credentials in Norse-related fields.

A more complicated relationship exists between the Heathen movement and contemporary scholarly work focused on Heathenry itself. Most Heathens remain remarkably open to those who wish to understand the movement more deeply. The Heathens I met were generally receptive to inquiries from outsiders and positive about scholarly interest and study. This was the case even though religious research conducted on and within the movement has received mixed reviews by Heathens. Some Heathens have resisted attempts to analyze and describe the movement. This attitude seems to arise from a couple of different motivations. There is the concern that scholars who do not share a Heathen perspective will be unfairly critical and misinterpret aspects of the movement. Others are sensitive to the misuse or disrespect of religious knowledge — publication of information that ought to remain within the Heathen community. Still, this research has had an effect on the movement. Heathens tend to be thorough critics of their own movement. Scholarly work contributes to the self-reflective evaluation in which Heathens are already engaged. The important point is that this work flows into the Heathen watershed as a tributary that shapes the movement. Practitioners of Heathenry are often quick to respond to new insights of the scholarly world. News stories of archaeological finds bounce around Heathen Facebook pages and listserv discussion groups online. This tributary signifies one important way that Heathens come to understand more deeply the culture and religion that inspires their religious pursuits.

## The Folkish/Traditionalist Tributary

An important interpreter of the Norse myth and culture tributary, the völkisch movement was an upwelling of German nationalist sentiment in the early twentieth century that took political, cultural, and religious forms. While the movement was diverse, it included the resurgence of Germanic and Norse Pagan ideas, images, religious, and occult practices. As the first "awakening" of Germanic Paganism in the modern world, this aspect of the movement has flowed into contemporary American Heathenry as an important tributary. This tributary influenced a race-based approach to Heathenry steeped in anti-Christian attitudes and race mysticism, a philosophical and cultural milieu from which both the Nazis and the Odinists selectively drew. It defines Heathenry as a religion for those of Northern European ancestry, encoded into the consciousness and subconscious soul of Northern Europeans, and manifested as a religious code of strength, power, and tribalism. It passed through a distinct and separate intellectual history: Guido List, Alexander Rudd Mills, Friedrich Marby, Else Christensen, Julius Evola, and others, all of whom maintained the salience of ethnicity, race, and warrior ethics. Religion for these writers is encoded in the blood, etched into the archetypes of the soul, only awaiting the right moment to awaken and surge forth in power and might. Völkisch esoteric philosophy, magic, and runework were developed by individuals such as Guido List and others in the early years of the twentieth century. List made important contributions to runic magic, finding in the runes the mystical philosophy of the German folk soul. Gardell describes a lineage of other writers and thinkers who developed and furthered the German völkisch ideology: the SS member and occultist Karl Maria Wiligut, the Italian Traditionalist philosopher Julius Evola, Savitri Devi, and Miguel Serrano among others.[287] This is a fascinating and diverse intellectual history in which the occult, runes, nature religion, hollow earth theories, and racial ideology are all intertwined.

These völkisch efforts and ideology were cut short by the World Wars, especially World War II, but have been carried forward by other groups, particularly the Traditionalist thinkers such as Evola and New Right founder Alain de Benoist. These writers make up the active reading lists of many folkish Heathens. Similarly the legacies of völkisch Heathen organizations are also being rediscovered and their relevance for contemporary Heathenry discussed. List's runic work and Friedrich Marby's system of runic yoga, have influenced the practice of many contemporary Heathens. Since the early 2000s,

---

287. Gardell, *Gods of the Blood*, 23–28, 165–90. In chapter 4 of his work, Gardell discusses several writers influenced by völkisch themes including List, Wiligut, Mills, Evola, Christensen, as well as others.

the Radical Traditionalist journal *Tyr* and to a lesser extent the *Journal of Contemporary Heathenry* are actively engaged in the ideological work of appropriating these ideas, becoming critical confluences in which folkish Heathenry, Traditionalist thought, and völkisch history flow together.[288] For instance, writing in the pages of *Tyr*, Markus Wolff locates the origin of many contemporary Heathen practices in the history of the *Germanische Glaubens Gemeinschaft*, a völkisch religious organization formed in pre-war Germany.[289] His interpretation rehabilitates völkisch history and suggests a direct causative relationship between it and American Heathenry. As folkish Heathens, including Stephen McNallen and Edred Thorsson, have become involved in this project, they are bringing völkisch history and Traditionalist ideas to the surface and interpreting them as important touchstones for contemporary Asatru. Through these efforts, the influence of the völkisch tributary continues to grow in importance.

A continent away from Germany during this same period, Alexander Rud Mills began developing an Anglo-Saxon-based religious program in the 1920s that took its inspiration from the continental Germanic völkisch movement. He was enamored by the Pagan developments in Europe and was significantly motivated by a keen disdain for Jewish and Christian religion. As Kaplan mentions, Mills saw both Judaism and Christianity as "vile Middle Eastern Abrahamic cults" and blamed these cultures for what he saw as the degeneracy of society.[290] Mills felt that a regeneration of Western culture could only be achieved by a return to the gods of the Nordic folk soul, the gods of Asatru. His system, however, mainly seemed to replace the Christian God with Odin, while maintaining many of the trappings of Anglican Christianity. While the initial impact of Mills' efforts was negligible, his writing was discovered by Else Christensen in the 1960s. Christensen was a Swedish political

---

288. Michael Strmiska, "Tyr: Myth—Culture—Tradition," *The Pomegranate: The International Journal of Pagan Studies* 12, no. 1 (June 2010): 118–21; Lauren Bernauer, "Modern Germanic Heathenry and Radical Traditionalists," in *Through a Glass Darkly: Reflections on the Sacred: Collected Research*, ed. Franco Di Lauro (Sydney: Sydney University Press, 2006), 265–74.

289. Wolff, "Ludwig Fahrenkrog and the Germanic Faith Community," 221–42. I discuss the GGG and include a quote from Wolff's article in chapter 1, "The Völkisch Movement."

290. Kaplan, *Radical Religion in America*, 15.

activist who had immigrated to the United States after World War II. Mills' work had a profound effect on her, leading to something of a political and religious awakening, which transformed her into the standard bearer for Odinism. Christensen became a more effective organizer than Mills and tirelessly promoted Odinism. She began publishing a long-running newsletter, *The Odinist*, which built the ideological basis for early Asatru and Odinist thought, primarily as a political/social system that challenged many of the assumptions and structures of modernity. Odinism served as the appropriate form of resistance to modernity for white people of northern European descent. She maintained a substantial correspondence, reaching out to other political and religious activists to build her movement, including neo-Nazi groups. She founded the first Odinist organization in America in 1971, the Odinist Fellowship, and found a ready audience by promoting Odinism among white prisoners in the federal prison system, an emphasis that continues to be prominent in both Odinism and Asatru.

Her work and personal influence extended into the lives of many early Asatru adherents who remain pivotal to the contemporary Asatru movement and who would develop her legacy in their own ways. These include Stephen McNallen, who would go on to found the Viking Brotherhood, the Asatru Free Assembly and the current Asatru Folk Assembly; Valgard Murray, leader and inspiration for the Ásatrú Alliance; and Jeff Heimgest Holley, a long-time member of the Odinic Rite and currently the Director of the Court of Gothar, the OR's leadership body. Although she was influential throughout the Heathen movement, Christensen's legacy tends to run particularly strong among Odinists. Christensen strongly influenced the leadership of the Odinic Rite, who venerate her as the Folk Mother. Proponents of folkish Asatru resonate with the political and anti-Christian elements of her work, a sentiment that can be traced from List to Mills to Christensen, Evola, and others.[291]

These early roots of Heathenry are crucial because they arose outside of the intellectual tradition that resulted in the growth of

---

291. List, *The Secret of the Runes*, 97. List wrote that his contemporary European culture was "caught up in the ascetic view of a life-denying religious system." Almost identical wording can be found among other writers such as Mills, Christensen, and folkish groups such as the Odinic Rite that are substantially influenced by the völkisch tributary.

American Witchcraft. These Germanic völkisch ideas came to the United States primarily through the work of Else Christensen, where they began to mingle with homegrown American white supremacy. Christensen developed substantial ties to American neo-Nazi groups. Had this situation continued to develop along these lines, there would not be an American Asatru movement. Odinism would have developed as a subset of radical, white nationalism, especially among the prison population into whom Christensen put so much missionary effort. However, something happened to change that trajectory: the explosion of contemporary Paganism into the American religious context.

## *The Wicca and Witchcraft Tributary*

America in the 1960s and 1970s was reverberating with a cultural event that some scholars have described as the Third Great Awakening. The American counterculture movement involved a widespread cultural revitalization that involved peaceniks and hippies but also included a diverse religious element. While both the charismatic Jesus Movement and the conservative political Moral Majority represented Christian aspects of this religious revitalization, it also involved a significant growth in alternative or new religious movements among these being contemporary Paganism. Paganism sought to revitalize religious life and spirituality through the appropriation of pre-Christian religious ideas, practices, and traditions. The Wiccan tributary has a long history that seems to originate in the literary tradition of the English Romantics who drew on images from classic mythology to develop spiritual themes involving Pagan deities and animism, closeness to nature, a spirituality of wildness and ecstasy. These ideas were taken up and developed by a series of intellectuals including Robert Graves, Margaret Murray, Aleister Crowley, Dion Fortune, and others, but are ultimately identified by their association with the figure of Gerald Gardner. It was Gardner, an Englishman working in the 1940s and 1950s who took advantage of the recently repealed laws against Witchcraft in Great Britain to introduce to the world the new/old religion of Wicca. Already substantially diversified in its British setting, Wicca provided the impetus for a broad Pagan religiosity when it came to America a decade later. The movement adapted quickly to the American context, with numerous innovative practitioners contributing to its eclectic ideological growth.[292]

The Witchcraft tributary is marked by its eclecticism, drawing on many forms of religion, philosophical, and esoteric ideas to create modern forms of religious practice. It tends to take a more playful and experimental approach to human identity, drawing as much on fantasy literature as historical texts for its ideal types, motivations, and goals.[293] Wicca and Witchcraft involves freeing the individual from the constraints of modernity through healing, magic, and ritual, with performance and drama seen as transformative endeavors. The ethical framework "An it harm none, do what ye will," reflects this highly individualized approach to religion, which encourages creativity, innovation, and self-expression. It is often associated with more liberal political and social values such as feminism, environmentalism, and an openness to diverse forms of sexual orientation and expression. Importantly, its ideas of deity are looser, more psychological, symbolic, and archetypal. Practitioners of the Craft see their spirituality as arising from an awareness of the enchanted world, awakening as it were from modernity's dour dream of disenchantment, a purely mechanical and naturalistic world. For Wiccans, the Goddess takes on many different names and many different guises. Their religious choices are part of a broad spectrum of religious options and tend to approach religious practice as something that happens within the setting of modernity. Wiccan spirituality enhances modern life, seeks healing from its abuses, and orients practitioners toward more healthy ways of living. Paganism is in many ways less politically than personally oriented, concerned with the construction of imaginative enchanted forms of modern identity. There are, of course, groups and teachers such as Starhawk who practice engaged Paganism, using magic and social protest to confront injustice and change society along Pagan and feminist lines.[294] Witches may incorporate and utilize various polytheist and Pagan religious traditions in this search for meaning,

---

292. Ethan Doyle White, *Wicca: History Belief, and Community in Modern Pagan Witchcraft* (Eastbourne: Sussex Academic Press, 2015), 34–64.

293. Pike, *Earthly Bodies*. Pike's book includes an extended discussion of playfulness and identity transformation in Paganism in chapter 6, "Serious Playing with the Self."

294. Sarah M. Pike, *New Age and Neopagan Religions in America* (New York: Columbia University Press, 2004).

healing, and transformation. Rather than making an exclusive mythological commitment, Witchcraft is much more likely to seek the similarities among polytheist traditions and drawn on all of them for inspiration. At a workshop I attended as part of a large Pagan festival in California, the stories, powers and characteristics of two deities, Brigid of Ireland and Sarasvati of India, were creatively compared and explored.[295] As an exercise both intellectual and devotional in its nature, such blending of traditions represents a theological style that lends to Paganism a source of creative energy. The mythological tributaries of Celtic, Norse, Egyptian, and even Hindu traditions are incorporated as means to further the Pagan search for freedom and transformation, re-magicking the self. Wiccan-influenced Heathenry reflects many of these qualities and characteristics (see figure 9). Rather than resurrecting an ancient repressed savage archetypal self and overthrowing the world in fire

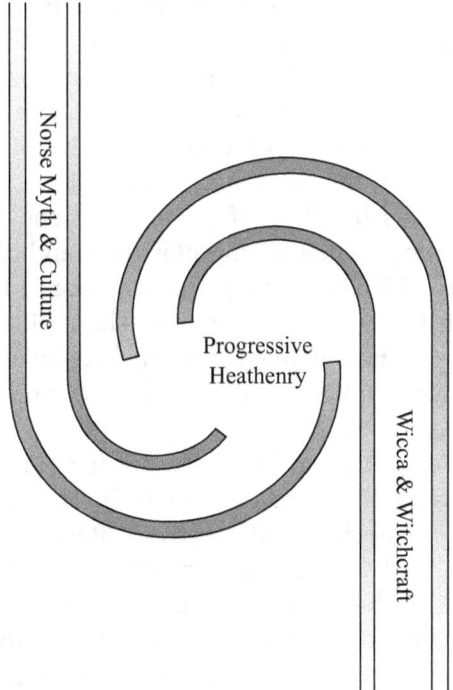

Figure 9. Tributaries of Progressive Heathenry.

295. Field notes taken by author, California, February 2013.

and blood, Wiccan-influenced Heathenry is much more focused on creating new contemporary identities within modernity, drawing on these ancient resources to build a religious identity that enhances an enchanted sense of self that is lacking in the modern world.

This intellectual tributary has been well documented by numerous sources, such as Hutton's *The Triumph of the Moon*, Adler's *Drawing Down the Moon*, Clifton's *Her Hidden Children*, Doyle White's *Wicca: History, Belief, and Community in Modern Pagan Witchcraft*, and others. The tributary has not remained static. While Gardnerian Wicca remains a part of the tributary, it has demonstrated a remarkable capacity to creatively and organically develop into related movements such as Witchcraft, Goddess traditions, groups oriented towards ceremonial and other types of magic, to name a few.

Although both the German völkisch and the contemporary Witchcraft tributaries developed in the same general historical moment, they are parallel movements. If one reads the intellectual history of the German völkisch movement and its subsequent torchbearers, as presented by Gardell in *The Gods of the Blood*, one will find no mention of the writers and themes associated with Wicca and Witchcraft. And if one reads Hutton's *Triumph of the Moon*, one of the most thorough of contemporary Pagan histories, it is entirely silent as to the runes, the Germanic gods, and the völkisch writers who developed this tradition of blood, race, and religion. While both may have roots in medieval esotericism, and both overlapped to some degree with Theosophy, it is important to note that they developed with fairly distinct histories. The political, ethical, and theological sensibilities of these two intellectual tributaries grow from different and at times conflicting presuppositions. When these two tributaries came together in America in the 1970s, they reacted not with a gentle syncretism, but with turbulent force.

That collision continues to be evident in Heathen life and has yet to resolve or subside. Instead, the waters continue to swirl. Every Heathen and Heathen group draws on and selects from these tributaries in their construction of modern Heathen identity and practice. The influence and interaction of these tributaries creates a diverse and often contentious landscape in contemporary Heathenry. The predominance of one tributary or the other matters significantly to the tenor and orientation of the individual or group. These characteristics cast the Heathen movement in a different light than other familiar forms of American Paganism. Heathenry has existed on the margins of the contemporary Pagan world. Wiccans and Witches have often avoided mixing with the Heathen movement, preferring to hold it at arm's length, while Heathenry often expresses itself in ways that seem out of step or at ideological odds with Wicca and Witchcraft. Interestingly, this incongruence leads to something of an identity crisis in Heathenry. Some adherents want to demonstrate to the contemporary Pagan community that they really fit within Pagan religious culture. Others want to stand apart and assert their difference and sometimes their superiority to Paganism. However, these different orientations or identities resulted from the particular historical processes by which modern Heathenry arose.

## The Tributary of Pop Culture

Our discussion of tributaries would not be complete without touching on the influence of popular culture on the contemporary Heathen movement. Unlike the other tributaries that are consciously chosen and incorporated, pop culture is a more omnipresent and often invasive influence. An impressive amount of Norse-related material circulates in American pop culture. This certainly influences the ways that Heathens understand and practice their religion, as well as public perceptions of Norse culture and religion. Many Heathens recall some aspect of pop culture—a book of Norse myths, a movie, a role-playing game—as a component of their conversion career. Jeffrey Kaplan found this to be true even in the 1990s, remarking that an important "entry point into Ásatrú flows from the influence of pop culture."[296] Widely consumed by Heathen practitioners, Tolkien's Middle Earth epic stands at the crossroads between the English literary tradition and American pop culture. As we have seen, it not only incorporates significant Norse themes but also has become one of the most prominent examples of a Secondary World. In the twentieth century, Secondary Worlds have transformed how Americans consume popular culture, as creativity, marketing, and technological platforms have multiplied the opportunities to participate in imaginative contexts. Even Secondary Worlds that are not particularly Norse may introduce important themes into the Heathen culture. For instance, the *Conan*

---

296. Kaplan, "Reconstruction of the Ásatrú and Odinist Traditions," 197.

*the Barbarian* book series, which originated with author Robert E. Howard in the 1930s, popularizes themes of heroic strength and action, a warrior ethic, a certain fantasy aesthetic, as well as magic, Pagan gods, and polytheistic religious beliefs practices. These themes were important enough to inspire as important a Heathen figure as Stephen McNallen, whose book *Asatru: A Native European Spirituality* includes a picture of himself pouring a libation on Howard's grave. Other contemporary pop culture artifacts engage their consumers more directly with engaging portrayals of Norse material. The 1999 film *The 13th Warrior*, starring Antonio Banderas as the Arab traveler Ibn Fadlan, imaginatively engages historical material to present a heroic vision of the Viking life. More recent movies released by Marvel focus on the comic book version of Thor, yet at the same time communicate elements of Norse mythology to their viewers. The range of portrayals is quite broad. The Norse material in Marvel's long-running superhero Thor series might be contrasted with the use of historical fiction to empathetically and complexly portray Viking life in Brian Woods' *Northlanders* comic book series. As youngsters, my children and millions of others were fond of the Viking-themed *How to Train Your Dragon* series of books and movies, which presented Norse material in an entertaining and relatable way. Watching *How to Train Your Dragon 2* with my children, I was impressed by the evocative Viking funeral scene in which Stoick, the main character's father, is given a ship cremation. Recalling the scene of Balder's cremation, the gathered warriors shoot flaming arrows into the ship while a prayer is intoned: "May the valkyries welcome you and lead you through Odin's great battlefield. May they sing your name with love and fury so we might hear it rise from the depths of Valhalla and know that you have taken your rightful place at the table of kings. For a great man has fallen: a warrior, chieftain, father, a friend."[297] While the quote would not pass muster for a serious Heathen reconstructionist, the scene carries considerable Norse themes and presents a Pagan, not a Christian, view of death and afterlife. For a child viewing this, the details are less significant than pop culture's power to create positive emotional impressions with Norse material. Similarly, the influence of music is located more in the impressionistic experience

---

297. *How to Train Your Dragon 2*, directed by Dean DeBlois (Twentieth Century Fox Film Corporation, 2014), DVD.

it creates. While the Norse themes found in some genres of metal music may or may not be historically or religiously accurate, the powerful experience of the music may create a positive connection to the Norse material.

Heathens consume these cultural artifacts and even celebrate them. Yet simultaneously, they are frustrated and sometimes appalled by the lack of historical faithfulness and the excessive use of creative license in how the gods and religious ideas are portrayed. Complaints about the portrayal of Norse material in pop culture abound among Heathens, who often see these portrayals as harmful to the healthy long-term development of Heathenry. Positive impressions, even enthusiasm, for Norse-related material may be stirred up in consumers of books, movies, and video games. Yet that enthusiasm may be shallow or fixated on popular images and ideas that Heathens consider inaccurate. Torsen says, "There's all this misinformation that's being put forth by the media. That is a detriment because anybody that is really serious about learning is not going to believe what they see in a movie or on TV."[298] Not only do Heathens tend to raise high boundaries against the naïve enthusiasm of those who blithely fixate on Norse-inspired pop culture, but they have also learned to be critical consumers of pop culture themselves. Bob Smietana writes about the complexity Heathens face in negotiating the influence of pop culture: "The pop culture success of the Norse gods can be a double-edged sword for today's followers. That's especially true for Heathens who are parents and want to pass on some of the lessons of their faith to their children."[299] For his article, Smietana interviewed Torsen, the prominent Heathen leader mentioned in earlier chapters and writes, "Like many Heathens, he's a fan of the pop culture versions of Thor. After all, he said, the Norse myths are great stories, even for non-Heathens. Still, he made a distinction to his kids between fiction and spirituality. 'I explain that Tor is our god and Thor is a comic book hero,' he said."[300]

---

298. Torsen, interview.

299. Bob Smietana, "The Spiritual Power of Thor," *On Faith* blog, December 2, 2012, www.onfaith.co/onfaith/2014/12/02/the-spiritual-power-of-thor/35213.

300. Ibid. In Smietana's article, Torsen's last name is spelled "Thorsson." In Smietana's quote from Torsen, I altered the spelling from "Thor is our god" in the published article to "Tor is our god." In my personal communication with Torsen, he indicated that he often uses a Danish spelling of the god's name to make a clear distinction between the comic book superhero and the god with whom he works.

Torsen expresses the ambivalence that many Heathens feel about representations of Norse culture and religion in popular culture when he discusses the *Vikings* television series. Created and written by Michael Hirst, *Vikings* was released by the History Channel in 2013. Set in an eighth- and ninth-century Norse context, the show is an intense and compelling drama that follows the lives of its Viking characters. Many of the main characters, such as Ragnar Lothbrok, are drawn from or at least inspired by the historical record. Rarely has a piece of pop culture explored Norse culture with such gritty realism, aesthetic detail, cultural competency, and psychological nuance. Many episodes have included significant Pagan religious themes, including an intense and intimate recounting of the Norse creation myth in "Raid," and portrayals of Viking religious practices such as the visually stunning depiction of a Norse Yule celebration in "Yol."[301] These scenes involve considerable interpretive license given that very little is actually known about the practical details of Norse religion. But as a result, the aesthetic power of the depictions, visual and musical, and their contrast with scenes of stilted, prudish Christian culture create an engaging and positive picture of Norse Paganism for a contemporary audience.[302] The immense popularity of the show has generated quite a bit of interest in Viking culture and religion. Writer Michael Hirst created a six-episode special, *The Secrets of the Vikings*, in which clips from the *Vikings* drama series were interspersed with featured archaeologists and scholars exploring Norse history and culture in engaging ways. Asatru adherents have been among its enthusiastic viewing audience. At the same time, some adherents will point out that enthusiasm can be shallow and the historical inaccuracies of the show perpetrate misconceptions about Norse religion.

I asked Torsen specifically about the show *Vikings* because of his comments in Smietana's article on pop culture. The question hit something of a raw nerve, tapping into Torsen's passion for Heathenry and its inevitable contact with this sort of entertainment

---

301. *Vikings*, "Raid," Season 1, Episode 5, directed by Ciarán Donnelly, written by Michael Hirst, *The History Channel*, March 31, 2013; "Yol," Season 4, Episode 4, directed by Helen Shaver, written by Michael Hirst, *The History Channel*, March 10, 2016.

302. Robert A. Saunders, "Primetime Paganism: Popular-Culture Representations of Europhilic Polytheism in Game of Thrones and Vikings," *Correspondence* 2, no. 2 (2014): 138.

culture. "Considering that all the crap shows and TV specials that keep coming on glorifying or romanticizing or doing whatever they can to continuously put forth misinformation. It just gets harder and harder every year. That stupid ass show, *Vikings*, comes on, then everybody was related to Ragnar Lothbrok, everybody."[303] Torsen goes on to discuss how he has occasionally had to deal with the Viking enthusiasm generated by the TV show: "But now, everybody's related to Ragnar, everybody wants to wear their hair like Ragnar. So, people are always asking me questions about it, and I'm just always like, 'If you really want to know history, stop watching this show, but if you just want it to be entertaining, then just go ahead and watch it.'" Popular culture has irrevocably shaped the Norse material in the minds of Americans. Torsen's experience shows that it has broadened the appeal of Norse culture and religion, while also reducing it in some cases to an aesthetic that can be worn like a hairstyle. Like many Heathens, he expresses concern with this media-induced reduction of Heathen religion to a cultural meme meant for consumption.

> So, the problem I see with the social media or the popular media is that a lot of people, and I say that 70 to 80 percent of the people who watch this, take it for granted. They love to be spoon-fed, and that's where they stop. Now, there are a few that it does spark their interest and they say, "Wow, that guy's pretty cool. I should dig into it and look at it a little bit more."

While pop culture tends to perpetuate misinformation and a distorted view of the Norse material, Torson recognizes its ability to provide a powerful and formative platform. These appealing images generated by pop culture function as cultural orientation, creating a context in which people are more likely to view Norse Paganism as a religiously attractive choice. When exposed to evocative Norse themes in pop culture some, particularly those predisposed to religious seeking, may become curious, leading them to pursue more information about the religious movement.

Helen Berger and Douglas Ezzy have addressed the religious-orienting effect of pop culture in relation to Witchcraft in their book *Teenage Witches*. Their research indicated that slick, youth-oriented portrayals of witches and magic in American pop culture

---

303. Torson, interview.

during the 1990s and 2000s reduced the social stigma around Witchcraft and contributed to a social context more conducive to its positive reception. They explain that "this [incorporation of supernatural, fantasy, and occult themes and images in mass media] has helped to create a world in which the magical, the mystical, and the paranormal are viewed as at least possibilities."[304] While their research focused on teenage participants in Witchcraft, their conclusions are quite applicable to Heathenry. On one level, popular culture may orient consumers to images, themes, and ideas broadly supportive of Heathenry. Examples include participation in the Society for Creative Anachronism and other LARPing events such as Renaissance Fairs, role-playing games such as Dungeons & Dragons, the many young adult novels and video games that include themes of magic, polytheism, and warrior ethics, perhaps even television shows and websites that emphasize knowledge of genealogy and connection to ancestors. Positive exposure to such themes may contribute to a context in which aspects of Heathenry "make sense" instead of being perceived as "weird" or socially marginal.

Other artifacts of pop culture may more directly contribute to a positive cultural orientation to Heathenry. The hit television show *Vikings* is such an example, having a great deal of cultural saturation at present. The Viking and Norse religious themes in heavy metal music are well known and continue to create a strong positive cultural orientation among those who consume that genre of music. Peter Jackson's movie productions of Tolkien's *The Lord of the Rings* and *The Hobbit* made Norse imagery, runes, and positive portrayals of magic and animistic themes available to a wide demographic of American consumers. On one occasion, I witnessed Peter Jackson being hailed and toasted in an Asatru blót for adapting these books into spectacular cinematic forms.[305] Another example of a piece of pop culture more directly orienting to Heathenry is the young adult book series *Magnus Chase and the Gods of Asgard* written by Rick Riordan. The first book in the series, *The Sword of Summer*, follows the main character Magnus Chase as he discovers his identity as an *einherji*, one of Odin's warriors in Valhalla. The story draws heavily on the Eddic lay *Skírnismál* as Magnus seeks to recover the lost

---

304. Berger, and Ezzy, *Teenage Witches*, 75.
305. Field notes taken by author, California, 2012.

sword of Frey before it can be used to start Ragnarok. The second title in the series, *The Hammer of Thor*, centers around a retelling of the Eddic poem *þrymskviða*, in which Thor must impersonate Freyja and be married to the giant Thrym in order to regain his stolen hammer.

Riordan had earlier written the very popular young adult series *Percy Jackson and the Olympians* and *The Heroes of Olympus* that engaged with Greek and Roman polytheism, as well as a series drawn from Egyptian mythology. Characters in these novels actively venerate and interact with Greek, Egyptian, and Norse deities, engage in divination and use magic within storylines driven by the myth cycles of these various cultures. All these books are set in the contemporary American context with approachable teenage characters, so that these appealing interpretations of polytheist and magical themes unfold in the reader's own world. Readers are immersed in a real yet enchanted world in which polytheism makes sense and the myths become accessible, realistic, and relatable. While Riordan takes considerable license with his stories, he also introduces his readers to myth, religion, and culture with remarkable detail. In the *Sword of Summer*, which I read with my children, we were introduced to the whole scope of the Norse religious world: numerous Norse gods, including less well-known deities such as Ran, all of whom were portrayed as realistic and captivating characters. Riordan explores the cosmology of the Nine Worlds and the world tree Yggdrasil. He engages with details about Valhalla, the einherjar, and the valkyries. He asks readers to empathize with a character learning rune magic, and to feel the dramatic tension of the impending possibility of Ragnarok. One of my favorite characterizations was Riordan's Ratatosk (ON *Ratatoskr*), the squirrel who inhabits Yggdrasil. Not only does the squirrel's raspy chitter pack impressive concussive force, but it is heard by the squirrel's targets as a barrage of personal insults and demoralizing criticism. To a person familiar with Norse myth, this subtle detail speaks to the role of Ratatosk in carrying insults up and down the world tree.

Despite including some silliness for his young audience, Riordan presents an imaginative world in which Norse Paganism makes sense and contributes to a positive cultural context for Heathenry. While books such as Riordan's and television shows such as *Vikings* may have a culturally orienting function, the impact of any cultural artifact is difficult to determine. While this sort of cultural orientation may predispose some to positive reception of Heathenry, a path to conversion and religious participation must be built over time by the religious seeker. As Berger and Ezzy point out in a comment applicable to Heathenry, "These broad cultural factors on their own do not result in conversion to Witchcraft, but they do provide a cultural context in which seekers can feel as though they have 'come home' to Witchcraft."[306] It is often the adult converts looking back over their spiritual journey, who give these cultural artifacts significance as part of their conversion careers.

It is very difficult to draw a causative line between the interest of popular culture in Norse themes and interest in the religious movement. None of this material is produced by or for the religious movement. However, its presence in the culture contributes to a familiarity with Norse themes. This familiarity may produce a cultural context that is positively oriented towards Asatru or predispose its consumers favorably toward Norse religious ideas. In the Heathen community, there is clearly a resonance with much of this mass media: positive portrayals of Norse material, even those that are wildly inventive, provide a sense of validation for many Heathens whose beliefs and practices are culturally marginal in many ways. At the same time, Heathens have become sophisticated critical consumers of pop culture, enjoying and being entertained while also critiquing elements that fall short of the movement's standards. It is the Lore, that loose canon of foundational texts, which provides Heathens a critical vantage point. For instance, the 2011 movie *Thor* raised a few eyebrows among Heathens for its portrayal of Heimdall by Idris Elba, a black actor.[307] No doubt, racial attitudes and complaints about political correctness fueled some of that ire. Yet, in every conversation I had about the movie, Heathens referenced the Lore in their critique contrasting the accuracy of the Lore with the director's frequent license with the Norse material. Heathens pointed out to me that not only was Heimdall not black according to the Lore, but that Thor was not blonde. Obviously, these references to the Lore might simply be diversions behind which racist attitudes are lurking, using the Lore to buttress a malignant racism. However, the fact that the critique of the movie

---

306. Ibid., 58.
307. Bob Calhoun, "The Misguided 'Thor' Race Controversy," *Salon*, April 20, 2011, www.salon.com/2011/04/20/thor_casting_viking_movies_open2011/.

was not based solely on personal opinion and bias but arose from an exegesis of the ancient texts indicates that a more complex analysis is taking place.

### The Turbulent Waters

During the period of the New Awakening, both the völkisch and the Wiccan and Witchcraft tributaries, different in so many ways, were joined together into the new Heathen movement. Like the confluence of two rivers, the fusing of two intellectual tributaries may create an area of violent tensions and muddy waters. Where two tributaries come together, there is often a disturbance, a roil. Each tributary is moving in its own direction, with its own force and power, resulting first in a collision even as the waters begin to mix. The two rivers seem to fight and struggle at the point of confluence. Such is the case in Heathenry. The tension generated by the confluence of these two tributaries became especially important and visible in the 1980s and 1990s, a period of development for the movement often interrupted by controversy and schism generated by the issue of racial attitudes.

The Asatru Free Assembly, which had grown out of Stephen McNallen's Viking Brotherhood, became the main organized American Asatru group in the 1980s. As the first active Asatru organization, "the only game in town" as some put it, the Asatru Free Assembly attracted a wide range of people and interests. Witnesses describe McNallen's meetings in Berkeley, California during this time as an explosive mixture of neo-Nazis and counterculture hippies.[308] McNallen attempted to hold these increasingly divergent perspectives together for several years. Yet the pull of the American radical racist movement was significant. To his credit, McNallen resisted overt ties with neo-Nazis and rejected the racist political agenda of white supremacist groups who were wooing the early Asatruars.[309] McNallen distanced the movement from racist politics, and more clearly positioned Asatru as a religious and spiritual movement.[310] However, by the mid-1980s the Asatru Free Assembly disintegrated amid leadership exhaustion and organizational politics. McNallen downplayed the role that racial attitudes played

---

308. Paxson, interview.
309. Kaplan, *Radical Religion in America*, 18–19.
310. Gardell, *Gods of the Blood*, 177–78, 260.

as a factor in the breakup of the Asatru Free Assembly. However a battle to define Asatru was underway. Even with the neo-Nazi element distanced from the religious movement, racial attitudes remained the most salient and divisive issue troubling the Heathen movement. Tension and partisanship over the issue of race hastened the collapse of the Asatru Free Assembly and left the movement in an angry wreckage. This fact is fairly incontrovertible, given the subsequent founding of two new organizations on different sides of the racial issue.[311]

During this period in the mid-1980s, distinct philosophies were enunciated concerning the nature of Asatru, drawing together intellectual tributaries within the Heathen milieu to form coherent ideological topographies. On one side of the growing divide were those who saw Asatru as a religion drawn from ancient northern Europe that could be authentically practiced by any sincere seeker, a position that came to be called "universalist." On the other side were those who saw Asatru primarily as an ethnic religion, a lifeway that manifested a Northern European "folk soul." This came to be known as the folkish position, ostensibly formulated as a middle way that avoided the extremes of either racism or universalism. As McNallen explains it, "on one hand, we were proud of our European heritage and we actively espoused the interests of European-descended people. On the other hand, we opposed totalitarianism and racial hatred."[312] One of McNallen's most important and controversial contributions to the Heathen milieu has been to formulate his theory of metagenetics, which provides an ideological underpinning for folkish Asatru, the implications of which will be further discussed in chapter 3.

By 1987, two new organizations had emerged from the implosion of McNallen's Asatru Free Assembly, a process that demonstrates the generative function of the cultic milieu in Campbell's theory. Not surprisingly each had a distinctly different stance on race, indicating that organizational forms were beginning to coalesce around these ideological points of confluence. Valgard Murray, who had former ties to white supremacy groups, took the reins of the folkish cause from McNallen and founded the Ásatrú Alliance.[313] He presented

---

311. McNallen, "Three Decades," 208.
312. Ibid.
313. Kaplan, *Radical Religion in America*, 20; McNallen, "Three Decades," 209.

the organization as a confederation of autonomous kindreds and tribes and championed a distinctly ethnic perspective of the religion. A longer-running folkish group, The Odinic Rite (OR), remained active primarily in Britain until the late 1990s when it expanded into North America under the leadership of Jeff Heimgest Holley, who became the leader of the organization in 1989. The OR fought its own battles over the racial issue in the early 1990s, leading to a split of the organization. Heimgest successfully steered the group toward a more cultural and esoteric focus. However, the OR retains many of the distinctions of Odinism, including the connection of ancestry and religion as part of the folk soul. The OR maintains a strong esoteric emphasis that focuses on spiritual evolution toward a higher state of awareness called Odinic Consciousness. The group's rhetoric has a revolutionary flair and decidedly political overtones and is often critical of mainstream Asatru as too religiously shallow, too concerned with dressing up like Vikings rather than pursuing the serious consciousness-raising that the OR advocates. The OR has continued the legacy of Else Christensen by remaining very active in prison work, establishing prison kindreds through the United States, particularly in California and a number of southern states. In addition to being a leading proponent of prison ministry, the OR has also been the most vocal Asatru group about environmental issues. However, the OR remains the most folkish of the Asatru groups and for that reason is often viewed critically as a racial organization. The tight centralized bureaucracy of the OR has provided stability and direction for the group, but has not facilitated rapid growth.

As McNallen tells it, Heathenry had always been folkish. The universalist persuasion first emerged in the 1990s with the growing influence of the Wiccan and Witchcraft tributary within the Heathen milieu. "I saw signs," he writes, "that a corrupt faction was making inroads into the Germanic religious movement in the United States . . . which denied the innate connection of Germanic religion and Germanic people, saying in effect that ancestral heritage did not matter. This error could not be allowed to become dominant."[314] As a response to the folkish AA, still considered by many to be overtly racist in its character, Edred Thorsson and several others formed the Ring of Troth, now simply the Troth, in 1987.[315] The founders

314. McNallen, *Asatru*, 65–66.
315. Kaplan, *Radical Religion in America*, 21.

emphasized the academic and magical aspects of the religion and enunciated a type of Asatru that was decidedly more inclusive than the folkish persuasion. The universalist perspective maintains that being Asatru is a religious choice that can be made by anyone who feels drawn to the movement, whether they interpret that as a spiritual call by the gods or simply an attraction to the Norse cultural aspects. The Troth welcomed the involvement of racial and ethnic minorities, LGBT persons, as well as those on the theological margins of Asatru. A network of Stewards represent the organization in all fifty American states and several international locations. In contrast to the tribal-emphasis of folkish Heathen, the Troth is a national organization that accepts and valorizes the place of the independent practitioner. The Troth has taken strong progressive political stances as well as focusing on scholarship, and creative and artistic development. Storytelling, drama, ritual innovation, and seið have all found a home in the Troth. While more tolerant of eclectic practice than folkish Heathens may be, the Troth still maintains a close watch over its intellectual tributaries. The Norse/Germanic tradition and sources remain of primary importance in the Troth, both intellectually and religiously. The organization also sees itself as a fount of the creative exploration of this tradition rather than the reconstruction of it. Diana Paxson, one of the Troth's long-time leaders, has had a significant role in the development of oracular seið, a magical practice further discussed in chapter 8. The leadership of the Troth has been routinized into a committee called the High Rede elected by the membership, and seems to have stabilized since the upheavals that rocked the organization in the 1990s. However, the more democratic nature of its governance and its openness to the eclectic aspects of the Wiccan tributary opens the Troth to recurring and potentially divisive controversies, such as that of the role of the god Loki in the organization's religious framework.

In the mid-1990s, sensing the growing influence of "universalist" Asatru, McNallen returned to active involvement in the religion. While McNallen maintained friendly ties with Murray and the AA, his active and charismatic presence led him to assume the role of the folkish torchbearer. Behind all that folkish earnestness, McNallen has a highly eclectic personality, fascinated by political, cultural, technological, and occult issues. As a result, he has explored numerous innovative directions as part of his Heathenry. He was heavily involved in the controversy surrounding Kennewick Man, discussed in chapter 3, and sought to claim the skeleton as a possible European ancestor of the American Asatru community. He began a guild within the Asatru Free Assembly that pursued the idea of space travel, colonizing other planets, and financially supporting the Asatru movement by mining asteroids. He served as the president of the European American Issues Forum, a political group that rode the dangerous margins of racist politics.[316] Through all these changes, his long-term survival as a religious leader in the contentious environment of the Heathen movement demonstrates his leadership capability. He formed the Asatru Folk Assembly (AFA) in 1994 with the combination of a clearly enunciated folkish perspective and a tight centralized organization, with him firmly ensconced as the charismatic leader of the movement. He sought to rescue the movement from the progressive politics that he saw as threatening to the essential nature of Asatru. McNallen was a folkish crusader with the mission to purify Heathenry from its Pagan drift and to re-establish it on a folkish foundation as the native religion of those of Northern European descent. While based on the West Coast, the AFA has sought to develop a nation-wide as well as international presence through a network of Folkbuilders, regional representatives who act as official contacts for the organization. In 2017, these Folkbuilders numbered about twenty, including two international Folkbuilders, one in New Zealand and another in Sweden. This strategy has proven successful as the California-based group began holding an annual event on the East Coast in 2011. Ritual has been an important part of McNallen's life and this has been reflected in the AFA. As the primary ritual leader of the AFA he engaged in innovative ritual experimentation, and published several ritual/devotional manuals such as his early *Rituals of Asatru* to his more recent *Twelve Nights of Yule*. As part of leadership development, the AFA has also focused heavily on clergy training through its Gothar Program. In 2016, McNallen retired from active leadership and sought to routinize leadership of the AFA within a triumvirate with Matt Flavel serving as the new Alsherjargothi, Pat Hall as Gythja, and Allen Turnage as Lawspeaker. This revitalized Asatru Folk Assembly has emerged as the primary ideological competitor to the Troth.

316. McNallen, "Three Decades," 214.

## The Wolves of Vinland

Just when Heathenry seemed turbulent enough, the Wolves of Vinland (WoV) group has emerged as new confluence drawing on other tributaries flowing into the turbid waters of the Heathen watershed. As with other new religious movements, the lifespan of such small schismatic groups is difficult to predict, although they are often short-lived without making long-term impacts on the larger group. However, the sudden release of energy into the movement from such a passionate and focused group can make rather large ripples or turbulences in the community. The Wolves have their origins in Virginia, and have grown from the ideas and activism of two brothers, Paul and Matthias Waggener, known respectively in the movement as Grimnir and Jarn-nefr. While the Wolves have been part of the scene since 2006, they have gained a good deal of public exposure since 2012 when Maurice Thompson Michaely, a WoV member also known as Hjalti, was convicted of an arson attack against a historically black church.[317] The group came to my notice gradually over the past two years, primarily through their appearances at the Heathen gathering Lightning Across the Plains, where their aggressive approach violated the trust and family-friendly expectations among the event's participants. They appeared as a young, raucous Pagan gang, exuding a type of adrenaline-infused masculinity described by one admirer referencing two popular television shows as "a cross between *Sons of Anarchy* and *Vikings*."[318] This persona of the aggressive, hard-partying, hyper-masculine Viking is a long-standing trope in Heathenry. Yet

---

317. The Wolves received significant criticism for the incident with Hjalti, particularly for continuing to support him during and after the conviction. Photographs of Paul Waggener visiting Hjalti in jail, combined with descriptions of Hjalti's continued involvement with the Wolves after his release, were re-posted on numerous websites to illustrate the Wolves' white power sympathies. However, the Wolves indicated that their support rested on their guiding philosophy of tribalism. The tribal ethos involves strong, binding commitments to members of the group characterized by frith. The word "frith" comes from the Old Norse verb *friða*, "to make or restore peace," and related noun *friðr*, "peace, love, or friendship." It is an important ethical term in Heathenry referring to the bond of fellowship among members of a kinship group, meant to be a relationship of loyalty and inviolable sanctity. The incident with Hjalti began a broader ethical conversation among some Heathens about the meaning and extent of frith and under what circumstances frith should be rescinded. See "What Are the Implications of Frith? A Real-Life Scenario," *Reddit* website, www.reddit.com/r/asatru/comments/3epiu5/what_are_the_implications_of_frith_a_reallife/.

318. Jack Donovan, "A Time for Wolves," *Jack Donovan* blog, June 14, 2014, www.jack-donovan.com/axis/2014/06/a-time-for-wolves/.

the Wolves have other characteristics that indicate a deeper level of sophistication and ideological nuance that made it challenging to fit the group into the typical dichotomy of folkish/universalist that has dominated the research on Asatru. The Wolves in their motorcycle gang form of tribalist collective challenged the family-oriented direction of the rest of contemporary Asatru. They are deeply involved in Germanic magic, yet reject the female-oriented magical paradigm of the Witchcraft tributary. Mix into this a penchant for body-fetishizing selfies riffing on the narcissistic and exhibitionist culture of power lifting, and a heavy presence on online social media. In fact, they may be one of the first Heathen groups to build their movement specifically around social media. Not that other individuals and groups are not using social media platforms—Heathens are heavy adopters of the Internet as a means to communicate information and to maintain relationships. However the Wolves were created by two millennials, the Waggener brothers. As digital natives, they have a more intuitive understanding of the power of the selfie: harnessing the aesthetic power of social media to produce an emotional affect in those who view their images online. From early on, the performance of their Heathenry and its presentation online have been inextricably intertwined. Utilizing Tumblr, Instagram, and Youtube, they present glimpses of a lifestyle in deliberately crafted memes, short video clips, and pieces of text that express their anarcho-primitivist philosophy of wildness, power, and brotherhood. These images use shock value and prominently placed symbols to communicate an ethos inspiring and appealing to Heathens who feel that a degree of depth or passion is missing in their religious practice, as well as other disaffected people who might respond to these images of masculine strength and camaraderie. A selfie of a guy flexing the muscles of his runic-tattooed torso may seem crass, but to its intended audience it inspires a romantic yearning for the magic and power of a barbarian tribe. Essentially they have been creating a brand through their careful use of social media, a style of Heathen expression that they are successfully exporting in the United States and Europe.

There has been a significant interest in the Wolves' association with the alternative right and white nationalism.[319] When asked

---

319. *Fools of Vinland*, a now-inactive blog set up to monitor the activity of the Wolves, has been their longest running critic. See http://foolsofvinland.blogspot.com/. Journalists have also criticized the Wolves as racists and white nationalists. See

pointedly about his and the Wolves' stance on race, Waggener tends to equivocate:

> We sort of have this bizarre stance with all these different groups where the Right doesn't think we're Right enough and the Left thinks that we're completely far to the Right . . . So, I don't know where we fall. We fall wherever we are. We're tribalists, certainly, and we're absolutely proud of who we are and where we come from, but not to the point where I'm interested in starting some kind of race war or doing something else crazy or wasting all my time talking about how supreme I am while I smash my way through another can of watery, shitty beer and get fatter and postpone the South rising again because there's a barbecue across the street. Those are the sort of groups that people think of when they hear the word "racially-aware" or whatever that means.[320]

Here, Waggener shows off his deft use of insults, a strategy he frequently employs to triangulate himself from others and avoid easy categorization. However, the Wolves clearly operate in the intellectual space of the alternative right, drawing heavily on the völkisch/ Traditionalist tributary. Waggener should be taken at his word when he enunciates his vision of a new "strength culture" and warrior ethic arising from the ashes of modern society. He is deeply invested in a völkisch-inflected approach to Germanic/Norse Paganism to fuel that vision. Ties to the racist right are abundant, with numerous Wolves connected to alt-right politics. These connections are most apparent in Waggener's close relationship with Jack Donovan. Donovan is best

---

also Cari Wade Gervin, "Vengeance Strength Kvlt Gym in East Nashville Has Links to Alt-Right," *Nashville Scene*, July 20, 2017, www.nashvillescene.com/news/pith-in-the-wind/article/20868176/strength-cult-gym-in-east-nashville-has-ties-to-altright; Betsy Woodruff, "Inside Virginia's Creepy White-Power Wolf Cult," *Daily Beast*, November, 12, 2015, www.thedailybeast.com/inside-virginias-creepy-white-power-wolf-cult; Rose City Antifa, "The Wolves of Vinland: a Fascist Countercultural 'Tribe' in the Pacific Northwest," November 7, 2016, https://rosecityantifa.org/articles/the-wolves-of-vinland-a-fascist-countercultural-tribe-in-the-pacific-northwest/; Robert Creekmore, "Nazis in Wolves Clothing, Part 1," April 5, 2016, https://robertcreekmore.com/2016/04/05/nazis-in-wolves-clothing-part-1/. In 2016, the Southern Poverty Law Center designated the Wolves as a white nationalist hate group. See www.splcenter.org/fighting-hate/intelligence-report/2016/active-hate-groups-united-states-2015#whitenationalist.

320. Paul Waggener, "Greg Johnson Interviews Paul Waggener" *Counter Currents*, February 3, 2016, www.counter-currents.com/2016/02/greg-johnson-interviews-paul-waggener-2/.

known for his books enunciating a philosophy of rugged masculinity, such as *The Way of Men*. He is also heavily involved with alternative right politics and white nationalist groups as a speaker and writer.[321] He is a charismatic and ambiguous character, who Waggener describes as "a guy who definitely keeps people off balance."[322] In 2014, Donovan wrote an article, "A Time for Wolves," in which he featured the Wolves as examples of his ideology of manhood.[323] Over the next three years, Donovan became increasingly involved in the group and its culture. He eventually patched in as an official member of the Wolves and now leads their Cascadia chapter in Oregon. Numbering between fifty and one hundred, the Wolves are not a large group but maintain a chapter in Virginia led by Paul Waggener, and one in Wyoming led by Matthias Waggener.

Their barbarian ethos, with its prominent anti-social, anti-civilization themes, sets the Wolves apart as a distinct group in the broader Heathen watershed. They see themselves as wolves living on the margins, rejecting civilization and escaping into the wild to find their true and primal selves. The wolf pack and its meritocracy maintained through displays of strength and violence symbolizes the communal yearning among marginal millennial males. The Wolves engage in ritual practices that are reminiscent of *Lord of the Flies* both in their primal excesses and juvenile predilections: guttural howling, aggressive wild galdr, cutting and blood-letting, and mixing blood with ash and mead as body paint for runic symbols and as sacrificial offerings in blót.[324] This is quite out of the social norm in Heathenry. While drinking, socializing, and carousing may be part of the social scene, the Wolves push this to an extreme by equating intoxication with the release of *wode*, wild untamed energy of Odinic inspiration. While Heathen rituals often take on an intense edge, they also tend to be more serious and orderly and do not encourage the sort of primal ecstasy sought by the Wolves.

---

321. Southern Poverty Law Center, "A Chorus of Violence: Jack Donovan and the Organizing Power of Male Supremacy," *Hatewatch*, March 27, 2017, www.splcenter.org/hatewatch/2017/03/27/chorus-violence-jack-donovan-and-organizing-power-male-supremacy.

322. Paul Waggener, "Interview."

323. Jack Donovan, "A Time for Wolves," *Jack Donovan* website, June 14, 2014, www.jack-donovan.com/axis/2014/06/a-time-for-wolves/.

324. The live blót, or animal sacrifice, is making a comeback among some American Heathen practitioners, including the Wolves of Vinland. See chapter 6 for more discussion.

I initially became aware of the Wolves by hearing about an occurrence at the Lightning Across the Plains folk sumbel, an informal and low-key event held around a campfire each year. Families relaxed in a large circle of camp chairs, children came and went, the horn was passed to whoever had a boast, a story to tell, or a gift to give. However, this time, the event had been hijacked when a visitor took the horn and began delivering a politically tinged rant, screaming and pacing, deriding the decadence of civilization and the weakness of Heathenry. Some guests were affronted at the display as it was uninvited and out of character from the usual family-friendly affair. Many of the details were vague and the story was shocking and confusing. It took some digging to begin to make sense of what had occurred. It was, I discovered, the Wolves who had recently expanded from their base in the mountains of Virginia to establish a satellite tribe in the woods of Wyoming. Their appearance continued to confuse me until I ran across a Wolves video that ended with the phrase "See you in the woods."[325] The gist of the video expressed the Wolves' ideology that modern humans have been weakened and domesticated by living in civilization. We have lost our natural wild, feral nature and our internal strength, our will, has atrophied. Here we find an important intellectual lineage drawing on Nietzschean ideas of the ubermensch and anarchist ideas that civilization is the root of the human problem. However, the key part of the lineage, clearly referenced in the line "See you in the woods," is Henry David Thoreau. In his book *Walden*, Thoreau famously sought to leave the corrupting influence of civilization by going into the woods and immersing himself in nature at Walden Pond. This reference connects the Wolves to the tributary of American anarchist-primitivism (see figure 10).

Anarcho-primitivism has been popularized and represented in the contemporary period by writers such as John Zerzan. Traces of the ideology originate with the French philosopher Jean-Jacques Rousseau, whose famous work *The Social Contract* begins with the dramatic statement that "Man is born free and everywhere he is in chains."[326] Rousseau can be interpreted as criticizing the Hobbesian

---

325. Galdr, "Wolves of Vinland: Community Building," YouTube video, posted December 7, 2011, www.youtube.com/watch?v= HBG5K29tLFY, now removed.

326. John Zerzan, *Against Civilization and Other Essays* (Los Angeles: Feral House, 2005); Jean-Jacques Rousseau and G. D. H. Cole, *The Social Contract and Discourses* (London: J. M. Dent & Sons, 1973), 181.

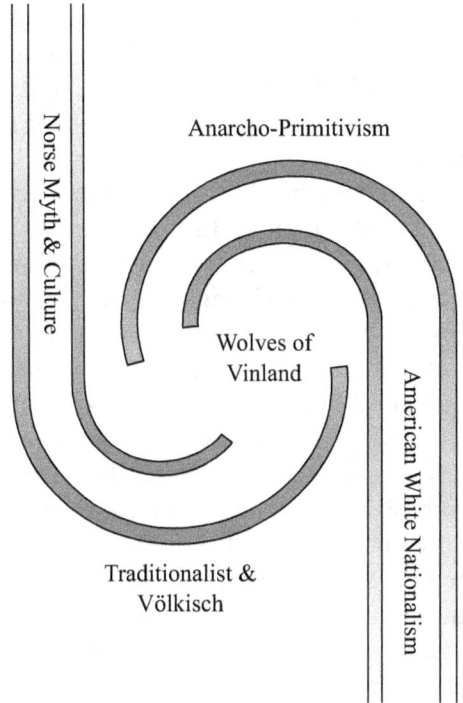

Figure 10. Tributaries of the Wolves of Vinland.

notion that the natural state of humanity was one of misery and warfare. Instead he pictured humanity in the state of nature, outside of or prior to civilization, as the noble savage. The noble savage, unmarred by civilization's influence represents all that is good about the human being. Before falling from the primitive condition and becoming enmeshed in society, humans were uncorrupted beings free from the chains of civilization. With this idea of the noble savage, Rousseau began to the rehabilitate the wild life and the wild man as a desirable state.

Approximately one hundred years later and a continent away, Henry David Thoreau sought to find a way to reclaim the wild life, with its vigor and clarity. He writes scathingly of society and its effects, both on human nature and the environment, and finds in Nature a vitalizing and ennobling element. In his most famous work, *Walden*, Thoreau writes: "We must learn to reawaken and keep ourselves awake," and states that by abandoning society we might shake off its stupefying effects, "I went to the woods because I wanted to live deliberately, I wanted to live deep and suck out all the marrow of life."[327] Thus Thoreau discovers a tool for reawakening himself, a method for regaining the vitality of life through adopting a lifestyle of primitivism: going into the woods. His essay "Walking," begins to develop the themes that will become so important in anarcho-primitivism: the decadence of civilization in contrast to the wild invigorating freedom of the outdoors. Thoreau writes about the softness of indoor life and the tameness that civilization and cultivation brings, "Nowadays almost all man's improvements, so called . . . simply deform the landscape, and make it more and more tame and cheap."[328] In contrast he lauds the wild, "In short, all good things are wild and free," that which is not subdued by civilization, but is wild is the most alive. Contemporary anarcho-primitivism continues to critique the modern reliance on technology and civilization as detrimental to the human condition.

Beginning with Thoreau's walk into the woods, a "rewilding" philosophy, a type of anarcho-primitivism, has developed suggesting that civilization has a "domesticating" influence that weakens, distorts, and corrupts the natural wildness of the human being. Miles Olsen, the author of the book *Unlearn, Rewild*, makes the connection with Thoreau clear, "I also read Thoreau and somehow I just got infected with the idea that this world is horrible. There is something incredibly sad at the core of everything about our lives, and I don't want to ignore it. And I think that the best way to get to something that is real and true is to go alone into the woods."[329] Olsen fuses Rousseau and Thoreau in his statement, longing for something real and essential, the strong noble life, and finding it by walking into the woods. A small economy has developed around the anarcho-primitivist rewilding philosophy such as a self-styled school called ReWild University. This school offers a variety of classes in a wilderness setting to help people strip off the

---

327. Henry David Thoreau and Brooks Atkinson, *Walden and Other Writings of Henry David Thoreau* (New York: Modern Library, 1992), 81–82.

328. Henry David Thoreau, "Walking," in *Walden and Other Writings of Henry David Thoreau*, 602.

329. Miles Olsen, "Unlearning and Rewilding: An Interview with Miles Olson," YouTube video, 9:09, posted by *Utne Reader*, January 19, 2014, interview by Suzanne Lindgren, www.youtube.com/watch?v=FLHG3qjkwgk. See also Miles Olsen, *Unlearn, Rewild: Earth Skills, Ideas and Inspiration for the Future Primitive* (Gabriola Island, Canada: New Society, 2012).

stupefying layers of domestication and civilization and have a real, unmediated, and cleansing encounter with nature and wildness. ReWild University describes four elements of the rewilding process, all of which are clearly evident in the Wolves of Vinland. These four elements include a natural diet, getting away from processed foods; a tribal lifestyle of "community, integrity, and connection with nature"; exercising in natural ways like "wild running," lifting, and climbing rather than the repetitive, mechanistic style of gym-based exercise; and regaining a wild mindset by uprooting the constraints imposed by a contemporary lifestyle. These elements serve as important "gateways into our wild selves" by providing a type of structure to the Thoreauean imperative of going into the woods.[330]

These elements also resonate with aspects of the German völkisch movement. In Germany contemporaneous with the völkisch movement, a back-to-nature movement was also popular. This "natural life" movement known as *Lebensreform* advocated a return to a more natural lifestyle and the healthy vitality, liberated mind, and social harmony it would produce. Germans were encouraged to take long hikes through the German countryside, exercise, eat healthy natural diets, engage in naturism, and pursue alternative therapies. Lebensreform appealed to many of those in the völkisch movement, who sought a return to strength, physical vitalism, and spiritual health. They saw this natural lifestyle as improving the vitality of the German people and connecting them spiritually to the German landscape.

The Wolves have drawn heavily on both the völkisch and the anarcho-primitivist tributaries, curating a confluence of Heathenry focused on strong individuals supported by ethnic tribalism and Germanic Paganism. The Wolves have a very developed sense of corpospirituality, seeing the physical and spiritual as deeply intertwined. In this light, the contemporary American diet comes under heavy critique. In a presentation at a Midwestern Heathen event, one WoV member described the processed food and sugary snacks that fill the pantries of America as poisons that fatten the bodies and weaken the spirit essence of those who eat them. Hinting at a conspiracy theory, he suggested that these foods are a means by which civilization tempts us, luring the weak into a vicious cycle

---

330. "What Is Human ReWilding?" *ReWild University* YouTube video, 10:00, September 24, 2013, www.youtube.com/watch?v=JH7kqmT7fIk.

that further debilitates them.[331] Resisting the temptation of highly processed foods both strengthens the will and purifies the body. The Wolves also seek to abandon civilization, finding in it a stultifying conformity and a social structure that strips the individual of his/her sovereign power and creative capacities, and that encourages passivity and consumerism. Their goal is to develop enough infrastructure to make such a separation possible: finding land, building primitive dwellings in the woods, and gathering a chosen tribe of selected people all of whom are dedicated to rediscovering and living out their wild feral selves. Taking Thoreau's disdain towards civilization to another level, they sneer about "the disease riddled whorehouse of modern culture," in which the vast majority of people have been stupefied by its convenience, consumerism, hedonism, a false sense of freedom that in actuality is only indulgence.[332] They are not simply social critiques. Acting on the Heathen motto, "We are our Deeds," they have been actively recruiting and established enclaves in Virginia, Wyoming, and the Pacific Northwest where they hope to create sustainable Heathen communities.

Along the lines of corpospirituality, the Wolves have embraced natural exercise as a way to strengthen body and soul. Bodybuilding has become integral for the Wolves, who promote a strengthening regime as part of their greater cultural work, Operation Werewolf. They have drawn intensively from the Centurion Method, a fitness program with Pagan, warrior, and Social Darwinist roots that involves natural exercises such as carrying heavy rocks, logs, and other outdoor exercises.[333] There is a strong connection between physical and spiritual strength for the Wolves: a weak and flaccid will, which is at the mercy of advertising and consumerist society, is mirrored in a soft and flaccid body. This Centurion Method idealizes the Germanic hero Sigurd as the strong heroic male ideal.

---

331. Matthias Waggener, "On Magic," field notes taken during oral presentation, Kansas, 2013.

332. Paul Waggener, "From Putrefaction To Purification," in *Operation Werewolf: The Complete Transmissions* (CreateSpace, 2016), 107–9. Waggener's *Operation Werewolf* book consists of his blog posts that have been collected and published. I had originally accessed all this material online from his ongoing blogs. In 2016, these blogs were removed from the Internet and the material later appeared in this publication.

333. Craig and Lucy Fraser, *The Centurion Method*, self-published, 2013.

Strengthening the will through bodybuilding is coupled with freeing the mind. This aspect of rewilding is especially important to the WoV who seek to return to a wild, free, and spiritually powerful state that they embody in the wolf image. The wolf is worn on clothing, tattooed on the body, and displayed as a totem of this inner feral and powerful will, which can be found through the process of rewilding. For the WoV, the wild mindset is discovered or reclaimed through engaging in self-discipline, Heathen ritual and Germanic magic. They perform typical Heathen ritual, the blót and the sumbel, with an ecstatic edge seeing the ritual as a way to create a wild communal mindset beyond the polite constraints of civilized behavior. One Wolf describes the communitas produced in the hallucinatory quality of these rituals: "The brothers I have chosen are wild Wolves. Sometimes I see them from the edge of our ritual circle in the forest, and I see their shapes change from men to animals, and back to men again, twisting in the firelight like strange beasts, unknown to the weak and civilized man."[334] The WoV emphasize magic, rune work, and seidr as vital Heathen pursuits through which the individual will is strengthened and projected into the world. Their magic is an eclectic mix of Aleister Crowley's emphasis on the will with the rune magic of the völkisch movement, which aimed to achieve higher awareness and Odinic consciousness and evolve the self into higher levels of being.[335] Drawing on the völkisch context of the occult, the Wolves avoid the feminization of magic and the tradition of female magic-workers that dominate the Wiccan tributary. Instead, associated with a strong, free, and disciplined will, magic is hyper-masculinized. The Wolves emphasize the role of the *vitki*, the Old Norse word for the male who masters the esoteric realm in order to control himself and his environment.

The Wolves introduce into the Heathen watershed a new tributary of anarcho-primitivism. It is an intellectual lineage stretching from Rousseau, through Thoreau, and into the contemporary niche of the rewilding movement. Among the Wolves, it mingles with Norse myth and iconography, and the racial and magical aspects of völkisch ideology, in order to create a new and distinctive form

---

334. Paul Waggener, "Living Myth," in *Operation Werewolf: The Complete Transmissions*, 57–59.
335. List, *The Secret of the Runes*, 46–48.

of Heathenry. The Wolves illustrate the fluidity and dynamism of the Heathen watershed, how new tributaries are brought in, combined with other long-standing approved Heathen sources to create new and possibly destabilizing confluences.

## *Conclusion*

The event described at the beginning of this chapter, of that eclectic group drawn together for stadhagaldr in the woods of Minnesota one morning, illustrates the power of religious innovation, not only to carry ideas and practices across time, but to incorporate them into new ideological topographies. The Heathen movement itself is a confluence of historical and intellectual tributaries that inform this new religion in creative and contentious ways. The Heathen milieu may be more ideologically bounded than some other new religions. However, it still draws on an eclectic bricolage of ideas situated around the strong core of Norse myth and iconography, and shows a remarkable tendency to evolve and adapt. As we have seen, one of the most important tensions in American Heathenry has been the issue of racial attitudes and the relationship, if any, between ancestry and religion. And perhaps the most important player in this ongoing struggle has been Stephen McNallen and his theory of metagenetics. It is to him and an analysis of the role of metagenetics in the movement that I now turn.

## Chapter 3

## Metagenetics

In the dawn light of Thursday, October 29, 1998, Stephen and Sheila McNallen stood in a museum parking lot in Seattle, Washington and raised a hammer and a horn in a ritual to bless the remains of Kennewick Man. Kennewick Man is a 9,000-year-old skeleton discovered on the bank of the Columbia River in Washington State. Much to the surprise of the investigating scientists, the remains did not match the physical characteristics expected of a Native American skeleton.[336] In fact, the archaeologist who initially examined the ancient skeleton, James Chatters, speculated that it was that of an early pioneer or trapper. In a talk he gave in 1999, Stephen McNallen remembered the discovery this way, "nine thousand three hundred years later [after Kennewick Man died] I got a phone call. 'Steve,' the caller said, 'the most astounding thing has just happened. They've found a skeleton up in Washington. It's ancient and it's a white guy!'"[337] The discovery seemed to challenge long-held notions of indigeneity—could it be that Caucasians had a significantly longer presence on the North American continent that traditionally thought, long enough perhaps to rival those considered "natives"? For McNallen, the discovery became a watershed event, a stage upon which he could enact his most tenaciously held tenet about Asatru—that it is a religion inextricably tied to race, the expression of the northern European folksoul, the ancient native religion of white Americans.[338]

---

336. Douglas Preston, "The Kennewick Man Finally Freed to Share His Secrets," *Smithsonian*, September 2014, www.smithsonianmag.com/history/kennewick-man-finally-freed-share-his-secrets-180952462/#JGEzFS1MfzJHOyqx.99.

337. Stephen McNallen, "Kennewick Man: Whites in North American B.C.," YouTube video, 1:02:44, posted by LastKaliYuga, October 12, 2012, www.youtube.com/watch?v=olszVUSJv1w.

338. From 1998 to 2017, Kennewick Man, known as the Ancient One to Native Americans, was under the care of the Burke Museum in Seattle, Washington. While there, he underwent a series of studies. DNA analysis by the University of

Standing in the parking lot on that early morning in 1998, the personal, the political, and the religious all conjoined in the Asatru ceremony performed by McNallen. He saw Kennewick Man as his ancestor, a European who had walked on the North American continent far longer ago than anyone had previously thought, who may have even venerated the gods of pre-Christian Europe. This challenged the traditional story of European and Native interaction: if Kennewick Man had been in America 9,000 years ago, significantly longer than any of the historical Native American tribes, then who was really native? Attired in ritual garb, "modern-day versions of clothing from the Viking era," as the press described at the time, the McNallens performed a blót, raising a horn filled with mead to the gods and to Kennewick Man, honoring him as an ancestor of northern European peoples on the American continent.[339] This was Stephen McNallen's moment in the spotlight, his dream of elevating Asatru to the national stage. It is a moment that in some way represented his struggle to bring Asatru to white Americans, to reintroduce them to their native religion, from his perspective the religion of their souls. It was a moment of deep significance, one that continues to motivate him, and one that he completely stands behind despite later recriminations both from the public and other Asatruars, many who remain abjectly embarrassed by the stance and theatrics of McNallen during this event.[340] The ritual carried out that day was the culmination of a dogged effort involving a long legal and media battle in which McNallen had sought to keep Kennewick Man from being repatriated to Native American tribes. McNallen saw the Kennewick Man discovery as a way to stake a claim for his long-held passion that Asatru was a religion of ancestry and blood.

Copenhagen demonstrated that he was most closely related to Native American populations. See Morten Rasmussen, et al., "The Ancestry and Affiliations of Kennewick Man," *Nature* 523 (July, 2015): 455–58. doi:10.1038/nature14625. He was repatriated to Native American tribes and reburied in a private ceremony in 2017, in accordance with the Native American Graves Protection and Repatriation Act. See Burke Museum, "Statement on the Repatriation of the Ancient One," February 20, 2017, www.burkemuseum.org/blog/kennewick-man-ancient-one.

339. Linda Ashton, "Indians, Pagans, Bless Kennewick Man," *The Spokesman-Review* (Spokane, WA) October 30, 1998, B4, http://news.google.com/newspapers?nid=1314&dat=19981030&id=0mJWAAAAIBAJ&sjid=4vEDAAAAIBAJ&pg=6688,8019382.

340. McNallen, *Asatru*, 66–68.

Two themes intertwine throughout this chapter: the life and thought of Stephen McNallen and the issue of racial attitudes in Heathenry. Of all the various leaders in Asatru, McNallen has made it his life work to represent American Asatru as a type of ethnic or native European spirituality: a religion for those of northern European descent. On the surface, McNallen's position seems remarkably similar to those of the ethnic and native religions emerging throughout Europe, which are not only inspired by a specific historical culture but are often seen as specific to a particular ethnicity.[341] In the American context however, McNallen's advocacy for Asatru as a *native* spirituality faces additional complications of its legitimacy. In contrast to the European movements' reconstruction of pre-Christian traditions in a setting of geographical and ethnic continuity, the claim that American Asatruars are practicing a "native" or indigenous spirituality is a much more ambiguous proposition. Exactly what it means to revive specific "local spiritual traditions" is unclear in the context of the American melting pot where cultural and genetic heterogeneity are the rule.[342] Additionally, McNallen's framing of Asatru as a native *European* spirituality is itself a complex abstraction. In McNallen's view of the world, white Americans *are* Europeans. He argues that being authentically European involves two characteristics. First, being European involves a genetic, or racial, heritage—a continuous genetic connection to ancient native Europeans. Second, it involves the awakening of a type of consciousness—the ancient Northern European religio-cultural consciousness lying dormant in everyone of Northern European heritage. While McNallen and other folkish Asatruar are Americans, their deep ancestral genetics and awakened ancestral consciousness makes them more European, *native* European in fact. McNallen's vision of Asatru as a native faith, led to his controversial theory of metagenetics and the creation of an ideological firestorm that continues to burn in contemporary Heathenry.

---

341. Scott Simpson and Mariusz Filip, "Selected Words for Modern Pagan and Native Faith Movements in Central and Eastern Europe," in *Modern Pagan and Native Faith Movements in Central and Eastern Europe*, 34–35.

342. Piotr Wiench, "A Postcolonial Key to Understanding Central and Eastern European Neopaganisms," in *Modern Pagan and Native Faith Movements in Central and Eastern Europe*, 10.

## The Legend, the Man

If there is one name associated with the birth, growth, and controversy of American Asatru, it is Stephen McNallen. And the Kennewick Man affair was only one moment in McNallen's storied career as an Asatru religious specialist. Within Asatru, he is hailed by some as the "father" of American Asatru, and begrudgingly recognized by many others for his important contribution to the development of Asatru as a religious movement. At the same time, other Heathens deeply criticize his personal faults and his commitment to a folkish interpretation of the faith. It is also important to recognize that many people have contributed to the development and growth of Asatru. The history of Asatru, as we have seen, does not revolve around one personality. Even if American Asatru did start with McNallen, it quickly grew into something well beyond his control and influence. Some of the frustration and vitriol that McNallen has expressed about the direction of contemporary Asatru arises from the fact that the movement has outgrown his immediate influence. Additionally, there are many young Asatruars for whom McNallen's legacy carries little significance. Asatru is not by any means a "cult movement" as Stark and Bainbridge would define it. It is not a religion built around allegiance and loyalty to one charismatic leader who is seen by his followers as a prophet. However McNallen's role and influence in Asatru is unique. We can learn much about the movement by understanding his contribution.

McNallen published an insightful article, entitled "Three Decades of the Ásatrú Revival," describing his own involvement in Asatru. The article is quite revealing, not only of McNallen's analysis of the history and future of the movement, but of his understanding of his own place in the movement's history.[343] The article begins by reminiscing about the early movement, when he first came to realize that the Norse gods could be worshiped. McNallen describes how he was first attracted to Norse mythology and the culture of the Vikings because it appealed to the adventurous and independent nature of his younger self. He was in his early twenties coming into a manhood that longed for the heroic, for an ethical and religious system that could inspire a life of derring-do. Not finding a supportive environment for rugged manhood either in Christianity

---

343. McNallen, "Three Decades," 203–19.

or in Wicca, he was drawn toward the Vikings, their warrior ethic and their gods who, as warriors themselves, were fierce and brave, not abstracted into some ultimate ground of being, nor ethically pacified by a turn-the-other-cheek softness, nor feminized within a religion of the Goddess. McNallen had found his calling, or as he might later put it: the gods had found him. He soon began to place ads in various magazines, seeking out others who were interested in Norse religion, and began to build a small following he called the Viking Brotherhood. It is interesting that one of his first instincts was to build a religious organization, a focus that has remained constant in his life for forty years. He soon began writing the first Asatru publication, *The Runestone*, printing a first edition of eleven copies on a mimeograph machine. At the same time, McNallen began active duty in the US military, which deeply curtailed the time he was able to devote to Asatru. This first attempt at organized Asatru religion would last three or four years, and consisted primarily of McNallen's self-published magazine, eventually reaching over a hundred people per issue.[344]

In his "Three Decades" article, McNallen nostalgically reflects upon a photograph of himself taken during the early 1970s, the Viking Brotherhood era. Writing about himself in the third person, McNallen describes the young man in the picture as serious, focused, and directed, with a scholarly bent betrayed by his eyeglasses. This young man, he writes, is both a romantic and a warrior, whose spiritual depths have yet to be understood or developed. He is a man awakening as it were, on the edge of a great destiny that has only begun to unfold. McNallen's reverie concludes with a telling line, "In a way, that photograph was not only Steve McNallen, it was the Viking Brotherhood itself."[345] This passage in the article is a striking scene in which McNallen, gazing at his own photo and seeing Asatru made in his own likeness, epitomized the early Asatru movement in the photograph of himself. McNallen betrays the sort of narcissistic self-involvement that might characterize the psychology of a charismatic religious leader, the founder of a religious movement. He sees the whole movement within himself, and equates the movement's identity and development with his own. In some ways, it does reflect history. The Viking Brotherhood

344. Ibid., 206.
345. Ibid., 207.

was the first organized attempt at a popular Asatru organization outside of Else Christensen's Odinist Fellowship, which was a mail-order journal primarily oriented towards prisoners. McNallen was undoubtedly central to the Viking Brotherhood's origin, vision, and success. At the same time the narrative, and his position in it, reflects McNallen's idiosyncratic vision of history, one in which he is the pivotal, literally the only figure of importance, so much so that his portrait is able to encapsulate Asatru.

A hint of narcissism is probably to be expected in leaders who have made significant contributions to movement building, compelled by a sense of destiny and often as a result of tremendous struggle and personal cost. There is a heroic element in this choice of life. McNallen deserves to be noted as one of many American religious dissenters who, because of strong personal conviction and vision, stood their ground in the face of hardship and opposition. What is more notable is that the sort of cult prophet personality associated with some new religious movements has not emerged in Heathenry. While McNallen has a reputation in the movement for his imperious moods, his demands for high degrees of personal loyalty, his difficulties in working with those outside of his own circle of authority, and his own sense of calling and destiny, neither he nor other Asatru leaders have sought to claim quasi-divine status. He makes no claims to be an "Asapope," expecting the allegiance and loyalty of all Heathens, nor has the Heathen movement ever consisted of a "following" that idolizes McNallen or any other leader.[346] While the fiercely independent spirit of Asatru contributes to this sentiment, contemporary Paganism as a whole evinces a lack of enthusiasm for charismatic leadership. Graham Harvey corroborates this characteristic of Pagan religiosity when he writes that "some groups form or divide around strong personalities but generally . . . Pagans are intolerant, skeptical or even cynical about leaders. They do not gather around 'Guru' figures."[347] As one Heathen put it, "because he is the leader of one group of Heathens does not make him the leader — or even the spokesman — of us all. Heck, no one can claim to be the leader of us all and we rather like it that way."[348]

346. Kaplan, "Reconstruction of the Ásatrú and Odinist Traditions," 202.
347. Harvey, *Contemporary Paganism*, 207.
348. Karl E. H. Seigfried, "Heathens in the Military: An Interview with Josh & Cat Heath, Part Three," The Norse Mythology Blog, February 2, 2013, www.norsemyth.org/2013/02/heathens-in-military-interview-with.html.

Yet McNallen *is* different, not only for his role in Asatru's founding, but also his propensity to identify the movement with himself, this sense that somehow he is in touch with the living heartbeat of the Heathen awakening, that his life embodies something of the true soul of Asatru. Stephen Flowers who has been a powerful influence on Heathenry himself states,

> I first met the leader of the AFA, Stephen McNallen, at the first AFA Althing in the summer of 1979. Meeting Steve was a life-changing experience for me. He is an embodiment of a kind of Germanic spirituality that puts words into action . . . Despite whatever history might have passed in the late 1980s and early 1990s, there can be no doubt that Stephen McNallen is the guiding light of American Ásatrú. I count Steve McNallen as a friend and colleague and very much value the fact that it was from him that I received my godhordh—or "authority as a godhi."[349]

McNallen is a genuinely charismatic man who commands a presence, and who is, as evidenced by his lifetime commitment to promoting Asatru, a man of both vision and perseverance.[350] He is the founder of three Asatru organizations, including the Viking Brotherhood that many recognize as the first Heathen religious organization in the United States. After many years of leadership and now into his retirement, he continues to hold a place of great respect in the Asatru Folk Assembly. He is officially recognized as the *Alsherjargothi* of the AFA, a term signifying both respect and authority, and one that is not used frequently in other American Heathen organizations.[351] His influence in the AFA should not be underestimated. The direction and goals, the theology and ritual, and even the membership of the AFA arises from McNallen's direction, leadership, and oversight.

And if that is the case, to be at odds with McNallen is somehow to be truly jumping off the Asatru longship. This fact is witnessed by

---

349. Michael Moynihan, "A Conversation with Dr. Stephen Flowers [aka Edred Thorsson]," *Renegade Tribune*, March 15, 2016, www.renegadetribune.com/conversation-dr-stephen-flowers-aka-edred-thorsson/.

350. By all accounts of those to whom I spoke about McNallen. Disappointingly, I attempted to contact McNallen numerous times, including emails and letters, all of which went unanswered.

351. Stefn Thorsman and Ed leBouthillier, "On Heathen Clergy: An Interview with Stefn Thorsman and Ed LeBouthillier," *Journal of Contemporary Heathen Thought* 2 (2011–2012): 207.

those Heathens who have been asked to leave the AFA for reasons ranging from theological variance, disapproved connections to other groups, and personal fallout with McNallen. As we have mentioned, McNallen is no stranger to acrimony and conflict, and he tells the tales of intra-movement conflict as larger-than-life dramas. There were the personality and ideological conflicts that tore apart the Asatru Free Assembly, started and run by McNallen in the late 1970s and 1980s; the ongoing conflict with the "politically correct faction" over McNallen's racial attitudes and politics in the 1990s, and a number of conflicts that rocked the AFA in the early 2000s, a time that McNallen writes about as being "under attack" through "infiltration and betrayal."[352] One of the most well-known feuds happened in the late 2000s between McNallen and Mark Stinson, one of the Folkbuilders for his AFA organization. In many ways, Stinson seemed to be an asset to the AFA. Intelligent, energetic, and charismatic in his own right, Stinson had a level of social and practical leadership skills that is rare in the Heathen world. Stinson served as an AFA Folkbuilder in the Midwest for two years and had made significant advances for the organization during that time. In a statement announcing his expulsion from the AFA, Stinson describes his contributions to the organization in this way:

> During my time as an AFA Folkbuilder for this region, the AFA memberships here have increased dramatically. I believe they've gone up almost 200%. Four of my kindred members are AFA members. I posted more on the Asatru Folk Assembly message board more than any other person . . . The Heathen Gods book I published supports a strong Folkish tribal approach to Heathenry. It encourages Folkish kindreds coming together, growing, and advancing our Folkway forward . . . My kindred hosted an event last year that brought together 120 Heathens from across our region in fellowship.[353]

The implication of Stinson's statement and the interpretation of other Heathen observers was that his removal was the result of a

---

352. McNallen, "Three Decades," 214. For a more detailed discussion of the end of the Asatru Free Assembly see Kaplan, "Reconstruction of the Ásatrú and Odinist Traditions," 202–5.

353. Mark Stinson, "Mark Stinson's Removal from the Asatru Folk Assembly," *Temple of Our Heathen Gods* website, June 3, 2010, www.facebook.com/notes/temple-of-our-Heathen-gods/mark-stinsons-removal-from-the-asatru-folk-ssembly/398657638955?comment_id=13016339&offset=0&total_comments=51.

power struggle between McNallen and Stinson. Stinson, a younger protégé of McNallen, represented a new generation of Heathen leadership and his success in building a Heathen infrastructure was interpreted as a threat by McNallen and the AFA, a turf war if you will.

For McNallen, these sorts of battle scars are part of an epic tale in which he plays the battered but stalwart hero. This, of course, is the Heathen ideal: the mark of a man is to live a valiant and noble life, a life that will be remembered. While Heathens steep themselves in the Icelandic sagas, epic lives are not merely meant to be tales from the past, but to be made and written in the present. Bold action, and the controversies that might arise as a result, are part of a heroic life. The life worth living is one that leaves a mark, a life in which an impact, an influence, was made. A type of immortality for Heathens, beyond that of children and descendants, is found in those deeds that are remembered. Of course, the deed itself matters: one would not want to be remembered as a fool. But a deed worthy of a tale ennobles one's life and seals one's reputation, and McNallen has done his share of memorable deeds.

## *Theory and Controversy*

For all his adventures as a spiritual leader, founder of religious movements, military man, soldier of fortune, writer, and teacher, one continual passion does make itself evident in his life: the promotion of folkish Heathenry. For all his other achievements and contributions to Heathenry, McNallen's most enduring legacy may be the publication of the essay "Metagenetics," his manifesto that sought to provide folkish Heathenry with an ideological underpinning.[354] Originally published in 1985, at the height of the controversy over racial attitudes that immolated the Asatru Free Assembly, it remains a current topic of conversation and controversy over thirty years later, making it one of the most discussed and enduring essays in Heathenry. McNallen himself seemed impressed by the dramatic and unanticipated response to his piece, "The shock wave

---

354. Stephen A. McNallen, "Metagenetics," in *The Philosophy of Metagenetics, Folkism and Beyond* (Nevada City, CA: Asatru Folk Assembly, 2006), 5-10. In his book, *Asatru: A Native European Spirituality*, p. 81, he writes that the essay was originally published in 1985.

from those three pages has caused more controversy than anything else I have ever written."[355]

McNallen's goal in writing "Metagenetics" was to provide folkish Heathenry with a theoretical basis that moved it away from racist ideology.[356] McNallen specifically states his position that the "foundations of metagenetics lie not in totalitarian dogma of the 19th and 20th centuries," that is, in Nazism, the Klan, and the racist dogma that sustained such groups.[357] Asatru was not to be coopted to support a supremacist vision of the white race nor fuel a campaign of aggressive rhetoric and violent action in an apocalyptic race war, such as that promoted by the Brüder Schweigen and their reliance on *The Turner Diaries* rather than the *Edda*. With this statement, McNallen took a stand against the racist political movements and moved Asatru in a different direction. With the American white supremacist movement laying claim to Asatru as a new theology for its racist political vision, McNallen saved the movement by breaking with the neo-Nazis and putting Asatru on a different trajectory. As part of that move, McNallen sought to place Asatru on a strong footing that established it as a religious and spiritual movement. Thus the original enunciation of "Metagenetics" served to give folkish Asatru a basis other than the specious racist reasoning that dominated the neo-Nazi and white supremacist movements.

Realizing that overt racism was a dead-end, McNallen's position was at least in part motivated by a desire to make Asatru acceptable to a wide range of Americans, a motivation that remains important to him. He dreamt not of a political movement, but of a new spirituality. In the counterculture, he perceived a crisis of identity and a growing spiritual restlessness among white Americans. He saw in Asatru a remedy, a religion that could answer this yawning spiritual hunger. McNallen truly believes that Asatru is the heritage of all northern-European-descended people and wants to make it accessible to as many as possible.[358] McNallen realized

---

355. Stephen A. McNallen, "Genetics and Beyond: The Ultimate Connection," in *The Philosophy of Metagenetics, Folkism, and Beyond* (Nevada City, CA: Asatru Folk Assembly, 2006), 11.

356. Kaplan, *Radical Religion in America*, 80–84.

357. McNallen, "Metagenetics," 5.

358. Edred Thorsson has also voiced such sentiments. Gardell writes that "Thorsson envisions Asatrú as a future mainstream American religion, 'something a local mechanic could be comfortable with.'" See Gardell, *Gods of the Blood*, 163.

that if Asatru was aligned with the perpetually marginalized and fractious American racist community, it would never become appealing to average mainstream white Americans. His vision all along has been that Asatru is the natural and native religion for the average American of Northern European ancestry: it expresses the authentic ethnic or folk identity of white Americans. Thus, his break with the racist right was not only an ideological repositioning of the movement, but perhaps more importantly, it was a way to maneuver Asatru closer to mainstream America. This break was clearly felt by the racial Heathens who were critical of metagenetics and found McNallen's position on race to be too weak. Those early members of the original Asatru Free Assembly who were committed to a racist interpretation of the Norse/Germanic legacy left the organization over McNallen's stance on race, aligning instead with Else Christensen's more overtly political and racial agenda.[359]

McNallen's basic argument in "Metagenetics" is simple: a people's group religious and cultural experience over thousands of years becomes encoded into their DNA. Not only physical characteristics but information usually considered cultural, such as religion, is stored in the organic database of the genetic code. This ancestral religion becomes, in a sense, part of one's genome and is passed down through the generations by biological descent. Just as ancestry is written into one's *physical* characteristics, e.g. "Oh, he has his grandfather's nose!" So mental, emotional, and *religious* ways of responding to the world are also passed down. One's mind, the way one thinks, is also part of one's genetic heritage, e.g. "She has her grandmother's soul," or in the deep genetic language of metagenetics, "She carries within herself the ancestral soul, the experiences and collective unconsciousness formed two millennia ago." For folkish Heathens like McNallen our true nature is not found in ephemeral social trends or the caprices of personality but in belonging to "a specific group of people sharing a common descent . . . bound by blood to a particular set of Gods and Goddesses."[360] The bonds of kinship transcend space and time," McNallen says, expressing this deep sense of connection. "Religion becomes a manifestation of our very essence, a part of us like our legs or our head. Asatru is not what we believe, it is what we are."[361]

---

359. Kaplan, *Radical Religion*, 81; Gardell, *Gods of the Blood*, 177-78.
360. McNallen, *Asatru*, 83.
361. McNallen, "The Nature of Folk Religion," in *The Philosophy of Metagenetics*, 2.

For McNallen the gods and traditions of one's ancestors are inscribed on the subconscious of their descendants: for those of Northern European descent, the gods and culture of the Norse; for those with a heritage in Mexico, the gods and culture of the Aztecs, etc.[362] McNallen writes, "We are more like our ancestors than we are like anyone else. We inherited not only their general physical appearance, but also their predominant mental, emotional, and spiritual traits. We think and feel more like they did; our basic needs are most like theirs."[363] This ancestral encoding is about access to a spiritual path, one's authentic relationship to a type of spirituality, gods, rituals, ideology, practices often referred to by folkish Asatru as the Heathen "lifeway." McNallen draws on Jungian psychology to argue that archetypes, as categories or predispositions that shape one's unconsciousness, are both unique to racial groups and passed down through genetics.[364] For McNallen, this means that the religious experience of one's ancestors, e.g. their gods, is passed down to their descendants as mental archetypes. Northern Europeans may have been Christians for a brief thousand years, McNallen argues, but they have been Pagans and polytheists for forty thousand years. By implication, one's authentic spiritual path is the deepest rut, encoded in one's ethnically specific genome over hundreds of generations and inherited through the biological connection with the ancestors. Ethnicity determines one's authentic religious path.

### The Problem of Cultural Essentialism

Before examining how the theory contributed to the Heathen watershed, let us briefly consider several concerns about metagenetics. The theory rests on a difficult to defend cultural essentialism that seems to defy the obvious reality of cultural change. There do seem to be characteristics of human nature, encoded in the genetic code, that remain constant or change very slowly over time. Culture and religion, however, do not seem to be part of those. Culture seems to be actually quite malleable and human beings with very similar

---

362. Stephen A. McNallen, "Wotan vs. Tezcatlipoca: The Spiritual War for California and the Southwest," *Asatru Folk Assembly*, www.runestone.org/about-asatru/articles-a-essays.html.
363. McNallen, *What Is Asatru?*, 2.
364. McNallen, "Metagenetics," 7–8.

genetic codes may have widely differentiated cultural expression. Culture changes for very good reasons, and human beings seem to adapt to cultural change fairly effectively. For most Americans, our identity is shaped by our occupation, education, the region in which we live, and the family within our living memory. McNallen, however, consistently shrugs off the last thousand years of history, suggesting instead that identity is rooted in an unchanging historical pattern tens of thousands of years old. "Behind these labels," he writes, "lurks an older, more essential identity."[365] His idea of an unchanging ethnic essentialism is not new, but comes to us from the racial science of the early twentieth-century völkisch movement. According to this thinking,

> the individual members of the Volk were fused together by ties of blood into what was effectively a biological and racial community. The fundamental natural qualities and characteristics of the Volk were thus racial qualities and characteristics. These had been determined in some primordial process of ethnogenesis and were fixed forever in an *Erbmasse* (or "genetic plasma") which was passed on from generation to generation and which set the absolute parameters for the Volk for all time. The genetic character of any given Volk-race was both absolutely unique and absolutely immutable.[366]

McNallen's attempt to tie Heathenry to this sort of discredited and dangerous view of human nature is not in the best interests of the religion.

I am somewhat persuaded that reconnection to a cultural heritage may be part of the solution for modern crises of identity and belonging, the lost-ness and wounded-ness that McNallen writes about.[367] He is not alone in suggesting that the conditions of life in modern societies may lead to identity crises. For example, sociologist Anthony Giddens proposes that modernity is uniquely disruptive to social and personal life and has produced distinct dislocations,

---

365. McNallen, *Asatru*, 1.
366. Mark Bassin, "Blood or Soil? The Völkisch Movement, the Nazis, and the Legacy of Geopolitik," *How Green Were the Nazis? Nature, Environment, and Nation in the Third Reich*, eds. Franz-Josef Brüggemeier, Mark Cioc, and Thomas Zeller (Athens: Ohio University Press, 2005), 175.
367. Ibid., 139–40. For further discussion of McNallen's deprivation theory of Northern European people, see Jefferson Calico, "Asatru: A Native European Spirituality," *The Pomegranate: The International Journal of Pagan Studies* 18, no. 1 (January 2016): 116–19.

"disembedding" people from traditional social contexts.[368] Reviving cultural traditions in a tribal school, teaching traditional folk art and music at an Appalachian settlement school, or celebrating a Kwanzaa event are examples of how identification with a cultural heritage may provide strength and meaning for contemporary individuals and groups. Yet, it is very difficult to find evidence to support the proposition of a cultural essence, the genetic code as a repository of archaic cultural information, or to locate that cultural essence thousands of years in the past. McNallen seems unconcerned with the question of which past culture to privilege, which point or stream in the ancestral line. He would, for instance, deny that the Viking period should be the primary source for Heathen practice and would draw instead on the cumulative cultural legacy cut short by the incursion of monotheism: the Vikings, the Migration Age peoples, the Bronze Age Indo-Europeans, the Neo- and Paleolithic, for religious inspiration. For McNallen, this does not consist of cultural appropriation. Metagenetics suggests a privileged access to the cultural essence: it cannot be appropriation if it is already part of yourself.

## The Problem of Race Mysticism

From the argument above, we see that McNallen's concept of indigeneity arises from this theory of metagenetics. Authentic identity, he argues, is rooted in the ancestral lineage, not necessarily in one's living culture. Therefore one's native home is the ancestral home, where this metagenetic legacy was originally brought together:

> We call ourselves Irish, or German, or Dutch, or European-Americans, and that is true. However, we are fundamentally indigenous Europeans. We may have migrated around the world, but our homeland is Europe. Its rugged environment shaped our bodies, our minds, and our souls; it is a part of us, and we are a part of it, forever. We are just as indigenous as are the Amazonian Indians, the Congolese, and Borneo tribesmen.[369]

---

368. Anthony Giddens, *Modernity and Self-Identity: Self and Society in the Late Modern Age* (Stanford: Stanford University Press, 1991), 89–90.

369. Stephen A. McNallen, "An Asatru Viewpoint—No More Mutts!" *Asatru Folk Assembly*, www.asatrufolkassembly.org/articles-essays/.

The implication is that an American, whose family has lived in the United States for generations and who may have no conscious cultural connection to Europe, can claim an indigenous European identity. This is because her essential self is connected to the native European home encoded within the deep ancestral line. Such reasoning stretches the idea of indigeneity to the breaking point, seeming to confuse it with nostalgia or a romantic longing for a remote and idealized past. In his original statement of the theory, McNallen proposed some quasi-scientific evidence for his idea of a metagenetic connection, stating that his theory brought together ancient wisdom with modern science. His argument was hardly convincing and quickly countered by his respondents and critics.[370] Since that time, he has gradually distanced himself from the attempt to provide a scientific ground for metagenetics. In a follow-up article written in 1999, he states that metagenetics is a hypothesis and makes a more philosophical presentation of the idea and its folkish implications.[371] Later in his 2015 book, while in no way backing down from his theory, he stated that the metagenetic connection between the individual, the ethnic group, and the gods is "intuitive, speculative, and personal. It is also very hard to verbalize."[372] What began in the 1980s as a scientific theory has gradually shifted towards the propagation of a race mysticism. This race mysticism seems to violate other more important and concrete aspects of Heathenry, particularly the importance of the very direct and living connections of family and proximity groups. More recently, McNallen has again sought scientific evidence for his racial theory. In a video released in March 2017, he again claims, "Race is real. It is not a social construct."[373] He then goes on to give examples about the behavior of newborn babies to indicate that race "effects deep psychology." In the video, he cites Nicholas Wade's book, *A Troublesome Inheritance: Genes, Race and Human History*, as a summary of the scientific evidence supporting his racial understanding of human nature and history.

370. For McNallen's supporting evidence, see McNallen, "Metagenetics," 5–9.
371. McNallen, "Genetics and Beyond," 11–15.
372. McNallen, *Asatru*, 82.
373. Stephen McNallen, "What Stephen McNallen Really Thinks About Race!" YouTube video, 12:37, posted by Stephen McNallen, www.youtube.com/watch?v=ewUuNO636ag&t=3s. Quoted sections appear at 1:05, 1:35 ff, and 4:05 ff. See also Nicholas Wade, *A Troublesome Inheritance: Genes, Race and Human History* (New York: Penguin Books, 2015).

## The Problem of Genetic Mélange

Earlier in the chapter, I raised the issue of the genealogical complexity found in the ancestry of many Americans. McNallen's theory seems to deal inadequately with this reality. Metagenetics values genetic specificity and suggests that one ancestral stream represents a person's authentic spiritual heritage. "All native religions are by definition centered on a particular *ethnos*," he writes, "and to deny this fact . . . is to be politically correct to the point of blindness."[374] Yet, political correctness is not the only problem. McNallen is less willing to acknowledge and contend with the complexities raised by his hypothesis. Average Americans likely have a culturally diverse family tree with several identifiable streams of ancestry, in other words a genetic mélange. They face the problem of which of their numerous ancestral streams represents the most authentic path. Does metagenetics give such people a practical way to determine which of those strands of ancestry is the proper one to follow? Should my father-in-law, who recently had his DNA mapped, follow the spiritual path of his Irish, Scandinavian, Greek, or Italian forebears? McNallen's solution to this obvious problem was to move away from specific notions of ethnicity. He created instead new highly diffuse categories, which he calls "eclectic Northern European" and "European-American."

On a practical level, it makes good sense for a reconstructionist Pagan religion to cast a fairly wide net of cultural sources, to consider and even include religious data from several closely related or neighboring cultures. Even if we could determine a specific ethnic strand of our DNA to follow, it would be difficult to adequately reconstruct the religion of a very specific ancient culture in a way that could be satisfactorily practiced by contemporary people.[375] However, even if we accept such a designation as European

---

374. McNallen, *Asatru*, 82.

375. Heathen reconstructionists have thought about these issues and continue to discuss the practical ramifications of reviving historically accurate forms of pre-Christian Norse and Germanic religion. How does one negotiate the tension between the values of maintaining historical accuracy, cultural specificity, and having a fully workable religious system for contemporary practitioners? See Bil Linzie, "Reconstructionism's Role in Modern Heathenry," July 13, 2007, www.angelfire.com/nm/seidhman/reconstruction-c.pdf. See also Joseph Bloch, "Towards a Theory of Reconstructionist Religion (Part 3)," *Jön Upsal's Garden*, August 2, 2015, http://jonupsalsgarden.blogspot.com/2015/08/towards-theory-of-reconstructionist.html.

American, would it still be proper to suggest that Asatru is the most authentic religious fit for this identity? Could not other European cultures such as Celtic, Hellenic, and Roman make a case for pan-European prevalence? Or should the practical application of his "eclectic Northern European" identity result in a similarly eclectic religion? The more glaring problem is that "Native European" is not an ethnos, a "folk" culture and community, any more than African American, Black, or White, for that matter. It ultimately rests on old racial categories associated with skin colors, which belie the real genetic and cultural complexity of those categories. The intriguing and powerful dimension of folkishness seems to be its potential to deconstruct these nineteenth-century racial categories and to create opportunities for new and more complex constructs of social and cultural elements. However, metagenetics falls short of providing a foundation for that sort of identity construction.

### *The Controversy Surrounding Metagenetics*

Metagenetics enabled McNallen to occupy a blurry middle ground between the specter of revolutionary American white supremacist movements and the "universalist" progressive Heathens who were beginning to enunciate an anti-racist religious vision. Still, metagenetics maintained a connection between race and religion. McNallen wanted to talk about race, to make it a fulcrum of his religion, while disavowing the ongoing racist overtones. Ann-Marie Gallagher notes that such discourse interfaces with the racist milieu,

> The edges of some Pagan philosophies blur dangerously with those that support racism and warn against what they see as racial and spiritual "miscegenation." The links made between fascist aspirations and Paganism appear to come from the provision . . . of the racial specificity of what some Pagans perceive to be their past and their cultural antecedents.[376]

As we will see, metagenetics generated quite a bit of heat for McNallen, who continued to be skewered as a racist by various factions, Heathen and non-Heathen alike. McNallen states in countless places

---

376. Ann-Marie Gallagher, "Weaving a Tangled Web? Pagan Ethics as Issues of History, 'Race,' and Ethnicity in Pagan Identity," in *Between the Worlds*, ed. Sian Reid (Toronto: Canadian Scholars' Press, 2006), 276.

that he is not a racist. A favorite tactic is to mention that he has fought side by side with ethnic freedom fighters from many different nationalities and supports the causes of ethnic groups, such as the Tibetans, for freedom and sovereignty. Because racists, by definition, hate other racial groups, no racist could support the cause of ethnic and racial groups, as McNallen suggests that he does. Another tactic that McNallen advances is to argue that his position does not cast blame on other racial groups. "Race is just family writ large," he states. "It doesn't have anything to do with hating other races or thinking of other races as inferior."[377] McNallen is inconsistent in this approach, at times interpreting other ethnic groups as threats.[378] More frequently, McNallen argues that the problems faced by whites are spiritual in nature, a sort of soul sickness resulting from the colonial oppression of Christianity upon native European people. He argues that a thousand years of Christianity has enervated the Northern European strength and vitality that was nourished by Paganism. "Rootless and stripped of their heritage and their sense of self-worth, they wander through the world bemused by idle entertainment and material delights," he writes. "We are a wounded people. Torn from our ancient tribes, riven by sword and burned by fire until we died or accepted foreign beliefs, stripped of our natural pride, filled with guilt—guilt about sex, guilt about power, guilt about the very color of our skin—we are brimming over with poison."[379] For McNallen, Heathenry's ethnic character, far from being racist, is part of recovering from this colonial experience and reclaiming the identity that had been lost. The complexities and weaknesses of McNallen's post-colonial argument are clearly identified by Thad Horrell, who notes that unlike other populations marginalized by colonialism, the former Heathens of Northern Europe, "became, through the power of Christendom, the very foot soldiers of the empire which had overrun them," and the "explorers and conquerors who subjugated Africa, Southeast Asia, the Americas, and elsewhere."[380] Despite this, the post-colonial argument is frequently found in folkish discourse.

377. McNallen, "What Stephen McNallen Thinks About Race!" Quote occurs at 6:00 minutes.
378. For instance, McNallen, "Wotan vs. Tezcatlipoca."
379. McNallen, *Asatru*, 139.
380. Thad N. Horrell, "Heathenry as a Postcolonial Movement," *Journal of Religion, Identity, and Politics* January (2012), https://jrip.scholasticahq.com/article/76-heathenry-as-a-postcolonial-movement, 10.

For McNallen, these concerns are quite distinct from an attitude of racial superiority. He attempts to make a distinction at the heart of his ideology between racial specificity and racial superiority. For McNallen, racial specificity is an obvious and demonstrable fact, part of the fundamental shape of the world. Disputing the reality of racial difference is simply a tactic of liberal social justice warriors. One's race, as part of an extended family, should compel loyalty and love. It is not racist to love your race.[381] A racist espouses a doctrine of racial superiority, believing that one race is better and should dominate others. Similarly, he distinguishes religious superiority from religious specificity. Religious superiority, with its ethos of conversion, missionizing, and proselytizing, considers other religions to be false or inferior and seeks to reduce them to the dustbins of history. Religious specificity takes the attitude of "to each his own," with each individual or group entitled to its own spirituality. Although, religious specificity may also lend itself to a puritanical position of purifying one's religion of extraneous and syncretic elements. With these distinctions in mind, McNallen's controversial move links *religious* specificity with *racial* specificity: authentically following Asatru requires being white, and the continuation of Asatru requires the preservation of white people. For McNallen, true religion is folk religion and requires racial specificity. He avoids an ideology of racial superiority, but continues to link race and religion in ways that many Americans and many Heathens find contentious, fallacious, and repugnant.

McNallen was right about one thing: ethnic groups often make use of religion as an important feature with which to define and distinguish their identity. In her analysis of Hinduism in America, Prema Kurien suggests that globalization has elevated the importance of ethnic identification in the United States. She describes how Indian immigrants gain a meaningful place in the American cultural landscape as well as a voice in American politics by identifying as Hindus.[382] Within a multicultural society, religions and religious organizations function as powerful symbolic carriers of ethnic identities. Not only does a religious identity provide a

---

381. McNallen, "What Stephen McNallen Really Thinks About Race!" See video at 4:45 minutes.

382. Prema A. Kurien, *A Place at the Multicultural Table: The Development of an American Hinduism* (New Brunswick, NJ: Rutgers University Press, 2007).

strong reference point for cultural identity, but it also acts to cushion the adherent from social pressure to "Americanize" or assimilate into the dominant society. Religion creates a social space within which ethnic and cultural distinctives such as history, food, dress, art, and music can be maintained and strengthened. Since religion is strongly protected by the First Amendment, it serves as "the most acceptable and non-threatening basis for community formation and expression." In the United States, religion is recognized as both a protected form of minority status and a legitimate way to express social otherness.[383] Thus religion becomes the "preferred means for immigrants to develop and maintain ethnic identity."[384] Kurien's thesis indicates that in a multicultural society, we should expect identity groups to form around religion, and to express ethnic/cultural differences through religious identities. Religious culture and identity function as a means for people to "take their place at the multicultural table.'"[385] For these immigrant communities, the religious/ethnic identities described by Kurien are primarily defined by culture and geography. They are rarely described as genetic and racial. However, Kurien acknowledges the potential for Hinduvta, far-right Hindu nationalism, to make use of religious identities in more race-conscious ways.

Kurien's argument essentially communicates the strategy at the heart of McNallen's metagenetics theory. In the multiculturalism of the American context, white Americans need strong ethnic identities to take an equal place in the changing society. McNallen asserts as much when he writes that the lack of an ethnic identity has put European-Americans in a socially disadvantaged position. "The results are clear for all to see," he writes, "more of us are dying than are being born, our children look to other peoples and cultures for their models, our heritage and history are steadily displaced. This is the road to marginalization and extinction."[386] Like a Hindu or a Sikh community, Asatru, defined in folkish terms, can be seen as an attempt to express such a cohesive and distinctive socio-religious identity, not as "white folks" but as the carriers of a more specific ethnicity, culture, and traditional folkway. Asatru adherents

383. Ibid., 6.
384. Ibid., 6–7, 143.
385. Ibid., 9.
386. McNallen, *Asatru*, 140.

achieve a personally meaningful life and claim a legitimate place in American society by appropriating or creating this ethnic religious identity. However, McNallen has consistently emphasized the primacy of race, of whiteness, instead of the religious and cultural aspects of metagenetics, demonstrating the continued ability of white nationalism to hijack the ethnic pole of Heathenry. If McNallen actually intended to unite an ideologically mainstream Asatru with "Metagenetics" and to create a socially legitimate form of religious identity, he miscalculated. What occurred instead was a predictable pushback.

McNallen's theory was modified by Edred Thorsson, writing in *Idunna*, the Troth's journal.[387] Thorsson accepted the basic outline of the theory, agreeing that an ancestral connection is a significant aspect of Asatru. However, Thorsson argued that genetic descent alone cannot provide a suitable foundation for the revival and growth of contemporary Asatru. Such a theory ends in the "absurd" and "unconvincing" conclusion that one's contact with the Germanic gods is determined solely by the degree of one's racial purity.[388] He introduced a more subtle argument that sought to distance metagenetics from the simplistic and erroneous reduction of religion to racial ancestry. Race, he argued, or the concept of *Volk*, did not form a significant category in the mindset of the arch-Heathens. It was the smaller socio-biological units, the family and the clan, which represented the genetic aspect of the society. Religion, he argued, was primarily associated with the tribe, which was a "super-genetic" social institution made up of many different family/clans. The tribe was a type of association that united disparate clans (genetic associations) through shared ritual practice and religious beliefs, (ideological associations): "From the 'racial' point of view, the thing that is most important to realize about the tribe is that as an institution it is super-genetic. It is not dependent upon genetic descent but upon belonging to a religio-political union, bound together by a common mythology (i.e. idealized paradigms of action) and purpose."[389] This religio-political union of the tribe was based on other shared characteristics, primarily a shared

---

387. Edred Thorsson, "Who Will Build the Hearths of the Troth: Are Racial Considerations Appropriate?" *Idunna*, no. 5 (1989): 16–24.
388. Ibid., 22.
389. Ibid., 20.

culture and language. He goes on to say that race should not be an issue in contemporary Asatru, writing that "since 'race' was never a real category of allegiance for the ancients, why should it be one now?"[390] Instead, contemporary Asatru should build its community primarily on non-genetic factors of culture, language, and shared interests. These, he suggested, are more appropriate and productive points of accessibility for those entering or drawn to Asatru. His development of McNallen's metagenetics clearly sought to move Asatru even farther away from racial implications by arguing that factors in addition to genetics allow people to connect with the gods of ancient northern Europe and enable them to authentically practice Asatru.

Thorsson's article essentially opened a floodgate through which criticism of metagenetics began to pour. Two additional and important writers entered the fray in the early 1990s publishing articles addressing the racial issue in the pages of *Mountain Thunder*, an independent Heathen journal published for two years by Wilfred von Dauster.[391] Kveldúlf Gundarsson and Alexander Jerome, a progressive Heathen from New Mexico known in the movement as Gamlinginn, were both part of the emerging intelligentsia closely associated with the Troth. Together, they began to enunciate what would become the anti-racist position in Heathenry. Garman Lord, the founder of Theodism, describes the time in a rather unflattering way:

> The Troth was beginning its courting dance with the wonderful world of Neopaganry, as well as introducing the element into the Asatru community that would come to be known in common slang Troth parlance as "Wiccatru." Soon the membership began to swell with a new kind of crossover Heathen, anxious to introduce ultra-Left values into the ethnically parochial, aridly xenophobic landscape of the new elder troth . . . Its highly vocal Ultra-Left contingent now could, and did, boldly hurl epithets of "racist" and "bigot" and "homophobe"

---

390. Ibid., 23.

391. Kveldúlfr Gundarsson, "Race, Inheritance, and Ásatrú Today," *Mountain Thunder* 5: 7–11. This article was published in an updated form as "Ancestry and Heritage in the Germanic Tradition," *Hrafnar: Thirty Years of Re-Inventing Heathenry*, www.hrafnar.org/articles/kveldulf/ancestors/. See also Gamlinginn, "Race and Religion" *Mountain Thunder* 5 (1993), www.thetroth.org/news/20170816-000204. For more on Wilfred von Dauster and *Mountain Thunder*, see Kaplan, "The Reconstruction of the Ásatrú and Odinist Traditions," 229, n. 24.

and the like at the Asatru Alliance and everybody else who didn't agree with them.[392]

What Lord describes here is the introduction of a new tributary into the Heathen conversation. The flow of these ideas created a confluence spinning against the direction McNallen and the folkish Heathens were going. Although Gundarsson does not mention metagenetics at all in his original article, it is clearly written as a response to McNallen's manifesto. Described by some as the most politically correct of Heathens, even Gundarsson is unable to entirely disassociate Asatru from ancestry. Like Thorsson, Gundarsson finds ancestry (although not race), to be a strong part of modern Heathenry, stating at one point in his article that "it appears that a person's own bloodline must be thought of as a meaningful guide to the path of her/his soul."[393] Many who are drawn to Asatru, he admits, come to it seeking to reclaim the lost heritage and religion of their ancestors. But does that mean it is *only* a religion of blood? Here both Gundarsson and Gamlinginn present a series of reasons why it is entirely possible for those of non-Germanic heritage to follow Asatru authentically. For instance, they make the sociological argument that the Vikings intermarried and interbred with other ethnicities, showing little interest in some abstract notion of racial purity. Appealing to mythology, they show that in the Norse mythological stories the gods themselves intermarried and bred with other "races" such as the *jǫtnar*, or giants, producing progeny who were accepted and played significant roles in the mythology.[394] Further,

---

392. Garman Lord, "The Evolution of Theodish Belief, Part 4: The Wider Folk," *Gerod Theod: The Official Website of Theodish Belief*, www.gamall-steinn.org/Gering/Evol-pt4.htm.

393. Gundarsson, "Ancestry and Heritage."

394. Jón Hnefill Aðalsteinsson, "Gods and Giants in Old Norse Mythology," *Temenos* 26 (1990): 7–22; Hilda Ellis Davidson, *Lost Beliefs of Northern Europe* (New York: Routledge, 1993), 83. The Old Norse *jǫtunn*, plural *jǫtnar*, a word meaning "one who eats" or "devours," refers to the giants of Norse mythology. They originated from the primordial being Ymir. In the Old Norse material, many of the jotuns are portrayed as powerful, wise, cunning, and beautiful. There seem to be several types of giants, with whom the gods may interact in different ways. Odin seeks after the wisdom of the giants, as we read in *Vafþrúðnismál* in the *Poetic Edda*. The gods have uneasy relationships with these beings. Some giants seem to live among and interact with the gods, even inter-marrying with them. Odin is known for his exploits with giantesses, and Frey loves the giantess Gerd. After the slaying of her father Þjazi at the hands of the Aesir, the giantess Skaði is offered the chance to marry any of

they read the *Völuspá* to suggest that all humans are descended from two original beings created by the Norse gods: Ask (Old Norse *Askr*) and Embla (Old Norse *Embla*). This implies that all people share a universal spiritual heritage. Gundarsson goes on to note that in the culture of the arch-Heathens, those who were not connected to a family through blood or genetics could be and frequently were joined to it through *ritual* means. Norse and Germanic cultures give significant evidence of arrangements such as blood-brotherhood, adoption, marriage, name-giving, and the practice of bestowing weapons upon a person, all as means of bringing outsiders into the family and the family's religion. Genetics, they argue, was only one of many ways that people came to be participants of the Northern European Pagan traditions. Both authors make the important point that Asatru is "not only ancestry," and build the ideological foundation for a non-racial form of Heathenry.

### Genetics and Beyond: Controversy Escalates

After almost a decade of distance from the world of organized Asatru following the collapse of the Asatru Free Assembly, something changed for McNallen in the mid-1990s, bringing an end to this period he calls his "wandering years." Alarmed by the growth of universalist, Pagan-influenced Asatru, McNallen returned to active participation in the movement, but this time with a mission to reclaim the religion from the "politically correct faction."[395] His re-entry into Asatru began with what McNallen does best: he started a new organization with himself as the leader and religious visionary, the Asatru Folk Assembly, which would become the flagship of folkish Asatru. What did McNallen see happening that precipitated his return? The Troth was becoming a substantial force to be reckoned with in the Asatru world, growing in its membership and adopting a stance that was more open to the American Pagan culture. Seið, a form of Norse shamanic practice discussed in chapter 8, had also come onto the scene, particularly the oracular seið developed by Diana Paxson. This practice became an important

---

the gods. However, the giants are also the perennial enemies of the gods. "Slayer of Giants" is a kenning for Thor, who is often at the forefront of hostile encounters with the jǫtnar.

395. McNallen, "Three Decades," 210–11.

practice for women, dramatically increasing the profile of women in the movement and causing alarm among conservative Asatru who saw in it an invasion of Wicca-derived magical practice. Furthermore, in 1994, the Troth had dismissed a member of the High Rede for comments made against the growing influence of Wicca-influenced Paganism in the movement.[396] Numerous independent kindreds had formed, such as Raven Kindred in the Northeast, which also rejected the folkish banner. Additionally, as we have seen, ten years of reaction against metagenetics had resulted in a clearly enunciated ideology of non-racial Asatru.

Meanwhile, with the growth of the Internet in the 1990s, a new generation of adherents was beginning to enter Heathenry. The conversation about metagentetics and folkish Asatru moved substantially to an online format in various Internet forums and discussion boards. The rising tide of non-folkish adherents was pushing back against the theory in these settings. For example, William Bainbridge, who served as the Steersman of the Troth from 1995 to 1998, was quite active on Internet discussion boards articulating a non-folkish approach to Asatru. As Bainbridge states in one online exchange,

> "Race" really is a disreputable topic in society as a whole. There seems to be the feeling that it should be OK in Asatru, because some people really seem to believe that it is the central thing about Asatru; but for the rest of us, it is still a disreputable topic, and identifying the religion with it brings disrepute on the whole religion. So no, we're not going to cooperate in letting people feel good about saying "Asatru is racial." For us, the notion is antithetical to "Asatru is spiritual."[397]

In response to all these factors, McNallen brought metagenetics back to the forefront as a rebuttal to his many critics. He released a new essay elaborating on his original theory, "Genetics & Beyond: Metagenetics—An Update," promoting the folkish position.[398] McNallen notes the particularly provocative nature of his revival of metagenetics, "The mere mention of metagenetics causes some people to go into a rage and a rant—so, both to inform my friends

---

396. Lewis Stead, "Huginn and Muninn," *Ásatrú Today* 1 (1994), www.ravenkindred.com/magazines.html.

397. William Bainbridge, *Asatru Discussion Forum*, November 3, 1996, https://groups.google.com/forum/#!topic/alt.religion.asatru/dli-RVa0f2I%5B1-25%5D.

398. McNallen, "Genetics and Beyond."

and infuriate my enemies, I decided it was time for an update on the subject!"[399] However, notably different this time around was the target at which the re-assertion of metagenetics theory was aimed. The critics and "enemies" to whom McNallen referred in his statement were not those of the racist right who he addressed in his original article in the 1980s. Instead, he aimed it entirely at the "politically correct faction," those Heathens who, as we now understand, take a perspective on religion much more like other contemporary Pagans. Thus the entire ground of the metagenetics argument had shifted and the ideological divide between folkish and non-folkish Heathens took on increasingly strident and acrimonious forms. In his article, "Genetics and Beyond," and a subsequent article, "In Defense of the Folkish View," McNallen directly counters the claims of Gundarsson and Gamlingenn, arguing that their view of history and Lore are misguided. In a flurry of intra-movement debate, Gundarsson and other members of the Troth fired back in the publication of *Our Troth*, a hefty two-volume work, part scholarly tome, part manifesto that serves as something like the Troth's official statement on the Asatru religion. In that work, the section on race and religion takes on McNallen's position with an impressive array of arguments ranging from discourses on modern science to interpretations of Norse lore.[400] Through this series of back and forth exchanges, the two camps of folkish and non-folkish Heathens face off and draw up ideological shield walls.

## Folkish Asatru

The Irminfolk Odinist Community, a folkish kindred in New York state and an AFA member kindred, provides a succinct definition of folkish Asatru in their statement of beliefs. Asatru is "an indigenous religion of a biologically distinct European ethnicity," it reads. "The Asatru religion appeals to the collective unconscious of people of ethnic European ancestry through a common ancestral bloodline."[401] It is a position that McNallen has described as "ethnocentric." In his study of racist Heathenry, Mattias Gardell stated unequivocally that McNallen's Asatru Folk Assembly was not a white supremacist

---

399. Ibid.
400. Gundarsson, *Living the Troth*, 25–60.
401. "Our Beliefs," *Irminfolk Odinist Community*, http://irminfolk.com/our-beliefs/.

group, a position that was appreciatively received by McNallen. However, Gardell somewhat ambiguously asserts:

> With rare exceptions, most pagans involved with ethnic Asatrú repeatedly assert their unequivocal rejection of racism, taking exception to racist paganism of the Wotansvolk variety. Still, the metagenetics theory is at its core racist, if racism is defined as an ideology that asserts that members of a specific race "by nature" share not only racially distinct physical features but also mental features.[402]

While metagenetics may be ostensibly racist, Gardell seems to indicate that it does not exhibit the dangerous and violent racial rhetoric that marks white supremacist groups, such as the overtly racist Wotansvolk. Folkish Heathenry may be exclusive, but it is distinct from racism in that it does not advocate or promote hatred for other racial groups. Making a distinction between ethnocentrism and racism is important for folkish Heathens. Stephen Borthwick states, "Ours is not a faith of conquest, nor one of domination, nor one of imperialism."[403] Along these lines, Gardell identifies McNallen and folkish Asatrú as a middle position on the spectrum of racial attitudes. Ethnic Asatrú is differentiated from both racist and inclusive forms of the religion. He goes on to distinguish the ideology of ethnic Asatrú from militant racism:

> When [militant racists] talk about Asatrú as an expression of the Aryan soul, they use an inclusive definition of a unified white race . . . Spokespersons of ethnic Asatrú revert to pre-WWII theories that distinguished between several white races . . . In the ethnic Pagan system of classification, humanity is divided into a multitude of genetically distinct folk groups whose different moral and spiritual characteristics are expressed in corresponding number of distinct folk-soul religions.[404]

Gardell observes that one foundational ideal of folkish Heathenry is that of genetically distinct folk groups, the idea that culture and religion are organic to distinct people groups. Prima facie, this seems to reject both the "white" and "European American" racial categories for a more culturally differentiated model. The idea of distinct folk

---

402. Gardell, *Gods of the Blood*, 271.
403. Stephen M. Borthwick, "Hermann Awakened: Folkishness vs. Racism," *Journal of Contemporary Heathen Thought* 1 (2010): 40.
404. Gardell, *Gods of the Blood*, 271.

groups is often found in conjunction with another foundational concept in folkish writings: the integrity and beauty inherent in each of these different folk expressions. Again Borthwick expresses such a viewpoint when he defines the folkish orientation as "the recognition of the uniqueness and exclusivity of social institutions to each individual Folk, just as no two flowers have the same petals and colours [sic], though they may be equal in beauty, they are tailored with a beauty unique to their species."[405] Is this attitude simply an expression of the separate but equal doctrine of pre-Civil Rights America and is folkishness then just a nostalgic attachment to the days of institutionalized American white supremacy? Or is this an attempt, however ineptly enunciated, to formulate a sort of post-racialism, to dismantle categories of race, i.e. "whiteness," and introduce new forms of social identity as Gardell suggests?

Ethno-pluralism emerged from the European New Right in the 1980s, and like folkish Heathenry, it takes an essentialist view of culture as a fundamentally formative aspect of human nature. Schnurbein notes that the ethno-pluralist approach allowed the New Right to shift their political conversation away from biological notions of race to a more socially acceptable discussion of the preservation of cultural identity and integrity.[406] Used in this way, she suggests, ethno-pluralism has become a rhetorical way to disguise a deeper racist agenda. The approach entered the American context through those intellectual connections between folkish Heathenry and the New Right, in this case the *Journal of Contemporary Heathen Thought*. While ideological connections between Odinism and the New Right have long been evident, this intellectual drift of folkish Heathenry has become more noticeable in recent years. It has been particularly evident in McNallen's thought, which at times seems to be playing with racial identity in very loose and dangerous ways. While he often writes about "particular cultural and biological groups," at others times he advocates a type of pan-European identity. "Sure, European cultures are all unique — unique, that is, as variants on the basic European pattern."[407] In this comment, McNallen seems to be reifying traditional racial categories, simply substituting "eclectic Northern European," as a new euphemism for white. Calling

---

405. Borthwick, "Hermann Awakened," 38.
406. Schnurbein, *Norse Revival*, 136–37.
407. McNallen, "No More Mutts."

himself a European American, in distinction to African, Asian, or Hispanic-American, is an obvious shot across the bow at current cultural manifestations of race in America. While Gardell describes McNallen and the AFA as ethnic Asatrú, a very different dynamic has emerged both on the ground and in the rhetoric that has dogged McNallen in the online world. McNallen's folkish Asatru is increasingly seen as the new Heathen racism.

## A Case Study: Dietsch and Deutch

One area of development in American Heathenry has been the growth of smaller culturally specific forms of Heathenry. These groups, often just a single kindred or even a single individual, specialize in an expression of Northern European Paganism such as Manx (Isle of Mann), Gothic, or Saxon variants of Heathenry. While these sub-movements have the potential to develop into religious movements of their own, they often maintain a strong connection with Heathenry and benefit from the ideological resources of the movement as well as from access to potential participants. The religious entrepreneurs who develop them build new sets of religious compensators by researching specific historical cultures and introducing variations on the gods, rituals, terminology, and iconography familiar to Heathens.

The Distelfink Sippenschaft kindred in Pennsylvania is an intriguing example of a culturally specific group. The kindred is reconstructing a variation of Heathenry from the Pennsylvania German tradition, a culture with more than three hundred years of history in the southeastern Pennsylvania region known as the *Deitscherei*, or Pennsylvania Dutch country. Most Americans would associate the area, its culture, and language with the Amish and Mennonites who emigrated from Reformation-era Europe to escape the rampant persecution of the Anabaptists. However, the seventeenth- and eighteenth-century emigration of German-speaking people was wider and more diverse than that, including Lutherans and Reformed Protestants, farmers, artisans, and merchants fleeing the economic devastation of the Thirty Years War, looking for land, and new opportunities.[408] "In America," writes Don Yoder, "the

---

408. The Historical Society of Pennsylvania, "German Settlement in Pennsylvania: An Overview," http://hsp.org/sites/default/files/legacy_files/migrated/germanstudentreading.pdf.

Pennsylvania Dutch, with their diverse European backgrounds, formed one people with a culture united except for religion." The folk cultures these emigrants carried with them contained fragments of pre-Christian beliefs and traditions, which melded into the living culture of the region. The Distelfink Sippenschaft kindred, which includes a native Pennsylvania German speaker, draws on the stories, folktales, and diaries of these immigrants as resources for rebuilding a viable Heathen spirituality. In many cases, pre-Christian spiritual practices are apparent within the living Pennsylvania German culture, such as hex signs or barn symbols, and the healing tradition of powwow or braucherei, which continues to be passed down from master to apprentice in lineages of practice.[409]

This emerging subset of Heathenry is called *Der Urglaawe*, or "the original faith" in the Pennsylvania German dialect.[410] Urglaawe has a number of correspondences with mainstream Asatru—recognizing similar gods, cosmology, seasonal rituals, and ethics. However, it also incorporates distinctive features from its Pennsylvania German origin, such as the continental European earth goddess Frau Holle, the symbol of the sickle rather than the Thor's Hammer, and the magical practice of braucherei rather than seið. Urglaawe has also emerged with a more fully developed earth-centered orientation than is commonly found in Heathenry. It is very much a nature religion that reflects the strong agricultural tradition of Pennsylvania German culture.

The relationship between Distelfink Sippenschaft and a local Pennsylvania mountain known as Hexenkopf illustrates the sorts of reconstructive practice involved in this group. Kindred members found references to this mountain in various historical sources that described it as a haunted mountain.[411] This folklore was several generations old, demonstrating that the local community had long perceived this mountain in spiritual terms, fearing it as the abode of evil spirits. Intrigued by these references, the kindred sought out the mountain itself. After securing permission from the landowners, the kindred spent time on the mountain, conducted rituals there,

---

409. Hrodulf, email to author, March 24, 2012. See also Don Yoder and Thomas E. Graves, *Hex Signs: Pennsylvania Dutch Barn Symbols & Their Meaning* (Mechanicsburg, PA: Stackpole Books, 2000).

410. Robert L. Schreiwer, *A Brief Introduction to Urglaawe* (Bristol, PA: Die Urglaawisch Sippschaft vum Distelfink, 2009), 7.

411. Ibid., 10.

and gradually discerned that it had a strong affinity with goddess Frau Holle. These experiences led the kindred to incorporate the mountain into their practice as a regular place of pilgrimage and ritual. Robert Schreiwer, the kindred leader, makes note of this reinterpretation, "Thus, a place that is associated with 'Witchcraft' in a negative connotation in Christianity becomes a splendid and positive location in which to honor our gods and goddesses."[412] The Hexenkopf story illustrates a process by which reconstructive practices enable religious entrepreneurs to transform historical folklore into creative new religious forms.

In addition, Distelfink Sippenschaft takes a distinctly "universalist" or inclusive orientation towards Heathen religious practice. Although its form of spirituality is rooted in a specific ethnic or folk identity, the kindred is explicitly non-folkish in its expression of Heathenry. It is open to those without a Pennsylvania Dutch heritage, drawing its members based more on proximity and affinity for Urglaawe as a spirituality. In addition, the kindred espouses the inclusive motto of the Troth, accepting members without regard to race, gender, and sexual orientation.[413] Schreiwer was involved in starting the In-Reach prison ministry, a distinctly anti-racist approach to Heathen chaplaincy operated by the Troth. The program began in response to ongoing concerns that incarcerated Heathens were being radicalized as racists in prison settings. According to an official statement, "the Troth is proactively undertaking efforts to thwart the racist agenda by increasing the availability of Heathen materials with positive, non-racist messages through the creation of a Heathen prison services program called In-Reach."[414] Since the early 2000s, Distelfink Sippenschaft and Urglaawe have taken an increasingly active and visible posture in relation to the community, adopting a cooperative approach to the greater Pagan community. This has included a leadership role at local Pagan Pride Days;

---

412. Ibid., 11. In addition to leading the Urglaawe kindred, Distelfink Sippenschaft, Schreiwer also became the Steersman of the Troth in 2016. See Cara Schulz, "Looking Toward the Future with the Troth's New Steersman," *The Wild Hunt* blog, June 21, 2016, http://wildhunt.org/2016/06/looking-toward-the-future-with-the-troths-new-steersman.html.

413. "The Troth Mission Statement," *The Troth*, www.thetroth.org.

414. "The Troth's Response to Evan Ebel and Asatru's Role in the Murder of Tom Clements," *The Troth*, May 6, 2013, http://thetroth.blogspot.com/2013/05/the-troths-response-to-evan-ebel-and.html.

numerous presentations, information sharing, and networking at Pagan festivals; and participation in community events such as annual food drives.

However, Urglaawe developed in a Heathen community in which tension between folkish and non-folkish adherents was a factor. In the late 2000s, another expression of Urglaawe Pennsylvania Dutch Heathenry began to emerge explicitly as a folkish rival to the inclusive Distelfink Sippenschaft. "Meanwhile, Germanic Heathenry in Pennsylvania had gotten ugly. Two camps had emerged," writes folkish Heathen and hexologist, Hunter Yoder.[415] In no uncertain terms, he contrasts the inclusive Dietsch (referring to the Pennsylvania German dialect) Urglaawe camp from the folkish expression he refers to as Deutsch, associated more with High German tradition. Urglaawe, he writes, "was largely Universalist despite its rooting in Deitsch culture. It also embraced cyberism and alternative lifestyles. It allied itself with the neo-Christian witchcraft, known as new-age Braucherei." As we have seen in the earlier case of Ralph Blum's *The Book of Runes*, this sort of rhetoric is designed to police the boundaries of the Heathen watershed, identifying and rejecting inauthentic variants. Here the folkish critique follows a similar pattern, specifically identifying those aspects that reflect disapproved tributaries.

This rival folkish kindred, Der Heidevolksstamm or "the tribe of Heathen folk," formed in 2009 specifically to counter what it saw as Urglaawe's universalism. Yoder writes that "a core group of folkish Germanic Heathens, unhappy with the universalist and pro-Christian stance of Urglaawe, formed Der Heidevolkstamm. Der Stamm, as it is affectionately known is unapologetically folkish with a Germanic bent."[416] It would be mistaken to see Der Stamm (the tribe) simply from a political perspective. Within Der Heidevolkstamm's folkish stance there is a creative world of religious culture-building. Like Distelfink Sippenschaft, Der Stamm holds rituals on the Hexenkopf, which Yoder describes in spiritual terms as "a strange piece of rock outcropping" where "Hexes or witches would congregate in colonial times in Pennsylvania. Not

---

415. Hunter M. Yoder, "The Reanimation of Germanic Tribalism in PA Deitsch Hexology," in *Heiden Hexology, Essays and Interviews* (Philadelphia: The Hex Factory, 2012), 79.
416. Ibid., 80.

a part of the Appalachian Mountains which are nearby, it is a distortion in the time/space continuum."[417] Not only Yoder but also several others of the tribe's members are serious herbalists. Art is also an important part of the tribe's culture, including needlework and Yoder's painting of hex signs as both folk art and magical work. Yoder has brought together his relationship with plants and völkisch rune magic into his hexology, incorporating the images of powerplants and runes into his hex signs. He continues to place his work within the context of Pennsylvania Dutch agriculture, "I believe my focus as a Hexologist is also the primary focus of the Berks County farmer — fertility and weather control. The essence of Pennsylvania Deutsch magic is fecundity. As farmers we seek to increase our yield and protect our farms."[418] Somehow, he considers this eclectic interplay of animistic nature religion, "the Galdrstafir of the Icelandic tradition, and the Hexology of Berks County," as folkish Heathenry.[419]

Drawing on a völkisch vision of culture, Yoder privileges folkish forms as more authentic versions of Heathenry. Regarding the founding of Der Stamm, he writes that "the purer, harder edged folkish aspects of continental European Heathenry coupled with the folk religious aspects of the Pennsylvania Germans was what we craved . . . Ultimately we wanted union with our European ancestors without the ancient imperialistic Mediterranean cultures' dilution."[420] This Deutsch tribe went on to form alliances with other folkish groups, including the Asatru Folk Assembly, the Irminfolk of New York State, and the Virgina-based Wolves of Vinland. Yoder writes,

> We all sensed an affinity for things wild, strong, and relentless. We three were producers, contributors, and creators; all forces of nature. Our magical sources were different, from an Icelandic death's pallid countenance approach to life perpetuating frank sexuality, drawing its inspiration from the German fertility gods and goddesses. And all three tribes shared a keen interest in Runology.[421]

---

417. Hunter M. Yoder, "Magic Plants Used Symbolically in Germanic Heathen Hexology," in *Heiden Hexology, Essays and Interviews*, 59–60.
418. Hunter M. Yoder, "Runic Symbology in Contemporary Deitsch Hexology," in *Heiden Hexology, Essays and Interviews*, 36.
419. Ibid., 39.
420. Yoder, "The Reanimation of Germanic Tribalism," 81.
421. Ibid.

In this instance, we see rival groups taking shape around the volatile confluence of folkish attitudes. Each was embodying a politicized form of Heathenry and vying for the high ground as the rightful representative of the Pennsylvania-Dutch tradition. Interestingly, both groups include eclectic elements, though they draw them from different sources. The folkish Der Stamm seeks a narrower vision of the past and higher tension with the contemporary world. In contrast, progressive Urglaawe seeks to balance its interpretation of the Heathen past with contemporary social concerns, lowering tension with the surrounding culture. These two movements illustrate the tensions of the tributaries in the Heathen milieu that occasionally escalate in creative and disturbing ways.

### *The Growing Divide: Online Heathenry*

While Heathenry on the ground has seen divisions take place, the online context of Heathenry has continued to be a battleground. In blogs and online forums, the discussion has escalated beyond the Heathen community, drawing non-Heathen Pagans, anti-facist groups, and media outlets into the battle against folkish Heathenry. Two particular incidents have raised the struggle to new heights of intensity. In a 2011 article, *The Wild Hunt*, a widely read and respected pan-Pagan media outlet, revealed that a number of AFA members had attended a meeting of the European Issues Forum, a group that caters to white supremacist and nationalist attitudes. In another incident in 2013, a controversy erupted over the AFA sponsored Stella Natura music festival, which included bands and musicians with radical right and Traditionalist connections. A Heathen anti-facist group called Circle Ansuz released a widely circulated exposé on McNallen that interpreted his ideology and actions as cover for a racist political agenda.[422] The series of articles meticulously connected McNallen to individuals who have been active in the radical racist right. While these friendships are well known, as are McNallen's own dabblings in right-wing politics, CircleAnsuz was unequivocating in their denouncement. The articles decry McNallen as "an active participant in the American neo-fascist radical traditionalist movement" who has

---

422. "Stephen McNallen and Racialist Asatru," *Circle Ansuz: A Heathen Anarchist Collective*, https://circleansuz.wordpress.com.

been "an unapologetic advocate for white nationalism."[423] In the interpretation of CircleAnsuz, McNallen has betrayed his elder position in the Heathen community, using his organization to broker a quiet deal with the racist underground. "His position in the Heathen community has enabled him to facilitate the infiltration of our community by neo-Nazis, corrupted our lore to justify a racialist agenda, and inflict grievous harm on the reputation of Heathenry due to these associations with organized hate."[424]

This conclusion about McNallen and the AFA reached by progressive Heathens was further inflamed by two events in 2016. The first was a Facebook post in which McNallen responded to news that migrant Arab men had sexually assaulted German women at a public New Year's event in Germany. McNallen posted "Germany — that is the German people, not sellout traitors like Merkel — deserve our full support ... Where are the Freikorps when we need them?"[425] The Freikorps were private right-wing militia groups that formed post-World War I, which perpetrated street violence and even political assassinations, and were associated with the later Nazi SA Brownshirts. McNallen's wording was either reckless or naïve, and it is difficult to believe the latter. Whatever McNallen meant by this choice of words, by invoking the Freikorps, he unleashed a storm of criticism. Numerous Heathen opinion makers spoke out against this statement, rehashing and examining every nuance of the post. And once again, beset by accusations that his deepest sympathies were colored by fascist and racist ideology, McNallen

---

423. "Stephen McNallen and Racialist Asatru Part 1: Metagenetics and the South Africa Connection," *Circle Ansuz*, August 19, 2013, https://circleansuz.wordpress.com/2013/08/19/stephen-mcnallen-part-one/.

424. "Stephen McNallen Part 4: Stella Natura and What Can be Done," *Circle Ansuz*, September 9, 2013, https://circleansuz.wordpress.com/2013/09/09/stephen-mcnallen-part-4/.

425. Joseph Bloch, "Hysteria and the Freikorps," *Jon Upsal's Garden*, January 11, 2016, http://jonupsalsgarden.blogspot.com/2016/01/hysteria-and-freikorps.html. McNallen's original Facebook post was removed from the Internet. It is preserved in Bloch's blog post. McNallen's follow-up statement was released through the same blog. See "A Statement from Stephen McNallen," *Jon Upsal's Garden*, January 12, 2016, http://jonupsalsgarden.blogspot.com/2016/01/a-statement-from-stephen-mcnallen.html. According to McNallen's original post, he was responding to an article that appeared in the *Daily Mail*. See Sue Reid, "Why Germany Can't Face the Truth About Migrant Sex Attacks," *Daily Mail*, January 8, 2016, www.dailymail.co.uk/news/article-3391075/Why-Germany-t-face-truth-migrant-sex-attacks-SUE-REID-finds-nation-denial-wave-horrific-attacks-reported-Europe.html#ixzz4wvpvewaZ.

simply dismissed the arguments of his critics by labeling them "the politically correct."[426] This tactic began to seem increasingly weak coming from someone as sophisticated as McNallen.

The second event happened in late August, several months after McNallen stepped down from day-to-day leadership of the AFA.[427] This time, a Facebook post by the new Alsherjargothi, Matt Flavel, created a seismic event in the online Heathen community. The post read in part, "The AFA would like to make it clear that we believe gender is not a social construct, it is a beautiful gift from the holy powers and from our ancestors. The AFA celebrates our feminine ladies, our masculine gentlemen and, above all, our beautiful white children." In the eyes of many observers, this statement crossed a line carefully maintained by McNallen by clearly advocating a racist, sexist, and homophobic ideology. Particularly appalling for many was the resonance of the post with the "14 Words." This statement attributed to white supremacist and Odinist David Lane has become a byword for the American white supremacist movement.[428] After this comment, the sheer volume of pushback was different, as well as its specificity and directness on Facebook, blogs, and websites among Heathens and Pagans alike. Unlike previous denunciations, which had originated from smaller groups and opinion-makers, this time a large number of Heathens spoke out online about the statement, denouncing the AFA in definite terms. Average Heathens had been loath to call out the AFA in any public way, primarily out of a sense of frith and grith—a stance of loyalty and goodwill with other Heathens.[429] After all, the AFA has been a prominent Heathen organization and its members are interconnected with the wider Heathen community. Yet after this statement was released, those lines of

---

426. Bloch, "A Statement from Stephen McNallen."

427. Stephen McNallen, "Words from the Alsherjargothi," *Asatru Folk Assembly* Facebook page, May 1, 2016, www.facebook.com/Asatru.Folk.Assembly/posts/1064986693576660.

428. "We must secure the existence of our people and a future for white children." David Lane's 14 Words have become a central ideological statement for American white supremacists.

429. Frith is commonly paired with "grith," from the Old Norse *grið* referring to a truce or peace. Grith is a Heathen ethical term referring to a temporary peace among extra-familial individuals and networks, a relationship of peaceful alliance in which all sit together without hostile intent. When paired together, "frith and grith" form a powerful idiom in contemporary Heathenry conveying a strong sense of friendship, peace, and commonality.

loyalty were dramatically redrawn with some Heathens taking the step of unfriending members of AFA and cutting off other ties with the organization. For the first time, the Troth made an official statement denouncing the AFA, stating that "the Troth stands against the AFA's vision of what Asatru should be, and we do not recognize their beliefs as representative of a majority of American Asatru (Heathenry)."[430] This statement was followed by another one encouraging AFA members to jump ship: "Folks who are essentially being cast out of the AFA should look into The Troth."[431]

The AFA did not back down from the post, standing by it as an accurate statement of its message and policies.[432] Folkish Asatruar denounced opponents of the AFA as social justice warriors (SJWs) who sought to undo the organization, calling them morons, traitors, and enemies. At this point it seemed that the Heathen world was becoming a microcosm in which the social tensions of the wider American polity were being played out. Tensions were further heightened shortly thereafter when a camp in Minnesota suddenly and unexpectedly canceled a scheduled AFA event.[433] Accusations circulated around the Internet that radical universalist Heathens had attacked the AFA by instigating the deplatforming of the event. The online discourse quickly became accusatory and inflammatory, drawing stark oppositional lines between the AFA and the Troth and raising the level of tension to an unprecedented level. Folkish spokespeople blasted universalist SJWs for launching a war against the AFA. McNallen surrogate Joseph Bloch responded with dire rhetoric and threats against radicals who had "drawn blood": "Make no mistake; if these radical regressive leftists had their way, every AFA member would be fired from their job, have their children

430. "Statement on Gender, Race, Nationality and Sexual Orientation," *The Troth* Facebook page, August 22, 2016, www.facebook.com/thetroth1/posts/1169835886409607.

431. "You Are Welcome in Our Hall" *The Troth* Facebook page, August 22, 2016, www.facebook.com/thetroth1/posts/1169561959770333.

432. For an example of the AFA's response, see Matt Sarver, "Interview with Matt Flavel, Asatru Folk Assembly," *Aesir Broadcasting Network*, September 13, 2016, https://soundcloud.com/aesirbroadcasting/abn-main-network-broadcast-matt-flavel-asatru-folk-assembly.

433. John Reinan and Paul Walsh, "Minnesota Camp Cancels Booking of Nordic Heritage Group with White Supremacist Bent," (Minneapolis) *Star Tribune*, September 2, 2016, www.startribune.com/camp-courage-cancels-festival-booking-of-nordic-heritage-group/392071771/.

taken away by the government, and be tossed out of their home. Literally. That's the mentality we are dealing with, and it's past time we respond."[434] The inclusive Heathen community responded to this veiled threat with another formal and decisive rejection of the AFA, essentially a boycott of the organization called Declaration 127. The Declaration invoked the Lore, *Hávamál*, stanza 127, to legitimate a radical break between these two Heathen camps, "When you see misdeeds speak out against them and give your enemies no frith."[435] Signed by numerous groups internationally, Declaration 127 labels the AFA as an enemy, an unprecedented move by such a wide variety of Heathens. The statement invokes the Lore against the AFA and utilizes the theological language of frith, which raises the gravity of the pronouncement. Essentially the statement draws the AFA outside of the goodwill of the community, pushing them into the utgarð beyond any sort of human congeniality. The Heathen community finds itself in a state of higher internal tension and discord than anytime in recent memory. One side has positioned itself in greater alignment with contemporary American Paganism, while the primary carrier of folkish ideology finds itself increasingly isolated, backed into a corner, and on the defensive.

We should not overlook the fact that this latest eruption of tension comes at a time of transition. McNallen, the founder of the AFA, had recently transferred authority to a new group of leaders. It is something of a truism in the study of new religions that the shift of power from a charismatic founder to other routinized structures often involves difficulty. In the increasingly hostile social context in which the AFA found itself every action was pressurized and every mistake magnified. The new leadership faced two alternatives: either open and liberalize, moving away from the stances of the past; or double-down on a hardline folkish position, adopting an increasingly entrenched stance against progressive Heathenry. The new leadership chose the latter. McNallen himself seems to have decided which path he will take as well. After months of silence,

---

434. Joseph Bloch, "The War Is Forced Upon Us," *Jon Upsal's Garden* blog, September 3, 2016, http://jonupsalsgarden.blogspot.com/2016/09/the-war-is-forced-upon-us.html.

435. "Declaration 127," *Huginn's Heathen Hof* blog, http://declaration127.com/. Declaration 127 states that signatories will "not promote, associate, or do business with the AFA as an organization so long as they maintain these discriminatory policies."

he spoke out in March 2017 in a YouTube video explicitly claiming his allegiance to the white race and racially oriented politics, as well as his identification with the 14 Words, confirming what many progressive Heathens had suspected all along.[436]

## Conclusion: Which Way Forward?

The Heathen community is more divided than ever. After forty years, the issue of racial attitudes continues to be the focus, the legacy of metagenetics. It is remarkable that Heathenry exhibits a continual problematic obsession over the issue of racial attitudes, while other forms of Paganism do not. The conflict is only understandable through the lens of the Heathen milieu and the clash of tributaries. This state of affairs exists because other forms of contemporary Paganism do not include the völkisch tributary and its deeper historical connections to racist ideologies and groups. The presence of both the völkisch/Traditionalist and the Wiccan and Witchcraft tributaries causes Heathenry to be existentially different from other American Paganisms, predisposed to this issue that will not be easily resolved. Folkish Heathenry carries ideas about the importance of ethnicity that are contested by numerous segments of the American population, including many Pagans and many in the Heathen community. Folkish Heathens are religious dissenters. At its best, the perspective refuses to accept contemporary notions of multiculturalism while at the same time rejecting antiquated generalizing categories of race. It pushes against modern constructions of identity along national lines, against the hyper-individualism that characterizes postmodern society, and against the reduction of religion to a shallow consumer choice. At the heart of folkishness, there is a yearning for connection and relationship. Folkishness searches for an alternative to the shallowness it experiences in modernity, to immerse itself into a more connected world, and to build identity from a foundation deeper than popular culture.

New religious movements often function as social spaces for experimentation and innovation regarding issues and tensions in their host societies. They experiment with marginal ideas seeking ways of

---

436. McNallen, "What Stephen McNallen Really Thinks About Race!" His comments on the 14 Words begins at 10:00 into the video.

resolving prevalent social tensions. In this sense, new religions can function as communities of dissent, rejecting certain social norms and expressing alternative ways of addressing social problems. It seems clear that Heathenry, whether knowingly or not, has functioned in this way in regard to the American struggle over the issue of race. Folkish Heathenry began as an attempt to navigate the social tensions and anxiety over race by reflecting on certain ideas within the Heathen watershed, to respond in a different way than either the racial theories of the nineteenth century or the progressivism of the Civil Rights era. In this light, the constant refrain from folkish Heathens that they are not racists needs to be heard with more nuance.

Folkishness was driven by the identity politics of the 1970s. McNallen sees himself as the Northern European equivalent to Vine Deloria, Jr., critiquing the oppression of his people and advocating a socio-religious path for white folk. As an ethnic identity, folkishness expresses a critique of an American dream that has evaporated in the lives of lower-class white Americans. As such, it is in touch with authentic sentiments, real fears, and actual social trends. There is something to McNallen's deprivation theory of cultural collapse and attending problems in white communities. There is increasing evidence that working-class and rural white communities are faring poorly in contemporary America. Many of these communities have faced a long-term struggle with poverty, educational deficits, rampant drug problems, a decline of positive family and community life, and the continued failure of government programs to deal with these seemingly intractable problems. Asatru is closer to these issues. McNallen draws attention to them within his narrative of folkishness. Although his narrative has strayed into racist thinking, Asatru as a whole and folkish Heathenry at its best may be posed to address these issues with creative religious and social solutions.

However, folkish Heathenry is rarely at its best. The folkish perspective has found itself increasingly at odds with the trajectory of American opinion as well as Pagan religious and ethical sensibility. McNallen himself, the most capable spokesman for folkish Asatru, has seemed to vacillate between a progressive vision of Asatru's role in the world as an innovative community and a more suspicious, inward looking, closed off, and hostile stance towards the broader society, one that inhibits growth and conversion. The reporting of Circle Ansuz and the ideological work of other inclusive Heathens arises from the laudable goal of rooting out racism from Heathen practice. It clearly demonstrates that folkish Heathenry remains connected to the world of racist ideology. This sort of ideological work, rooting out the remnants of racism, may determine the future success or failure of the Heathen movement. It may influence whether Heathenry continues to grow in visibility in the ongoing Pagan resurgence in America or moves into the shadows of the alternative right. While it seems that McNallen is now revealing himself as an "unapologetic advocate for white nationalism," as Circle Ansuz has claimed, that is not necessarily the case for all folkish Heathenry. At present, the degree of polarization, vitriolic language, and level of distrust crowd out the development of a more nuanced and complex position: a folkish but truly non-racist approach to Heathenry. If the folkish community responds by drawing away from broader participation, taking on a sentiment of victimization and isolation, and defining itself by increasingly high tension with society, these Heathens may migrate towards a friendlier reception in the darker networks of radical racism.

Granted, it is the Heathen way to stand one's ground and aggressively defends one's honor. But McNallen is so embedded in his war against inclusive Heathenry that he dismisses his Heathen critics as politically correct, short-circuiting discussion. In times of crisis and tension, the range of acceptable positions tends to become polarized into two rigid camps or positions: one is either for or against a social issue. It may actually be that, at their best, some folkish Asatruar are attempting to envision and enunciate a third way between the camps of racist and progressive Heathens, and to think about the issue of race and ethnicity along new lines that are not easily reduced to one point or another. Yet the question remains whether folkishness can evolve into something that is neither angry nor exclusive and can function positively in a multicultural context? Or will it gradually succumb to racial tendencies, slide toward an isolated and angry social posture, and migrate more fully towards the cultic milieu of the radical racist subculture? Both the Troth and the AFA have clearly poised themselves as the heirs to true Heathenry. But it is just as likely that these groups have become so embedded in this conflict that neither will be viable and attractive as a new generation of Heathen adherents emerges. Racial attitudes will become the baggage of the old guard as ideological space opens in Heathenry for a new tributary or tributaries to form that are not so weighed down by the controversy of the past.

What new Heathen directions will emerge? Tribalism is a form of social arrangement that is increasingly discussed among Heathens and practiced in various manifestations. In its best forms, tribalism eschews categories of race and draws on Edred Thorsson's more inclusive definition that envisions the tribe as a "super-genetic" social entity.[437] Snook, Horrell, and Horton suggest that tribalism may represent an emerging form of Heathen social practice that avoids the polarizing politics of the folkish/universalist controversy: "Those wanting a middle way between the extremes have turned to 'tribalism' in an attempt to reconcile the desire to be inclusive and avoid accusations of racism, while maintaining a degree of exclusivity through an 'authentic' historical social structure."[438] The tribe blends small biological family units with others who share mutually agreed-upon values and customs, those who prove their usefulness and worth to the group. By drawing on a type of merit or worth-based system, tribalism both maintains Heathen exclusivity while avoiding the fault lines of race. John T. Manier, a member of the Troth's High Rede, acknowledges that Heathenry is an exclusive community while maintaining that this exclusivism should be based not on skin color but on worth, the Heathen moral concept of the virtuous individual:

> Everyone is not welcome in our community. Our own are welcome here, however other people would describe them. There is not a colour that gets you in the door, nor one that bars you from it . . . Our ancestors were masters of community building; and they built those communities of the people they found of whatever tribe, race, or nation they met, who could share their sense of worth . . . their actions . . . judged individually by standards to which they held, or aspired to, themselves.[439]

As conceptualized by Manier and others, tribalism based on moral worth is a meritocratic form of social organization that prima facie avoids racial distinctions, as Thorsson suggested twenty years previously. People enter the tribe, the innangarð, by proving themselves based on their actions, and conforming to virtues and

---

437. Thorsson, "Who Will Build the Hearths of the Troth," 20.
438. Snook, Horrell, and Horton, "Heathens in the United States," 53.
439. John T. Mainer, "Diversity in Heathenry," *The Troth* blog, posted January 2015, http://thetroth.blogspot.com/2015/01/perspectives-on-racial-issues-in-united.html.

standards maintained by the tribal group. In many ways, tribalism looks toward the strength of small local communities of the past and seeks to restore the vitality of local, situated community to the lives of contemporary Americans.

McNallen, however, is a true believer. For all his thoughtful critique of the history of the Asatru movement and his own role in its development, despite all of McNallen's desire to appeal to the wider community with the beauty and power of Asatru, the AFA has never been able to turn the corner. Perhaps this is the reality of almost every new religious movement. McNallen is simply unable to grow outside of a certain subculture or effectively evaluate metagenetics and the controversial, even deleterious impact it has had on the movement. In this sense he remains an ideologue, more concerned with purity than pragmatism. He is a man both inspired and trapped within the constraints of his own vision, convinced of the fundamental importance of his tenaciously held tenets. McNallen is a man of action, but driven by a firmly held ideal. And, depending on one's perspective, that ideal has either been dangerous and disruptive to the growth of the movement, or the last handhold of its purity. Three decades has become four, while the turbulence stirred up by metagenetics has continued to churn. Meanwhile folkishness has evolved to become more of an attitude, a presupposition that is not seeking a justification, a meme circulating in unpredictable ways in the broader Heathen worldview.

## Chapter 4

## Spears and Shieldwalls

The Self and the Struggle of Life

On the outskirts of a small southern American city, a mixed crowd of about ten people, Heathens and their Wiccan hosts, had come together in a double-wide in the middle of a sprawling trailer park to celebrate Charming of the Plow. The contemporary practice of Charming of the Plow takes its inspiration from other ancient rites that took place at the very beginning of the agricultural year, when the fields were ready for plowing. In northern climates, this first plowing was intended to hasten the thawing of the frozen ground and encourage its latent fertility.[440] An earlier planting meant a better harvest. In this sense, Charming of the Plow was not simply a rite venerating Nature and her fertile power. Instead, the rite focused on the first human work of the agricultural year, asking that the gods favor this human effort with productivity. As much as it acknowledged natural fertility, the ritual highlighted the challenge of survival for the human community as it emerged from the darkness and cold of winter. The rite represented the struggle of the human community in the midst of nature's unforgiving realities. For the societies living in the harsh northern climates with their short growing seasons, an early planting might hold off the threat of winter starvation. The ancient rites awakened the community to the cycles of work necessary for survival in marginal agricultural environments.

None of the participants of this contemporary ritual were farmers preparing to plow their fields, one significant way in which the contemporary Heathenry community differs from its arch-Heathen model. As the ritual started, people reached into their purses, bags, and pockets. Cell phones, car keys, a laptop, knitting needles, a pair of jewelry pliers, wallets, and pocketknives clattered as they

---

440. Gundarsson, *Living the Troth*, 365–66.

were placed on and around the altar. The tools were representative of the daily lives of students, teachers, artisans, and food service workers, the sort of work they depended on for their livelihood and survival.[441] While the implements may have changed since Norse times, the work necessary for human survival is no less paramount for modern people. This is especially the case for the Heathens gathered on this occasion, many of whom work and live on the margins of the American middle class, vulnerable to downturns in the economy, for whom making a living wage may be comparable to coaxing fertility out of the frozen northern ground. Seen in light of these economic and social tensions, Charming of the Plow appears as a ritual of marginality and dissent. These Heathens were celebrating the basic goodness of their work, but also acknowledging the struggles of survival, the frustrations faced by the middle and working classes of society in a time of American economic hardship. The rich rarely petition the gods for survival. In the trailer park, however, the contingencies of survival become crystal clear, struggle and striving take on heightened value. The cosmology of the North and its sanctification of struggle appeal to this group of people who live with economic challenges and seek to mitigate the harsh realities of American society. Not only did the ritual call forth their own determination and perseverance, but also invoked powerful cultural themes and supernatural resources to assist and bless the struggle to thrive.

As we will see, Norse mythology contains many stories that sanctify the striving individual, envision life as a sacred struggle, and enlist the help of supernatural entities in the process of survival. In turn, the contemporary Heathen movement has thoroughly incorporated these themes. One of the most important symbols within the modern Heathen movement is Mjolnir, the hammer of Thor. Worn around the neck as a pendant, the symbol is the most recognizable and most widely utilized symbol of Heathen religionists. The popularity and significance of the hammer sign reflects a similar prominence in the Pagan practices of the Viking Age. The hammer was a significant presence and a potent symbol,

---

441. Field notes by author, Lexington, KY, February, 2012. At this meeting, things were a bit disorganized. The intention for the ritual had not been well communicated ahead of time, and we waited for quite a while as the group leaders made last minute plans. As a result, several participants had not brought work-related items but made do by just pulling things out of their pockets.

found in the mythology, displayed in the great temple in Sweden and perhaps used to simulate the sound of thunder there, carved into stone monuments, and present physically and symbolically in life-stage rituals associated with births, weddings, and funerals.[442] In fact, the practice of wearing the Mjolnir as a pendant first emerged during the Viking Age, a practice confirmed widely in archaeological sites from the period. Evidence suggests that Thor featured prominently in the conflict between the Heathen North and the growing influence of Christianity. William Craigie explains, "It was Thor whom the believers in the old faith expressly put forward as a rival to the God of the Christians."[443] Thomas DuBois also notes that the increasing friction between Heathen and Christian cultures was expressed by directly and innovatively juxtaposing Thor with Christ, such as through the invention of new myths.[444] In one fascinating example, a mythological story circulated among Viking Age Heathens in which Thor challenged Christ to a fight, an invitation to which the cowardly Christ demurred. The hammer pendant was another such innovative response that evolved as a symbol by which Viking Age Heathens visually depicted their resistance to Christianity. The Thor's Hammer pendant may have developed in imitation of the Christian crosses worn by priests and other Christian adherents, but was worn by Heathens as a challenge to the presence of the new faith, functioning as something of an "anti-cross," in DuBois' words.[445]

These examples demonstrate the emergence of a new Heathen identity in response to growing Christian cultural pressure. Prior to the Christian presence in Northern Europe, such a pan-Heathen symbol never developed. That is not to say that there were not historical instances, perhaps even a social trend, towards some sort of common Heathen identity. DuBois, for instance, argues that the temple at Uppsala represented a developing sense of religious unity among otherwise distinct and varied local religious cults.[446] However, this ancient "Heathen" identity, referring rather loosely

---

442. Davidson, *Gods and Myths*, 80–81.

443. William Alexander Craigie, *The Religion of Ancient Scandinavia* (Freeport, NY: Books for Libraries Press, 1969), 10.

444. Thomas A. DuBois, *Nordic Religions in the Viking Age* (Philadelphia: University of Pennsylvania Press, 1999), 59–60.

445. Ibid., 159.

446. Ibid., 43.

to all the non-Christian northern people, was actually a construct forged in the clash with Christianity. The emergence of the hammer pendants demonstrates how those who retained the old ways gradually forged a dissenting pan-Heathen identity against the encroaching Christian culture.

Developed in the conflict of ancient cultures, these dissenting symbols now shape how Heathens experience the contemporary American religious landscape. For instance, the ancient rivalry between Thor and Christ remains an accessible theme in the Heathen movement. A contemporary song known by many Heathens on the East Coast, contrasts Red Thor and the White Christ in ways that would seem familiar to Viking Age Heathens.[447] The verses, carried by a tentative phrasing and lightly arranged instrumentation, ask listeners if they will succumb to the dominant cultural pressure to exhibit a Christian religiosity:

> Will you follow?
> Will you follow the White Christ of the cross?
> Will you follow when he says your soul is lost?

These searching questions are answered resolutely in the rhythmic chorus with a declaration of allegiance to the Heathen gods:

> And I will lead and hold the raven's banner high.
> And I will stand and pray with my fist held to the sky . . .
> And I will stand alongside Red Thor.[448]

The contemporary movement makes use of these figures, the White Christ and Red Thor, to communicate their own struggles as a minority religious group. Heathens identify with the historical conflict and appropriate it to express their stance of resistance to the dominant religious culture in their own American context.

Similarly, Heathens have adopted the Thor's Hammer as the most universally accepted symbol of their identity. It continues to hold multiple meanings in modern Heathenry. It marks the identity of a Heathen adherent, communicates theological significance, and asserts the presence of a dissenting minority religion in the

---

447. Jonathon Cyr and Ingmar Lauer, "Red Thor," recorded 2008, on *A Gift for a Gift*, Trú. Spirit Music, compact disc.

448. Ibid. Lyrics for *A Gift for a Gift* are available at http://truspiritmusic.com/html/a_gift_for_a_gift.html.

American religious and social milieu. All these meanings were apparent in the campaign undertaken to gain approval for the Mjolnir as an official religious symbol on military grave markers. This work had been ongoing for years by various Heathen groups such as the Asatru Folk Assembly, the Odinic Rite, the Troth, and perhaps most notably the Open Halls Project, an independent Heathen group that serves and advocates for Heathens in the military. As a result of these efforts, the Veterans Administration approved the Mjolnir for use on military grave markers in 2013 and according to some media sources the hammer adorns the grave markers of at least two veterans.[449] The symbolic value of military headstones engraved with the Mjolnir should be not overlooked. It communicates not only the Heathen values of bravery and loyalty, but also permanently enshrines the Heathen identity as part of the American religious landscape.

## *The Hammer of Thor and the Precariousness of Life*

Symbols of violence abound throughout the world's religions: from the club of Heracles, to the Sikh *khanda* and the martial hymn of evangelical Christianity, "Onward Christian Soldiers." Like them, the Heathen hammer has a distinctly militant significance. Mjolnir is a weapon of war and on the surface at least a symbol of violence. The militancy is not a latent symbolism but is often actively encouraged, through song lyrics for instance. Although in no way associated with racist Heathenry, the Swedish heavy metal band Amon Amarth is well known in Heathen circles for its songs inspired by the violent themes of Norse mythology. Many of the band's lyrics play into the aggressive images and apocalyptic aspects of the Heathen milieu.[450] For instance, the band's song "Annihilation of Hammerfest" from their 2001 release *The Crusher* envisions Mjolnir as an instrument of war wielded against Christian opponents. In the lyric, Thor, called the warlord of the gods, retrieves his hammer and wields it menacingly against his foes:

---

449. Jason Pitzl-Waters, "More on the VA Thor's Hammer Emblem Addition," *The Wild Hunt: A Modern Pagan Perspective*, May 14, 2013, http://wildhunt.org/2013/05/more-on-the-va-thors-hammer-emblem-addition.html.

450. Karl E. H. Seigfried, "Interview with Johan Hegg of Amon Amarth, Part One," The Norse Mythology Blog, July 29, 2010, www.norsemyth.org/2010/07/interview-with-johan-hegg-of-amon.html.

> Dark and grim he appears
> The warlord of the Gods comes with force ...
> Frozen by fear
> They gathered stand and stare
> And what they see is death.[451]

Whatever the intention of lyrics such as this, they provide validation for an interpretation of the hammer as a symbol of anti-social violence. The hammer that crushes its enemies plays into the apocalyptic worldview of racist Norse Paganism, that loose collection of people who find that Heathenry offers legitimation for their fantasies of violence and destruction. While such views are limited in their appeal, the symbolic prominence of the hammer reifies the potentially oppositional values that it represents. There is just no getting away from the fact that the hammer signifies a hard edge to contemporary Heathen religion and the valorization of an aggressive approach to social conflict.

However, like the Sikh *khanda*, the militant interpretation does not exhaust the symbolic domain of the hammer. A more significant value to Mjolnir, one more reflective of Asatru in general, is that of striving and protecting. As the Lore suggests, Thor wields the hammer in defense of what is good, something like peace through strength. Thor carries the hammer because he must defend Asgard, and the mortal realm Midgard for that matter, against the constant threat of the jǫtnar and *þursar*, the elemental beings who lurk on the edge of the civilized world and threaten its collapse.[452] Thor's role, and that of the hammer, is to vigilantly protect the small, civilized space that the gods have managed to create and maintain by striving against forces that oppose and would destroy it. The gods of Heathenry do not exist serenely in the world. They must constantly strive to maintain themselves in a potentially chaotic

---

451. Dark Lyrics, "Amon Amarth Lyrics Album: The Crusher," www.darklyrics.com/lyrics/amonamarth/the crusher.html#7.

452. Davidson, *God and Myths*, 80–81; DuBois, *Nordic Religions*, 159. See also *A Dictionary of Old Norse Prose*, s.v: "Þurs," plural Þursar; Lafayllve, *A Practical Heathen's Guide*, 79, 91. A thurs is a type of giant, a subset of the jǫtnar. Thursar are closely associated with danger and catastrophic destruction, distinguishing them from jotuns who may be thought of as powerful land-vaettir. The *hrímþursar*, frost giants, are hostile beings who represent a constant threat to the Aesir. The word is related to *þurisaz, a rune associated with the power of the giants or the destructive capability of the thorn.

world, against beings who seek to erode the carefully guarded balance. The necessity and value of striving, modeled by the gods and symbolized by the hammer, is deeply ingrained into the Heathen approach to the world. Mjolnir symbolizes an attitude of fierce and serious struggle for positive social change. A noble, worthy life is one that strives against opposition to create and build something of value. While this noble pursuit may entail violence, it always involves asserting one's will as a force in a world in which survival is neither guaranteed nor easy. From the world-affirming Heathen perspective, life is precious, valuable, and good, yet under constant assault. It must be protected and defended. This precarious quality of life, and the necessity of struggle to maintain it, is exemplified in the lives of the gods and also in the most fundamental cosmological stories of the great world tree, Yggdrasil.

At first glance, the world tree may seem to represent the strength and vitality of the cosmos. Yggdrasil rises from the *Ginnungagap*, the primal abyss of Norse myth, as the greatest of living beings and holds within itself all the realms of the multiverse. Its roots grow deeply into the underworld and provide the superstructure upon which the cosmos is extended. However, on closer inspection, the Heathen world is neither stable nor safe. Dangerous forces stress the cosmos and "the tree was continually threatened even as it grew and flourished."[453] The Norse myths depict this condition of cosmic struggle by means of several beasts that attack, prey upon, and threaten the tree's existence, such as the deer and goats that devour the leaves of the tree and the serpent *Niðhoggr* who gnaws upon its roots.[454] Another beast, the world serpent *Jormungandr*, encircles the tree and strains against it. Describing the symbolic value of Yggdrasil, another writer states, "The Tree that supports all that is and all that will be is under attack."[455] The giants who inhabit the worlds of fire and ice seek the destruction of the orderly cosmos that gods and humans have created, a constant threat delayed only the by vigilance of the gods. This struggle against chaos and disorder comes to a climactic resolution at Ragnarok, the battle of the gods and giants in which the cosmos is virtually destroyed.

---

453. Davidson, *Gods and Myths*, 26–27.
454. Bauschatz, *The Well and the Tree*, 25.
455. Krasskova, *Exploring the Northern Tradition*, 31.

The Heathen cosmos is unstable and at any moment, the balance of power could shift. In fact, the underlying tendency is one of destabilization or disintegration: the cosmos is only tenuously held together by effort. The Norns, the mythological figures of Time, stand at the cosmic well and water the Tree to nourish it. Odin searches for knowledge and information that will help him maintain the balance of power and delay Ragnarok. Heimdall ceaselessly watches and listens from the Bifrost Bridge for signs of danger. Thor maintains order by constantly fighting back the aggressive efforts of the giants with his weapon Mjolnir. Similarly, human beings are understood to be partners with the gods in their efforts to stabilize and prolong the existence of the orderly cosmos. As Davidson writes,

> By supporting them [the group of two or three powerful deities ruling the world—namely Odin, Thor, and Freyr] men helped to maintain the existing order, and so ensure the continuing survival of themselves and their descendants in a precarious world . . . They were very much alive to the threats constantly menacing them, and aware that the order of the world and the prosperity of the community would not endure forever . . . their awareness of possible destruction; it was something deeply engraved into the framework of their religion.[456]

This sense of life as a struggle against external threats plays an important role in the worldview of many contemporary Asatruar. Jorvik, a kindred gothi in Colorado, sees Heathenry as a worldview suited to resisting the challenges and threats of the world, whether they be physical, economic, political, or spiritual. For him, courage, strength, and perseverance are significant Heathen values encoded in the Nine Noble Virtues and within his own ancestral heritage. These values inspire a constant and valiant struggle against the forces of disorder and disintegration. The very name of his kindred, Fimbul Winter, meaning "great" or "terrible" winter, is evocative of this mindset of struggle.[457] For Jorvik, Heathens must work hard

---

456. Hilda Roderick Ellis Davidson, *Myths and Symbols in Pagan Europe: Early Scandinavian and Celtic Religions* (Syracuse: Syracuse University Press, 1988), 221.

457. *A Dictionary of Old Norse Prose*, s.v. "*fimbulvetr.*" "Fimbul winter," meaning "great" or "extreme" winter, is a phrase from the *Prose Edda* used to describe a catastrophic environmental event in which the human population of Midgard experiences three years of constant winter and related hardships prior to Ragnarok. "First will come the winter called Fimbulvetr. Snow will drive in from all directions; the cold will be severe and the winds will be fierce. The sun will be of no use. Three

and sacrifice to make their own way in the world, in such contemporary activities as surviving economic recession in the United States and running a small business in tough economic times. Jorvik also seeks to embody these values of struggle, self-discipline, and sacrifice in his role as a mixed martial arts fighter. The intense training and fighting situations he faces strengthen his understanding and practice of the Asatru virtues. Courage and perseverance are directly applicable when facing an opponent in the ring. Fighting also functions metaphorically for Jorvik by picturing life as a struggle overcome by disciplined strength, the deeper symbolic value of Mjolnir.[458] The *trú* individual approaches life with a self-reliant attitude and embodies the values of courage, discipline, and perseverance against challenges.[459]

This orientation of struggle carries with it accompanying attitudes of valiant striving or, in different circumstances, a forceful combative approach to life. The heroes of the sagas exemplify that the good life involves rising up to meet challenges. Being beaten is better than never fighting at all, a perspective to which Jorvik holds not only himself but also his children. I observed these values in action at a Heathen event in the Midwest. Many Heathen weekends feature "Viking games" in which participants compete in archery, axe throwing, tug-of-war, and other events. At Lightning Across the Plains, one of the most interesting events was called "Steal the Wench." It is a game consisting of a vigorous wrestling match between a male and a female, who engage in both comedic play and brutal struggle for the cheering and taunting audience.[460] The match takes place in a "house," a small square marked off for the

---

of these winters will come, one after the other, with no summer in between," Snorri Sturluson, *Gylfaginning*, 51, in *The Prose Edda*, trans. Jesse L. Byock (New York: Penguin, 2005), 71.

458. Jorvik, interview.

459. The term "trú" is used in Asatru to refer to those who live according to the ethical virtues of the religion, who have "worth" or a good reputation, and demonstrate loyalty to the gods.

460. The enactment of the game dramatizes the ideal of fierce independence for both men and women and the necessity of struggle to defend and actualize it. Participants either must fight to win, to make their own way in the world, or become subject to forces greater than themselves, subject to the will of others. However, issues of gender and sexual violence are also clearly apparent. Snook rightly suggests that the game reinforces a pattern of patriarchal relationships in conservative Heathenry. See Snook, *American Heathens*, 130.

contest. The male tries to drag the female from the house, while the female attempts to pull the male into the "kitchen," represented by one corner of the house. Jorvik's young teenage daughter faced up against a young man, grappling and sparring for all she was worth, eventually taking a hard fall and an elbow to the face as she was dragged to defeat. As the girl dusted herself off, Jorvik's wife, who served as chieftain of the kindred, brought her over and said, "Jorvik, she got elbowed in the eyeball." In most situations, this might have resulted in panic, distraught hovering parents, and calls for first aid. As a mixed martial artist himself, Jorvik was familiar with evaluating blunt force trauma injuries. He bent down and looked at his daughter's eye, surveying the damage. Then giving her a high five he said, "A black eye is a medal you have to earn."[461] None of this exchange was callous or neglectful — Jorvik acted the supportive dad throughout. The interaction was a teaching moment in which he evaluated the events that had occurred: the fight, the injury, and the defeat, in a very Heathen way. The high-five was an example of socializing his daughter into the values and worldview of Asatru. Jorvik did not castigate his daughter for losing, but commended her for fighting hard, for taking the risk and not backing down, and interpreted her swollen eye as a badge of honor and worth.

In addition to passing these values to his children, Jorvik also incorporated the themes of striving against challenges and facing tests of one's mettle into his rituals. Lightning Across the Plains traditionally featured an Odin blót and one year Jorvik served as the ritual leader. The blót began with Torsen, the gothi, lighting the ritual fire "the old way," i.e. with a flint, then invoking Odin as "All-Father, One-Eye, and Lord of the Gallows." After blessing the mead horn, Jorvik instructed the crowd of participants to walk around the ritual space through a series of preparatory stations. Participants first came to a woman holding a horn who said, "As Odin gave his eye for knowledge at Mimir's Well, think about what you would give for knowledge." Handing the horn to each person, she commanded, "Drink from Mimir's Well!" We were surprised to raise the horn and drink consecrated water instead of mead. This slight shift in the usual blót pattern intensified the experience and the connection with the myth that provided the structure for this blót. Participants then moved around the circle and approached another

---

461. Field notes by author, Kansas, September, 2013.

woman holding the blessing bowl. She dipped a leafy oak branch into the liquid and sprinkled us with the mead, recognized by its tangy smell where the droplets stung our faces, a symbol of both cleansing and blessing. Then the moment of challenge was at hand and the ritual reached its tense apex as participants found themselves facing Jorvik, spear in hand, its very real point glinting red in the firelight. Every Heathen knows the symbol of the spear, Odin's weapon Gungnir. So participants approached with their own set of emotions: hesitantly with nervous laughter, or grimly and seriously with faces set as if approaching death. With a flourish, Jorvik took aim and pressed the spear point to their chests demanding, "What will you sacrifice for Odin?" In the ritual performance, the god who had sacrificed his own eye for a drink of the wisdom and knowledge of Mimir's Well, now challenged each person with the cost of their own growth and insight. Only those who strive hardily can wrench enlightenment from its hiding place. There at the point of the spear, each participant answered, declaring what they would do or sacrifice as a response to the god's challenge and Jorvik would not let them pass until they had answered satisfactorily. With the bite of the spear tip still stinging the flesh, we made our way to the edge of the circle. A woman stood holding a basket from which each participant drew a rune tile. Here was the reward of the testing, the wisdom and guidance of the god won through his own ordeal.[462]

Of all the Asatru rituals I have participated in, the elements of testing and challenge were particularly strong in this event. To some extent, the challenge at spear point reflects the ideology of reciprocal exchange—a gift for a gift, which underlies Asatru theology. The sacrifice of Odin for the gift of knowledge requires a similar sacrifice from the adherent for the blessing of Odin. Yet at the same time, in facing the spear the individual faced an existential challenge. The blót forced participants to confront themselves and their willingness to forge ahead along a potentially costly spiritual path. It was not a call to war, but a test of the individual's inner strength and perseverance: can he or she stand courageously against

---

462. The elements of this ritual bear a strong resemblance to Stephen McNallen's Winter Finding ritual. See Stephen A. McNallen, *The Rituals of Asatru: Volume 2 – Seasonal Festivals* (Payson, AZ: World Tree Publications, 1991), 19–21. Jorvik adapted the ritual, reordering the elements in an effective way to introduce the familiar pattern of separation, liminality and reintegration into the ritual. It was interesting to see McNallen's ritual script come to life.

Figure 11. Preparing for Ritual at Lightning Across the Plains. (Photo by the author.)

the challenge, the obstacles in his or her path? The spear serves as a symbol for the challenges that the individual must confront on her own merits to achieve success in life. While Odin and the gods protect, they also issue the challenge. The ritual presented life as a series of challenges that must be confronted by the individual's own strength and virtue.

To push against the challenges of life, to act consistently and reliably under pressure, to uphold and protect those around you, these actions build "worth." Worth represents an important moral category in Heathen circles, indicating a person's standing in the community.[463] Inclusion in Heathen communities, with the respect, dignity, and voice that implies, is closely guarded. Those come only through the communal awareness of an individual's actions and contributions. A person of worth has proven herself and earned the respect and esteem of others. Worth is not a matter

---

463. John R. Clark Hall, *A Concise Anglo-Saxon Dictionary*, 2nd edition (New York: Macmillan, 1916), s.v. "weorð," meaning "value" or "honored," "noble," "of high rank."

of one's achievements in the professional world. Heathens do not care that much for a person's resume. Rather, it is a relational virtue that valorizes deeds done towards others, especially within a particular Heathen community. It is a fragile virtue: once achieved, it is easily lost. And the movement is fractured enough that worth in one group's estimation might earn derision in another's. But Heathens, at their best, tend to recognize strong individuals and respect honesty, loyalty, and tenacity. The value of worth indicates that Heathens prize individuality tempered by strong communal connections. Heathens draw on resources within the Lore to create this innovative, dissenting sense of self to counter the weakness perceived in the indulgent hyper-individualism of modernity.

### *The Heathen Self-Concept*

In Norse mythology, the creation of human beings by the gods receives little fanfare. It is merely one of many acts of creation, described in two short stanzas in the *Völuspá*. It follows a long passage concerning the making of the dwarves, also called the *svartalfar* or dark elves, from the body and blood of the primordial giant, Ymir. The passage includes several lists of the various dwarves created by the gods, stanzas that were later mined by J. R. R. Tolkien for the names of his dwarvish characters.[464] Snorri Sturluson's Prose Edda is similarly terse, summarizing the account in one short paragraph. Despite their brevity, the powerful evocative language has generated intense interest among contemporary Heathens.

> To the coast then came,    kind and mighty,
> from the gathered gods,    three great Æsir;
> on the land they found,    of little strength,
> Ask and Embla,    unfated yet.
>
> Sense they possessed not,    soul they had not,
> being nor bearing,    nor blooming hue;
> soul gave Óthin,    sense gave Hœnir,
> being, Lóthur,    and blooming hue.[465]

---

464. O'Donoghue, *From Asgard to Valhalla*, 183–88. See also Lafayllve, *A Practical Heathen's Guide*, 77.

465. Lee M. Hollander, *Völuspá*, stanzas 17, 18 in *The Poetic Edda* (Austin: University of Texas Press, 2016), 3. The Hollander translation has a long history of use within American Heathenry. One reason for this is Hollander's methodology

In stanza seventeen the phrase "from the gathered gods," likely refers to the assembly of the gods mentioned earlier in stanza six of the poem. The gods gathered to order and name things in the world; they constructed their homes and halls and set about creating the dwarves. Then these three great gods come to explore the world, to walk along the coast of Midgard (ON *miðgarðr*), the human world in Norse cosmology. The seeress names them as Óthin, Hœnir, and Lóthur. Scholars and Heathen commentators have debated about their identities. Óthin is clear enough, the chief of the Norse gods known to most Americans as Odin. Speculation has revolved around whether the other two gods represent aspects of Odin himself or two other individuals. Hœnir is an obscure figure, known to appear in other contexts with Odin and Loki, leading to the idea that Lóthur is another name for Loki. These three walk along the shore, the sea that forms the boundary between Midgard and Utgard (ON *útgarðr*), the home of the giants. There they come across what seem to be two trees, an ash and an elm, perhaps living trees, tree trunks that had fallen over or, as Larrington suggests, driftwood washed up on the shore. Hollander describes them as "of little strength" and "unfated," phrases that are translated in various ways to indicate an unformed state, in comparison to the richer, fuller existence that the gods are about to bestow. According to the *Völuspá*, the gods "found" or "came across" these beings, indicating a spontaneous or circumstantial event that resulted in the creation of humankind. The gods shape these trees into living human beings by endowing them with certain qualities, more of a transformation than a creation. This mode of creation was not unknown in ancient times. There are references in ancient Greek literature to humans originating or being born from trees or, alternatively, being turned into trees. Our own ways of talking about ourselves also imply a similarity to trees, for instance we sometimes describe the human body as having a trunk and limbs. The Eddic text emphasizes that humans came into being through this divine intervention in which life was shared and instilled in them. For all its spontaneity, the action of these gods reflects a creative and thoughtful generosity that shaped the fundamental nature of humans.

---

of privileging English words of Germanic origin for his translation. See Hollander, *Poetic Edda*, xxviii.

## Pagan Cosmology and Identity: Ways of Framing the Self

Heathens with a theological bent often treat this account to a vigorous exegesis, honing a model of human nature from this and other texts from the Lore. Formulating a working conception of selfhood is an important part of any religion, especially a new religion that consciously diverges from the cultural mainstream. As a dissenting religious culture, contemporary Heathens seek a self-concept that contrasts with various contemporary ways of constructing identity. Being Viking requires drawing upon the Norse mythological resources to reconstruct an ancient vision of the self, uncorrupted by the body/soul dualism that has characterized the Christian ethos. While Heathens would not see themselves in conflict with science, the self they describe is more than the purely materialist entity of scientific naturalism. Heathen visions of human nature imagine a type of Pagan selfhood that is also distinct from the erotic self of the Wicca and Witchcraft traditions.

Poets, mystics, and occultists have long used erotic metaphors to describe the cosmos. In contemporary Paganism, Wiccans and their successors codified the metaphor in the Wheel of the Year and important practices such as the Great Rite in which sexual intercourse serves as a primary cosmological metaphor. Over time, it has been broadly influential in contemporary Pagan thought and experience. While other sorts of theologies exist within the Pagan family of religions, erotic theologies are prevalent. A very basic description of Pagan erotic theology suggests that a paired duality of energies, traditionally understood as feminine and masculine in nature, animate the cosmos. The interplay of these energies is the source of the joyful, creative, and fertile dynamic of the cosmos. They are embodied as the Goddess and Horned God, in the living qualities of nature, as well as in the masculine and feminine aspects of human beings. Pagan theologian Christine Kraemer describes this energy of life as the "union of the God and the Goddess, seen as primal powers whose interactions underlie the ongoing creation of the universe."[466] Religious cultures that draw on erotic theological metaphors often take a positive approach to sexuality, seeing it as a way to participate in these divine energies. The Charge of the

---

466. Christine Hoff Kraemer, *Seeking the Mystery: An Introduction to Pagan Theologies* (Englewood, CO: Patheos Press, 2012), Kindle e-book. See "Erotic Theology and its Origins," chapter 4.

Goddess suggests this connection between erotic cosmology, ritual, and sexuality: "ye shall be naked in your rites; and ye shall dance, sing, feast, make music and love, all in my praise."[467] By celebrating, raising, focusing, and channeling this life energy, humans partake in the divine cosmos and participate in its creative power. In human experience, Kraemer writes, the erotic "describes a state of intimate, embodied relationships that puts the participants in touch with the flow of divine life force."[468] In this way, sexual energy may be experienced as sacred divine energy, the body and its sexuality as ways to experience the divine.[469]

Heathens make use of these erotic themes in their discourse criticizing Wiccans as sensuous and indulgent. While this critique may over-simplify or misrepresent Pagan approaches to sexuality, it has become a boundary used to distinguish a Heathen approach to the self. Heathens have a basic understanding of the cosmos that rests on a decidedly different theological metaphor—the dynamic energy of the past. Struggle, not sexuality, is a sort of rapture that sanctifies the Heathen body, defining a decidedly non-erotic theology. Instead, the connection of the body to the past is emphasized. The human body consists of, is shaped by, and is intimately connected to the past. In this Heathen sort of embodiment, the body becomes holy and healthy through its connection to the mythological past in the divine capacities given by the gods. Human beings participate in the ancestral past through the influence of *ørlög*, *wyrd*, and *hamingja*, as well as other aspects of the soul. Of particular interest in the Ask and Embla story is the phrase "without fate," a reading of the Old Norse *ørlöglausa* in strophe seventeen.[470] The words "fate"

---

467. Doreen Valiente, "The Charge of the Goddess," *The Doreen Valiente Foundation* website, www.doreenvaliente.org/Doreen-Valiente-Poetry-11.php.

468. Ibid.

469. Clifton, *Her Hidden Children*, 65.

470. Zoëga, *A Concise Dictionary of Old Icelandic*, s.v. "or-lygi"; Cleasby and Vigfusson, *An Icelandic-English Dictionary*, s.v. "Örlög." These three concepts appear throughout the book. The Old Norse "*ørlög*" is a composite of two words: the prefix "*ör-*" designating "old" or "primal," and the noun "*lög*" meaning "law." The word is translated as "primal law" or "fate," though Heathens prefer to use the ON term. Wyrd, from the Old English *wyrd*, cognate to the Old Norse *urðr*, is a closely related term. It functions as both a philosophical concept and a mythological being. *Urðr* is one of the Norns, three numinous beings who care for the world tree Yggdrasil and carve or weave the events of human lives. Heathens use the term wyrd in a more impersonal sense to indicate the past—what has been and how the past shapes emerging events. The Old Norse hamingja is commonly translated as "luck" by

or "destiny" tend to have future-looking implications, as if there is a future written or woven for each individual. For Heathens, the word has more to do with looking backward: ørlög refers to the law or pattern that has been laid down by the past, layers of past that now nourish and shape the individuals who grow from them. This might call to mind a forest floor, upon which leaves have fallen year after year, building up layers of rich detritus from which new plants and trees grow. In some sense, the living trees are new formulations of the past, rooted and arising from that soil formed by layers of fallen leaves. It is the connection to the past, having a past, that creates the individual. A person's nature is found by looking into the past, the line of events and deeds that shaped one's life and give it meaning. We might read the phrase *ørlöglausa* just as validly as "empty of or lacking a past." Without a past, these two trees are without the defining characteristic of life. Identity, power, and purpose arise in connection to the past. In fact, we might understand American Heathenry in one sense as a longing for ørlög, a search for a meaningful past.

For some Heathens, these different ways of constructing identity have become a point of religious distinction, an easy way of contrasting the Heathen self from the "fluffy bunny" Wiccan self. I saw this contrast enacted at a Heathen event that took place at a Midwestern Pagan campground. Holding a Heathen event at a Pagan campground seems a perfectly natural thing to do. The campground is secluded and already prepared to protect the alternative religious practices of its guests. On this occasion, however, the campground facilities became a means for Heathens to highlight and perform their perceived differences with other sorts of Pagans. Just prior to the ritual of land-taking, which opened the event, the camp organizers held a short orientation during which they explained the shower house situation.[471] The event leader described how the shower houses at this particular campground

Heathens and refers to an ancestral power that guides, protects, and empowers the life of the individual. See Cleasby and Vigfusson, *An Icelandic-English Dictionary*, s.v. "Urðr," and "hamingja."

471. Land-taking is a ritual by which Heathens claim rights to a piece of land. Modeled on descriptions in several Icelandic sagas, the ritual involves walking the perimeter of the land with fire. Participants at this event formally opened the gathering by presenting a torch at each compass point around the camp, declaring their peaceful intent, and petitioning the land spirits for their goodwill.

were not gender specific: the shower house consisted of one room with several showerheads in which men and women showered together. The fact that this particular campground had been a nudist resort goes some way in explaining the shower house. However, the arrangement in itself is not entirely unknown for Pagan campgrounds.[472] S. Zohreh Kermani, in her book *Pagan Family Values*, describes a similar shower house at another Pagan campground with "a half dozen showerheads in a large communal room in which the only semblance of privacy is one small curtained showerhead in a corner. Both rooms are used by people of all genders, except for certain designated hours each day when the two shower rooms are gender-segregated."[473] From shower houses to skyclad rituals, Paganism tends to be a religious culture that supports those cultivating a more open approach towards nudity and sexuality, "Pagans tend to hold and proudly proclaim relatively positive, progressive, and liberal views on sexuality, alternative sexual lifestyles, and sexual ethics."[474] Kermani paints with a broad brush here. Those familiar with contemporary Paganism understand that participants take diverse approaches toward sexuality and the body. Attitudes and practices have shifted as the movement has grown. She expresses a more generalized feel for this world-affirming religious culture and its level of comfort with the human body.[475] Pagans are not the first to approach sexuality in affirming ways. Sexual liberation has strong roots in secular movements and philosophies as well. Scholars have shown that these secular movements have influenced the development of Pagan views of sexuality.[476] As American culture was entering a period of more openness to sexual

---

472. Jon Niccum, "Gaea Retreat: Music, Environmental Awareness, Spirituality Collide in New Festival," *Lawrence.com*, July 18, 2008, www.lawrence.com/news/2008/jul/18/music_environmental_awareness_spirituality_collide/.

473. S. Zohreh Kermani, *Pagan Family Values: Childhood and the Religious Imagination in Contemporary American Paganism* (New York: New York University Press, 2013), PDF ebook, 176.

474. Ibid., 174. "Skyclad" refers to ritual nudity occasionally used in some forms of Wiccan practice.

475. Nikki Bado-Fralick, *Coming To the Edge of the Circle: A Wiccan Initiation Ritual* (Oxford: Oxford University Press, 2005), 99–101. Bado-Fralick reflects on the cultural place of nudity in Wicca and the dynamics of tradition, personal preference, sexuality, experience, and concerns about objectification and power that complicate it.

476. Chas S. Clifton, "Sex Magic or Sacred Marriage: Sexuality in Contemporary Wicca," in *Sexuality and New Religious Movements*, eds. Henrik Bogdan and James R. Lewis (New York: Palgrave Macmillan, 2014), 149–63.

expression in the 1960s, Wicca provided a theological approach that sacralized sexuality. The result was a religious culture with a particularly celebratory approach to the human body. Nudity can be used to enact a sense of unity with nature or as an expression of freedom from repressive social norms, and sexuality can represent a potential way into the divine. As Kraemer writes, "lovemaking and celebration can be devotional acts," whether they are performed literally or symbolically.[477] Similarly Sarah Pike notes that contemporary Pagan communities "see the body as sacred and beautiful, a site for healing and a source of power" and the diverse spectrum of sexuality as potentially healing and liberating.[478] Rediscovering, reclaiming, and expressing sexuality is one mode by which Pagans construct a more holistic and sacred embodied identity, experience their spirituality and magical nature, and heal from the suppressive and dysfunctional identities of modern life. In some sense, the shared shower house may reflect an ethos in touch with the erotic dynamic that animates and flows through life and nature.

For the Heathens at this event, the shower house presented a problem to be solved, not a religious solution to be enjoyed. The event leader shared a ribald comment and everyone got a laugh imagining Wiccans frolicking together in the showers. The leader then went on to explain that during this *Heathen* event, the shower house was to be strictly gender segregated: women-only during even hours and men-only during odd hours. He then warned the Heathen participants that campers in other areas of the grounds may be engaging in public nudity. Should they encounter someone wandering around in the nude, he suggested that they "just be polite."[479] Heathens look on this proclivity for displays of nudity and sexuality with attitudes ranging from bemusement to active hostility, a tendency also noted by Snook during her fieldwork. "Heathens," she writes, "do not hesitate to mock the liberal stance that Wicca takes toward sexuality and the body."[480] One Heathen leader described a Pagan event he attended in which the ritual leader was completely nude except for a jester hat and a set of bells tied around his penis.[481] From his perspective, the display of

477. Kraemer, *Seeking the Mystery*, chapter 4.
478. Pike, *New Age and NeoPagan Religions*, 137–39.
479. Field notes by author, Kansas, 2012.
480. Snook, *American Heathens*, 45.
481. Anonymous, telephone interview by author, February 2015.

nudity did not facilitate a genuine religious experience but reduced religiosity to a joke. It suggested a dysfunctional approach to religious identity, one that exhibited the pitfalls of the modern age. The event became a decisive turning point on his religious journey in which he rejected the contemporary Pagan scene and embraced Heathenry as something different. This sort of discourse creates strong boundaries distinguishing Heathenry from other ways of being Pagan, particularly concerning how Heathens construct the self. As reflected in the discourse about the shower house, the issues of nudity, sexuality, and theology of the body are fault lines, points where the American Heathen and Wiccan-influenced ideologies diverge.

The erotic self of Wicca and the past-oriented self of Heathenry are themes broadly characterizing their respective religious cultures and reflective of the ideological tributaries that contributed to each. Yet in the larger picture, these two positions represent two points around which lie a diversity of approaches to theology and identity construction. Regina Smith Oboler has shown that the whole paradigm of erotic theology is in transition.[482] The gender essentialism and hetero implications of Gardnerian theology have been challenged as newer Pagan perspectives on cosmology, magic, and sexuality have gained greater prominence. In response, the erotic metaphor has been evolving and growing in complexity instead of remaining static as Heathens often take it to be. Wiccans and practitioners of Witchcraft also draw on non-erotic theological resources for religious identity, such as meditation and breath control, as well as past-oriented memes such as political/psychological identification with women oppressed during the Burning Times or with a primal European goddess religion.[483] Meanwhile other streams of Paganism, Druidry for instance, represent long-standing Pagan traditions in which eroticism does not act as the primary religious metaphor. Interestingly, tensions between Heathenry and Druidry did not arise as issues during my research. In fact I met several Heathens with a dual-trad Heathen/Druid identity.

---

482. Regina Smith Oboler, "Negotiating Gender Essentialism in Contemporary Paganism," *The Pomegranate: The International Journal of Pagan Studies* 12, no. 2 (2010): 159–84.

483. Bado-Fralick, *Coming to the Edge of the Circle*, 79. Bado-Fralick describes breath control as "the gateway to all other embodied ritual practices within my lineage of Wicca."

While it is important to acknowledge that there is just nothing like the Great Rite in Heathenry, that is not to say that erotic metaphors are entirely absent from Heathen thought. Odin is well known for his own sexual exploits. Loki mixes shape-shifting and gender-bending with interesting sexual consequences. Heathenry has a Lord and Lady, Frey and Freyja, who are closely associated with fertility and sexuality, making possible an erotic theology similar to that of Gardnerian Wicca. Davidson suggests that Thor and Sif may represent a similar pair of fertility gods.[484] Although Heathens are well aware of these theological possibilities, they remain secondary or tertiary to other emphases. There are also many Heathens who take more progressive views on sexuality, gender, and family, reflecting the influence of Wicca and Witchcraft tributaries. The clash between the AFA and more progressive groups such as Heathens United Against Racism during the summer of 2016 occurred in part because of the resurgence of gender essentialism within the AFA's ideology. At issue was the AFA's Facebook comment referencing "our feminine ladies, our masculine gentlemen," which seemed to reify traditional notions of gender and sexuality in ways that felt marginalizing to many Heathens. As we have seen, these sorts of Heathens have found a stronger voice and have spoken out against a gender essentialist religious vision. Meanwhile the AFA and other Heathens influenced by the folkish/Traditionalist tributary continue to express more essentialist views, valorizing heterosexuality, and patriarchal gender roles. Among the racist fringe, the 14 Words Heathens who mix Norse religious themes with white supremacist ideology, there may even be the possibility of a racist erotic theology that sees the coupling of white Heathen bodies as sacred, or sanctifying, in contrast to other inter-racial configurations that are interpreted as defiling. Such opinions have been decidedly rejected by the majority of those who pursue the old ways.

## Embodying the Past

This past-oriented self of Heathenry has its own rituals and practices by which it is constructed and reified. Heathen thinking about the self and its relationship to the world begins with the individual

---

484. Davidson, *Gods and Myths*, 84.

striving or struggling to build and maintain a life in a dangerous and sometimes hostile world. The individual and her autonomy are of paramount importance in both anthropology and ethics. I have often heard Asatruar state that they do not bow to anyone, even the gods. Gundarsson declares that "the Gods are most pleased with someone who stands on their own two feet. This is one of the reasons for the Asatru 'rule' that we do not kneel to the Gods during our ceremonies."[485] A pronounced libertarian value exists in contemporary Asatru, an attitude that corresponds well with the historical American virtue of rugged individualism expressed by the famous Gadsden Flag, the Revolutionary War banner that stated "Don't Tread On Me." Several of the Nine Noble Virtues emphasize the importance of individuality, especially the virtue of free-standing or self-reliance, described as "individualism or free will, the freedom to be one's own man (or woman) . . . to make their own way in the world and not to lean on others for their . . . needs."[486]

The free-standing individual does not burden others with his or her own needs and responsibilities: not their families, communities, nor their gods. Nor do individuals easily subordinate themselves to others. This value that may account for the sentiment against national organizations as well as some of the divisive behavior and in-fighting that has troubled the Asatru movement. In a talk given at an event on the East Coast, an influential Asatru leader addressed this problematic dynamic,

> The same things that draw us to this faith: the individuality, the freedom, the resistance for a central authority, those things are also the characteristics that can divide us. Our ancestors had this issue as well. You read the sagas, there were a lot of blood-feuds going on around the very tiny island of Iceland. And our ancestors were very first warriors, but whenever they got together as an army to fight another army, consistently they did not win. The Battle of Ashdon, they lost; the battle of Stamford Bridge they lost, because they were unable to act as a cohesive unit, as a community.[487]

Individuality is a significant, but not an uncontested, value. As important as individualism may be, the individual as commonly

---

485. Lewis Stead, and Raven Kindred, *The Raven Kindred Ritual Book*, 1995. See "Self Reliance" in chapter 8 "The Values of Asatru," www.ravenkindred.com/Ravenbok.html.
486. Gundarsson, *History and Lore*, 536.
487. Jarl, oral presentation, audio recording by author, Pennsylvania, July 2012.

conceived is weak, isolated from others who can provide companionship and aid in the struggle for life. Weakness, as mentioned in the quote above, produces defeat. As the Viking battle tactic of the shield wall indicates, the individual is strengthened by those around him. So too the Heathen vision of the individual is buttressed by a number of other aspects of selfhood that connect the individual to the dynamic past (see figure 12). For instance, the striving of the individual must be directed by an ethic that allows deeds of worth to be pursued. Individuality works best when accompanied by other community-oriented virtues, such as truth, honor, loyalty, self-discipline, hospitality, and industriousness, also part of the Nine Noble Virtues. Practicing these nine virtues together produces a strong robust individualism conditioned by openness to others and a willingness to extend mutual support to those around oneself. This sort of life is an ideal sought in the tension between individualism on one hand and the well-being of the community on the other, expressed in the values of kindred and frith. A strong approach to individualism tempers that virtue with the interests of the community.

The Heathen vision of the self does not stop with this rugged individualism. Heathens reject the modern notion of the individual as an autonomous human being bound in time and space, deriving their anthropology neither from the Lockean *tabula rasa* nor the Sartrean individual creating herself from her own choices.[488] The anthropological vision of Asatru is decidedly more complex. The individual may be against the world, but is never alone in the world. Instead, a specific individual could be thought of as the point of the spear: while the spear's point is of immediate concern, it is everything *behind* the point, the weight and heft of the shaft, which allows the spear to be aimed, thrown, and to strike effectively. What is *behind* the point gives the spear its power and effectiveness. Just so, it is what is *behind* the individual that gives an individual life its strength. Additional metaphysical realities within the Heathen soul complex enhance individuality and connect people to the past in ways that matter.

---

488. Simon Blackburn, "Existentialism," and "Individualism," in *The Oxford Dictionary of Philosophy* (New York: Oxford University Press, 2005), 125, 184.

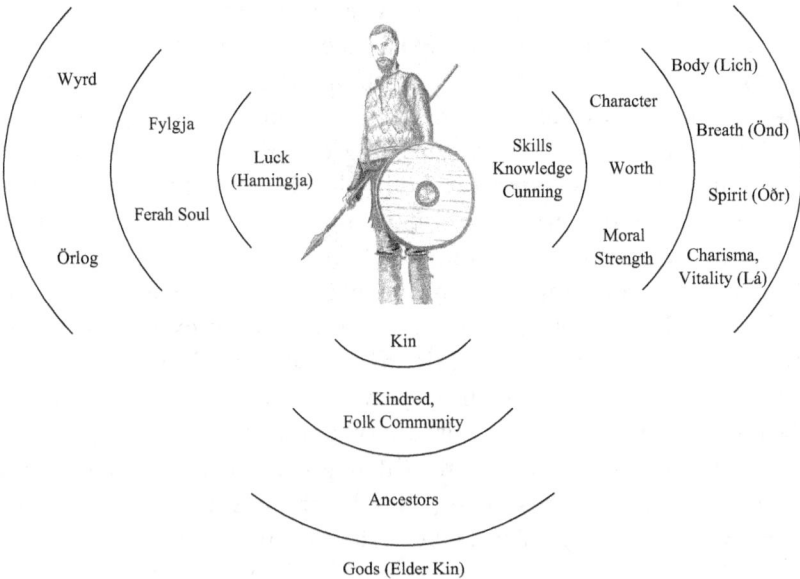

Figure 12. Heathen Soul Complex and Its Connections to the Past. (Image of warrior by Emily Hecker, used with permission.)

## *The Heathen Soul Complex*

The Heathen self-concept posits an enhanced individualism, a soul complex that strengthens the individual being in his or her struggle to thrive in the world. A soul complex is a composite soul of many integrated parts, "multiple spiritual essences that serve different functions."[489] The gods imbued Ask and Embla, and human beings more generally, with powerful natural capabilities, which the individual must seek to improve, develop, and master. This concept of the soul complex has generated significant interest among Heathens, resulting in a good deal of work to reconstruct a Norse Pagan understanding of soul anatomy. Paxson, who has written much on the topic herself, refers to this type of theology as hyge-cræft, the study of the soul.[490] Heathen scholars have mined

---

489. Kraemer, *Seeking the Mystery*, chapter 4, "The Multiple Soul."

490. Diana L. Paxson, "Hyge-Cræft: Working with the Soul in the Northern Tradition," *Idunna*, no. 28 (1995), also available at https://hrafnar.org/articles/dpaxson/norse/hyge-craeft.

the Lore to develop a systematic account from ancient Norse sources. This soul anatomy work seems somewhat abstract at times, a perennial problem of systematic theology, with Heathens identifying and discussing nine or more souls, or soul-parts, from various sources and with varying degrees of clarity. These writers draw on numerous sources in both Old Norse and Old English to create their own maps of the soul, and to develop a vocabulary of soul-parts. In my discussion that follows, I am not seeking to systematize a comprehensive model of my own. I do not attempt to fully describe or replicate any of those soul complexes constructed by Heathen authors. Rather I describe a schema showing how the Heathen soul complex illustrates a type of identity-building tied to the past. Because of this, my discussion of the soul complex will look rather different from those of the theologians. Heathen discourse on the soul complex seems to engage with the past and manifest it in three ways: as an aspect of the body, as a living force or energy, and as a network of familial relationships. Within each of these dynamic categories, I introduce various soul-parts discussed by Heathens.

Heathens have been exploring ideas about the soul for over thirty years. In the late 1980s, Thorsson published a robust model of a body–soul–mind complex in his *A Book of Troth*, writing that "the Germanic peoples had a bewildering number of names for the 'soul,' 'spirit,' 'mind.'"[491] For Thorsson and Heathen scholars following him, the detailed Norse vocabulary of soul anatomy proves that the arch-Heathens had a sophisticated understanding of human nature. "That they had many [words]," writes Thorsson, "shows an intimate knowledge of the thing ... a deep understanding implicit in the very language." He goes on to identify several types of souls or aspects of the soul-complex. The material component of the soul is the body, the *lyke* or *lich*. It is closely related to the *hyde*, which is its shape or form, the energy field of the body. The body is animated by the *athem*, the "breath of life." What we might call "the mind" is made up of several souls: the *hugh*, "the intellectual and analytical" mind; the *myne*, which is the "well" of memory, both deep ancestral memory and the personal memories of the individual.

---

491. Edred Thorsson, *A Book of Troth* (Smithville, TX: Rúna-Raven Press, 2003), 56. Fifteen years later, Thorsson's work remained central to Heathen thinking. See also Gundarsson, *History and Lore*, 499. Gundarsson's discussion of the soul draws heavily on Thorsson's 1989 description, calling it the "most precise version of such a model."

*Wode* is the ecstatic state of mind, the soul of inspiration. Thorsson also describes two ancestral souls that attach to the individual. The *fetch*, frequently called the *fylgja* by other Heathen writers, is an ancestral spirit being, an entity that acts as a guardian of sorts. The second, *hamingja* or luck, is the storehouse of ancestral deeds and power.[492] Thorsson's terminology mixes Old English and Old Norse words to build up a picture of the soul. Although many of these concepts and soul words are comparable, later writings such as Gundarsson's *Our Troth* more clearly distinguish between two cultural models.[493] The components described by Thorsson remain the basic framework for Heathen discourse about human nature, though Heathen scholars have continued to develop more thorough and complex ideas.

Despite its rather abstract nature, discourse on the soul complex is not without its practical implications. Heathens working to create a robust contemporary understanding the self are identifying applications that could have an impact on mental and physical health, magical practice, ritual work, and ideas about death. Eric Sjerven, a goði and Heathen scholar, notes that "understanding the way the ancient Heathens viewed the soul will grant us deeper insight into the functioning of the mind, illnesses, and our own growth and development."[494] Among other things, he has in mind the growth of a specifically Heathen version of religious counseling informed by the intricacies of the soul complex. Along these lines, Kari Tauring, a völva or female staff-carrier and magic-worker in the Midwest, has been working for several years on physical and emotional healing techniques that combine scientific knowledge about brain function with a Heathen concept of the multiple soul.[495] Additionally, the concept of the multiple soul could have a bearing on the ongoing

---

492. Luck, *hamingja* in Old Norse, is an important metaphysical concept for Heathens, who understood it as an ancestral force that enables success in life. It is similar in function to *barakah* in the Sufi tradition, or anointing in the Christian Pentecostal tradition. However, unlike those examples, luck derives from the past, a storehouse of the accumulated noble deeds performed by one's ancestors.

493. Gundarsson, *History and Lore*, 499–508. Gundarsson includes a section on Anglo-Saxon soul lore and another on Norse soul lore.

494. Eric Sjerven, "Musings on the Heathen Soul Complex," *The Well*, January 24, 2013, http://word-weaver.tumblr.com/post/41411661902/soul-complex.

495. Tauring sums up her techniques under the rubric of Völva Stav, discussed further in chapter 8. More information about her work is available at http://karitauring.com/völva-stav/.

debate regarding the usage of sacred sites. One type of claim to those sites derives from the idea that contemporary Pagans have an ancestral link to ancient people buried at those sacred sites. Michael Cooper argues that Pagan ideas of reincarnation work against such claims: once reincarnated, an ancestor could no longer be thought of as in the gravesite.[496] However, the concept of the multiple soul suggests that the dead can inhabit multiple places simultaneously, with some parts of the soul in the spirit world and reincarnated into the world of the living, while other parts may indeed be in the ground. This work on multiple souls could potentially add an interesting twist to the legal debates on rights of use if Heathens could theologically substantiate a claim that ancestral souls continue to occupy those sites.

When we think of a soul complex, we might imagine a machine with many parts or an organic body with many organs working together. For Heathens, the soul complex is more like connective tissue, connecting the individual to the past, to entities and powers beyond itself. The soul complex might be thought of as roots sunk into the past, sustaining the individual by drawing nourishment into the present. First, we see the past manifested in the body. The body carries in itself the physical characteristics of the family line, spiritual characteristics such as character and moral values, knowledge and patterns of life stored up in us from our upbringing. The soul also contains essences of the ancestral past, connecting the individual to a living shieldwall, a network of familial relationships enmeshing the living and the dead. Heathens see the individual as born into concentric circles of relationships that are vital and definitive for identity. While some of these relational bonds are forged volitionally during one's life, the strength of this network lies in its connection to the past. Four levels of kinship provide continuity and support and supplement the individual life. These consist first of one's immediate kin and family relationships; second, "fictive kinships" or voluntary relationships of loyalty and friendship represented primarily by the Asatru kindred; third, ancestors and relationships with the living dead; and fourth, the gods, who are understood as "elder kin" to human beings. These relationships of kinship lend power and effectiveness to life, bulwarking individuals in their struggle for survival. So vital are these social relationships that a

---

496. Cooper, *Contemporary Druidry*, chapter 5, section titled "Contemporary Druids and Ancestors."

person can hardly be thought of apart from them. To be severed from this network is an unnatural and a highly undesirable state. It is to have a part of oneself torn off, literally a rending of the soul. Every individual is born into a web of relationships, linked to other beings in ways that are meant to bring strength and wholeness. Heathens believe that all humans come into the world carrying these active qualities of soul and ancestry. Relationships form a seamless and integral part of the self. In addition to this shieldwall of relationships, Heathens conceive of the past manifesting as a living force in the lives of individuals. Heathens commonly use religious terminology derived from the Lore such as wyrd, ørlög, and fylgja to identify and describe these aspects of the soul complex.

## Wyrd and Ørlög

I was sitting in a coffeehouse with Mika and Helga, the leaders of Well of Wisdom kindred. We were meeting for the first time after I had contacted them by email about attending one of their kindred's monthly meetings. They wanted to check me out, get to know me, and understand my motivations before granting further access to the kindred. Such a meeting is a standard part of Heathen culture—any kindred leader would expect to develop a relationship with a stranger before allowing them into kindred gatherings. After chatting awhile and understanding how new I was to Asatru, Mika looked at me grimly and warned me not to cross them. "This is not a religion of forgiveness," he said, shifting from a friendly to a serious even threatening tone. "Christians think that the past can be wiped away, that you can be forgiven and start from nothing. But that's not true. The past cannot be undone, it is always with you." Part of this was just Mika's dramatic flair, wanting to put a little fear into the newbie by driving home the hard edge of his faith. But his words were grounded in the Heathen cosmology defined by ørlög and wyrd. Like the idea of karma in Indic religions, these Heathen terms describe a world in which we cannot escape from our actions. The deeds of the past have consequences for the present.

These are related two concepts that, like many theological terms, are widely utilized but not always clearly defined.[497] In fact, Stephen

---

497. Snook, *American Heathens*, 213, 215. Snook's definitions of these terms show their ambiguity or interrelatedness in common Heathen usage.

McNallen tends to conflate these two terms as functional equivalents: ørlög an Old Norse term and wyrd from Old English both referring to the "fate we fashion for ourselves" out of the circumstances and conditions inherited from the past.[498] Most Heathens distinguish the two terms to indicate slightly different aspects of cosmology. The term *wyrd* is associated with *Urðr*, one of the mysterious Norns who are "responsible for shaping lives out of ørlög, the layers of the past."[499] Wyrd is the Norn, the past personified, the mythological Well where the past accumulates, and the Web, the interconnected energy field or matrix of actions past and present. For American Heathens, an important source for cosmology has been Bauschatz's book, *The Well and the Tree*.[500] Bauschatz's perspective has been formative for Heathens, who have treated it essentially as part of the Lore, wholeheartedly embracing its description of the pre-Christian Germanic worldview. The book's influence is felt in older works, such as Gundarsson's *Teutonic Magic* from 1990, as well as newer ones, like McNallen's 2015 *Asatru: A Native European Spirituality*. And most of the important Heathen authors across the Heathen ideological watershed incorporate it: Wódening, Paxson, Karlsdóttir, and Lafayllve to name a few, representing a remarkable continuity of usage. Bauschatz describes how the world tree Yggdrasil, which holds the Nine Worlds of Norse cosmology, grows from the Well of Wyrd. Actions done within the cosmos drip like dew from the leaves of the Tree and fall in the Well, creating a cosmic loop of wyrd. Wódening draws directly from Bauschatz in his description: "These actions form the seething layers of the past contained within the Well Tree. These actions also create an energy source which moves back through the Tree's root like water, to influence the present of the worlds within the Tree."[501] Wyrd is the fundamental cosmological energy and organizing principle in the worldview of Heathenry. It is the past as energy, the creative potential of the present moment, defining its limits but also giving rise to its possibilities.

---

498. McNallen, *Asatru*, 212, 207.

499. Arlea Æðelwyrd Hunt-Anschütz, "What Is Wyrd?" *Cup of Wonder* 5 (October 2001), www.wyrdwords.vispa.com/heathenry/whatwyrd.html.

500. Bauschatz, *The Well and the Tree*, 11. Bauschatz defines ørlög as "primal law . . . the earliest things laid down," the layers of past action. Wyrd is a more active principle that "governs the working out of the past into the present (or, more accurately, the working in of the present into the past)."

501. Wódening, *We Are Our Deeds*, 57.

Patricia Lafayllve takes care to clearly distinguish between ørlög, the layers of the past that are fixed, and wyrd, the dynamic and evolving present, the loose threads that are being woven and can be influenced by strong actions and will. Using the metaphor of a river, she describes ørlög as the river's watershed—the watershed is fixed, a given, it defines the essence and nature of the river. No matter what the river does, it cannot change its watershed. Wyrd, however, is like the river's channel—more fluid and pliable, liable to shift and change given a powerful enough event. Wyrd is what *ought* to happen given all the present factors if nothing acts to alter the movement and flow of events. However, most American Heathens do not see the wyrd as fixed and unchangeable. Powerful heroic ørlög may wield significant influence on the wyrd. Similarly, strong decisive actions can change patterns that have been set in the past, reworking the threads of wyrd, adding new layers of ørlög. In his discussion of fate, McNallen also brings up the interaction of will and wyrd, suggesting that an individual's or group's ability to affect the present depends on the strength of will. People can do whatever they want within the limitations of their strength to struggle and strive against the imposing structure and weight of the past. Not only McNallen, but many American Heathens with some consistency resist the idea of fate as a fixed destiny, instead emphasizing the ability of choice and actions to alter and shape the future. This too seems to come from Bauschatz, who takes care to differentiate wyrd from fate,

> The dangers in translating ørlög as "fate" are now clearer. To us, man's fate or destiny is likely to suggest present knowledge of what is to be, of what we believe to be preordained to occur. The Norns, however, speak of what has been, of what is already known. Explicit mention of predestination or foreknowledge is absent from the passages given and from the Norse universal myth itself.[502]

Over time, consistent disciplined action—the concentrated will and focus of one or many people— might substantially alter the wyrd. Some events such as Ragnarok take on an irresistible energy, to the point of inevitability. Once set in motion, they roll over even the most powerful. There is no concerted strength and effort in the Nine Worlds, not even that of the gods, to alter its course.

---

502. Bauschatz, *Well and the Tree*, 7.

Wyrd involves more than one's own choices. Decisions and actions have consequences for all those in proximity, whose lives are connected to one's own. The Norns weave the individual threads of wyrd together into the tapestry of the past. This "web of wyrd" reflects the deeper principle of cosmic interconnection. The decisions, actions, and events caused by others affect the conditions and context within which one's wyrd is woven. Heathens by and large would be completely comfortable with the allusions or comparisons to karma. In fact, a strong correspondence exists between the concepts of ørlög and wyrd and the Indic/Buddhist concepts of karma and *pratītyasamutpāda*, or dependent co-arising. No surprise, some Heathens argue. Those concepts are the shared inheritance from the religious world of the Proto-Indo-Europeans.[503] Like Buddhists, Heathens point out that accepting the concept of interconnection necessitates ethical considerations, though compassion for all beings is rarely one of them.

> With an understanding of wyrd comes a great responsibility. If we know that every action we take (or fail to take, for that matter) will have implications for our own future choices and for the future choices of others, we have an ethical obligation to think carefully about the possible consequences of everything we do.[504]

Heathens tend to guard their wyrd. They avoid crossing threads and conjoining wyrds in a careless or inadvertent fashion.

Many Heathens describe ørlög as something like one's personal past, one's own strand of wyrd specific to each individual being, "our contribution to the wyrd," as Heathen theologian Sara Axtell puts it.[505] Ørlög is the past laid down by actions, choices, and deeds of one's family line. It is inherited and intimately shapes the life of the individual, a thread woven by one's ancestors that forms the individual in all his or her specificity.[506] In this sense, our identity is strongly tied to the past. Generations of learned behavior within a family and the habitual patterns of action through time by social groups are passed to each person. These patterns determine the

---

503. Thorsson, *Book of Troth*, 63; McNallen, *Asatru*, 87.
504. Hunt-Anschütz, "What Is Wyrd?"
505. Sara Axtell, "The Heathen Soul: A Balance of the Individual with the Collective," *Idunna*, no. 87 (Spring 2011): 18.
506. Snook, *American Heathens*, 160.

current conditions from which individuals live and make choices.[507] The concept of ørlög, the primal law, indicates that the past is a fixed and inherited reality. An individual cannot easily escape its consequences or be severed from its influence. A powerful ørlög built from a history of family success, status, and effective relational patterns may work to one's personal advantage in life. In this sense, ørlög is a gift, the true family inheritance — the personality traits, skills, insight, and wisdom from the ancestors brought into the present as a resource for us. Thorsson expresses this view when he writes that "the great THEN is there to strengthen our hands and sharpen our blades to be here in the NOW and to enable us to go forward with good speed."[508] At the same time, it can cripple, limit, and be painful for us as well, as the traumas of the past remain with us, embedded in our ørlög. One's "story" is part of what Heathens mean by ørlög — the stories passed down that inform our self-concept, who we are and where we came from. But ørlög also works at a deeper, precognitive level. The forces of the dim past acting upon us, the inner strengths and foibles that we carry around and live with every day, are aspects of reality that operate outside of the range of ordinary awareness. The deepest influences and motivators in our lives may be hidden deep in our ørlög, the flaws, traumas, and gifts that stay beneath the level of consciousness, yet come out in actions and patterns of life. Yet ørlög is not only psychological. It is a corpospiritual concept that manifests in ways we might not expect. Ørlög is written into nature and the landscape, whose shape, appearance, and characteristics have been drastically altered by the actions of living beings. The strip-mined landscape in the Appalachian Mountains and the farm developed into condominiums and strip malls are corporeal manifestations of ørlög, as well as the community garden in the middle of urban sprawl, or a beautifully terraced apple orchard. These affect the possibilities of the present and shape our wyrd. Our own bodies are visible ørlög — the inheritance of our ancestry sculpted into the lines of our faces, the shapes of our hands, the way we walk, passed along through the generations from grandparents, to parents, to children, and so on.

As Heathenry matures as a religious movement, so does its conception of the self. Many Heathens are moving beyond the

---

507. Wódening, *We Are Our Deeds*, 57. Paxson, *Essential Ásatrú*, 137.
508. Edred Thorsson "The Edge of the Sword," *Idunna*, no. 4 (1989): 3-4.

hotheaded Viking ideal of early Asatru and contemplating what it may mean to build and protect healthy ørlög. For instance, in his essay "Protecting Our Heathen Children from Divorce," Mark Stinson discusses the role of ørlög in Heathen ethical decision-making. He lists several reasons to avoid divorce but, most compellingly for our discussion, he argues that divorce damages the ørlög of one's children. Divorce entails breaking an oath that has been spoken into the Well of Wyrd. He argues that "if they break their marriage oath ... their Luck will wane ... and they will likely bring unnecessary and disruptive complexity and chaos into their Wyrd." Not all Heathens would agree with Stinson's conclusion, though he reaches it by reasoning from these cosmological principles. I have met other Heathens who have made oaths to refrain from alcohol for periods of time in order to alter that thread of ørlög. Thinking of ørlög as thread woven on a spindle, one could say that negative, harmful, or antisocial actions introduce knots, frays, or weak points in the thread of ørlög. Children who inherit this damaged ørlög will struggle with disruptive and dysfunctional patterns in their own lives. Thus, deeds may have metaphysical consequences that are serious and multi-generational, a type of soul damage defined by a Heathen understanding of human nature. Stinson's ethical solution reflects the belief that actions have consequences: "So, honor your Oaths. Protect your Wyrd. Preserve your Luck. Pass good Ørlög onto your children. If you find yourself having marital problems, tackle the challenge like Heathens tackle any challenge ... intelligently, fearlessly, generously, honorably, and with lots of hard work."[509] Here again we see the role that struggle plays in shaping the Heathen self-concept. People build luck and ørlög by striving nobly against life's challenges. In turn, these resources of the soul come to the aid of the individual in the struggles he or she faces. While damaged ørlög can be rebuilt, it "takes years of right action and deeds of worth. That is how one repairs one's Ørlög, and becomes a man of Worth."[510] Here we see the working out of an ethic built from Heathen worldview principles and consistently applied.

We are only aware of a tiny bit of the wyrd and ørlög that shapes the conditions of our reality and flows around us and within us. Divination is a tool that Heathens use to sharpen and deepen their

---

509. Mark L. Stinson, "Protecting Our Heathen Children from Divorce," in *Heathen Families: Fables and Essays*, 50.

510. Stinson, *Heathen Gods*, 122.

## The Self and the Struggle of Life

awareness of these forces. The runes are cast and consulted to search for the shape of wyrd in the present moment, the choices that are in play, and the specific forces that are influencing our lives. The runes also give insight into the internal psychological dynamics that may be cloudy to us, bringing to awareness aspects of ourselves upon which we can act. In the months before and after the death of my father in the summer of 2016, I found myself struggling to move forward, unable to get significant work done and feeling emotionally walled-off. One day while sitting at my child's sports practice and feeling particularly low, I remembered that I had downloaded Tauring's rune app on my smartphone. The app was sophisticated, with three different types of castings all linked to Tauring's rune interpretations. I pulled up the app and choose the Odin casting, in which a single rune tile is selected. The rune that revealed itself was Isa, the ice rune. The simple vertical stroke of Isa accurately diagnosed the frozen emotional and psychological pattern in which I found myself.[511] This confirmation provided much needed comfort. Soon after, looking for insight in how to break free from this frozen state, I again tried the app. Drawing one tile like before, I turned over Eiwaz (see figure 13).[512]

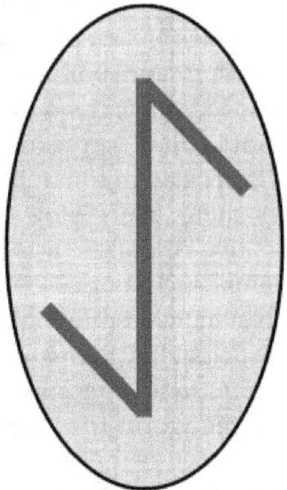

Figure 13. Eiwaz Rune.

511. The rune *isa* is one of the most well attested of the runes historically.
512. This is the "ė" or "ei" rune, reconstructed as *ī(h)waz* or *eihwaz*. It is commonly written as Eihwaz by Heathens, or Eiwaz as Tauring names it in this case.

As an answer to my question, the shape of this rune in the Elder Futhark seemed particularly instructive.[513] Tauring associates the rune with the yew, the world tree linking the nine worlds. Eiwaz begins with a single vertical stroke, simply the Isa rune, then adds an angled stroke at the top and bottom, connecting both to the world above and the world below. In this case, Tauring's app functioned as a stopgap, providing enough interpretative resources to guide my thinking in the moment of crisis. A skilled rune caster takes the information supplied by the runes and acts as a spiritual counselor, interpreting it and making recommendations to actualize this knowledge in the life of the querent. This personal example illustrates one way that Heathens may use the runes to gain insight into these cosmological forces of the past. Because of this unknown and mysterious quality of wyrd and ørlög, Heathens use forms of divination to "see" the connections between past and present, to visualize how the past is unfolding and influencing the present. Future decisions and actions are best made by first understanding and learning to act within the dynamic shape of the past.

### Ferah: The Tree Soul

Written into the account of the Ask and Embla story is the implication that human beings are deeply related to trees. As noted above, ancient Greek writers and philosophers have assumed a similar thing. Aristotle conceives of the human being as composed of multiple souls or a soul complex, one of which is the nutritive or vegetative soul.[514] The vegetative soul represents the basic living property that all beings share, and bestows on living beings their reproductive and appetitive impulses. It is part of human nature that is shared with plants, such as trees. Heathens approach the tree/human connection somewhat differently. The human body is like a tree. Humans participate in the natural world through this close connection with trees, and in cosmic nature by the further analogy with Yggdrasil, the world tree. Carole Cusack notes that

---

513. "Futhark" is an acronymic term designating a runic alphabet. The term is derived from the first six runic letters: *fehu, *ūruz, *þurisaz, *ansuz, *raidō, and *kēnaz. The Elder Futhark, consisting of twenty-four runes, was used prior to the ninth century CE. Linguistic and cultural changes eventually led to the adaptation of other futharks, such as the Gothic and Old English runic alphabets. The Younger Futhark was a Scandinavian futhark consisting of sixteen runes.

514. Aristotle, *De Anima* 2.4.

this tree/human/cosmos homology is a prevalent feature of Indo-European mythology and ritual.[515] She develops the theme in detail in the Norse sacred stories, showing important resonances among the creation stories, the sacrifice of Odin on Yggdrasil, the fate of Yggdrasil in Ragnarok, and other mythic instances.

Völkisch thinkers took a different approach to the human/tree homology in their concept of *Dauerwald*, "eternal forest."[516] They theorized that as the individual tree was part of the forest, so the human individual was part of the nation. The forest/nation, both seen as organic and perpetual entities, had lives and identities all their own, greater than the transitory individuals of which they were composed. Furthermore, völkisch thought entailed that the Dauerwald should consist only of native trees, with foreign or invasive species eliminated. At one level, these ideas are ecological in nature. They envision the forest as an integrated ecosystem, which biologists have since proven to be the case. As a system of forest management, the approach elevated the health of forests over commercial and economic concerns. However, the ecology was entwined with the racism and Social Darwinism of the völkisch context. Nazi propaganda exploited the homology to encourage "their ideal of a classless, racially pure, and 'eternal' *Volksgemeinschaft* or national community" and to legitimize excising from German society what they considered foreign, weak, and sick.[517]

Winifred Rose Hodge, a Heathen theologian who has done a great deal of work on the soul-complex, takes another approach. She goes on to develop this homology *within* the human being. She examines implications of the tree soul, what she calls the *ferah* soul in human beings.[518] She begins, as many Heathen scholars do, with linguistics, sampling words in various Germanic languages. She borrows *ferah* from Old High German, translating it as "life-soul" and relates it to other words, such as Old Norse *fjörr* (tree) and *fjör* (soul) and Old English *feorh* (soul), to indicate a relationship between the concepts of tree, soul, and body. This tree soul is expressed mythologically

---

515. Carole M. Cusack, *The Sacred Tree: Ancient and Medieval Manifestations* (Newcastle upon Tyne: Cambridge Scholars, 2011), ebook, 12, 147-70.

516. Michael Imort, "Eternal Forest—Eternal Volk: The Rhetoric and Reality of National Socialist Forest Policy," in *How Green Were the Nazis?*, 43.

517. Ibid., 56, 52.

518. Winifred Hodge Rose, "The Ferah Full-Soul Born of Trees and Thunder: Heathen Soul Lore Part 2," *Idunna*, no. 68 (2006): 27-37.

in the human affinity for trees: the first two humans were brought to life from trees, and in the apocalyptic story of Ragnarok the two surviving human beings take refuge from the destruction in the world tree, returning to their essence. The ferah not only gives life but also connects humans with other living beings and the world around us, orienting humans to the natural world. Hodge writes that "a well-developed Ferah confers power and wisdom" attuned to the patterns of nature, and is perceptive, aware, and responsive to physical, social, and divine cues in the environment.[519] Rose poetically describes how the ferah creates a connection to supernatural powers as well: "Like trees, people are nourished and sustained by Gods of earth and sky. Like trees, we are sometimes struck by lightning—God-power, and if we do not burn to death, then we burn with life as conduits of God-power into the world."[520] Like the world tree that survives the conflagration of Ragnarok, so this soul lends to human beings a degree of perseverance against the pressures and stresses of the world. The ferah provides this strength by connecting humans to a deep past in the natural world rooted in their mythological origin.

### Fylgja and Hamingja

With the fylgja or fetch, the past is manifested as a sort of personal energy or being. It is another aspect of the soul complex understood as "an independent being attached to one's soul for life," a spirit guardian that is a manifestation of ancestral power.[521] The past comes to life and acts to protect their living kin. This spirit guardian protects and guides the individual, manifesting as a female spirit or a spirit animal that can be discovered and known through meditation and self-reflection. A related concept is *hamingja* or luck, another important anthropological concept of force or power that connects the individual to his or her ancestral inheritance. Luck is made from the cumulative deeds of one's ancestors that shape that quality and potential reflected in one's life. Lafayllve calls it "a kind of ancestral or 'folk soul' that flows from generation to generation, every

---

519. Ibid., 35–36.
520. Ibid., 37.
521. Gundarsson, *History and Lore*, 502; also field notes taken by author, Minnesota, 2012.

member of the family contributing to it with their actions in life."[522] We have this modern notion of luck as the experience of "things going our way," our daily lives somehow enhanced by moments of ease, fortuitous coincidence, or unexpected lucky breaks. This colloquial idea is a reflection of the Heathen understanding of luck as a metaphysical force attached to human souls that facilitates their efforts and makes their way through life more easy and productive. Krasskova explains the effects of luck this way, "In many ways, our Hamingja determines the quality of our lives, the degree of difficulty we will have to expend to reach our goals, and our chances of success."[523] Luck is a characteristic of human beings, part of the soul, "our store of psychic power," as Gundarsson explains it, amplifying the individual's or community's efforts and striving in the world.[524] Luck is understood to be inherited from our ancestors, grown from the cumulative effect of their honorable deeds, "Hamingja is a reality that surges forth from the dense darkness of the ancient past . . . It is the sum-total of all . . . deeds done in the family line before . . . and moves through each person, and through each family."[525] Luck is a dynamic force that is continually being shaped. Heathens see themselves as building luck for their descendants through their own actions, "the luck we gather in our own lives gets folded into the family hamingja for our next generations."[526] Thinking about his own family, another Heathen writes,

> I am the father of a family; my wife is the mother of a family. In our children lies the entire hamingja-legacy of both our lines, and in us, the lines that came before us. In us gathers the whole family-soul to which our children belong . . . Through my wife and I, the ancestors watch over our children and join us in raising them and impart wisdom and protection to them.[527]

In this sense, both the fylgia and hamingja are also aspects of familial or ancestral religion. Both suggest that the family of the past

---

522. Lafayllve, *A Practical Heathen's Guide*, 60.
523. Krasskova, *Exploring the Northern Tradition*, 129.
524. Gundarsson, *History and Lore*, 506
525. Alfarrin, "Bringing Forth the Gods of My Kin" *Cauldron Born: The Journal of Hofstadr Hearth*, June 9, 2011, http://cauldronborn.blogspot.com/2011/06/bringing-forth-gods-of-my-kin-heathen.html.
526. Patricia Lafayllve, email to author, April 9, 2011.
527. Alfarrin, "Bringing Forth the Gods of My Kin."

is active in the present in the life of living people, enhancing our individual lives.

### *Ancestors*

If these soul-parts function as the metaphysical connection with the past, Asatru also strongly encourages an active practical connection between individuals and their ancestors. Ancestral veneration features prominently in the spiritual lives of many Asatruar. It is hard to find a Heathen who does not have a strong emotional connection to his or her ancestors and many will recount dreams and other religious experiences in which ancestors have played a role. For Lafayllve, this aspect of Asatru is similar to other religious traditions of ancestor worship. "Ancestor worship is probably the oldest form of religion in human history, so we Heathens are a lot like traditional cultures—we keep their mementos, remember them by telling their stories, and pray to them for guidance and support."[528] Perhaps Asatru is tapping into a broader cultural phenomenon. Tauring senses a crisis among contemporary Americans who are longing to strengthen their sense of identity by connecting to an ethnic past:

> There is a global urgency to identify, understand, and heal ourselves as individuals and as part of a cultural root group illustrated by the popularity of television shows about tracing DNA, migrations . . . Genealogy has become a national hobby. Americans have a deeper urgency because we are removed from the continent that holds the bones of our ancestors and the memories of the landscapes that contributed to the development of our various folksouls.[529]

Several American television shows, such as *Finding Your Roots with Henry Louis Gates Jr.* and *Who Do You Think You Are?*, are dedicated to telling lost stories of ancestors and uncovering forgotten family history.[530] Companies providing genetic services offer to reconnect

---

528. Lafayllve, email.
529. Kari Tauring, email to author, May 5, 2011.
530. The show *Finding Your Roots* is hosted by Harvard professor Henry Louis Gates, Jr. and produced by the Public Broadcasting Service. The National Broadcasting Company initially produced the show *Who Do You Think You Are?* from 2010 to 2012. It was picked up by the TLC network where it continued to run through 2015.

Americans to their lost ethnic and geographic past, reading the mystery of the DNA to tell the genetic story of their identity. Many Americans, not only Heathens, feel a sense of loss regarding their heritage and experience deep, even spiritual, emotions about connecting to their ethnic past. For instance, Vigen Guroian, an Orthodox Christian theologian, shares his emotional experience of returning to Armenia, the homeland of his ancestors, for the first time at the age of forty:

> I mean, the first time I ever stepped foot in Armenia, it was next to a mystical experience. I arrived early, early in the morning as the sun was coming up. I had flown in from Moscow, and I felt as if I landed on a different planet. Maybe it was just the climate or something, but there was something else going on inside of me. I've never had that, quite that experience again going back to Armenia. But that first time—I don't mean to make too much of it, collective memory or whatever it might be—but, yeah, it was like I returned home.[531]

This experience made him realize that he had been living in a state of "exile" from his Armenian identity.[532] This wording, indicating a state of being pulled out of or removed from a native context, vividly recalls Gidden's "dis-embedding" thesis. Guroian's experience of going to Armenia as a person of Armenian ancestry was a transcendent experience of homecoming, of discovering new dimensions of his identity by connecting to these ethnic or folk roots. Such journeys to a European homeland are not particularly common among American Heathens. Reasons for this include the difficulty of reliably tracing one's ancestry, connecting that ancestry to a specific geography, and of course issues of finances and time. However, for those who have been able, these experiences are often remarkably meaningful. Tauring is one of those who has traveled to reconnect to her ancestral home in Norway, her Mother roots as she calls it.[533] She has been able to visit the family's farm and to stay

---

531. Vigen Guroian, "Restoring the Senses: Gardening and Orthodox Easter," transcript, *On Being*, interview by Krista Tippett, April 21, 2011, www.onbeing.org/program/restoring-senses-gardening-and-orthodox-easter/transcript/4521#main_content. Quoted section begins at 35:58 minutes into the interview.

532. Guroian, interview.

533. Kari Tauring, "In the Footsteps of My Mothers," *Kari Tauring: Norse Roots Author, Educator, and Performer*, July 15, 2015, http://karitauring.com/in-the-footsteps-of-my-mothers/.

in the ancestral family home and longs to return to a particularly sacred place, the mountain where her great-great-grandmother's family lived. On those journeys to Norway, Tauring felt her ancestral memories coming alive and as an artist, she has written movingly of those experiences. Many of her poems and songs reflect on the power of standing in that ancestral homeplace.

Integral to this longing for ancestral roots is the search for meaning and personal identity, a discovery of "who we really are." For Heathens, the connection to the ancestral past becomes more than, or perhaps, other than genealogical in nature. In fact, for all their interest in ancestors, few Heathens I have met show more than a passing interest in genealogy. Instead, Asatruar seek out a sense of emotional connection with the familial past as well as living relationships with ancestral beings. Many can in fact describe significant experiences of relating to ancestors. And in each case, these experiences with ancestors serve to endow the person with strength, purpose, and direction for their lives. Ancestral veneration in Heathenry makes a significant contribution to religious identity: it bulwarks the sense of self by giving the individual an experience of connectedness, a family line from which comes strength and purpose. This sense is powerfully evoked in a moving story related at East Coast Thing in 2012, in which an adherent described being on the brink of suicide. In a moment of final despair, he called out to his ancestors. He described being immediately caught up in a vision in which an ancestor came to him and led him out of his apartment, through the city streets, to a playground that transformed into mystical landscape. While waiting there alone and in terror, he began to notice that other beings were gathering around him and sensed that these were supportive presences. He soon realized that these were his ancestors, encouraging him and lending him the spiritual strength to go on with life. When he awoke from his vision, he continued to feel their presence and knew he was not alone. His grief and loneliness lifted; the depression gradually faded away and he experienced a renewed sense of healing and wholeness. Now, he begins each day with a meditation to connect with the living presence of his ancestors and their strength.[534]

Experiences such as these provide affirmation and direction in the lives of Heathens. During a period of religious seeking, another

---

534. Field notes taken by author, Pennsylvania, 2012.

adherent described a dream that was vital to his journey into Asatru. In the dream he was outside alone in the middle of the night. He came across a group of Viking-like men who spoke a language he could not understand but accepted him into their fellowship. One of these warriors offered him a handshake and at once, he felt an emotional connection with this man. He followed the men to a beach where a large wooden ship had been pulled up on shore. There, they joined more warriors who were gathered around a fire. They began to pass around a horn of mead, a practice with which he had not been familiar before the dream:

> From what I remember, there was a loud thunder crack and I woke up in a cold sweat. It was like I had been sitting too close to the fire for too long and I still had that smoky smell in my nostrils. That just put this weird impression on me that nothing else ever had. Because I don't usually dream. And it wasn't like a dream; it was like I could seriously remember being there on this beach . . . I think that those men were my ancestors from long ago basically welcoming me home. I didn't feel like I as a stranger; I felt like I kinda belonged.[535]

The vague quality of the ancestral beings experienced by this adherent is notable. Almost all Heathens could name and discuss the impact of specific family members on their lives. However, the more important goal is emotional and psychological: a sense of belonging and connection with the familial past, a sense that one is known, encompassed, and supported by these family members. The emotional wholeness obtained from the ancestral experience is heard in the rhetoric of belonging and homecoming used by these adherents. While the two circumstances were quite different, these encounters with an ancestral past caused a change in self-identity, a deeper understanding of self as connected to a greater whole. For the Heathen adherents, the relationship with ancestral beings was a significant aspect of that greater self.

Heathens commonly integrate these sorts of experiences into their religious lives through the practice of ancestor veneration, facilitated by an ancestor altar in their home or other sacred space (see figure 14). The altar acts as a focal point for ancestral rites and

---

535. Dave Carron and Sandi Carron, "New to Asatru," *Ravencast* podcast, Episode 7, 2007, www.digital podcast.com/feeds/51432-ravencast-the-asatru-podcast?page=7. Quoted section appears 5:50–10:26 minutes into podcast.

Figure 14. Ancestor Altar at Lightning Across the Plains, 2012. (Photo by the author.)

practices, where adherents may display photos, give offerings, and engage in prayer. For instance, the ancestral altar maintained during the regional Lightning Across the Plains gathering was representative of this Heathen approach. Participants were encouraged to bring significant items to include on the altar for the weekend. Photographs placed on the altar represented ancestors who were personally significant to a participant's life, as seen on the left-hand side of the LATP altar in figure 14. Adherents would actively commune with these personalities, talking and praying to them, engaging in meditative acts of remembrance, speaking their names, and giving toasts to them with offerings of sacred mead or food. The bowl seen on the LATP altar in figure 14 acted as a receptacle for these offerings, facilitating these acts of communion and veneration. On the right-hand side, several small statutes or images are displayed. Figures such as these often represent the ancestoral line, including unnamed and unknown ancestors whom the adherent wants to honor. The LATP altar also included a book for recording thoughts, memories, and stories of one's ancestors.

Heathens often feel close to their ancestors through work and hobbies. I met Krueger at several Heathen events and got to know his reputation for home-brewing. He always had several varieties that he brought and shared with friends. When discussing his approach to brewing, the conversation quickly turned to ancestors. His ancestry, he said, included a long line of brewers, a connection apparent in his name, which he suggested was related in meaning to brewer or tavern-keeper in German. When he took up brewing, almost by accident, he said he immediately felt the presence of his ancestors. He now is an avid amateur brewer and sees the hobby as a religious practice.[536] Similarly, Thora describes how she feels connected to her ancestors while making jam:

> I'll tell you, the most spiritual thing I do is making jam . . . I have a canner that was my grandmother's and then my mother had it and I remember as a kid we would can strawberry jam in it. And then she gave it to me, so now I have it. I love it because it has so much history. And I definitely feel when I am making jam . . . my dísir are totally there. And they're keeping me company and giving me that positive vibe that's awesome, that only the dísir can give you.[537]

The dísir that Thora mentions are the female ancestors of her family line. The word derives from the Old Norse *dís*, plural *dísir*, with a wide domain of meaning from "sister" to "goddess."[538] Patricia Lafayllve, a gythja who has worked extensively with ancestral worship, describes the dísir as "helping spirits . . . traveling directly with their descendants, offering help, volunteering advice, and generally maintaining the family's hamingja."[539] The dísir enhance and support the individual in all these ways, providing companionship, wisdom, and guidance as well as protecting the hamingja or luck that produces positive momentum for daily life. Heathens tend to their dísir in various ways, including meditation, ritual, prayers, and offerings of food and drink at an ancestral altar. In an ancestral ritual I observed on a couple of different occasions on both the East and West coasts, Lafayllve guided participants to connect with ancestors by making use of Heathen practices like

---

536. Field notes taken by author, Pennsylvania, 2012.
537. Thora, interview by author, Kansas, 2011.
538. Zoëga, *A Concise Dictionary of Old Icelandic*, s.v. "dís."
539. Lafayllve, *A Practical Heathen's Guide*, 60.

galdr, meditation, and offerings of mead.[540] The "o" rune, Othila in Lafayllve's runic system, is the ancestral rune that embodies and expresses one's ongoing connection with the past. It became a refrain within the ritual, its syllables drawn out and intoned as a galdr at every transition point. While chanting the rune, participants visualized its shape and listened for the voices of their ancestors, creating a corpospiritual event that linked body, mind, and spirit world. Between each rune chant, Lafayllve poured an offering of sacred mead and said a prayer to the ancestral beings, first the dísir, then the *alfar* (from the Old Norse *álfr*, meaning elf or fairy but representing here the male ancestral spirits), and finally the ancestors, the family dead themselves. "Ancient ones. Hallowed ones. Ancestors whose bones are our bones and whose blood sings in our veins. Dísir, alfar, shining ones. We ask that you share your wisdom with us now. We listen in silence to your words."[541] Lafayllve then encouraged participants to sit in silence, listening for the voices of their own departed relatives, "Listen to your heart, to the emotions that stir you, to the wind as it blows or the whispers that touch your ears. Hear the words of the ancestors in silence." Her words created a moment charged with expectation, a strong sense that the ancestors were present, moving around the participants, whispering and speaking in a polyphony of silent voices, eager to be heard by their living kin. For myself, this part of the ritual was thick with impressions from a passage in *Eirik the Red's Saga* popular among Heathen magic workers. It depicts a seeress named Thorbjorg, a *seiðkona* gifted with far-sight, who has been invited to a farmstead for a divinatory rite. As part of Thorbjorg's ritual, a woman was encouraged to sing a *varðlokur*, "a chant required for carrying out magic rites," particularly the divinatory practice of *seið*.[542] The song seemed effective. "The seeress thanked her for

540. I participated in Lafayllve's ancestral ritual on two occasions. In both events, the ritual remained very consistent. Field notes taken by author, California, 2012, and Pennsylvania, 2012. I used her book, *A Practical Heathen's Guide to Asatru*, which substantially reproduces the ritual, for the quotations in this section.

541. Lafayllve, *A Practical Heathen's Guide*, 69.

542. Keneva Kunz and Gísli Sigurðsson, *The Vinland Sagas: The Icelandic Sagas About the First Documented Voyages Across The North Atlantic: The Saga of the Greenlanders and Eirik the Red's Saga* (London: Penguin, 2008), 32. The Old Norse *varðlokur* is difficult and has been translated in several different ways. It may refer to a spell that entices the spirits to speak as Kunz's translation suggests, or a warding spell that weaves a protective aura around the seeress allowing her to interact safely with the spirits.

her chant. She said many spirits had been attracted who thought the chant fair to hear—'though earlier they wished to turn their backs on us and refused to do our bidding.'"[543] The magical song seemed to draw the spirits near. They became willing to communicate with seeress and share their knowledge with the human community. There are many differences between this passage and Lafayllves' ritual to be sure; for one, the spirits that communicate with Thorbjorg are not ancestral but spirits of nature and place. But I, and perhaps other Heathen participants, had a powerful connotative moment in which Lafayllve's ritual resonated with this ancient magical event. The intention of the ritual was to create this resonance; the chant, the ritual, the prayers were meant to draw the spirits close, so that they surrounded us, willing to speak in that moment of silence as we strained to listen for them.

Lafayllve's ritual encouraged participants to construct an identity supplemented and enhanced by the past through a conscious interaction with ancestral beings. For Thora, and many Heathens like her, the connection with ancestors happens on a more personal and less formal basis. She finds her awareness of the dísir opened particularly by the activity of cooking. The rituals of daily life, what Ronald Grimes calls ritualization, are pathways through which the ancestors make themselves known in her experience.[544] As an experienced and accomplished cook, Thora talks about jam-making as a religious activity that creates a living point of connection with her female ancestors whose ørlög and experience were so intimately connected to cooking. At one level, making jam is simply a utilitarian act, one that she does not pursue primarily for religious reasons. Yet folded into the work and its sensory qualia: the colors, smells, the patterns of work that have remained largely constant through generations of her family, come the comforting and strengthening presence of her dísir. Her story also demonstrates how Heathens utilize ancestor relics in their veneration practices. Objects that have been owned, touched, and used by one's ancestors may retain a memory of them, their work, deeds, and power. In

---

543. Ibid.
544. Ronald L. Grimes, *Ritual Criticism: Case Studies in Its Practice, Essays on Its Theory* (Columbia: University of South Carolina Press, 1990), 10–11. Grimes explains the term, "Ritualization ... includes processes that fall below the threshold of social recognition as rites, but nonetheless take on some of the qualities of ritual." Grimes mentions housework, with which I include cooking, as a type of ritualization.

Thora's experience, not only is the activity of making jam a type of ancestral veneration, but the canner itself acts as a powerful object that holds ancestral ørlög. As Tauring says about her experiences with ancestral beings, "They may show up in dreams or as feelings and thoughts when we look at their photos, prepare their recipes, sing the songs they taught us, pray their prayers."[545] Rather than feeling alone or isolated, Heathens may be strengthened by personal relationships with both living and dead, present and past. Heathens find these relationships with ancestral beings to be positive and comforting experiences. Rather than pursuing ancestor worship out of fear, fear of reprisal from angry spirits and hungry ghosts, Heathens seek the ancestors in order to broaden their experience of family, ground their own sense of identity, and gain strength from the past for facing life's challenges. As another Heathen adherent told me, "I feel lucky because I get to interact with my [deceased] grandmother and the rest of my family doesn't."[546] Heathens seek after the presence of their ancestors, drawing on them for strength and guidance, and structure their identities in relation to their ancestral past.

## Conclusion

From the ancient symbol of Mjolnir to the idiosyncratic practice of jam-making, Heathenry envisions and enacts a rich sense of self connected to the world in ways that enhance individuality. The Heathen self-concept dissents from the enervated sense of individuality that Heathens perceive as taking hold in the modern Western world, as well as in other types of religious identity-making. Heathenry orients adherents toward the past, seeing the individual as a complex intersection of family relationships of living and dead, soul-parts, and metaphysical forces within the human frame. In a world that is potentially dangerous and chaotic, the individual must make a home, a space of its own in which to thrive. Success and thriving are not guaranteed. Adherents seek after these goods by acting and struggling in the world, building

---

545. Kari C. Tauring, *Völva Stav Manual* (Minneapolis: Kari Tauring, 2010), 34.
546. Nertha, telephone interview with author, January 2, 2013. She suggests that the Christian beliefs of her family kept them from pursuing these ancestral experiences.

and maintaining an innangarð connected to the past. Individuals are supported, strengthened, and enhanced by a shieldwall of the various relationships and powers to which they are connected as parts of their selves. Having examined some of the non-theistic religious resources of Heathenry, the next chapter will continue by paying attention to the theistic side of the culture—the gods and goddesses.

## Chapter 5

## Hard Polytheism in a Soft World

In the summer of 2012, I attended a Heathen gathering tucked away in the Pocono mountains of northern Pennsylvania. Along the perimeter of one large field, participants had brought and set up several outdoor shrines. This sort of shrine, sometimes referred to as a *vé*, is a distinctive Heathen sacred space set off by ropes or a small fence and devoted to a particular god or spiritual entity. The arrangement of these sanctuaries created a small circuit through which participants could move and enact something of a pilgrimage, walking from one shrine to another paying homage to the many different deities who were represented. Freyja's shrine stood out because of the amount of amber it contained. An irminsul engraved with a Tiwaz, ↑, stood in Tyr's shrine.[547] One vé held two shrines: a wain or wagon that carried a statue of Thor and served as a mobile shrine, and Odin's shrine marked by the distinctive one-eyed godpole. To the Heathens strolling along or sitting thoughtfully in these sacred spaces, each one represented a powerful entity, distinct and unique. Throughout the weekend, rituals were held to honor the gods at their vé or one of the fire-rings on the campgrounds. These were often very emotional events during which worshipers spoke passionately and made dramatic displays of devotion. The large vé dedicated to Odin had been set up by the Laerad kindred from New York, who held a faining there on Friday evening

---

547. An "irminsul" refers generally to a type of sacred wooden column, often shaped like a capital T, and symbolic of the world tree. Historically, the Irminsûl featured prominently in religious practice of the Saxons and was associated with the god Irmin. Charlemagne notably cut down the Saxon Irminsûl in 722 CE. See Davidson, *Myths and Symbols*, 21–24; Claude Lecouteux, s.v. "Irminsûl," *Encyclopedia of Norse and Germanic Folklore, Mythology, and Magic* (Rochester, VT: Inner Traditions, 2016). The "T" rune, reconstructed as *tiwaz, or *teiwaz is often written as Tiwaz or Tyr by Heathens. Tauring also associates it with Zisa, a consort or twin deity of Tyr. See Kari C. Tauring, *Runes: A Human Journey* (Minneapolis, MN: Kari C. Tauring, 2015).

(see figure 15).⁵⁴⁸ Earlier in the day, they had announced that a basket had been placed outside the shrine to collect offerings for Odin. During the subsequent hours, visitors to the shrine had deposited small gifts for the god. As night fell, kindred members lit torches around the *vé* and sounded a horn, its warm sustained tone calling the worshipers from the surrounding campground and alerting the god to the worship that was about to take place. A fire was kindled in the *hörg* and the kindred goði Josh Rood stood illuminated by the flickering firelight as he began to recount the story of Odin, Odroerir, and the mead of inspiration to the gathered crowd.⁵⁴⁹ In the context of the ritual, the performance of the story served to prepare the worshipers for the faining, creating a shared experience of the god.⁵⁵⁰ Rood recounted how one of the jǫtnar, a giant named Suttungr, had obtained the mead and secreted it in his mountain stronghold, guarded by his daughter Gunnlöð. Through his cunning, Odin wooed Gunnlöð, stole the mead and fled the wrath of Suttungr by escaping in the form of an eagle. As he flew, some of the mead spewed from his mouth over Midgard, Odin's gift shared with humans in the form of spiritual and creative inspiration. Neil Gaiman writes that "ever since then, we know that those people who can make magic with their words, who can make poems and sagas and weave tales, have tasted the mead of poetry."⁵⁵¹ The worshipers reflected on Odin's heroic action that brought enlightenment and inspiration to humanity, a divine or magical ability experienced in meditation, in writing and reciting poetry, and in artistic creativity. To engage in such activity is to receive and enjoy the gift of the god.

---

548. Since mead served as the primary offering to Odin that night, this event was technically a "faining," a worship event in which no blood sacrifice is offered. The term blót is frequently used to designate a variety of acts of worship in which offering are made to gods or other beings. However, more Heathens are making distinctions between fainings and blóts as worship practices and religious terminology develop.

549. Cleasby and Vigfusson, *An Icelandic Dictionary*, s.v. "*hörgr.*" A hörg is a Heathen altar, often made of stone, and used for the blót sacrifice. In this case, no live blót was performed and the hörg was represented by a raised braizer in which a fire was lit.

550. Sturluson, *Skaldskaparmal*, 2 in *The Prose Edda*, 83–86. While mentioned in the Völuspá, Sturluson recounts the more complete version of the tale. Ódrœrir refers to the cauldron in which the mead was made, or alternatively the mead of inspiration itself.

551. Neil Gaiman, *Norse Mythology* (New York: W. W. Norton, 2017), 151.

Figure 15. Odin and Thor Vé at East Coast Thing. (Photo by the author.)

Rood exuded this passionate inspiration as he spoke, ending his account by hailing the heroic god. His kindred members brought forth a decorative wooden cask of mead painted with a Norse design. Rood described how the kindred had brewed the mead of the best ingredients and aged it for a year specifically for this blót, "No mortal lips will ever taste it. It is for Odin alone," he said.[552] With that, he took an axe and busted the cask. The sacrificial fire hissed and sputtered as the mead was poured in, releasing a heavy column of steam but not going out, which seemed like a good omen to all. Another kindred member then took the basket full of offerings, gifts from the community, and placed it in the fire. The weekend included several of these large-scale blóts, in addition to other smaller and more private acts of devotion. Earlier on Friday afternoon, participants had hiked through the woods to a small clearing where a faining for Tyr was held. And on Saturday night at the camp's central fire pit, several female gythjas led an elaborate and creative ritual honoring Freyja. The Thor worship, fittingly held on Thursday night, heightened the sense of drama and pageantry by incorporating a procession. Processions have been an important

552. Field notes by author, Pennsylvania, August, 2012.

part of religious observance in Pagan cultures past and present, and Heathen worship has begun to make use of the practice in certain settings. Processions tend to be more effective with a large number of people, costumes, noisemakers, and other paraphernalia. Not all of this was available for the Thor ritual and many of the participants, never having been part of a religious procession and uncertain about what to do, ended up standing around watching the event. Yet, the procession added a new level of energy to the ritual, offered an opportunity for participants to be physically involved in the worship, and graphically illustrated the invocation of Thor's protection over the camp. Again the Laerad kindred led the ritual. After lighting the ritual fire, a small wagon or wain displaying an image of Thor (see figure 16) was drawn around the large field where the Thor shrine was located.[553] Several participants pulled the wagon while the other participants followed behind in a long torch-lit procession under the night sky. I climbed the nearby hill overlooking the large field in order to watch the spectacle. Setting out into the darkness, those pulling the wagon began a song praising Thor. It was difficult to catch the words, but after every few lines, the song was punctuated by the crowd yelling, "Ride, Thunder, Ride!" the phrase echoing through the campground. The scene was raucous and powerful, calling to mind the sort of revelry that must have characterized such processions in Heathen worship in the Norse age. The singing and shouts of devotion marked the progress of the wain around the camp, the line of torch-bearing worshipers circling the field in the warm summer night. As the procession returned to the vé, participants were invited to come forward and approach the image of the deity one by one. As each person stepped forward to the vé's opening, they were sprinkled with mead, purified and blessed before entering the sacred space and praying before the image of Thor. This entire experience was not only passionately felt but also a deeply theocentric event. Evocative worship experiences such as this bring home to the participants the personal and real nature of the gods.[554]

---

553. A wain is simply a wagon or cart upon which the image of a god would ride. There are several references in the Lore to Norse gods riding on carts. For instance, Tacitus describes how during the religious festival of Nerthus, the image of goddess made a circuit of the countryside on a cart or chariot pulled along by cattle (Tacitus, *The Agricola and the Germania*, 134–35). Thor is thought to have traveled at times in a cart pulled by two goats. Sturluson refers to him as Ökuþórr, Thor the Charioteer, in *Gylfaginning*, 44 in the *Prose Edda*.

554. Field notes by author, Pennsylvania, August, 2012.

Figure 16. Thor Statue Carried in a Wain at East Coast Thing. (Photo by the author.)

## *Encountering Heathen Polytheism*

When I first began to become familiar with Heathenry, the highly theocentric nature of Heathen culture caught me by surprise. The gods were everywhere: in books and conversations, invoked in rituals, portrayed in images, and on altars. British academic Graham Harvey, a long-time and careful researcher of Pagan religious practice, makes a generalization about Pagan religion that is important to note in this context. "Paganism," he writes, "is not centred around the worship of deities ... Ask Pagans what is most important, attractive, enjoyable, profound or Pagan about their Paganism and they will not begin by describing their beliefs about deities."[555] While plenty of Pagans venerate gods as part of their practice and certain types of Paganism are very focused on deities, Harvey's comment reflects the diversity of spirituality within Paganism. In the broad scope of contemporary Paganism, veneration of deities takes its place alongside magical disciplines, shamanic practice, divination, animism, veneration of

---

555. Harvey, *Contemporary Paganism*, 165.

nature, geomancy, and other important spiritual pursuits. This is also the case in Heathenry. Heathens, like other Pagans, make use of a wide variety of spiritual practices, some of which are non-theistic in their approach, emphasizing ancestral practice, ethical values, ontological concepts, and the prevalent community dimensions of Heathenry.

Yet a general impression of American Heathenry suggests the centrally important place of the gods. While polling data point toward an ongoing decline in both religious practice and belief in the divine among Americans, Heathenry presides over a vibrant rebirth of theocentric practice.[556] Many American Heathens, if asked about their spirituality, will respond by talking about the gods, perhaps not their "beliefs" about the gods but definitely about their connection to and experiences with the gods. For many Heathens, an awareness of numinous powers outside of themselves, gods with names, stories, and personalities, is a core orientation of religious experience. Harvey makes note of this distinctive Heathen approach, suggesting that in contrast to the diversity of Pagan approaches to deity, Heathens demonstrate more particularity. "Heathens," he writes, "tend to be much more definite about theology. Since the deity-talk of feminist-influenced Pagans uses a female form, the*a*logy, perhaps it would be appropriate for Heathen deity-talk to use a plural form, the*oi*logy, that is if Heathens did not have a strong preference for north European words and strong antipathy towards southern European ones."[557] Harvey's comment emphasizes the degree to which Heathen spirituality is god-focused and culturally specific, as well as the strongly polytheistic mode of Heathen theology. As he suggests, perhaps we should coin a new word to describe Heathen god-talk, perhaps *regintal* or *goðatal*, speaking of and about the gods. This gods-talk or regintal among Heathens often occurs in stories, retellings of the stories of the gods or accounts of one's own experience with the gods, rather than in an abstract or philosophical mode.

In my discussions with Heathens, their accounts of significant religious experiences were often oriented towards the gods. A

---

556. Michael Lipka, "Religious 'Nones' Are Not Only Growing, They're Becoming More Secular," *Pew Research Center*, November 11, 2015, www.pewresearch.org/fact-tank/2015/11/11/religious-nones-are-not-only-growing-theyre-becoming-more-secular/.

557. Harvey, *Contemporary Paganism*, 67–68.

Heathen in the Northeast described how even as a child, before he knew anything about Heathenry as a religion, he sensed the reality of powerful spiritual entities and began spontaneously offering to the gods. The young age that marked his god-awareness is uncommon; most Heathens I spoke with found Heathenry and the gods as adults. However, there is widespread interest among Heathen parents and some kindred leaders in teaching children about the gods.[558] At a workshop for Heathen parents that I attended, parents traded tips and suggestions for how to engage children's interest and imagination with the gods through story, art, and ritual. Many Heathens have experiences in which they perceive the god's activity in their lives. Heathens may engage in highly personal types of devotion, such as one Heathen's experience of formally declaring himself a Heathen while talking and praying to Thor during his commute on the freeway. For many, the gods or signs of the gods appear in dreams or visions. Magically-oriented Heathens may bump into gods while involved in journey work. Several Heathens talked about becoming drawn toward the gods through the occurrence of physical ailments. In one particularly strong account, Radulf described how he had been studying the gods for some time and felt particularly interested in Tyr. But he was "just reading," and not actively worshiping them. His study remained fairly detached and intellectual. During this time however he "totaled the work truck," injuring himself in such a way that he lost the use of his "sword arm" for a couple of months. Reflecting on this, Radulf stated, "I'm not saying that the gods come down and mess you up if you don't listen, but I get a lot of significance from that."[559] Of course, in Norse mythology, the god Tyr lost his own sword arm when the wolf Fenris bit off his hand. Radulf did not want to assert that Tyr called him in some way. Heathens tend to be fairly circumspect about claims of direct personal experiences with the gods. However, through the injury, he became aware of an affinity for Tyr, understanding and connecting to the god in a new way that changed his life. Radulf continues to be strongly god-oriented in his religious practice.

---

558. See for instance, Su Eaves, "Raising Children with the Gods," *Idunna*, no. 102, (2014): 18–21. Eaves is a good example of a Heathen who has focused on children's spirituality. In addition to her writing, she has led an annual summer camp specifically geared towards Heathen children and their Heathen families.

559. Observations taken from numerous interviews with Heathen practitioners with the author.

Not only do the gods inform the religious identities of American Heathens, the veneration of the gods remains a central focus of religious activity at this stage in the development. The bold nature of Heathen reginal (gods-talk) was on clear display in a sumbel in Minnesota, in a small hall filled to bursting with over a hundred Heathens representing a variety of kindreds and groups from all over the Midwest. During the first round of sumbel, the horn circulated through the hall to each kindred leader, each of whom called upon a different deity: Odin, Thor, Frey, Tyr, Frigg, Freyja, and other deities were invoked throughout that night sumbel.[560] Many of the kindreds had a special affinity for, or relationship, with the god they invoked that night. Some Heathens take this even further into a *fulltruí* relationship in which they feel bound to a god in a close working relationship and often make vows to devote themselves to this patron deity.[561] Yet none of the groups assembled for the sumbel would have understood their affinity for, involvement with, or dedication to a god to imply a relationship of exclusivity. In fact, the opposite is true: the invocation of multiple deities in the sumbel signifies a community that understands itself to be living in the midst of a diversity of gods, in relationship with many distinct, living, and powerful gods and goddesses. This strongly felt experience of polytheism is at the core of Heathen spirituality.

The very intense human/divine relationships known as fulltruí, in which an adherent binds her/himself to a god by oath, may sound at first like a sort of Heathen henotheism. However, in the highly polytheistic context of Heathenry, these relationships are better described as "closest friends or allies" in which the god becomes "first among many" to the adherent. A Heathen may work closely with a god for life, or move sequentially through a series of intense god-relationships as a part of his or her path of spiritual development. Torsen describes how his initial dedication to Thor slowly shifted to include a relationship with Odin:

---

560. Field notes taken by author, Minnesota, June 2012. I discuss the sumbel ritual further in chapter 7.
561. Fulltruí, translated as "patron," "well-beloved friend," or "protector" refers to a close relationship between a god and a devotee. The god becomes the patron deity or friend of the devotee. The Norse tradition has a few examples of fulltruí, a couple of the most well known include Thorolf's committed devotion to Thor in *Eyrbyggja Saga*, chapter 4; and that of Glúm and the god Frey in *Víga-Glúms Saga*, chapter 9.

> I had grown too comfortable in my role as a Tor's goði, that it was time for me to be uncomfortable again, and that it was time for me to take on the blue cloak, to put the hammer down and take up the blue cloak. So I thought about this for a while, and what that meant was that it was time for me to change the way I looked at things and start following more of an Odinic path. And so, I dedicated to Odin for the next part of my learning.[562]

Another experienced and thoughtful Heathen describes how her experiences with seið led her from involvement with Odin towards being sworn to Freyja: "When I started working seið I got closer and closer to her. But I also had this connection with Odin and I still do, you know. But slowly it became clear over years that I was closer to Freyja."[563] Lafayllve sees it as an act of service to be particularly dedicated to the interests of one god and that god's involvement with the Heathen community. While their lives are deeply intertwined with one god, neither would describe themselves as henotheists, in the sense of worshiping only one god while recognizing the existence of many. They are through and through polytheists who happen to be working closely with one divine being. Lafayllve chuckled as she described the complexities of the relationship, "so what that means to me is basically I am fulltruí to her [Freyja] but I still work with the rest of the pantheon. Polytheism is a lot like polyamory, you can have more than one."

For those whose orientation towards the divine has been predominantly shaped by the prevailing monotheism of the American ethos, the emerging polytheism found within the Pagan revitalization may be difficult to comprehend. The opportunities to misunderstand polytheistic religious practice are manifold. One common misunderstanding is simply to overlook polytheism or to see it as an odd exception to monotheistic hegemony, a strange curiosity or a rare holdover from a past age. Monotheism exercises such a profound cultural influence that its adherents are often imperceptive to the ongoing presence of polytheism, overlooking the growth and spread of polytheistic religions in the contemporary period. Contemporary Pagan polytheisms make up part of this growth. But other traditions like Santeria and Hinduism, whose temples now dot the American landscape, have slowly changed the

---

562. Torsen, interview.
563. Patricia Lafayllve, interview with author, February 19, 2012.

Figure 17. The Mobile Freyja Shrine at East Coast Thing. (Photo by the author.)

American religious context. Polytheistic religious practices remain an important dimension of lived experience for millions, often in communities where it represents an unbroken tradition hundreds or thousands of years in the making. Classics scholar Page duBois points out that the myth of America as a monotheist nation fails to recognize that America is bursting with gods. Multitudes of gods cohabitate and compete in a religious mosaic on every street corner in a de facto polytheistic context. DuBois goes on to argue, as many Heathens have suggested, that the monotheistic traditions themselves contain lingering echoes of polytheism.[564]

When monotheistic societies have noticed these living polytheistic traditions, they tend to be uncompromising in their evaluation of these religious cultures, seeing them as sinful, deluded, or degenerate. Pagan polytheism receives a good deal of vitriol within the Jewish, Christian, and Islamic sacred texts, and these ancient condemnations

---

564. Page duBois, *A Million and One Gods: The Persistence of Polytheism* (Cambridge, MA: Harvard University Press, 2014).

influence the perspectives and worldviews of contemporary believers. For an observer socialized within that perspective, misinterpreting polytheism by failing to see it as an authentic religious tradition or misunderstanding the rational, emotional, and social dimensions of its practices becomes a very real possibility. For the researcher, the stakes in getting contemporary polytheism right are even higher. In his book *The Deities are Many* scholar Jordan Paper raises just this critique—a monotheistic bias could cloud or distort the interpretation of polytheistic forms of religion.[565] According to Paper, the monotheist bias tends to get polytheism wrong in a couple of important ways: either by disparaging it as a morally, intellectually, and spiritually inferior position; or by reducing it to something else, such as a proto-monotheism.

This sense that polytheism is wrong or sinful is quite evident in the history of the dominant monotheistic traditions. Paper writes, "There is a great misunderstanding of these cultures in monotheistic ones, for Western religions are based on the premise that polytheists are either inferior human beings or the most despicable of enemies."[566] Scholars like Paper and Dubois make a good case that this bias rears its head in the study of Pagan religions, perhaps akin to the Orientalism noted by Edward Said in the Western perception of the Middle East and Asia. Too often, we have read into religious traditions our own prejudices and stereotypes and made polytheists into exotic wonders, primitives, or despicable idolaters. In the Bible Belt, where I live and work, it is not at all uncommon for Wiccans to be associated with devil worship. Nor is it surprising to hear the term "heathen" used as a derogatory put-down directed toward unruly children or adults who violate the social norms of polite company. Paper writes that the term "heathen" is commonly used to refer to a non-monotheist, but also a social and moral degenerate, an "unenlightened person . . . lacking in culture or moral principles."[567] Such usage reveals biases that hamper one's ability to accurately understand polytheism.

I commonly encounter a second distortion among otherwise well-meaning people, who have difficulty wrapping their minds

---

565. Jordan D. Paper, *The Deities are Many: A Polytheistic Theology* (Albany: State University of New York Press, 2005).
566. Ibid., 4.
567. Ibid., 104.

around the experience of a robust hard polytheism. The many gods with their powers, specialties, and domains are seen as pre-scientific explanations for natural and psychological phenomena such as weather phenomena or internal emotional states. At times, polytheistic religions are interpreted as proto-monotheistic traditions: Hindus who really worship one God, *Ishvara*; or Native Americans who actually worship one God, the Great Spirit. All of these approaches in some way deny or downplay the polytheistic or animistic dimensions of these cultures. About this sort of interpretation Paper writes, "in effect, such theories deny that there is any living polytheistic tradition."[568] Reading Paper's warnings early in my research, I tried to enter into Heathen polytheistic contexts aware of the potentially distorting effects of my own cultural bias, and willing to bracket them as a means to authentically appreciate Heathen spirituality. To the researcher, Paper gives a couple points of advice "to avoid the effects of one's ethnocentrism on one's analyses of culture and religion."[569] First, learn the language of the culture, which for Paper means Chinese or whichever language the religious tradition uses. For myself this meant internalizing as much as possible the religious vocabulary of Heathen people, to read the sources and to become fluent in the religious technology. Second, Paper emphasizes a practice familiar to those of us trained in ethnographic methodology: "One needs to fully participate in its religious rituals, that is, participate with the mindset that these rituals are utterly meaningful. If one can do this without losing one's original cultural ways of thinking, then one has two or more paradigm systems."[570] I have tried more or less successfully to follow both of his practical prescriptions.

Some practitioners and scholars push back against the monotheistic bias by making use of theological or apologetic approaches. In his book *Pagan Theology*, Michael York uses the discipline of comparative religion and theology to set contemporary Paganism side by side with the other world religions. Christine Hoff Kraemer adopts the approach of systematic theology in *Seeking the Mystery* in order to recover a theological language for Pagans and polytheists, reclaiming vocabulary long monopolized by the

---

568. Ibid., 107.
569. Ibid., 108.
570. Ibid., 108-9.

Abrahamic traditions to bring clarity and voice to Pagan theologies. Author and Druid John Michael Greer also attempts to make room for polytheism in the broader theological conversation in his book, *A World Full of Gods*.[571] In the book's first section, he attends to the well-known philosophical arguments for and against theism, such as the ontological, cosmological, and teleological arguments, as well as the argument from evil, which have been a part of Christian theological discussion and education for centuries in the West. He rehearses each argument in some depth, suggesting in each case that polytheism stands up as well as or better than monotheism. These books are examples of a developing fluency among Pagans and polytheists in the Western tradition of theology and apologetics. Heretofore, polytheism may have been regarded as fringe and trivial, dismissed by observers in the mainstream of American culture. However, as practitioners begin to move into these fields and continue to enunciate their practice in terms familiar to a broader audience, polytheism will be poised to emerge as a more seriously regarded religious orientation.

Because of the scholarly dimension of reconstructive Paganism, Heathens have a strong history of theological discourse: explicating passages from the Lore, developing and exploring important Heathen religious concepts such the soul, etc. Most of the work has been descriptive and practical, such as discussing the characteristics of a god or developing a working system of rune magic or seið. Enunciating a Heathen theology of hard polytheism has been slower to develop, yet some Heathens are beginning to think along these lines. I stumbled into an amazing conversation at a Heathen event in which a group of people were discussing the question "Is my Thor the same as your Thor?"[572] I was immediately intrigued and even though the conversation did not last long it stuck with me. To a monotheist, the question sounds ridiculous and reflects the comical absurdity of polytheism, but what I noticed in the conversation was a hint of emerging polytheist theology. Consider Hinduism for a moment. Interpreted by and for monotheists, even the gods of polytheistic Hinduism take on a transcendent and transcultural persona—Shiva is systematized. Surely Shiva is the same wherever

---

571. John Michael Greer, *A World Full of Gods: An Inquiry into Polytheism* (Tucson: ADF, 2005).

572. Field notes taken by author, Pennsylvania, 2012.

he appears: one god with a consistent personality, story, and way of interacting. But the living Hindu tradition within the experience of practitioners and localities suggests much more ambiguity, more resistance to a reductive approach to the deity. Shiva is more complex than he is often presented in a world religions classroom. Even as Shiva is one of many gods, Shiva himself is not one. What appears at the phenomenological level are numerous Shivas: local forms of Shiva, each with its own temples, worship practices, traditions, names, and salient stories. The concept of a unified and transcultural Shiva arises from the myriad of local manifestations of this god. Perhaps this is not so different from the early Semitic experiences of divinity: a close reading of the biblical Abraham cycle of stories reveals a number of names and manifestations that defy easy reconciliation: *El Roi* of the south, Abraham's *YHWH Jireh, El Elyon*, and Jacob's House of God, *Beth El*, and the *YHWH* of Mamre. On the face of it, this myriad of narratives and experiences does not easily provide a consistent and cohesive picture of one distinct god. Rather than are many religious experiences manifesting many *El*s of many places. It is interesting to note that the monotheistic impulse of the Israelite King Josiah coincided with the destruction of these sacred localities and shrines, where *baalim, asherim, elohim*, and *elat* had been worshiped. Similarly, the conversion of the Heathen North involved the desecration or cooptation of the many shrines to the gods. The emerging dominance of one transcendent form of deity often involves the destruction or minimizing of more diverse instances.

The question "Is my Thor the same as your Thor?" reveals a few Heathens who are thinking about and seeking out the deeper logic or theology of polytheism. The question refuses to skim too quickly over the differences apparent in multiple experiences of deity. In their rush to create a unified picture of Thor, Heathenry 101 books run the risk of reducing Thor to a character epitomized by a few standardized stories and lists of personality traits. In the process, such efforts fall prey to a sort of bias that can only be characterized as monotheistic. The harmony is only achieved by minimizing differences in the experience of who Thor may be. The polytheistic impulse, on the other hand, seems to be more open to a diverse set of experiences, to allowing differences and tensions to stand unresolved. It may be that a robust polytheism allows for a transcultural understanding of a god, while not erasing or sanitizing the many different regional or local manifestations. So asking and pursuing that question may be a sign of a theological strength and robustness in American Heathenry, a sign that a deeper polytheist sensibility may be evolving. Indeed, it should not be assumed that Thor of the Catskills and Poconos would be the same as Thor of the Redwoods. Like the Shaivite who goes on pilgrimage to the diversity of shrines in India, Heathens traveling among different Heathen communities might encounter and worship Thor of the Colorado Rockies in distinctly different ways than the Thor of the Everglades or Thor of the Upper Peninsula. In some ways, Thor will always be the same, with each of these Thors sharing some commonalities, all the while maintaining distinct regional and local understandings and practices regarding Thor. In some sense, each instance is like meeting a new person who you have known all along.

### Polytheism as Qualitative Experience

Another reductive approach to polytheism is to regard it as the *belief* in many gods. While belief plays a role, polytheism involves a qualitative experience as well as a living and holistic culture. In this regard, introductory books to Asatru can be somewhat disappointing in their portrayal of Heathen polytheism. Many of these Asatru 101 books contain static lists and staid descriptions of the Norse gods that one might find in compendiums of mythology or the *Deities and Demigods* manual from Dungeons & Dragons.[573] While this work may be necessary in trying to introduce Heathenry to interested observers or new adherents, it is only a first step in defining or describing a living polytheism. For Heathens, recognizing Thor or Odin or Freyja and their attributes is important.

---

573. These lists of characteristics found in "Asatru 101" books often strike me as pedantic, shallow, and inauthentic in the attempt to provide a systematic description of the gods. However, compendiums have their uses. There are examples in the Lore of comprehensive descriptions of the gods. Lokasenna for instance may represent "a kind of dictionary for mythology, a compilation listing the gods and the major myths associated with each one" (Philip N. Anderson, "Form and Content in Lokasenna: A Re-Evaluation," in *The Poetic Edda: Essays on Old Norse Mythology*, ed. Paul Acker and Carolyne Larrington [New York: Routledge, 2002], 143). These lists also reinforce the god-oriented nature of Heathenry for new Heathens and the value of becoming fluent in Heathen reginal (gods-talk). Knowing the names of Frigga's handmaidens, or some of the many heiti or bynames of Odin, is a type of fluency that not only gives one credence within the Heathen community but also provides a complexity and depth to religious experience.

Discerning the shape, scope, and personalities of the numinous powers is a serious part of polytheistic practice, part of the process of spiritual maturity. Yet, these books have the effect of reducing polytheism to a rationalized set of categories, as if the most important thing is to know facts about the gods. But existentially, polytheism is a way of experiencing the world, the qualitative experience of living in the presence of many compelling numinous powers and negotiating a world in which these powers live and breathe.

Some of the most compelling thinking about the gods is reflected in Heathen work such as the writing and dramatic story telling of Steven Abell, whose *Days in Midgard: One Thousand Years On* reimagines Norse myth and divine personalities from a modern perspective.[574] For example, his short story "The Physics of Summer" recounts a few hours spent by William, a high school chemistry teacher, at a late afternoon cookout in a park with his difficult and acerbic mother-in-law.[575] While thumbing through a magazine, William finds that a group of children has arrived. They play in the park, watched over by a man sitting at a nearby picnic table. To William, distracted and agitated by his mother-in-law, the nearby man seems to be at peace, embodying a sense of calm mastery. William muses, "At the other table, the man sat, looking out over the evening and all it contained . . . What would it be like, he wondered, to be lord of a summer evening, and all the warmth and growth and ripeness in it?" Later, the children find a peach in a tree and take it to the man, their guardian or teacher, as William calls him. "Extending his arm, [he] raised the peach up into the last shaft of sunlight filtering into the park . . . The peach glowed hotly there, yellow and orange." One of the children then brings the peach over to William, who "hesitated, then reached for it and took it . . . [he] looked at the peach, running his fingers over the cleft between the two full hemispheres. It was neither hard nor soft, but just firm, and very ripe. It was perfect. Holding it up to his nose to inhale its thick, sweet aroma, he could almost feel the life waiting in the seed inside." Though never directly identified as such, the man is of course Freyr, the Norse lord of summer, frith (peace), and

---

574. Steven T. Abell, *Days in Midgard: A Thousand Years On — Modern Legends Based on Norse Myth* (Denver, CO: Outskirts Press, 2008). Abell also served as Steersman of the Troth from 2013–2016.

575. Ibid., 103–20.

*arð*, (bounty, fertility, and abundance).[576] Freyr's blessing enlivens William's perception of the peach.

In his story, Abell invites the reader to observe the character William as he moves from idleness, distraction, and worry toward an experience of peace and wholeness. The climactic moment is underplayed—William simply holds a peach in his hand, but that peach is lush with the vitality lacking in William's drab life. The story asks us to consider what it might be like to live in the presence and reality of this god, who is not a superhero but a god of the real world. Abell's thoughtful portrayals of divine/human interaction are full of psychological subtlety, instead of pedantic descriptions of characteristics. Divine beings are rarely identified outright. They appear instead as enigmatic and appealing figures from the perspective of the modern human characters with whom they engage. Their arrival in the stories always catalyzes the mundane lives of those who encounter them, sometimes in thrilling and erotic ways like William's peach, and often by introducing dangerous, threatening, and unsettling change. The gods in Abell's stories are complicated but always vivifying. Although Abell may not be intending to undertake theology, his stories can be read as creative excursions into the Heathen theological imagination. Avoiding stodgy flat descriptions, he invites readers vicariously to experience interactions with divine powers in personal rather than ritual ways and to reconsider the odd and poignant moments of their lives as brushes with the divine. In doing so, he posits a modern world filled with gods.

## Polytheism as Culture

Polytheism relies upon a robust cultural element, a socio-religious context involving a complex set of religious sensibilities, practices, and institutions. Within the Pagan blogosphere, a few writers have been exploring trends and trajectories for the development of new contemporary polytheist cultures. Ryan Smith notes that current practitioners are the "formative generation" for this polytheistic revival and should consider how their actions and choices will affect the development of the traditions. He suggests that developing

---

576. Many of the god's names end with the Old Norse masculine nominative "-r," such as Freyr, Heimdallr, and Njörðr. In everyday Heathen usage, these names are often anglicized and the final "-r" dropped, resulting in Frey, Heimdall, and Njord or Njorth.

polytheisms must be relevant for contemporary society, not isolated "in an idealized world that is sealed off from what is around us."[577] In attempting to reconstruct a polytheistic spirituality in the midst of a dominant monotheistic culture, American Heathens are among those engaged in a religious experiment, part of a new phase in the history of religion. Most American Heathens are discovering polytheism for the first time without the benefit of a long-standing living tradition to step into or from which to learn. The issue is more complex than just *being* polytheists; it requires *becoming* polytheists, building a culture and exploring a type of spiritual experience for which there are few landmarks. In America, this continues to be a spirituality of dissent, a way of ideologically separating from a dominant monotheistic culture. Heathen polytheism is a religious mode of shaping a dissenting identity that rejects the mainstream and seeks to build a new type of American identity outside of the traditional Christian ethos. The challenge for a dissenting religious movement is to move from the apophatic declaration "We are not monotheists," toward the development of a polytheistic religious and social infrastructure, a culture.

This sort of living polytheistic culture has been slow to develop in Heathenry, hampered by the small number of adherents, its geographically diffuse nature, and the contentious reality of the social scene. As John Beckett mentions, "for a large number of Pagans and polytheists, the desire for community is outweighed by the price of community. We don't want to invest the time and energy into creating and maintaining a group, and we don't want to make the compromises necessary to get along."[578] For these reasons, much of the polytheistic culture of Heathenry occurs within long-running kindreds. These groups have developed consistent leadership and ritual practice as well as suitable infrastructure, such as a sacred space in a backyard or a room that serves as a meeting space. The scope and scale of these religious cultures are quite small, however, accessible only to the members of the kindred and their innangarð. Unfortunately, the kindreds that I observed on a regular basis simply did not develop the contributing factors for a robust polytheistic

577. Ryan Smith, "Polytheism's Future," *Through the Grapevine* blog, August 21, 2016, www.patheos.com/blogs/throughthegrapevine/2016/08/polytheisms-future/.

578. John Beckett, "Building our Polytheism," *Under the Ancient Oaks*, September 8, 2016, www.patheos.com/blogs/johnbeckett/2016/09/building-our-polytheism.html.

Figure 18. Communing with the Goddess at Frigg's Vé, East Coast Thing. (Photo by the author.)

practice, instead bouncing from one space to another with limited resources and patched-together ritual.

The development of an actual living polytheistic culture in Heathenry was more apparent, in my experience, at the regional *moots* and *things*, the weekend gatherings that bring together Heathens and kindreds usually broadly dispersed throughout the region. These events became important hubs for shaping and building a polytheistic culture shared by a diverse mix of Heathens. For a few days at these gatherings, a small polytheistic world takes shape, putting on display the numerous experiential, ritual, and intellectual means Heathens utilize to develop their religious cultures. Differing expressions of religiosity are enacted and encountered at the rituals conducted during these events (see figure 18). Workshops allow Heathens to discuss theological and social questions raised by polytheistic practice. Thoughtful engagement with varieties of divine experience are seen as Heathen struggle over figures such as Loki and the jǫtnar and their appropriate roles in Heathen religiosity. Cultural skills such as mead-making and blacksmithing are taught and encouraged. Songs and stories are shared, learned, and remembered. This cross-pollinating dimension of regional gatherings is so important for the development of Heathen culture.[579] Events such as Lightning Across the Plains, last held in 2014, brought together Heathens from across the country in (mostly) productive ways in which real learning and growth occurred. The loss of such events and the closing of other gatherings to a members-only basis represent real detriments to the development of the religion.

In an article entitled "What Is Heathenry Missing?," Dagulf Loptson suggests that Heathen spirituality and religious practice lack both depth and breadth. He observes that,

> the deeper one digs into modern Heathenry, the more one starts to realize that its waters are actually very shallow compared to the depth possessed by traditions with literally thousands of years of unbroken history ... I find more and more that the people who have been at this religion for a long time eventually will hit a plateau in their spiritual development and relationships with the gods.[580]

The gist of this argument hinges on the idea of polytheism as a complex culture with numerous religious technologies to enrich an adherent's experience of the divine. Loptson draws particular attention to the lack of "sacred song, sacred dance, intense (and accurate) divination, sacrifice, a consciousness of tradition lineage, magic that actually works." Galina Krasskova offers a similar criticism of Heathen polytheism, pushing back against Heathenry for what she sees as a staid approach to the gods. She suggests that American Heathens acknowledge the polytheistic nature of their religion intellectually while avoiding devotional interaction with the gods, a tendency she attributes to "a rampantly white, middle-class, Protestant pseudo-rational modernity."[581] In its place, she argues for

---

579. Bado-Fralick, *Coming to the Edge of the Circle*, 31–32. Bado-Fralick describes how Pagan festivals performed a similar function among Wiccans, Witches, and other Pagans, "The Pagan festival movement not only exposed us to an amazing variety of Pagans and Witches, but likely created new forms of Pagan religious practice as well."
580. Dagulf Loptson, "What Is Heathenry Missing?" *Ørgrandr Lokean*, January 19, 2016, http://polytheist.com/orgrandr-lokean/2016/.
581. Galina Krasskova, "Toward a Heathen Theology," *Wyrd Ways: Building a Better Heathenry*, November 23, 2015, http://polytheist.com/wyrd-ways/2015/11/23/toward-a-heathen-theology/#fnref-2027-3.

a more engaged theology. "We need to begin discussing Heathen theology, and not in the 'oh look how much lore I can quote' way," she writes. Heathens need to develop a robust devotional approach to polytheism, seeing "religion as a language and protocol for maintaining right relationships with the Gods." This devotional polytheism represents a more authentic Norse approach to religion, "we can look at it the way our ancestors actually did: as a necessary, god inspired protocol for engaging with the sacred and illuminating our daily lives."

These critiques are important to notice. In my experience, many Heathens do suffer through a rather limited religious repertoire, as the authors suggest. They may not venture far beyond discussing a piece of Lore and talking about the gods, or standing in a circle for a brief and awkward invocation with a horn of mead. Too often, practitioners supplement this shallow religious practice with the performance of their Heathen identities online through Facebook or other social media, short-circuiting the development of a thick Heathen culture. Both Loptson and Krasskova critique the fear of syncretism that has kept Heathens from learning from long-standing polytheistic traditions and cultures of the world. Heathens tend to be concerned that drawing substantially from other cultures will dilute the essential Norse nature of Asatru. This conservative inclination fears that cross-pollination and devotional UPG lead inevitably along a slippery slope to dancing naked around a fire and howling at the moon. Loptson suggests that such concerns are overblown, "rather than diluting some imagined purity of my Heathen practice, my journey into Africa, India, and Hawaii actually brought me closer to the Norse gods, and inspired me to take what I had learned and use it as a way to flesh out [what] our surviving scraps of lore have left us with."[582] Again, the authors lob a relatively accurate criticism at strict reconstructionism—it limits the development of living religion because it remains suspicious of looking beyond the Lore for source material.

However, the authors go too far in suggesting that Heathenry completely lacks these cultural resources and devotional practices. As the movement continues to develop, numerous Heathens are filling out these spaces in Heathen religious culture. This work can be seen in the devotional contributions of Heathen artists and

---

582. Loptson, "What Is Heathenry Missing?"

craftspeople, the folk songs and dances of people like Kari Tauring, the religious dramas written and performed by Hrafnar Kindred, and in the ongoing work on the ritual calendar, runework and the practice of magic. Yet the panoply of these emerging Heathen practices is rarely experienced outside of the regional and national gatherings, during which participants are exposed to and make use of a richer variety of religious technologies. For instance, at one regional Heathen event, I attended a workshop led by goði Rod Landreth before his untimely death. He was experimenting with and teaching a devotional, puja-like approach to Heathen worship. I also encountered creative approaches to the holidays, food, art, and worship practices. However, this required substantial travel and interaction with a variety of people. While the growth of spiritual practices may seem slow, Heathens are generally a cautious people, weighing the cost of each innovation and attempting to avoid unapproved sorts of syncretism.

The truth is that Heathen polytheism for all its genuineness and robustness is a young polytheistic tradition in a process of development. While some Heathens were raised in secular, Paganish, or folk-magic family contexts, (used by some as a badge of pride, "I was never Christian!"), the movement is primarily composed of people who have culturally Christian backgrounds. For the last fifty years, its adherents have been shedding the remnants of their socialization into a predominately monotheistic culture. Replacing that with a new polytheistic culture takes time. Heathens are people seeking to take on polytheism, learning and experimenting with what it means. They have not been "mentored" in polytheism, relying instead on English translations of the Lore and their own UPG. Heathens have been protective of their tradition. As a result, they have tended to turn away from, rather than learn from, the experiences of older, established polytheistic traditions. A second generation of Heathens raised exclusively within a polytheistic culture, who see and experience the culturally Christian American ethos from the outside, is beginning to come of age. It will be interesting to see how Heathen polytheism develops or evolves within this second generation of Heathen young people. However, for now Heathenry is *developing* a polytheistic tradition, building a new culture from the ideological basis of this emerging polytheism. As that culture grows, it becomes a reinforcing factor in the lives of Heathen people.

## Hard Polytheism

The theology and practice of polytheism has become a topic of significant interest in the American Pagan world. Heathen polytheists have sometimes experienced this as a conflicted theological space in which tensions form around "soft" and "hard" perspectives on the nature of deity. Think of these like cooking an egg. A soft position oozes, yolk and albumen flow together, with little definition or boundaries. Likewise soft polytheism envisions the nature of deity as more fluid, with less distinction among the divine personalities. The energies of the Goddess and God stream through the numerous forms and faces of the world's gods. In contrast, imagine an egg cooked hard, yolk and albumen firm and set, with clear boundaries and distinctions. Hard polytheism understands the many gods as distinct, personal beings as individuated as human persons are from one another.

American Heathens have associated soft polytheism with the milieu of Wicca and Witchcraft, the theological tributary that flows from the poetry of the English Romantics through the practical systematizing of Gerald Gardner and the further feminist developments of Goddess worship. Soft polytheists note that there are many occurrences of similar deities in the ancient world, patterns of divinity among various cultures. These particular expressions of deity are archetypal or metaphorical representations of deeper, more essential realities: natural forces, aspects of the human psyche, or embodiments of the Goddess and the God. "Soft polytheism," as Christine Kraemer explains it, "is the idea that there are many Gods, but they are aspects of one God/dess, or sometimes a Goddess and a God."[583] In this case, the goddesses of the Norse tradition are beings who reveal or embody some aspect or dimension of the Great Goddess. They are cultural instances of the Goddess herself. This soft understanding of deity explains the multiplicity of gods as the multicultural manifestations of the binary polarity of divine masculine and feminine. York writes that "the plethora of names for goddesses and gods often used by contemporary Western Pagans of the neopagan school does not represent independent, substantially

---

583. Christine Kraemer, "Three Legs on the Pagan Cauldron, or Must Pagans Be Polytheists?" *Dowsing for Divinity: Pagan Theology, Poetry, and Praxis*, January 11, 2013, www.patheos.com/blogs/sermonsfromthemound/2013/01/must-Pagans-be-polytheists/#ixzz3RZx69b00.

or cosmically distinct entities but, rather and simply, designations for either its Goddess or God."[584] Here the ontological status of the various gods and goddesses is over-shadowed by the emphasis on the duotheistic conception of the divine nature.

The harder Heathen perspective often vociferously resists soft positions of polytheism, seeing in them an implicit dilution or adulteration of the real and personal nature of the gods. Heathens have pushed back against the depiction of their gods as coinciding with natural energies, existing as instances of archetypal figures, as "aspects" of a transcultural duotheistic reality, or as conflations with deities from other cultural contexts. All these soft approaches in one way or another tend to obscure the hard nature of the gods, who are distinct persons in their own right. While doing field research at contemporary Pagan festivals, Sarah Pike recalls how a ritual was opened by invoking the various names of the Goddess without consideration for cultural or ethnic boundaries, "'Artemis!' 'Kali!' 'Ogun!' 'Isis!' 'Pan!' and 'Great Spirit!'" all of which expressed different aspects or cultural manifestations of a great goddess.[585] Such an invocation would, and at times has, caused an uproar at a Heathen gathering. While Heathenry maintains a highly polytheistic ethos, the boundaries of its gods-talk remain tightly controlled. In fact, at a Heathen event, one would hear specific warnings against the invocation of non-Norse deities, and perhaps even some Norse ones! Every public blót I have attended has incorporated some sort of "warding" or bounding of the ritual to prevent the invocation of deities outside of the Norse tradition, protecting as it were the domain of the family.

In contrast to other types of Pagans, Heathens often describe themselves as hard or true polytheists. Most share the perspective of Thora who says, "I'm a true polytheist. And I like all the gods and I'll work with them if they need me."[586] Hard polytheists like Thora view the gods as ontologically real beings each with his or her own distinct, specific, and individual nature. As Gundarsson writes, they are "real and mighty beings, as free-standing and as individually aware as we who work their wills upon the Middle-Garth."[587] Pagan

---

584. York, *Pagan Theology*, 64.
585. Pike, *Earthly Bodies*, 123.
586. Thora, interview.
587. Gundarsson, *History and Lore*, 131.

theologian Christine Kraemer states that hard polytheism represents a more straightforward reading of the Lore, which suggests "the gods are objectively existing, independent personalities."[588] As such, the gods are individuals, "volitional and unique beings much like individual humans, and should be treated as such."[589] This view implies that, just as individual humans exist within specific times, places, and cultural contexts, the deities have contexts and qualities specific to themselves. "Hard polytheists," Kraemer explains, "experience the gods as powerful presences with distinctive desires and behaviors, as well as historical ties to particular traditions, cultures, and lands."[590] This is certainly the case in Heathenry, in which the gods are highly enculturated and some degree of cultural fluency is concomitant with venerating them.

The depiction of the gods is an important dynamic of most polytheistic religions, including contemporary Heathenry. Images of the gods serve both devotional and heuristic functions, referencing the stories of the gods and revealing their important individuating characteristics. These images, as well as the religious literature of the Lore, frequently anthropomorphize the gods. Heathens take these descriptions to represent metaphorical, not literal, depictions of their unique personalities.[591] Norse and Germanic cultures must have depicted the gods in a variety of ways, but one style from these cultures has received a good deal of attention in contemporary Heathen culture—the godpole (see figure 20). The godpole has a very particular and simple aesthetic. It consists of an upright wooden pole into which the god form is carved, emerging subtly and only slightly distinguished from the pole itself. Carole Cusack mentions that these godpole depictions are reminiscent of trees.[592] Indeed they are trees and carry the tree-human-world homology important to the Norse myths. The iconography is compelling, de-emphasizing the human-like characteristics and depicting the gods in a mysterious and powerful way. The face staring from the godpole signifies the otherness of the gods: not quite human, nor

---

588. Kraemer, *Seeking the Mystery*, "Hard Polytheism."
589. Kraemer, "Three Legs on the Pagan Cauldron."
590. Kraemer, *Seeking the Mystery*, "Hard Polytheism."
591. Within Asatru, there exists a diversity of views on the nature of the gods. Some Heathens view the gods as archetypal realities, while others take a non-theistic approach to Heathenry, seeing the gods as symbols of its ethical and cultural aspects.
592. Cusack, *The Sacred Tree*, 94, 167–68.

reducible to the details of human form, the anthropomorphized images are the human-facing aspect of the numinous, recognizable but unknowable and obscure at the same time.

The tangibility of the gods in these images draws them close to human awareness. Veneration practices include sprinkling the images with sacred liquid such as mead or blood from a sacrifice, burning incense, saying prayers and leaving offerings in front of them. Many Asatruar will have images of the gods in their homes, particularly on a home altar or outside in a sacred space. These images range from hand-carved semi-anthropomorphic godpoles to expensive resin statues available from dealers in Pagan items. At the Heathen gathering in Pennsylvania mentioned above, campers pulled the image of the god Thor in the wain around the field every morning and evening, symbolically circumambulating the camp.[593] This twice-daily procession, reminiscent of the twice-daily pujas to the *murthi*s in a Hindu temple, represented the protective power and presence of the deity protecting the *wael*, the well-being, of the gathered Heathens and the frith, the peace of the community.[594]

At the experiential level, it may be that soft and hard polytheists are not as different as it may appear and that the theological lines gets fuzzy. Hard polytheists may have *experiences* of the gods that are quite variable. At times, these experiences may resemble the approaches of soft polytheists. Paper suggests that polytheistic religious systems tend to be comfortable with a variety of experiences and viewpoints about the gods. "Both unitary and multiple understandings of the numinous," he writes, "can be found side by side, either separately or in a complementary fashion in a number of religious traditions."[595] His statement suggests that within mature polytheistic systems, a colorful variety of theological positions may exist even within one person's range of experience. In this case, clear ideological boundaries between "hard" and "soft" polytheism may represent the growing pains of new polytheistic cultures. Hard polytheism that rejects "soft" experiences and a soft polytheism that has difficulty with "real" gods both may represent positions that are ideological responses to the dominant monotheist creeds, and the struggle between spiritual experience and the rationalities of

---

593. Field notes by author, Pennsylvania, June 2012.
594. Field notes by author, Pennsylvania, August 2012.
595. Paper, *The Deities Are Many*, 122.

modernity. While these basic positions remain part of the conversation, the polytheist movement has grown more complex. Numerous voices are engaged in a vibrant exploration of polytheism and its contemporary revival occurring especially on the Internet at sites such as Polytheist.com and other Pagan religious sites and blogs. It has become something of an interdisciplinary project, focused more on the polytheist experience itself than any particular Pagan traditions.

The emergence of hard polytheism in Heathenry poses an interesting problem, because it is not obvious that Heathens should hold such a view. Neither the influence of völkisch Paganism nor the magical approach of the Wiccan and Witchcraft tributary would predispose the movement to hard polytheism. The origin seems to lie in three other factors: the American religious context, the Lore-oriented nature of the movement, and the sociological impetus to define a religious identity distinct from that of Wicca. A conservative perspective on religion and deity remains an important dynamic in many American communities that perpetuate a Christian theology of "hard" monotheism. For Americans socialized within those conservative cultural contexts, there exists a predisposition to imagine deity in a hard way, which may go a long way to explain the predominance of hard polytheism among Heathens in the American heartland. Furthermore, the socioeconomic location of Heathenry might also be a consideration. A working-class religion may reject literary or metaphorical interpretations of deity in favor of something more solid and real, like a god who wields a hammer. Similarly, the Lore portrays the gods as distinct persons, and a straightforward reading of the Lore lends itself to hard interpretations. The theological material in the Lore consists primarily of the mythological stories themselves. Commentary and interpretation of this material comes later, including the theologically dismissive approach of Christian missionaries, the euhemeristic tendencies of some historians, and the various scholarly approaches of the modern period. Interpretations arising from within ancient Norse Paganism is lacking, unlike the ancient Greek cultures in which surviving plays, poetry, essays, and philosophical works shed light on evolving interpretation of the gods and their stories from within the tradition. The most important factor pushing Heathenry in a hard theological direction remains the long-running tension with Wicca and Witchcraft, a point made by Lewis Stead in his article

"The Pentagram and the Hammer" published in the mid-1990s. In it, he contrasts the pantheistic orientation of Wicca with the polytheist approach of Heathenry. For Stead, this difference has important implications that lead to distinctly different approaches. Wiccans, he suggests, see spiritual development in terms of achieving balance, while Heathens see it a result of conflict. Wiccan cosmology is based on the fertility cycles of the earth, while the Heathen cosmos hurtles toward the impending cataclysm of Ragnarok. Wicca is a mystery religion, while Heathenry is a votive religion. "In analyzing conflict between Wiccan and Ásatrú communities," he writes, "this particular concept [the theological differences] cannot be underestimated."[596] These factors have contributed to a religious culture in which hard polytheism is a predominant approach as well as a distinctive feature important to Heathen identity.

## Heathen Polytheistic Culture

The gods, goddesses, and other divine beings of Norse mythology play an enormously important part in the Asatru worldview and experience. Heathens dedicate time and attention to becoming well versed and knowledgeable about the Norse deities. Most Heathen books contain descriptions and discussions of the gods, their histories, natures, and techniques to facilitate interaction with them. Heathen authors are writing and publishing monographs focused on exploring one specific god or goddess in depth.[597] Those who are even casually acquainted with Norse myth will recognize that the corpus is complex, with a great variety of names, places, events, and relationships represented. Odin himself has many names, which may reveal or hide his identity. Each is reflective of his many attitudes and adventures. Despite its complexity, many Heathen adherents become deeply knowledgeable about the Lore and its content. References to Norse mythology abound in the casual conversation of Heathens. Many personal Heathen names taken by adherents reflect their affinity for gods and goddess. Kindred

---

596. Devyn Gillette and Lewis Stead, "The Pentagram and the Hammer," *Raven Kindred* website, www.ravenkindred.com/wicatru.html.
597. These monographs often combine elements of scholarship, the writer's UPG or personal experience of the god, and devotional material. Examples of this Heathen genre include Patricia M. Lafayllve, *Lady, Vanadis: An Introduction to the Goddess* (Denver, CO: Outskirts Press, 2006); and Sheffield, *Frey: God of the World*.

names frequently reference the Lore, such as Jotun's Bane, which refers to either Thor himself, or his hammer Mjolnir; Gladsheim Kindred and Bifrost Kindred, both of which refer to distinct locations within the Norse cosmology. At one event, I noticed kindred members wearing shirts emblazoned with what appeared to be a chicken. When I inquired about the image, one member told me it represented Gollinkambi. I must have appeared puzzled, having no idea who that was. He kindly explained that Gollinkambi referred to the golden rooster of Asgard who crows a warning at the outbreak of Ragnarok. Heathenry abounds with such examples of detailed familiarity with Norse mythological names. Heathens study and memorize the many names of the gods, drawing on them during blót and sumbel, and using them during personal meditation to invoke their many different facets. It is not merely knowledge of the names and bynames that is important, although such mastery of the Lore earns a Heathen much respect. These divine names open up new dimensions of experience and understanding, not only of the gods but also of the adherent's own internal states. While the polytheism of the arch-Heathens did not produce a systematic theology, the names function in that capacity as cues for theological concepts as well as for the values and cosmology of the Norse mythological system.

At most Heathen events, the children in attendance form quick friendships. They spend the weekend exploring and running around in small packs of juvenile energy while their parents take part in the religious events. There is often a row of vendors' tables set up outside under canopies, displaying their items. At one Heathen event, I watched as a pack of young boys paused in front of a vendor's table full of small figurines of the deities, items that an adherent might add to a home altar. In a back and forth discussion with the vendor, the boys began to identify the various gods, mentioning their stories and adventures. Although the boys could not remember the names of Odin's wolves, they knew that he had two as well as two ravens.[598] I was impressed not only with the fluency in the Norse myths displayed by several of the boys, but also their excitement in talking about it. The experience brought home the way that Heathen polytheism was coalescing as a culture. As they ran off, I wondered how their relationship with the gods

---

598. Field notes by author, Kansas, 2013.

would change over time as they reflected more deeply on their own spirituality.

In his definition of Paganism, Michael York pointed out that Pagans tend to understand gods and humans as codependent and interrelated. Heathen hard polytheists express this reality in their description of the deities as "elder kin" and "beloved friends" to humans, indicating that a family relationship exists between humans and the gods.[599] This awareness of divine/human kinship derives from *Rígsþula*, one of the Norse creation stories found in the *Poetic Edda*. Often called a lay, a type of narrative poetry that recounts a story of adventure or heroics, *Rígsþula* follows the adventures of the god Ríg, "a wise god ancient, rugged and mighty."[600] In contemporary Asatru, Ríg is commonly identified as Heimdall, who is best known as the guardian standing watch over the Bifrost Bridge. As Ríg, he wanders across Midgard and enters into three homes — that of a poor, elderly couple; an industrious, neatly dressed, middle-class couple; and a finely-dressed, noble couple, enjoying their plenty in leisure. He stays with each couple for three days sharing their hospitality, including the sexual favors of the wives with whom he sires sons. These sons become the progenitors of the three human castes: the thralls or servant caste, the free landholders, and the nobility.[601] The caste implications of this story are downplayed by most Asatruar. However, folkish Heathens often take note of this theme, giving more credence to the idea that human communities should reflect a hierarchical structure. Interpreted as a value intrinsic to properly ordered Germanic societies, hierarchy has long been a value practiced within Theodism. Theods, the small-group structure of Theodish Anglo-Saxon Heathenry, incorporate the practice of sacral kingship into each small group. Many folkish Heathen groups model the *primus inter pares* leadership of the Germanic warband, in which a chieftain takes leadership over a band of strong equals. Many folkish Heathens want to take caste more seriously and push against the dynamic of low power distance that shapes the informal and egalitarian nature of contemporary American society. Stephen

---

599. Gundarsson, *History and Lore*, 135; Gardell, *Gods of the Blood*, 268.

600. Hollander, *The Poetic Edda*, 120. Hollander notes that Vösluspá refers to all humans as Heimdall's children. This reference leads to the idea that the name Ríg in *Rígsþula* is a kenning for Heimdall. However, the name does not appear in Sturluson's list of kennings for Heimdall in *Skaldskaparmal*.

601. Paxson, *Essential Ásatrú*, 57.

McNallen observes, "Asatru today has too many mediocre men and women who, believing 'we are all equal,' have no notion of the bond between leaders and followers so central to Germanic society . . . where the chieftain, the aristocracy, and the freemen existed in an interplay of powers."[602] His understanding of Germanic society, drawn primarily from Dumézil's descriptions of a tripartite social structure in Indo-European culture, seems to lack a desired critical perspective. Other than a Romantic attachment to hierarchy, these folkish writers give little indication of how they would enact such a caste system.

For most Heathens, the important consideration of Ríg's story is not the need to return to a caste-based society, but the notion of a relationship of kinship with the gods. The story suggests an organic, even biological relationship with the gods. As one Heathen author writes, "The important thing to remember is that humankind is kin of the gods, first crafted by Their own hands, then imbued with Their own lifeforce, and later descended directly from Them."[603] This idea has become fundamental to Heathen reginal (gods-talk). Humans interact with the gods as kin, neither as their subjects nor as their creatures. Not only the souls and minds, but also the physical bodies of Heathens in some way share a connection to the divine beings. This creates a different paradigm for human nature than the body/soul dualism typically associated with the monotheistic traditions. This idea of divine kinship came to be interpreted in a racially exclusive way by the völkisch predecessors of the movement, and continues to exert its influence over racist Heathens. For most, it symbolizes a closeness and a commonality between gods and humans, expressing a continuity of being rather than two completely distinct ontological categories. Similarly, the familial theology of hard polytheistic Heathenry influences how practitioners conceive of their religious goals. The emphasis of Heathen theology and practice is not soteriological but social: the reestablishment of this kinship relation, based on acknowledging, enacting, and maintaining relationships through the practice of mutual and reciprocal exchange.

---

602. McNallen, "Three Decades of the Ásatrú Revival," 216.
603. Krasskova, *Exploring the Northern Tradition*, 33.

## The Heathen Gods

The Norse gods are members of two distinct divine families: the Aesir (Old Norse *Æsir*) who some describe as deities of mind and culture, and the Vanir who represent the chthonic powers of earth and fertility. After a brutal war between these two tribes of gods, a truce was formulated and the two united to maintain the cosmos since that time. While some contemporary Asatruar consider themselves specifically "Asatru" or "Vanatru," i.e. connected with one family of gods in particular, most practitioners venerate all these gods equally. A third group, the jǫtnar, represents the elemental forces of nature, the underworld, and the fire and ice from which the primeval cosmos emerged. Some contemporary practitioners consider these beings as a third divine family and choose to work with or venerate them, a persuasion of Heathenry sometimes called Rokkatru. This is a decidedly controversial position since the giants are also the initiators of Ragnarok and the destruction of the gods. Followers of the Rokkatru path, which might include devotees of Loki, often take on a marginal and dissenting identity and form an interesting sub-community within Heathenry.

Figure 19. Altar for Freyja Blót at East Coast Thing. (Photo by the author.)

While Odin may be considered chief of the family of gods, the divine feminine is also emphasized and both male and female deities play important roles. Goddesses are considered the equals of the gods, "no less holy are the *asynjur* [the goddesses] nor is their power less."[604] While observers describe early Asatru as a Viking boys club, this situation has dramatically changed in recent years with women becoming a significant presence and taking important leadership roles.[605] Not only are women now more numerous and prominent in the movement but the visibility of the goddesses has increased as well. Heathen polytheism has fully integrated the worship of female spiritual powers into its religious culture, though *how* fully is closely associated with the tributaries informing any particular Heathen event or group. Veneration of Iðunn, goddess of new life, opens each annual Trothmoot.[606] At East Coast Thing, there are often multiple rituals devoted to goddesses each year. In 2012, East Coast Thing featured a nighttime faining to Freyja as the main ritual (see figure 19). The gythjas who officiated the ritual handed out small pieces of amber, recalling for participants the mythological account of Freyja's tears.[607] As horns of mead circulated through the crowd, participants were instructed to speak softly and privately to the goddess in contrast to the loud and often verbose orations given to the gods at most blóts. After these prayers had been made, worshipers were given an opportunity to approach the hörg and offer the amber pieces as a gift to the goddess by placing them in the fire. After this faining, there was such an emotional response that several ritual leaders remained behind to counsel with participants. In other years, rituals have been held for Frigg; Eir, a healing goddess and one of Frigg's maidens; Hel; and Skaði, a jotun who married into the family of the gods.

While it is often the case that Heathen men primarily venerate the male warrior gods and women worship the female goddesses,

---

604. Paxson, *Essential Ásatrú*, 77.

605. Paxson, interview; Eowyn, email to author, June 6, 2011.

606. Iðunn is the keeper of the apples of youth and wife of Bragi, the god of poetry. Her name is commonly written as Idun, or Idunna, with the ending added to denote her feminine status. The names of several other goddesses are treated similarly: Frigg and Frigga, the mother goddess and Odin's wife; Hel and Hella, the keeper of the underworld Helheim and Loki's daughter.

607. Sturluson, *Gylfaginning*, 35, in the *Prose Edda*. Freyja is said to weep tears of red gold, often interpreted as amber, for her wandering husband Óðr.

this is not a universal rule by any means. Many women look to male gods and Asatru men are gradually opening to the experience of the divine feminine. In an essay titled "A Conversation with Frigga," Mark Stinson writes about his experiences with the goddess Frigga and suggests that male Asatruar should more actively venerate the goddesses:

> I think male Asatruars tend to talk a lot to Odin, Thor, Tyr, Freyr, and the other male Gods. We tend to honor them more, and not pay enough attention to the Asyniur. But, those of you with families, wives, and children . . . I would encourage you to begin talking with Frigga . . . and offering her gifts. In this day and age of "disposable marriages" and "temporary families," a Heathen husband should turn to Frigga for guidance.[608]

In Stinson's remark, we see the important way that polytheism functions, as the variety of gods and goddesses bring resources to the diverse aspects and experiences of life. Asatru culture will become more distinctly and authentically polytheistic as this broadening of veneration continues to develop. While most Heathens can describe personal experiences with the gods, Odin is by far the most ubiquitous subject of veneration among contemporary practitioners. No contemporary Asatru movement would exist without the presence of Odin. For many Heathens, their first foray into the religion came as a result of dreams or other experiences in which they interacted with the gods, particularly Odin. As one practitioner told me, "Odin is the gateway drug for modern Heathenry."[609]

The reasons for Odin's prominence have much to do with the transmission of the Norse material into the American context. Odin is simply the most well known of the gods, so it is no surprise that he might be the first that adherents become aware of. It is clear that in the religious practice of the ancient Norse cultures, gods were more or less prominent in any region or time period. One of the strengths of polytheism is the flexibility of the religious system, allowing for shifts of veneration and visibility of gods without disrupting the entire religious culture. So while Odin may be ubiquitous in contemporary Heathenry, the gradual broadening

---

608. Mark L. Stinson, "A Conversation with Frigga," in *Heathen Families: Fables and Essays*, 52–53.
609. Nertha, interview.

of devotion is a sign of religious vitality. The diversity of gods allows worshipers to orient towards the gods who correspond most closely to the needs or goals of life. Each deity is known for his/her spheres of power and skill and contemporary worshipers are often attracted to specific gods for this reason.[610] As Stinson stated above, Frigg may be especially important for those who are building a household, raising children and working on their marriages, as well as crafters and practitioners of the arts of domestic life. Odin is known for wisdom, poetry, but also magic and battle fury. Thor is the god of protection and might. Tyr, who sacrificed his hand so that the Aesir could bind the terrible Fenriswolf, is known as the god of the polestar with an unwavering sense of justice. Freyr is the god of fertility and virility. Freyja is the goddess of sexuality, the "witch" goddess who is the source of magic and venerated by seið workers. At the same time, she is a war goddess who gathers half the battle dead. In addition to the major gods of Norse tradition many Heathens call upon less well-known entities when given the opportunity. The sun goddess Sunna, Mani who steers the moon across the sky, Bragi the god of poetry, the sea goddess Rán, some of the various handmaidens of Frigga, and many others all have their place in Heathen religiosity. To name the gods is to forge relationships with them. At the same time, hard polytheists resist the tendency to reduce a god to a "sphere." While one may want to call on Thor in particular circumstances of life, he is not the god "of" protection, or battle or lightning, or the god "of" anything in particular. He is ultimately and irreducibly Thor. He, like the other gods, is a complex and sophisticated being to whom one must relate personally.

This complexity extends into the moral sphere as well. As Harvey clearly states, "Pagan deities do not have to be 'nice,' compassionate or even provident."[611] Odin is neither good, in some traditional moral sense, nor predictable. In fact the gods of Heathenry can be demanding and challenging, deceptive and manipulative, ominous and threatening. During a powerful moment in a Trothmoot workshop, Kveldúlf Gundarsson warned his Heathen listeners not to grow too complacent and comfortable with their gods. "The hall of Odin," he reminded them,

---

610. Paper, *The Deities are Many*, 139.
611. Harvey, *Contemporary Paganism*, 160.

is a terribly frightening place. Instead of hounds, he has wolves; instead of hawks he has a corpse-eating eagle; instead of pillars supporting the roof, he has spears. The women who carry ale in this terrible place are not soft and beautiful, but choosers of the slain, dripping with blood. And this is appropriate because those who are feasting there are the dead, a zombie feast.[612]

The statement grabbed the attention of the participants, many of whom audibly expressed their agreement about Odin's more terrifying aspects. The vividness of his description brought home the point that the gods do not conform to our suppositions about what is appropriate and comfortable. It was a warning to the participants to avoid overly domesticating their gods and minimizing their complexity and mystery. This complex nature of the gods may be difficult at times for Heathens. Perchta who sees herself as a devotee of Odin also expresses her personal emotional struggle with the god, whom she holds responsible at some level for taking children from her through miscarriages. At times, she feels something akin to love for him, while at others she struggles with anger toward this difficult god. Heathens revel in the fact that the gods are willing to go to great lengths to achieve their goals in the world, striving against the odds and against the limits of their own natures to grasp and gain the objects of their desires. Like the gods themselves, humans are meant to struggle courageously towards worthy goals and for those to whom they have relationships of responsibility.

But generalizations like this do not fit comfortably with a hard Heathen conception of the gods. Each god approaches and works in the cosmos in his or her own distinctive way. Odin responds to the world differently than Tyr or Freyja might, for instance. Similarities are apparent on the surface of the myths, for example both Odin and Tyr sacrificed themselves for the greater good. Odin gave up an eye, and Tyr his forearm. Yet the motivations for those actions, the values they express, and the solutions gained are individual to each god involved. Recognizing and appreciating those differences are important aspects of Heathen spirituality. For the humans working with these beings, there are distinctive "ways," lifestyles, values, and forms of interaction, which accompany or are associated with the gods. To say that the gods "represent" ways of being is too abstract. Rather, as divine exemplars, they make possible multiple

---

612. Field notes taken by author, Pennsylvania, 2012.

ways of being holy. To "put down the Hammer and take up the cloak," as Torsen said earlier in the chapter, represented a shift in his approach to life, shaped by the "way" of the god. In its directness and forthrightness, a Thor-like approach to problem solving will be decidedly different than a life lived in the domain of Odin. There may be several different approaches inspired by Odin, but all might emphasize a questioning and questing approach, a search for knowledge, using testing, subtlety, and cunning over force and forthrightness. Steven McNallen engaged in a similar exploration in a pamphlet entitled *Thunder from the North*, in which he identified six "warrior" types based on Norse gods. "So what kind of warrior are you? To find out, take a stroll through the family tree of our mighty Gods," he writes. He goes on to profile the warrior models of Odin the mystical warrior, Thor the fiery defender, Frey who is creative and aesthetically refined, Tyr who is honest and dutiful, and Balder, "the unproven warrior," who is still naïve about his capabilities.[613] While it comes across like a kitschy personality profile at times, a deeper reading suggests that McNallen has in mind six different expressions of masculinity each based on the domain of a Norse god.[614] Similarly the numerous goddesses have their own ways of being, providing patterns that shape, influence, and inspire the lives of their followers. For adherents who are open to learning from and living within the domains of particular gods, Heathen polytheism provides a range of gender expressions and multiple ways of being in the world.

### *Hard Polytheism and the Blót*

Polytheism is as much a system of practice as it is a belief in many gods. In the discussion of hard and soft polytheism, the relationship between belief and practice may be overlooked. Beliefs are expressed through and supported by practices, and may in fact arise from practices. The exact relationship may be hard to pin

---

613. Stephen A. McNallen, *Thunder from the North: The Way of the Teutonic Warrior* (Nevada City, CA: Asatru Folk Assembly, 1993), 8–10.

614. Scott Simpson, "Men Constructing Masculinity in Polish Rodzimowierstwo: Tradition and Nature," *Pantheon* 10, no. 1 (2015): 3–20. Simpson has noticed similar occurrences in the Polish reconstructionist religion known as *Rodzimowierstwo*. In gods such as Perun and Veles, male adherents discover different expressions of manhood and find new models for their lives and roles in society.

Figure 20. Godpole at East Coast Thing. (Photo by the author.)

down: do beliefs give rise to corresponding practices, or do practices generate theological ideas? Hard polytheism and the practice of the blót, the Heathen sacrificial ritual, are interrelated. If the gods are distinct personalities and ontologically real beings, then hard polytheism necessitates the need for a ritual of relationship. In turn, the practice of blót supports and confirms the experience of the deities as distinct personal entities. As Kraemer states, when hard polytheists invoke a deity, "they see themselves as calling someone very specific."[615] Heathen performance of blót emphasizes venerating the gods as honored kin, but not the subjection or submission of the self. According to Harvey, Pagans "rarely describe their approach to deities as worship, which they often see as a form of

---

615. Kraemer, *Seeking the Mystery*, "Hard Polytheism."

self-denigration and servile dependence. They honour their deities, and respect them for their more-than-human abilities in some area, or for their care, concern and guidance."[616] The basic understanding of human interaction with the gods is that of reciprocal exchange, a theology summed up in the ubiquitous Heathen phrase "A gift for a gift," and concretely enacted by practitioners in the ritual of blót.[617] Humans give gifts and offerings, particularly and most commonly mead, the sacred beverage of Heathenry. Animal sacrifice remains a decidedly minority activity among Asatru adherents, however the practice of "live blót" is nevertheless being practiced by some on special occasions and seems to be increasingly so by serious reconstructionists.[618]

A blót usually begins with some sort of hallowing of the space. Early in the Heathen movement, this hallowing was often performed with the Hammer Rite or Hammer-Working that may have first been described in Thorsson's *Book of Troth*.[619] The Hammer Working ritual borrowed substantially from Wicca's calling of the quarters as well as from Native American practice. It consisted of raising the symbol of Mjolnir, representative of Thor's protective power, in each of the six directions, "Hammer in the North, hale and hallow this holy stead!" and so on. As Heathenry increasingly articulated its differences with Wicca, the Hammer Rite dropped out of favor and has been used less and less within Heathen ritual. More frequently, rituals are opened by addressing the land spirits and the gods, asking for their beneficent company, and inviting their participation. Mead, poured into a horn, is "charged" with the invocations of the participants, whether the ritual leader alone or all those in attendance. Words spoken while holding the horn are especially significant. Jarl, an experienced goði, says that "when

---

616. Harvey, *Contemporary Paganism*, 160.

617. Paper, *The Deities are Many*, 14. Paper writes in more detail about reciprocal relationships with deities.

618. Field notes taken by author, Kansas, September, 2012; Michael Strmiska, "Putting the Blood Back into Blót: The Revival of Animal Sacrifice in Modern Nordic Paganism," *The Pomegranate: The International Journal of Pagan Studies* 9, no. 2 (2007): 154–89. See chapter 6 for my discussion of animal sacrifice.

619. In the same work, Thorsson also described a "hammer-signing" in which the practitioner drew the shape of the hammer across the body with a fist, from forehead to mouth, to solar plexus, and across the shoulders. Seemingly a mixture of chakras and the Roman Catholic sign of the cross, this practice did not seem to catch on with many Heathens.

you have the horn and you are passing it around, I think it is like an intercom. So that you're talking to the gods. Not that they can't hear you without the horn. But when it is formalized that way, that's how it is working."[620] The words of praise, request, and sincere emotion are ritually infused in the mead. This sacred liquid becomes a libation, an offering to the gods poured out at the base of a sacred tree, into a sacred fire, or given by other means. Physical gifts of various sorts are also dedicated to the gods and goddesses during blót. These offerings might be hung on trees in a sacred outdoor space or burned in a fire.[621]

These rites are moments of great sanctity for Heathens. At times, they can become moments of great vulnerability. This happened at a Heathen event held in a state park in Oklahoma. As the Iðunn blót ended, the ritual leader took the bowl of mead and other offerings to a stream on the park grounds to place the offerings into the running water. Her decision reflected the Heathen understanding of nature as alive and sacred. By placing the offerings into the stream, the participants venerated and expressed appreciation to the goddess but also to the indigenous land spirits of the area. As it turned out, that section of the stream was also near a popular swimming hole for local inhabitants. Several families as well as some sunbathing teenagers were wading and lying out along the rock-lined stream. When the ritual leader and another female approached the stream, both wearing Norse-styled apron dresses as part of their ritual garb, they were greeted at first by stares from the bathers. As they laid the offerings at the edge of the stream into the quickly flowing water, a woman from one of the families began yelling at them, "Demon worshipers!"

For Heathens, giving offerings to the gods and spirits is a concrete enactment of the ongoing relationship with these beings. In response to these offerings and the petitions and prayers of the worshipers, the gods and goddesses are thought to reciprocate with both tangible and intangible gifts, blessings for their human kin and friends. While these blessings are primarily experienced

---

620. Jarl, telephone interview with the author, February 23, 2015.
621. These practices have precedents in the Norse tradition. For a well-written and evocative description of a contemporary blót that included these sorts of offerings, see Josh Heath, "Two Yule Rituals: One Heathen's Experience in the Northeast US," *Óðrærir: The Heathen Journal* 2 (2014), http://odroerirjournal.com/two-yule-rituals-one-heathens-experience-in-the-northeast-us/.

psychologically and internally, they are also manifested physically such as when the ritual leader sprinkles the participants with sacred mead that has been blessed by the gods or when participants drink from the ritual horn.[622] During the Iðunn ritual, leaders distributed apple slices dipped in honey that participants ate as tangible symbols of the goddess' blessing. In a sense, all these examples of concrete, tangible, and consumable blessings are reminiscent of Hindu *prasad*. This reciprocal exchange is symbolic and involves more than obtaining tangible results. It should not be minimized to a "tit for tat" theology of either divine appeasement or bribery. Again, the monotheistic bias may cause misinterpretation of this pattern of reciprocal exchange as crassly materialistic, impersonal, or manipulative. For instance, Jan Baal argues that the early scholars of comparative religion, such as Edward Tylor and others, interpreted sacrifice as a primitive and unsophisticated practice, more like manipulating or bribing a deity for one's own gain than real religion.[623] While any form of worship may devolve over time into a rote practice lacking intellectual vigor and emotional vitality, such a degraded form is hardly a fair representation of the ideal intent of the act.

Blót, as Heathens see it, is about relationship. The ritualized act symbolically traces the network of relationships of loyalty and trust. When the ancient Heathen tribal leader presented gifts to his followers, it was not the physical gift itself that was foremost. Most importantly, the gift signified the relationship between them, a relationship of belonging, honor, and mutual dependence. Similarly, exchanging gifts is seen as religiously efficacious in establishing and maintaining ongoing relationships with divine beings.[624] As Swain Wódening, an influential Theodish author, indicates, "the exchange of gifts between Gods and men creates a bond between the two," humans and gods are brought together through the dynamic of reciprocal relation.[625] As Michael York points out, this is a bond of "co-dependent" and mutual cooperation. The gods relate to humans

---

622. Strmiska, *Modern Paganism in World Cultures*, 130. Field notes taken by author, Kansas, 2011, 2012.
623. Jan van Baal, "Offering, Sacrifice, Gift," *Numen* 23 (1976): 161–78.
624. Wolfe, "The Blót," 72.
625. Swain Wodening, "Connecting with the Gods," *Theodish Heathen*, September 16, 2010, https://theodishHeathen.wordpress.com/2010/09/16/connecting-with-the-gods-2/.

as autonomous beings, not perhaps as equals, but at the same time not as submissive and dependent slaves. Diana Paxson dismisses this "sheep model," of divine relationship, referring to the Judeo-Christian metaphor of God as a shepherd guiding his helpless sheep. Continuing with the ovine metaphor, Mark Stinson states, "I am not a lamb. I am an adult human being, and the Gods expect us to make our own decisions, fight our own battles, and make things happen for ourselves."[626] Heathens commonly make this distinction between Asatru and Christian theology. The Heathen gods are not shepherds of the dumb and defenseless flock. Mark Stinson draws heavily on familial themes as he describes how the arch-Heathens "honored their Gods, they respected their Gods . . . but their Gods were seen as their kin — part of the Folk — or part of their village or tribe. They treated the Gods as mentors, or elders in their tribe. Many saw them and treated the Gods like honored Ancestors."[627] Similarly, Raven Kindred North, a prominent and long-running kindred in the Northeast, speaks about the gods as "older members of a family who have worked and continue to work at strengthening that family physically, emotionally, and spiritually."[628] Far from manipulating or bribing, or reducing a spiritual relationship to one of crass materiality, the blót enacts and maps out, through corpospiritual means, the mutual and ongoing sets of relationships that exist between the gods and the human community. Humans are not alone in their struggle for survival and thriving; they may cultivate relationships with the numinous powers of the world. For Heathens, the gods stand alongside them.

## Conclusion

"What few westerners seem to realize is the possibility that polytheism fits the human mind and experience so comfortably," notes Jordan Paper.[629] In areas where monotheism represents the dominant religious model, polytheism has been reduced to an oddity or an outrage in the experience of most. Some Westerners, however, are seeking to rediscover that once-comfortable relationship

---

626. Stinson, *Heathen Gods*, 8.
627. Ibid.
628. Raven Kindred North, "The Gods and Goddesses," *Raven Kindred North* website, www. ravennorth.org/?page_id=12.
629. Paper, *The Deities are Many*, 4.

between humans and the many numinous powers around them. The emerging new Paganisms such as Heathenry are gradually building new cultures that give place to the old gods. Heathenry is on the cutting edge of this act of culture making. It is not an easy task. What does it mean to become a Heathen polytheist? What are the gods like and what do authentic numinous experiences look and feel like? How does one appropriately go about relating to divinity? Were the arch-Heathens "hard," "soft," or otherwise in their understanding and experience of the gods? These and many questions like them bear witness to the birth pangs of a new religious identity. Although hard polytheists abound in Heathenry, there is no one Heathen view of the gods. Heathens are striving to carve out an experience of the numinous consistent with their Lore that also works in contemporary life. The various theological and philosophical issues that arise from hard polytheism remain to be worked out by another generation of Heathens. For now, the Norse gods gradually take their place in the pluralism of American religion. The next chapter will further examine the blót and its developing relationship with Heathen culture by looking specifically at animal sacrifice in Heathenry.

## Chapter 6

## Animal Sacrifice and the Blót[630]

Animal heads on poles. Such was the sight that greeted a visitor to Hedeby in the tenth century. Hedeby was a sizeable Danish settlement on the Jutland peninsula on the boundary between Charlemagne's Christian empire and the Heathen north. It served both as an important center of trading as well as part of the Danevirke, the massive system of ramparts and forts built to protect Denmark from Frankish incursions. Accustomed to the more refined environs of Andalusia's cultured city of Cordoba, the visitor, Ibrahīm ibn Ya'qūb al-Isrā'īlī al-Turtūshī, evidently experienced a good deal of what we would now call "culture shock." In his writing, he left a brief description some of the sights and sounds that made him uncomfortable, such as singing that sounded like barking dogs or wild animals, noise and filth, the exposure of infants, and the freedom of women to divorce.[631] He also took note of animal sacrifices of oxen, rams, goats, and pigs performed by the Heathen residents of the town. These sacrifices were made in conjunction with feasts held in honor of a god, then displayed on poles in front of homes. What exactly al-Turtushi witnessed is open to conjecture. However, Jacqueline Simpson describes the well-attested practices in the ancient Pagan north of ceremoniously exhibiting the head of a sacrificed animal on a pole, and of flaying sacrifices in such a way that the head, with the full hide and hooves attached, could be displayed together.[632] During important Heathen blóts, the meat of the animal was eaten in the communal feasting that was

---

630. Portions of this chapter were first included in a paper presented for the Religion and Ecology section of the Southeastern Commission for the Study of Religion, Atlanta, GA, 2014.

631. Anders Winroth, *The Conversion of Scandinavia: Vikings, Merchants, and Missionaries in the Remaking of Northern Europe* (New Haven, CT: Yale University Press, 2012), 89; Davidson, *Myths and Symbols*, 37, 52.

632. Jacqueline Simpson, "Some Scandinavian Sacrifices," *Folklore* 78, no. 3 (1967): 192.

the centerpiece of Heathen spirituality. It seems that as part of the sacrificial process, the head was offered to the gods and publicly displayed as a record of the offering.[633]

The head on the pole served as a powerful symbol of piety for the Hedeby Heathens. This may seem counterintuitive to many modern American observers, as the aesthetics of the display do not comfortably conform to those typically associated with piety and religious observance. That realization accentuates the fact that our cultural formation, biases, and suppositions may initially form a barrier to deeper understanding of its spiritual significance. Consider the aesthetics of more contemporary practices, such as the performances of self-mutilation during the mourning for Ali that may take place in some Shi'ite Muslim communities on the ninth of Muharram. For participants, these are spiritual acts, although they may seem appalling to those who see them without understanding or sharing the cultural context. The crucifix, an important Christian religious symbol, is similarly a display of sacrifice—in this case, a human hung on a pole. The image, in its typical modern presentation, is softened and sanitized of the more grisly elements that would have accompanied a Roman crucifixion. However, it remains a depiction of torture and sacrifice. Even so, the social formation of many Christians enables them to interpret this image of horror as communicating significant religious values and generating profound spiritual emotions. Again, someone who does not share the value system or is unaccustomed to this presentation of human suffering might find it offensive. Similarly, the display of the sacrifice by the northern Heathens seems to have been an important component of their spirituality. The animal head was a symbol of piety, blessing, and relationship to the gods. It is comparable in some ways to other religious displays and performances of piety that we are accustomed to in our world and time.

It may also be helpful to consider the public display of Hedeby sacrifices as evidence of a dissenting religious attitude. I am reminded of driving along the roads of the rural American South a few years ago and seeing home after home displaying cardboard placards of the Ten Commandments in their front yards. During a particular political season that saw a great deal of conflict over

---

633. The practice of displaying sacrifices on poles may also correspond to the tree/human/world homology discussed in chapter 4.

the display of the Ten Commandments in schools and government spaces, the presentation of these placards became an innovative and effective way of publicly stating the piety of the household and taking a stand on a contentious social issue. More than a simple display of piety, the placards carried a dissenting message: a refusal to budge in the face of encroaching secular values. In the tenth century, Hedeby was also a location of religious conflict. The public presentation of the sacrifice made a similar statement for the Hedeby Heathens living on the border of Christian lands during a time of aggressive Christian expansion. The display of the animal head was an instantly recognizable declaration of a household's piety to the Heathen gods *and* a public declaration of a family's uncompromising stance in refusing to give up its religious values, even under encroaching social pressure to convert. While the display of the sacrifice might have been a traditional practice for Norse Heathens, traditions may appropriate dissenting connotations during times of social pressure and tension. In our own contentious times, contemporary Americans can relate to religious displays that serve as potent symbols of both piety and dissent.

This chapter concerns the religious and ethical dimensions of animal sacrifice or live blót in the religious culture of American Asatru.[634] Does the example of Hedeby help us in any way toward understanding the growing practice of animal sacrifice in contemporary Heathenry? Perhaps it takes us some distance in teaching us not to stop merely in response to our initial confusion over imagery and practices that are at first exotic to us. It reminds us that to understand a religious practice, we must first gain access to the religious values that inform it. That is not to minimize the "yuck factor" involved in animal sacrifice — it is not by any means a tidy religious rite and, very likely, would inspire a sense of revulsion for most contemporary observers. At the same time, that emotional response is, in part, what infuses the practice with awe and spiritual power for those who undertake it as part of serious spiritual and religious work. While sacrifice has long been a part of religious practice, contemporary Heathens face concerns about animal sacrifice that their arch-Heathen predecessors never had to

---

634. The word blót may be related to the Old Norse word for blood, blóð, giving it the more specific meaning of a "blood sacrifice," the offering of animal blood as a gift to the gods. See Wolfe, "The Blót," 71.

consider. Some of these concerns include the relevancy or usefulness of animal sacrifice, the pain involved in sacrificial death, and the moral status of the animal itself.

In the revival of ritual animal sacrifice, Heathens have not ignored these objections. Concerning the relevancy and efficacy of sacrifice, two points are particularly important. The first is that the skeptical and naturalistic suppositions of modernity create an intellectual context in which sacrificial religion seems passé. Many ancient religious societies, notably the Greek, Roman, and Norse, recognized and practiced animal sacrifice as an important component of their religious repertoire. However, in the modern West, the secular values and critical culture of modernity smirk at the idea of the efficacy of animal sacrifice. In the early development of religious studies, suppositions about the religious evolution of human civilization led to a critique of sacrifice as a primitive and out-moded practice. Accordingly many Americans, shaped by these modern beliefs, may struggle to understand sacrifice, failing to see how killing innocent animals could be effective for achieving spiritual and religious goals. Those Heathens who have begun to practice sacrifice turn this reasoning on its head. They locate the crisis of modern religion precisely in its overly spiritualized, sanitized, and abstract character. Religion removed from the gritty realities of life and death falls short, fails to engage and inspire. Sacrifice returns something vital to religious practice. The participants must confront the reality of death and its place in the ongoing life of the world. The act of sacrifice focuses the attention, draws in all the senses, and grabs the emotions. It presents a challenging spectacle in which the participants know that something important has occurred.

Heathens make a second point that has to do with the nature of the gods themselves and the reciprocal way in which humans relate to them. In the hard polytheism to which many Heathens hold, a relationship with real gods requires real gifts. The exchange between Heathens and their gods is an exchange of items of real value. The offering to one's gods must be costly, ideally an item to which the worshipers have contributed or made themselves, and therefore carrying part of the worshipers with it. Something of quality made with one's own hands is by far the best gift that worshipers can give to their gods. This aspect of value and connection is amplified in the case of a life that the worshiping community has fed, raised, and cared for. In the case of this living being, the wyrd and luck of the worshipers are bound up and intertwined with the animal, making the sacrifice that much more vital, costly, and powerful.

## *The Social Context*

Forty years ago in 1975, Peter Singer advocated vegetarianism as the only sufficient solution to the various moral issues associated with eating animals. Singer wrote, "Practically and psychologically it is impossible to be consistent in one's concern for nonhuman animals while continuing to dine on them." He drew the conclusion that "becoming vegetarian is the most practical and effective step one can take toward ending both the killing of nonhuman animals and the infliction of suffering upon them."[635] His absolutist argument rejecting meat as a morally legitimate food was the shot across the bow in a growing cultural divide. The idea that the only way to be an ethical eater is to be a vegetarian has been reflected in much of the literature and activism that followed.

How has that argument fared? When we examine actual eating practices over the last thirty years, we find that the vegetarian argument has not been persuasive, leaving mainstream American culture little changed. The rate of vegetarianism among Americans has remained flat for at least the past ten years. As Gallup polls indicate, "vegetarianism in the United States remains quite uncommon and a lifestyle that is neither growing nor waning in popularity."[636] Research by the Vegetarian Resource Group indicates that 97–99 percent of Americans sometimes eat meat, while research by Yale School of Medicine suggests that less than 1 percent of Americans are true vegetarians.[637] And at the same time, data indicate that the growth of consolidation within the American agricultural industry, i.e. factory farming, continues and the average meat consumption of Americans has increased.[638] Natural and

---

635. Peter Singer, *Animal Liberation: A New Ethics for Our Treatment of Animals* (New York: Random House, 1975), 172–73.

636. Frank Newport, "In U.S., 5% Consider Themselves Vegetarians; Even Smaller 2% Say They are Vegans," *Gallup*, July 26, 2012, www.gallup.com/poll/156215/consider-themselves-vegetarians.aspx.

637. Hal Herzog, *Some We Love, Some We Hate, Some We Eat: Why It's So Hard to Think Straight About Animals* (New York: Harper, 2010), 191.

638. Jennifer Mueller, "Data Shows 20 Percent Growth in Factory Farming In Past 5 Years," *Care 2 Make a Difference*, 2010, www.care2.com/causes/data-shows-20-percent-growth-in-factory-farming-in-past-5-years.html; National Cattlemen's Beef Association,

organic meat accounts for only a small percentage of retail sales of meat in the United States.[639] In comparison, the fast food industry has expanded exponentially in the last forty years, with revenue growing "from $6 billion in 1970 to $160 billion last year, an 8.6 percent annualized rate," according to industry reports in 2014.[640] Thus a significant divide exists between a minority who recognize the ethical unsuitability of animals as food (e.g. by activists, ethicists, and some religious groups) and the practical food choices of most Americans. These trends demonstrate one of two things: either that after considered reflection, most Americans find the commercial meat industry to be an ethical way of eating; or more likely, that the issues involved in ethical eating do not rise to a level of significance. Advertising, convenience, and the cost of food seem to be the primary factors shaping American eating habits and not ethics at all. The practice of eating continues to be bereft of ethical context, despite the arguments of Singer and other ethicists and the vegetarian movement. In fact, in contrast to ethical eating, it is "healthy eating" that seems to be the most prominent dissenting response to the commercial food industry. The rhetoric of healthy eating, however, seems to avoid issues concerning the ethics of meat eating. For these sorts of alternative viewpoints, we need to look to new religious movements.

New and alternative religions often address areas of social tension by acting as sites of social experimentation. Using religious ideas and practices, these groups create social spaces in which alternative approaches to mainstream norms can be proposed and developed. Given the social tension that now exists around eating animals, we would expect some new religious groups to express alternative conceptions of the relationship between animals, food, and morality. For example, the International Society for Krishna Consciousness has long advocated for animal rights and practiced vegetarianism.

"Annual Per Capita Consumption of Meat," *Beef USA*, www.beefusa.org/CMDocs/BeefUSA/Resources/Statistics/annualpercapitaconsumption-meat-retail.pdf. See also Herzog, *Some We Love*, 191.

639. Catherine Greene, "Organic Market Overview," *United States Department of Agriculture*, 2012, www.ers.usda.gov/topics/natural-resources-environment/organic-agriculture/organic-market-overview.aspx; Christopher Doering, "American Consumers Hungry for Organic Beef," *Organic Consumers Association*, 2004, www.organicconsumers.org/madcow/organic-beef.cfm.

640. Matt Sena, "Fast Food Industry Analysis 2014—Cost & Trends," *Franchise Help*, 2013, www.franchisehelp.com/industry-reports/fast-food-industry-report/.

On the other hand, the Asatru movement, quite carnivorous in its eating preferences, is slowly and carefully reviving the practice of animal sacrifice as part of its religious expression. Clearly, sacrifice is a decidedly marginal practice that appears shocking to mainstream considerations, yet the Asatru practice of animal sacrifice envisions a moral approach toward animals and food that rejects the ethical extremes of factory-farmed meat on one hand and vegetarian or vegan lifestyles on the other. Sacrifice is a special death, an ideal type that creates and enacts a web of ethical relationships in which the animal's life and death "counts" in social, moral, and religious ways.

### Sacrifice and Asatru

I considered animal sacrifice to be a marginal Asatru practice until an incident during the summer of 2012 while I was attending a large Asatru event in the Midwest. While standing in line for the opening feast that fed about two hundred, my son, who was attending the event with me and was something of a picky eater asked what was being served for supper. I answered, "Pulled pork." Overhearing my son's question, a member of the kindred hosting the event turned and said, "Blótted pig."[641]

This quick exchange represented the kind of moment that researchers occasionally experience in fieldwork in which a seemingly minor offhand comment sinks in and changes our entire perspective. It was a moment of revelation for me into the Asatru worldview that continues to unfold. The kindred member's use of the religious terminology "blótted pig" implied a completely different way of seeing what was happening than was reflected in my response of "pulled pork." The use of such discourse framed the event in a way that made the animal itself apparent, and the meal undertaken in the conscious awareness that a living animal had been religiously sacrificed that we might eat together. Since that time, I have come to realize that among those Heathens practicing live blót, some basic patterns of practice and belief are beginning

---

641. Field notes by author, Kansas, 2012. I did not attend a Heathen animal sacrifice during my research. The accounts presented here reflect the first-hand observations of Heathens who wrote and told me about their experiences with blót. I thank them for their willingness to share their insights about such significant and controversial experiences.

to emerge. These patterns include connections to farms where sacrificial animals are ethically raised, a concern for animal suffering, and a ritual cycle that includes common practical and theological elements. While the basic blót pattern remains essentially the same whether the offering is an animal, mead, or some other object, we will note important points of difference. The primary goal of this chapter is to discuss the ethical aspects of live blót and to describe how the sacrifice intensifies the act of eating among these Heathen kindreds and tribes, necessitating a heightened ethical awareness and sensitivity. Eating the sacrifice becomes a sacred as well as a dissenting act that calls into question and occasions a critique of secular, mainstream American eating practices.

Figure 21. Gothi Addressing Worshipers at Lightning Across the Plains. (Photo by the author.)

For most practitioners, however, social or ethical motivations do not serve as the primary reasons for reviving animal sacrifice. Drawing attention to animal rights or animal cruelty, subverting American consumption patterns and the techno-industrial food industry, even creating new religious networks—none of this is a significant factor behind the turn toward animal sacrifice. The primary motivation is the desire to be Viking, to embody religious practices from the past in the contemporary moment. Of course, the issue of restoring a Heathen practice untarnished by Christian ideas and practices is always present. Christianity obviously influenced the range of practices considered socially acceptable forms of worship. However, for most Heathens the reconstructive tendency is neither completely corrective, nor merely mimetic. Rather, Heathens who pursue the practice of sacrifice think, "There must be something to it," and set about discovering the reason or experience behind the practice. The past contains the pattern for the wholeness of humans and their communities. As part of the ancient religious pattern of life, it must have enriched the lives of the arch-Heathens. In the case of sacrifice, Heathens might approach it as a more authentic way of relating to the "hard" gods, a deeper recognition of reciprocity, or a religious practice that is more existentially alive and compelling.

However, it is the *implications* of sacrifice that interest me here. Engaging in a new religious practice in a consistent and significant way creates social and ethical possibilities that did not exist before. In addition to reordering specifically "religious" aspects of life, sacrifice also provides opportunities for re-evaluating one's relationship with animals, experience of eating, and involvement with the land, agriculture, and farming people. These possibilities remain out of reach for Americans whose consumption of food remains fully embedded in the mainstream American food system, the techno-industrial global food economy.

## The Sacrifice

The comment about "blótted pig" that sparked my interest in Heathen sacrifice occurred while standing in the food line at a feast. But the full story of the feast begins much earlier. Prior to hosting the gathering, this particular Midwestern Asatru kindred traveled to a farm operated by another Heathen family. There they held a sacrificial rite in which a pig was slaughtered as an offering to the gods. This cooperative effort represented an alliance or relationship between these two kindreds. The sacrifice took place in the context of a community network of urban kindreds and the rural farming kindred, a network of relationships built around and maintained by the material culture of sacrifice. The killing of the pig was embedded in the religious ritual of the blót, which as we have seen begins by consecrating the ritual space with the invocation of land spirits, ancestors, and gods. The invocation, in the description of one participant, clearly emphasized the treatment of the animal, "That evening we held blót, offering this gift in sacrifice to our Gods and Goddesses. We told them how well this animal had been treated, how well it had been fed and cared for, how it made a fitting offering to them and, in return, we asked that they watch over us and all our guests."[642] Participants each laid a hand on the animal and spoke to it with a kind phrase, a word of thanks, a message for the gods, a wish for a good journey, or blessing. The idea of the animal as a messenger for the human community is decidedly different from the theology of propitiation and expiation often associated with animal sacrifice in the Judeo-Christian worldview. The animal is not considered to be substitutionary sacrifice that removes sin or assuages the potential anger of a deity. Instead, it is part of a reciprocal exchange that traces the ongoing relationship of the human and divine communities. The death of the animal translates it into the spiritual realm. In some Asatru rituals, the animal is explicitly referred to as a "traveler" and the killing is liturgicized as sending the animal on a journey to the gods, as a gift, a messenger, and a witness.[643]

A very similar pattern is found in other examples of live blót. For instance, in a live blót held during the Heathen Yule holiday on the East Coast, the sacrifice also took place on a farm, where the animal had been raised, and to which urban kindreds had been invited to participate. In another example, this time in Michigan's Upper Peninsula, we again find the connection between blót and farm, "We arrived at the farm and things began to move quickly. There was a reserved silence by now. Not the fake enforced kind of silence that

---

642. Hvitt, "Account of Blót," *Temple of Our Heathen Gods*, September 2012, www.Heathengods.com/forum/discussion/60.

643. Eric Ferguson, "Animal Sacrifice at Winter's Hof," *Volkshof* blog, August 2010, https://volkshofkindred.wordpress.com/2010/08/28/august-2010.

you would see in a church or library, but a silence of expectation. For most of us, this would be our first live blót. They were two lambs, a ewe, and a ram, farm-born and hand-raised."[644] This farm-to-altar connection functions on one hand as an act of pilgrimage. Since most Heathens are urban, these events may require a road trip, so a narrative of pilgrimage often accompanies the accounts of live blót. The urban kindred journeys out of the city into a simpler, more beautiful, more isolated setting, an idealized place where the sacred event itself occurs. Perhaps more importantly, the farm-to-altar connection functions ethically and ceremonially (the two dimensions are quite tightly linked in the live blót as we shall see.) It carries the implication that the farm raised sacrificial animal has been raised humanely, has had a good life, and has received ethical or honorable treatment from the human community. This point is made expressly clear above in Hvitt's description of the Midwestern blót. For an animal obtained commercially from an unknown source, such treatment cannot be assumed. And while meat obtained at a grocery store could be sacrificed, a point often made by Heathens who advise novices to avoid live blót, the anonymity of the animal works against the full ritual and theological meanings.

In its death, the animal is considered to be transferred to the spirit world; its loss of availability to humans is understood to effect its availability to the gods.[645] The animal is understood as a gift, whose value is found not in its physical perfection, as a blemish-less specimen, but in a moral dimension, in being a special animal that has been well treated by the human community. The animal is understood to bear witness to the moral integrity of the human community who gifted it, informing the gods about the treatment it has received and indicating the "worth" of the human community. Thus the value of the sacrifice is determined by the moral integrity of the human community. The animal itself does not have to be physically perfect, but the treatment it has received from the human community must be honorable. I encountered a similar practice and theology at the Heathen gathering Lightning Across the Plains.[646] At the start of the event, the children stuffed a shirt and pair of pants

---

644. Ibid.
645. Kimberly Patton, "Animal Sacrifice: Metaphysics of the Sublimated Victim," in *A Communion of Subjects: Animals in Religion, Science, and Ethics*, eds. Paul Waldau and Kimberly Patton (New York: Columbia University Press, 2006), 399.
646. Field notes taken by author, Kansas, 2011, 2012, 2013.

with straw to form a figure called Alviss.[647] This figure was then hosted by the community throughout the weekend: brought to events, given food and drink, shown hospitality at different campsites, which often led to hilarity and comical situations. At the end of the weekend, he was burned in order to release him as a messenger to the Gods who would witness the frith, hospitality, and moral worth, of the Heathen community. In this light-hearted practice, the theology of live blót is enacted.

The metaphysical question at the heart of sacrifice is: How do you give something to a god? How can a physical being present or transfer or gift: a physical concrete object that is a product of his or her work and effort, to a god who is a more-than-natural being? The answer in many cultures, especially ancient cultures with a theology of sacrifice, has been to devote it: to destroy the object, to render it useless, or remove it from temporal and physical efficacy. By removing from an object the possibility of temporal use and ownership, by making it physically "use-less," the object or entity is made spiritually or supernaturally useful. Its functionality is transferred from the physical to the spiritual world. Thus a person at death is burned or buried as a way to hasten their arrival in the spirit world. This understanding also explains the large number of weapons, kitchen utensils, and other items that have been found in lakes and bogs in northern Europe that were bent or broken before being offered.[648] Destroying the object: bending a sword or punching a hole in a pot or bowl, activates that object in the spirit world. Similarly with sacrifice: to give an animal to the gods, one must sacrifice it.

In the Midwestern blót, after being greeted and welcomed by the human community, the pig was killed, in this case with one rifle shot. Dispatching an animal with a knife or sword has been attempted by some Heathens and might demonstrate a flair for the theatrical, but those methods are slower and less reliable. Many Heathens choose a gunshot specifically to minimize any potential suffering the animal might experience. A consideration of animal suffering marks almost every account of live blót, as Heath makes clear, "It was over incredibly quickly, and efficiently. Taking care

---

647. Named for Alvís, "All Wise," a svartalf or dwarf, whose story is found in *Alvíssmál* in the *Poetic Edda*. In order to avoid a marriage between Alvís and his daughter þrúðr, Thor tricks him into reciting his knowledge all night long until the rising sun turns him to stone.

648. Davidson, *Myths and Symbols*, 62–63.

that the animal is in as little pain as possible is essential. We expect our meat to be butchered humanely and safely."[649] In this East Coast blót, the pig was fed mead-infused fruit prior to the sacrifice in order to induce a relaxed state in the animal and further reduce its anxiety. In an additional layer of ritual complexity, the gothi dispatched the pig with a gun that had been passed to him by his grandfather, a family heirloom that according to Heathen ontology was imbued with the luck of the family.[650] In the Upper Peninsula blót, lambs were sacrificed instead of pigs, yet the same consideration is reflected in almost exactly the same language used by Ferguson in his description: "Each lamb was placed on the altar and dispatched with skill. The point is to cause as little pain for the animals as possible. Causing unnecessary pain would be both cruel, and cause the Gods to reject the gift. However that was not the case, and the end came quickly."[651] Thus, in three distinct regions of the country, we encounter among Heathens an awareness of and concern for animal suffering.

After the animal is dispatched, live blót requires attention to the carcass itself, first ritually and later physically in preparing the meat for the feast. In all cases, ritual use focuses on the animal's blood, which is collected and used as a means of blessing and sanctification. In both the Midwestern and the Michigan blót, the ritual leader applied the blood to the forehead of each participant as a blessing, the application of blood being a common part of sacrificial ritual. Other Heathens sacralize the blood in similar ways. Heath describes how the sacrificial blood was caught in a bowl then used in ceremonial ways: the gothi "began to stain the idols with our blót's sacrifice . . . took a *hlaut* twig and sprinkled the attendants from the

---

649. Josh Heath, "Two Yule Rituals: One Heathen's Experience in the Northeast US," *Óðrærir: The Heathen Journal* 2 (2014): 116, http://odroerirjournal.com/two-yule-rituals-one-heathens-experience-in-the-northeast-us/.

650. These details were added by the gothi, mentioned above, who discussed the sacrifice in an episode of Raven Radio, a Heathen radio show. "Usually the animal has been fed with some mead-laced fruit, corn—what have you—to get the animal in a relaxed state. In the two blóts we have done, the animals have been dispatched with a single shot, in the case of Jul it was two shots, from my grandfather's, 22. The next blót, I'm going to attempt to just use a knife. I think I'm a little bit more comfortable now in actually doing it." Gothi, "Sacrifice" Raven Radio, episode 83, accessed October 10, 2017, www.ravenradio.info/blog/2012/02/12/sacrifice-pt-1. The pertinent portion begins at 34:30 minutes into the program.

651. Ferguson, "Animal Sacrifice at Winter's Hof."

bowl with the sacred blood. A portion of the blood was poured into a horn, mixed with mead and would be offered to [the] Odin Pole which sat outside the grove."[652] This sacrificial blood is understood to be extraordinarily efficacious and powerful, a belief common to several religious traditions. Kimberly Patton notes, "The blood of the animal is so numinous a substance that it is splashed on the sides of the altar of the Holy of Holies, as it is similarly used in ancient Greek sacrifice."[653] Ancient Norse uses of blood as a sacred substance included "reddening" runes and sprinkling altars, hof (temple) walls, and the worshipers themselves as a means of venerating, sanctifying, or blessing them.[654] Ethnographic accounts of animal sacrifices in the Pagan-like folk practices of modern Orthodox Christians in rural Greek villages indicate similar use of the blood,

> the blood that gushes from the victim's neck has a universally strong positive value for the faithful. Its flow inspires no revulsion; its contact has a beneficial effect on men and animals. Everyone dips a finger in it to make the sign of the cross on his or her forehead or to leave a fingerprint... the victim's blood also possesses fecundating virtues.[655]

The East Coast Heathens offered the remainder of the sacred blood to the gods as a libation, a process that Heath observed and described as part of the reciprocal nature of the relationship enacted in the blót: "The blood is offered to the gods, it shows both our dedication to them, and it acts as a vessel for the symbolic circulation of luck between god and man. The gothi takes a portion of the blood from the bowl, once it has been sanctified by the gods, and he symbolically spreads the luck that they imbue it with around to those in attendance."[656] The offering of the blood and the blessing

---

652. Heath, "Two Yule Rituals," 116. *Hlaut* is an Old Norse word referring to the blood of a sacrifice. In mead-based blóts, the mead is either ingested by participants, or sprinkled/flicked over them using a leafy branch, a ritual action sometimes called asperging.

653. Patton, "Animal Sacrifice," 395.

654. Davidson, *Myths and Symbols*, 58; Snorri Sturluson, *Heimskringla: A History of the Kings of Norway*, trans. Lee M. Hollander (Austin: University of Texas Press, 1992 [1964]), 107.

655. Stella Georgourdi, "Sanctified Slaughter in Modern Greece," in *The Cuisine of Sacrifice Among the Greeks*, eds. Marcel Detienne and Jean-Pierre Vernant (Chicago: University of Chicago Press, 1989), 190.

656. Heath, "Two Yule Rituals," 116. Heath notes that luck can be circulated among the kinship relationship of deities and human communities through the ritual of the blót.

of the participants, the exchange of luck, brings the blót ritual itself to an end. The participants move on to butchering the animal and preparing its meat to be served later at the communal feast.

## Two Objections

Two important objections are often expressed by animal rights activists in relation to factory farming and slaughtering: animal objectification and animal suffering. While the issue of animal suffering is quite clear, animal objectification is a subtle way of defusing the ethical issues of meat consumption. In most cases of carnivorous eating, while people may be dimly aware that eating meat necessitates the killing of an animal, both the animal itself and the acting of killing tend to remain out of sight, hidden from view and therefore removed from conscious consideration as moral subjects. First, the presence of the animal is hidden through discursive objectification as a meat product, as food object rather than living subject: take for instance my comment about "pulled pork" in comparison to the kindred's "blótted pig." In the former, the animal is obscured, denied its identity and recognition by referring to it as a food product, while the "blótted pig" accentuates and makes apparent the animal identity. Second, the animal is hidden simply through the material separation engendered by industrial technicalization. Contemporary urban Americans will rarely encounter a food animal outside of a petting zoo. In their paper "The Conceptual Separation of Food and Animals in Childhood," Kate Stewart and Matthew Cole point out that our economy utilizes the "material and discursive practice of separation, of instrumentalization, of literally and metaphorically hiding [animals] from view." The practice of intensive animal farming, known as factory farming, has "led to a progressive removal of animals from public view, through relocating farms, increasing security measures, and the use of trespass laws." And animals are an "absent referent . . . definitionally absent through being misnamed, not as killed animals, or the body parts thereof, but as euphemisms like 'pork,' 'hamburger' and so on."[657] When consumers interact only with the food product, the animal itself is obscured, leaving the animal and

---

657. Kate Stewart and Matthew Cole, "The Conceptual Separation of Food and Animals in Childhood," *Food, Culture and Society* 12, no. 4 (2009): 461.

its life morally unaccounted for in the eating process. Hiddenness and objectification create a conceptual distance between food and animals that functionally perpetrates the mistreatment of animals.

However in some cases, particularly these events involving live blót and communal eating, Heathens resist this specific tendency by consciously making the body of the animal visible. For instance, a kindred donated a pig for the feast at East Coast Thing in 2012. While the pig had already been slaughtered, disemboweled, and cleaned, the entire body was brought into the camp in a public but informal way, spit mounted, and cooked in a portable roaster in the sight of all. In Michigan's Upper Peninsula, the farming family actually completed the butchering process, simply because they had the necessary experience and skill set. During the feast on the following evening, the two blót-animals were given special prominence and recognition by the participants, "The evening feast featured the two lambs, as well as potluck. It was delicious. Each kindred contributed something, and everyone ate their fill."[658] In Heath's East Coast experience, those involved in the ritual also butchered the animal. He writes, "The blot-swine was carried back to the shed and we began the process of cleaning, skinning, and butchering . . . Set behind the house, this shed was . . . often used it to clean and butcher animals he had hunted. It had been years since I'd witnessed this process, and it was amazing to me."[659] For Heath, being involved in the butchering reversed this dynamic of hiddenness and called the participants' attention to the significance of the animal's life and the act of sacrifice.

The hiddenness of the animal in the industrial food economy not only objectifies the animal but also denatures human eaters as moral agents, leaving them without an opportunity to act morally towards the animal. The sacrificial context, however, reverses this objectionable dynamic by bringing both the living animal and the act of killing to the fore: visible, apparent, and included in the conscious act of eating. The sacrifice necessitates accountability by making the living animal present with the eating community, and empowering participants to take a moral response to the killing and eating of animals. The structure of the sacrifice requires the human community of eaters to encounter and interact with the full scope of

---

658. Ferguson, "Animal Sacrifice at Winter's Hof."
659. Heath, "Two Yule Rituals," 116.

the act of eating, maximizing, not minimizing the moral dimensions of eating, and necessitating human moral agency. The sacrificial rite provides a context in which human people must address the moral dimension of killing and eating another being. Josh Heath puts it this way:

> Knowing the animal your meat comes from bothers some people enough to stop eating it. For me it's the opposite, I respect the animal that has given its life so that we can eat. It lived a good life and was treated well, killed well, and had a purpose. Factory farming animals has removed us from the beauty of life in so many ways.[660]

Further, the religious context in which this takes place is important. In the Asatru sacrifice, the living animal is present with the eating community not only at the moment of sacrifice, but also over a longer period of time. Because of the religious use of the animal, the intensified religious context of the sacrifice, the raising of the animal becomes a salient moral issue. The animal is not *just* for eating but also for sacrificing. For the Heathen blót, it is precisely the moral treatment of the animal—not merely its physical quality—that is significant. The worshiping/eating community proves its worth to the gods by its long-term treatment of the animal, caring for the animal during its life as well as the moment prior to sacrifice in which the animal is brought into the company of humans who bless it and speak to it, and even memorialize the animal in poetry. Whatever this may mean to the animal, it obviously serves a purpose to the humans involved by providing a context for eaters to act morally toward this animal.

In all three live blóts examined in this chapter, the sacrifice takes place on a farm operated by a Heathen family and with animals that had been raised by those families. There is evidence that the revival of animal sacrifice, and its accompanying Heathen theology of sacrifice, motivates the creation of Heathen social networks in which the long-term ethical treatment of the blót-animal is addressed. That is not to say that animal husbandry is being widely enunciated as part of Heathen ethics. Indeed, it is not, nor is there yet any significant "back to the land" movement in which young Heathens are actively seeking to farm or raise animals as an expression of their religious

---

660. Ibid., 117.

commitment. However, in these three separate geographical areas, in which live blót is occasionally practiced, the Midwest, Upper Peninsula, and the Northeast, Heathens are forging social networks that support the ethical raising and care of blót-animals. The Heathen understanding of blót, it is argued, drives the need for the ethical treatment of animals. A worthy animal is one that has been treated well by its human community over the length of its entire life from birth to the moment of death.

## *Asatru Response to Suffering*

As we have already begun to see, Heathens who practice live blót are concerned and attuned to the problem of animal suffering. The concern for animal suffering is heightened by the intensely religious nature of the sacrifice and expressed in Asatru narratives of sacrifice gone wrong. In addition to responding to the objections levied by outsiders, the Asatru community has begun to develop its own critical discourse about sacrificial ritual. Stories about the "botched sacrifice" serve as contrasts within Asatru discourse to the solemn religious and moral practice that the blót represents. There may be several ways in which an animal sacrifice ritual can go wrong. Ronald Grimes' discussion of "infelicitous performances" gives us access to a typology and a vocabulary for these sorts of occurrences.[661] In most cases, a blót is marred through some sort of mistake made by those involved in the sacrifice, which Grimes would understand as a misfire or flawed performance of the rite. In conversation with Asatru adherents, no one has ever described a botched sacrifice going wrong through a liturgical mistake, such as saying the wrong words or facing in the wrong direction. Botched sacrifice always involves a story about animal pain and suffering, which represents the Heathen understanding of "unnecessary suffering."[662] While animal sacrifice necessarily involves some degree of pain inflicted on the animal, we can imagine a rite of sacrifice in which participants deliberately cause animal suffering or seemed callous about it occurring, or in which the death of the animal is exploited in some way. Such an event would be understood as a ritual violation in Grimes' typography, a rite that was intentionally degrading,

---

661. Grimes, *Ritual Criticism*, 191–209.
662. Strmiska, "Putting the Blood Back into Blót," 169–70.

demeaning, or harmful. Joking or bragging about animal suffering is something I have rarely encountered in Asatru. However, in one incident, the Wolves of Vinland posted photographs on social media in which members were posing with bloody animal parts in ways that struck observers as exploitative and demeaning to the animal and the sacrificial process. Those crude images reflected a rather immature stage in the group's presentation of its "barbarian" ethos. Later photographs of their sacrificial rituals have been more respectful, indicating that they have refined their brand somewhat as well as their practice of sacrifice. Yet that incident represents a type of violation, a deliberate misuse of the Heathen blót.

A more typical example of botched sacrifice involves inadvertent animal suffering. In the example we will examine below, a gunshot failed to kill the animal immediately, literally a misfire that caused animal suffering. Asatru practitioners almost universally react to such events with the aesthetic response of disgust, horror, and revulsion. As Eric Ferguson noted above, animal suffering renders the sacrifice not only *ritually* ruined but also *morally* defiled, polluted by the failure of the human community to act in a noble and honorable way. Thus a concern for animal suffering is quite apparent in Asatru practice, situated in relation to the Heathen ethical imperative of noble and honorable behavior. In the context of the blót, the dishonor of unworthy action spills over to reflect on all participants, raising the fear of pollution, of being contaminated by the dishonorable behavior. In Heathen terminology, the participants share to some degree in the dishonorable action, the luck of all the participants now bound to it and its consequences in an irrevocable way. The moral consideration is not that of animal rights, such as an inherent right not to suffer that is so crucial for Peter Singer. Few Heathens would concede even an inherent *human* right not to suffer. Instead, it is located in the Asatru notion of innangarð, which is the obligation to live nobly and honorably with those beings within one's care, with whom one is bound through reciprocal relationship. Animal suffering is not only polluting but also violates the category of innangarð that calls for the moral uprightness of human conduct towards the animal under one's care.

The East Coast blót that we have been discussing provides an interesting test case for a flawed performance, because in this event the sacrifice went slightly wrong. Heath, an able writer, describes the incident with intimate detail as the gothi prepares to sacrifice the pig: "At the moment [the gothi] took the shot, she moved her head. The bullet struck, but not in the spot intended . . . He apologized to the pig, and took aim again. This shot was perfect and it went down immediately."[663] As Heath continues his narrative of the blót, it is apparent that the incident had impacted both the gothi and the participants, and the responses are important to note. The gothi "seemed a little worried about not hitting his mark correctly the first time."[664] In his anxiety and concern, we can read the Heathen theology of sacrifice, the connection of ceremonial and ethical considerations around the botched sacrifice. The participants address those very considerations in their responses to the gothi:

> I and many others assured him that his skill and his steady nature was what mattered. Nothing could be done about the pig moving her head. That was her choice to make, and [he] took the absolutely correct actions when this occurred. Historically, blót would likely not have been as clean, but we wanted to ensure the most humane treatment we could provide.[665]

The pig's movement caused the shot to go amiss, wounding but not killing the animal and creating a situation potentially charged with ritual and religious danger. As Heath describes, the gothi handled the situation in a noble, reverent, and humane fashion, avoiding or at least recovering from a botched sacrifice. Heath gives credit to the experience and character of the gothi in preventing the situation from spiraling out of hand, "I know many that would have been terrified at this occurrence, so much that they would have failed to take action. [This gothi] is not one of those people."[666] This statement describes the care with which the experienced gothi successfully handled the situation with all its potential ritual, spiritual, and ethical danger. The most evocative moment in his account is when the gothi apologizes to the animal before taking the second and fatal shot. That gesture captures the complex Heathen understanding and approach to the ethics and theology of sacrifice, in which the moral behavior of the human community is deeply intertwined with concern for the animal's suffering and the god's acceptance of the gift.

663. Heath, "Two Yule Rituals," 3.
664. Ibid., 4.
665. Ibid.
666. Ibid., 3.

## *Special Death*

### *The Religious Significance*

Despite the inundation of our culture with death and the images of death, the emotionally deadening impact of viewing countless murders as entertainment in movies and television, and of virtually enacting them in video games, Heathen participants of live blót report the spiritual saliency of the event (see figure 22). For those Heathens who have shared their experience of live blót with me, the experience was one of emotional profundity. While the intensity of the event generates a good deal of excited anticipation, solemnity, silence, and a loss of words characterize the sacrifice itself. Trivial human banter is temporarily silenced, not by the sight of death, but by participating in the sacrifice, by being bound up in it. Heath writes that after the East Coast sacrifice, "there was a feeling of reverence and a deep emotional effect on those there," a sentiment also shared by participants in the other blóts.

The powerful ritual churns up emotions in the participants: a profound sense of sanctity, but not one free from emotional conflict and turmoil. Heath, and other Heathens, indicate that when the live blót goes well, there is a shared feeling that something right and appropriate has been done. It is not that these are bloodthirsty gods satisfied only by death. Joe Marek, an experienced and thoughtful gothi who has long served the Heathen community in the Northeast, points out that the mead sacrifice remains potent and viable and that the live blót should only be done on significant occasions.[667] The sense of "rightness" has more to do with the live blót as the utmost expression of human veneration, a human community that has given its all, its best and most noble gift, to the shining deities with whom they are in relation. Questions of animal agency have yet to be formally addressed in Heathen discourse on sacrifice: can an animal "give" its life and is the animal in some way a "willing" participant in the act? Scholars of Greek and Roman sacrifice note that animal assent became part of the sacrificial ritual in these cultures: flicking water on the face of the animal caused it to nod its head, taken as its assent to the sacrifice. For Heathens, the gods signify their acceptance of the sacrifice both through this feeling of

---

667. Marek, interview.

rightness and omens that might accompany the offerings.[668] That the animal has been accepted and received by the gods assures the human community that the animal's death was not in vain, wasted, or otherwise without value.

## The Ethical Significance

Millions of animals are slaughtered anonymously for food every year. In contrast to these ignominious and ugly deaths, the sacrifice sets apart one animal and one moment of killing as a special and sacred death. As Kimberly Patton states, sacrifice involves the elevation and individuation of the victim: "Sacrifice results ... in a kind of magnification of what had been quite ordinary: an animal, a 'typical' member of a domesticated species, becomes atypical, a player in a sacred drama."[669] It becomes the ideal type of animal death, the exemplar, which represents Asatru's highest ideals about life and death. In some instances, these exemplary or special deaths are memorialized by Heathens in various ways, such as by utilizing parts of the animal in significant ways. For instance, after the sacrifice of a prized ram named Ottar, Heathen farmer Jon Cyr, who had raised and cared for the ram for years, had its horns fashioned into a pair of ritual drinking horns. Cyr, who is also a poet, also memorialized the ram in a poem written in *fornyrðislag*, a traditional form of Old Norse verse, one stanza of which illustrates the special sanctity of the ram Ottar's death:

> I cannot conceive,
> Or call to mind,
> A better way,
> This one to thank.
> Gods and Goddess,
> Gifted with feast,
> A tribute to Ottar,
> To honor the lord.[670]

To understand the full significance of this memorial, we must remember that, for Heathens, words spoken in the formal ritual

---

668. Heath, interview.
669. Patton, "Animal Sacrifice," 397, 399.
670. Jon Cyr, "Ottar's Tribute," *Óðrœrir: The Heathen Journal*, August 8, 2014, http://odroerirjournal.com/ottars-tribute-jon-cyr/.

setting of blót or sumbel carry religious weight; they become part of the wyrd, the metaphysical force of history, of deeds and actions that shape the future. In this way, through the poem and its performance in sumbel, Ottar's death is marked as an existentially powerful moment that continues to positively impact and benefit the luck of all those who shared it in, a moment in which the gods and the human community were powerfully joined together in relationship.

The feast, however, is the most significant expression of this special death. If the blót can be understood as an ideal type of animal death, it also represents an ideal type of food, a moral way of eating. The community can utilize this ideal act as an evaluative tool for other acts of using animals as food. The sacrifice and the feast, the gathering of people to eat, are irrevocably linked. We hear it when a participant states, "It was an extremely generous gift ... not just the pig itself, but also the opportunity to gather with good Folk and join with them in the holiest of rituals which will, in turn allow us to gift all our guests with a sacred meal that serves to further connect us with the Elder Kin."[671] Another adds, "We go into [the event] ready to serve a meal to everyone there from a pig that was sacrificed to our Gods. A Holy gift. A circle of gifts. [The farm] gifted the pig to [our] kindred. [We both] gifted the pig to the Gods and paid them honor. And in return, an amazing feast has been gifted back to the Folk from our Gods."[672] The sacrificial meal is ontologically rich. The gift of the animal in its death is the gift of human community and relationships. The sharing, distribution, and eating of the sacred meat creates the human community, calls it together from its disparate constituents and creates a zone of peace and cordiality. The idea that animal sacrifice is directly related to eating and eating as commensality, eating together or the act of community building, is well established. Detienne notes that in ancient Greek sacrifice, the sacrificer was also the cook, the acts of killing and eating indissolubly linked in one physical body.[673] Regarding the folk practice of sacrifice by a community of Greek Orthodox Christians, Georgourdi writes, "all these ritual acts [of sacrifice] seem only the preliminaries to the heart and essence of the

---

671. Hamilton, "Account of Blot."
672. Mark Stinson, "Sacrifice of the Pig," *Temple of Our Heathen Gods* discussion forum, September 2012, www.Heathengods.com/forum/discussion/60.
673. Marcel Detienne, "Culinary Practices and the Spirit of Sacrifice," in *The Cuisine of Sacrifice Among the Greeks*, eds. Marcel Detienne, and Jean-Pierre Vernant (Chicago: University of Chicago Press, 1989), 8.

festival: the distribution of food and the shared meal." The apex of the ritual is not the act of killing but the commensality of the human community, the greater purpose of community building. Like the Greek festival, the Asatru gathering is "really a village festival, a noisy and joyful event where everyone gathers, not only to eat and drink together but also to laugh, sing, and dance."[674] The shared meal both creates and sanctifies communal life.

This meal is unlike other meals. The sacred nature of the death imbues the food with power and significance. It becomes special food linking the human community to the land, animals, each other, and the gods, evoking and creating this larger range of relational connections. This special food embodies the Asatru ideal of peaceful and harmonious community. More than just a symbol, eating together in this way enacts the innangarð. The feast is explicitly presented as such—frith and grith are evoked prior to the meal and the community eats together with this state of peace. By sharing the blótted pig, participants represent and experience the blessing and approval of the gods on this human community.

One additional aspect is important. As an ideal type, the sacrifice becomes the mode from which other animal deaths and interactions between humans and animals can be evaluated, furnishing "a conceptual framework into which all cases can be brought for analysis."[675] The sacrifice is a manner of death that demands subjectivity, visibility, and care from every instance of animal death. Thus it is a "special death" in which the ethical implications of all acts of eating are revealed and accentuated. Eating the sacred sacrificial meal, experiencing the sacred community that it brings into being, compels us, or at least raises the potential in us, to evaluate other acts of eating in its light. How does the experience of eating at the McDonalds drive-thru compare to the ideal type as represented in the blót, when individuals are at their best, most attentive, and most unified as a community?

## *Conclusion*

The practice of Heathen animal sacrifice stands in tension with two other attitudes toward animal death commonly found in our society:

---

674. Georgourdi, "Sanctified Slaughter," 192.
675. Daniel Pals, *Eight Theories of Religion* (New York: Oxford, 2006), 156–57.

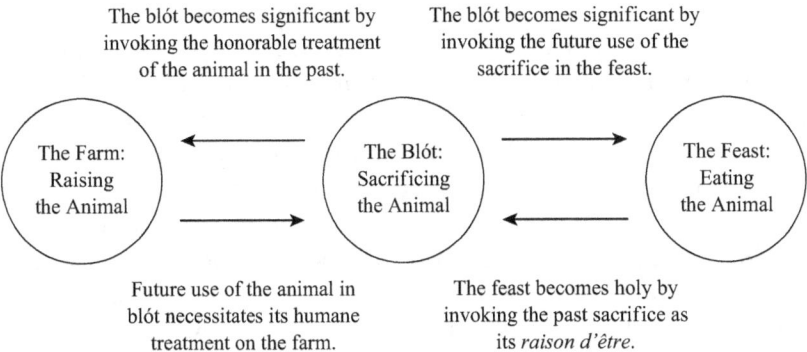

Figure 22. Creation of Meaning in the Blót.

the moral idealism of vegetarianism and the complete abstinence from meat, and the moral vacuity of the techno-industrial food industry in its systematic, merciless degradation, mass slaughter, and consumption of animals. I have tried to make the case that the Asatru sacrifice acts to ameliorate the human use of animals by potentially functioning as an ideal type of animal death that accentuates the conditions in which humans might legitimately use animals as food. It models the desirable patterns of human action toward animals and eating that is at the heart of Asatru religion. The context of the blót offers a unique vantage point from which the moral agent can look both backwards and forwards in time to evaluate the ethics of sacrifice and eating.

Those who raise the animal, on the farm, look forward in time to the blót in which the animal will become a gift to the gods, the exemplar who carries the moral worth of the human community to the deities. This perspective calls forth and even morally obligates them to the humane treatment of the animal. Those who blót the animal not only are concerned to treat the animal well during the sacrifice, by reducing as much as possible any suffering of the animal, but also invoke the humane care provided to the animal by the human community. The luck of the community is bound with the ethical raising of the animal in the past. At the same time, during the blót, those who sacrifice the animal look forward in time toward the creation of the sacred community in the sacrificial feast. The sacrifice of the animal is given value and significance, legitimated and sanctified, because it will be eaten as part of the sacred feast, enacting the sacred kinship and community of gods and humans. Those who participate in the feast are called to awareness by the sacred nature of the meat they share. In my experience at the Heathen gathering in the Midwest, I was suddenly called to attention, made aware of the sacred quality of the event by hearing it called "blótted pig." By framing the feast in light of the sacrifice, its sacred dimension comes to light. It is not just any other meal, but the meal of a sacred community in the presence of and in kinship with the gods. The feast is the gift of the gods, which calls the human community together as a sacred community. The implication of eating the blótted meat is that we must act in frith and grith. We must be or become the sacred community, living up to the gift and blessing that the gods have shared with us. By "re-sanctifying" the raising, slaughtering, and eating of animals within a religious context, this contemporary Asatru sacrifice potentially functions to regulate relationships to animals and eating in a way that protects animal communities and calls this religious community to a moral consideration and inclusion of animals.

The further discussion of foodways in American Heathenry is an important topic that has yet to be addressed thoroughly. For the most part, I found that Heathens are not pursuing the reconstruction of Norse dietary practices broadly speaking. Reconstruction is notably a selective process and in this instance, Heathens are choosing to reconstruct a specific religious practice that has dietary and ethical implications. However, an incipient food culture is present in the movement. Heathen feasts often feature menu items that reflect German-styled food, particularly modern Continental fare. Recipes for these types of food can be found in Heathen recipe collections, several of which have been published.[676] As we have seen in the Heathen accounts of animal sacrifice, practitioners of live blót are sometimes creating small networks of local food producers to support the religious practice. Heathen mead producers are often farther ahead in putting together networks of local producers of

---

676. For a good example of emerging Heathen foodways, see "An Interview," *My Cat Cries*, January 4, 2012, www.mycatcries.com/blog/an-interview/. Jesse and Rebecca Radcliff, members of Der Heidevolkstamm discussed in chapter 3, share recipes and discuss the foods they cook for several Heathen holidays. The Troth has published an *Old Heathen's Almanac* that contains recipes for Germanic fare. The Odinic Rite published a cookbook, *The Odinic Rite Cookbook*, described as "a collection of member recipes celebrating European culture through cooking."

honey and locally grown herbs for varieties of infused mead known as metheglin. Admittedly such efforts are nascent, but the conditions exist for the development of a Heathen food culture that challenges mainstream American assumptions about the production, eating, and meaning of food.

## Chapter 7

## Kith and Kin

### Asatru as Family Religion[677]

Children were everywhere! It felt a little chaotic but fun and festive at the same time. Packs of boys and girls ran through the campground, disappearing among the tents only to re-emerge from the edge of the woods moments later. Some of the older teens hung out with each other in the shade, talking quietly, reading, or drawing. A few little ones played around the large firepit building castles and eating sand, much to the consternation of their parents. I had brought my own kids to Kansas for this long weekend, and they had already disappeared, whether into the woods or among the vendors' booths, I was not sure. I wanted to get a feel for the experience of Heathen parents, both the joys and stresses of bringing children to this religious event. And I was also interested in what children saw, felt, and learned by being immersed in this intense weekend of Heathen religious life. After all, events such as these may be formative influences on this second generation of Heathenry. Bringing my own children was the perfect opportunity to gain insight into these questions. My son, who had already made the trip with me the two previous years, had come home with epic stories about the "Viking camp," as he called it. This year, my daughter enthusiastically joined us. From their perspective, the long drive, camping out, and the many new faces were just part of a grand adventure. It was already reassuring knowing that my kids could run and play without worry. They were old enough, nine and ten, to fit in and handle themselves without constant supervision and they quickly took to the freedom and fun of the camp.

The best moment of the weekend was the troll battle. The kids, armed with foam swords and battle-axes, faced off across the field

---

677. Portions of this chapter were presented to the Contemporary Pagan Studies Group of the American Academy of Religion, Chicago, IL, 2012.

of battle from a group of adults playing "trolls." At the signal, the children sounded a war cry and charged at their opponents, ready for battle. A swirling melee ensued with groups of children surrounding the trolls and taking them down in a flurry of strikes. Parents and other onlookers stood along the field, laughing, taking photos with their phones and cheering on their young combatants. Two refreshment stands had been set up on the sidelines, one representing Folkvangar, the home of Freyja who gathers half the slain according to the Lore, and the other Valhalla, where Odin collects the rest of those courageous warriors. As the children "fell in battle" or just tired out under the hot sun, they came in to cool down and enjoy cookies and Kool-Aid. Was I concerned about adults inciting their children into violence? While I did consider the gladiatorial overtones, the tone of the event was jovial and even comic as the "trolls" hammed up their roles—no harsh words or ill feelings. I have seen far worse displays of parental provocation at the average children's sporting event and this was far from the grim war games that engage children on video game platforms. What I saw, while cheering my own children, was children and parents, young people and adults engaged together in interactive play that reinforced the religious worldview of Heathenry.

This sort of family-friendly environment characterized most, though not all of the weekend Heathen gatherings I attended. Often there were workshops specifically for children, short plays or skits around religious themes that the children would work on. At East Coast Thing, the children built rockets and launched them from the field in the middle of the camp, chasing the parachutes as they slowly floated to the ground (see figure 23). Yet this Heathen family ethic did not develop overnight. A gradual transformation has occurred regarding the understanding and importance of family in the movement. American Asatru began as a new religious movement (NRM) in the 1970s in which young men sought to recapture an experience of rugged heroic individualism modeled on the Viking warrior. Stephen McNallen, who was there at the very beginning of American Asatru remembers:

> When I first approached Asatru back in the late 1960s, what attracted me was the panache, vigor, and passionate assertiveness of the Vikings. Bold and free, it attracted my testosterone-laden teenage soul like a magnet ... and it still calls to me, after all these years ... Underlying

the insistent Viking freedom was a deeper validation of a heroic view of human individuality, and for me this was an essential.[678]

However, as these men grew older and began to start families and as new adherents joined the movement bringing families with them, the situation began to change. The re-interpretation of ideology resulted not in the abandonment of the heroic warrior ethic but its supplementation with an increasingly prominent family ethic.[679] Diana Paxson describes this noticeable cultural shift:

> In the early days of Heathenry, Heathens were unmarried young men. You know in the eighties, it was these young guys. And two women would go to a Heathen gathering and the guys would say, "Oh wow, we have so many women!" Of course eventually the unmarried young men attracted young women and now we have the "Faith, Folk, Family," thing and a lot of Heathens are "It's family, it's family!"[680]

Scholars have shown that the presence of children in new religions leads to adaptive responses within these movements.[681] While these changes involve addressing the practical needs of the children themselves, such as how to educate, retain, and discipline children, they also may initiate a re-evaluation of the role and understanding of family in a movement's ideology.

Religious groups have often been the source of ideals about family and have provided rationale for family structure and its role in American life. As Penny Edgell notes, "Historically, religious institutions in the United States have been centrally concerned with the production of familism, or ideals of family life."[682] Religious familism has idealized certain forms and functions of the family, defining them as legitimate, valuable, and morally correct, even essential for a healthy social order. Mainstream forms of Christianity

---

678. Steve McNallen, "Fire and the Fog," *Asatru Folk Assembly*, www.runestone.org/about-asatru/articles-a-essays/140-fire-and-the-fog.html.

679. Paxson, *Essential Ásatrú*, 162.

680. Paxson, interview.

681. Susan J. Palmer and Charlotte Hardman, *Children in New Religions* (New Brunswick, NJ: Rutgers University Press, 1999), 1. See also James D. Chancellor, *Life in The Family: An Oral History of the Children of God* (Syracuse: Syracuse University Press, 2000), 205-6.

682. Penny Edgell and Danielle Docka, "Beyond the Nuclear Family? Familism and Gender Ideology in Diverse Religious Communities," *Sociological Forum* 22, no. 1 (2007): 27-28.

have often embraced the predominant cultural schema for the family in America since the 1950s—"the 'Ozzie and Harriet' ideal" of a "married male-female couple oriented to the bearing and raising of children."[683] This nuclear family model itself resulted from the effects of modernity, which dis-embedded most Americans from an older more traditional extended family context. This modern ideal of the nuclear family has been challenged from all sides and continues to undergo rapid change as seen in the cultural shifts in American society toward single-parenthood, cohabitation, same-sex marriage, singleness, and other configurations of family structure. New religions have vigorously participated in the critique of the modern American family. These dissenting voices draw on their ideological resources to create and introduce their own religious visions of family. Their religious spaces function as "creative cultural arenas where new understandings of the meaning of religious traditions, doctrines, and teachings are forged . . . They are places to look for the innovations that may lead to larger changes over time."[684] These alternative models have often pushed the boundaries of popularly accepted notions, creating and advocating solutions outside of mainstream ideals.[685]

Susan Palmer discusses three types of responses that groups often make in creating new forms of familism: dissolving the family, sacralizing the nuclear family, or creating a superfamily. New religions run the gamut of these responses. For instance, the Raelian and Rajneesh movements have advocated dissolving the family as an outmoded, superfluous, and oppressive social arrangement. These groups seek to liberate individuals from the bonds of nuclear families, the damaging psychodynamics, and oppressive gendered roles that limit their spiritual advancement.[686] Groups that sacralize the nuclear family generally theorize the family as a natural or divinely ordained structure. They elevate the status of the married heterosexual couple, and advocate strengthening

---

683. Ibid., 28.
684. Ibid., 46.
685. Ibid., 28. "Mainstream religious institutions in the United States have promoted the SNAF [Standard North American Family] model, emphasizing the importance of stable, monogamous, heterosexual marriages which produce children; supporting parental authority; and discouraging premarital and extramarital sex."
686. Susan J. Palmer, *Moon Sisters, Krishna Mothers, Rajneesh Lovers: Women's Roles in New Religions* (Syracuse, NY: Syracuse University Press, 1994), 164, 222-23.

and preserving the family as the primary socializing context for children. The Unificationist (Moonie) and Latter-Day Saints (Mormon) movements, both of which valorize the nuclear family as a potentially eternal and righteous family unit, might illustrate this approach.[687] In contrast, the well-known aphorism, "It takes a village to raise a child," reflects the approach of building superfamilies. Groups such as the Messianic Community and the Family (Children of God) consider the nuclear family insufficient to nurture children into healthy adults. The model seeks to resolve tensions experienced by nuclear families by expanding the supportive social network. The nuclear family exists within, or is dissolved into, a larger community structure that may either resemble an extended family or take the shape of a communal living situation.[688]

## *Pagan Family Values*

American Pagans have also reflected deeply on the role of family. Over forty or fifty years, Pagan approaches to family and children have been diverse. Some Pagans have offered a critique of the nuclear family model as a social entity that has been damaging to parents and children. In their experience, the authoritarian structure of the American family has too often stifled the psychological and emotional health of children and suppressed their magical natures. This discourse about the family reflects Palmer's first category, advocating the dissolution or transformation of the patriarchal family model. By deconstructing authoritarian and patriarchal roles and normalizing the "feminine" values of caring and nurturing relationships, these Pagans seek to enact a more egalitarian vision of family. In such a family, the natural magical creativity of children finds room to grow, while adults are free to explore new dimensions of their own identities. At the same time, Pagans often encourage the "village" approach to family, supplementing but not supplanting the nuclear family with close bonds within the religious community.

In *Pagan Family Values*, Kermani explores notions of childhood in contemporary American Paganism, although her focus is really on a particular Wiccan culture. It is an important topic because perceptions of childhood are in dynamic relationship with other

---

687. Ibid., 212.
688. Ibid., 215, 217.

aspects of life: adult identities, family structures, raising children, and religious practice. She describes a Wiccan approach toward family very much like that described above—egalitarian and free from constraint. Men in particular are encouraged to cultivate less-authoritarian roles, while children are given more freedom and elevated as voices of wisdom. She recalls attending a Pagan festival that provided a supervised play area for children while their parents were busy attending workshops. She volunteered for a shift supervising children at the playground and was paired with another volunteer, a middle-aged male who she calls Mike. At one point, a disagreement arose among the children and they ran to Mike to resolve the squabble. Mike responded by playfully asking, "Why are you looking at me? I'm not a grown-up. The grown-ups I've known are always tired and unhappy. That's not me."[689] His words suggested for Kermani an underlying ambivalence about adult roles and authority in Wiccan culture, downplaying typical adult authority and looking to the children to address problems in more consensual ways.

Mike's approach enacts a critique of family structure, a way to subvert traditional adult roles that is motivated in part by the magical worldview of Paganism. His words indicate the sense that modernity's disenchantment has entrenched itself particularly with how we understand adulthood. Before their socialization as adults into this disenchanted world, children are naturally open, sensitive, and aware of the magic all around them. Children exhibit not only a joy and wonder in the world, but an ability to work magically, intuitively making connections with the natural world, and thinking outside of the practical mundane rationality that characterizes mainstream adulthood. Kermani writes, "Contemporary Paganism sees children as more spiritually 'open' than adults, with a direct, unmediated access to the divine that adults lack. This spiritual 'openness' and flexibility is often understood as the natural state of humans before we learn to deny fantasy and spirit in favor of rationality and the physical world."[690] As children grow older and take on worldly responsibilities, they are required to conform more and more to the strictures laid upon them by modernity. They quickly lose this sensitivity and receptivity to the magical cosmos.

689. Kermani, *Pagan Family Values*, 71.
690. Ibid., 58–59.

Easy for children in their innocence and naiveté, magic becomes difficult for adults. However, there is a sense in Paganism that health and wholeness may be found by re-enchanting of one's experience of the world.

This has at least two consequences for understanding childhood and family. Children, on one hand, should be free from the dulling and disenchanting effects of adult constraints in order to explore their magical nature. Children in touch with these inner magical selves are "old souls" who not only exhibit an affinity for magic but, as Kermani notes, might also "demonstrate a somber, exaggerated maturity."[691] In order to craft a family environment friendly to the magical nature of children, this Wiccan model encourages adults to shed the roles forced upon them by modernity, finding and reconnecting with the inner child, a magical receptive self that has been buried under stereotypical adult roles and responsibilities. According to Kermani, the Wiccan context encourages adults to resist "adulthood" as typically understood and to cultivate a playful childlike persona. Like Mike, these magical adults "have no place in the sad, serious, conservative world of adults . . . their place, instead, is in the magical world of childhood imagination, fantasy, and joy."[692] Parents and other adults exercise responsibility, while also subverting the dichotomy between child and adult behaviors and roles. The playful and non-authoritarian values of enchanted adulthood modify and mollify the relationships between adults, parents, and children. For Kermani, this family structure represents the emergence of a new "Pagan-American" parenting paradigm that "emphasizes fantasy, 'childlike' wonder, and a complex and ambivalent relationship with authority."[693] These Pagan attitudes work to question, restructure, and transform the traditional American nuclear family.

### Heathen Family Values

Heathen leader Mark Stinson's book, *Heathen Families*, serves as a contrast to Kermani's insights into Pagan notions and practices of

---

691. Ibid., 86.
692. Ibid., 71.
693. Ibid., 88.

childhood and family.[694] Although Stinson's book enunciates the perspective of only one participant in Heathenry, it is an influential perspective that corroborates many of my field observations of the roles played by children and adults in Heathen life. As I have mentioned, there are a spectrum of attitudes and understandings at work in Heathenry and the notion of the naturally magical child is not completely absent. In language very reminiscent of that encountered by Kermani among practitioners of the Craft, Stinson reflects on the sensitivity and awareness of his young daughter to the spiritual world. When she was about six years old, he wrote that of all his children, she is "the one that most connects with the unseen. She seems to have a real connection with our House Wight, one that has developed independently of me. She does things with the House Wight that I do not even hear about until weeks later . . . I couldn't be prouder of her."[695] Stinson describes the ease with which his daughter relates to the enchanted world, exhibiting a natural affinity for spirituality, magic, and unseen beings. He describes her playful interactions with the house wight, who seemed to engage in games of hide and seek with her hairclips, and her interest in connecting with her ancestors, especially Stinson's deceased father who appears in her dreams.[696]

At least in part, her spiritual awareness "has developed independently of me," he writes. Even as Stinson describes the childhood openness to magical experience, his words convey the importance of the mature serious adult in guiding and shaping religious experience for children. Indeed, the account of his daughter's spiritual experiences is set within a larger narrative of Stinson's active involvement in shaping, guiding, and participating in the process of spiritual maturity. Stinson takes the lead, guiding his daughter in how to relate to the house wight and discussing with her the importance of relating to ancestors. For instance,

---

694. Mark L. Stinson, *Heathen Families: Nine Modern Fables for Heathen Children and a Collection of Essays Regarding Heathen Families* (Kansas City, MO: Jotun's Bane Kindred, 2011).

695. Ibid., 37. A "house wight" is simply a house spirit, a spirit being that lives in one's house or homestead. The Heathen term "wight" derives from Old English word *wiht*, referring to a living being of any sort. Heathens commonly refer to spirit beings that inhabit the land, water, or dwellings as "wights." See Joseph Bosworth and T. Northcote Toller, *An Anglo-Saxon Dictionary* (Oxford: Oxford University Press, 1921), http://lexicon.ff.cuni.cz/texts/oe_bosworthtoller_about.html, s.v. "*wiht*."

696. Ibid., 34, 37.

Figure 23. Families Launching Rockets at East Coast Thing. (Photo by the author.)

Stinson shares his own ancestral experiences, "I told her that Dad visits me in dreams, and that when she goes to bed that night, she should think of him and ask him to visit her."[697] It is through this process of parental guidance that his daughter begins to report that her grandfather has appeared in her dreams.

While most of this experience is compatible with Kermani's discussion of Wiccan parenting, Stinson is nothing like her example of Mike. Stinson enunciates a Heathen paradigm of parenting quite unlike the Pagan family values associated with Mike's ambiguous role. Rather than the idealization of childhood among the Wiccans that she observed, my observations of Heathen culture revealed an emphasis on training children to take on adult roles. A phrase I heard repeatedly in Heathen conversations about family and parenting is the need to "raise up strong Heathen children." Stinson explicitly incorporates this emphasis on guiding children toward maturity in one of his essays entitled "The Transition from Childhood to Adulthood." He begins by lamenting the blurred lines of childhood

---

697. Ibid., 36.

and adulthood in modern America. From his viewpoint, this epidemic of status confusion manifests itself in an extended period of immaturity, young adults who act like perpetual children and fail to take upon themselves the duties and responsibilities of adulthood. Rather than accepting this status quo, the values of Heathenry are especially suited to addressing this social issue by developing for children a "guided process that logically and inevitably leads to their roles and responsibilities as adults."[698] He suggests a "worthing" process that would teach the practical skills, religious knowledge, and social dexterity that are necessary for successful adulthood, incorporating rites of passage that signify the movement from childhood and into this new phase of life. Such a process draws on the Heathen themes of struggle and testing to endow the individual with strength, identity, and purpose. The process must be gender specific, expressing the tendency towards gender essentialism that is a significant part of the Heathen ethos, "it should have a male and female path. Boys growing into men need different knowledge, responsibilities, and experiences than girls growing into women."[699] Proper human development follows a trajectory that leads to mature and competent adulthood: "The whole process comes down to preparing our children to fulfill their adult responsibilities, and to be mature enough to enjoy adult privileges without abusing them."[700] It is important to note that for Stinson the process he outlines is not merely one of individual development and actualization. Rather, worthing should enable a young person to become a functioning and contributing member of the family and kindred, the Heathen socio-religious human community. Childhood is not idealized. The proper goal of life is not to remain childlike or cultivate childlike states, but to take one's place as a skilled and strong member of the adult family. While appreciating childhood for its magical possibilities, Heathens tend to see it as a state of immaturity, a state that should be rightly abandoned for adult roles. Rather than valorizing childhood, the Heathen ethos emphasizes the importance of adulthood and the desirability of assuming its mantle of authority and responsibility. While Kermani's idealized Pagan adult *takes off* adulthood to experience a child-like liberation and magical, ecstatic

698. Ibid., 38.
699. Ibid., 40. This is not unlike the rites of passage that Oboler describes for Wiccan boys. See Oboler, "Negotiating Gender Essentialism," 181.
700. Ibid., 41.

individuality, the idealized Heathen joyfully *puts on* adult maturity in order to create and maintain the order and structure necessary for a strong and vital family, to act in strong, noble, and significant ways.

These examples represent two ends of a family values spectrum within Pagan religiosity. Kermani presents a progressive vision of children and family as a predominant Pagan model, while I present a particular Heathen family ethos that is a counterexample in some ways, particularly in its emphasis on the desirability of adult roles and authority. The reality is more complex, I would suggest. While these models may represent influential ideas and perspectives, there are Heathens whose families would strongly resemble the egalitarian family model, while many Wiccans might resonate with Stinson's vision of childhood as a preparatory time for adult responsibility. Most American Pagans, including Heathens, will fall somewhere in between, working to reconcile and align their religious ideas and practices with the pressures that families find themselves under in America. The tributaries flowing into Heathen culture encourage families to negotiate between two religious values: the Wiccan emphasis on the magical curiosity and freedom of children, along with a folkish, Traditionalist tributary that valorizes a traditional family with its gender-specific identities as core values of Heathen culture.

However they sort out these values, many Heathens express interest in strengthening the family. Mark Stinson, for instance, warns against the weakening of the family bond that is symptomatic of American society: "It is a sign of our decaying culture that parents have abandoned their own children."[701] Despite the conservative tone of his statement, Stinson is not perpetuating a set of values modeled on the familial myth of the 1950s. From a Heathen perspective, the Ozzie and Harriet ideal itself is a sick and enervated version of family, one that is all too conformist, consumerist, bourgeoisie, and spiritually sterile. Stinson's folkish-oriented Heathenry tends to value the social function of the family: that of raising mature, skillful, and religiously trained children, and tends to believe that families are the best context for developing "strong Heathen children." However, Stinson and many other Heathens remain critical of the nuclear family model, which has failed from their perspective to produce happy, healthy families. Instead it has given way to a culture in which children are neglected for reasons

---

701. Ibid., 26.

of work, entertainment, and convenience, producing generations of increasingly alienated young people and distracted self-serving parents. The progressive sexual and family ethic associated with Wicca proves equally unattractive for these Heathens. They perceive it as sharing in the same contemporary ills that have weakened the family and left children without a sense of identity and maturity. Instead, Heathens are actively developing spiritual solutions that draw on Asatru theology.[702] Stinson clearly expresses this goal when he writes optimistically that "Heathenry is the answer to the widespread emotional abandonment of children within our failing culture, and our children are the future of our native folkway."[703] He and other Heathens look toward Palmer's third type of response — the enactment of Heathen superfamilies — as part of that answer.

## Heathen Superfamilies

As I described in chapter 4, Heathens envision the individual as embedded in a network of supporting entities and forces. The Heathen superfamily is an extension of this idea. Heathens are supportive of the nuclear family; no Heathens that I am acquainted with seriously advocate dissolving the nuclear family in favor of a completely communal living situation. Yet Heathens sense that as an isolated unit, the family is weak — a position that the Lore supports. Families build strength through nourishing and supportive connections with others, by surrounding oneself with a superfamily. In order to encourage the growth of these superfamilies, Heathens draw on three types of religious resources: theological, sociological, and ritual. The theological resource involves the use of ancestor worship to create superfamilies. As we have seen, ancestral beings are considered living presences connected to our lives through ørlög. The Heathen self-concept understands the individual life as formed and continually influenced by a deeper past of known and unknown ancestors, the extended ancestral family. Heathens enact this theological awareness in the practices of ancestor veneration.[704]

702. Palmer, *Moon Sisters*, 209.
703. Stinson, *Heathen Families*, 27.
704. Stinson, *Heathen Tribes*, 197. Stinson advocates learning about one's family predecessors through genealogy, remembering and honoring them through meditation and ritual practices, and making them proud by living honorably and raising healthy children by passing on good ørlög to them. In these ways, ancestor worship has theological, sociological, and ethical implications.

These practices cultivate a sense of closeness to the ancestors, generating psychological and emotional connections that constitute part of a supportive superfamily.

The sociological resource for the superfamily focuses on the kindred, tribe, or hearth, the basic organizational unit of Heathenry. The nomenclature used to describe these social units carries familial connotations. Early in the history of American Asatru, the kindred came to represent an alternative family that shared a faith and set of values, in addition to or in place of one's family of origin. While acting as a center of religious activity, the kindred also fulfills or approximates some of the functions of family life. Stinson directly builds on the superfamily model when he describes the kindred as, "coming together as an extended family. Caring for each other, looking out for each other's interests, coming to each other's aid . . . The children should . . . come to see each as brothers and sisters."[705] While kindreds often start as groups of religiously interested individuals, there is significant interest in the expansion of kindreds into "tribes," multigenerational groups consisting of several families that function as a religious and social community. Many Heathens now identify themselves neither as universalists nor folkish, but as tribal Heathens who desire to build small-scale socio-religious networks around intimate organic familial bonds of affection and loyalty. The goal is to establish a shared history and culture, a thew, among a group of families from which a new tribal identity emerges. Some Heathens are quite serious about building these superfamilies and are putting into place specific practices to accompany and enact this ideal. For instance, several Midwestern kindreds are pursuing the practice of fostering, in which children from one family/kindred spend extended visits with another family/kindred, developing long-term relationships. Fostering is a relatively new innovation being reconstructed from examples found in the Lore, which describe Viking Age families raising or fostering a child from their extended relations. These exchanges, which are carefully monitored by parents and occur only between families who know each other well, function to create a superfamily dynamic in which adults outside of the nuclear family are instrumental in socializing children.

The ritual resource for building superfamilies is the sumbel. As discussed in chapter 6, the most fundamental ritual in Heathen

---

705. Stinson, *Heathen Gods*, 54–55.

life is the blót, in which veneration and offerings are exchanged for the intangible gifts of the gods as part of the ongoing human/god relationship. Of the Asatru rituals, blót has received the most attention as the ritual most directly concerned with the worship of the gods and other spiritual beings. Swain Wódening states that the blót provides the highpoint of Heathen *religious* experience, while the sumbel provides the highpoint of *social* or *community* experience.[706] This distinction between the two rituals is helpful and instructive, although we should note that both are deeply religious in a broad sense. The sumbel is not a sacrificial rite, but a complex and formal drinking ritual that honors the gods, ancestors, and other beings. In a typical sumbel, a horn of sanctified mead or other beverage is passed among the participants each of whom makes a toast or verbal invocation over the horn.[707] This ritual and its setting, the mead-hall, constitute the most evocative and nuanced expression of Heathen religiosity, picturing a structured cosmological community of kinship, a superfamily composed of both divine and human beings living and dead. As we will see, the sumbel is a potent ritual in which Heathens draw on powerful symbols to create and experience sacred families and communities.

## The Sumbel Ritual

There are several reasons for privileging the sumbel as a means to understanding American Heathen religious experience. First, the sumbel frequently takes the climactic position in Heathen gatherings, often occurring at the height of the festival experience along with a feast, entertainment, and accompanying practices.[708] Second, the sumbel best expresses the complex cosmology and polytheism that is so vital to Heathenry. As we will see, participants make toasts or speeches venerating the gods of their choice. These heartfelt speeches of thanksgiving to a multitude of Heathen gods and goddesses emphasize the importance of devotional plurality

---

706. Swain Wódening, email message to author, July 22, 2012.
707. Mead is an alcoholic beverage made by fermenting honey in water. It is one of the oldest forms of alcoholic drink.
708. For example, Stinson writes, "From a religious and spiritual standpoint, the High Symbel is the main focus of LATP [Lightning Across the Plains]," Stinson, email. Lightning Across the Plains was a regional Heathen gathering hosted by Jotun's Bane Kindred in Kansas.

within the community. Third, the sumbel makes apparent the essential family aspect of Heathen religious experience. As Mark Stinson pointed out, "Heathenry is about community."[709] Similarly, Rod Landreth explained that "Heathenry is ultimately a communal religion."[710] According to these and other Heathens, the fullest expression of Heathen spirituality is achieved within the group setting when humans experience the gods as *part of* that community of kinship. Scholars like Steven Pollington shape and reinforce these ideas when describing the ancient Heathen religious vision as "particularly communal—not personal and private. The activities are about sharing with others—not personal communion with the divine. The divine is experienced in the context of the gathered community."[711] For these reasons, we should see the sumbel as the ritual most evocative of Heathen religiosity.

I became aware of the cultural importance of the sumbel while participating in regional and national Heathen gatherings in which the ritual often represented one of the event's high points (figure 24). Prior to the ritual, I frequently noticed a shift in the atmosphere and activity of these events. For instance, at a Heathen gathering in the Midwest, the sumbel was held in a large picnic shelter. Preparations began hours before with an announcement that participants should not go near the shelter while it was being prepared. Meanwhile the participants dispersed and began changing clothing into their Heathen garb—Norse-inspired clothing often worn during rituals.[712]

---

709. Stinson, *Heathen Gods*, 39.
710. Landreth, email.
711. Pollington, *The Meadhall*, 226.
712. At almost every Heathen event I have attended, some participants wear Norse-inspired garb. During a formal ritual it is very common to see people dressed in garb. Garb carries a good deal of symbolic weight. However, it is loosely defined, its aesthetic function being more important than its historical accuracy. For most men, a Norse-like tunic worn over jeans suffices, while others may add elements such as leather gauntlets, boots, bits of armor, and weapons. Women most frequently wear a Norse-style apron dress with jewelry. While widely practiced, garb can be controversial. Heathens do not want to be pegged as Viking reenactors or as indulging in fantasy role-playing known as LARPing. While that dynamic never completely disappears, practitioners emphasize Heathenry as a faith for contemporary people. For that reason, some groups reject the use of this quasi-historical clothing. From my observations, garb is treated fairly haphazardly by most Heathens. I have met several Heathens who design and sew garb and put a great deal of attention and historical accuracy into their work, though this is not the norm.

# Asatru as Family Religion

Figure 24. Author and Son Prepared for Sumbel. (Photo used with permission.)

Over the course of an hour or two the scene changed visually as well as thematically. As the heat of the day faded and the horn was sounded calling participants to the sumbel, we were clearly in a different space. No longer a picnic shelter, the building had been transformed to recall an ancient Viking longhouse or mead-hall, a gathering place for the tribes, with altar, banners, and shields. It had become a liminal space, undergoing its own temporary transformation into a sacred site where the ritual was about to commence. This process of transition caught my attention and raised the question in my mind, "Why is this picnic shelter being re-imagined in this way?"

## Sources and Symbolism of the Heathen Sumbel

The combination of activities that I witnessed that night were replicated to one degree or another at various sumbels that I attended throughout the United States. This indicated that to me that an underlying pattern was at work structuring the way Heathens were approaching the ritual. Many cultures utilized drinking practices for various purposes, the Greek symposium being a notable example. In Germanic societies, drinking customs have been associated with the formal reception of guests, the celebration of successful battles or seasonal festivals, as well as informal social bonding, such as the drinking parties among common folk called *beorþegu* or *gebeorscipe* in the Old English sources.[713] In the development of American Heathen culture, a particular interpretation of Germanic drinking customs and traditions has become salient. This interpretation, enunciated most clearly by Bauschatz, argues that Germanic custom involved a formal drinking ritual called a *symbel* (in the Old English sources) or *sumbl* (in the Norse sources).[714] Bauschatz takes a robust approach to the symbel custom. The ritual, he suggests, was practiced across northern Europe as an important and formal socio-religious ritual informed by the Germanic cosmological symbols of Urth's well and Yggdrasil, the world tree. This set of shared symbols, and other symbolic actions, were enacted by Germanic communities as a rite of membership. Among Heathens, his ideas about the ritual have taken on great significance and have been widely incorporated into the religious culture.[715]

Heathens in America have incorporated the work of several scholars to form a powerful synthetic symbol of the sumbel and

---

713. Pollington, "The Mead-Hall Community," 24.

714. Bauschatz, *The Well and the Tree*.

715. Scholars have had mixed responses to Bauschatz's ideas. See Bruce Lincoln, "Of Time and the Brunnr," *History of Religions* 23, no. 1 (1983): 84–87; Anatoly Liberman, "The Well and the Tree (Book Review)," *Germanic Review* 58, no. 4 (1983): 158–59; Ernst S. Dick, "Review: The Well and the Tree: World and Time in Early Germanic Culture by Paul C. Bauschatz," *Speculum* 59, no. 3 (1984): 616–19. Lincoln finds much to be admired in the work, calling it "clear, readable, scrupulous in its scholarship, and compelling in its argumentation." Liberman suggests that too much is made of the well and the tree as the central mythological images of Germanic culture, though he is interested Bauschatz's analysis of drinking and feasting rituals. Dick takes a more negative position, questioning the quality of scholarship and suggesting that the term symbel simply refers to a feast, and not a formal ritual. Bauschatz himself never followed up on his work in *The Well and the Tree*.

its setting in the mead-hall. Three works have been particularly important to the development of the ritual: *The Well and the Tree* by Paul C. Bauschatz, a scholar of English literature who taught at University of Maine; *Lady with a Mead Cup* by Michael Enright, a historian of medieval Europe; and *The Meadhall* by Stephen Pollington, an independent scholar of English history, culture, and language.[716] While each of these works has been influential in its own way, Bauschatz's *The Well and the Tree* has functioned in Heathenry as an authoritative source for information about the sumbel. Its primary contribution was a thorough exploration of the ritual featured in the Old English poem *Beowulf*. Prior to the publication of his book, American Heathens were not practicing the sumbel. As late at 1985, when Stephen McNallen published the first comprehensive guide to American Heathen ritual, the sumbel was not mentioned at all, indicating that it was not yet part of the religious world.[717] By 1986, a couple of short articles had appeared in *Vor Trú*, the magazine of the Ásatrú Assembly, introducing and describing the sumbel.[718] In both these articles, the language and ideas used to describe the ritual closely resembled those of Bauschatz. In his capacity as a scholar of Germanic languages and medieval studies, Edred Thorsson (Stephen Flowers) encountered and read *The Well and the Tree*. He incorporated the sumbel ritual into his Austin, Texas kindred. Thorsson's Asatru manual, *A Book of Troth*, which arose from the practice of his kindred, included one of the earliest sustained treatments of the sumbel as a contemporary practice.[719] Through these entry points, Bauschatz's interpretation came to be the formative influence in the development of this important ritual in Asatru.

Heathens have made use of Michael Enright's concept of "fictive kinship" to think about the ways that the sumbel creates and

---

716. Michael J. Enright, *Lady with a Mead Cup: Ritual, Prophecy and Lordship in the European Warband from La Tene to the Viking Age* (Portland, OR: Four Courts Press, 1996).

717. Stephen A. McNallen, *The Rituals of Asatru* (Payson, AZ: World Tree Publications, 1991).

718. Helga Larsson, "On the Meaning of the Sumbl," *Vor Trú* 18 (1986): 3; "A Sumbel Summary," *Vor Trú* 20 (1986): 4. The latter article, "A Sumbel Summary," includes language that closely resembles McNallen's description of the ritual. See McNallen, *Asatru*, 145–49.

719. Thorsson, *A Book of Troth*, 85–87.

formalizes enduring bonds of loyalty and friendship.[720] Enright draws on historical and literary sources, such as Tacitus' *Germania* and the epic *Beowulf*, to describe the development of the sumbel itself. According to Enright, the sumbel or "liquor ritual" as he calls it, served as a religio-political rite at the heart of the Germanic warband, forming its extra-tribal members into a cohesive and effective unit. He argues that powerful symbols from pre-Christian Germanic culture were combined over time to create this ritual intended to bind unrelated people together into a quasi-familial relationships. This concept was quite applicable to the creation of superfamilies within the contemporary Heathen movement, since the tribal ideal is in tension with the fact that most adherents are not related.[721] Drawing on Enright, contemporary Heathens saw the sumbel as efficacious in creating social unity from its disparate participants, and investing that fictive family with religious significance.

Heathens have also been interested in Stephen Pollington's suggestion that the historical sumbel was a place-specific ritual. He described it as inextricably linked to the mead-hall, a prominent feature of Germanic communities for hundreds of years.[722] So important was the mead-hall that Northern European architecture continued to preserve its form even beyond the survival of traditional Pagan societies. "The concept of the hall as the community's centre remained constant to the end of the Anglo-Saxon period, even though by the ninth century there were new social and economic forms of secular community," he writes. The longevity of the hall

---

720. Enright, *Lady with a Mead Cup*, 76. Enright's term "fictive kinship" refers to a non-biological relationship that is perceived or articulated in biological terms. According to Enright, the relationship of a leader and his warband was conceived of as a father to son relationship, with the leader's wife acting as mother. This is applicable to contemporary Heathens because many kindreds are composed of non-biologically related individuals who seek to function as a family.

721. Ibid., 16. Enright discusses how intoxicating drink and an authoritative female figure are linked as important religious symbols in Germanic culture, going so far as to say that "the incidence of usage . . . is so high as to indicate that it reflects a deep-seated attitude, a pattern of thought which lies at the basic core of the culture," Enright, *Lady with a Mead Cup*, 80. These two symbols are brought together in the "liquor ritual," to form a powerful religio-political event, or at least the potential for such an occasion in which marriages, alliances, coming of age, bonds of fealty and other community-building were enacted and formalized.

722. Pollington, *The Meadhall*, 147.

indicates that its cultural importance was more than functional.[723] Its place in Germanic and Norse cultural life was celebrated and idealized in the *Beowulf* poem. *Heorot*, the hall Beowulf fights to defend from the ravages of the monster Grendel, stands as the epitome of civilized life, a symbol of human culture at its pinnacle. The poet describes the hall in ideal terms as a "wonder of the world forever . . . a timbered hall, radiant with gold. Nobody on earth knew of another building like it. Majesty lodged there, its light shone over many lands."[724] Those who gathered in the hall enjoyed the blessings that were the result of community life: food and drink, finely crafted objects, culture and art, and companionship.[725]

While not all halls lived up to the high ideal presented in the Beowulf poem, Pollington shows that the hall was "physically replicated in most Anglo-Saxon communities, even small ones seemed to have had a 'hall' even if it was simply a room in the leadman's house."[726] The hall's ubiquity and longevity indicate its important metaphorical value in the culture. The hall represented a sort of ideal Germanic lifestyle, "hall life," which "invoked the ideal of human togetherness."[727] Hall life encompassed the moral/political/social order of the community as well as the enjoyment of its abundance, the "pleasures of the hall," which included "friendship, hospitality, fellowship, brightness, and warmth. They represent the 'indoor' aspects of men's lives, the world of shelter, hierarchy, and comradeship."[728] The metaphor was also used to represent the supernatural world, Pollington suggests. For instance, pre-Christian Norse mythology described Valhalla, the hall of the slain, as a mead-hall. In later Christian Anglo-Saxon culture, heaven and the Christian afterlife were occasionally depicted as sitting in sumbel in the mead-hall.[729] So in several ways, the mead-hall long functioned as a metaphor for ideal life.

723. Ibid., 31.
724. Seamus Heaney, trans., *Beowulf: An Illustrated Edition* (New York: Norton, 2008), lines 70, 307–11.
725. Ibid., lines 88–99, 1010–18.
726. Pollington, *The Meadhall*, 226.
727. Ibid., 31.
728. Pollington calls the mead-hall the "idealised epicenter of social and political life," see Pollington, "The Mead-Hall Community," 28, 33.
729. Bauschatz, *The Well and the Tree*, 73; Pollington, *The Meadhall*, 116.

The setting of the sumbel within the mead-hall signifies that the rite was communal in nature. If Pollington is right, the mead-hall functioned historically as something of an *axis mundi*, symbolizing the sovereignty of the community geographically, politically, and spiritually. The sumbel ritualized that function. It reinforced the boundaries and bonds of the community and served as the means by which outsiders could be included.[730] Pollington writes that "by sitting with their peers to share food and drink, men and women publicly affirmed membership of the group. The drinking horn circulating around the mead-hall benches described a path which was effectively the boundary of that community."[731] The basic image of the sumbel is simply the family sitting together at table. This image of family informed the rite by which the tribal group, consisting of an extended family, formalized and renewed its bond as a single unit.[732] It eventually came to function as a religio-political ritual within the Germanic war-band, in which the familial-like bonds of "fictive kinship" were invoked in order to bind together the extra-tribal members of the community.[733] As the site of this efficacious ritual, the mead-hall came to symbolize the ideal community, a kinship forged from sacred bonds and vows of loyalty. It was both a means of community-making and the symbol of community.

Moreover, Bauschatz points out that the historical sumbel resonated with Germanic cosmological concepts. In Bauschatz's interpretation, the ørlög of all beings was contained or collected in Urth's Well, also called the Well of Wyrd, at the base of the world tree, Yggdrasil. Bauschatz symbolically connected Urth's Well with the horn of mead at the sumbel. The act of holding the horn, speaking into it, and drinking from it represented the placing and layering of the person's words into Urth's Well.[734] As words are spoken over the horn, "they disappear into the drink; as it is drunk, the speaker of the speech, his actions, and the drink become one, assuring that all now have become part of the strata laid within the well."[735] These words have been spoken to me almost verbatim by Heathens. In the sumbel, the understanding and awareness of this connection

---

730. Enright, *Lady with a Mead Cup*, 76.
731. Pollington, *The Meadhall*, 226.
732. Enright, *Lady with a Mead Cup*, 86.
733. Ibid., 17, 128, 283.
734. Bauschatz, *The Well and the Tree*, 70.
735. Ibid., 77.

between the horn and the Well of Wyrd forms an important part of the ritual consciousness. Participants will speak solemnly into the horn, knowing that their words shape the cosmological pattern of time and potentiality, and influence the lives of those who share in it. To speak and drink from the same horn binds the ørlög of those who share it.

In addition to the mead-hall, the drinking horn itself is a powerful and evocative symbol in Heathenry. The horn is certainly ubiquitous within the movement. It is often carried by adherents or worn on the body on a belt strap and serves in a functional capacity as a vessel for all kinds of beverages. Horns are also status symbols with those bearing intricate carvings, fitted with rims or metal ends often garnering attention and pride. Some kindreds pride themselves in having very large horns used for public ceremonial purposes. I have drunk from horns in sumbel that threatened to engulf my entire head and experienced thoughts of sincere apprehension about the amount of mead that might gush from it. The horn is a multivocal symbol with significant religious meanings as well: the mundane love of a good drink, the connection to an ancestral and cultural past, the source of divine inspiration, and a cosmological symbol of the Well of Wyrd. Perhaps most importantly the horn functions as a metaphor for community, particularly in the willingness to *share* a drink. Since its physical shape prevents it from being easily set down, the horn is passed from hand to hand, and a horn is rarely filled solely for private consumption. In a sumbel, the ritual horn is usually passed among the participants by a woman, a role often referred to as a "valkyrie" among Heathens. Here again, we see the importance of contemporary scholarship in shaping the real practices of the movement. In his discussion of the *Beowulf* sumbel, Bauschatz notes the role of a socially powerful female in serving the sacred mead and Enright's work thoroughly developed this theme.[736] Heathens have fully adopted this practice, in some cases making it a point of orthopraxis. While the horn carries all these meanings, only its ritual use in the context of sumbel elevates the horn to its full metaphoric potential within Heathenry.

736. Ibid.

## The Contemporary Sumbel

Heathens draw specifically on all these ideas, images, and historical patterns of the drinking ritual noted by these authors in order to create a significant religious event for contemporary practitioners.[737] Mark Stinson writes, "From a religious and spiritual standpoint, the High Symbel is the culmination of Lightning Across the Plains. It is the holy moment where all of the community and bonds we have built are celebrated before our Gods, our Ancestors, and the Folk."[738] Before continuing to discuss the sumbel as a "significant religious event," it is worth noting that some American Heathens take a dissenting position on the practice and its meaning. At a discussion of Heathenry at Mystic South, a Pagan conference held in Atlanta, Georgia in 2017, one Heathen mentioned that "the idea that the horn is the Well of Wyrd is simply not there in the Lore."[739] He represented a demographic of Heathens who take a strong reconstructionist approach, as well as an emerging generation of young Heathens who are less likely to take conventional Heathenry at face value. From his perspective, the sumbel is an important practice of social religion and community-building, but not a mystical event. These Heathens, a small but vocal minority, push back against what they see as the over-sacralization of the sumbel in its predominant form and argue for a reformation of these first-generation concepts.

The basic pattern of events making up the contemporary sumbel includes a time of preparation and three rounds of drinking and toasting, often following a time of communal feasting (see figure 25).[740]

---

737. Academic work on ancient Germanic culture is often closely and consciously appropriated, as well as critiqued, by contemporary practitioners who use it as a guide for Heathen practice. For example, at an event in Minnesota, I was told that the order of the sumbel would draw on Pollington's reconstruction of the Anglo-Saxon sumbel ritual from *Beowulf*. The actual ritual closely followed Pollington's outline. Field notes taken by author, Minnesota, June, 2012. See Pollington, *The Meadhall*, 42–48.

738. Stinson, email. Lightning Across the Plains was an annual regional Heathen gathering hosted by Stinson's Jotun's Bane Kindred and at the time one of the largest in the United States. Stinson uses the Old English spelling, symbel, showing the influence of both Bauschatz and Pollington.

739. Field notes taken by author, Atlanta, 2017.

740. Thorsson provides the earliest Heathen liturgy for the sumbel with six distinct movements: (1) seating "in right/holy order"; (2) bringing in the horn and "holy liquid"; (3) beginning by invocations; (4) first boasts "honoring gods and heroes"; (5) other boasts; and (6) leaving, which closes the round. See Thorsson, *A Book of Troth*, 86.

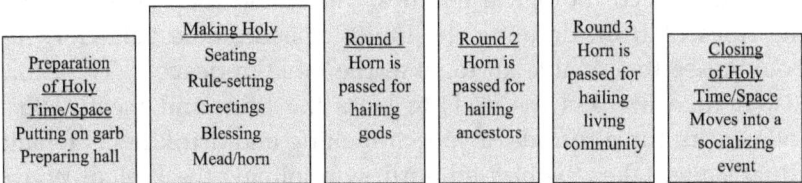

Figure 25. Order of the Sumbel Ritual.

As mentioned earlier, a transition may occur prior to the sumbel, envisioning a type of sacred space. First, the physical environment itself may be manipulated to create a Viking aesthetic resembling a historical mead-hall. An altar, kindred banners, shields, and other accessories such as tapestries and table coverings evoke an idealized version of the ancient mead-hall, an atmosphere furthered enhanced by the Norse garb often worn by participants.[741] One notices a shift in rhetoric as well, as participants and leaders refer to the site of the ritual as the "hall," setting the space apart linguistically.[742] The sumbel often begins with some type of sitting ritual. The host occupies a high table at the front, while other participants are seated in hierarchical order from front to back, often according to kindreds led by a chieftain.

A ritual leader then performs an opening ritual, often calling upon the gods, ancestors, and land spirits to sanctify and protect the hall. This gesture accounts for the wider audience of the ritual and invites the presence and participation of those beings, creating a mood or awareness among the Heathen participants of certain

---

741. The garb worn by some participants serves as part of the liminal transformation that reveals and displays the real or ideal self. The special clothing demonstrates a type of self, one's "trú" self, which is often obfuscated or downplayed in daily life. A secular example might be the dress robes donned by university professors during a graduation ceremony, revealing their status as "masters" of their academic disciplines. Modern dress in our society has a homogenizing or denaturing effect, which cuts us off from ethnic, cultural, and religious identity. By wearing garb, participants temporarily imagine, create, and reveal this deeper self, a cultural-religious self that is formed in relation to the Germanic worldview.

742. I noticed this rhetorical shift during the introductory speeches at several sumbels I attended, which frequently referenced the ritual space as "the hall." Leaders used this rhetoric to re-cast the space in metaphoric and ritualistic ways. Field notes taken by author, Oklahoma, Kansas, Minnesota, 2012-2013. Some Heathens have constructed a ritual room in their homes that they refer to as a hall, Stinson, email.

spiritual and cosmological realities. The leader may also establish the rules of frith, defining the limits of acceptable behavior, the boundaries that enable all to sit at the table in peace.[743] The ritual leader then invokes the gods to bless the horn and mead. What follows are three rounds of speech-making and drinking. A female ritual leader takes the blessed horn, symbolizing the Well of Wyrd, around the room. Each participant stands, takes the horn, and gives a short speech that is generally greeted with a loud cry of "Hail!" by the participants. Mark Stinson describes it this way,

> In the first round, participants toast a God or Goddess of their choice. In the second round participants toast an ancestor or hero with great meaning for them personally. In the third round, participants can boast of their own accomplishments, toast other Heathens for their accomplishments, or even make oaths about future deeds they will accomplish. As the gathered group says these words over the horn, they are putting them into the horn. This is akin to putting layers in the Well.[744]

Each round adds a new layer onto the Heathen superfamily. At the end of each round of speech-making, the mead now laden with sacred words is poured into an offering bowl. The horn is refilled for the next round. After all the rounds are completed, the ritual is formally closed and a leader will pour the sanctified mead as a libation offering to the land spirits and gods. This complex ritual can often last for several hours at a large gathering, though most instances are smaller, shorter, and simpler. Important variations can occur, such as the use of apple juice in place of mead when children or adults who abstain from alcohol are participating. The core of this basic pattern, involving acts of sacred speech-making accompanied by ritual drinking of a sacred beverage, always remains constant.

---

743. These rules define the limits of frith, the boundaries within which peace and ritual decorum is maintained. The walls of the hall are a physical metaphor for the sacred cosmos, the realm of frith, while the rules of behavior designate the metaphysical boundaries of frith, the terms of inclusion in that sacred community. The rules often prohibit certain types of discourse during the ritual. For instance, oaths are forbidden in many instances, especially in large settings in which not everyone knows each other. Another common rule forbids the hailing of Loki or other malicious beings. Transgressing a rule might result in a warning from the warders. More serious penalties are occasionally enacted, such as expulsion from the hall or even terminating the rite itself as happened at Trothmoot 2010.

744. Stinson, email.

## Creation of the Sacred Community

The sumbel is best described as a rite of intensification, This type of ritual reinforces the social structure of a community by providing a "dramatic representation of the habitual relationships of the individuals in the sets of which the system is composed."[745] The ritual manifests and legitimates the roles and relationships between members. Most interactions among Heathens are casual and egalitarian and social hierarchy is muted. The sumbel, however, is a moment in which hierarchy and special relationships between individuals and groups are emphasized, clearly pictured, and affirmed as cosmologically significant. The sumbel encodes these values in a notable dyadic ritual structure. Victor Turner noted this aspect of ritual when "pairs of opposed values lie along different planes in ritual space."[746] His insight is useful in identifying three such dyads within the sumbel.

### Dyad One: Order and Chaos – Within and Without

The physical structure of the hall itself signifies an inner/outer dyad, a microcosm of the Heathen cosmology (see figure 26). Unlike the blót, the sumbel typically takes place inside. The walls of the hall represent the metaphysical boundaries of sanctity. A communitas of fellowship, the innangarð or the "hall life" described earlier, exists within the hall. Outside the hall lays the outer darkness, the unordered chaos known as útangarð. These are important moral distinctions. The innangarð is equivalent to the good, the trusted. The útangarð represents what does not belong, what is disruptive and cannot be trusted. This is a picture of the sacred cosmos. In large rituals, experienced participants known as warders protect the sanctity of the space. They watch over the internal mechanisms of the ritual, ensuring an orderly process and guarding access and egress from the hall. Usually, participants do not leave without permission from the warders and do not enter without their consent and direction. Disruptions may cause the warders to suspend the ritual until the issues are resolved. This dyad emphasizes the

---

745. Eliot Dismore Chapple and Carleton Stevens Coon, *Principles of Anthropology* (New York: Henry Holt, 1942), 507.

746. Victor Turner, *The Ritual Process: Structure and Anti-Structure* (Ithaca, NY: Cornell University Press, 1969), 38.

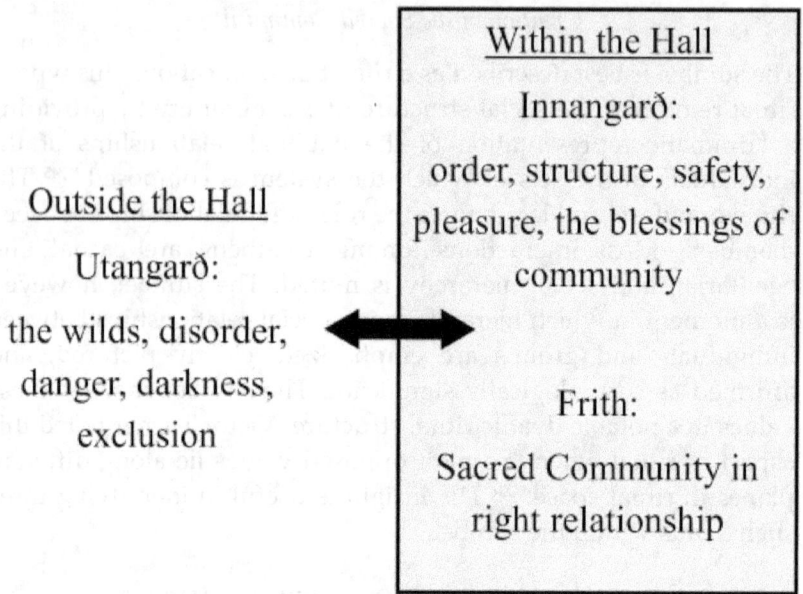

Figure 26. The Inner/Outer Dyad of the Sumbel.

dynamic of belonging: within the mead-hall participants are part of the sacred community.

### Dyad Two: Status and Hierarchy – Front to Back

The seating order within the hall follows a dyad indicating the status or worth of participants (see figure 27). Status is spatially represented by the opposition of the high table at the front of the hall and the benches leading into the back of the room. Participants are seated along this longitudinal axis, signifying rank within the gathered community. The hosting kindred or leaders preside from the high table, while other participants are seated at the benches according to the host's determination of their worth and the quality of their relationship. An individual's location in the hall corresponds to his/her role in the superfamily and relationship to the host. The variety of approaches to seating create interesting dynamics along this dyad. In the Midwest, the host kindred occupied the high table, allied kindreds were seated closest, and other guests were seated in successively distant tables. At Trothmoot, the High Rede holds the position of rank at the high table, while participants seated

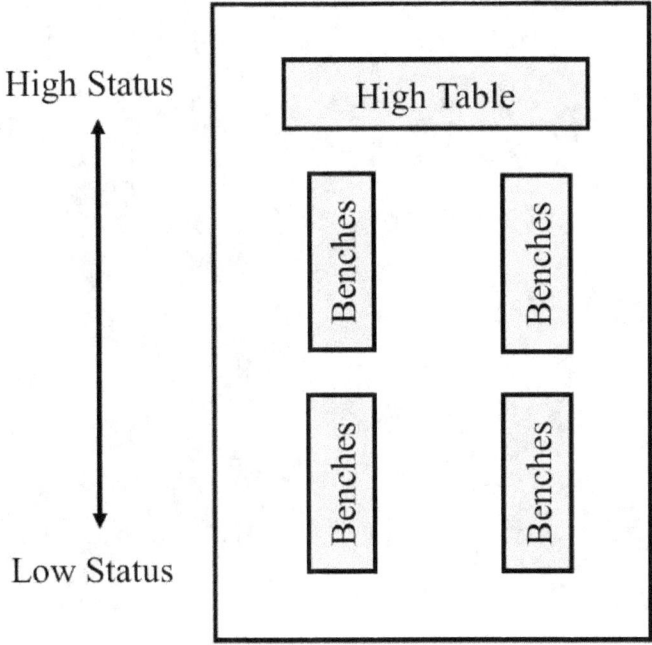

Figure 27. The Longitudinal Dyad of the Sumbel.

themselves in the benches with less regard to gradations of status. At times, these arrangements lead to disgruntlement. As a back-bencher myself on several occasions, I frequently commiserated with those who felt snubbed by their placement in the hall. However, within this context, the sumbel seeks to achieve a communitas of sorts that acknowledges and reinforces the underlying hierarchical nature of the Heathen movement. This dyad portrays the community as a rightly ordered family, structured according to rank or worth.

## Creating the Sacred Community

The preparatory period and the seating ritual embed participants within a structured ideal society. The invocation and blessing of the mead draw the attention of the gods and other spiritual beings to the event, marking the onset of the sumbel. At this point, the participants are now gathered in a sacred place/time as a sacred community. During the three rounds of speech-making, layers of cosmological community are added through the repetitive ritual cycle of speaking, listening, and affirming each other's words. With

Figure 28. The Community Gathered for Sumbel at Lightning Across the Plains. (Photo by the author.)

each round, participants invoke a different set of relationships—deities, ancestors, and other living people. As the assembly receives these invocations by a chorus of loud hails, these beings are understood to be joined to the community, sitting with the family at the table as kin. In this way, a "fictive kinship" is established that transcends the visibly gathered community.

In round one, participants invoke the gods, recognizing the human/god relationships that exist in the community. These speeches are not structured as petitions, but as acts of veneration. Participants speak the names of the gods and voice the bonds of familiarity between human and gods. This focuses attention on the family relationship that exists between the human and divine communities. The gods are understood to participate in the gathering through their attentiveness and awareness of the words spoken by their human kin.[747]

---

747. Stinson states, "If there is any time that the gods are paying attention, it is tonight at High Symbel." Mark Stinson, "Symbel as a Complex Social and Religious Practice," workshop, recorded by author, Kansas, September 21, 2012.

During the second round, participants name and toast their ancestors. This brings the ancestors into the assembly's shared awareness and makes them present as part of the community of kinship. Just as the recognition of kinship with the gods blurs theological distinctions between divine and human, so the recognition of ancestors blurs existential distinctions between the living and the dead. The ancestors are invoked and included as part of the Folk, the living Heathen community. Jonathan Z. Smith describes the complexities of this relationship: "It is, on one hand, crucial that the dead remain in the sphere of the dead . . . On the other hand, it is equally crucial that there be controlled contact with the dead, that there be a continuity of relationship and appropriate modes of the dead's presence."[748] The ancestor round offers exactly that opportunity to Heathens. A participant might present or introduce a deceased relative to the community and then proceed to interpret that ancestor's legacy. This involves a discursive process of appraising the quality of the ancestor's life. The speech act is a type of revision or reinterpretation that casts the ancestor in a light acceptable to the Heathen community, precisely as one who the community can accept as its own. As the participant speaks, she constructs an extemporaneous narrative that emphasizes the ancestor's commitment to Heathen values. In doing so, the participant interprets the ancestor (who in life may or may not have been approving of Heathen religion) as supportive of the Heathen community and its values. For example a speaker might say, "She may have been a Christian but she lived out our values of honor, independence, and hard work." Or similarly, "My grandfather went to church his whole life, but he was always giving me books about mythology and encouraged my curiosity." This places the relative within the participant's own narrative of becoming Viking. The "Hail!" voiced by the assembly validates and approves the ancestor's place of significance in the participant's life.

The speech-making function presents an opportunity for this interpretive process by which the relative becomes a Heathen ancestor. As the name is spoken and the tale told, re-imaging the

---

748. Jonathan Z. Smith, "Here, There, and Anywhere," in *Prayer, Magic, and the Stars in the Ancient and Late Antique World*, eds. Scott B. Noegel, Joel Thomas Walker, and Brannon M. Wheeler (University Park: Pennsylvania State University Press, 2003), 26.

relative in Heathen categories of value, the ancestor is received into the frith and welcomed to take a seat at the table. Throughout, we see the importance of controlled contact with the dead, which takes place in the act of interpretation and revision. The Christian ancestor poses a dangerous discontinuity for Heathen adherents, a source of psychological dissonance. Heathens may be estranged from their families or in tension with relatives because of their choice to pursue an alternative religious path. They may experience nagging doubts about how a beloved grandparent might have dealt with their religious choices. Larger theological and existential issues are also at stake, as adherents may question their ability to draw on the ancestral power, the ørlög and luck, of that individual. All this can be resolved in the interpretive act of the sumbel. Once received and accepted in such a way, the ancestor takes a comfortable and positive place in the adherent's religious life as part of the religious superfamily.

The third round adds the final layer of kinship as friendships and relationships between members of the living human community are recognized and celebrated.[749] Very frequently, participants share gifts in addition to words to signify and formalize bonds of friendship. At a sumbel in Minnesota, two kindreds brought gifts to exchange as part of an alliance with each other. Sitting across from each other in the ritual, the leaders shared bottles of mead and home-brewed soda for the kids. They read a statement of friendship in which both kindreds promised to be there for each other, with hugs and back-slapping for all involved. "Songs will be sung about this night!" said one of the ritual leaders, indicating the significance of this new quasi-familial bond.[750] At a different sumbel, this one in Kansas, late at night and deep into the third round, I saw a man stand and raise the horn to two people who had befriended and encouraged him as a new Heathen. He brought out a bottle of mead to give them and praised them for their strong moral characters and kindness to him. Unfortunately, both women had left the sumbel

---

749. Landreth described how sumbel is "a happy affair, but also extremely more solid, more real because the words spoken are going into the Well, our deities, ancestors, and the vaettir around are also 'present' and listening. In many ways, for a short time . . . that Hall becomes the most important place in the world for Heathens." Landreth, email.

750. Field notes taken by author, Minnesota, June 2012.

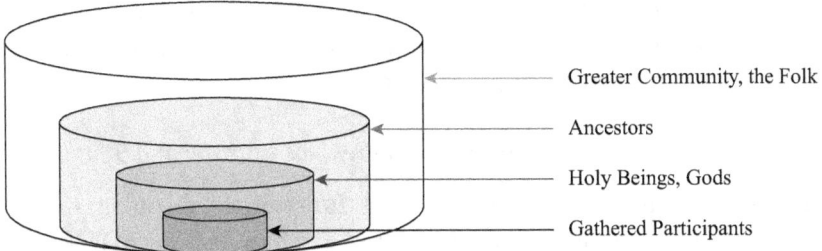

Figure 29. The Asatru Superfamily.

and gone to bed, missing the significant moment.[751] Their absence noticeably disappointed the man, but he recovered and finished his speech and the familial emotions he expressed towards them were affirmed and hailed by the group. The lengthy ritual and late hour conspired to create a moment of infelicitous performance in this sumbel, a hitch that kept the rite from fulfilling its intended purpose.[752]

These three rounds trace the boundary of a community greater than the individuals, families, and kindreds present (see figure 29). The bonds of kinship manifested within the sumbel express the Heathen concept of "the Folk." As described in chapter 2, some groups may define the term along ethnic or racial lines. But for many Heathens, the term has evolved beyond its völkisch connotations. Like "church," "sangha," or "ummah," the Folk is a deeply important idea that signifies the human community in right relationship with the transcendent world, in this case the superfamily of ancestors and elder kin, the gods. The cosmology of the sumbel evokes Michael York's description of the Pagan worldview as an "organic perception of the world, the supernatural, and humanity in which gods and humans are seen as interrelated components of a single cosmic system."[753] Through this ritual process, the sumbel builds a microcosm within the roof and walls of the hall. The hall becomes a cosmological symbol of the world structured by these sacred relationships.[754] The Well of Wyrd symbolized by the horn becomes

---

751. Fields notes taken by author, Kansas, 2013.
752. Grimes, *Ritual Criticism*, 200.
753. York, *Pagan Theology*, 38.
754. Pollington, *The Meadhall*, 226.

the *axis mundi* around which the sacred hierarchal community assembles—a cosmic superfamily of divine, human, and ancestral beings in right relationship with each other.

*Dyad Three: Creation of the Sacred Individual – Sitting and Standing*

The three rounds of speech-making function to create a sacred superfamily, a network of quasi-familial relationships that serves to enhance individuality. The Heathen individual does not face the world alone, but as part of a family, embedded within and strengthened by the bonds of relationship with gods, ancestors, and other living persons enacted in the sumbel. Simultaneously with the creation of the superfamily, this complex and sophisticated ritual serves to valorize the individual (see figure 30). To observe how this occurs, we must focus on the ritual horn that moves through the hall during each round. The female ritual leader ("valkyrie" is a contested term for this role) navigates among the benches carrying the horn to each individual, male and female, for the speech-making act. When a participant's turn arrives, he or she stands and takes the horn. Standing elevates the participant above the seated assembly, enacting the vertical axis of the third dyad. The basic posture of sumbel involves sitting at a table. Standing noticeably breaks this pattern. The hierarchical distinctions of the second dyad are temporarily suspended. At that moment, the attention of the assembly becomes focused upon the one who stands and takes up the sacred horn.[755]

This attentiveness is not merely a religious ideal, but is enacted with remarkable consistency. During the course of my field research, I attended numerous sumbels and have always been struck by the degree of attentiveness actually demonstrated by real Heathens in this setting. For instance, the sumbel rituals at Lightning Across the Plains notoriously ran late into the night. Numerous factors worked against attentiveness, such as the duration of the event, participants' increasing drowsiness, and the biting cold of the Great Plains on those autumn nights. One memorable night towards the end of a long sumbel, a man took the horn and rose to speak. As he did so, the officiants at the high table were distracted by their own

---

[755]. In a talk given about the ritual, Mark Stinson pointed out the important role of attentiveness in the sumbel, "An important part of the sumbel is listening." Field notes taken by author, Minnesota, June 16, 2012.

Figure 30. The Vertical Dyad of the Sumbel.

conversation. Noticing this, he lifted the horn and addressed them in a loud, clear voice. Instantly, the conversation stopped and all heads turned, returning their focus to the sacred moment at hand.[756]

### Giving Voice, Limiting Voice

When standing and speaking over the horn, each individual is elevated over the seated group. Words spoken over the horn at this time are significant because they are ritually deposited into the Well of Wyrd.[757] This connection is considered metaphysical in nature, not merely symbolic. In that moment, each speaker's words carry equal weight, influencing the wyrd of the whole assembly. Each participant who stands at the *axis mundi*, holding the mead horn and speaking words of religious and social weight, is clearly framed as a sacred individual.

The disruption of the hierarchical structure during speech-making is not a subversive act. Within the boundaries of the sumbel it is sanctioned and affirmed by the assembly. Each individual is given their sacred moment. There is even a subtext at work of

---

756. Field notes taken by author, Kansas, 2013.
757. Stinson, email. The significance of the moment is also communicated through body language and elocution. People speak up in a declaratory tone of voice. They peer into the horn, speak over the horn, or hold the horn aloft. While there may be other horns in the hall, those do not carry the same weight or importance as the ritual horn holding the sanctified mead.

friendly competition regarding who can speak most eloquently and movingly. At the same time, the hieratic position assumed by each participant is temporary and dependent upon the goodwill of the assembly. If the individual speaks in a way that is seen as inappropriate or dangerous, the speech will be cut short by ritual leaders.[758] When ritual leaders deem that false, insincere, or transgressive speech acts are taking place, they typically deal with it quickly and decisively. While the individual is recognized in the moment as a spiritual equal, that freedom is subject to the authorization of the sacred community. The sacred individual must keep frith by acting within the accepted bounds of family behavior in order to be given license to speak and express him/herself in this binding way. This caution protects the assembly from whatever potentially hazardous metaphysical implications might be engendered by careless or malicious words.

The oath is a type of speech act that receives particular attention among Heathens. Oaths are binding promises about future behavior that must be fulfilled once they are formally spoken. They are vows placed into the Well of Wyrd to which the future and luck of individuals is tied. Oaths are made in various ways but a common practice involves speaking the oath into the horn at sumbel. This method involves and binds not only the individual speaker, but all those who affirm the oath during the ritual. Because of their collectively binding nature, oaths are frequently ruled "out of bounds" or beyond the bounds of frith during the ritual. During a sumbel I attended in 2012, a man took the horn and began speaking emotionally about an ancestor who was a war veteran, a very appealing sort of ancestor among Heathens. The participants were engaged and listening attentively as he told a moving story about this man's death in the war. With tears running down his cheeks he loudly declared, "And I swear by the ancestors . . .!" Suddenly from around the room, shouts of alarm rang out. Warders ran towards him from the corners of the room and in the moment of confusion the man stopped speaking. After a brief consultation, he was allowed to continue, "but without the oath."[759] By preventing the oath, the

---

758. Landreth, email. Also in field notes taken by author, Pennsylvania, June 2012.

759. Field notes taken by author, Pennsylvania, 2012. Sumbels can be affected by rash words even more dramatically than this incident, such as Trothmoot 2010 in which the ritual was disrupted and canceled when a group of participants violated

sacred community avoided becoming metaphysically bound to whatever words he might have spoken in the heat of the moment. On one hand, this incident exemplified the religious intensity that can be generated by the sumbel and the importance that words carry in Heathenry. Yet it also illustrates that the freedom of the sacred individual is a gift from the community and is subject to its authorization. Hierarchy reasserts itself as the underlying structure of this superfamily.

## Conclusion: Sumbel as Superfamily

In Heathenry, the sumbel is a powerful symbol of family. Those who sit in the hall and share the sumbel horn are bound together as loyal kin. That picnic shelter in the Midwest was reimagined as a mead-hall in order to activate this metaphoric meaning in the lives of contemporary Heathens. The sumbel portrays the ideal community as a familial relationship between divine and human participants, living and dead. Divine and human beings are seen as part of an innangarð, a bounded community of identity and relatedness, kindred beings and members of a family.

What does sumbel really achieve? In some ways, the ritual is useful for post-modern people. It creates the felt experience of family without entangling people in the actual difficulties of close familial relationships. Yet for many Heathens, this would represent the failure of the ritual. A cathartic experience of community, an imagined family that fails to substantially alter the state of modern individualism, would be insufficient. Sumbel is meant to be a Heathen response to individual loneliness and family breakdown. It enacts the innangarð, the family enclosure, a social space of belonging.[760] As with any rite, it is more or less effective in any given enactment. Participants do say important words, share personally significant moments, and express themselves in ways they ordinarily would not. Deep emotions are felt and shared during the

---

the terms or boundaries of frith. A similar event happened at Trothmoot 2014, when a young participant invoked Loki in a sumbel ritual. However, in this incident, a process of negotiation allowed the ritual to continue without a complete collapse of frith.

760. Wódening, *We Are Our Deeds*, 9. For example, Stinson stated that "The individual is only a small part of something greater." Field notes taken by author, Kansas, September 21, 2012.

rounds of the horn. Relationships are enacted with the hope that they will be meaningful and lasting. The elusive quality of frith is sought in the family-like atmosphere of closeness and caring. The act of disparate people sitting together in peace holds profound and life-changing possibilities. In these ways, the ritual emphasizes and drives home what contemporary Heathenry is in part about—calling together a new type of sacred family within a world perceived as sacred and blessed. Because of the dispersed and often fractious nature of contemporary Heathenry, some metaphor is necessary to communicate a sense of greater unity. This metaphor is found in the mead-hall and its ritual, the sumbel, which can function to unite Heathens from different localities and different theological perspectives. It can create a temporary experience of harmony and unity, even new friendships and lasting bonds. Not only is the community seen, but it is created as individuals and groups are called and bound together by the rite. The creation of this familial bond is the intent and potential of the ritual; achieving the ideal is something toward which the movement continues to struggle.

# Chapter 8

## Asatru as a Magical Religion

A völva, a woman with the power of second sight, sits beneath a yew tree in the Teutoburg Forest, Germany, eyes closed with her back to the trunk.[761] Three powerful forces are conjoined there as she breathes slowly and attunes her mind to her surroundings. First, the forest: the Teutoburg forest is a potentially powerful site, a place of death and victory, where an army of unified Germanic tribes wiped out three Roman legions. In Heathen thinking, burial places are nexus points, sites of connection to spirits and ancestral beings. Second, the tree holds a special place in Heathen religious thought. The yew tree in particular is thought to be sacred and powerful. It is associated with the ancient shrines of the old gods, as well as with the rune Eihwaz, ᛇ, or Eoh in the Old English rune poem.[762] The old massive yews that grow in the churchyards of northern Europe are thought to be survivors of the sacred groves and ancient Pagan shrines that once occupied those lands.[763] Third, the magic worker herself, who goes by many different names in the Heathen tradition: völva, *seiðkona*, seeress, is a powerful presence whose mind and body have been trained and primed to focus her consciousness, to enter trance states extending her awareness and will, and to peer or travel into the Nine Worlds. With her back against the trunk, she stretches out her awareness into nature, grounding her energy. From the tree with its roots sunk deep in the earth, she draws strength up into her own body, regulating her breath and slowing her heart rate.

---

761. Yngona Desmond, *Völuspá: Seiðr As Wyrd Consciousness* (BookSurge, 2005), 48. Desmond is a well-known figure and a long-time practitioner of Heathen magic. The scene described here is a composite illustration that draws significantly from an experience described in Desmond's book, while also drawing on conversations with other practitioners of seið.
762. This is the "ė" or "ei" rune, reconstructed as *ī(h)waz* or *eihwaz*. It is commonly written as Eihwaz or Eiwaz by Heathens. The Old English rune poem preserves the rune as *ēoh*, meaning "yew."
763. Thorsson, *Futhark*, 45.

While trance is difficult to obtain for many, the experienced völva quickly enters into an altered state of mind, in which she feels her consciousness amplified by the energy of nature, quickly ascending, even rocketing upward, only tenuously anchored to her body. Other seers experience this journey as a descent, spiraling down, following the spreading roots of the world tree towards the underworld. Images flash around her, growing in speed and intensity, racing through her mind beyond the speed of conscious thought, as if her awareness is escaping the clutches of gravitational pull. Then suddenly she experiences a puncturing into a new state of consciousness, she has transcended ordinary limitations and has taken on a new perspective, "wyrd consciousness," in which she is present to the raw structure of the cosmos where the emerging edge of events are unfolding. She describes this enhanced awareness in stream-of-consciousness prose, "There were threads everywhere, everywhere coiling and knotting, coiling and un-knotting, vibrating and shimmering, 'singing' as they moved. There were threads of sun and moon and season, threads of All Worlds humming, threads of unwounding and of wells bubbling from deep nowhere springs, and runos and life and death."[764] It is not that she has left the world, indeed she is more deeply open to the world, embedded in it. It is the world that sings around her. But she perceives it at another level, with its layers, connections, and flowing living energy revealed. The tree at her back is still there, but is now experienced in its multidimensional layers, not only a sacred tree but also "The Tree," Yggdrasil the world tree itself, the spine of the cosmos. The ordinarily limited human awareness of the physical cosmos has been frayed so that the völva sees through the cracks; it has given way to this awareness of the wyrd, the transcendent reality that lies underneath and continuous with the physical world. In the account of her esoteric experience, the völva passes through the natural world into the direct awareness and experience of the wyrd, the living energy that lies behind and animates the natural world. This living Past, the wyrd, is directly perceived in the ecstatic trance-enhanced vision of the seiðwoman.

As she rockets along the spine of the world, she passes imperceptibly into the more-than-natural world, a cosmic nature connected to the natural world but of a different order and

---

764. Desmond, *Völuspá*, 50.

magnitude. The natural world partakes of this cosmic nature, is shaped and defined by it, and can be a gateway into it. In turn, what happens in the natural world builds, adds to, and shapes the wyrd, while the wyrd thrums underneath as the living energy of the past that pushes into the present. The wyrd is the interconnected nature of reality, threads entwined with threads. This Heathen experience closely resembles what Clifton has described as Cosmic Nature, "not the Gaian nature of animals, trees, and flowers, but a more abstract nature whose laws generations of astrologers, magicians, philosophers, and the founders of occult schools and orders perceived as demonstrated in the movement of heavenly bodies."[765] Whereas the astrologers and ceremonial magicians of high magic peered into the workings of cosmic nature through the movement of heavenly bodies, the Heathen shamans use seiðwork to extend consciousness into this esoteric realm. In her trance state, the will of the völva is able to interact with this higher order of nature, seeing it and describing it. In some cases, she may participate in it, potentially manipulating and influencing it from within, like a genetic scientist who manipulates the hidden layer of genes to produce a new outworking of their potential. These aspects of the seiðkona's experience: her trained will, her expanded participatory consciousness, and the possibilities of transformation opened to her are the core components of magic.

Magic in Heathenry is a complex phenomenon that defies easy categorization. In one sense, magic has developed as the natural outworking of a particular Heathen cosmology, a worldview that lends itself to magical practice with concepts such as wyrd, objects such as the runes, and techniques such as galdr or runic incantation. At the same time, the role and place of magic in Heathenry is highly contested. Heathenry has a complicated relationship with magic, a tension that sets Heathenry apart from Wicca and Witchcraft, forms of contemporary Paganism in which magic plays a vital role. According to many of its adherents, Heathenry is first and foremost a votive religion, having to do with worshiping the gods, while magic is only of marginal importance. Yet despite this opinion, magic is everywhere in Heathenry. After an attempt to define the phenomenon of magic, I will explore the contested place of magic within Heathenry, discovering once again the uncomfortable

---

765. Clifton, *Her Hidden Children*, 46.

confluence of two different ideological tributaries. A deeper look at Heathen magic will focus on *seið*, specifically three distinct ways in which *seið* is currently understood and practiced within the movement: as a magical process of self-transformation, as epistemic magic seeing the world in a new way, and as a technique of magical healing.[766] While sharing many characteristics, such as the distinctly Heathen worldview and religious technologies of runes, trance, and galdr, these three types of seið magic reveal differing purposes that yield widely divergent practices.

## Misunderstanding Magic

With wry insight into the modern confusion over magic, Diana Paxson notes that "Modern English has very few words to describe magical practice."[767] She contrasts this with the "rich magical vocabulary of the Germanic languages" that provided the conceptual framework for a widely varied magical repertoire.[768] The lack of linguistic resources available to even talk about magic reflects the degree to which modern people have been dis-embedded from the magical worldview that was predominant in the pre-modern period. Magic is almost always something imagined from the outside, through the lens of other cultural frames of reference. Perhaps the most powerful and lingering connotation of magic in the minds of many mainstream Americans has been its association with Witchcraft and, by implication, with occult or demonic powers. This picture of magic as satanic, evil, and dangerous has a decidedly medieval flavor and a well-documented cultural history with its roots extending back even earlier than the witch trials of the fourteenth through the seventeenth centuries. The association continues to have considerable power within the American Christian sub-culture and those who are influenced by it. A search of online Christian booksellers will quickly reveal a number of texts that approach magic through this particular theological lens. With titles such as *Dancing with the Devil*, *Escape from the Cauldron*, or *Taken from the Night: A Witch's Encounter with God*, these books dwell on the

---

766. Seið is a category of magic that utilizes trance states of consciousness for divination, psychic journeying, and other practices. It transliterates the Old Norse *seiðr* and is pronounced "Sayth" or "Seeth."
767. Paxson, interview.
768. Paxson, *Essential Ásatrú*, 117.

dangerous yet seductive power of the occult that lures people into a trap of demonic activity. Perhaps the most thoughtful member of this genre is Catherine Sanders' *Wicca's Charms*, published in 2005. Sanders recognizes how this perspective entirely misunderstands the contemporary Pagan approach to magic. Although she herself evaluates Wicca from a Christian theological perspective, seeing it ultimately as a false spiritual path, she does not sensationalize magic nor promulgate the occult mystique. Instead she argues that Paganism authentically addresses certain contemporary spiritual needs that are neglected by much of modern Christianity: a connection to nature, to the divine feminine, and to more embodied forms of spiritual expression. Despite her contribution, associations with the demonic continue to cloud the ability of many to understand the resurgence of magic in contemporary Pagan religions.

An entirely different cultural trend grows from the depiction of magic in popular books and movies. "I love magic," declares Harry Potter in one memorable scene from the famous movie series.[769] Ducking under the flap of a small unassuming tent set up in a field at the Quidditch World Cup, Harry is stunned when he steps into a luxurious multi-roomed mansion "magically" fitted with all the amenities of home. The camera draws into a close-up of Harry's beaming face as he utters the words that ignited a beatific childhood fantasy of magic in the hearts of his admirers. While the demonic theme still lingers in the form of Voldemort, whose frightening death magic continues to threaten Harry's world, the magic that Harry and his friends share is bright and fantastical, a world of self-washing dishes and displays of aesthetic beauty, jelly beans, fireworks, and acrobatic broom-riding. But this Hollywood magic is more than simply innocent, playful, and powerful: Harry Potter's magic signifies a longed-for freedom. The automobile, which once figured prominently as the symbol of social freedom for pent-up teenage dreams, has been replaced by Harry on his broomstick. Magic, packaged by Hollywood for the coming-of-age American youth, indulges the fantasy of freedom, freedom from the boredom and constraints of mundane middle-class life. Even as the demonic connotations are stripped away or distanced from magic, this Potterized portrayal remains a parody of magic, a type of childhood utopian fantasy rather than something to be really practiced.

769. *Harry Potter and the Goblet of Fire*, Warner Brothers, 2005.

A third predominant outsider approach to magic has its roots in the scientific and technological ideology of modernity. Whereas a religious worldview posits supernatural beings who must be appeased and supplicated to effect change in the world, magic might be seen as a more secular approach attempting to produce results through the application of natural laws. Sir James Frazer, an early scholar of religion, enunciated this view over a century ago, explaining magic as a pre-scientific attempt to manipulate the world. According to Frazer, magic is essentially distinct from religion: "Religion assumes the world to be directed by conscious agents who may be turned from their purpose by persuasion . . . Magic [on the other hand] takes for granted that the course of nature is determined, not by the passions or caprice of personal beings, but by the operation of immutable laws acting mechanically."[770] Frazer defined magic as a system that manipulates impersonal natural forces to accomplish an end. Magic in this way resembles a quasi-scientific worldview, one that recognizes the reality of cause and effect. Magic "assumes that in nature one event follows another necessarily and invariably without the intervention of any spiritual or personal agency . . . Underlying the whole system is a faith . . . in the order and uniformity of nature."[771] According to Frazer, the natural laws of magic arise from a pre-scientific and therefore flawed understanding of the world. He enumerated two of these magical laws in his work: the law of sympathy, which supposes that performing a ritual action will produce a similar cosmic action; and the law of contagion, which supposes that objects once in contact continue to maintain a psychic or magical connection that can be manipulated by the magical practitioner. Despite the rational appearance of these laws, Frazer suggests that they failed to grasp the actual dynamics of nature that have been discovered through the work of experimental science. Magic is "primitive" in that social Darwinist mode of thought. The efficacy of the scientific endeavor, its empirically proven capacity to achieve real results, has displaced magic as a worthy human undertaking. Where science succeeds, magic fails. In an age of science and technology, magic is simply irrational and impractical.

770. Frazer, *The Golden Bough*, 49.
771. Ibid., 51.

Of course, the contemporary growth of Pagan and magical religion confounds Frazer's expectation of magic's increasing redundancy and irrelevancy. Why then are magical practices and worldviews finding such a ready audience among contemporary Pagans in the contemporary West? Tanya Luhrmann's study of magical practice, *Persuasions of the Witch's Craft*, was one of the first anthropological studies to seriously address the question.[772] She observed that questions such as "What allows people to accept outlandish, apparently irrational beliefs?" and "Why do people find magic persuasive . . . in the face of constant failure?" simply misunderstand its place and function in the lives of contemporary Pagans and practitioners of magic.[773] Most Pagans do not evaluate magic solely according to standards of external verifiability and strict empiricism, and have a more complex relationship to scientific and magical suppositions than this "intellectualist" approach admits. Similarly, Síân Reid argues that by indicting magic as a "reasoning pathology" this approach makes two mistakes.[774] First, it takes a reductive approach to the complexity of the human mind by suggesting that "the only valid mode of thinking is literally, logically, and linearly." And second, it misapprehends magic as actually practiced by contemporary Pagans by reducing magic to instrumentality. Reid writes that "in conflating magic with . . . an end-oriented, instrumental tunnel-vision, interpreters are missing the point."[775] She describes magic as much more about self-creation than about externally verifiable results, and frames magic as more akin to a therapeutic process than a scientific one. Magic draws practitioners into the experience of an interconnected cosmology with which a person can meaningfully interact, restoring to practitioners a strong sense of agency and positive sense of self. Magic is about growth, healing, and self-actualization that leads to an experience of "wholeness, connections, self-knowledge, and personal agency."[776]

---

772. T. M. Luhrmann, *Persuasions of the Witch's Craft: Ritual Magic in Contemporary England* (Cambridge: Harvard University Press, 1989).
773. Ibid., 7–8.
774. Síân Reid, "As I Do Will, So Mote It Be," in *Magical Religion and Modern Witchcraft*, ed. James R. Lewis (Albany: State University of New York Press, 1996), 161.
775. Ibid., 160.
776. Ibid.

## The Tension of Disconnection

Perhaps alluding to Wittgenstein's language games, Luhrmann states that "it is as if magicians learn a new language in which to talk about their world, and gain a new set of possibilities for organizing it."[777] She called this "interpretive drift," the gradual adoption of new beliefs to validate experiences. Other scholars have critiqued Luhrmann's theory and have developed more holistic models to account for magic's modern allure. For instance, Helen Berger and Douglas Ezzy point to the dual role of cultural orientation and individual seekership to explain the appeal of magical religion to young people.[778] Their model has been formative for my own thinking about Heathenry. However, Luhrmann is correct to suggest that magic involves a process of self-transformation and discovery, a re-making of the self. In this sense, magic is a re-envisioning, a way of talking about the nature of things that encodes the world with expanded meaning, a re-enchanting approach to the self as much as the world. In my time spent with Heathen practitioners of magic, I noticed very little inclination to justify magic in the face of scientific rationalism. Rather than evaluating their own practice against it, the Heathens I have met tend to critique and question the ability of modernity to fully explain the world and see magic as a necessary supplement to correct the damage done by Occam's razor. There is a strong sense among Heathens, and Pagans more generally, that modernity, both in its scientific and Christian forms, disconnects or numbs modern people to the possibility of deep spiritual interaction with the world that is reflected in the experience of Pagan people in the past. Berger and Ezzy's idea of cultural orientation suggests that some people, those who have engaged with Secondary Worlds for instance, are already primed to expect more from the world than scientific materialism can deliver. Diana Paxson recalls attending a Christian communion service during college and feeling an energy or power in the ritual that was different from her previous experiences with religion: "What I was always looking for was a spiritual path that would allow me to make contact with the divine and I didn't get that very often in Christianity . . . The chaplain at college was a man of great spirituality and when he did the

---

777. Luhrmann, *Persuasions of the Witch's Craft*, 244.
778. Berger and Ezzy, *Teenage Witches*, 58.

communion service, you could feel the energy. And I went "Okay that's what I want. I want that energy."[779] This sense of searching for and returning to an experience of power pervades the Pagan worldview. The "mechanical philosophy" that dominates modern Western civilization has stripped away our experience of the world as "alive, animate, and interconnected," leaving modern people with a disenchanted world.[780] Pagans believe that it is possible to have a deeper and fuller experience of reality and the sacred than is ordinarily found in modern life. They believe there is more to know about the world and the self than what modern science and religion have described and envision a past in which a connection to that power and energy still existed in human society. Pagan and magical traditions are new religions that seek to reconstruct "older, once-enchanted cosmologies" in part as a response to this perceived modern disconnection from the world.

The narrative of disenchantment is widely accepted by Heathens. As Adrian Ivakhiv explains, magic once constituted a sustaining worldview that supported the life of human communities, "in traditional societies, myth, storytelling, and ritual activities . . . served to maintain a sustainable relationship between the different structural elements of the cosmos: human society and the gods, conscious ego and unconscious underworld."[781] This worldview saw a cosmos alive with beings, forces, relationships, and magical correspondences that were vitalizing for humans and their societies. Magical religion kept the unknown "within the reaches of the society itself," and capable of being accessed at significant moments. The spiritual mediators of these societies—"shamans, sorcerers, witches, and the like" as well as community rituals such as rites of passage—served to bridge this boundary and brought people into temporary but creative and meaningful contact with larger, natural, and supernatural forces around them.[782]

---

779. Paxson, interview.
780. Helen A. Berger, *A Community of Witches: Contemporary Neo-Paganism and Witchcraft in the United States* (Columbia: University of South Carolina Press, 2005), 23.
781. Adrian Ivakhiv, "The Resurgence of Magical Religion as a Response to the Crisis of Modernity: A Postmodern Depth Psychological Perspective," in *Magical Religion and Modern Witchcraft*, ed. James R. Lewis (Albany: State University of New York Press, 1996), 240.
782. Ibid., 239.

However, through the process of modernization, this function was "shifted out beyond the society's margins," delegitimizing contact with these forces and beings.[783] Modernity in Western society no longer tolerated these magical practices now thought of as occult, a situation arrived at through social and legal pressure applied by the Christian state, as well as the social upheaval caused by industrialization and the development of the capitalist economy. Ivakhiv states that "contemporary Euro-American society finds itself . . . in the dilemma" of being dis-embedded or disconnected from this traditional context that brought meaning to people's lives by connecting them to the natural world. In the context of modernity, we have "lost the sense of sacredness in our relationship with the world about us" and live in a "disenchanted" world, "disconnected (or at least, not *meaningfully* connected)" with the people and world around us.[784] As scholars of religion know well, this thesis has been somewhat overstated. The enchanted experience has never been fully suppressed. For many moderns, however, the scope of mundanity has grown to encompass large swaths of life, making enchantment more complex and difficult to find. From a Pagan perspective, this situation of disconnection is a sign of a "maladapted or 'diseased'" society.[785] It surfaces, among other ways, in the psychological angst of modern individuals who "don't know what it is we should do or what our rightful place amidst it all is meant to be."[786] Caught in the tension of desiring a deeper connection to the world but unable to find it in modern society, Pagans look back to the enchanted, magical cosmologies of pre-Christian, pre-scientific cultures. Magical religions such as Wicca, Druidry, and Heathenry arise to "fill the gap," to find the elements of connection again and re-embed modern people back into fuller ways of knowing and interacting with the world around them.

### *Defining Magic*

In the study of religion, defining magic has proven to be an ongoing and notoriously difficult endeavor. The literature on magic is

783. Ibid.
784. Ibid., 242.
785. Ibid., 241.
786. Ibid., 242.

voluminous, reflecting the difficulty of defining magic and the diversity of magical practices, the many "colors" of magic that confound attempts at systemization.[787] Definitions seem to fall into three categories: essentialist, which seek to define the fundamental nature of magic; functional, which seek to describe what magic does; and family resemblance definitions which identify magical phenomena according to a set of characteristics.[788] For instance, Ivakhiv draws on this model when he writes, "Whatever definition one favors, it is clear that magic has something to do with *imagination* (a word that shares etymological roots with 'magic'), with *patterns* (of images, symbols, correspondences between the human, natural, and macrocosmic worlds), and with some sort of *efficacy*."[789] This attempt to triangulate the phenomenon proves helpful by enabling observers to recognize magic when they see it and because it takes seriously the values of participants and practitioners. While his conceptual categories of imagination, patterns, and efficacy are thoughtful starting points, we will focus on three elements particularly salient in the ways that practitioners write and speak about magic: will, participatory consciousness, and transformation.

## *The Will*

Perhaps the most well-known description of magic comes from Aleister Crowley's *Magick in Theory and Practice* and expresses an essentialism that focuses on personal will in contrast to Frazer's natural law theory of magic. Crowley famously defined magic as "'The Science and Art of causing change to occur in conformity with Will,'" a definition that has been incredibly influential among contemporary Pagan practitioners.[790] On the face of it, the will is simply the power of the mind focused and concentrated. Mind, properly disciplined, can control and manipulate matter, a conception of magic reflected in nineteenth-century Romantic anthropology and the American New Thought movement.[791] Grimnir, a Heathen

787. Harvey, *Contemporary Paganism*, 90–91.
788. Cusack, *Invented Religions*, 20.
789. Ivakhiv, "The Resurgence of Magical Religion," 244.
790. Aleister Crowley, *Magick in Theory and Practice* (New York: Castle Books, 1960), xii. See also Pike, *Earthly Bodies*, 13; Joyce Higginbotham and River Higginbotham, *Paganism: An Introduction to Earth-Centered Religions* (Woodbury, MN: Llewellyn Publications, 2006), 163–64.
791. Albanese, *Nature Religion in America*, 112.

magic worker who prefers the Old Norse term vitki to emphasize his specifically Germanic approach to magic, follows Crowley in understanding the will as a personal esoteric power. He writes, "Magic 'works' by a vitki summoning his Will, the numinous energy that drives our existence, and using that force in a very direct and focused way."[792] This power can be built up or accumulated by disciplined individuals through the use of various spiritual practices and tools, similar to the Vedic understanding of *tapas*, the inner heat acquired by ascetic practice.

Magic is a system of tools and techniques that amplifies and focuses this personal will and releases it into the world, an emphasis that is inevitably read by some in a Nietzschean sense as the strong individual's Will to Power. Enacting one's will in the world raises the specter of force and the dangers of the ego—asserting one's agenda upon others. Think of the evil vizier Jafar in Disney's *Aladdin* who seeks magical power in order to dominate, declaring "the ABSOLUTE power! The universe is MINE to command, to control!"[793] However, magic as it is actually practiced by contemporary Pagans rarely has to do with a solitary sorcerer forcing his will upon the world. A more contextual reading of Crowley suggests that "will" has more teleological connotations. The use of will is not "a license to self-indulgence," but involves a "challenge ... to find out what your destiny is and fulfill it."[794] The will, far from being an excuse to exercise one's personal whim or ego upon others, should reflect one's place and role in relationship to the cosmic scheme of things. More contemporary versions of this definition move beyond notions of willful Romantic individualism to draw on democratic and populist images of will. For instance Starhawk, the popular author, ecofeminist and Pagan priestess, has advocated an understanding of magic focused on non-hierarchical power and "the actions of many consciousnesses voluntarily working together."[795] This egalitarian understanding of will is fundamental, for instance, to the magical practice of raising and releasing a cone of

---

792. Paul Waggener, "On Magic," in *Operation Werewolf: The Complete Transmissions*, 115.

793. *Aladdin*, Walt Disney Pictures, 1992.

794. Chas S. Clifton, "What has Alexandria to do with Boston? Some Sources of Modern Pagan Ethics," in *Magical Religion and Modern Witchcraft*, ed. James R. Lewis (Albany: State University of New York Press, 1996), 271; Harvey, *Contemporary Paganism*, 95.

795. Adler, *Drawing Down the Moon* (2006), 164.

power. As Margot Adler described it, the "cone of power" is really the combined wills of the group, intensified through ritual and meditative techniques, and focused on a collectively agreed-upon end. "When it has been raised, it is focused and directed with the mind and shot towards its destination."[796]

All these versions of the will focus on agency, whether personal or communal in nature, the ability to act effectively in the world. The will lends to magic a potentially transformational quality, to produce change both in the self and in the world. Along these lines, Joyce and River Higginbotham have a simple explanation for the role of will in magic. At its simplest, a magical working involves forming an intention, projecting it into the universe, and letting it go.[797] The exercise of intention or will has the potential to produce change. While much of the literature on magic is focused on the practitioner and her will, the will alone is not enough. Practitioners also focus on the context or environment in which magic happens. The worker of magic enters into a relationship with the world, its beings and energies, working with the world rather than subjugating it to her will. The effectiveness of one's will depends on a participatory consciousness.

## Participatory Consciousness

In her work on magical experience, Susan Greenwood describes the magical mindset as the expansion of one's awareness into a participatory relationship with the world.[798] Imagination, a word that both she and Ivakhiv use, has been trivialized in the modern cultural context, implying daydreaming, flights of fancy, fantasy, and fiction. This usage creates a false distinction between the analytic/practical mind focused on the tangible and measurable physical word, and the phantasmagorical mind lost in the "imaginary," reverie, illusion, or worst yet delusion. Greenwood uses the term in a broader sense: the imagination is a mindful capacity, indicating a "pliable and responsive" mental state that is able to "range freely beyond the usual constrictions of everyday thinking"[799] What is "imagined" or "imaged" in one's mind is not

---

796. Ibid., 106.
797. Higginbotham and Higginbotham, *Paganism*, 170.
798. Susan Greenwood, *The Anthropology of Magic* (Oxford: Bloomsbury, 2009).
799. Ibid., 64, 65.

necessarily fantastic or unreal. Imagination is not an escape from reality, but opens up the possibility of creatively and broadly exploring reality unencumbered by socially constructed boundaries of whatever passes as acceptable or normal thinking.

As we observed in the völva's experience earlier in the chapter, participatory consciousness is a "magical mindset" that involves shifting the consciousness into altered states to create or discover previously unseen associations among things. The shift, usually but not always consciously induced, enables the participant to become receptive or open to the esoteric interconnections that are purported to exist in the world beyond normal human perception.[800] Magic workers use various techniques to produce these shifts of consciousness: visualization and meditation; repetitive or rhythmic actions such as drumming, chanting, or dancing; ritual and environmental cues; sensory deprivation; entheogens, and more. Having achieved an altered state, the magic worker perceives layers of association among entities and apprehends the world in relational ways. Participatory consciousness is an "inspirited world view," as Greenwood puts it, in which the world seems to be alive with energy and power, full of encoded meaning to those who are open to it.[801] Like the völva's perception of the yew tree, the physical world and the spiritual cosmology of the imagined world merge and coincide, a vision of the world overlaid with connections across time and space. Greenwood describes cultivating a participatory mindset while on a visit to the Welsh countryside, near the Preseli Hills. Reaching out with her awareness, she surveyed the physical prominence of the hills while at the same time, as if superimposed upon them, she perceived another layer, the entrance to Annwn, the Welsh underworld.[802] Diana Paxson relates a similar experience, giving a Heathen account of these participatory layers of experience while performing seið in a Pagan festival: "With doubled vision, I see the hotel function room, where sixty people are thinking about how to word their questions, and the mighty gate to Helheim, its timbers banded with iron and graven with runes of power."[803] In the altered state of consciousness, two conjoined levels of reality can be seen together:

---

800. Higginbotham, and Higginbotham, *Paganism*, 165–66; Nertha, interview.
801. Ibid., 31.
802. Ibid., 29.
803. Diana L. Paxson, *The Way of the Oracle: Recovering the Practices of the Past to Find Answers for Today* (San Francisco: Weiser Books, 2012), xi.

the awareness of the hotel room is overlaid by its participation with the supernatural reality of Helheim, the Norse underworld and abode of the dead.

These participations or correspondences are found in all magical systems from high ceremonial magic to natural kitchen magic and turn on the idea of an esoterically interconnected cosmos. Words, sounds, and symbols might link physical objects and entities with their spiritual counterparts. "These patterns," states Goodrick-Clarke, "concern correspondences between a higher divine reality, the universe, the earthly realm, and human beings."[804] Because of the interconnected nature of the magical cosmos, a practitioner of magic uses her will to influence one part of the cosmos expecting to produce change in another. Modern practitioners frequently reject Frazer's critique that magic misapprehends the laws of nature. Instead, thousands of years of magical practice suggests that the universe *is* naturally interconnected and that there *are* forces of nature and types of natural connections and correspondences between objects, which science has not yet described.[805] Explanations for this conclusion seem to arise from two different sets of presuppositions. A preternatural orientation towards magic suggests that esoteric forces exist of which modern science is simply ignorant, subtle energies that cannot be discovered through scientific means. A natural orientation explains that the esoteric forces of the cosmos are discoverable in the new science of quantum physics, where the boundaries between matter and energy are observed to break down. However it is explained, magical practitioners believe that if one can manipulate those correspondences through the exercise of one's will then, "Like a lever, a small magical spell can shift the world," a statement that brings us to the element of transformation.[806]

---

804. Nicholas Goodrick-Clarke, *The Western Esoteric Traditions: A Historical Introduction* (New York: Oxford University Press, 2008), 15.

805. See Berger, *A Community of Witches*, 19; and Luhrmann, *Persuasions of the Witch's Craft*, 118–19. According to Luhrmann, these forces may be "rather badly defined," but it serves us to note that while metaphoric descriptions of esoteric realities often lack a scientific precision, this does not preclude their usefulness. For instance, the runes and tarot pictures symbolically represent and differentiate these energies with a degree of specificity.

806. Luhrmann, *Persuasions of the Witch's Craft*, 118.

## Transformation

Contemporary Pagan practitioners undertake magical work in order to effect change, to transform the world in some way in response to human need. As indicated by our earlier discussion of the will, the instrumental understanding of magic forms an important part of the Pagan and Heathen worldviews. Later in the chapter, we will discuss three distinct instrumental goals of Heathen magic: the magical evolution of the self into higher levels of consciousness, the magical acquisition of knowledge, and the magical process of emotional healing. However, many observers of contemporary magic have also noted its important role in the process of developing or constructing the self. Practitioners of magic focus on building and developing their will by using such techniques as meditation and visualization. At the same time, they come to know themselves, individuate themselves, and develop a stronger sense of personal agency. In this sense, focusing on the will is a therapeutic undertaking: a transformative process.

Helen Berger takes such an experiential perspective, enunciating a functional definition of magic as a type of self-transformative experience. Pagans contend that magic has a "direct effect on the world" and is "efficacious in solving a wide variety of problems."[807] However, Berger notes that magic most clearly works to alter or transform the practitioner's identity, "Magic is seen, at least in part, as a process of awakening one's own psychological mechanisms."[808] She draws on Anthony Giddens' critique of modernity, which argues that the modern individual is dis-embedded from traditional identity structures, such as family, caste, or geographical place.[809] Loosened from these structures, self-identity becomes a narrative that must be shaped, altered, and redefined within the rapidly changing circumstances of modern life.[810] Magic functions as a technique by which a type of self, a new magical self, is constructed and maintained. Sarah Pike's understanding of magic is quite similar, focusing on the functionality of identity creation. She writes that "the explanations that NeoPagans give for the concept of magic almost always include 'change' and 'transformation.'" Magic can

---

807. Berger, *Community of Witches*, 18–19.
808. Ibid., 34.
809. Ibid., 28, 36.
810. Ibid., 28.

be anything that involves "consciously separating oneself from the world of the everyday and moving into a realm where possibilities are open for physical or psychological transformation."[811] She describes the practice of fire dancing at Pagan festivals as a magical event imbued with "the potential to create powerful experiences, to transport participants to 'higher states of consciousness,'" which "liberate participants from the 'selves' they bring with them."[812] In this magical liminal experience, participants are empowered to try on new types of selves and reshape their identities in alternative forms, beyond the limited and limiting categories available within modern society. Along these same lines, Síân Reid finds that magic "has a great deal more in common with therapies described in self-help literature than it does with the sort of quasi-scientific instrumental methods for producing change in the external world."[813] Magic in the contemporary world takes on an important therapeutic role as practitioners use its tools and techniques to reconstruct holistic selves out of the fractured individualism of modern life. Now with a clearer view of what defines the phenomenon of magic, we can explore the practice of magic within Heathenry.

## Is Asatru a Magical Religion?

Magic has an important role in the Pagan worldview, as Graham Harvey states, "Not all Pagans engage in magic, but a significant number do."[814] Wicca, for instance, is essentially a magical religion in which all initiated participants are considered priestesses and priests whose practice consists almost entirely of magical work. Asatru, unlike Wicca, is not an initiatory magical religion. There are magical specialists in Asatru, such as the seið workers, völvas, vitkis, and rune casters who we will discuss in this chapter. However, the majority of Asatru adherents are lay people who participate primarily in the exoteric aspects of the religion: its ethical, cultural, and ritual elements. Diana Paxson is a very magically oriented Heathen herself and recognized as an elder in the Troth, which may be the most magic-friendly of the Asatru groups. She has

---

811. Pike, *Earthly Bodies*, 13.
812. Ibid., 185–87.
813. Reid, "As I Do Will," 161.
814. Harvey, *Contemporary Paganism*, 87.

been a central figure in developing the Heathen magical practice of oracular seið. Yet, she writes that "magical workings are not central to Heathenry in the same way that they are to Wicca," a revealing statement from someone so deeply involved with Pagan magic of all sorts.[815] Similarly, in a popular Heathen podcast, the hosts Dave and Sandi Carron introduced the subject of magic in Asatru in this way:

> Dave: What we are putting forth . . . is that Asatru is first a religion.
> Sandi: Yeah, a religion, folks. That, as much as this may scare people, means dogma, rules, ideals. So, there's an emphasis on tradition, what our ancestors did, what people in our family have done, and trying to stick to those things or at least try and keep the spirit if not the letter of those sorts of teachings. There's an emphasis on self-improvement, on improving the world around us, and most importantly . . . on ethics and morals.
> Dave: These are the big concepts. We are dealing with spirituality first. We are dealing with what it means to have a connection with the divine. So in other words it [magical practice] is like salt: you can add it to things to make things better.[816]

These comments suggest that Heathenry is a form of contemporary Paganism in which the role of magic is ambiguous and disputed. In fact, as we will see many Heathens have an uncomfortable relationship with magical practice.

While a person's first act as a Wiccan would likely involve a magical working, Asatru adherents can be officially and thoroughly Heathen without ever participating in any practice of a magical nature. In fact, an attitude of reservation toward magic dominates the movement: magic is often deliberately downplayed. Mark Stinson, an influential Heathen leader in the Midwest, relativizes magic as a minority practice in Asatru, "a majority of our Heathen

---

815. Paxson, *Essential Ásatrú*, 117.
816. Dave Carron and Sandy Carron, "Asatru 101: Religion vs. Magic," *Ravencast: The Asatru Podcast*, October 29, 2007, http://ravencast.podbean.com/2007/10/29/asatru-101-religion-vs-magic/.

Ancestors weren't involved in Seidhr/Spae work," adding that only "a small minority were involved in these specialized 'magical' areas of our faith."[817] He reasons that a reconstructed religion ought to resemble the antecedent and therefore magic should remain a minority practice in contemporary Asatru. Stinson calls himself a "blue collar Heathen" who has little interest in esoteric pursuits. Continuing Dave and Sandi's culinary imagery, he states that magic ought to be like "gravy," added only after the "core knowledge and beliefs" have been mastered.[818] Although anyone familiar with Southern cooking knows that no meal is complete without both salt and gravy!

Stinson's comment about blue-collar Heathenry reflects the fact that first-generation Heathens convert from different backgrounds, often bringing particular religious orientations and preconceived attitudes about magic with them. Those who emphasize Norse magic often come into Heathenry from a background steeped in magical practice, such as involvement in Wicca or ceremonial magic. Background is often determinative for interest in magic, indicates Lorrie Wood, who notes that the core group of magical Heathens came from "a very magically aware population of ex-Wiccans as opposed to a less magically conscious population of former Protestants."[819] For these Heathens, magic often came first and only later did Asatru become a comfortable context to situate their practice.

Stinson's comment takes this a step farther by alluding to the intriguing element of economic and class background. He suggests that a practical realism characterizes the worldview of working-class Heathens, making them less inclined to pursue magical solutions. In Heathenry, they find a religion that coincides with blue-collar values of practicality, hard work, and self-reliance. Stinson's observation comes from his own experience of meeting many different Heathens and noting a generalized distinction between them. Anecdotally, there are cases that confirm his observation. While much has been written about magic as a response to the experience of deprivation, such analysis overlooks the fact that the characteristics of magical consciousness are similar to those acquired through exposure

---

817. Stinson, *Heathen Gods*, 15.
818. Ibid., 15.
819. Wood, interview with author.

to social privilege and its institutions, while the contemporary working class bears the brunt of modern de-enchantment. Pursuing the possibility of a correlation between magical practice and class among Heathens is something that necessitates further work. Still, my own anecdotal evidence of discovering Heathen magic in apartments and trailer parks in the working-class neighborhoods of Kentucky suggests that Heathens of all sorts draw on magic as a way to enhance their religious practice.

While these distinctions are found on the level of personal practice, what is true for individuals is also true on a larger scale. Heathen gatherings also exhibit more or less openness to magical practice. On one hand, at the annual meeting of the Troth, magic is clearly visible. Trothmoot workshops often include magical topics such as rune magic, seið, and amulets. In addition, a session of oracular seið always features prominently on one night of the moot and many rune workers and seers are available to do personal readings.[820] As one Troth member put it, "You can't swing a dead cat at Trothmoot without hitting a seeress."[821] At other events, such as East Coast Thing held in Pennsylvania and Lightning Across the Plains held in Kansas, magical practice can be more difficult to find. Workshops rarely feature magical topics and magical performances of oracular seið are less prominent or nonexistent. While magically oriented Heathens attend these gatherings, their own magical and esoteric practice usually takes a backseat during the event to the cultural and ritual exotericism on the official agenda.

Opinions on the subject of magic can be rather strong, often arising from the reconstructionist imperative found in much of Asatru and the authoritative role of the historical record and Lore. The importance of the reconstructionist agenda was on display at an informative workshop on Norse poetic meter that I attended at East Coast Thing, led by a writer and self-taught student of Norse poetry. During the workshop, we were introduced to a particular poetic form called *galdralag* or incantation meter—an Old Norse poetic form associated with magical practice. Without dwelling on the technicalities of Old Norse poetry, *galdralag* adds an unexpected extra poetic line at the end of a stanza, often repeating the previous line with a slight

---

820. Field notes taken by author, Pennsylvania, June 2012.
821. Nertha, interview.

change.[822] The repetition with a twist forms the incantation, extending the poem's effect beyond describing reality toward shaping and transforming it. In this way, the writer of *galdralag* verse subtly inserts his or her will and bends the poem toward an intended purpose. The presenter pointed out that *galdralag* is one form of magic clearly preserved in the Norse tradition and Lore: "We have examples of it. We can see how they used it and we can replicate it."[823] With an air of exasperation and incredulity, he noted that "while I have seen plenty of contemporary books on rune magic and seið, I have not found any that included a discussion of *galdralag*." Although he did not point fingers, his statement clearly indicated a frustration that historical forms of magic were neglected for others he perceived as less authentic, less substantiated, modern practices. The presenter's reconstructionist orientation to Heathenry values authenticity and seeks to adhere as closely as possible to the Norse Tradition tributary of Heathenry, avoiding adulteration by contemporary Pagan, völkisch or other influences.

The confluence of intellectual tributaries is also evident in the sometimes conflicting views of the runes among Heathens. The reconstructive question revolves around the historical usage of runes by the arch-Heathens—were runes used in magical ways? and if so, what specific practices were involved? Some Heathens argue intensely that the runes were simply an alphabet for practical use, "There's many logical thinking Heathens who just don't think magic is real . . . Rune magic isn't legitimate because runes are just an alphabet and it's used for an alphabet and it's not magical, so don't magic it!"[824] All Heathens consider the runes to be special, even if that is only as a historical writing system that developed uniquely in the Norse context. At the very least, runes are evocative symbols of Norse tradition and many Heathens use runes for types of writing that resonate with that tradition, have religious significance, or demand a Heathen aesthetic. For instance, kindreds may publicly display banners at Heathen gatherings that often

---

822. Anderson, "Form and Content in Lokasenna," 139-58. From a Heathen practitioner, Eirik Westcoat, "The Goals of Galdralag: Identifying the Historical Instances and Uses of the Metre," *Viking Society For Northern Research* (University College London, 2016), www.academia.edu/28802822/The_Goals_of_Galdralag_ Identifying_the_Historical_Instances_and_Uses_of_the_Metre.

823. Field notes taken by author, Pennsylvania, 2012.

824. Thora, interview.

Figure 31. Friedenhof Kindred Banner Written in Runes. (Photo by the author.)

include the kindred name or motto written in the runic alphabet (see figure 31). Runes are commonly incorporated into Heathen tattoos for magical as well as symbolic and aesthetic reasons.

Runic tattoos are examples of where the aesthetic and the magical overlap. Many Heathens argue that the historical record demonstrates the frequent magical use of runes. Some believe that the runes were *primarily* a sacred alphabet used for magical purposes. Paxson compares the runes to the Hebrew alphabet in this regard: "As a sacred alphabet, runes are much more like Hebrew letters, each having a meaning in itself that transcends its function as a representation of sound . . . each rune has a name of its own and serves as a focus for a constellation of meanings, associations, and symbols."[825] Furthermore, Paxson emphasizes the historical evidence for other magical uses of the runes, such as in divination, spell-casting, charm-making, and rituals of healing.[826] Vital to Paxson's interpretation is the mythological history of the runes. Runes have both an "earthly" or exoteric history discovered through

---

825. Paxson, *Taking Up the Runes*, 2.
826. Ibid., 2–3.

archaeology and linguistic studies for instance, and additionally an esoteric history attested in Norse mythology. An adherent's perspective on the nature of the runes is largely determined by which of these histories is given the most weight.

In the mythological account, the runes are not created by humans as an alphabet, but discovered by the god Odin as magical forces. In his unceasing search for knowledge and wisdom, Odin is sometimes given to acts of great self-sacrifice, such as plucking out his own eye for a taste of the Well of Wisdom.[827] In the *Havamal*, the Norse wisdom book, Odin describes his ordeal upon the world tree — hanging for nine nights, longing for occult knowledge:

> I know that I hung on a windswept tree,
> nine long nights,
> wounded with a spear, dedicated to Odin,
> myself to myself,
> on that tree of which no man knows
> from where its roots run.
> With no bread did they refresh me nor a drink from a horn,
> Downwards I peered;
> I took up the runes, screaming I took them,
> Then I fell back from there . . .
> Then began I to quicken and be wise,
> And to grow and to prosper.[828]

Heathens magical and non-magical alike are deeply moved by this mythological event, which exemplifies the struggle of both gods and humans in wresting order and knowledge from the chaotic wildness. The story describes the discovery of the runes through ecstatic religious practices involving fasting and physical trial, and presents the runes as sources of esoteric knowledge that give wisdom to those who master them. This mythological history is often ritualized by Heathen practitioners. For instance, Paxson's primer of rune magic, *Taking Up the Runes*, ends with a runic initiation ritual, which calls to mind Odin's self-sacrifice on the world tree. More often, devotees of Odin and Heathen rune magicians will perform their own rituals, such as the eastern Kentucky Asatru healer I met who described tying himself to a tree for an all-night vigil to seek deeper cosmic

---

827. Larrington, "Seeress's Prophecy," stanza 29, in *The Poetic Edda*, 7.
828. Larrington, "Sayings of the High One," stanzas 138, 138, 141, in *The Poetic Edda*, 32.

insight. Rituals such as these allow participants to experience their own journey into knowledge and relationship with the runes.[829]

In this mythic telling, however, the runes did not originate even with Odin, but were only discovered when he was able to look "downwards" into the depth of cosmic mystery. The runes, therefore, pre-existed Odin's ecstatic experience and represent for magical Heathens the primordial energies of the cosmos.[830] Thorsson describes them as part of the participatory cosmos of correspondences, "ideographs expressing a process and flow of force and energy . . . related to the self, to the planet, and ultimately to the multiverse."[831] Yet, in the animate cosmology of Asatru the runes are not "forces" in a purely mechanistic sense. To those who can rightly interpret them, the runes are living and conscious energies that express the shape of the wyrd and potentialities for future events. Lorrie Wood, a California Heathen, illustrates this understanding with a twenty-first-century metaphor when she compares the runes to hypertext transfer protocol, HTTP, the layers of rules and mechanisms that govern and facilitate the flow of information on the Worldwide Web.[832] Michaela Macha expresses a similar insight in a poem titled "The Runatal for Geeks":

> I know that I hung
> On the internet line
> All of the nights nine . . .
> Download I did,
> Took up the source code, Took it up screaming,
> Then I powered down."[833]

The runes are like a cosmic source code through which rune magicians interact with the cosmos, not only reading and comprehending wyrd but also focusing and directing it.

Paxson further indicates the living quality of the runes in her directions for making a set of homemade rune stones. After inscribing the ideographs on small tiles, the rune magician is instructed to bless the newly cut runes. The rune worker intones, "With Önd I

---

829. Paxson, *Taking Up the Runes*, 404–8.
830. Gundarsson, *Teutonic Magic*, 23–24.
831. Thorsson, *Futhark*, 2–3.
832. Lorrie Wood, "The Well and the Web," *Seeing for the People*, www.hrafnar.org/articles/lwood/well-and-web/. See also Harvey, *Contemporary Paganism*, 100.
833. Michaela Macha, "The Runatal for Geeks," *Odin's Gift*, www.odins-gift.com.

awaken you, with *Odhr* I inspire you, with *Lá* and *Læti* and *Litr* I enliven you."[834] These words invoke the creation of Ask and Embla from the *Völuspá*: as the gods bestowed these gifts onto the first humans, investing Ask and Embla with life, so the magician calls the forces of life into the runic forms. Paxsons' ritual of consecration is closer to an act of quickening than to a blessing, symbolically creating the runes as living beings. The tiles are "awakened" not simply as ideographs but as conduits of living spiritual energy, with each rune a specific cosmic personality.

The runes have a cherished place in Asatru as a uniquely northern European alphabet associated closely with ancient Norse culture. Yet at the same time, for many they exemplify the esoteric mysteries of the Heathen religion. These two interpretations can sometimes come into tension, reflecting the confluence of esoteric and non-esoteric tributaries that influence the approach of the practitioner. Heathens seek to avoid a drift toward eclectic magical practice unmoored from historical accuracy, and for reconstructionists this becomes a priority. Yet, Heathens are also wary of the disenchanted rationalism of modernity and see magic as integral to a more holistic and realistic worldview. The tensions and conflicts over magic represent the struggle to find a balance between these two extremes.

## *The Varieties of Heathen Magic*

Pointing to the root of magical practice in contemporary American Asatru can be difficult, and the decisive history of modern Heathen magic, in the vein of Hutton's *Triumph of the Moon*, has yet to be written. Magic has been a part of Norse and Germanic culture for centuries, including the folk magic of prehistory, the healing magic of the farmhouse, and the ceremonial, alchemical, and occultist

---

834. Paxson, *Taking Up the Runes*, 26. Paxson's blessing is adapted from Voluspa stanza 18, here from the Codex Regius and Carolyne Larrington's translation:

| | |
|---|---|
| ond þau ne attu    oð þau ne hofðu | Breath they had not, spirit they had not |
| laa ne læti    ne litv goða. | blood nor bearing nor fresh complexions |
| Ond gaf oðinn    od gaf henir | breath gave Odin, spirit gave Hænir |
| laa gaf loðvR    ok litv goða. | blood gave Lodur and fresh complexions. |

See the Codex Regius, www.germanicmythology.com/works/codexregiusvoluspa.html, and Carolyne Larrington, *The Poetic Edda*, 6. See Bellows' translation of this passage in chapter 4.

magic of the Medieval and Renaissance periods. One important tributary contributing to contemporary Heathen magic is the esoteric revival of the völkisch movement, in which runic and ceremonial magic mingled with racial mysticism and fascist politics in Germany during the early decades of the twentieth century. Its most prominent exemplar is Guido List, a writer and esotericist who developed an occult system based on his Armanen runes, a system of eighteen runes adapted from the ancient futharks, the runic alphabets of the Norse period. According to List, the esoteric secrets of these runes were revealed to him during a spiritual epiphany experienced while convalescing from eye surgery. To be properly understood, these runes must be interpreted according to List's theory of *kala* in which each rune carries three layers of increasingly esoteric meaning.[835] When read in this way, they express the lost wisdom of the ancient Germanic world.[836]

Followers of List's work continued to develop his legacy through the popular Guido von List Society and the Armanen Order, a circle of those initiated into List's system of runic magic. Other important ariosophic groups continued to develop ideas of mysticism, rune magic, and Aryan supremacy, such as Jorg Lanz von Liebenfels' Ordo Novi Templi.[837] While World War II dramatically interrupted the development of rune magic as well as other völkisch trends, many of these esoteric ideas were revived in the contemporary period. Mattias Gardell traces the influence of pre-war racial and political ideals into the contemporary American Odinist scene through Alexander Mills, Else Christensen and others.[838] It is certainly the case that esoteric occult societies of völkisch inspiration were active in post-war Europe. In fact, Jeffrey Holley, known as Heimgest and the current leader of the Odinic Rite (OR), had his magical beginnings in such a group. This esoteric focus influenced the OR through its own esoteric circle of initiates, the Circle of Ostara. The OR eventually brought its European magical practice to North America as the group expanded in the 1990s, with Heimgest himself relocating to the Pacific Northwest to better serve the OR's growing North American presence. According to Heimgest, "I would say

835. List, *Secret of the Runes*, 72, 78.
836. Gardell, *Gods of the Blood*, 23.
837. Nicholas Goodrick-Clarke, *Black Sun: Aryan Cults, Esoteric Nazism and the Politics of Identity* (New York: New York University Press, 2002).
838. Gardell, *Gods of the Blood*, 165–90.

that esoteric practices play quite an essential role in Odinic Rite practice and progress."[839] The most pervasive influence has been the Rune-Gild, an international initiatory lodge founded in the 1980s by Edred Thorsson and focused on reviving esoteric practice in a Heathen context.[840] Thorsson states that a German magician named Karl Spiesberger revived the Armanen system after World War II, dismantling its more racist elements and providing the basis for modern Germanic magic.[841] Thorsson has clearly framed his own goals in a similar fashion, as much of his work has involved the reintroduction of ideas and practices from these völkisch magicians. The prolific research, publishing, and organizing efforts of Thorsson and the Rune-Gild has influenced a wide variety of Heathens including McNallen and Heimgest, firmly establishing the legacy of European occultism within American Heathenry.

The esoteric idea most prominently associated with the völkisch tributary is that of evolution of the self into higher states of consciousness, giving this magic a decidedly mystical flavor. Völkisch-influenced magic is only secondarily about obtaining knowledge, healing, or working change in the world; it is primarily about self-transcendence of which Odin's trial on the world tree serves as the emblematic text. What Odin achieved there was not only the knowledge of the runes, as in the magical letters, but a breakthrough in consciousness in which his mind expanded to take in the mysteries of the cosmos. Odin achieved enlightenment on the tree in an experience akin to dying: Odin died to his limited individuality, his ego, and by this death achieved access to a greater reality, reborn into a cosmic state of awareness. List writes that Odin sunk into non-being and by doing so won the awareness of the secrets of life, "an eternal 'arising' and 'passing away,' an eternal return, a life of continuous birth and death."[842] Odin becomes All-father, who strives for "eternal change through the transformation from arising through being toward passing away for a new arising throughout all eternity." In this Odinic mode, life is the continual striving for self-transcendence into higher levels of awareness—Odinic Consciousness. In its more insidious forms, Odinic Consciousness has been associated with

839. Heimgest, interview.
840. Thorsson, *Futhark*, 18.
841. Ibid., 16.
842. List, *Secret of the Runes*, 46.

race consciousness, conceptualizing the racial group as an organic living entity evolving into higher forms. Odin is interpreted as the primal energy of the Germanic soul, the drive towards self-mastery that motivates the Folk. However, for most American Heathens influenced by these ideas, it serves as an example of the possibilities for the individual consciousness to evolve into higher states. As the master of this process, Odin pushed to the point of breakthrough, the dissolution of his ego, to cosmic consciousness. The point is not to worship Odin as a divine being, but to strive towards this divinization oneself. This expresses the spiritual path and goal of völkisch magic: to follow Odin's example towards enlightenment.

While these tendencies remain a strong undercurrent, a second and more visible tributary to American Heathen magic has involved the resurgence of contemporary Pagan magical religion in Wicca and Witchcraft since the 1970s. American Asatru grew in the context of the vibrant, diverse, and rapidly growing American Pagan movement and the development of Heathen magic included a sizeable download from the Wiccan tradition. Many of the traditions, rituals, language, and tools of early Heathen magic were simply adapted from Wicca and other Pagan groups for use in a Norse context. As the Heathen movement has matured, considerable pushback against Wiccan influence has emerged with some practitioners seeking to distill a more fully and authentically Heathen magic. This boundary tension is noticeable in the disdain some Heathens express towards what they perceive as Wiccan or even New Age magic, as noted in the earlier example of the Blank Rune.

Neither does seið, another important form of Heathen magic with roots in the Lore, escape from the turbulence of these contrasting tributaries. Yngona Desmond expresses her view on the mix of tributaries involved in its contemporary practice: "Unfortunately, shamanic tradition has been infected by Harnerism, which has further corrupted those in Heathenry today who claim to practice and teach Seidr."[843] At issue is the oracular seið of Diana Paxson, which is quite popular with Heathens and Pagans alike. When I attended Pantheacon, a pan-Pagan convention held in California,

---

843. Yngona Desmond, "Core-Shamanism, Oracular Seid, and What Seidr Really Is," *Vinland's Völva*, http://vinlands-volva.blogspot.com/2011/03/core-shamanism-oracular-seid-and-what.html.

the line for the Oracular Seið session led by Paxson's Hrafnar Kindred, stretched down the hall, beyond the capacity of the room where it was to be held. I only just avoided the cut-off to attend the session myself. As noted by Desmond, one of Paxson's influences is Core Shamanism, a system of trance-induced magical working developed by Michael Harner from his experiences with traditional shamans in South America.[844] As we will see, Paxson is strongly rooted in the Norse tradition but also confident in the benefits of a cross-cultural approach. However, she and others such as Galina Krasskova are often made to serve as a counterpoint to those who seek to reconstruct a more pure, culturally specific Heathen magic as Desmond describes her magical work:

> For the past thirty plus years I have been delving deep into the historical record to discern from the many Northern European tribes the very nature of their most intimate connection to the divine. And I have been a diligent gardener; for, as a Seiðwoman—a culturally specific "magic" user—not only have I carefully weeded out, at every turn, the external influences and interpretations, but have been ever mindful to exclude a biased interpretation (or to reimagine Seiðr in my own image).[845]

Although Desmond has become a controversial figure for her strong opinions and uncompromising critique of other Heathens, the culturally specific approach to reconstructing magic has become an important and widespread trend in Heathen magic.

The confluence of Heathenry and Witchcraft produced an enduring lineage of magical practice that can be traced back to the early development of the Troth in the late 1980s. The Troth, then known as the Ring of Troth, its founders and many of its early members such as Edred Thorsson, Kveldúlf Gundarsson, Freyja Aswynn, and Diana Paxson all contributed substantially to the development of modern Heathen magic, often collaborating and referencing each other's work. Much of the contemporary understanding and practice of magic among American Heathens derives from original work on Germanic and Norse lore by these authors themselves, combined with substantial inspiration and experience in the Wiccan magical worldview.

---

844. Michael J. Harner, *The Way of the Shaman* (San Francisco: Harper & Row, 1990).
845. Desmond, "Core-Shamanism."

Edred Thorsson might be considered the preeminent Asatru magician. His book on rune magic, *Futhark*, proved to be foundational for all that followed.[846] In it, he laid out a system for esoteric use of the runes focusing on *galdr*, the chanting or vocalization of runes; runic stances, body postures that imitate the rune staves; and ritual, all substantially set within a Norse context and worldview. This book caught the attention of other magically oriented Asatruar. Diana Paxson mentions that the book "had impressed me because he had managed to present a spiritual system based on the northern material that had some scholarly backing and a knowledge of [ceremonial magic]."[847] Another important book on contemporary Heathen magic was Gundarsson's *Teutonic Magic*, published in 1990.[848] Drawing heavily on Thorsson, he focused on the runes as the core of Heathen magic. Somewhat eclectic in style, the material is a synthesis of Gundarsson's own considerable expertise in Norse and Germanic Paganism and modern ceremonial magic. His runic meditations reflect the style of Pagan path-workings: highly detailed and inspired by fantasy literature, yet they often eloquently express the Pagan experience of ancient natural power. For instance, this example from Gundarsson's meditation on the Othala rune, ᛟ, captures many of the themes we have discussed about race and ancestry, the soul, magic, and the earth:

> You feel power thrumming up into your bare feet through the earth; you know that it is part of you, earth filled with the bones and blood of your forefathers and foremothers for generations. Their might is passing into you from the ancestral soil, filling you with their magic and strength. You feel that you bear the waxing power of a thousand generations within you, might like a great wave sweeping through you and filling your mind with secrets, wisdom lay hidden in the blood and soul that has ghosted down the ages from father to son, mother to daughter, your true heritage coming forth at last.[849]

---

846. Paxson also comments on the influence of Thorsson's work, see Paxson, *Essential Ásatrú*, 120.
847. Paxson, interview.
848. Gundarsson, *Teutonic Magic*.
849. Ibid., 156–59. The "o" rune, reconstructed as *ōþila or *ōþala, is usually written as Othala or Othila and associated with ancestry or inherited wealth. Gundarsson relates the rune to the boundaries of property, gaining wealth, and the wisdom and power found in the ancestral line of the past. The rune has gained a reputation because of its use by racist Heathens.

Gundarsson's work and example have profoundly influenced a generation of Heathen magic workers especially those associated with the Troth, an organization that he has served in many roles. Gundarsson now acts as a scholar and statesman within the Troth, accepted as a mediating presence and provider of wisdom.

Despite the magical environment of the early Troth organization, Diana Paxson describes the first time she held a seið session at Trothmoot as a real showstopper. Seið is a type of Norse magic with similarities to shamanic practice, utilizing an induced trance state of consciousness. In the Lore, seið is utilized to achieve various ends such as weather-making, spells of protection or harm, healing, and success in hunting or battle and communicating with spirits.[850] Paxson's specialty, however, is oracular seið, a form of magic in which a seer—or more often a seeress—goes into trance to see visions and to confer with ancestors, spirits, and gods.[851] She recalls the first time Hrafnar performed seið at a Troth event:

> I brought a lot of my kindred to the second Trothmoot and we did seið. Nobody in the Heathen community had ever seen anybody do anything like that. That was serious "woo." And poor Ingrid, who was the person I had as seeress at that one, is a very dramatic personality, a very powerful and very good seeress and the poor thing, the next day nobody would talk to her. They all kind of edged around her. So that made quite a splash.[852]

From that first introduction, seið has grown to become an important, though contested, form of Heathen magic and still regarded with suspicion in many Heathen circles. One seið worker remarked, "the fact that there are many women who are interested in it and want to do it, I don't think we'll ever be accepted in the larger Heathen community."[853] As she suggests, the practice of magic is complicated in Heathenry. Gender and magic have always been linked in Heathenry and lingering patriarchal attitudes compound the substantial skepticism about magic. In 2017, Heathen women took to the virtual streets with the hashtag #HavamalWitches,

---

850. Paxson, *Essential Ásatrú*, 123.
851. "Seeress" is a term commonly used for a woman who practices the oracular magic known as seið. Other terms for female magic workers include völva, seidkona, and spakona. For male practitioners, terms include seer, seidmadhr, and spamadhr.
852. Paxson, interview.
853. Thora, interview.

raising and addressing the issue of misogyny and sexism within Heathenry.[854]

At its current stage of development, magic in Asatru continues to evolve, growing in the depth and diversity of practice. In addition to the runic arts, hexology, plant lore and herbology, and the creation of amulets and talismans, called *taufr*, are all important developments. Utiseta, the Norse practice of sitting outside under a cloak or upon a mound in order to attain insight, is a type of ascetic practice that may have similarities with the Native American vision quest. Oracular seið is usually practiced only occasionally, at special moments or more formal settings. Spae is a related practice associated with "far-seeing," the divinatory ability to look into the wyrd and read the direction of events, though not necessarily "predict" the future. Galdr is the vocalization of runes, often sung in long low chant-like intonations by Heathens as a means to open or close a ritual, focus power, or aid in meditation. Some Heathens are beginning to incorporate technology into these practices in interesting ways. With the help of a smart phone, one can access several rune divination apps developed by Heathens, with which practitioners can cast and interpret runes as part of a regular spiritual practice to seek guidance about their lives.

## *Magic and Women's Roles*

If one of the effects of modernity has included the dis-embedding of people from a holistic context, then this disconnection has particularly altered the roles of women in society and family. Susan Palmer, whose work has focused on women in new religions, indicates that "women's conversion to unconventional religions can be interpreted as a response to 'rolelessness' resulting from dramatic upheavals in the structure of society."[855] Palmer's analysis affirms many of the struggles enunciated by contemporary women: while the social freedom to live outside of traditional structures of marriage and family brings numerous advantages, there are also additional tensions. Disembedded from traditional social roles,

---

854. Dodie Graham McKay, "#HavamalWitches Hashtag Earns Applause and Backlash," *The Wild Hunt*, July 20, 2017, http://wildhunt.org/2017/07/havamalwitches-hashtag-earns-applause-and-backlash.html.

855. Palmer, *Moon Sisters*, xiii.

women must negotiate the fragility and ambiguity of modern relationships, the weakening of the parent/child bond due to work and school schedules, and the economic vulnerability that may accompany being a single parent. Palmer describes modern women as feeling "insecure as a wife . . . undervalued as a mother, and 'stressed out' as a worker-wife-mother-housekeeper."[856] I am not completely comfortable with the deprivation theory implicit in Palmer's analysis. However, the social tensions she identifies as affecting women have influenced the Heathen critique of American society.

Pagan and Heathen women have paid attention to the spiritual disconnection in the lives of modern women, noting that women's bodies, roles, and work have been disenchanted and secularized, stripped of their traditional religious contexts. For instance, they argue that in traditional pre-Christian European cultures the menstrual cycle of the female body was positively associated with fertility, magic, and women's power.[857] In the context of modernity, however, society has devalued the menstrual cycle and socialized women to perceive their period as an inconvenience and annoyance. This modern interpretation disconnects women from the idea that their bodies and menstruation cycles may have deeper religious significance. In contrast, many Pagan and Heathen women have sought to reclaim the female reproductive cycle as a particularly powerful occurrence and menstrual blood as magically efficacious.

Similarly, the process of modernization has clearly disrupted the traditional domestic role of women. The logic of global capital has changed the way American women live and is now filling Chinese and Mexican factories with young women "dis-embedded" from their own traditional contexts, a change interpreted variously by some as freeing and liberating for women, and by others as bewildering and damaging.[858] One effect of this valorization of paid work within the modern industrial economy has included a devaluing of traditional housework. While modernization has failed to decisively uproot from our society the association between women and the duty of housework, it has degraded the status of

---

856. Ibid., 6–7.
857. Paxson, *Taking up the Runes*, 25. See also Eowyn, "Attracting Women to the Rite—Some Considerations," *The Odinic Rite*, November 30, 2010, www.odinic-rite.org/main/attracting-women-to-the-rite-some-considerations.
858. Palmer, *Moon Sisters*, 218; Kari Tauring, interview.

such work. Activities such as cooking, cleaning, clothing the family, spinning, and weaving were reduced to "chores" while the skills associated with these tasks, especially their religious and magical dimensions, were lost. While Heathens are not suggesting a return to the days in which women bore the brunt of household labor, there is a resurgence of interest in the magical and religious dimensions of that work.

In the Heathen analysis, many of these activities were traditionally embedded in magico-religious contexts. Domestic chores were valorized with religious significance and were important means by which women exercised religious and social power. For instance, there is strong evidence that domestic weaving was long associated with women's magic. As they made clothing for their families, women wove into their work a kind of protective magic, as Michael Enright observes, "spells were being worked into the fabric. Actually this category of magic appears to have been very nearly routine."[859] Similarly, Kari Tauring describes how evidence of the magico-religious function of the tools of women's daily work, such as spindles, looms, bowls, or churns, is preserved in the folksongs and stories of Northern Europe. She writes that there are "many examples in the lore about women creating magical clothing, imbued with protection through chants to the rhythm of the spinning or weaving ... Churning, spinning and stitching spells and charms abound in folk songs."[860] For contemporary observers, the repetitive and monotonous actions associated with much of this work may be seen as mind-numbing drudgery. Yet from a sacral/religious perspective, the rhythmic, even hypnotic, nature of the work embeds opportunities for altered states of consciousness within the context of women's work. The swish of the broom, the fall and spin of the drop spindle, usually and ordinarily tedious, might also at times subtly shift a woman's consciousness into a trance state and open her to magical experience.

Marion Zimmer Bradley includes such a scene in her important novel, *The Mists of Avalon*, which has served as a formative book for many contemporary Pagans. In one passage, Bradley depicts with remarkable authenticity the consciousness of her character Morgaine as she slips into a trance state. Morgaine is a priestess of the

---

859. Enright, *Lady with a Mead Cup*, 118.
860. Kari C. Tauring, *Völva Stav Manual* (Minneapolis: Kari C. Tauring, 2010), 22.

Goddess and also has the Sight, an ability to see future possibilities in the evolving web of events and choices. In the passage, a group of women sits spinning and chiding Morgaine for not doing her share. Morgaine avoids the ubiquitous female activity of spinning not because of its drudgery or monotony, not because she is bored by the tedium, as the reader might first assume. She avoids it because the activity too easily triggers a state of trance. As Morgaine begins to spin, she thinks to herself,

> True—she hated spinning and shirked it when she could . . . twisting, turning the thread in her fingers, willing her body to stillness with only her fingers twisting as the reel turned and turned, sinking to the floor . . . down and then up, twist and twist between her hands . . . all too easy it was to sink into trance.[861]

Bradley accentuates the rhythmic, hypnotic qualities of the work. Focused on the rotational motion of the spindle, Morgaine's thought process becomes looser and more open, "her mind roaming as her fingers moved . . . as the thread turned, it was like the spiral dance along the Tor, round and round . . . as the thread went round itself over and over, spinning like a serpent." The spinning rhythm relaxes her mind, her grounding in the existential realities of the present, and opens her consciousness to a visionary experience. Bradley's description illustrates the many levels, functional and experiential, that overlap in the activity of spinning. The women gather to spin thread that will help clothe the family in the coming winter. They enjoy a moment of social interaction created by the shared work. Yet this is not just watercooler small talk, the chitchat and gossip shared in the interaction does the serious work of community-building, social regulation, and the passing along of female survival skills. At another level, the spinning becomes the context for trance and vision. The magico-religious possibilities of spinning may not have been a universal experience, yet for countless real women, spinning provided an opportunity for drawing on the deeper aspects of the personality and consciousness.

The point is not that these domestic activities were highly humanizing and fulfilling. Surely tedium, monotony, and frustration were regular and prominent aspects of women's lives and domestic

---

861. Bradley, *Mists of Avalon*, 305.

work. The twentieth-century revolution in labor-saving devices and its promised freedom from domestic chores were enthusiastically received by women who could afford the application of modern technology to housekeeping. But by approaching domestic tasks only from the perspective of their mundaneness, we too quickly overlook the complex functionality of these tasks in the personal and social lives of women. For many contemporary Heathen women, such evidence suggests that women's minds, bodies, and work were or at least *could be* enhanced and hallowed by these activities. Through household work, women found a way to connect with the supernatural and exercised vital religious roles in their families and communities.

During the period of Christian conversion in Northern Europe, laws designed to eliminate Pagan practice targeted the magical aspects of women's work. Tauring writes, "It was so prominent a magic that early Christian laws directly forbade this fusion of spiritual and mundane tasks."[862] As authorities outlawed women's "kitchen magic," these domestic activities lost their religious context, resulting over time in their disenchantment and secularization. With the onset of the twentieth century, women's work was redefined as a mundane and undesirable array of activities that held neither personal nor religious significance. While cognizant of the benefits and freedoms that modernity affords to women, many Heathens feel that those benefits came with too high a cost, as Eowyn of the Odinic Rite notes, "in the alienation of our folk from their natural organic religion, the feminine has been deliberately disempowered."[863] In order for McDonalds' fast food and cheap clothing from Asian factories to appear acceptable to a culture, women's work must first be dis-embedded from the religious meaningfulness and power it had in traditional contexts. As Tauring states, "When everything is coming wrapped in plastic from Walmart you're in big trouble. Big trouble. There's no connection and we need to start having a connection again."[864]

---

862. Tauring, *Völva Stav*, 22. See also Enright, *Lady with a Mead Cup*, 115–16; Eowyn, "Attracting Women to the Rite"; Vivianne Crowley," Women and Power in Modern Paganism," in *Women as Teachers and Disciples in Traditional and New Religions*, eds. Elizabeth Puttick and Peter B. Clarke (Lewiston, NY: Edwin Mellen Press, 1993), 130.

863. Eowyn, "Attracting Women to the Rite."

864. Kari Tauring, interview.

Vivianne Crowley writes that women take three main routes into Paganism: feminism, ecological awareness, and "a desire for occult power or knowledge: the way of the witch."[865] From the perspective of many contemporary Asatru women, the answer to this tension is found in re-embedding their lives in a magical context. By looking back to older models of femininity, models in which women were empowered by magical roles, these contemporary Heathens are developing new ways of being women that seek to repair the sense of disconnection they experience in their own lives. Writing specifically about Asatru, Crowley states, "The followers of the Norse Gods, for example, worship a strongly patriarchal group of deities. However, even in these groups the role of the seeress—the *völva* or *seidkona* (a priestess practitioner of magic and divination)—is of growing importance."[866] While Crowley sees the co-existence of a patriarchal pantheon and the rise of the völva in Asatru as a discrepancy, these two phenomena are closely related.

## Gender Essentialism in Asatru

Masculinity and femininity have been strongly held ideals in Asatru life, with a strong assumption of gender essentialism influencing Heathen perspectives. Many Heathens see these distinct male and female natures as positive and valuable and manifested in different but compatible social roles. While there are variations, gender roles in Asatru exhibit the characteristics of sex complementarity, in which men and women are considered equal but "endowed with different spiritual qualities."[867] The collaboration of men and women in practical and religious pursuits is valued. Men have often been looked to as leaders, chieftains of kindreds while women may take on caregiving roles. The Norse-inspired garb sometimes worn

---

865. Crowley, "Women and Power," 126.
866. Ibid., 127.
867. Palmer, *Moon Sisters*, 10. Palmer's model of Sex Complementarity interprets marriage as "uniting two halves of the same soul to form one, complete androgynous being." Religious communities that teach Sex Complementarity may also look to a "dual or androgynous godhead," who sanctions this social structure. The Norse pantheon exhibits several examples of divine male and female pairs: Odin and Frigga, Thor and Sif, etc. However, I would argue that Norse polytheism, with its emphasis on male and female divine power and its distribution of divine authority and responsibility among a family of gods is a suitable theological context for the Asatru understanding of gender roles and marriage as a partnership between equals.

by Heathens in ritual contexts emphasizes gender difference, not androgyny. There remains quite a bit of social currency around the idealized Viking male: bold, assertive, and rugged. While assertiveness is also valued in women, females are also associated with ideals of caretaking, motherliness, and emotional and intuitive attributes. These qualities do not preclude women from leadership, but shape the ways in which their leadership functions. In Asatru, women embody qualities that are "positively feminine and beneficial for authority" such as "practicality, intuition, tenderness, body-affirmation, caring, healing, devotion, forgiveness, holism, social engagement and social mysticism."[868]

The gender essentialism of Heathen culture has not exhibited an accompanying doctrine of male superiority, female subordination or submissiveness, female impurity or sexual deviancy, all of which Puttick identifies as aspects of religious patriarchy.[869] Looking at gender roles in the Icelandic sagas, Heathens tend to remark on the equality of the husband and wife in the household and the power and authority of women who helped manage the farming estates. This sense of equality is important to many Heathens. For instance, during his Asatru marriage ceremony, a Heathen entrepreneur and small business owner presented his wife with the keys to his business, symbolizing the equality and partnership of their relationship. As he said, if he was not able to run the business, he fully trusted his wife to run it in his place.[870] Heathens often attribute the historical development of gender discrimination and anti-female bias in Germanic and Norse society to the influence of Christianity, a theology interpreted as particularly discriminatory against women. However, with the discussion around #HavamalWitches, Heathens are coming to terms with the sexism and alienation experienced by women in less formal ways within the movement.[871]

As might be expected, the mix of intellectual tributaries within Heathenry creates the potential for sociological tension and a clash

---

868. Elizabeth Puttick, "Women in New Religious Movements," in *Cults and New Religious Movements: A Reader*, ed. Lorne L. Dawson (Malden, MA: Blackwell, 2003), 241.

869. Ibid., 238–39.

870. Jorvik, interview.

871. Stevie Miller, "#HavamalWitches Make Their Magic," *Huginn's Heathen Hof*, July 10, 2017, www.heathenhof.com/havamalwitches-make-magic/.

of values over the question of gender roles and sexuality.[872] Wicca and Witchcraft have more rapidly embraced progressive politics and attitudes around gender and sexuality, while Asatru has remained more conservative and cautious. The strong folkish tributary tends to emphasize gender essentialism and structured gender roles. Such a strong sense of sex complementarity is readily apparent in Juleigh Howard Hobson's discussion of women's roles: "Our equal gender footing in Midgard was based on the healthy respect of each for each. Respect for the warrior, respect for the weaver, respect for the father, respect for the mother."[873] This clear delineation of gender identity is reflected in the importance of family structure, "We need our men to be successful as fathers and husbands, we need our women to be successful as mothers and wives. We need our children brought up at home with values and spirituality that reflect our age-old folk ways."[874] However, folkish thinking about gender has not always been so rigid. McNallen presents what could be a range of acceptable male gender identities in his *Thunder from the North* pamphlet discussed earlier in chapter 5. His explication of god-types makes room for different but potentially legitimate versions of masculinity: a "Thors-man" and a "Bragis-man" are two of several distinct representations of what it means to be a Heathen male.

In practice, Heathenry has been slow to adopt this sort of gender complexity and a dualistic gender essentialism has characterized the wider culture. Expression of gender and sexual transgressivity have been pushed into subsets of Heathenry, such as the community of Loki devotees — linking progressive attitudes with theological marginality. Some who are in proximity to Heathenry, such as Raven Kaldera, go even further into gender transgressivity. Kaldera, a writer and shaman who works within the Northern Tradition, argues that the Old Norse term *ergi* represented a third-gender category found among shamans, characterized by cross-dressing and gender-transgressive sexual activity.[875] He suggests that this *ergi* identity and accompanying behaviors were sources of power for the shaman. Kaldera and others actively push the boundaries of the

---

872. Paxson, *Essential Ásatrú*, 153.
873. Juleigh Howard Hobson, "The Feminine in the Post-Modern Age: How Feminism Negates Folkways" *Journal of Contemporary Heathen Thought* 1 (2010): 97.
874. Ibid., 99.
875. Raven Kaldera, "Ergi: The Way of the Third," *Northern-Tradition Shamanism*, www.northernshamanism.org/ergi-the-way-of-the-third.html.

Heathen milieu to create a social space radically inclusive, not only of *ergi* seið magicians, but even transgressive religious paths such as Rokkatru, the veneration of the jötnar who Heathens generally regard as enemies of the gods. However, the ideology of gender essentialism may be increasingly in flux since the crisis over the AFA's leadership transition and the now-notorious Facebook post referencing "our masculine men and feminine ladies." In opposition to this post, progressive Heathens have become more vocal in their opposition to essentialist ideals of gender. The groundswell of progressive Heathenry may well represent a permanent cultural shift bringing Heathenry more in line with contemporary Pagan attitudes.

In regard to magic, Heathen magical practice developed in this context of gender essentialism and role differentiation. The magical culture actually draws on gender essentialism to empower, not subordinate, women. As Paxson has said, her practice of oracular seið arose as a solution for giving the women something to do while the men played Viking games at Heathen gatherings. It draws on the qualities of femininity that sex complementarity valorizes: women's receptive, relational, caring, therapeutic nature, to create a niche of autonomy and innovation for women. Diana Paxson's book on oracular magic originally had the working title of "Seeing for the People," emphasizing the community function of oracular seið. The seeress performs her magic out of caring for the community, presenting seið magic as a type of women's ministry that builds on the ideology of women as caretakers and maintainers of relationships, "weavers of frith."[876] Seið workers frequently describe their motivations using a discourse of caring for others and service to the community.[877] Kari Tauring invokes feminine qualities when she draws on the emotional intuitiveness of women in healing trauma. At the same time, the magical role expands the reach of those female qualities beyond the limits of the nuclear family, the home, and the authority of a husband or male leader. Magical women can avoid the more oppressive consequences of patriarchy, such as "rigid control of sexuality, work and worship by husbands and elders, loss of status and opportunities for direct

---

876. For more on women's role as "frith-weaver" see Winifred Hodge, "On the Meaning of Frith," *Frigga's Web*, www.friggasweb.org/frith.html.

877. Paxson, Wood, Thora, and Nertha, interviews with author.

spiritual advancement, and a high incidence of wife and child abuse."[878]

Central to this vision of a woman liberated by her magical role is the historical figure of the "little völva," þorbjörg, the female seer who appears briefly in *Eirik the Red's Saga*.[879] In Heathenry, she is the tantalizing image of a real historical woman who held the "sacred office of womanhood."[880] This figure, referenced in every discussion of seið almost without fail, captivates magical women in Asatru. She was the last of the *völur*, the sole remaining representative of a sisterhood of women who had practiced this magical art for centuries in service to their community. In the saga, she arrives at a farmstead community devastated by a lingering winter. She is dressed distinctively in finery and magical garb. Her meal consists of a selection of various animal hearts. Only one person in the gathering, a young Christian girl, knows the old magical songs (ON *varðlokkur*) that can draw the nature spirits to the place of prophecy where the völva will listen to them. After she sings, the spirits are favorably inclined and whisper to the völva, assuring her that the winter will soon give way to spring. þorbjörg then answers the questions of all the community members who have gathered to seek her knowledge. She is a powerful and independent presence, who is clearly free from the command of any male. From the few clues provided in this and other texts, contemporary Asatru women try to tease out the intricacies of her life, history, and magical practice. The work of several, such as Diana Paxson and Kari Tauring, has led to the development of systems of seið magic for the contemporary Asatru movement.

## *Three Variations of Heathen Magic*

Magic continues to be an area of experimentation and innovation in Heathenry. As a result, the movement functions as a context for numerous magical systems and practitioners who draw on range of similar techniques but whose motivations and outcomes are often quite different. Three variations of Heathen magic—the radical mystical path of the Wolves of Vinland, the oracular seið

---

878. Puttick, "Women in NRMs," 238.
879. Kunz and Sigurðsson, *The Vinland Sagas*.
880. Kari Tauring, email to author, January 19, 2013.

of Diana Paxson, and the Völva Stav of Kari Tauring—illustrate some of this variation. The Wolves work primarily with the will and use magical techniques to transcend individuality, culminating in a mystic unitive experience called Odinic Consciousness. Diana Paxson's oracular seið draws on the shamanistic and oracular techniques found in Pagan cultures worldwide to reconstruct a specifically Heathen approach to divination. Through advanced training in trance work and psychic journeying, she seeks to find answers and provide insight to guide querents along their life-paths, framing oracular seið as a type of alternative epistemology. Kari Tauring's practice of Völva Stav, on the other hand, uses trance states to seek out and repair wounded emotions and psyches, soul-damage woven into the ørlög of her clients through multiple generations of deprivation and dysfunction. She describes the role of the völva in therapeutic terms, positioning Völva Stav as a type of healing magic.

## The Magical Mysticism of the Wolves of Vinland

In the broad culture of Heathenry, women are most often portrayed as the magical gender. The hyper-masculinized culture of the Wolves, however, valorizes the esoteric role of the male. In the spirit of völkisch magic, the Wolves are actively creating and disseminating a male magical spirituality, the way of the vitki, which takes its cues from Odin and embodies the themes of völkisch magic touched on earlier in the chapter.[881] In the *Havamal*, the book of Norse wisdom, Odin declares that he will never share his esoteric wisdom with a female, and several times obtains insight through tactics that seem to involve the coercion or deception of women. The sexism of this perspective characterized the magical culture of the völkisch movement, which was decidedly masculine. Similarly the Wolves believe in different esoteric paths for men and women. The stories of Odin, the god who plucks out his eye, who hangs himself on the tree, who becomes a snake and slithers into the heart of the mountain, who leads the frenzied Wild Hunt through the winter storms, exemplifies the mystical path of the male vitki. The völva, the female magical path, is guided by and modeled on the goddess Frejya.

---

881. Vitki is an Old Norse word referring to a "wizard," a male magic user. See *Concise Dictionary of Old Icelandic*, s.v. "vitki."

The Wolves work with a definition of magic that focuses on the accumulation of will, described in strongly worded masculine terms. The male is meant to be a wolf, which the Wolves interpret to mean wild, strong, predatory, and aggressive, yet disciplined enough to use his strength in a tactical way. Thus the magic of the Wolves begins with the accumulation of this willful power, engendered by various ascetic practices that include the standard magical techniques of meditation and visualization. In addition, physical strength training is incorporated as an element in the overall discipline of mastering indulgence and becoming a person whose will controls the self.[882] Male magic works by hardening the will, pushing relentlessly against obstacles, especially the depravity, slothfulness, and weakness that erode male spiritual strength.

This strong will is created through self-discipline for the purpose of transformation into higher states of consciousness. The Wolves maintain a radical bent toward the goal of spiritual evolution, interpreting other magical projects as the indulgence of weak selves. Paul Waggener, also known as Grimnir, who is both the founder of the Wolves and their esoteric master, expresses nothing but derision for the culture of contemporary Pagan magic. In a statement dripping with sarcasm, he writes:

> If you're looking to make traffic lights change for you/magically get a raise at work/seduce your boss/improve your sex life/whatever . . . pick out any number of amazing and intelligent books by authors with names like Silvershine RavenMoonWolfSongbird and join a Wiccan coven . . . I'm sure your wildest dreams will come true.[883]

In contrast to what Grimnir sees as the soft, feminized, banalities of Witchcraft, the magical culture of the Wolves has a hard edge: "True magic . . . is self-sacrifice. It is a fanatical devotion to self-transformation and self-improvement: learning, acting and growing." The path is one of ascetic discipline. "In order to be a vitki . . . he must dedicate himself to long years of study, practice, frustration, confusion, failure, craftsmanship and finally Understanding." Stephen McNallen's vision of the spiritual life shares much with the masculine völkisch culture of the Wolves. He

---

882. Matthias Waggener, workshop on magic, field notes taken by author, Kansas, 2013.
883. Paul Waggener, "On Magic," 114.

describes the male path of magic in similar terms: "It is war with that-which-we-are, that we may become something higher. It is the use of will to overcome inertia and to change ourselves despite everything inside us that wants to stay comfortable. The Path of Odin is not so much the opening of a delicate flower as it is the forging of a fine steel sword."[884] This is the disciplined, renunciatory path of the vitki, who incorporates the various techniques of Germanic magic: runes, galdr, seið, utiseta, hexology, as tools to push the consciousness toward higher states, the same state as Odin as he grasped the secrets of the runes. The Wolves interpret Yggdrasil, the world tree, esoterically as a map of the mystical soul-states of the vitki.[885] Yggdrasil is both cosmological as well as interior and mystical, a macrocosm that corresponds to the microcosm of the inner self. The cosmological map is also a spiritual map, which guides the vitki in his ascension into mystical union with the esoteric forces of the cosmos, the Runa. Beginning with the mastery of the body, shaping it into a tool controlled by the fires of the will, the vitki eventually becomes able to transcend the physical, activating the esoteric dimensions of the Heathen soul-complex: connecting to the collective past, the wyrd, the hamingja, using seið to project one's self into other realms. In clear and succinct prose, McNallen describes the goal of this mystical path in words that the Wolves would embrace: "The promise of Odin is that by certain practices, men and women can become Sovereign, Wode-Filled, and Immortal beings free from the limitations of space, time, and mortality."[886]

Odin, however, is not just Wisdom, but also Madness. "I am not a follower of Odhinn—I am Odhinn. His name means the ecstasy, the frenzy, the fury, the wild," writes Grimnir.[887] This ecstatic nature of Odin opens another dimension to the Wolves' magical practice: the cultivation of ecstatic states as a means of transformation. While some contemporary Pagans look toward the inner child as the magical ideal, the Wolves would draw on other metaphors and look for an ancient, primal self. The magic of Odin is not that of an innocent child, but that of the berserker. In the hands of the Wolves, the rituals

---

884. Stephen McNallen, "Spirituality Is Strength and Practicality!" *The Path of Odin*, October 30, 2014, www.stephenamcnallen.com/.

885. Matthias Waggener, workshop on magic.

886. Stephen McNallen, "The Promise of Odin," *The Path of Odin*, August 28, 2014, www.stephenamcnallen.com/.

887. Paul Waggener, "Living Myth," 58–59.

of blót and sumbel are transformed into ecstatic magical practices meant to devolve the minds of participants into more primal states. In a short but evocative description of a blót written by Galdr, a member of the Wolves, the ecstatic elements are clearly evident.[888] The ritual takes place in an aesthetically primal setting: the woods under cover of darkness with Mani, the personified moon of Norse cosmology, riding overhead. Within the heightened awareness of participatory consciousness, Galdr senses the living qualities of his natural surroundings. The woods are enlivened with the eyes of other spirit beings, "world-spectres and grave-kin" gleaming from the dark. The Wolves incorporate practices into the *blót* to shift consciousness away from individuality in order to generate a primal and communal experience, the identity of a pack of wolves. Galdr describes how the Wolves mark their bodies with ash and blood, often in runic patterns, and engage in rhythmic drumming and the guttural chanting of runic syllables, which becomes a "symphony of drone and growl," all designed to produce a communal trance state. Invoking the land spirits, gods, and ancestors from the four directions takes on added intensity: "Four of their number separate from the rest, abide awhile at the cardinal points of the world. Rage-roughened voices echo . . . The very air reverberates with the power of their howls, the stamp of their bare feet shakes the earth of this forest which has glutted on so much of their blood and sweat." At the height of the ritual, an ecstatic communitas is reached, described by Galdr as "Odin walking among them, driving frenzy-spikes deep into heart and mind." The "cleansing blaze" of the sacrificial fire is a layered reference, describing the fires that burn on the horg but also the ecstatic frenzy induced by the ritual, the "*od*-tinged madness" that cleanses weakness and uncertainty from the soul.

The ritual creates the experience of transformative power, perhaps similar to that which Sarah Pike experienced at the fire-dancing circle at Spirit Quest. Galdr describes the transformative experience in explicitly magical terms, "power snaps and swirls as these gore-maddened woods-witches sing ancient mysteries to the night; mysteries of blood and Tribe and bund. The sorceries growled by these vitkar snake into all gathered, wrap tight around their

---

888. Galdr, "Wolves Take What Wolves Will," in *Operation Werewolf: The Complete Transmissions*, 121–23.

hearts, strangling weakness in its crib."[889] In Grimnir's experience, the ecstatic state takes on animistic qualities,

> the brothers I have chosen are wild Wolves. Sometimes I see them from the edge of our ritual circle in the forest, and I see their shapes change from men to animals, and back to men again, twisting in the firelight like strange beasts, unknown to the weak and civilized man. I look at them, covered in blood and ash, wild eyes, pupils dilated from a mixture of mead and mushroom. I hear their songs ring out through the changing of the year, and I know that THIS is Paganism.[890]

Many Heathens would dispute his conclusion that the Wolves' represent the true essence of Pagan religion. As their profile has grown in Heathen culture, the Wolves have become controversial. Observers of the far right see the slow creep of crypto-fascism in their movement.[891] The aesthetic of the Wolves is outwardly aggressive, intensely tribal, often misogynistic, and disparaging of much of Heathen culture. For instance, Galdr writes derisively of other Heathen groups: "What palsied sheep can truly claim kinship with the slavering Wolf? They heap derision and shame upon the milling, tunic-wrapped flock of Heathenry with its pork-belly faith, cumbrous with desert moralities. Let them gather in their impotent masturbatory pubmoots."[892] Here the Wolves' anarcho-primitivist ideology pushes them toward this radical critique as outsiders even on the edges of Heathenry, a radical revitalization movement willing to burn Heathenry to the ground. It is from this position that their edgy mix of renunciation and ecstasy takes shape as a magical path towards self-transformation.

### *Oracular Seið: Seeing Deeper, Obtaining Knowledge*

To witness a performance of oracular seið is to be impressed by it as a women's moment. This perception has held true almost every time I

---

889. Galdr's terminology, "blood and Tribe and bund," all resonate with the völkisch discourse of race.
890. Paul Waggener, "Living Myth," 59.
891. "The Wolves of Vinland: a Fascist Countercultural 'Tribe' in the Pacific Northwest," *Its Going Down*, December 11, 2016, https://itsgoingdown.org/wolves-vinland-fascist-countercultural-tribe-pacific-northwest/.
892. Galdr, "Wolves Take What Wolves Will."

have observed the practice in a public setting.⁸⁹³ In seið, women take center stage and assume extraordinary roles of authority. A "high seat," the chair from which the oracle presides in her trance state, is the focal point and in formal settings, it can take the appearance of a throne, a tall wooden stately chair often draped in furs.⁸⁹⁴ The seeresses gather up front, each carrying a staff as the sign of her authority and often wearing elaborate "robes of office" — ritual garb such as Norse apron dresses luxuriantly decorated with strings of amber. While there may be men involved, they often take secondary supporting roles as warders and assistants who facilitate the gifts of the women.

While there are numerous independent practitioners of oracular seið, the practice is significantly the result of innovative and pioneering work done by Diana Paxson. In this sense, seið could be seen as a woman-founded NRM in and of itself.⁸⁹⁵ Many Heathens might be more comfortable seeing it this way, as an ancillary development to Heathenry. Paxson has been the intellectual source, primary author, and organizer of this movement that has influenced hundreds of people to varying degrees through her workshops, books, and personal interaction. Her work has involved developing reliable shamanistic and oracular practices and teaching them to others. In doing so, Paxson is tapping into prominent trends in contemporary Paganism, engaging a confluence of witches, Pagans, and Heathens interested in these practices. In her study of Pagan practice, Gwendolyn Reese reports that nearly 60 percent of her respondents engage in shamanic work and 54 percent are involved in oracular practices.⁸⁹⁶ For these reasons, Paxson ought to be better recognized among contemporary Pagans for this work than she often is. After years of practicing ceremonial magic, she became interested in Michael Harner's "Core Shamanism"

---

893. Of course, male-led oracular seið does occur in specific contexts. For instance, in the Well of Wisdom kindred in Lexington, KY, two men, one of whom was heterosexual, regularly led the kindred in Hrafnar-style seið. Field notes by author.

894. For an example, see the "Great Chair" pictured in Paxson, *The Way of the Oracle*, 34.

895. Elizabeth Puttick, *Women in New Religions: In Search of Community, Sexuality, and Spiritual Power* (New York: St. Martin's Press, 1997), 185.

896. Gwendolyn Reece, "Prevalence and Importance of Contemporary Pagan Practices," *The Pomegranate: The International Journal of Pagan Studies* 16, no. 1 (2014): 13.

movement.[897] While attending one of Harner's workshops, she had an experience during trance-work in which she encountered the god Odin, who invited her to learn seið magic. This event led her to begin researching the historical practice of seið in Norse culture as well as oracular practice in other ancient Pagan religions. Through years of experimenting and testing with her kindred Hrafnar, she fleshed out a workable Asatru context for practicing oracular magic. While continuing to perform and teach her "Hrafnar method" of seið, she has since gone on to develop a transcultural method of oracular practice which she believes can be successfully adapted to any religious system.

Oracular seið has developed in contemporary Asatru as a *de facto* type of woman's magic. While I have witnessed men performing oracular seið, these have been a minority of occasions and usually associated with local kindreds with a male seið practitioner. Most seið workers point out that both males and females can be effective and that there are no "rules" or "theology" that would limit the practice to women. It is primarily women who have developed and maintain this type of magic, however. Paxson points out that straight men practice seið and that the Lore indicates that men were often involved with the practice during the historical period. However, in her experience of the contemporary Asatru movement, she finds that "the people who have continued and made it a part of their permanent practice have pretty much all been women or gay men."[898] And while no theological prohibition exists for men's involvement, the earlier discussion of gender essentialism may imply the existence of cultural standards of masculinity in Asatru that would inhibit men from making this a regular practice.

The issue of gender in regard to seið arises from the use of the term *ergi* to describe seið in the Icelandic sagas as a disreputable and shameful activity, with "unmanliness" being a common but disputed translation of the term. Jenny Blain discusses the term extensively in her book, *The Nine Worlds of Seid-Magic*, in which she suggests that the unmanliness of seið is associated with homosexuality,

---

897. Michael Harner created the Core Shamanism movement with his book *The Way of the Shaman* (San Francisco: Harper One, 1990). Drawing on fieldwork with indigenous shamans, Harner identified principles of shamanic practice from which he extrapolated a trans-cultural shamanic method. Many Pagans, including Diana Paxson, have learned the method in workshops held throughout the United States.

898. Paxson, interview.

whether real or metaphorical in which the seer took on a passive, receptive, or vulnerable state in relation to the spirit world. In this analysis, ergi often carries a distinctly homophobic connotation.[899] In Blain's assessment, the homophobic discourse within contemporary Heathenry limits the appeal of seið. However, I suspect that the male avoidance of seið results more from the underlying gender essentialism of the Heathen ethos and that the fear of homosexuality is an outgrowth of that highly gendered way of discerning the world. Dubois, on the other hand, avoids the implication of homosexuality by suggesting that seið was seen as an underhanded way to deal with conflict, relying on magic rather than a fair and open fight.[900] Ergi, in his view, is similar to cowardice: "In a society that valued a forthright male manner and a ready embrace of outward conflict, a ritual allowing the secret manipulation of another's will would violate ideals of proper masculinity." Whatever the meaning, the association of seið with the term ergi continues to shape attitudes about the practice.

The seið workers use various means to produce or enter a trance state. Diana Paxson's method utilizes drumming and singing, a common method associated with core shamanism.[901] In the Hrafnar method of seið, the system developed by Paxson's West Coast kindred, the seer trains or conditions herself to quickly enter trance with the use of certain cues: donning certain elements of Heathen garb, taking up her staff, hearing the beat of the shamanic hoop drum, hearing or singing certain songs. Each seer might create her own cues. The training involved should not be underestimated, as Patricia Lafayllve writes, "It is a difficult art to work, and even more difficult to master. Seið should be considered a lifelong discipline."[902] Paxson has developed a rigorous training program with exercises that participants can do to grow in their ability to enter and work in trance states. In the Hrafnar method, the ritual leader or warder guides the entire audience of participants in a visualization exercise, a path-working that

---

899. Jenny Blain, *Nine Worlds of Seid-Magic: Ecstasy and Neo-Shamanism in North European Paganism* (London: Routledge, 2002), 120–41.
900. DuBois, *Nordic Religions*, 136–37.
901. Diana L. Paxson, "The Return of the Völva: Recovering the Practice of Seiðr," *Seeing for the People*, www.seidh.org/articles/seidh/. In this article, Paxson gives a complete description of the Hrafnar ritual associated with oracular seið.
902. Lafayllve, *A Practical Heathen's Guide*, 140.

takes them on a journey through the Norse cosmos from Midgard, down along the trunk of the world tree and into the underworld, Helheim, the realm of the dead. In the vision, the audience is seated outside the gates of Hel, while the seeress herself approaches and enters the gates to speak with the spirits. Alternatively, the visualization might involve journeying to the Well of Wyrd into which the seeress will peer, seeing and interpreting the threads and visions of the Wyrd. Once the seer is situated, then the real work of oracular seið begins.

The core of the ritual involves a series of questions asked by audience members to the seeress in an orderly and formal process supervised by the warders. One by one, audience members approach the high seat and ask their questions, inquiring information from the seeress. At times, they will request the seeress to look for and address a particular ancestor or Norse god. As part of Paxson's thoroughness and dedication to developing her system, she has over the years collected and analyzed the types of questions that are commonly asked in sessions of oracular seið in a database she calls "The Seidhjallr Files."[903] Questions are often of a practical nature: people ask about work, financial problems, health, travel, relationships or guidance along their personal spiritual path. Her conclusions are confirmed in my own informal analysis of questions: for the most part, querents seek information that will allow them to make productive life choices and solve problems.[904] Many seers understand their role as serving the community by providing this means of practical insight and guidance.

The entire process of oracular seið must be interpreted as a pursuit of knowledge and information. The oracle assumes the trance state in order to gain information and impart it to the gathered community. She does this by "seeing"; an oracle looks, sees, and speaks. She looks into the wyrd, she receives impressions imparted to her from a variety of sources. The trance state is simply a technique to attune the seer to this data available in the cosmos. In this sense, oracular seið exhibits epistemological implications concerning what we can know and how we can know it. E.O. Wilson, an evolutionary biologist, points out that human beings are epistemically challenged by having only a "narrow channel of

---

903. Paxson, *The Way of the Oracle*, 61–73.
904. Field notes taken by author at various Heathen events.

human cognition," which limits our ability to sense and know most of the world around us. He writes,

> Our sensory world, what we can learn unaided about reality external to our bodies, is pitifully small. Our vision is limited to a tiny segment of the electromagnetic spectrum . . . We can see only a tiny bit in the middle of the whole, which we refer to as the "visual spectrum" . . . Of sound frequencies all around us we hear only a few. Bats orient with the echoes of ultrasound, at a frequency too high for our ears, and elephants communicate with grumblings at frequencies too low.[905]

He goes on to write about the highly evolved capacities of some animals to sense electrical impulses and magnetic fields, or to taste and smell acutely. "We are idiots compared with rattlesnakes and bloodhounds," he states, "forced to stumble through our chemically challenged lives in a chemosensory biosphere."

His description of our limited physical epistemic range parallels the critique of our spiritual epistemic ability offered by seið magic. For Diana Paxson and other seið workers, the vast majority of people have an incredibly limited perception of the spiritual world, which prevents us from seeing and making use of information. While this information is all around us, we are unable to access it because of our limited epistemic range. Along these lines, Bil Linzie, a long-time seið worker states, "The only difference between a seiðman and an ordinary man is that the seiðman operates in a world with all the doors and windows open, and the ordinary man doesn't know that the windows and doors even exist."[906] The open windows and doors he mentions represent the expanded sensory and epistemic awareness attained by the seið worker. In "ordinary" states of consciousness, we are cut off from sensing and making use of a whole range of spiritual information that exists around us.[907] Seið magic provides a method to enhance a human being's sensitivity, the ordinarily limited range of ability, and open a practitioner to a more epistemically holistic reality. The training and practices developed by Paxson are designed to open those doors and windows, and to

---

905. E. O. Wilson, "On the Origin of the Arts: Sociobiologist E. O. Wilson on the Evolution of Culture," *Harvard Magazine* 114, no. 5 (2012): 32–37.
906. Bil Linzie, "Where Does a Seiðman Go?" *The Seidhman Rants*, www.angelfire.com/nm/seidhman/seidgo.html.
907. Diana L. Paxson, *Trance-Portation: Learning to Navigate the Inner World* (San Francisco: Red Wheel/Weiser Books, 2008), 5.

provide the oracle with the discipline to use them productively. Once she obtains proficiency, the seeress can see with enhanced sensory ability beyond the confines of ordinary consciousness to gain additional and useful data. Just like the biologist uses a microscope or an astronomer a telescope, the seið worker is a spiritual scientist peering into an unknown or unavailable aspect of reality with the magico-religious technology of trance and extracting information that is useful for living.

### Völva Stav: Healing the Soul

Kari Tauring (see figure 32) refers to her method of seið magic as Völva Stav. The völva is the magic-working women of the Norse world, one who sees into the wyrd, and her stav, or staff, is the emblem of her religious office. Tauring has adapted this emblematic aesthetic from the work of various scholars. Historian Michael Enright makes the case that the staff-carrying woman was an important religious figure in northern Europe, finding a "common denominator linking women, staffs and magic over a very broad cross-cultural context lasting more than a thousand years."[908] He interprets the staff as symbolizing a weaving beam, the top beam on a warp-weighted loom from which the weaving was hung. As we have seen, weaving was a powerful Norse cultural symbol of women's magic and carried connotations of the weaving of wyrd, thus associating the staff-carrying woman with prophetic, divinatory, and magic abilities. He writes,

> Peoples of Germanic culture always associated such looms with the warp and woof of fate and the women who worked them were often associated with magic. Weaving implements like distaffs, spindles and whorls were thereby associated with prophecy and prophetesses ... and such women are often described as carrying them. A weaving beam is therefore an appropriate symbol of divine prophetic talent.[909]

For Tauring, the völva was a vital part of the pre-Christian Norse culture, a religious specialist who maintained the health of the community through her magic-laden activities of storytelling, singing, dancing, and healing. In order to reconstruct a healthy

---

908. Enright, *Lady with the Mead Cup*, 116.
909. Ibid., 111–12.

Figure 32. Kari Tauring with Author, Trothmoot, 2011. (Photo used with permission.)

Asatru belief system and religious practice, Tauring believes that the office and practice of the völva must also be reconstructed and restored. She has given herself fully to this work of learning the Norse folk songs, dances, and magical practices associated with runes and seið and passing these on to the women who she personally trains. She has developed the ability to transition almost imperceptibly from performance to magic working, as I have witnessed on several occasions.

Although Tauring begins her *Völva Training Manual* with a nod to gender inclusivity, she specifically refers to völva work as "women's magic."[910] While Paxson's *seið* is contextually female-oriented, Tauring's practice is deeply female-based. She situates magic within the experience of the female body. This became particularly notable to me in a staving workshop in which I participated. Having interviewed Tauring the year before and being impressed with her seriousness, depth, and insight, I was determined to experience her techniques firsthand. I found myself as the only male in a circle of women swaying and rhythmically striking the ground with their stavs. I felt and immediately recognized the female-centric orientation of Völva Stav. In contrast to the interrogative nature of Oracular Seið, Völva Stav has a physical organic quality driven by the pulsing beat of the stavs, the percussive clatter in which the staver is immersed, and the close proximity of the moving bodies. However, as Tauring began to chant and instruct the circle, I increasingly felt out of place, decidedly *ergi* if you will. The staver is rooted with the earth, visualizing her legs and her root chakra of the perineum connected to the natural energy of Mother *Jorth*. Meanwhile with her staff, she taps out a rhythm, particularly the *pols* or pulse rhythm, which mimics the rhythm of the heart, "a magical rhythm that wakens the Nordic soul in a deep way."[911] This rhythm focuses the staver's awareness in her body, synchronized with the energy of the earth. Stavers feel the energy rising within them and collect it in the pelvic girdle, the natural cauldron of the woman's body, as Tauring calls it. The magic grows there, the place of mystery formed by the women's hips, where growing life is cradled within the womb. Pagan traditions frequently observe correspondences between the power of female fertility and the natural rhythms of the earth and associate the female body with magical potential.[912] As one Pagan writer puts it, "Bodily experience is the very essence of feminist spirituality and is seen as the locus of women's power," a sentiment clearly echoed in Tauring's understanding of magic.[913]

In Tauring's method, the work of the völva in the modern age revolves primarily around healing. At the root of her practice is the concept of the *hael* person, informed by Heathen soul concepts

---

910. Tauring, *Völva Stav Manual*, 18.
911. Ibid., 33.
912. Puttick, *Women in New Religions*, 226–27.
913. Susan Greenwood, "Feminist Witchcraft: A Transformatory Politics," in *Practising Feminism: Identity, Difference, Power*, eds. Nickie Charles and Felicia Hughes-Freeland (New York: Routledge, 1996), 114.

to encompass a holistic understanding of physical, spiritual, and social health.[914] Tauring's healing work centers on the emotions, which Tauring describes as the "point of power" and the "carriers of memory."[915] The trance state induced by staving is a form of participatory consciousness, which she sometimes calls seið consciousness. While in that space, the völva is able to follow the strands of emotional ørlög into a client's inner life to find the origin of emotional hurt and trauma: "As Völva, we seek to repair and heal broken lines of orlag in order to co-create the future through our choice making ... To stav into the moment of trauma and sing healing runes into that point changes the emotional body's response to the trauma. Through this process we can create functional and healed orlag for the future."[916] In this way, Völva Stav works with the Heathen model of the soul-complex: the grief and trauma of past generations is stored in the ørlög and passed into the future along the family line. Many of the problems faced by modern people, Tauring feels, originate in unresolved trauma experienced by their ancestors. This historical trauma is encoded in their ørlög and manifested in the lives of living people in terms of psychological and social dysfunction, a phenomenon Tauring calls "inherited cultural grief."[917] Not only do we carry the Luck of our ancestors, we also carry their dysfunction. In trance, the völva becomes aware of this damaged ørlög and can follow it into the past, tracing the threads of ørlög to the historical source of the trauma. A powerful völva may be able to obtain access to these ancestral memories and in some sense relive it in her own body, organically and magically "processing" the trauma.

Tauring recounts the dramatic experience of encountering an ancestral memory—an account that illustrates the emotional sophistication essential to her method.[918] One day, she felt a powerful sense of shame and fear welling up inside her. Recognizing that these feelings did not come from her own circumstances, she fell into trance, reaching into her ørlög to seek out the origin of the

914. Dubois, *Nordic Religions*, 94.
915. Tauring, interview; Tauring, *Völva Stav Manual*, 33.
916. Tauring, *Völva Stav Manual*, 21
917. Tauring, email. See also Sorcha Feilnar, "Return of the Völva," *Witches and Pagans*, June, no. 30 (2015): 27-32; David de Young, "Kari Tauring: Digging Deep Nordic Roots," *Sing Out!* 55, no. 3 (2013): 4-9.
918. Tauring, *Völva Stav Manual*, 34.

feeling. Realizing that the emotion was the ancestral memory of a young boy, she shifted her response and sent waves of loving energy towards the feeling, singing and rocking as if she was a loving parent holding a child. As she did this, Tauring felt the memory of trauma resolving itself: "I felt his being inside me relax. Warmth spread over me, contentment and relief. I began to rock, grounding and aligning with the world tree. I began to hum a lullaby. I felt my ancestor move through my legs and into the roots of the tree where this once fractured part of his soul could join the rest of him in wholeness." By allowing the grief to be expressed through herself, the inherited trauma was resolved. As a völva, Tauring seeks to apply the practice to others as a culturally specific method of healing the threads of ørlög and allowing her clients to overcome inherited patterns of debilitating behavior.

Her emphasis on human well-being and physical, psychological, and emotional health places Tauring within the more than one hundred-year tradition of American healing religion, of which animal magnetism, hydrotherapy, homeopathy, and chiropractic have all played a part. In this tradition, which Catherine Albanese calls physical religion, "acts of caring and curing constituted the central ritual enterprise for believers" with a healed or whole individual as the religious goal.[919] Although widely displaced by modern Western medicine in the lives of many Americans, the association of spirituality, religion, and healing has never been lost in American religion. The healing tradition, in which "healing works as sacred manifestation, and healers work as religious officiants," has become an important dimension of contemporary Pagan magical practice.[920] Reece describes healing work as "part of the constellation of pervasive practices within contemporary Paganism," with 85 percent of her respondents engaging in healing practices and close to a third of professional Pagan religious workers identifying as healing specialists.[921] Like other Pagans who engage in magical healing, the power of the mind to "alter the physical pattern" is on display in Tauring's work.[922] In reconstructing the völva role for contemporary Asatru, Tauring has situated this healing tradition within the

---

919. Albanese, *Nature Religion in America*, 123.
920. Ibid., 121.
921. Reece, "Prevalence and Importance," 12.
922. Albanese, *Nature Religion in America*, 183–84.

Norse magical worldview and made it available to contemporary Heathens. This context provides a coherence for Tauring's work with concepts such as seið consciousness, wyrd, and ørlög, which give her magical vocabulary a specificity and lineage. Her model shows us what is possible when a tradition such as healing religion borrows or becomes situated within the reconstructed context of an ancient Pagan worldview.

## Conclusion

Despite being frequently misunderstood in the popular imagination, magic comprises an important part of contemporary Pagan and Heathen cultures. Although magic, and seið magic in particular, remain contested areas of Asatru practice, the confluence of tributaries of Norse Culture, folkish/völkisch, and contemporary Wiccan and Witchcraft ideas and practices have created a rich magical culture in Heathenry of which we have only touched the surface. It serves as a creative outlet for self-expression, a means of effecting change in the world, and a deeply meaningful system of world and identity construction for the many Heathens who pursue magical practice.[923] While gender essentialism may exercise a limiting function on women in many ways, Asatru women have drawn on "feminine qualities" to create a sub-movement of magical practice. This sub-movement has been a protected sphere for women to exercise a degree of creativity, innovation, and autonomy that may be slower to develop in the broader Asatru movement. While women have also been active in developing and leading Asatru ritual, the almost exclusively female contribution to seið magic sets it apart in the Asatru world. By capitalizing on gender essentialist understandings of feminine nature, women have created for themselves an empowering role in the movement. But more importantly, the practice of seið provides contemporary adherents, male and female, a way to address the disconnections from their own bodies, families, and theology, which they may have experienced as a result of modernity.

---

923. Peter L. Berger, *The Sacred Canopy: Elements of a Sociological Theory of Religion* (New York: Anchor Books, 1967).

## Chapter 9

## The Windswept Tree

### Nature Religion in Asatru

From the third story window of the university library, the vibrant green of late spring is on full display. Gazing across the quadrangle, I see the grass is lush and neatly mowed and the trees that line the campus pathways are carrying their rich dark crown of leaves. In front of the table where I am working is a spectacular wall of glass, which opens to a view of a great old oak tree, like those that grace the lawns of so many college campuses. At this height, I can peer into the canopy, its topmost branches reaching out of sight toward the sun and its spreading limbs almost brushing the library windows. As I watch, a squirrel busily makes its way down the wide trunk, spiraling around from branch to branch towards the earth thirty feet below. From its base, the tree's roots spread out in gnarled knots before disappearing into the earth, straining into the unseen depths of the world. The tree in its entirety is an integrated ecosystem that extends beyond ordinary human perception, incorporating sky, ground, and the earth beneath, and the animals that dwell upon and around it: a biosocial community entangled in mystery and power. Musing upon the living system of the tree in this way, it is no great surprise that great trees such as this oak have been mythologized in nature-oriented cultures throughout the world.

The scene at the window is evocative of Yggdrasil, the tree that symbolizes the Heathen cosmology. The world tree is a massive living entity that nourishes and integrates the nine worlds of Norse myth, the ecosystems of the multiverse, and serves as a home to so many diverse life forms. The tree is one of the important orienting symbols of the religion. In 2012 in a large hotel meeting room in California, I participated in a ritual lead by gythja Patricia Lafayllve that evocatively expressed the orienting function of the world tree in

Heathen life.[924] Stretching out her arms, she gestured to the left and right, "To the north, ice; to the south, fire," she said as if Niflheim, the cosmic pole of ice, and Muspelheim, the pole of fire, were just there beyond the tips of her fingers. "There between them yawned the gap, Ginnungagap," the cosmic potency in the swirling confluence of fire and ice. From the creative tension of Ginnungagap's infinite void, she envisioned the emergence of the cosmos, "the mighty Ash rose, Yggdrasil, three great roots anchoring it, its branches spreading forth touching all the nine worlds."[925] At the center of the Heathen worldview stands Yggdrasil, the world tree, in which the cosmos exists. "The world ash Yggdrasil is taken to contain within its branch and root structure the worlds of the gods, giants, dwarves, and most importantly Midgard, the world of men," writes Paul Bauschatz.[926] The world tree forms the conceptual framework for understanding the contemporary cosmology of Asatru. While Heathens have no qualms with a scientific understanding of origins and tend to be evolutionist in their perspective, it is the religious concepts of Norse myth that deeply inform their thinking about and relationship to the world around them.[927] It is an animated universe, alive and interconnected. The cosmic squirrel Ratatosk climbs up and down its trunk; the gods, such as Odin on his eight-legged steed Sleipnir and Freyja in her falcon cloak, travel along the tree from world to world. It is a universe full of flowing energy with Midgard, the physical world, as the very nexus through which sacred power moves.

With her body mirroring the shape of the tree, Lafayllve directed the attention of her listeners into the present moment and location. "Here we stand at the base of the great tree," she intoned, "Here we stand in sacred Midgard." In the ritual process, the hotel meeting room had become *axis mundi*, poised at the creative center of the careful harmony of the Norse cosmos. By drawing on the natural imagery of the tree, Lafayllve oriented her listeners physically as

---

924. Field notes by author, 2012, 2013. The ritual invocation is reproduced in part in Lafayllve, *A Practical Heathen's Guide*, 68.
925. Field notes taken by author, California, February 2013.
926. Bauschatz, *The Well and the Tree*, 5.
927. "It is important to note that we Heathens have no issue with science or the scientific method. We understand science and believe in its evidence, same as most people—we just also have a spiritual component, and that is the kind of thing you'll see the most of in our conversations." Lafayllve, email.

well as religiously revealing the hotel room as a place of power and potency. If the monotheist goes to God to learn about the creation, then the nature religionist goes to nature to learn about and understand life. As Anna Bramwell describes, "Nature is seen as a path which leads somewhere; it is a teacher. One goes to the natural world to learn from it, and returns with a series of lessons."[928] The nature religionist is one who goes to nature to find not only what is divine, but what is ultimately real, who rejects idealism in favor of nature's enduring truth. Who needs scripture when you have the witness of the tree?

Heathenry and many other forms of contemporary Paganism take nature as one of the central organizing themes that shapes everything from an aesthetic sense to a sacred sense of time and place. To a great extent, the ideologies of Pagan religions are inspired by their encounter with the natural world, though Nature might mean many things from the esoteric correspondences of cosmic nature to the wild reaches of one's own body. In the case of our hotel-bound Pagan religionists meditating on the image of the world tree, nature may exist ideally, in the space of one's religious imagination. This use of nature calls to mind Graham Harvey's discussion of the "Greenwood," a modern mythological construct of a magically potent nature reminiscent of fairy tales.[929] By meditatively journeying into the Greenwood, a Pagan religionist participates in a special, enchanted experience of Nature, where unexpected encounters may bring healing, challenge, or insight. Despite its idealistic qualities, "its purpose is not primarily to entice people away to a fantasy, a never-never land," but instead to reorient people to the real world in new re-enchanted ways. Changed on personal, social, and political levels by these imagined or magical experiences of the Greenwood, a person sees and acts in the actual world from a new frame of reference. The Greenwood is one of many ways in which nature is re-exerting her presence back into the experience of contemporary people, whose lives are often characterized by alienated and disconnected relationships with the real physical world of nature. In a similar way, the imagined experience of Yggdrasil in the hotel conference room

---

928. Anna Bramwell, *Blood and Soil: Richard Walther Darré and Hitler's "Green Party"* (Bourne End, UK: Kensal, 1985), 11.

929. Harvey, *Contemporary Paganism*, 158–59.

asked participants to see their current lives as charged with the holy power of cosmic nature.

In her work *Nature Religion in America* Catherine Albanese defines nature religion quite broadly as religion that takes nature as its symbolic center.[930] Religion, according to Albanese, consists of a system of symbols that orient people in the world, including their beliefs, rituals, and patterns of everyday life. What people "believe and do is generated by the kind of 'center beyond' that Mircea Eliade has called the sacred," expressed by the "symbolic center and the cluster of beliefs, behaviors, and values that encircles it."[931] Nature religion enshrines "nature" as the central orienting symbol of the sacred around which religious meaning and practice is structured. For some Heathens, nature is central to their religious experience, while for others themes of nature run throughout their worldview as the source of a rich set of orienting symbols. There is a strong natural aesthetic in the Heathen world, found in the abundance of animal iconography, the use of fur, bone, and leather in art and fashion, the ubiquitous drinking horns, and nature-inspired path-working. In addition, Heathens have a strong connection and orientation to the outdoors. Heathens follow a seasonal calendar, organizing time around the solar and agricultural cycles. Heathens seek out powerful sacred spaces in nature, honor nature spirits in their rituals, and use the natural imagery of the world tree to construct their cosmology. These and other characteristics place Asatru within the sphere of nature religions. However, to more fully understand the interaction of Heathen religion with nature, we must ask what "nature" means to Heathens and to locate it among the varieties of nature religion that have been described by others.

## *Four Models of Nature*

For many scholars of religion and participants in the Pagan movement, contemporary Pagan religions represent some of the clearest and most visible expressions of nature spirituality in contemporary America. Graham Harvey notes that "Paganism is a spirituality in which the world . . . and the body are central and celebrated.

---

930. Catherine L. Albanese, *Nature Religion in America: From the Algonkian Indians to the New Age* (Chicago: University of Chicago Press, 1991).
931. Ibid., 7.

It is fundamentally 'Green' in its philosophy, taking seriously the understanding that 'everything that lives is holy.'"[932] Chas. S. Clifton shows that Paganism emerged in the United States as a popular movement just as nature-based spirituality was reaching a critical mass with the first Earth Day celebration in 1970. Of course, nature-oriented spirituality was not new to America in the cultural revolution of the 1970s. Such ideas, movements, and spiritualities had percolated in American society throughout its history, as Clifton writes, "In America, nature had spoken with a holy voice for at least two hundred years."[933] The nineteenth century had seen well-developed philosophies, churches, and organized religious movements that included robust involvement with nature. The twentieth century witnessed a continued expansion of nature-oriented ideas among the American populace. Natural health and healing therapies, the conservation movement and the creation of national parks, the hiking and outdoors movement manifested in hiking clubs and the Boy and Girl Scouts, homesteading, and the *Whole Earth Catalog*, all demonstrate the continued attraction with nature.[934] By the twentieth century, however, much of American engagement with nature lay outside the realm of mainstream organized religion. American Christianity was slow to respond and often hostile to the awakening of this ecological consciousness and its spiritual implications. However, people with many different visions of nature and nature-oriented spiritualities found a receptive religious context in the Pagan movement.

Numerous scholars have contributed to the work of delineating the religious modalities of nature in Paganism, how Pagans have organized and expressed different approaches to nature. And that body of work is fascinating and insightful. In his article "Nature and Ethnicity in Eastern European Paganism," Adrian Ivakhiv provides a useful model, helpful in both its simplicity and its comprehensiveness.[935] He outlines four different approaches to nature, or as he calls them, "cultural constructions of nature"

---

932. Harvey, *Contemporary Paganism*, 122.

933. Clifton, *Her Hidden Children*, 42.

934. For more on American hiking clubs, see Silas Chamberlin, *On the Trail: A History of American Hiking* (New Haven, CT: Yale University Press, 2016).

935. Adrian Ivakhiv, "Nature and Ethnicity in East European Paganism: An Environmental Ethic of the Religious Right?" *The Pomegranate: The International Journal of Pagan Studies* 7, no. 2 (2005): 194–225.

(see figure 33). He begins by suggesting that "two main traditions of thinking about nature have arguably dominated popular Anglo-American discourse since the middle of the twentieth century."[936] In the first tradition, nature stands apart from human civilization, a separate "realm that is more or less autonomous from human society, a primary material realm," against or in relation to which human society is posited. This approach informs two different models. It can been seen in a "pastoral tradition" that idealizes a past time when humans lived in closer harmony to the land, or a "wilderness sublime" tradition that "privileges an imagined past in which nature was undefiled by human presence." The second tradition, derived from science and ecological sensibilities, envisions nature as a "realm of untamed biological interrelationships," or a "set of nested and interdependent physical and biological systems."[937] This ecosystemic model includes humans and their social systems as part of these ecologies. In addition to these three perspectives, Ivakhiv argues that a fourth approach to nature is prevalent in Eastern European Paganism. Nature, in this perspective, came to be seen as an organic biosocial system consisting of a sacred land, people, and culture. This construction, he suggests, has been downplayed or lost in the West due to the differing intellectual histories of the two regions. Yet, as we will discuss later in the chapter, American Heathenry is one socio-religious location that retains some aspects of this organic biosocial approach.

Ivakhiv's model provides a helpful structure for thinking about Pagan expressions of nature. However, the work of other scholars adds important nuances and categories to this basic picture.[938] Albanese provides the additional category of Native American constructions of nature, characterized by a continuity among sacred, natural, and human worlds, and a vision of nature as a personal world inhabited by numinous nature beings. She summarizes, "The material world was a holy place; and so harmony with nature beings and natural forms was the controlling ethic, reciprocity the recognized mode of interaction."[939] In fact, the sense of nature as

---

936. Ibid., 197.
937. Ibid., 198.
938. My discussion is not a chronological account of these sources. Ivakhiv's model summarizes other scholarly models in order to contrast them with the Eastern European construction of nature.
939. Albanese, *Nature Religion in America*, 23.

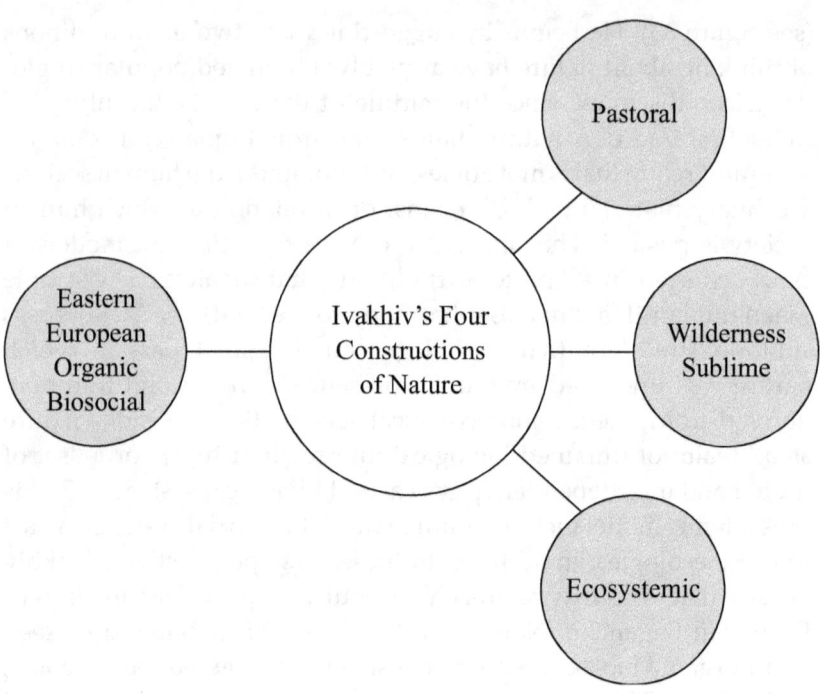

Figure 33. Ivakhiv's Four Constructions of Nature.

Other among the European colonists was formalized in some ways by their observation and astonishment at this Native American approach to the natural world. For instance the Puritans in New England notoriously saw the woods as sublimely horrible, a God-forsaken wildness of Witchcraft and devilry, and found beauty in the ordered pastoral ideal of a land tamed to European agricultural uses.[940] By the time of the American Romantic movement in the mid-1800s, a transition was underway in the American imagination of nature and wilderness.

In his novel *The Scarlet Letter*, Nathaniel Hawthorne elucidates this period of transformation. He first pictures nature within the older Puritan perspective as an ominous threating wilderness.[941] Pearl, Hester Prynne's young daughter, quotes an old Puritan dame who imagines the forest as the domain of the devil, who haunts

---

940. Ibid., 35.
941. Nathaniel Hawthorne, *The Scarlet Letter* (New York: The Modern Library, 1950).

the forest as an "ugly Black Man" with a book and an iron pen in which his victims write their names with blood. Pearl teasingly questions her mother whether the old dame's allegation is correct that Hester's scarlet letter "glows like a red flame when thou meetest him at midnight, here in the dark wood."[942] In a later scene, Hawthorne envisions nature in a new way, as a refuge from the harsh moral judgments and merciless scrutiny of human society, a place where forbidden love could flower, and full humanity could flourish. Deep in the forest, Hester and her lover, Arthur Dimmesdale sit on a mossy tree, sharing their deepest inner feelings and speaking truthfully and freely. Hester takes off her scarlet letter and lets down her hair, freed from social constraints and restored to youthful beauty and happiness. At that moment,

> as with a sudden smile of heaven, forth burst the sunshine, pouring a very flood into the obscure forest, gladdening each green leaf, transmuting the yellow fallen ones to gold . . . Such was the sympathy of Nature—that wild, heathen Nature of the forest, never subjugated by human law, nor illumined by higher truth—with the bliss of these two spirits![943]

Hawthorne's description of this mysterious and sacred experience of nature foreshadows the possibilities of a new wilderness sublime orientation among the American Transcendentalists like Emerson, Thoreau, and Muir. They continued to re-imagine wilderness as a place where the human spirit could thrive unbounded by society's constraints, and where a holy and divine light shone to illuminate the human heart and intellect. Meanwhile in the novel, as Hester and Arthur Dimmesdale converse, Pearl wanders in the forest communing with the animals and gathering flowers and plants. Hawthorne describes the slow transmutation of the girl as she adorns her hair and body with violets, anemones, columbines, and twigs, seemingly becoming "a nymph-child or an infant dryad, or whatever else was in closest sympathy with the antique wood."[944] She becomes one of the wild things of nature, taking on the appearance of a nature spirit herself. Hawthorne writes, "the mother-forest, and these wild things which it nourished, all recognized a kindred wildness in the

---

942. Ibid., 212.
943. Ibid., 233.
944. Ibid., 236.

human child."[945] In Pearl's sensual, embodied wildness, Hawthorne anticipates another experience of nature, the Embodied nature described by Chas S. Clifton.

In his history and analysis of American Wicca, *Her Hidden Children*, Clifton describes three ways in which nature acts as a central orienting religious symbol in Paganism: Embodied, Cosmic, and Gaian natures.[946] Embodied nature roots the experience of nature in the wild body, its passions and energies. I discussed this theme earlier in relation to the erotic theology of Wicca and its approach to magic. The embodied experience of nature is expressed not only in sexuality but also in many body-oriented religious technologies that deal with life energies, healing religion, or even Primal Scream therapy.[947] The Cosmic construction of nature comes from the alchemic and magical traditions and is seen in the practice of astrology and ceremonial magic in the Western esoteric tradition. Although very different in some ways, both of these approaches, Embodied/Erotic and Cosmic nature, share qualities of the ecosystemic approach mentioned by Ivakhiv. Cosmic nature describes the world as interconnected through correspondences between the natural and the supernatural worlds—earthly nature participates and interacts with transcendent nature, a sort of esoteric ecosystem. Meanwhile, Embodied nature expresses a sense of an energetic or sensual ecology, the body receptive and interconnected to the cosmos and its living energies.

Gaian nature on the other hand seems to be most at home within Ivakhiv's wilderness sublime category. This construction attributes divinity to the earth and its beings, experiencing and venerating the earth and its ecosystem as a goddess. From a Pagan perspective, the holiness of nature is nothing new and had long been associated with the goddess figures of ancient cultures. As Ronald Hutton describes, "all classical goddesses were different aspects of 'Great Nature' or 'Earth,'" in the incipient Paganism of English Romantic poetry.[948] However, the new Pagan nature religion that began to develop in America in the 1970s moved beyond the literary goddess of the poets. The influence of the environmental movement on Wicca led to a

---

945. Ibid., 235.
946. Ibid., 44–45.
947. Ibid., 63.
948. Hutton, *The Triumph of the Moon*, 35.

growing willingness of Pagans to adopt an *ecological* understanding of Goddess, consciously identifying her with the earth and giving "to planet Earth the status of a goddess."[949] The Goddess is all around us in her sublimity and power. Pagan adherents experience the Goddess by going out into nature, the sunlight and moonlight, the forests and streams, the cycle of the seasons. There are clearly influences of the ecosystemic approach here as well. By the late 1960s, both ecologists and Pagan religionists were describing the earth as an interconnected natural system. Clifton points out that Tim Zell, the founder of the Church of All Worlds had enunciated a vision of the earth as a living organism before James Lovelock proposed his own now-famous Gaia Hypothesis.[950] The scientific establishment was reluctant to embrace such a notion, but alternative religions such as Wicca and other Paganisms were eager to accept this view of nature and breathe the soul of the Goddess into it. And while this view of nature was new, contemporary Pagans felt its resonance with ancient perceptions of nature, the Native cultures of the American continent, and the indigenous Paganisms of the deep European past.[951]

This Gaian experience of nature became an important component of Pagan religiosity, and has received further treatment by Bron Taylor. In his book, *Dark Green Religion*, Taylor presents a typography of nature-oriented religion that includes essentially a further development of Clifton's Gaian Nature category.[952] Taylor first distinguishes "green" from "dark green" nature religion. Green religions build on ecosystemic constructions of nature. They express theological motivations for valuing and caring for the earth, and advocate environmentally friendly behavior. Many Pagans see green lifestyles as natural consequence of their religious perspective. And increasingly, the monotheistic traditions are discovering ecological themes within their respective traditions that are supportive of environmental attitudes and practices. Such themes might include the Jewish teaching of *bal tashchit* and the *shmita*

---

949. Clifton, *Her Hidden Children*, 51.
950. Ibid., 55.
951. Prudence Jones, "The Native European Tradition," in *Nature Religion Today: Paganism in the Modern World*, eds. Joanne Pearson, Richard H. Roberts, and Geoffrey Samuel (Edinburgh University Press, 1998), 77–88.
952. Bron R. Taylor, *Dark Green Religion: Nature Spirituality and the Planetary Future* (Berkeley: University of California Press, 2010).

year, Christian interpretations of environmental stewardship in the Genesis creation accounts, and Muslim concepts of vice-regency and corrupting the earth (*fasad fil-ard*).

Dark green religions on the other hand are developments of the "wilderness sublime" category, in which nature itself is experienced as a sacred other. Taylor describes dark green expressions of nature religion as falling somewhere along two spectrums.[953] The first spectrum has to do with the attribution of transcendence to the earth and its beings, running from supernaturalist to naturalist. Supernaturalist orientations attribute a more-than-natural dimension to nature, seeing it as enlivened by soulful intelligences of one sort or another, while naturalist perspectives are purely materialist in orientation. For example, to a naturalist, the "green fire" in the eyes of a wolf indicates its vital life-energy, perhaps even personhood, what Taylor terms "lifeforces." The supernaturalist, on the other hand, sees in that green fire the spirit being of the wolf, the "spiritual intelligences" of beings who transcend a merely natural existence. The second spectrum, running from animistic to Gaian, concerns the level at which divinity is located in the natural world.[954] Animism attributes divinity to each natural being, while a Gaian perspective sees it as occurring at the holistic level of the planetary system. For example, an animist encounters each tree as an individual spirit being, such as dryad or vaettir, and each flowing spring as the home to its own naiad or nykken. For a Gaian religionist, the forest, seas, and plains are components or organs of a larger integrated and conscious being: what is alive is the greater holy organism, Mother Earth.

### *Heathen Experiences of Nature*

Reading *Nature Religion in America* in graduate school was my introduction to the idea that social groups construct different visions of nature. Albanese's narrative about the development of important American approaches to nature helped me to realize the formative influence these perspectives have. Looking at Heathenry through this lens, it became clear that Heathens were the inheritors of these two hundred years of American experience. Nature forms

---

953. Ibid., 15.
954. Ibid., 15–16.

# Nature Religion in Asatru

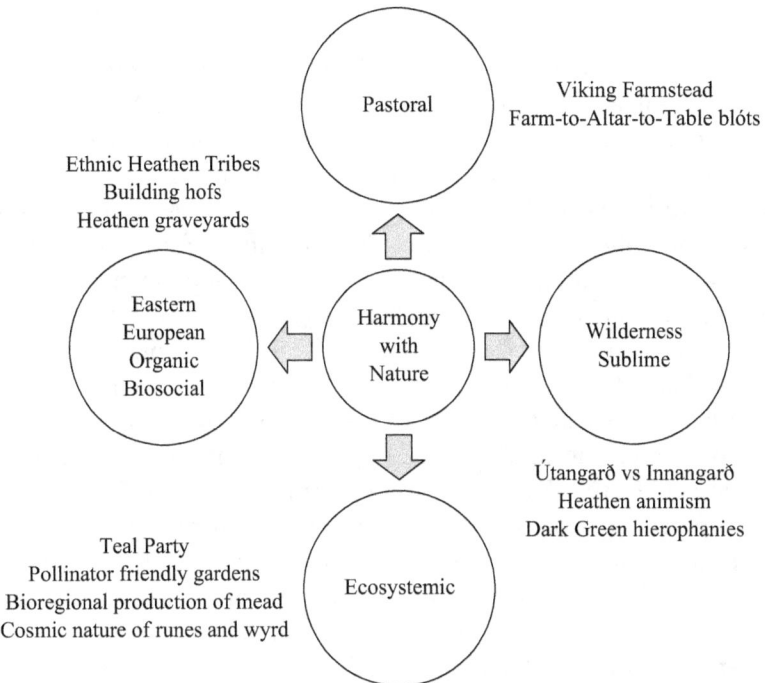

Figure 34. Four Constructions of Nature with Heathen Exemplars.

an important value within American Heathenry. Most American Heathens would include nature as part of the "symbolic center" of their religious orientation. "How to live in harmony with nature" is a central guiding question that most Heathens will ask and turn to their religion to provide answers. However, any thoughts of identifying a uniquely Heathen approach were quickly scattered by the reality I encountered among Heathens and their communities. Rather than one perspective of nature, there are many (see figure 34). The varieties of nature religion described by Albanese and other scholars continue to shape various Heathen experiences and orientations toward nature, recapitulating the American experience within the Heathen context. Furthermore, Ivakhiv's description of an Eastern European construction of nature made it clear that a particular view from outside the American context was an additional influence. This organic biosocial construction that originated in Europe flowed into Heathenry through the folkish/Traditionalist tributary.

## Pastoral Nature

American Heathens have placed relatively little emphasis on the pastoral ideal. Despite its recognized place in Norse culture and the Lore, farming and the reconstruction of a Norse pastoral experience has not proved particularly important. The Viking farmstead has served as a source for theological reflection in some cases. For instance, it figures in Eric Wódening's formulation of the útangarð and innangarð concepts, and in Nigel Pennick's thinking about sacred space, the "Norse heathen sacred enclosure called the Vé."[955] The most important expressions of the pastoral ideal come in the Farm-to-Altar-to-Table blóts described in chapter 6. The Heathen farmstead figures prominently in these religious events, and preserves the motif of the happy Heathen homestead in the religious culture. This dimension of nature religion informs only a small percentage of actual Heathen practice at present. However, the practice of live blót represents one opportunity for it to take a larger role in Heathen life. More likely, it will remain a minority experience for a couple of reasons not specific to Heathenry. In the American context, it falls outside of the usual *religious* conceptions of nature. The value of agriculture has suffered such attenuation in American life, and the agrarian voice has been so marginalized, that the spiritual dimensions of farming are lost to most. Like other Americans, this cultural trend has influenced Heathens so that "the farm" is not seen as an important way to experience nature. Similarly, the structure of the American society and economy puts farming out of reach for most Americans. Small-scale agriculture remains a niche occupation and is simply beyond the reach of most Heathens economically and practically.

## Wilderness Sublime Expressions of Nature

Ivakhiv's "wilderness sublime," Clifton's "Gaian nature," and Taylor's "dark green religion" categories together describe important varieties of Heathen nature religion. Some Heathens are naturalist in their perspective, preferring a scientific and materialist approach to nature while still regarding it as holy Midgard. Most Heathens assert a supernaturalist perspective, claiming to encounter a transcendent

---

955. Wódening, *We Are Our Deeds*, 1–6; and Pennick, "Heathen Holy Places," 139–49.

element within the natural world and taking the notions of supernatural beings such as elves, dwarves, and nature spirits more seriously. Heathen approaches to nature occasionally encompass a supernaturalist Gaian perspective, encountering the Earth as Mother Jorth. At times, Asatruar may refer to the Earth in anthropomorphic terms as a Norse earth goddess, Jorth or Jord, from the Old Norse *jörð*, meaning the earth or land.[956] The Old Norse term and its cognate *erda* in Old High German became *eorthe* in Old English from which our modern English "earth" derives. In Norse myth, she is a giantess, "the personified Earth, the planet we stand on," one of Odin's lovers who gives birth to the god Thor.[957] For instance, the environmental writings of the Odinic Rite, a Heathen organization with a long track record of ecological thinking, frequently reference "Mother Jorth, the Earth, our home." Asrad, a member of the OR's Court of the Gothar, expresses a Gaian perspective when he points to the environmental degradation caused by those who "have no love for Mother Jorth, no respect or understanding for our home, our great Mother. No understanding that we are part of nature, not its owners."[958] While these theological resources hold forth the possibility that a dark green planetary consciousness could arise among Heathens, such an awareness is still latent and ultimately unlikely. As Jenny Blain points out, "Mother Jorth is not *The* Goddess, but *a* goddess," one among many in the hard polytheistic culture of Heathenry.[959] Nor is she a deity who has achieved a position of prominence in the practical side of Heathen life, its ritual and iconography. For many Heathens, Mother Earth is too abstract, too "fluffy," resembling the diffuse notions of divinity they associate with contemporary Pagans.

More commonly, Heathens experience nature from an animistic perspective by venerating holy beings within nature. For instance, it was near Midsummer when I received a text from a former member of the old Well of Wisdom kindred inviting several kindred members

---

956. Cleasby and Vigfusson, *An Icelandic Dictionary*, s.v. "Jörð."
957. Lafayllve, *A Practical Heathen's Guide*, 53; Paxson, *Essential Ásatrú*, 152.
958. Asrad, "Ragnarok" *The Odinic Rite*, November 29, 2010, www.odinic-rite.org/main/ragnarok/.
959. Jenny Blain, "Heathenry–Ásatrú," in *The Encyclopedia of Religion and Nature*, eds. Bron R. Taylor, Jeffrey Kaplan, Laura Hobgood-Oster, Adrian J. Ivakhiv, and Michael York (London: Thoemmes Continuum, 2005), 753.

Figure 35. Hailing the Land-Vaettir at Lightning Across the Plains. (Photo by the author.)

for a gathering at her new apartment. The kindred had been led by one particular couple whose recent break-up had resulted in a good deal of turmoil and the cessation of kindred meetings for a while. The former member had moved to a small apartment in a nearby town and invited us for a house-warming and Midsummer event. The apartment complex was situated between the interstate ramp and a busy highway with businesses on either side. It had been built on a small hill, leveled by bulldozers and filled with the cast-off from the bypass construction. Above the apartment complex rose another hill, also leveled, where the flashing "Checks Cashed Here" sign glowed from the strip mall. In between ran a narrow ravine, woody and grown up, with a small creek trickling through it, the only surviving natural remnant that the bulldozer had left untouched. Too steep to mow, it sat neglected, though "unintentionally preserved" might be a better description for this type of space to which no one pays much attention. Seeing the little ravine, a civil engineer might note the necessity of directing and channeling run-off water. But if you were a nature religionist your heart would leap to find this survivor, a small wild place of relatively untouched natural space tucked away in the midst of suburban sprawl.

At some point while we were eating, I saw Jordsvin, a long-time Heathen, seið practitioner and kindred member, slipping out of the apartment with a horn and plate of food. This caught my attention because a horn is an important symbol in Heathenry associated with the blót. To leave with horn in hand indicated that Jordsvin had a ritual intention. He walked across the heat-blighted parking lot and down into the little wooded ravine. Until that moment, I had not given the ravine a second thought but now it suddenly took on a huge importance. He was going there, I realized, to make offerings to the nature spirits, the land-vaettir who make their homes in natural, wild places. Jordsvin made his short, personal, and informal blót as a gift of reverence and recognition to the nature spirits of the ravine, the spirits of that specific locality. In performing the ritual, he enacted a type of nature spirituality, which recognized a sacred value to the marginal land clinging to survival between the apartment complex and the strip mall. His blót was directed not towards a theological generality but a concrete specificity, not to the Earth but to that ravine and its forgotten denizens. The act was motivated by several Heathen ideas: that humans share spaces with other communities of beings; that these beings are individuated and specific to a location or habitat; and that a holy and healthy human life is lived in relationship to these beings. Significantly, Jordsvin used Heathen religious structures as the means with which to interact with nature. The horn and the libation poured from it, the food offering, and the structure of the blót all provided him with the resources to see nature as sacral and to engage with nature in a spiritually meaningful way.

Like Jordsvin, many Heathens express views of sacred nature in continuity with Taylor's typology of supernaturalistic animism.[960] Heathens approach nature with a distinctly animistic perspective as a living world inhabited by a diverse set of spirit beings. The natural cosmos is an interconnected multiverse inhabited by living beings with a spiritual dimension or soulful intelligence. These entities share the world, populating their proper habitat, and forming their

---

960. Taylor, *Dark Green Religion*, 15.

own communities characterized by culture, knowledge, skill, and power. For Heathens, these beings deserve acknowledgment, as well as respect and reverence and quite possibly fear or avoidance. While not all these beings are benevolent, humans should attempt to live in proper relationship with the other non-human spirit beings in their vicinity. With some effort on the part of human beings, these personalities can be known and befriended through various religious means including offerings, meditation, and ritual (see figure 35). Relating to one's unseen neighbors can bring blessing to the human community. This animistic orientation is significantly closer to the experience of nature found in the myths and sagas of Heathen Lore than to a Gaian perspective of Mother Earth. It fits comfortably within Heathen theology and predominates in the lived experience of Heathen people. Trees, mountains, streams all have their spiritual aspects, but one does not have to venture far to encounter them. One's own backyard is home to unseen beings of wild nature, alive and endowed with personalities, who inhabit its nooks and crannies. Heathens may reach out to discover and form relationships with these beings wherever they are as part of a rich religious approach to the world.

*Reconstructing an Animist Worldview*

Jordsvin is hardly alone in performing his personal and spontaneous ritual to the land spirits. The re-enchanting of the land, by means of ritual and personal experience, is a significant trend within the Heathen movement. Invoking nature spirits in ritual, creating spaces and leaving offerings for them are common and frequent actions Heathens perform as part of daily life. We have already mentioned that large events, moots and things, are generally opened with a ceremony focused on greeting and appeasing the land spirits by offering gifts, such as the birdseed at East Coast Thing or the (much less environmentally friendly) Skittles candy thrown into the woods by the children at Lightning Across the Plains. Giving gifts to land spirits (whether the nymphs of ancient Greece or the vaettir of Iceland) was a ubiquitous practice in ancient Pagan religions.[961] By incorporating these practices, contem-

---

961. Jennifer Larson, "A Land Full of Gods: Nature Deities in Greek Religion," in *A Companion to Greek Religion*, ed. Daniel Ogden (Malden, MA: Blackwell, 2007), 61–62; Davidson, *The Lost Beliefs*, 113, 117.

porary Asatruar show their intention of reconstructing a religious culture of animism, hallowing the earth in ways similar to these ancient examples of nature religion. This involves moving beyond modern disenchanted understandings of land and nature and envisioning a landscape alive with spiritual beings. The lived culture of animism attempts to re-embed awareness in a pattern reminiscent of the ancestors.

For many Heathens, these religious practices express the primal and intuitive connection they have to nature. Take Sten, a Heathen practitioner on the East Coast, who describes how a sacred orientation toward nature was instilled in him at an early age:

> We had no formal practices, but I began to spontaneously offer to the gods and spirits at a very young age. We also, as a family, always showed great reverence for our forebears as well as both reverence and respect for the wild places in the world ... On one [camping] trip my dad commented to me that this, the wilderness, was our cathedral and our pilgrimage was to our sacred place.[962]

Similarly, Hege describes having a natural connection with nature spirits, which she has developed by actively working with the spirits, learning to know and be sensitive to them.[963] This type of personal, experiential knowledge of spiritual realities comes into play to supplement other sources of information about animism among Pagans and Heathens. Hege led a well-attended workshop on nature spirituality at Lightning Across the Plains, which sought to actively engage other Heathens in the religious practices of supernatural animism, i.e. working religiously with nature spirits. Her talk indicates the existence of a larger-scale cultural movement within Heathenry to re-enchant or re-animate nature. Heathens interact with the beings of nature in personal and localized ways, creating backyard shrines and habitats for nature spirits in which offerings are made and blóts can be held. In her workshop, Hege described in detail the personalities of nature spirits, and the subtleties involved in relating to them, the sorts of environments that attract them, and the types of offerings they like. She even had creatively decorated spirit houses for sale. A few of her suggestions had

---

962. Sten, telephone interview with author, March 19, 2015.
963. Hege, "Working with the Wights," oral presentation, field notes taken by author, Kansas, 2013.

an ecological bent, such as composting and incorporating gardens into the backyard environment.

This "instinctive" sense of nature's sanctity, such as Sten's youthful experience of the cathedral of nature, indicates a strong connection to an environmental tributary stretching from Thoreau's hierophanies of nature, to John Muir's spontaneous spiritual Paganism, and Aldo Leopold's deep ecology.[964] Furthermore, the folkish/Traditionalist tributary of Heathenry draws on the strong ecological themes of the völkisch movement, which sought spiritual renewal within a hallowed German landscape. These traditions of ideas and experiences influence the reconstruction of Heathen nature spirituality. Heathens long for a more primal experience of nature, something reminiscent of indigenous animistic experiences of nature. The practice of giving offerings to land spirits produces within adherents a participatory orientation to the land, a consciousness that one is a guest within a larger ecosystem that has its own needs, purposes, and inhabitants. While ancient Norse Pagans certainly were immersed in such an experience, reconstructing that experience from the context of modern middle-class American lifestyles may be significantly more difficult than it was for Thoreau and others who tried to reclaim it. The advantage that Heathens have over Thoreau and Muir is their avid connection to an indigenous European culture and the descriptions in Lore and in archaeology that give Heathens an ancient vocabulary and pattern that might be revitalized. First-generation Heathens are engaged in very self-conscious attempts to experience the landscape as animistic; their children, second- and third-generation Heathens raised within that context, may exhibit a much more organic, precognitive experience of animism in years to come. At the same time, the increasingly technological world of this second generation presents additional challenges and changes to the experience of nature. It will be interesting to see how these factors interact. Can technological and animistic worldviews synthesize into a coherent perspective? Can Heathens reconstruct social networks, such as the urban–rural connections mentioned in our discussion of the blót in chapter 6, to

---

964. Thoreau and Atkinson, *Walden and Other Writings*; John Muir, *Nature Writings: The Story of My Boyhood and Youth; My First Summer in the Sierra; The Mountains of California; Stickeen; Selected Essays* (New York: Literary Classics of the United States, 1997); Aldo Leopold, and Charles Walsh Schwartz, *A Sand County Almanac, and Sketches Here and There* (New York: Oxford University Press, 1987).

further support a direct experience and knowledge of the natural world? Will Heathen projects such as hof building and the interment of bodies in Heathen cemeteries create new sacred landscapes accessible to future generations? Such questions underscore the fact that the project of reconstructing a quasi-traditional animistic religion is a highly complex and multi-generational undertaking.

### Are the Norse Gods Deities of Nature?

The divine beings venerated by Pagans often represent elemental and natural forces. Writing specifically of Greek gods but applicable also to the pantheon of the ancient north, Jennifer Larson states, "All the Greek gods were connected in one way or another with natural phenomena, so in some sense all are nature deities."[965] As we observed in our discussion of hard polytheism, many contemporary Heathens are wary of the idea that the gods are personifications of nature. For the most part, it is the jotuns who are related to nature.[966] For instance, Jord is the giantess of the earth. Ran and Aegir make their home in the sea and are closely related to its activity, their daughters even described as the waves.[967] Several of the Norse gods, even central ones such Thor, retain some of the characteristics of nature deities in contemporary Asatru practice. For instance, Heathens strongly associate Thor with lightning and thunderstorms. Some interpret Thor's wife Sif as related to the growing of crops and the earth's bounty, making the pair an example of fertility gods.[968] In a contemporary prayer for Thor, practitioners invoke him as the storm god, "Thor, we hear your might in the booming crash of the thunder, and see your power in the blazing bolt of lightning."[969] The invocation is likely influenced by McNallen's Thor blót, which also draws on similar imagery from the domain of nature, "Thor, we hear you in the might of the crashing thunder, and we sense your

---

965. Larson, "Land Full of Gods," 58.
966. Aðalsteinsson, "Gods and Giants," 20.
967. Sturluson, *Skaldskaparmal*, 6, in *The Prose Edda*. The reference to Aegir's daughter as waves of the sea is found in *Helgakviða Hundingsbana I*, stanza 29, in *The Poetic Edda*. See Larrington, "First Poem of Helgi Hundingsbani," in *The Poetic Edda*, 114.
968. Lafayllve, *A Practical Heathen's Guide*, 37.
969. Steve Wilson, "Thor Blot," *Jordsvin's Norse Heathen Pages*, http://home.earthlink.net/~jordsvin/Blots/.

presence in the growing fields which sustain us."[970] And when a thunderstorm began brewing during a Thor blót at East Coast Thing in 2007, it was not seen as an interruption as much as an indication of Thor's favor. One participant reported it as a good omen that, "as he was raising his sacrifice and making the sign of the Hammer, the most brilliant streak of lightning raced across the sky directly above us."[971] But even while the gods are associated with nature in some ways, gods are not subsumed into the natural world, nor reduced to natural phenomena wrapped in the guise of personality.[972]

Even if the Heathen gods are "in some sense" nature deities, the worship of deities is qualitatively different from the veneration of the earth and its ecology. God worship is only indirectly concerned with nature: the god is the focus of devotion. The supernatural layer of deity, especially in a hard polytheistic mode, draws attention away from nature itself. Bron Taylor emphasizes this distinction between naturalistic and supernaturalistic forms of nature religion in his typography. He suggests that the supernaturalistic forms of religion will fail to produce truly ecological cultures. In an interview with the editors of *Journal of Contemporary Heathen Thought*, Taylor commented specifically on the ecological efficacy of Heathenry and other deity-oriented religions. Perhaps to the disappointment of his interviewers, Taylor dismissed the idea that Heathenry might become a viable ecological actor: "I mean no disrespect to those who represent supernaturalistic forms of Paganism, but I think the naturalistic forms are the ones that will have the greatest long-term cultural traction."[973] Taylor seems correct in his observation that while a religion might be dark green in its orientation to the earth, it very well may not be effectively ecological, simply because the adherent is oriented towards the transcendent dimension of the relationship. The act of offering food and drink to a nature spirit is not a straightforward ecological act. This may be a little like the lovers in Gabriel Garcia Marquez's novel, *One Hundred Years of Solitude*, who make love while the house falls down around them, their

---

970. Stephen A McNallen, "Thor Blot," in *The Rituals of Asatru, Volume 1 – Major Blots*, (Payson, AZ: Worldtree Publications, 1985, 1992), 7.

971. Rick, "East Coast Thing 2007," *Raven Kindred North*, http://rick-of-rkn.livejournal.com/19493.html.

972. Clifton, *Her Hidden Children*, 57.

973. Bron Taylor, "Green Heathenry: An Interview with Bron Taylor," *Journal of Contemporary Heathen Thought* 2 (2011–2012): 226.

amorous affections for each other so engulfing their attention that everything else is neglected.[974] However, we should note that such supernaturally directed practices may engender attitudes, actions, and cultures that are ecological. As we will see in our discussion of sacred spaces and Heathen Greens, the supernaturalistic mode of nature religiosity has encouraged the preservation of wild spaces and in some cases the development of environmental consciousness within Heathenry. For instance, Hege's suggestion that the landvaettir may like offerings of compost in addition to Irish whiskey is suggestive of the incipient ecological possibilities of animism.[975]

## Heathen Hierophanies of Nature

Mircea Eliade used the term hierophany to describe a type of religious experience in which the divine appears or manifests directly to an observer. Eliade wrote that "Man becomes aware of the sacred because it manifests itself, shows itself, as something wholly different from the profane. To designate the *act of manifestation* of the sacred, we have proposed the term *hierophany* . . . [indicating] that *something sacred shows itself to us.*[976] Hierophanies should be understood as important elements of nature religion when the sacred is revealed in and through Nature, "The sacred tree, the sacred stone . . . are worshipped precisely because . . . they show something that is no longer stone or tree but the *sacred.*"[977] The experience seems insepar-able from the Pagan corpospirituality that we have described, in which physical and spiritual aspects of being are intertwined and often indistinguishable, clarifying the more-than-symbolic relationship that exists between the natural and the supernatural in Pagan religion. The manifestation of the sacred *in* nature, such as the appearance of a land spirit in or as a rock or tree, or the presence of Thor signified by a lightning bolt, is a significant aspect of that experience.

These encounters with the sacred cosmos, which might be described as nature mysticism, have played a role in the American

---

974. Gabriel García Márquez, *One Hundred Years of Solitude* (New York: Avon, 1970), 372–73.
975. Hege, "Working with the Wights."
976. Mircea Eliade, *The Sacred and the Profane: The Nature of Religion* (New York: Harcourt, 1959), 11.
977. Ibid., 12.

experience of nature. Catherine Albanese describes John Muir as having this sort of experience during a stay in the sequoia groves of Yosemite in 1870.[978] At one point, Muir experienced a transformative mystical union with the sequoias in which a great tree rapturously appeared to him as a sacred entity he call the Lord Sequoia. He found himself immersed in the tree's presence, an ecstatic experience of communion he described as drinking "Sequoia wine, Sequoia blood." Despite being encoded in quasi-Christian language, the experience seems to represent a profoundly earth-based hierophany, in which the tree appears not as a symbol for the sacred, but sacred in itself. Albanese writes that for Muir, "nature religion meant nature *worship*."[979] While clearly not a traditional indigenous experience, Muir's immersion in wilderness and his ecological sensibility merge to elevate his awareness into this peak experience of sacred nature.

Heathens have also experienced hierophanies of nature. William Bainbridge, the Steersman and leader of the Troth from 1995–1999, drew upon the evocative language of nature worship to describe a mountain hike in Arizona. He framed his hike in religious ritual, the journey wrapped in layers of religious imagery from beginning to end. Before starting out up the mountain trail, Bainbridge poured a libation at the mountain's foot to venerate the land spirits that inhabited the place and when he reached the peak he prayed to *Jörð*, the Old Norse earth goddess. But in between those two points, it was the mountain itself that beguiled him. He described his encounter with the mountain in mythic terms as a metaphor for life and for the "Germanic soul." He felt a personal connection to it as an "old friend, and the divine giver of gifts." The hierophany, the ecstatic moment of his experience, came at the peak. As he spoke the words of Brynhildr's prayer, a break in the clouds suddenly opened up the mountain panorama. The clouds surrounding him appeared as the swirling mists of wyrd and when they parted, he saw the "snowy crags of three mighty peaks . . . ancient, brave and indomitable giants in formation . . . symbols of earth's grandeur, suddenly revealed in terrible majesty."[980] In that moment, the spiritual dimension of

---

978. Albanese, *Nature Religion in America*, 100.
979. Ibid., 101.
980. William Bainbridge, "Forest Ásatrú," in *Living the Troth,* 12. Brynhildr's prayer appears in *Sigrdrífumál*. See Larrington, "The Lay of Sigrdrifa," stanzas 3–4, in *The Poetic Edda*, 162–63.

the physical world was apparent to Bainbridge, the mountains revealing themselves as the giants, the jotuns of the Norse Lore. Caught up in the manifestation of sacred nature, Bainbridge felt welcomed by the mountain beings as a friend and awed by the "terrible majesty" of the vision that pierced through the wyrd to reveal the multidimensional fullness of the natural world.

The feeling of oneness or communion with nature apparent in Bainbridge's account is a familiar theme of nature spirituality. Thora had a similar experience during an outdoor ritual for the land spirits. Her kindred had performed rituals in the same outdoor space at a local park several times before. However, on this particular occasion she remembered being overwhelmed with a sense of the absolute beauty of the area, seeing it shimmer with intensity as if the landscape had come alive. She suddenly felt the presence of the land spirits, the personified beings that inhabited the park, but also experiencing the earth itself as awake and conscious and communicating to her in waves of emotion. She described the feeling as excitement, sensing that the spirits were "thrilled that we were there." At the same time, she felt a great sadness emanating from the spirits "because so few people ever experience it, appreciate the land in this way."[981] In some sense, both Thora's and Bainbridge's experiences of the numinous in nature recall Rudolph Otto's sense of *mysterium tremendum et fascinans*.[982] An encounter with the mystery and power of the numinous produces dread and awe, as well as fascination and bliss. Both felt at home in nature, drawn to the living earth as a majestic, welcoming presence. At the same time, in the raw power and cosmic scale of Bainbridge's hierophany, he felt the sense of wonder that humbles the human at the revelation of nature's sacred and majestic presence. In Thora's account, she felt overwhelmed by the yearning relational need of her experience, the terrible sadness that flooded through her in the presence of the Earth distraught and mourning the alienation of her human children.

This theme of majesty, fear, and awe in the presence of divine nature is recalled by Jorvik who like Bainbridge also sought out the mountains as a source of religious experience. Jorvik, a gothi in Colorado, planned a Thor ritual for the Yule season, which is

---

981. Thora, field notes taken by author, Kansas, September, 2012.
982. Rudolph Otto, *The Idea of the Holy* (New York: Oxford University Press, 1958), 12-13, 31-35.

celebrated during the month of December in America. Wanting to experience Thor in his ferocity, his kindred waited for a winter storm to blow in, then drove up into the mountains to hold a ritual in the midst of the weather, perhaps an example of religious fervor overriding practical sense. They went ahead with the plan but once in the mountains the snow-covered roads proved too much. The cars slid off the road into the deep drifts. Stuck in the fury of the alpine storm, they performed a short ritual but were then forced to hike out to find help. Jorvik recalled that the surprising, almost terrible, power of nature in the mountain blizzard was something for which even these Colorado residents were unprepared. It tested them and forced them to the limits of their endurance.[983] Here the storm's potentially deadly power revealed the *mysterium tremendum* of the human encounter with living nature. Otto described this as "creature-feeling," writing that "it is the emotion of a creature, submerged and overwhelmed by its own nothingness in contrast to that which is supreme above all creatures."[984] Otto's ideas about religious experience show their usefulness in describing the human response to the driving winter storm, revealing something of the fury of the Wild Hunt. But his sense of creature-feeling, arising as it did from his reading of biblical texts, seems to overstep the Heathen experience. As we have seen in chapter 4, Heathens emphasize the human relationship with nature, as part of nature, and would not usually describe it with Otto's stark dichotomy between "nothingness" and "supremacy." In each case, these experiences are set within a clear Heathen frame of reference, in which human beings share in a holy cosmos with the divine beings, jotuns, and land spirits. At the same time, they are shaped by the visions of nature tempered by two hundred years of American experience.

### *EcoSystemic Nature: Heathen Green Religion*

Some observers of the Pagan movement have argued that Paganism should be considered a nature religion because it exhibits an ecological consciousness. Harvey comments that Paganism "is fundamentally 'Green' in its philosophy and its practice."[985] Other observers of contemporary Paganism have shared similar sentiment,

---

983. Jorvik, field notes taken by author, Kansas, 2012.
984. Otto, *The Idea of the Holy*, 10.
985. Harvey, *Contemporary Paganism*, 126.

"seeing Nature as an expression of divinity means that Pagans naturally have an ecological awareness of the globe."[986] However, in some instances the common-sense correlation between earth-based religion and ecological practice fails to develop in lived religions.[987] In practice, nature religion is not always green religion. Albanese also clearly demonstrates that "environmental" or "ecological" religion is only one of many denominations of nature religion and a particularly modern strand at that. As Mark Stinson sees it, very few Asatruar exhibit a clear connection with an ecological version of nature religion: "Heathenry has no central organized dogma, no central authority, and thus there is a wide variety of beliefs on many topics. One such topic is environmentalism. Some Heathens are hard core environmentalists, some Heathens aren't, and every degree in between exists as well."[988] There is neither an environmental agenda nor an organized form of environmental religion common to all stripes of Heathenry. While this may be the case, green attitudes and inclinations are growing in Heathenry as more adherents work to develop an ecological consciousness to inform theology and practice. One example might be the members of Distelfink Sippschaft, the Urglaawe kindred in Pennsylvania mentioned in chapter 3, who have focused extensively on gardening, herbs, and natural remedies, combining nature and healing magic with green practices. At Trothmoot in 2012, the kindred led an informative and enjoyable nature walk around the campground, pointing out a surprising number of medicinal and edible plants along the way and discussing their properties and uses. For each participant, they put together a booklet containing a collection of plant specimens found on the walk (see figure 36). Over time, this kindred has begun to develop an ecological form of religion, including growing a pollinator-friendly flower and herb garden.

The Teal Party is a Heathen environmental initiative that originates with the Hrafnar Kindred led by Diana Paxson and Lorrie Wood. The Teal Party bases its environmentalism on a "new view of Ragnarok" that interprets the material from the Lore in an ecological

---

986. Dennis D. Carpenter, "Emergent Nature Spirituality: An Examination of the Major Spiritual Contours of the Contemporary Pagan Worldview," in *Magic Religion and Modern Witchcraft*, ed. James R. Lewis (Albany: State University of New York Press, 1996), 63.
987. Clifton, *Her Hidden Children*, 56–57.
988. Stinson, email.

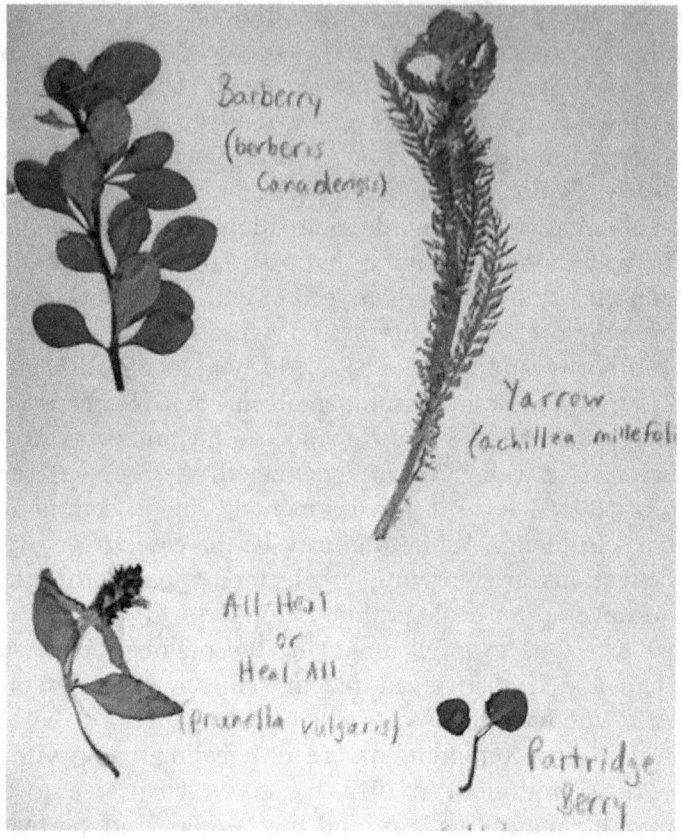

Figure 36. A Page from the Trothmoot Nature Walk Booklet. (Photo by the author.)

vein.[989] The account of Ragnarok derives primarily from the *Völuspá*, in which the god Odin summons a prophetess from her rest in order to acquire information from her. As their conversation develops, the völva gradually describes a cataclysmic event taking place at the end of the age. Thus Ragnarok, foreseen in the vision of the völva, is an apocalypse in both the original sense of revelation as well as in the more popular sense of a destructive end of the world.[990] The

---

989. Diana Paxson, and Lorrie Wood, "The Teal Party: A New View on Ragnarok," *Hrafnar*, www.hrafnar.org/about-us/teal-party/.

990. Catherine Wessinger, "Millennialism With and Without Mayhem," in *Millennium, Messiahs, and Mayhem: Contemporary Apocalyptic Movements*, ed. Thomas Robbins and Susan J. Palmer (New York: Routledge, 1997), 50.

## Nature Religion in Asatru 455

story unfolds in this way: Loki, often presented as the trickster god of Norse myth, has schemed to carry out the murder of Balder, Odin the All-Father's son and the most beautiful and beloved of the gods. For this crime he is perpetually bound, as are two of his progeny: a great sea serpent, Jǫrmungandr, who encircles the world at the bottom of the ocean and a terrible wolf, Fenris, whose great mouth has been muzzled. The giants of fire and ice are safely contained in their homelands by the vigilance of the gods, who hold in check the chaotic potential of the universe and tenuously maintain the cosmic order. However, a series of events unravels this precarious balance and unleashes the forces of chaos in the world. Fenriswolf and the world serpent break their bonds and the cosmos roils under their attack. Loki escapes his imprisonment and seeks his revenge against the gods, bringing with him the dead from the underworld. The *hrímþursar*, frost giants, sail in on a cosmic ship. Surtr, the fire giant, comes riding with the sons of Muspell across the Bifrost Bridge invading Asgard, the fortress abode of the gods. Heimdall, the guardian of Asgard, sounds a warning blast on his horn and the gods rush into battle with their armies of the valiant slain. In the ensuing clash the majority of gods are killed while vanquishing their enemies. The cosmos itself is saved but only at great cost. Snorri Sturluson, the thirteenth-century compiler of Norse myth, describes the cataclysm in classic apocalyptic language,

> The sun grows black, the earth sinks into the sea.
> The bright stars vanish from the heavens. Steam surges up and the fire rages.
> Heat reaches high against heaven itself.[991]

In the aftermath, a few young gods survive as well as two humans who take refuge within the world tree and live to repopulate an empty devastated world.

Paxson and Wood read the mythological descriptions of cataclysmic destruction as a warning about environmental collapse driven by global warming.[992] They describe the destructive giants of Norse myth, the þursar, as the "personified forces of nature" and see Ragnarok as an apocalyptic event in which the balance

---

991. Sturluson, *Gylfaginning*, chapter 51. See Sturluson, *The Prose Edda*, 75.
992. Paxson, and Wood, "The Teal Party."

of nature unravels resulting in worldwide environmental crisis. Current indices of global warming foretell the incipient disaster, giving rise to the Teal Party's other name "Gjallarhorn Alliance," which references the horn sounded by the god Heimdall at the outbreak of Ragnarok. The Teal Party seeks to raise awareness of the environmental crisis and call Heathens and other Pagans to action on behalf of the earth and its ecosystems. For Paxson and Wood, living an environmentally conscious Green life means to "stand by my gods" in the fight to delay the onset of Ragnarok's ecological crisis, imbuing ecological behavior with religious significance. The Teal Party advocates simple Green lifestyle adjustments such as buying locally grown food, shopping with reusable bags, and voting for environmentally conscious legislators. Paxson and Wood meld myth and science, using religious language to give significance to the scientific scenario of global warming. Recasting it in a mythological mode invigorates the Green lifestyle not merely as a type of moralism, but as a religious reorientation towards nature. The Teal Party is a good example of a green environmentally oriented nature religion calling for the kind of activist response that characterizes environmental Paganism.[993] However, the movement seems to have had little traction in producing an ecological awareness in the wider Heathen community. So while contemporary Heathenry provides a religious context that is conducive to the development of ecological consciousness, the practice of Green Heathenry remains limited to individuals and progressive kindreds such as Hrafnar.

Another example is the emerging ecological awareness of Stephen McNallen, former leader of the AFA. McNallen has come to promote Asatru as an environmental religion. In language similar to that of the Teal Party, he suggests that environmental collapse is a real possibility, "The unrestrained victory of the nihilistic force we call the giants would be the devastation of all that we know ... and would leave our planet lifeless. It follows, then, that one of the great tasks of Asatru in the years to come will be the preservation of Earth as a place hospitable to life ... including our Folk and all humankind."[994] McNallen calls for Heathens to adopt life-

---

993. For a definition of environmental Paganism, see David Chidester and Edward Tabor Linenthal, *American Sacred Space* (Bloomington: Indiana University Press, 1995), 99.

994. McNallen, *Asatru*, 184.

styles of recycling, reduce their carbon footprint, and engage in political activism on environmental issues. He goes on to suggest that Heathens should become early adopters of green technology and put themselves at the forefront of environmental practices such as organic gardening and energy-efficient home construction.[995] Like the Teal Party, McNallen's advocacy has yet to result in a widespread adoption of environmentalism in the Heathen movement. However, the fact that prominent and influential Heathens across the spectrum of Heathen life are engaging these issues may indicate the beginning of a groundswell and a cultural shift within the movement.

## Organic Biosocial Expressions of Nature

Earlier in this chapter, I introduced four constructions of nature described by Adrian Ivakhiv, one of which he identified as influential in Eastern Europe Paganism. This view, which I call an organic biosocial expression of nature, works with a set of ideas that most Western thinkers have pushed to the margins of discourse. In the modern West, individualized conceptions of human nature, civic notions of the state, and instrumental ecologies have largely replaced the notions of ethnic primordialism, collectivist ideas of the state and nation, and mystical ecologies found in this approach. Ivakhiv sums up the Eastern European construction of nature as a complex human–nature continuum in which "humans are not [perceived as] distinct from nature, but as culturally or ethnically 'rooted' within the natural world. Humans are seen less as a single, unified species, and more as inherently differentiated into blood-related collectivities that emerge out of specific histories of interaction with the natural environment."[996] Nature involves the land and its ethnos. The ethnos is a "tightly knit, biologically related community" united by a common ancestry, shared history, language, values, and customs. This people group is inseparably intertwined with its native homeland in a sacred relationship of care. Distinctive peoples and cultures are thought to grow organically from their interaction with the landscape, a process called ethnogenesis. The resulting native religious cultures maintained the powerful bond between the people and the land, integrating them into an organic whole.

995. Ibid., 189.
996. Ivakhiv, "Nature and Ethnicity," 195.

Ivakhiv is primarily interested in tracing the development of this organic biosocial view in Eastern Europe, particularly Ukraine. However, he notes that its origins lie in Western Europe. He suggests that it took shape in the mid-nineteenth century as the ecological thought of the German Ernst Haeckel fused with the earlier ethnic nationalist philosophy of the German philosopher Johann Gottfried von Herder.[997] Herder had described a mystic ethnic collective, the *Volk*, as a biosocial entity, "the carrier of traditions that emerged out of a close interaction with an environment." The concept of *Volk* laid the foundation for the human–nature relationship so important to emerging European nationalist thought.[998] This organic biosocial entity of land, people, and religion became formative for the "blood and soil" ecology of the German völkisch movement of the early twentieth century, as well as the Green fascism enunciated by some members of the Nazi government.[999] Excised from mainstream scientific and environmental thought in the West after World War II, ideologues of the Traditionalist movement and the New Right carried these ideas forward. Ivakhiv writes, "Neo-traditionalists and ethnic nationalists draw on the writing of Western European radical traditionalists, including René Guénon and Julius Evola, and on writers associated with the French Nouvelle Droite (New Right)."[1000] Evola, for instance, describes how the moral character of Aryan people evolved through their interaction with the rugged mountain

---

997. Ibid., 203–4.
998. Ibid., 203.
999. For more discussion of ecofacism in völkisch and German National Socialist contexts, see Brüggemeier, Cioc, and Zeller, *How Green Were the Nazis?* and Bramwell, *Blood and Soil*. Bramwell provides a sympathetic account of Richard Darré, who served as a Nazi official and Hitler's Minister of Agriculture for a time. She presents him as a champion of a nostalgic German agrarianism, valuing small-scale agriculture and the moral virtue of the landed peasantry. In Bramwell's view, Darré was a völkisch environmentalist, whose values ran counter to the destructive industrialism of the Nazi war machine. Most scholars contest this view and see Darré as much more complicit in Nazi ideology and war effort. Gesine Gerhard rejects the notion that Darré was primarily an environmentalist, arguing that "the racial 'renewal' of the German people, the elimination of the Jews, and the conquest of *Lebensraum* (living space) in eastern Europe for Germans," were foundational to his ideology. See Gesine Gerhard, "Breeding Pigs and People for the Third Reich," in *How Green Were the Nazis*, 130. Bramwell's approach attempts to distinguish völkisch ideals from Nazism, and in that way rescue the völkisch movement. A similar tactic is used by American Asatruar who legitimize völkisch sources by noting that the Nazis disliked and rejected völkisch Pagans.
1000. Ivakhiv, "Nature and Ethnicity," 209.

heights and cold northern climes of the European landscape. He writes that "if there is a natural environment that might encourage the emergence of an analogous inner form, this is the mountainous environment—especially those areas where great glaciers and high peaks are to be found."[1001]

The Native Faith movements of Eastern European are not the sole heirs of this ecological tradition. The view has a place in the spectrum of Heathen expressions of nature as well. An example is the ecology of the Odinic Rite, which expresses a deep affinity for the English countryside and a sense of protective stewardship over its sacred sites. The OR sees England as the land of the Folk, manifesting a sort of mystic attachment to the land expressed in the Odinic ideal of "odal" lands. One member of the Odinic Rite states that their aim is "to bring Odin's folk back in touch with the land. Our land. The Odal lands."[1002] The term, from the Old Norse óðal, referred to property held by inheritance, the "homestead of the original settler," a freeholding unbeholden to any social superior.[1003] Among the Odinist community, odal lands call to mind the longing for a homeland, the organic connection between an ethnicity group and its ancestral land, the landscape in which the ethnic identity is rooted.

In the context of American Heathenry, these ideas moved from the völkisch/Traditionalist tributary through Odinism and into the thought of folkish Asatruar. While decidedly a minority perspective, McNallen's framing of Heathenry as a "native European religion" is profoundly indebted to organic biosocial ideas about nature. His theory of metagenetics, discussed in chapter 3, attempts to redefine contemporary white Americans as an organic biosocial ethnicity, linked by genetics to a Heathen religious culture and its Northern European homeland. In his essay "No More Mutts," McNallen makes an argument based in a Herderian view of ethnogenesis, "We are fundamentally indigenous Europeans. We may have migrated around the world, but our homeland is Europe. Its rugged environment shaped our bodies, our minds, and our souls; it is a

---

1001. Julius Evola, *Meditations on the Peaks: Mountain Climbing as a Metaphor for the Spiritual Quest* (Rochester, VT: Inner Traditions, 1998), 32.

1002. Redwald, "Live—Breathe—Grow," *Odinic Rite: Odinism for the Modern World*, March 18, 2012, www.odinic-rite.org/main/live-breathe-grow/.

1003. *Oxford English Dictionary Online*, s.v "udal, n.," www.oed.com.

part of us, and we are a part of it, forever."[1004] This human-nature interrelationship is furthered strengthened by the native religion that links the land and people together. He goes on to state that "folk religions—native religions, indigenous religions, whatever you want call them—are inherently linked to a particular cultural and biological group . . . a people."[1005] Thus for McNallen, nature consists of the unity of land, people, and the sacred customs that bind them together—a view entirely consistent with Herder's conception of *Volk*. Of course, this perspective is out of step with the rest of American ecological thought. So McNallen also turns to another source to support his perspective: Native American traditions, particularly Vine Deloria, Jr., the Native American theologian and activist. As we saw earlier, Catherine Albanese described a Native American construction of nature that has similarities to the organic biosocial model in its sense of a people group embedded in a sacred land to which they are bound through their primal sacred customs. Deloria describes Native American religion in similar terms, writing that "most tribal religions make no pretense as to their universality or exclusiveness. They came to the Indian community in the distant past and have always been in the community as a distinct social and cultural force. They integrate the respective communities as particular people chosen for particular religious knowledge and experiences."[1006] He emphasizes the importance of the ethnically defined community, a tribe or a people, and its exclusive right to its own native culture. Deloria published *God is Red* just as McNallen was emerging as a religious leader, and the book contributed to his understanding of folkishness. Throughout his career, McNallen has referenced Deloria as a touchstone to bring legitimacy to his own metagenetic perspective.

The organic biosocial construction of nature is particularly difficult for most American Heathens, who recognize their lack of native connection to North America. As we saw in chapter 3, McNallen had hoped that Kennewick Man would provide a link to the primal American past, substantiating a claim of indigeneity for white Americans. More recently, McNallen and other folkish

---

1004. McNallen, "No More Mutts."
1005. Stephen A. McNallen, "The Nature of Folk Religion," in *The Philosophy of Metagenetics*, 1.
1006. Vine Deloria, Jr., *God Is Red: A Native View of Religion* (Golden, CO: Fulcrum, 2003 [1973]), 210.

Heathens have proposed a sort of "re-indigenizing" project. By "sinking our roots into the soil," American Heathens can become a new indigenous ethnicity. McNallen takes up this theme in his essay "Wotan vs. Tezcatlipoca," arguing that, "we must sink down roots into the soil, and insist on our right to be here . . . Our forebears fought and died to carve out this place in the world, and we will not give it up."[1007] In later writings, he develops these thoughts more thoroughly, describing a vision for a new Heathen ethnicity deeply integrated with the land. These ethno-religious communities would buy and share land, establishing themselves on new homelands through farming, shared religious practice at multigenerational sacred sites, evolving a tribal thew of Germanic customs and laws, and creating a "burial place for our dead."[1008] Of all these recommendations, the creation of Heathen burial places in these tracts of Heathen land is most telling. Nothing links a people to a land more powerfully than the inhumation of their dead. Reading into McNallen's perspective, I suppose that when future archaeologists dig in North America and find Heathen burials, the link of indigeneity will be complete.

## Symbols of Nature

Heathens have many ways of encountering and venerating nature. Some Heathens encounter the gods and other spiritual beings in nature; others work with the animistic powers of plants and their spiritual and healing qualities. Many find sources of power within natural holy places, while others seek out esoteric interpretations and magical experiences of nature. Others gravitate toward the use of natural materials in handicrafts. In addition, Heathens utilize symbols of nature. For instance, the sun wheel, consisting of a circle with two internal crossbars, is a symbol used throughout Asatru (see figure 37). It is an ancient symbol associated with the sun's movement, fertility, and power, and found on rune stones and petroglyphs in Northern Europe.[1009] At East Coast Thing 2012, ritual leaders fashioned harvest garlands from straw and set them up on poles during the land-taking ceremony, a ritual done to hallow the

---

1007. McNallen, "Wotan vs. Tezcatlipoca."
1008. McNallen, *Asatru*, 188.
1009. Davidson, *Gods and Myths*, 82; Davidson, *Myths and Symbols*, 166.

campground for the weekend. Participants placed garlands, shaped like sunwheels, at the four corners of the camp while scattering birdseed and bread as offerings to the land spirits (see figure 38). Nigel Pennick points out that these circular harvest garlands displayed on poles are also reminiscent of ᛃ, the "J" rune, *jera, preserved in the Old English futhorc as gēr, referring to the harvest or year.[1010] The sun wheel also figured prominently in rituals for the god Thor performed in Kansas on the fall equinox. The rituals were held in the morning just as the sun rose on the last day of Lightning Across the Plains. The gothi brought a wooden sun wheel around the circle of participants, each of whom said a few quiet words, a prayer, traced a rune, or meditated over the wheel for a few moments before passing it on. In the ritual held in 2011, the gothi ceremonially placed the wreath on the altar in the camp's central vé, or sacred place. In the 2012 ritual, the wreath was placed on the central fire and burned as an offering for the god.

Figure 37. The Sun Wheel. (Image used with artist's permission.)

1010. Nigel Pennick, *The Complete Illustrated Guides to the Runes* (Boston: Element Books, 1999), 55.

The sun wheel is not the only, nor even the main symbol in Asatru. It exists side by side with a host of other symbols: nature symbols such as the raven, anthropomorphic images of the gods, and cultural symbols such as the drinking horn. Perhaps the most important is the symbol of Mjolnir, Thor's hammer, found ubiquitously in contemporary Asatru and frequently worn on a necklace by adherents as a symbol of their faith. While nature is not the only symbolic center of Asatru, the movement does make significant use of symbols drawn from a Traditionalist type of nature religion. As Albanese writes, "Nature provides a language to express cosmology and belief; it forms the basis for understanding and practicing a way of life; it supplies materials for ritual

Figure 38. Harvest Garland at East Coast Thing. (Photo by the author.)

symbolization; it draws together a community."[1011] What does the sun wheel mean to contemporary Heathens? It is, first of all, not a modern symbol, a tribute to commercialism, or some other cultural artifact of modernity, but a symbol significant to the arch-Heathens. It is an ancient symbol drawn from the tributary of Norse culture connecting contemporary Heathens to an imagined ancestral past. Second, the sun wheel signifies the power of life in nature, connecting Heathens to the cycles of nature and the sun itself, the direct experience of sacred nature.

In Asatru, several of the major holidays are agricultural and earth-based as well as solar in their orientation, fitting for a religion that originally developed in a northern climate where the longest and shortest days are dramatically different. However, most Heathens follow a seasonal ritual calendar that retains the structure of the Wiccan Wheel of the Year. Stephen McNallen first adapted and introduced this Heathen Wheel of the Year based on the four solar quarters, rather than alignment with the religious observances noted in the Lore or the seasonality of the Scandinavian north.[1012] Midsummer recognizes the summer solstice and Yule, the winter solstice; Ostara is celebrated as a major holiday around the spring equinox, while Haustblot, referring to a "harvest sacrifice," is held around the autumn equinox, late September in the northern hemisphere and celebrated as Mabon by most Pagans. Meanwhile, the cross-quarter days are named for other holidays more agricultural in nature: Charming of the Plow is also commonly referred to as Dísablot, involving a sacrifice to the female ancestors; May Day, or Walpurgisnacht; Freyfaxi at the beginning of August; and Winter Nights, a harvest festival in late October around the time of Samhain, round out these holidays. This pattern of holidays has the advantage of being widely recognized by Pagans, and therefore very accessible to many who come into Asatru from these traditions, and conforming to something like a shared

---

1011. Albanese, *Nature Religion in America*, 155–56.

1012. McNallen has consistently identified his calendar as the "Wheel of the Year" that it best fits with the "broad sweep of native European religious tradition." He considers it a better alternative to a calendar pieced together from "the historical bits and scraps available to us from European prehistory" or a more historical Icelandic calendar that "recognized only two seasons" and "had little to do with the ordering of things in England or on the Continent." Stephen A. McNallen, *The Rituals of Asatru: Volume 2 – Seasonal Festivals* (Payson, AZ: World Tree Publications, 1985), 2; and McNallen, *Asatru*, 150–58.

Pagan "holiday season." The calendar is also earth-based, aligning religious observance, human work, and internal psycho-emotional states to the changes in nature and the seasons. Thus, the calendar establishes a basis for an earth-centered Heathenry oriented toward the sacredness of nature.

It will come as no surprise that some Heathens resist, or are at least uncomfortable with, the idea of a Wiccan-derived ritual calendar. One writes,

> If you were to go back in time and show this calendar to a Viking Era worshiper of Odin, they would have no idea what you were talking about. The ancient Norse didn't base their year on the solstices and equinoxes, and a number of these holidays are actually Christian celebrations with a Heathen veneer on them. For example, Walpurgisnacht is the celebration of a Christian Saint, not a Heathen festival. Again, this is not to say that those who use this calendar are somehow wrong, or bad, just that the calendar itself has nothing at all to do with any ancient Heathen traditions.[1013]

Critical observations such as these raise the question of how Heathens can authentically respond to these felt tensions. Douglas Ezzy, writing about Australian Paganism, has observed several different responses to received calendars that are pertinent to the Heathen situation.[1014] Wicca and Witchcraft came into the Australian context from Europe, bringing with it a northern hemispheric Wheel of the Year. This set up a disconcerting misalignment between the calendar and the seasons as they are actually experienced in the southern hemisphere. Beyond inverting the northern hemispheric calendar, Ezzy notes two more sophisticated approaches taken by these southern hemisphere witches. "These adaptations moved in two directions," he notes. "First, they became more localized, attuned to the seasons and 'nature' of where practitioners lived. The second trend was toward a greater sensitivity to the European folklore and traditions that nurtured Pagan practice."[1015]

---

1013. Xander Folmer, "Ranting Recon: What Are the Heathen Holidays?" *Huginns Heathen Hof*, April 28, 2016, www.heathenhof.com/ranting-recon-what-are-the-heathen-holidays/.

1014. Douglas Ezzy, "Cosmopolitan Witchcraft: Reinventing the Wheel of the Year in Australian Paganism," in *Cosmopolitanism, Nationalism, and Modern Paganism*, ed. Kathryn Rountree (New York: Palgrave Macmillan, 2017), 201–19.

1015. Ibid., 211.

Like these Southern Hemisphere witches, Heathens who felt that the Wiccan calendar did not work well for them have utilized two of these approaches. The first involved accepting the received calendar while making minor changes to align it with one's practice. Like inverting the calendar in Australia, Heathens have generally adopted the Wheel of the Year model, retro-fitting it with Heathen-specific names for the holidays and incorporating Heathen-style rituals. As the movement has matured, some Heathens have taken the second approach of looking with increased rigor at the "folklore and traditions" that nurtured Heathen practice, namely the Lore, and deriving a Heathen calendar from those sources. Xander Folmer's calendar, published on the Huginn's Heathen Hof blog, organizes the year around the three major annual sacrifices mentioned in *Ynglinga Saga*. These blóts include Sigrblót held on April 21 to open the summer season with an offering to Frey; Alfarblót, held on the first day of winter, October 22, as a harvest celebration in the homestead; and Jól or Yule associated primarily with Odin and held, according to his reading of the Lore, on November 21. The common practice of celebrating Jól in December came about during the Conversion Period, he suggests, when the original date was changed to coincide with Christmas.[1016] Around these main events, Folmer includes other holidays: þorrablót, a mid-winter sacrifice celebrated on January 22; Góublót, a sacrifice for wives and other important women on February 21; Midsummer observance, held on the summer solstice, June 20 or 21; and Dísablót, the sacrifice for female ancestors held either at the beginning or end of the winter season according to different sources.

There is much to be admired about this work as it exemplifies the value given both to the Lore and to the acquisition of historical knowledge in American Heathenry. But in either approach, nature takes on an idealized or stylized façade, either as nature idealized in the Wiccan Wheel of the Year or an Old Norse blót calendar. What has been less evident is the first response described by Ezzy: the adaptation of the religious calendar to localized experiences of nature, structuring time and religious observance around the lived experience of nature in the practitioners' vicinity. For most Heathens, the regularity of the stylized calendars works better. Since few Asatruar live in agricultural communities or pursue

---

1016. Folmer, "Ranting Recon: What Are The Heathen Holidays?"

agricultural professions, there is little need for increased sensitivity to local cycles of nature. These idealized earth-based holidays allow for a more abstract approach to nature and the flexibility to take on the intonations of modern suburban life. While these may be types of genuine nature-oriented practice, they do not exemplify ecological or bioregional approaches to nature religion.

Local adaptations are occurring, however, on the individual and kindred levels. For the most part, they involve slight adjustments of the dates on which celebrations occur. For instance, Ale Glad exemplifies this approach when he writes about Winter Nights:

> For me, I aim for something that fits my lifestyle. I know that in the South East there is still more time to harvest the remaining crops and in some areas where apple orchards are common, they would normally be working to get things in before it gets much cooler. This year has seen a rather mild September after an early warming. This has thrown things off a little, but so goes the world. Now, you'll notice I didn't say it was cold yet, but we have had a few night time lows under 60°F. This is the key reason that I don't celebrate Haustblót and Vetrnætr at the same time. I prefer to put Winter Night near the end of October, which is when it looks like it would have been. By then, we will be feeling the coming of winter.[1017]

In this statement, Ale Glad tries to balance the received calendar with both the Lore and the realities of his local weather. He wants to situate Winter Nights "when it looks like it would have been," acknowledging historical accuracy and the Lore. Yet he also takes into account the importance of lived experience, associating the holiday with "feeling the coming of winter." These sorts of considerations and the willingness to alter practice away from tight applications of the Lore could allow groups of Heathens to evolve in the direction of bioregional, earth-based practice.

### Nature and Heathen Sacred Space

As we have seen, the animistic aspects of the Asatru cosmology lend a sense of sanctity to the whole cosmos. The world is full of sacred beings and Heathens stand in the midst of the holy without a sense

---

1017. Ale Glad, "Haustblót 2012," *An Ásatrú Blog: Exploring the Northern Troth*, September 22, 2012, www.asatrublog.com/2012/09/22/haustblot-2012/.

of division between physical and spiritual, ordinary and sacred worlds. Midgard stands as a hub between the realms, through which divine beings pass and energies flow through the material world. An action as simple as chanting a rune is thought to direct, attract, and focus the numinous energy already present and circulating in the world. Any drinking horn hallowed through a simple prayer, or a rune chanted or traced above it becomes a portal into the Well of Wyrd. Norse mythology describes bridges and gates linking the Nine Worlds of the cosmic multiplex. These features serve not as obstacles to accessing those realities but as connective apparati that facilitate travel among the worlds. Thus within Asatru cosmology, there is a great sense of openness to spiritual realities and little sense of separation from them.

Space, set apart and sacralized, provides a religious axis around which the world turns, "an opening to the holy or divine, a place where communication with sacred power is made possible."[1018] Sacred space provides an organizing center for a religious community and becomes a symbol for its identity. While long-standing American religious traditions may have recognized religious spaces, new religions face the important challenge of creating and establishing new sacred spaces that are authentic and functional. Like other forms of Paganism, Heathens often look to the natural world for sacred spaces where the divine can be experienced. The most basic manifestation of this instinct may be the fact that Heathens and other Pagans frequently meet and hold rituals outdoors, drawn towards nature as the context closest to the sacred.[1019] Heathens regularly hold blóts and fainings outdoors and any natural space, briefly sanctified, is suitable for a ritual even during inclement weather such as a thunderstorm or a cold Yule night.

Most Heathen kindreds will have some local outdoor space set aside for ritual use. At the same time, they look for significant aspects of landscape as indications of energy and power. In doing so, Heathens distinguish between places of more or less spiritual power. Not all outdoor spaces are equal. Diana Paxson underscores this when she compares Old World sacred sites in Europe to the temporary sacred spaces of American Asatru,

---

1018. James C. Livingston, *Anatomy of the Sacred: An Introduction to Religion* (New York: Macmillan, 1989), 56.
1019. Pike, *New Age and Neopagan Religions*, 32.

If you go to a spot that is already a European sacred place, the energy levels are there waiting to be tapped. And you get "whoosh" [indicating a rush of spiritual energy] and if you are used to taking any old piece of ground in the US and making it your sacred space and raising your energy and so forth, you get more than you anticipate.[1020]

Adherents make these sorts of distinctions in the American context as well. Significant landscape features indicate the presence of potentially sacred and powerful space. In Pennsylvania, both Der Heidevolkstamm and Distelfink Sippenschaft kindreds identified the local mountain Hexenkopf as a sacred place.[1021] The significant presence of the Rocky Mountains represents spiritual power for the Fimbul Winter kindred located in Colorado. When Jotun's Bane Kindred in the Midwest was seeking a location for ritual, they found it beneath the largest oak tree in a nearby Pagan campground. The tree, named *Forn Halr*, the Old Man, by the kindred, is accessible by means of a narrow path winding through the forest's edge.[1022] The path opens into a small clearing where benches and a stone altar have been set up beneath the tree. In the massive girth of its trunk and the spread of its branches, Forn Halr embodies the dignity and wisdom of its years and is recognized as an elder spirit being by the kindred. The tree stands witness to the rituals held under its canopy, representing not only the sentience and soulfulness of the animistic natural world, but a safe and welcoming space within nature for the Heathen community. It functions to symbolize and actualize a new type of relationship between nature and contemporary Heathens, reminiscent of the guardian tree custom found in German and Scandinavian tradition.[1023] These notable instances, as well as the countless backyard shrines and spaces of Heathen adherents, exemplify the Pagan notion that the visible and invisible are linked, "In traditional polytheistic cultures, aesthetic appreciation of nature is inseparable from awareness of the sacred in the landscape; special beauty means that the spot is the abode of a god or gods."[1024] The natural world itself is alive with divinity. While Larson points out that natural beauty is often a marker of this

---

1020. Paxson, interview.
1021. Schreiwer, *A Brief Introduction to Urglaawe*, 11.
1022. Stinson, *Heathen Gods*, 152.
1023. Davidson, *Myths and Symbols*, 170.
1024. Larson, "Land Full of Gods," 58.

concentration of spiritual power within the landscape, beauty is not the only category of aesthetic appeal. Any exceptional feature of the landscape might indicate to the Pagan observer that spiritual power is present.

For the most part, Heathens have created sacred spaces by utilizing temporary space and creating movable rituals. In an insightful article, Carolyn Prorok describes several other methods by which religious groups create sacred space in contexts where none currently exist.[1025] While she focuses on the transplanted pilgrimage traditions of American Catholicism and Hinduism, her findings are particularly applicable to Heathenry. Heathenry is simultaneously a new religion as well as a "transplanted" religion. Its sacred origin is European, its sacred stories take place in Europe, and sites with religious significance to Heathens are still extant throughout Europe. Prorok discusses two strategies that find little support in Heathenry: "co-opting indigenous sacred sites," and "replicating homeland sites" in the new context.[1026] Asatru adherents may recognize the significance of indigenous American Indian sites but dispute or reject their relevance as sacred places to Asatru. This strategy has been entangled in the debate surrounding the issue of cultural appropriation, which is regarded by most of the Pagan community as "stealing" someone else's cultural property and generally avoided for that reason.[1027] The replication of homeland sites strategy is exemplified in the practice of some groups of the Hindu diaspora who construct religious sites to resemble the ancient temples and sacred landscapes of India. Similarly, American Christian groups may indicate significant sacred sites by constructing European-style cathedrals. However, I know of few examples of this strategy in contemporary American Heathenry. While Heathens certainly borrow historical cultural features such as clothing, objects, words, and aesthetic elements as part of a Heathen "style," or a Norse "feel," this does not amount to "recreating" an authentic Icelandic model. Heathens seem uninterested in creating a miniature Þingvellir, rebuilding a working model of the Pagan temple at Uppsala, or investing in a Viking theme park!

---

1025. Carolyn V. Prorok, "Transplanting Pilgrimage Traditions in the Americas," *Geographical Review* 93 (2003), 292–94.
1026. Ibid., 288, 291.
1027. Pike, *Earthly Bodies*, 124–25.

The strategy of pilgrimage, which uses travel to connect with the sacred sites of the original religious homeland, is more visibly part of the American Heathen experience.[1028] Pilgrimage is a viable, if underutilized, possibility in American Asatru.[1029] Numerous sites connected to pre-Christian Norse and Germanic Paganism are still extant in Europe such as Þingvellir in Iceland, Old Uppsala in Sweden, runestones throughout Scandinavia, megalithic sites in Great Britain, as well as numerous archaeological finds throughout Europe. A few Heathens have made pilgrimage-like journeys to Europe and have documented those trips in various ways. For instance, Victoria Clare, who served as Steer of the Troth from 2010–2013, described a trip to her ancestral country of Norway in an article published in the organization's journal *Idunna*.[1030] Kari Tauring explores her significant spiritual involvement with the Scandinavian, particularly Norwegian, landscape on her album *Nykken & Bear* as well as in other articles.[1031] In his book *Heathen Gods*, Mark Stinson reflected upon a trip with one of his kindred members to Iceland. The trip included a visit to Þingvellir, the volcanic plain where the pre-Christian Viking society of Iceland held their annual parliament.[1032] At Þingvellir, Stinson and his friend performed a blót, raising horns filled with consecrated mead, the sacred drink of Heathens, and calling upon the gods and land spirits. They dedicated their own Heathen work in America to the gods and left offerings (brought from America) for the Icelandic land-vaettir. The intentional religious nature of their activities implies that they treated the visit as a pilgrimage. Similarly, comments made on

---

1028. Prorok, "Transplanting," 289–90.

1029. An exception may be the Odinic Rite, which because of its trans-Atlantic structure and membership remains actively involved with Old World sites in Britain, such as the White Horse Stone megalith in Kent. OR members have been active in preservation efforts regarding the stone. The stone serves as a place of memory, pilgrimage, and ritual, "The stone is a sacred place for Odinists and people have travelled from around the world to make oaths, get handfasted (married), or to scatter the ashes of loved ones." See "About the White Horse Stone," *Guardians of the White Horse Stone*, www.whitehorsestone.org/.

1030. Victoria Clare, "Norge 2008!" *Idunna*, no. 80 (2009): 5–15.

1031. Kari Tauring, *Nykken and Bear*, Omnium Records, 2013, CD OMM2109. See also Tauring, "In the Footsteps of My Mothers."

1032. Stinson, *Heathen Gods*, 176. See also Jesse Byock, "The Icelandic Althing: Dawn of Parliamentary Democracy," in *Heritage and Identity: Shaping the Nations of the North*, ed. J. M. Fladmark (Donhead St. Mary, Shaftesbury: The Heyerdahl Institute and Robert Gordon University, 2002), 1–18.

Facebook and other online sites by American Heathens indicate an interest in pilgrimage to the Ásatrúarfélagið's temple in Iceland, once it is constructed.

Despite these exemplary experiences, most American Heathens seem curiously unattached to European sacred sites. For instance, American Heathens do not turn to the northeast when praying or performing blót in order to recognize the sanctity of the aboriginal homeland. Nor do they mention these sites in their invocations, such as the invocation "Next year in Jerusalem!" that caps the Jewish Passover. Rather, their eyes and emotions are connected fully to sites in their own local American context. There is just no overriding sense that a pilgrimage strategy is important or necessary for a fully expressed Heathenry. At a meeting of the American Academy of Religion, I was asked how Asatru can be practiced in the United States since the gods are in Scandinavia. But the answer is that American Heathens do not feel that the gods are in Scandinavia, nor is their spirituality connected to specific Old World sites. These gods are as mobile as their worshipers and connection with them is possible throughout the sacred cosmos.[1033] Many adherents express a strong desire for more permanent sacred spaces for Heathenry. Many of these are already taking shape in the American landscape, such as the camps, shrines, backyard horgs, and indoor altars that are recognized by Heathen kindreds.[1034] A prominent example was the purchase of land and the opening of a hof in 2016 by the Asatru Folk Assembly, which was hailed by some Heathens as the first permanent Heathen temple in the United States. On their Indiegogo fundraising page, the AFA described their achievement by proudly announcing, "This is a historic event. There has been no temple, shrine, or other structure like this in almost a thousand years. It is a hallmark in the revival of our indigenous European faith!"[1035]

While many of these sites orient Heathens toward the natural world, the instinct to find the sacred in nature is balanced by the special significance Heathens give to the indoors. At times, indoor space can have significant religious symbolism. Perhaps because the

---

1033. The Icelandic sagas reflect this idea of divine mobility. When Norse settlers first came to Iceland, they brought their gods with them without any sense of cognitive dissonance or religious complication.

1034. Marek, interview; Prorok, "Transplanting," 291–92.

1035. "NewGrangeHall – AsatruHof," *Indiegogo*, www.indiegogo.com/projects/newgrange-hall-asatru-hof#/.

severe northern climate in which Norse religion developed made indoor space vital to human survival, the indoor experience as a place of warmth, comfort, and blessing was encoded into religious experience. Nature outdoors, wild nature, is in tension with nature indoors, the social nature of human civilization. We have seen how during the sumbel ritual, contemporary Heathen religiosity involves leaving the wild and going into the innangarð, the cultivated protected space of human culture. The garð, or enclosure, is a type of safe space that offers protection from the potential hostilities of wild nature, a place to escape from nature. The garð of the gods is built to provide protection from "mountain trolls and frost giants," i.e. the hostile elements of wild nature.[1036] According to the Lore, the enclosure proved its worth on several occasions, such as when a blazing fire lit at the walls of Asgard stopped the giant þjazi.[1037] The space of human habitation, especially the hall where the local community gathered, functioned as the sacred microcosm signifying the human/divine cooperation that maintained order in Midgard. Instances of synthesis between outdoor and indoor nature emphasize this sacred role of human habitation. King Völsung's hall, in the middle of which a great tree grew, is a powerful cosmological symbol of the world of human habitation in relationship to or as an extension of the world tree, Yggdrasil.[1038] These ideas of innangarð, what lies within the enclosure, and útangarð, what lies outside of the enclosure, are rich terms carrying ethical and social significance. They may also have important implications for a American Heathen approach to ecology.

## Latent Ecological Implications Within Heathenry

The elements of instability and danger inherent in life give rise to a pair of important ethical concepts in Asatru: innangarð and útangarð. Derived from the agricultural basis of Norse society and the layout of Icelandic farmsteads, the innangarð represents that which was within the farmstead boundary: the farmhouse, barns, and fields representing orderly human society regulated by law and

---

1036. Sturluson, *Gylfaginning*, chapter 42, in *The Prose Edda*, 50.
1037. Sturluson tells the story of *þjazi*, the powerful shape-shifting jǫtun, in *Skaldskaparmal*, chapter 1, in *The Prose Edda*, 82.
1038. Cusack, *Sacred Tree*, 154.

custom. The innangarð also represented the boundaries of the moral community, defining those toward whom its human occupants must exercise care and ethical consideration. The land that lay between the farmsteads was wild land, útangarð, consisting of everything beyond the boundary fence: the wild, forces and beings potentially disorderly and disruptive.[1039] Recognizing wildness and instability as the basic state of the cosmos, Heathens seek to establish innangarð, sacred spaces of order and community. If the cosmos is primarily útangarð, a concept with which the English philosopher Thomas Hobbes might agree, then humans must build these enclosures of society and custom that hold disorder at bay and prevent the cosmos from destabilizing. In doing so, humans emulate the gods who have established Asgard, literally the "enclosure of the gods," as a fortress of order, light, and culture bulwarking the holy community against the elemental forces of chaos represented by the giants. Similarly, Midgard itself, the realm of human beings in the cosmos, is set apart as an enclosure suitable for orderly human life. This religious emphasis on achieving and maintaining order differs significantly from worldviews associated with a type of contemporary Pagan experience that advocates escaping order, at least temporarily, and losing oneself in ecstatic wildness. Unlike this sort of search for liminal experience, the Heathen ethic is one of order creation, a more conservative tendency. If a stereotypical image of Paganism is one of individuals dancing ecstatically around a fire in the night, the image of Asatru is of an orderly community gathered together and sitting at the family table. Within the wilderness of útangarð, boundaries of orderly habitation are maintained through the cooperation of divine and human effort.

This vision has important implications for the way the Norse tradition thought about nature and wildness. The wild was, on one hand, a place to be ventured into to prove one's mettle, to obtain resources, and perhaps to be colonized for new human habitation. On the other hand, it was the domain of immensely powerful and dangerous spiritual entities.[1040] These beings are formidable enough to challenge the gods themselves. For instance, during Thor's journeys through the wild, he has a frightening encounter in the darkness of night with the jotun Skrýmir, whose snore was like an

---

1039. Wódening, *We Are Our Deeds*, 2.
1040. Ibid., 5.

earthquake and whose glove seemed to Thor and his companions like a large cave in which they sheltered for the night.[1041] Symbolized by this tremendous and unpredictable being, the wild represents a place of potential danger, where unexpected encounters might prove deadly. Wild nature was regarded as powerful and uncontrollable, something that must be approached with caution and skill, boldness and luck. At the same time, it is important to recognize that the innangarð consisted of more than buildings and indoor spaces. It also included nature, specifically nature that had been claimed and put to human uses. The innangarð may also have included zones of wild, small spaces that were set apart as "no man's land," ground left untilled and untouched, apportioned and guarded as habitat for the land spirits.[1042] This preservation of small wild spaces demonstrates an innovative Norse use of religion as a form of hospitality for wild nature within the zone of human utilization.

## A Heathen Land Ethic

The concepts carry two important implications for a contemporary Heathen environmental ethic. First, they seek to balance the sacred wild with the hallowedness of human use. Recalling Thoreau's experience of walking into nature, dark green religion commonly looks for the holy outside of civilization, in the wilderness sublime. In contrast to cultivated space, the wild is a place of spiritual potential. But in Heathen nature religion, it is the boundaries of innangarð, domesticated space, which is first recognized as holy. The homestead, which is at once a natural place as well as the site of human work, is the place where blessing is experienced. The cultivation of nature within limits, the garð, provides a place for human thriving, in which the blessings of the gods are found and made available. Human work is not seen as perverting or destroying the sanctity of nature, but a type of cooperative involvement in which the fertile potentiality of nature is turned, adapted, made use of for human good.

The second implication has to do with the recognition of human limits. The boundary simply marked the end of human work, the extent of the land of which one family could make productive use.

---

1041. Sturluson, *The Prose Edda*, 55.
1042. Pennick, "Heathen Holy Places," 139.

But this boundary is porous: humans go into the wild and the human community accommodates and preserves the wild in its midst. The value of hospitality marks the human relationship with the wild: the vé, the corner of the garden left untilled, the holy spot roped off from human use, invites the wild and its untamed spirits into the innangarð. As a religious domain, the vé recognizes nature as more than a resource for human use. Nature is not wholly given over to human dominion. Instead, the limits of human use are marked. The garð should not only be understood as a barrier to prevent the wild from encroaching, but also as a barrier against human expansion and degradation of nature, the recognition that human activity must have limits. The innangarð mediates human interaction with wild holy powerful untamable nature. It stakes a claim against the possibility that nature will sweep away the tenuous human perch on the edge of a windswept fjord. It also protects nature against the spilling over of human hubris.

## The Innangarð as Bioregion

The environmental application of these concepts is suited to the development of a bioregional ethic within Heathenry. Bioregionalism is an ecological approach that recognizes the need for human communities to live in harmony with the specific characteristics of their local ecosystem. The local food movement, which seeks to eat locally grown foods in season, is one example of a bioregional practice. Bioregionalism, at its root, suggests that human communities have specific habitats. Whereas American Anglo-European modernity has marshaled the power of technology to suppress the constraining limitations of these bioregions on human lifestyles, a truly ecological approach recognizes that a long-term sustainable lifestyle must abide within the capacities and characteristics of the local ecosystem. The concept of innangarð, as a localized and defined network of relationships, has much in common with the concept of ecosystem or bioregion. In contrast to the generalized abstraction of "Mother Earth," it is precisely the specificity of the innangarð and the localized nature of Heathen concern that enables Asatru to accommodate a bioregional approach. One only needs to define the local ecosystem as innangarð, as the location of ethical concern and the limit of human activity. The result would be a religious bioethic of place and community linking humans and their local ecosystem, a Heathen bioregional approach to the environment.[1043] McNallen's language resonates with this approach, "We must intimately know the land, plants, animals, and weather of the place we inhabit. We will learn to listen to the unspoken wisdom of these places," he writes.[1044] While we need to be cautious of the "blood and soil" echoes of völkisch thought, it is also fair to note the bioregional outlook that informs his environmentalism.[1045]

Regionalism already influences the emerging cultures of American Heathenry. As I visited different parts of the country during my fieldwork, the regional distinctiveness of Heathen communities, from food to ritual practices, was clearly noticeable. Heathens increasingly recognize and celebrate these regional distinctions and think about the contours of Heathen life in regional ways.[1046] For instance, an episode of Raven Radio, a popular Heathen radio show, noted the inclusion of the chili pepper into the Heathen celebrations and feasts of many kindreds in the Southwest.[1047] During a discussion that focused on the distinctive ritual approaches and customs that have developed among regions of Heathenry, someone pointed out, "Look at what we do here in the Southwest . . . we celebrate around food, our traditional food. That is our norm here. There is always something hot in our blót, our feast." In contrast, when I shared in the feast at a Heathen gathering in Minnesota, there was not a chili to be found. The distinctively German and Scandinavian dishes had been prepared from recipes passed down in those families and reflected the culture of the region. While the basic format of the blót and sumbel remained similar, these differing cuisines demonstrate the developing sense of regionalism. Whether this religious and cultural regionalism might grow into an ecological approach remains to be seen. Despite Taylor's pessimism about the ecological

---

1043. For more on Pagan bio-regionalism, see Chas S. Clifton, "Nature Religion for Real," in *The Paganism Reader*, eds. Chas S. Clifton and Graham Harvey (New York: Routledge, 2004): 335–41.

1044. McNallen, *Asatru*, 188.

1045. Janet Biehl and Peter Staudenmaier, *Ecofascism: Lessons from the German Experience* (San Francisco: AK Press, 1995). The völkisch "blood and soil" theme represents a racial interpretation of bioregionalism. However, bioregionalism in no way necessitates an ethnic or racial definition of local human communities.

1046. Marek, interview.

1047. *Raven Radio*, "Progression of Asatru," Episode 136, 1:23:39, July 7, 2013, www.ravenradio.info/blog/2013/07/07/episode-136. The quote occurs 27:00–27:58 minutes into the broadcast.

potential of supernaturalist religions, it is precisely religious cultures such as Heathenry that are equipped with the ethic and ideological resources suitable for an ecological bioregionalism.

## Conclusion

There is a deep reverence and resonance with nature found in Heathen culture. It is quite possible that Heathenry could develop a more consistent and integrated form of nature religion. The shift would provide an alternative foundation to that of an ethnic-based folk religion. As Clifton points out, the re-orientation of Wicca around nature-oriented themes expanded the breadth of American Paganism beyond a close identification with either ethnicity or magical practice, thereby activating new intellectual and theological possibilities.[1048] In a similar way, Heathenry might grow to include a holistic orientation toward nature derived from northern European precedents. Such a religious perspective has the potential to appeal to a significantly larger demographic.

Interest in more environmental forms of Heathenry also seems to be growing across the diverse American context. McNallen seems serious about shaping Asatru as an environmental religion.[1049] The issue of environmental degradation, McNallen argues, is one of the most pressing issues facing humanity and only Heathenry has the answer. He points to the Christian ideology of human dominion over the world as the primary factor in creating the environmental crisis, a perspective more famously raised by Lynn White, Jr.'s article "The Roots of our Ecological Crisis." In contrast to the unmitigated consumption of the world, McNallen suggests that the Heathen value of reciprocity provides an ideological resource conducive to environmentalism. He argues that reciprocity extends to the relationship between human communities and the ecosystems that they inhabit. A contemporary environmental Heathenry would adopt a reciprocal approach to living with the earth that would result in a health and wholeness for both. This idea closely resembles to the Teal Party's desire to live with the earth in a balanced way, to fend off

---

1048. Clifton, *Her Hidden Children*, 44.

1049. Stephen McNallen, "How Asatru Will Recover the European Soul and Heal Our People!" *Asatru Rising*, March 6, 2015, http://asatrurising.podbean.com/e/how-asatru-will-recover-the-european-soul-and-heal-our-people/.

"the ecological overbalances that humanity has caused."[1050] A sense of balance is central to reciprocity. As Heathens often say, "a gift for a gift." The "G" rune, *gifu*, written as two diagonally intersecting lines, X, represents a balanced exchange, a relationally balanced way of life. For both McNallen and the Teal Party, reciprocity is the value that points toward a more balanced, ecological approach to life. Of course McNallen's folkishness and the Teal Party's progressivism represent two Heathen confluences that have been enmeshed in significant tensions. The organic biosocial ideas that McNallen plays with never arise in the Teal Party's ecosystemic approach to nature. However, reciprocity represents a shared value, widely agreed upon in American Heathen culture. It provides an ideological point from which a more widespread Heathen ecological consciousness could arise. Reciprocity, animism, the ethical concept of innangarð, the growth of regional identity, even urban/rural networks formed around the practice of sacrifice all have the potential to contribute to the greening of Heathenry.

---

1050. Paxson and Wood, "The Teal Party."

# Conclusion

In the cosmological visions of Norse mythology, a confluence of fire and ice churns at the center of the universe. From the mixing of these potent elements into a salty brine, all living things emerge. The image is remarkably pertinent to the approach taken towards the Heathen movement in this work. Heathenry is a confluence of disparate elements, tributaries of distinct ideas, symbols, and practices that, like fire and ice, often exist in contention and conflict. As these tributaries flow together, a religious movement emerges and takes shape. One can see this confluence either as a chaotic turmoil or a creative tension. Summarizing her perspective on the diversity of the Heathen community, Diana Paxson writes:

> Although there are plenty of Heathen liberals, and at various points the Heathen spectrum merges into the Goth, biker, and ceremonial magic communities, the average Heathen group is more aligned with middle America, with a strong emphasis on family values, and many Heathens are conservative both politically and socially.[1051]

The basic themes of my discussion are implicit in Paxson's comment. What she calls the "Heathen spectrum" is the Heathen milieu—the watershed of ideas and practices that inform Heathenry. It is more than a spectrum, more than a linear scale of liberal to conservative or left to right. While a Heathen might be liberal or conservative on any one issue, the shape of Heathenry is altogether more diverse and three-dimensional. As Paxson points out, the Heathen spectrum "merges" with other influences, which are the various social and intellectual tributaries that flow into and contribute to the Heathen watershed. I have attempted to definitively outline several of those tributaries and to discuss the ways in which they influence and shape the Heathen community. I identify the three most important as the

---

1051. Paxson, *Essential Ásatrú*, 159.

Norse cultural tributary, the Wicca and Witchcraft tributary, and folkish/Traditionalist tributary. The confluence of these three has contributed substantially to the creativity of the Heathen movement as well as to its tensions. These tributaries in turn branch off and connect to further ones — philosophical and theological, magical, environmental, and familial. I have mentioned several of these secondary tributaries, such as American white nationalism, anarcho-primitivism, and the corpus of queer and transgender theory that informs the work of Raven Kaldera. These tributaries influence smaller confluences within Heathenry, making the American scene both fascinating and complicated indeed. The fact is that every Heathen and Heathen group draws on a diverse set of tributaries to inform their own practice of Heathenry. By identifying and mapping out these confluences, I hope that the contours of the movement have become clearer. By no means can Heathens be appropriately reduced to a bunch of racist thugs, "large, angry, heavily-tattooed white guys wearing hammer necklaces," as a 2015 article suggested.[1052] These modern "Vikings" are incredibly diverse. Their family resemblance involves a shared ritual form, a few worldview beliefs, an aesthetic sense, but most importantly their willingness to accept the Norse tradition as a source of living spiritual values. In his 2005 analysis of Asatru, Michael Strmiska came to a similar conclusion, "What unites Nordic Pagans, whatever their different understandings of the gods, is their common conviction that the Norse myths and related Nordic traditions provide a coherent set of values for how to live in our world in an honorable and successful manner."[1053] What distinguishes them, however, are the many ways in which Heathens tap into differing tributaries and use them to construct the particularities of their practice. The resulting confluences give rise to the diversity of forms of Norse Paganism. Thus, part of the ongoing project of researching Heathenry must involve mapping more of these intersecting tributaries and reflecting on how they contribute to Heathen attitudes regarding modernity, religious pluralism, race, gender, and class. Of particular interest is the coming of age of the second generation of Heathens, children raised exclusively within a Heathen framework. How will they build, transform, and develop

---

1052. Rick Paulas, "How a Thor-Worshipping Religion Turned Racist," *Vice*, May 1, 2015, www.vice.com/read/how-a-thor-worshipping-religion-turned-racist-456.
1053. Strmiska, *Modern Paganism in World Cultures*, 143.

these confluences? After forty years of development, Heathenry continues to change, grow, and transform. Heathenry has not yet decided what it will become. Will it drift towards one modality or another, congealing more fully as a contemporary Pagan form of religion or take shape as something more folkish and exclusive?

We are observing contemporary Paganism during a period of intense religious change. Globalization, technology, migration of people, and shifting values toward human diversity in the contemporary world have all contributed to new forms of religious consciousness. Some scholars have even characterized this as a fourth Great Awakening.[1054] Lorne Dawson has argued that this new religious consciousness reflects a type of "hyper-modernity" as new religions respond to these changing conditions. Modernity is characterized by individualism, flexible social connections, the value of personal experience, and globalized consumer choices. The new religious consciousness arises from these values. Dawson identified six features that characterize these new religious adaptations: a pronounced individualism, a focus on personal religious experience, charismatic rather than routinized authority, tolerance towards other traditions and syncretic borrowing from a diversity of sources, holistic theologies that reject dualistic distinctions, and greater organizational openness.[1055] Rather than rejecting modernity, the new religious consciousness enfolds itself into the characteristics of modern life.

In many ways, contemporary Paganism fits into Dawson's outline as a type of new religious consciousness. Yet Paganism also involves a strong critique of the modern world. Heathenry in particular expresses a dissatisfaction with hyper-individualism, reliance on personal religious experience or UPG, syncretism and cultural blending, and other aspects described by Dawson. In response, the movement draws on its tributaries including ancient Norse sources to create innovative roles and experiences that re-embed adherents into a more holistic context. Its strong ethnocentric identity seems to be one aspect of Heathenry clearly at odds with Dawson's description of the new religious consciousness. Asatru is representative of a renewed interest in ancestral, ethnic identities. As Strmiska observes, "efforts to revive traditional, indigenous, or native religions are occurring around the world; modern

---

1054. Dawson, *Comprehending Cults*, 62–66.
1055. Ibid., 183–85.

European-based Paganism is but one variant of a much larger phenomenon."[1056] These new ethnic faiths are local in their focus, specific in their theologies, and resistant to syncretic borrowing. They are past-oriented and nativist, focused on the natural community to which an individual organically belongs. They attempt to deeply embed adherents into one specific cultural experience and may at times express somewhat of a fundamentalist approach, in spectacular contrast to the eclectic, universal, syncretic, and progressive faiths of the new religious consciousness.

Ironically, the conditions of modernity make these new reconstructive religions possible. In one sense, the new ethnic faiths represent a particularly modern phenomenon. Ethnic identities have become mobile and have even gone viral as they move around the globe and online. Being Viking no longer requires living on a Scandinavian or Icelandic farmstead. These identities have become unmoored from their traditional contexts and made available for a global audience of religious innovators. Similarly, living in modern conditions may considerably loosen, or erase almost completely, close ties to one particular ethnicity. This gives Americans and others as well, the particular freedom to select ethnic identities that suit them emotionally and socially.

These religious choices may result in identities and ideologies that are decidedly at odds with modernity. The new ethnic faiths are ambivalent about modern identity and look for the transformation of modern society. They organize around a more human scale, tribe and family rather than national identity or citizenship, more environmental and rooted, more enchanted and magical than scientific and rational. Though they may be more prevalent in Europe, Heathenry represents the most successful of these new ethnic faiths in America. These faiths are both modern and anti-modern, innovative and reactionary, global and local at the same time. They express the desire of modern people for a deeper, more intimate experience in which identity, religion, culture, nature, epistemology, and health are all closely bound together. Whether new ethnic faiths will become a vital part of the American religious context is yet to be seen. But if the growth and evolution of Asatru are any indication, they may garner a small but growing share of religious adherents.

1056. Strmiska, *Modern Paganism in World Cultures*, 2.

What chance does American Heathenry have of becoming a mainstream religion or contributing meaningfully to the public discourse? America seems to stir with dissent: the Tea Party, the Occupy movement, Black Lives Matter, Greens all represent growing segments of dissent. It seems that if an alternative dissenting religion stands any chance of garnering attention and having its voice heard in a meaningful way, this would be the cultural moment. However, most scholars seem pessimistic about such an occurrence, especially for the mainstreaming of contemporary Paganism.[1057] Piotr Wiench adequately summarizes the conditions that limit the impact of Pagan religions in Europe and America:

> Most of the Neopagan groups are entrenched in small niches, built around close-knit circles of followers. They have also remained marginal and nonexistent in mainstream public discourse. While occasionally they enjoy some brief interest from the media, this interest is mostly limited to the sensationalist media coverage, whenever journalists venture to explore fringe phenomena to arouse the curiosity of the general public.[1058]

The diversity of the American context renders unlikely the possibility that Asatru could act as a unifying religious influence. The lingering associations with racism also pose significant barriers to the public acceptability of Heathen religionists. The skepticism about religion in America also poses a barrier to it representing any significant amount of the social unrest that is bubbling in American society. While dissent and social critique abounds, there seems to be less interest in funneling those sentiments into religious forms.

If Heathenry is to make a difference, its impact will be slower and of a smaller scale. Despite its lack of popular appeal, Asatru has developed into a producer of significant religious meaning. Let me briefly tell about a moment when Asatru made sense for me. The story has two parts. The first takes place in my grandmother's house when I was a young man in my early teens: my great-uncle, brother to my grandmother and whose name I share, had given a pistol to me that had belonged to his father. He had arranged two chairs in a room in which we sat facing one another and strategically placed a video camera to record us as the exchange took place. He presented

---

1057. Dawson, *Comprehending Cults*, 179–80.
1058. Wiench, "A Postcolonial Key," 13.

the gun while telling the story of how his father had carried the pistol during the Great Depression and had used it to protect his family during those precarious years. He told me about a couple of drifters who had shown up at the house one night and how his father had driven them off, brandishing but not firing the weapon. In the telling he was reduced to tears, quickly got up and left the room, while I was left awkwardly sitting in the chair holding the pistol and not knowing how to respond, not understanding what had just happened as the video camera recorded my embarrassed and baffled expression.

The second part of the story took place years later, by which time the memory of the pistol presentation was buried in the recesses of my mind. In this episode, I was at a state park in Oklahoma sitting on the floor of an air-conditioned cabin to escape the summer heat. I was there interviewing Kari Tauring, who has been featured in this book, in what turned out to be almost a four-hour conversation ranging widely over many Heathen-related topics. At one point, talking about the concept of ørlög, she mentioned that ørlög could adhere to or be carried by objects that had been used by the ancestors. Objects such as weapons had often been passed down in families and were thought to carry the power of the brave and noble deeds that had been done with them. As she was talking about this, I thought about how a very similar pattern was observable in my own context. In the culture of the rural southern United States, families and men in particular often treated weapons as heirlooms. They were collected, along with stories of war or hunting, and passed down from one generation to the next. Just then, the presentation of my great-grandfather's gun, forgotten for all those years, suddenly flooded back into my conscious memory. For the first time, I understood what had happened and why it was emotional for my uncle. Heathenry provided an interpretive framework to explain that significant moment.

Tauring's explanations, applied to this personal memory, transformed my years of bewilderment about the event into clarity and significance. I understood that the presentation was not just about the physical gun but the gun as a spiritual object. For my great uncle, it represented the legacy of manhood represented by his father and other influential men in his life. As a young boy on the verge of manhood, he wanted me to emulate that example of masculinity, bravery, and strength that had been so formative in his own life.

From the Heathen perspective, that gun was a potentially powerful religious object that carried the virtues, the force of character, even the ancestral presence of the men of my family who had handled it. What my great-uncle had presented to me was a talisman of our family ørlög and luck. In that moment I understood the power that Asatru has to speak to modern people. I saw what thousands of Heathen people have also experienced over the last forty years: the power of Asatru to instill meaning into modern life, to take situations that fell outside of the range of modern interpretative categories and re-enchant them with spiritual significance.

# Bibliography

Abell, Steven T. *Days in Midgard: A Thousand Years On: Modern Legends Based on Northern Myth*. Denver, CO: Outskirts Press, 2008.
Adler, Margot. *Drawing Down the Moon: Witches, Druids, Goddess-Worshippers, and Other Pagans in America*. New York: Penguin Books, 2006 [1986].
Aitamurto, Kaarina, and Scott Simpson (eds.). *Modern Pagan and Native Faith Movements in Central and Eastern Europe*. Durham, UK: Acumen, 2013.
——. "The Study of Paganism and Wicca: A Review Essay." In *The Oxford Handbook of New Religious Movements*. Vol. 2, edited by James R. Lewis, and Inga B. Tøllefsen, 482–94. New York: Oxford University Press, 2016.
Albanese, Catherine L. *Nature Religion in America: From the Algonkian Indians to the New Age*. Chicago: University of Chicago Press, 1991.
——. *Reconsidering Nature Religion*. Harrisburg, PA: Trinity Press International, 2002.
Allhoff, Fritz, and Dave Monroe (eds.). *Food and Philosophy: Eat, Think, and Be Merry*. Malden, MA: Blackwell, 2007.
Aloi, Peg, and Hannah E. Johnston (eds.). *The New Generation Witches: Teenage Witchcraft in Contemporary Culture*. Aldershot, UK: Ashgate, 2007.
Anderson, Philip N. "Form and Content in Lokasenna: A Re-Evaluation." In *The Poetic Edda: Essays on Old Norse Mythology*, edited by Paul Acker and Carolyne Larrington, 139–57. New York: Routledge, 2002.
Aðalsteinsson, Jón Hnefill. "Gods and Giants in Old Norse Mythology." *Temenos* 26, 1990: 7–22.
Asprem, Egil. "Heathens Up North: Politics, Polemics, and Contemporary Norse Paganism in Norway." *The Pomegranate: The International Journal of Pagan Studies* 10, no. 1 (2008): 41–69. doi: 10.1558/pome.v10i1.41.
Aswynn, Freya. *Leaves of Yggdrasil: A Synthesis of Runes, Gods, Magic, Feminine Mysteries, and Folklore*. St. Paul, MN: Llewellyn Publications, 1990.
Axtell, Sara. "The Heathen Soul: A Balance of the Individual with the Collective." *Idunna*, no. 87 (Spring 2011): 16–20.
Baal, Jan van. "Offering, Sacrifice and Gift." *Numen* 23 (1976): 161–78.
Bado-Fralick, Nikki. *Coming To the Edge of the Circle: A Wiccan Initiation Ritual*. Oxford: Oxford University Press, 2005.
Bainbridge, William. "Forest Ásatrú." In *Living the Troth*. Vol. 2 of *Our Troth*, edited by Kveldúlf Gundarsson, 9–14. Charleston, SC: BookSurge, 2007.
Barkun, Michael. "Conspiracy Theories as Stigmatized Knowledge: The Basis for a New Age Racism?" In *Nation and Race: The Developing Euro-American*

*Racist Subculture*, edited by Jeffrey Kaplan and Tore Bjørgo, 58–72. Boston: Northeastern University Press, 1998.

Barstow, Anne Llewellyn. *Witchcraze: A New History of the European Witch Hunts*. San Francisco: Pandora, 1994.

Bassin, Mark. "Blood or Soil? The Völkisch Movement, the Nazis, and the Legacy of Geopolitik." In *How Green Were the Nazis? Nature, Environment, and Nation in the Third Reich*, edited by Franz-Josef Brüggemeier, Mark Cioc, and Thomas Zeller, 204–42. Athens, OH: Ohio University Press, 2005.

Bauschatz, Paul C. *The Well and the Tree: World and Time in Early Germanic Culture*. Amherst: University of Massachusetts Press, 1982.

Behrens, Kevin. "Tony Yengeni's Ritual Slaughter: Animal Anti-Cruelty vs. Culture." *South African Journal of Philosophy* 28 (2009): 271–89.

Bellows, Henry Adams. *The Poetic Edda*. New York: American-Scandinavian Foundation, 1923.

Benario, Herbert W. "Arminius into Hermann: History into Legend" *Greece & Rome* 51, no. 1 (2004): 83–94. www.jstor.org/stable/3567880.

Berger, Helen A. *A Community of Witches: Contemporary Neo-Paganism and Witchcraft in the United States*. Columbia: University of South Carolina Press, 2005.

Berger, Helen A., and Douglas Ezzy. *Teenage Witches: Magical Youth and the Search for the Self*. New Brunswick, NJ: Rutgers University Press, 2007.

Berger, Helen A., Evan A. Leach, and Leigh S. Shaffer. *Voices from the Pagan Census: A National Survey of Witches and Neo-Pagans in the United States*. Columbia: University of South Carolina Press, 2003.

Berger, Peter L. *The Sacred Canopy: Elements of a Sociological Theory of Religion*. New York: Anchor Books, 1967.

Bernauer, Lauren. "Modern Germanic Heathenry and Radical Traditionalists." In *Through a Glass Darkly: Reflections on the Sacred: Collected Research*, edited by Franco Di Lauro, 265–74. Sydney: Sydney University Press, 2006.

Biehl, Janet, and Peter Staudenmaier. *Ecofascism: Lessons from the German Experience*. San Francisco: AK Press, 1995.

Blackburn, Simon. "Existentialism," and "Individualism." In *The Oxford Dictionary of Philosophy*, 125, 184. New York: Oxford University Press, 2005.

Blain, Jenny. "Heathenry-Ásatrú." In *The Encyclopedia of Religion and Nature*, edited by Bron Raymond Taylor, Jeffrey Kaplan, Laura Hobgood-Oster, Adrian J. Ivakhiv, and Michael York, 751–54. London: Continuum, 2008.

———. *Nine Worlds of Seid-Magic: Ecstasy and Neo-Shamanism in North European Paganism*. London: Routledge, 2002; Thoemmes Continuum, 2008.

Blum, Ralph H. *The Book of Runes Twenty-Fifth Anniversary Edition*. New York: St. Martin's Press, 2008 [1982].

Borthwick, Stephen M. "Hermann Awakened: Folkishness vs. Racism." *Journal of Contemporary Heathen Thought* 1 (2010): 35–40.

Bosworth, Joseph and T. Northcote Toller. *An Anglo-Saxon Dictionary*. Oxford: Oxford University Press, 1921. http://lexicon.ff.cuni.cz/texts/oe_bosworthtoller_about.html.

Bramwell, Anna. *Blood and Soil: Richard Walther Darré and Hitler's "Green Party."* Bourne End, UK: Kensal, 1985.

———. *Ecology in the 20th Century: A History*. New Haven, CT: Yale University Press, 1989.

——. *The Fading of the Greens: The Decline of Environmental Politics in the West.* New Haven, CT: Yale University Press, 1994.

Brüggemeier, Franz-Josef, Mark Cioc, and Thomas Zeller (eds.). *How Green Were the Nazis? Nature, Environment, and Nation in the Third Reich.* Athens, OH: Ohio University Press, 2005.

Byock, Jesse. "The Icelandic Althing: Dawn of Parliamentary Democracy." In *Heritage and Identity: Shaping the Nations of the North,* edited by J. M. Fladmark, 1-18. Donhead St. Mary, UK: Heyerdahl Institute and Robert Gordon University, 2002.

Calico, Jefferson. "Asatru: A Native European Spirituality." *The Pomegranate: The International Journal of Pagan Studies* 18, no. 1 (January 2016): 116-19. doi: 10.1558/pome.v18i1.30932.

Callahan, Richard J. Jr. *Work and Faith in the Kentucky Coal Fields: Subject to Dust* Bloomington: University of Indiana Press, 2008.

Campbell, Colin. "The Cult, the Cultic Milieu and Secularization." In *The Cultic Milieu: Oppositional Subcultures in an Age of Globalization,* edited by Jeffrey Kaplan and Heléne Lööw, 12-25. Walnut Creek, CA: AltaMira Press, 2002.

Cardeña, Ivette. "On Humour and Pathology: The Role of Paradox and Absurdity for Ideological Survival." *Anthropology & Medicine* 10, no. 1 (2003): 115-42. doi: 10.1080/1364847032000094540.

Cargle, Josh Marcus. "Contemporary Germanic/Norse Paganism and Recent Survey Data." *The Pomegranate: The International Journal of Pagan Studies* 19, no. 1 (2017): 77-116.

Carpenter, Dennis D. "Emergent Nature Spirituality: An Examination of the Major Spiritual Contours of the Contemporary Pagan Worldview." In *Magic Religion and Modern Witchcraft,* edited by James R. Lewis, 35-72. Albany: State University of New York Press, 1996.

Chamberlin, Silas. *On the Trail: A History of American Hiking.* New Haven, CT: Yale University Press, 2016.

Chancellor, James D. *Life in the Family: An Oral History of the Children of God.* Syracuse: Syracuse University Press, 2000.

Chapple, Eliot Dismore, and Carleton Stevens Coon. *Principles of Anthropology.* New York: Henry Holt & Company, 1942.

Chidester, David, and Edward T. Linenthal (eds.). *American Sacred Space.* Bloomington: Indiana University Press, 1995.

Clare, Victoria. "Norge 2008!" *Idunna,* no. 80 (2009): 5-15.

Clark Hall, John R. *A Concise Anglo-Saxon Dictionary,* 2nd edition. New York: Macmillan, 1916.

Cleasby, Richard, and Vigfusson, Gudbrand. *An Icelandic-English Dictionary.* Oxford: Clarendon, 1957.

Clifton, Chas S. *Her Hidden Children: The Rise of Wicca and Paganism in America.* Lanham, MD: AltaMira Press, 2006.

——. "Nature Religion for Real." In *The Paganism Reader,* edited by Chas S. Clifton and Graham Harvey, 335-41. New York: Routledge, 2004.

——. "Sex Magic or Sacred Marriage: Sexuality in Contemporary Wicca." In *Sexuality and New Religious Movements,* edited by Henrik Bogdan and James R. Lewis, 149-63. New York: Palgrave Macmillan, 2014.

———. "Smokey and the Sacred: Nature Religion, Civil Religion and American Paganism." *Ecotheology* 8, no. 1 (2003): 50–60.

———. "What Has Alexandria to do with Boston? Some Sources of Modern Pagan Ethics." In *Magical Religion and Modern Witchcraft*, edited by James R. Lewis, 269–75. Albany: State University of New York Press, 1996.

Clifton, Chas S., and Graham Harvey (eds.). *The Paganism Reader*. New York: Routledge, 2004.

Connors, Sean M. "Ecology and Religion in Karuk Orientations toward the Land." In *Indigenous Religions: A Companion*, edited by Graham Harvey, 139–51. New York: Cassell, 2000.

Cooper, Michael T. *Contemporary Druidry: A Historical and Ethnographic Study*. Salt Lake City: Sacred Tribes Press, 2010. Kindle e-book.

Craigie, William A. *The Religion of Ancient Scandinavia*. Freeport, NY: Books for Libraries Press, 1969.

Crowley, Aleister. *Magick in Theory and Practice*. New York: Castle Books, 1960.

Crowley, Vivianne. "Women and Power in Modern Paganism." In *Women as Teachers and Disciples in Traditional and New Religions*, edited by Elizabeth Puttick and Peter B. Clarke, 125–40. Lewiston, NY: Edwin Mellen Press, 1993.

Cusack, Carole M. *Invented Religions: Imagination, Fiction and Faith*. Burlington, VT: Ashgate, 2010.

———. *The Sacred Tree: Ancient and Medieval Manifestations*. Newcastle upon Tyne: Cambridge Scholars, 2011. PDF e-book.

Davidson, Hilda Roderick Ellis. *Gods and Myths of Northern Europe*. London: Penguin, 1990 [1964].

———. *The Lost Beliefs of Northern Europe*. London: Routledge, 1993.

———. *Myths and Symbols in Pagan Europe: Early Scandinavian and Celtic Religions*. Syracuse: Syracuse University Press, 1988.

———. *The Road to Hel: A Study of the Conception of the Dead in Old Norse Literature*. Cambridge: Cambridge University Press, 2013.

Davy, Barbara Jane. "Definitions and Expressions of Nature Religion in Shamanic Traditions and Contemporary Paganism." In *Between the Worlds: Readings in Contemporary Neopaganism*, edited by Siân Reid, 79–89. Toronto: Canadian Scholars' Press, 2006.

Dawson, Lorne L. *Comprehending Cults: The Sociology of New Religious Movements*. Ontario: Oxford University Press, 2006.

de Young, David. "Kari Tauring: Digging Deep Nordic Roots." *Sing Out!* 55, no. 3 (2013): 4–9.

Deloria, Vine Jr. *God is Red: A Native View of Religion*. Golden, CO: Fulcrum, 2003 [1973].

Desmond, Yngona. *Völuspá: Seiðr as Wyrd Consciousness*. Charleston, SC: BookSurge, 2005.

Detienne, Marcel. "Culinary Practices and the Spirit of Sacrifice." In *The Cuisine of Sacrifice Among the Greeks*, edited by Marcel Detienne and Jean-Pierre Vernant, 1–20. Chicago: University of Chicago Press, 1989.

Dick, Ernst S. "Review: The Well and the Tree: World and Time in Early Germanic Culture by Paul C. Bauschatz." *Speculum* 59, no. 3 (1984): 616–19.

Douglas, Mary. *Purity and Danger: An Analysis of the Concepts of Pollution and Taboo*. New York: ARK, 1984.

DuBois, Page. *A Million and One Gods: The Persistence of Polytheism.* Cambridge, MA: Harvard University Press, 2014.
DuBois, Thomas A. *Nordic Religions in the Viking Age.* Philadelphia: University of Pennsylvania Press, 1999.
Eaves, Su. "Raising Children with the Gods." *Idunna*, no. 102 (Winter 2014): 18–21.
Edgell, Penny, and Danielle Docka. "Beyond the Nuclear Family? Familism and Gender Ideology in Diverse Religious Communities." *Sociological Forum* 22, no. 1 (March 2007): 26–51.
Egeler, Matthias. "A Retrospective Methodology for Using *Landnámabók* as a Source for the Religious History of Iceland? Some Questions." *The Retrospective Methods Network Newsletter* 10 (2015): 78–92.
Eliade, Mircea. *The Sacred and the Profane: The Nature of Religion.* New York: Harcourt, 1959.
———. "The Yearning for Paradise in Primitive Tradition." *Daedalus* 88, no. 2 (1959): 255–67.
Elliott, Ralph W. V. *Runes: An Introduction.* Manchester: Manchester University Press, 1959.
Enright, Michael J. *Lady with a Mead Cup: Ritual, Prophecy and Lordship in the European Warband from La Tene to the Viking Age.* Portland, OR: Four Courts Press, 1996.
Evola, Julius. *Meditations on the Peaks: Mountain Climbing as Metaphor for the Spiritual Quest.* Translated by Guido Stucco. Rochester, VT: Inner Traditions, 1998.
Eyerman, Ron. "Social Movements." In *The Cambridge Dictionary of Sociology*, edited by Bryan S. Turner. Cambridge, UK: Cambridge University Press, 2006.
Ezzy, Douglas. "Cosmopolitan Witchcraft: Reinventing the Wheel of the Year in Australian Paganism." In *Cosmopolitanism, Nationalism, and Modern Paganism*, edited by Kathryn Rountree, 201–19. New York: Palgrave Macmillan, 2017.
Ezzy, Douglas, and Helen Berger. "Witchcraft: Changing Patterns of Participation in the Early Twenty-First Century." *The Pomegranate: The International Journal of Pagan Studies* 11, no. 2 (2009): 165–80. doi: 10.1558/pome.v11i2.165.
Feilnar, Sorcha. "Return of the Völva." *Witches and Pagans*, June, no. 30 (2015): 27–32.
Ferguson, Robert. *The Vikings: A History.* New York: Penguin Books, 2009.
Flowers, Stephen Edred. "Runes and Magic: Magical Formulaic Elements in the Elder Tradition." PhD diss., University of Texas at Austin, 1984.
Fraser, Craig, and Lucy Fraser. *The Centurion Method.* Self-published, 2013.
Frazer, David. "Caring for Farm Animals." In *A Communion of Subjects: Animals in Religion, Science, and Ethics*, edited by Paul Waldau and Kimberly Patton, 547–55. New York: Columbia University Press, 2006.
Frazer, James G. *The Golden Bough: A Study in Magic and Religion.* New York: Macmillan, 1951.
Gaiman, Neil. *Norse Mythology.* New York: W. W. Norton, 2017.
Galdr. "Wolves Take What Wolves Will." In *Operation Werewolf: The Complete Transmissions*, 121–23. CreateSpace, 2016.
Gallagher, Ann-Marie. "Weaving a Tangled Web? Pagan Ethics as Issues of History, 'Race,' and Ethnicity in Pagan Identity." In *Handbook of Contemporary Paganism*, edited by Murphy Pizza, and James R. Lewis, 577–90. Leiden: Brill, 2009.

Gamlinginn. "Race and Religion." *Mountain Thunder* 5 (1993). www.thetroth. org/news/20170816-000204.

Gardell, Mattias. "Black and White Unite in Fight?" In *The Cultic Milieu: Oppositional Subcultures in an Age of Globalization*, edited by Jeffrey S. Kaplan, and Heléne Lööw, 152–92. Walnut Creek, CA: AltaMira Press, 2002.

——. *Gods of the Blood: The Pagan Revival and White Separatism*. Durham, NC: Duke University Press, 2003.

Georgoudi, Stella. "Sanctified Slaughter in Modern Greece." In *The Cuisine of Sacrifice Among the Greeks*, edited by Marcel Detienne, and Jean-Pierre Vernant, 183–203. Chicago: University of Chicago Press, 1989.

Gerhard, Gesine. "Breeding Pigs and People for the Third Reich." In *How Green Were the Nazis? Nature, Environment, and Nation in the Third Reich*, edited by Franz-Josef Brüggemeier, Mark Cioc, and Thomas Zeller, 129–46. Athens: Ohio University Press, 2005.

Giddens, Anthony. *Modernity and Self-Identity: Self and Society in the Late Modern Age*. Stanford: Stanford University Press, 1991.

Gimbutas, Marija. *The Language of the Goddess: Unearthing the Hidden Symbols of Western Civilization*. San Francisco: Harper & Row, 1989.

Girard, Rene. *Violence and the Sacred*. Chicago: The University of Chicago Press, 1989.

Goodrick-Clarke, Nicholas. *Black Sun: Aryan Cults, Esoteric Nazism and the Politics of Identity*. New York: New York University Press, 2002.

——. *The Western Esoteric Traditions: A Historical Introduction*. New York: Oxford University Press, 2008.

Granholm, Kennet. "The Rune-Gild: Heathenism, Traditionalism, and the Left-Hand Path." *International Journal for the Study of New Religions* 1, no. 1 (2010): 95–115. doi: 10.1558/ijsnr.v1i1.95.

Graves, Robert. *The White Goddess: A Historical Grammar of Poetic Myth*. New York: Farrar, Straus, & Giroux, 1978.

Gray, Thomas. "The Descent of Odin." In *Eighteenth-Century Poetry and Prose*, 2nd edition, edited by Louis I. Bredvold, Alan D. McKillop, and Lois Whitney, 603. New York: The Ronald Press, 1956.

——. "The Fatal Sisters." In *Eighteenth-Century Poetry and Prose*, 2nd edition, edited by Louis I. Bredvold, Alan D. McKillop, and Lois Whitney, 602. New York: The Ronald Press, 1956.

Greenwood, Susan. *The Anthropology of Magic*. Oxford: Bloomsbury, 2009.

——. "Feminist Witchcraft: A Transformatory Politics." In *Practising Feminism: Identity, Difference, Power*, edited by Nickie Charles, and Felicia Hughes-Freeland, 109–34. New York: Routledge, 1996.

Greer, John Michael. *A World Full of Gods: An Inquiry into Polytheism*. Tucson, AZ: ADF, 2005.

Grimes, Ronald L. *Ritual Criticism: Case Studies in Its Practice, Essays on Its Theory*. Columbia: University of South Carolina, 1990.

Gundarsson, Kveldúlf (ed.). *History and Lore*. Vol. 1 of *Our Troth*. Charleston, SC: Booksurge, 2006.

Gundarsson, Kveldúlfr. *Living the Troth*. Vol. 2 of *Our Troth*. Charleston, SC: Book Surge, 2007.

Gundarsson, Kveldulf. "Race, Inheritance, and Ásatrú Today." *Mountain Thunder* 5 (1993): 7–11.

———. *Teutonic Magic: The Magical and Spiritual Practices of the Germanic People*. St. Paul, MN: Llewellyn Publications, 1990.

Harner, Michael J. *The Way of the Shaman*. San Francisco: Harper & Row, 1990.

Harvey, Graham. *Animism: Respecting the Living World*. New York: Columbia University Press, 2005.

———. *Contemporary Paganism: Religions of the Earth from Druids and Witches to Heathens and Ecofeminists*. New York: New York University Press, 2011.

Hawthorne, Nathaniel. *The Scarlet Letter*. New York: The Modern Library, 1950.

Heaney, Seamus, and John D. Niles. *Beowulf: An Illustrated Edition*. New York: W. W. Norton, 2008.

Heath, Josh. "Two Yule Rituals: One Heathen's Experience in the Northeast US." *Óðrærir: The Heathen Journal* 2 (2014): 114–21. http://odroerirjournal.com/two-yule-rituals-one-heathens-experience-in-the-northeast-us/.

Herzog, Hal. *Some We Love, Some We Hate, Some We Eat: Why It Is So Hard to Think Straight About Animals*. New York: Harper, 2010.

Higginbotham, Joyce, and River Higginbotham. *Paganism: An Introduction to Earth-Centered Religions*. St. Paul, MN: Llewellyn Publications, 2002.

Hobson, Juleigh Howard. "The Feminine in the Post-Modern Age: How Feminism Negates Folkways." *Journal of Contemporary Heathen Thought* 1 (2010): 91–100.

Hodge Rose, Winifred. "The Ferah Full-Soul Born of Trees and Thunder: Heathen Soul Lore Part 2." *Idunna*, no. 68 (2006): 27–37.

Hollander, Lee M. *The Poetic Edda*. Austin: University of Texas Press, 2016.

Hope, Murry. "Practical Rune Magic." *Fate* 38, no. 3, issue 420 (March 1985): 88–93.

Horrell, Thad N. "Heathenry as a Postcolonial Movement." *Journal of Religion, Identity, and Politics*, January (2012). https://jrip.scholasticahq.com/article/76-heathenry-as-a-postcolonial-movement.

Horton, Kristen An. "Why Aren't More Heathens Eco-Pagan Vegetarians? The Intersection of Gender, Politics, and Spiritual Environmentalism." Master's Thesis, University of Mississippi, 2014.

Hutton, Ronald. *The Triumph of the Moon: A History of Modern Pagan Witchcraft*. Oxford: Oxford University Press, 2005.

Imort, Michael. "Eternal Forest—Eternal Volk: The Rhetoric and Reality of National Socialist Forest Policy." In *How Green Were the Nazis? Nature, Environment, and Nation in the Third Reich*, edited by Franz-Josef Brüggemeier, Mark Cioc, and Thomas Zeller, 43–72. Athens: Ohio University Press, 2005.

Ivakhiv, Adrian. "Nature and Ethnicity in East European Paganism: An Environmental Ethic of the Religious Right?" *The Pomegranate: The International Journal of Pagan Studies* 7, no. 2 (2005): 194–225.

———. "The Resurgence of Magical Religion as a Response to the Crisis of Modernity: A Postmodern Depth Psychological Perspective." In *Magical Religion and Modern Witchcraft*, edited by James R. Lewis, 237–65. Albany: State University of New York Press, 1996.

Jenkins, Philip. *Mystics and Messiahs: Cults and New Religions in American History*. Oxford: Oxford University, 2000.

Johnson, Philip, Gus DiZerega, and John Morehead. *Beyond the Burning Times: A Pagan and Christian in Dialogue*. Oxford: Lion Hudson, 2008.

Jones, Prudence. "The Native European Tradition." In *Nature Religion Today: Paganism in the Modern World*, edited by Joanne Pearson, Richard H. Roberts, and Geoffrey Samuel, 77–88. Edinburgh: Edinburgh University Press, 1998.

Jung, C. G. *Civilization in Transition*. Vol. 10 of *The Collected Works of C. G. Jung*. London: Routledge & Kegan Paul, 1964.

Kaplan, Jeffrey. *Radical Religion in America: Millenarian Movements from the Far Right to the Children of Noah*. Syracuse: Syracuse University Press, 1997.

———. "The Reconstruction of the Ásatrú and Odinist Traditions." In *Magical Religion and Modern Witchcraft*, edited by James R. Lewis, 193–236. Albany: State University of New York, 1996.

Kaplan, Jeffrey, and Heléne Lööw, eds. *The Cultic Milieu: Oppositional Subcultures in an Age of Globalization*. Walnut Creek, CA: AltaMira Press, 2002.

Kermani, S. Zohreh. *Pagan Family Values: Childhood and the Religious Imagination in Contemporary American Paganism*. New York: New York University Press, 2013.

Kirkpatrick, R. George, Rich Rainey, and Kathryn Rubi. "Pagan Renaissance and Wiccan Witchcraft in Industrial Society: A Study of Parasociology and the Sociology of Enchantment." *Iron Mountain: A Journal of Magical Religion* Summer (1984): 31–38.

Kraemer, Christine H. *Seeking the Mystery: An Introduction to Pagan Theologies*. Englewood, CO: Patheos Press, 2012. Kindle e-book.

Krasskova, Galina. *Exploring the Northern Tradition: A Guide to the Gods, Lore, Rites, and Celebrations from the Norse, German, and Anglo-Saxon Traditions*. Pompton Plains, NJ: New Page Books, 2005.

Kunz, Keneva, and Gísli Sigurðsson. *The Vinland Sagas: The Icelandic Sagas About the First Documented Voyages Across the North Atlantic: The Saga of the Greenlanders and Eirik the Red's Saga*. London: Penguin, 2008.

Kurien, Prema A. *A Place at the Multicultural Table: The Development of an American Hinduism*. New Brunswick, NJ: Rutgers University Press, 2007.

Kurlander, Eric. "Völkisch-Nationalism and Universalism on the Margins of the Reich: A Comparison of Majority and Minority Liberalism in Germany, 1898–1933." In *German History from the Margins*, edited by Neil Gregor, Nils H. Roemer, and Mark Roseman, 84–103. Bloomington: Indiana University Press, 2006.

Lafayllve, Patricia, M. *Lady, Vanadis: An Introduction to the Goddess*. Denver, CO: Outskirts Press, 2006.

———. *A Practical Heathen's Guide to Asatru*. St. Paul, MN: Llewellyn, 2013.

Larrington, Carolyne. *The Poetic Edda*. Oxford: Oxford University Press, 2014.

———. "Sayings of the High One (Havamal)." In *The Poetic Edda*, 22. Oxford: Oxford University Press, 2014.

Larson, Jennifer. "A Land Full of Gods: Nature Deities in Greek Religion." In *A Companion to Greek Religion*, edited by Daniel Ogden, 56–70. Malden, MA: Blackwell, 2007.

Larsson, Helga. "On the Meaning of the Sumbl." *Vor Trú* 18 (1986): 3.

———. "A Sumbel Summary." *Vor Trú* 20 (1986): 4.

Lecouteux, Claude. *Encyclopedia of Norse and Germanic Folklore, Mythology, and Magic*. Rochester, VT: Inner Traditions, 2016.

Leopold, Aldo, and Charles Walsh Schwartz, *A Sand County Almanac, and Sketches Here and There*. New York: Oxford University Press, 1987.
Lewis, C. S. *Surprised by Joy/The Four Loves*. Boston: Houghton Mifflin Harcourt, 2011.
Lewis, James R. "The Pagan Explosion: An Overview of Select Census and Survey Data." In *The New Generation of Witches: Teenage Witchcraft in Contemporary Culture*, edited by Hannah E. Johnston, and Peg Aloi, 13-23. Burlington, VT: Ashgate, 2007.
———. "The Pagan Explosion Revisited: A Statistical Postmortem on the Teen Witch Fad." *The Pomegranate: The International Journal of Pagan Studies* 14, no. 1 (2012): 128-39.
Liberman, Anatoly. "The Well and the Tree (Book Review)." *Germanic Review* 58, no. 4 (1983): 158-59.
Lincoln, Bruce, "Of Time and the Brunnr." *History of Religions* 23, no. 1 (1983): 84-87.
———. *Theorizing Myth: Narrative, Ideology, and Scholarship*. Chicago: University of Chicago Press, 1999.
Lincoln, Yvonne S., and Egon G. Guba. *Naturalistic Inquiry*. Beverly Hills, CA: Sage, 1985.
List, Guido. *The Secret of the Runes*. Translated by Stephen E. Flowers. Rochester, VT: Destiny Books, 1988.
Livingston, James C. *Anatomy of the Sacred: An Introduction to Religion*. New York: Macmillan, 1989.
Luhrmann, T. M. *Persuasions of the Witch's Craft: Ritual Magic in Contemporary England*. Cambridge: Harvard University Press, 1989.
McCloud, Sean. "The Ghost of Marx and the Stench of Deprivation." In *Religion and Class in America: Culture, History, and Politics*, edited by Sean M. McCloud and William A. Mirola, 91-107. Leiden: Brill, 2009.
McCloud, Sean, and William A. Mirola (eds.). *Religion and Class in America: Culture, History, and Politics*. Leiden: Brill, 2009.
McNallen, Stephen A. *Asatru: A Native European Spirituality*. Nevada City, CA: Runestone Press, 2015.
———. "Genetics and Beyond: The Ultimate Connection." In *The Philosophy of Metagenetics, Folkism, and Beyond*, 11-15. Nevada City, CA: Asatru Folk Assembly, 2006.
———. "How the Gods Came to North America." In *Asatru: A Native European Spirituality*, 61-69. Nevada, CA: Runestone Press, 2015.
———. "The Nature of Folk Religion." In *The Philosophy of Metagenetics, Folkism and Beyond*, 1-2. Nevada City, CA: Asatru Folk Assembly, 2006.
———. *The Philosophy of Metagenetics, Folkism and Beyond*. Nevada City, CA: Asatru Folk Assembly, 2006.
———. *The Rituals of Asatru*. Payson, AZ: World Tree Publications, 1991.
———. *The Rituals of Asatru: Volume 2 – Seasonal Festivals*. Payson, AZ: World Tree Publications, 1991.
———. "Thor Blot," in *The Rituals of Asatru, Volume 1 – Major Blots*, 7-9. Payson, AZ: Worldtree Publications, 1992 [1985].
———. "Three Decades of the Ásatrú Revival." *Tyr: Myth, Culture, and Tradition* 2 (2003-2004): 203-19.

——. *Thunder from the North: The Way of the Teutonic Warrior*. Nevada City, CA: Asatru Folk Assembly, 1993.

——. *What Is Asatru?* Nevada City, CA: Asatru Folk Assembly, 1985.

Magnusson, Magnus, and Hermann Pálsson. *The Vinland Sagas: The Norse Discovery of America*. Baltimore: Penguin Books, 1965.

Márquez, Gabriel García. *One Hundred Years of Solitude*. New York: Avon, 1970.

Mees, Bernard. *The Science of the Swastika*. New York: Central European University Press, 2008.

Melton, Gordon J. "Perspective: New New Religions—Revisiting a Concept." *Nova Religio* 10, no. 4 (2007): 103–12. doi:10.1525/nr.2007.10.4.103.

Moynihan, Michel. "Odinism." In *The Encyclopedia of Religion and Nature*, edited by Jeffrey Kaplan, Bron Raymond Taylor, Laura Hobgood-Oster, Adrian J. Ivakhiv, and Michael York, 1218–20. London: Continuum, 2008.

Moynihan, Michael, and Didrik Søderlind. *Lords of Chaos: The Bloody Rise of the Satanic Metal Underground*. Los Angeles: Feral House, 2003.

Muir, John. *Nature Writings: The Story of My Boyhood and Youth; My First Summer in the Sierra; The Mountains of California; Stickeen; Selected Essays*. New York: Literary Classics of the United States, 1997.

Murray, Margaret Alice. *The God of the Witches*. London: Oxford University Press, 1970 [1931].

——. *The Witch-Cult in Western Europe: A Study in Anthropology*. New York: Barnes & Noble Books, 1996 [1921].

Nasström, Britt-Mari. "Healing Hands and Magical Spells." In *Old Norse Myths, Literature and Society: Proceedings of the 11th International Saga Conference*, edited by Geraldine Barnes, and Margaret Clunies Ross, 356–62. Sydney: Centre for Medieval Studies, University of Sydney, 2000. http://sydney.edu.au/arts/medieval/saga/pdf/0000-all.pdf.

Nelson, Timothy J. "At Ease with Our Own Kind: Worship Practices and Class Segregation in American Religion." In *Religion and Class in America: Culture, History, and Politics*, edited by Sean McCloud, and William A. Mirola, 45–68. Leiden: Brill, 2009.

O'Donoghue, Heather. *From Asgard to Valhalla: The Remarkable Story of the Norse Myths*. New York: I. B. Tauris, 2008.

Oboler, Regina Smith. "Negotiating Gender Essentialism in Contemporary Paganism." *The Pomegranate: The International Journal of Pagan Studies* 12, no. 2 (2010): 159–84. doi: 10.1558/pome.v12i2.159.

Olsen, Miles. *Unlearn, Rewild: Earth Skills, Ideas and Inspiration for the Future Primitive*. Gabriola Island, Canada: New Society, 2012.

Otto, Rudolph. *The Idea of the Holy*. New York: Oxford University Press, 1958.

Page, Raymond Ian. *Runes*. Berkeley: University of California Press, 1987.

Palmer, Susan J. *Moon Sisters, Krishna Mothers, Rajneesh Lovers: Women's Roles in New Religions*. Syracuse: Syracuse University Press, 1994.

Palmer, Susan J., and Charlotte Hardman (eds.). *Children in New Religions*. New Brunswick, NJ: Rutgers University Press, 1999.

Pals, Daniel L. *Eight Theories of Religion*. New York: Oxford, 2006.

Paper, Jordan D. *The Deities Are Many: A Polytheistic Theology*. Albany: State University of New York Press, 2005.

Patton, Kimberly. "Animal Sacrifice: Metaphysics of the Sublimated Victim." In *A Communion of Subjects: Animals in Religion, Science, and Ethics*, edited by Paul Waldau and Kimberly Patton, 391-405. New York: Columbia University Press, 2006.

Paxson, Diana L. *Essential Ásatrú: Walking the Path of Norse Paganism*. New York: Citadel Press, 2006.

———. "Hyge-Cræft: Working with the Soul in the Northern Tradition." *Idunna*, no. 28 (1995): 24-32.

———. *Taking Up the Runes: A Complete Guide to Using Runes in Spells, Rituals, Divination, and Magic*. Boston: Redwheel/Weiser, 2005.

———. *Trance-Portation: Learning to Navigate the Inner World*. San Francisco: Red Wheel/Weiser Books, 2008.

———. *The Way of the Oracle: Recovering the Practices of the Past to Find Answers for Today*. San Francisco: Weiser Books, 2012.

Pehl, Matthew. *The Making of Working Class Religion*. Urbana: University of Illinois Press, 2016.

Pennick, Nigel. *The Complete Illustrated Guides to the Runes*. Boston: Element Books, 1999.

———. "Heathen Holy Places in Northern Europe: A Cultural Overview." *Tyr* 2 (2003-2004): 139-49.

Pike, Sarah M. *Earthly Bodies, Magical Selves: Contemporary Pagans and the Search for Community*. Berkeley: University of California Press, 2001.

———. *New Age and Neopagan Religions in America*. New York: Columbia University Press, 2004.

Pollington, Stephen. *The Meadhall: The Feasting Tradition in Anglo-Saxon England*. Ely, UK: Anglo-Saxon Books, 2010.

———. "The Mead-Hall Community." *Journal of Medieval History* 37 (2011): 19-33. doi: 10.1016/j.jmedhist.2010.12.010,

Pope, Liston. *Millhands and Preachers: A Study of Gastonia*. New Haven, CT: Yale University Press, 1965.

Prorok, Carolyn V. "Transplanting Pilgrimage Traditions in the Americas." *Geographical Review* 93 (2003): 283-307.

Puttick, Elizabeth. *Women in New Religions: In Search of Community, Sexuality, and Spiritual Power*. New York: St. Martin's Press, 1997.

———. "Women in New Religious Movements." In *Cults and New Religious Movements: A Reader*, edited by Lorne L. Dawson, 230-44. Malden, MA: Blackwell, 2003.

Rahden, Till van. "Germans of the Jewish *Stamm*: Visions of Community between Nationalism and Particularism, 1850 to 1933." In *German History from the Margins*, edited by Neil Gregor, Nils H. Roemer, and Mark Roseman, 27-48. Bloomington: Indiana University Press, 2006.

Rasmussen, Morsen et al. "The Ancestry and Affiliations of Kennewick Man." *Nature* 523 (July 2015): 455-58.

Reece, Gwendolyn. "Contemporary Pagans and Stigmatized Identity." *The Pomegranate: The International Journal of Pagan Studies* 18, no. 1 (2016): 1-36. doi: 10.1558/pome.v18i127917.

———. "Prevalence and Importance of Contemporary Pagan Practices." *The*

*Pomegranate: The International Journal of Pagan Studies* 16, no. 1 (2014): 1–20. doi: 10.1558/pome.v16i1.1.

Reid, Síân. "As I Do Will, So Mote It Be." In *Magical Religion and Modern Witchcraft*, edited by James R. Lewis, 141–67. Albany: State University of New York Press, 1996.

Rountree, Kathryn (eds.). *Cosmopolitanism, Nationalism, and Modern Paganism*. New York: Palgrave Macmillan, 2017.

Rousseau, Jean-Jacques, and G. D. H. Cole. *The Social Contract and Discourses*. London: J. M. Dent & Sons, 1973.

Rubin, Rachel Lee. *Well Met: Renaissance Faires and the American Counterculture*. New York: New York University Press, 2012.

Saler, Michael T. *As If: Modern Enchantment and the Literary Pre-History of Virtual Reality*. Oxford: Oxford University Press, 2012.

Salomonsen, Jone. "Methods of Compassion or Pretension? Conducting Anthropological Fieldwork in Modern Magical Communities." *The Pomegranate: The International Journal of Pagan Studies* 8, May (1999): 4–13.

Saunders, Robert A. "Primetime Paganism: Popular-Culture Representations of Europhilic Polytheism in *Game of Thrones* and *Vikings*." *Correspondence* 2, no 2 (2014): 121–57.

Scheiwer, Robert L. *A Brief Introduction to Urglaawe*. Bristol, PA: Die Urglaawisch Sippschaft vum Distelfink, 2009.

Schnurbein, Stefanie von. *Norse Revival: Transformations of Germanic Neopaganism*. Leiden: Brill, 2016.

Scott, James C. *Domination and the Arts of Resistance: Hidden Transcripts*. New Haven, CT: Yale University Press, 1990.

Seigfried, Karl E. H. "Interview with Hilmar Örn Hilmarsson of the Ásatrúarfélagið, Part Three." The Norse Mythology Blog (July 12, 2011). www.norsemyth.org/2011/07/interview-with-hilmar-orn-hilmarsson-of.html.

——. "Interview with Johan Hegg of Amon Amarth, Part One." The Norse Mythology Blog (July 29, 2010). www.norsemyth.org/2010/07/interview-with-johan-hegg-of-amon.html.

——. "Heathenry in Iceland, America and Germany: The mainstream and the fringe." Iceland Magazine (August 14, 2015). http://icelandmag.is/article/heathenry-iceland-america-and-germany-mainstream-and-fringe.

——. "Heathens in the Military: An Interview with Josh & Cat Heath, Part Three." The Norse Mythology Blog (February 2, 2013). www.norsemyth.org/2013/02/heathens-in-military-interview-with.html.

——. "Worldwide Heathen Census 2013: Results and Analysis." The Norse Mythology Blog (January 6, 2014). www.norsemyth.org/2014/01/worldwide-heathen-census-2013-results.html.

Sheffield, Ann Gróa. *Frey: God of the World*. Raleigh, NC: Lulu.com, 2007.

Simek, Rudolf. "Hrungnir's Heart." In *Dictionary of Northern Mythology*, 163. Cambridge: D. S. Brewer, 1993.

Simpson, Jacqueline. "Some Scandinavian Sacrifices." *Folklore* 78, no. 3 (1967): 190–202.

Simpson, Scott. "Men Constructing Masculinity in Polish Rodzimowierstwo: Tradition and Nature." *Pantheon* 10, no. 1 (2015): 3–20.

Simpson, Scott, and Mariusz Filip. "Selected Words for Modern Pagan and Native Faith Movements in Central and Eastern Europe." In *Modern Pagan and Native Faith Movements in Central and Eastern Europe*, edited by Kaarina Aitamurto and Scott Simpson, 27-43. Durham, UK: Acumen, 2013.

Singer, Peter. *Animal Liberation: A New Ethics for Our Treatment of Animals*. New York: Random House, 1975.

Smith, Christian, and Robert Faris. "Socioeconomic Inequality in the American Religious System: An Update and Assessment." In *Religion and Class in America: Culture, History, and Politics*, edited by Sean McCloud and William A. Mirola, 27-43. Leiden: Brill, 2009.

Smith, Jonathan Z. "Here, There, and Anywhere." In *Prayer, Magic, and the Stars in the Ancient and Late Antique World*, edited by Scott B. Noegel, Joel Thomas Walker, and Brannon M. Wheeler, 21-36. University Park: Pennsylvania State University Press, 2003.

Smith, Wilfred C. *Towards a World Theology: Faith and the Comparative History of Religion*. London: Macmillan, 1981.

Smith, William. *The History of Rome: From Earliest Times to the Establishment of the Empire*. Luton, UK: Andrews UK, 2010.

Snook, Jennifer. *American Heathens: The Politics of Identity in a Pagan Religious Movement*. Philadelphia: Temple University Press, 2015.

———. "Reconsidering Heathenry: The Construction of an Ethnic Folkway as Religio-Ethnic Identity." *Nova Religio: Journal of Alternative and Emergent Religions* 16, no. 3 (2013): 52-76. doi: 10.1525/nr.2013.16.3.52.

Snook, Jennifer, Thad Horrell, and Kristen Horton, "Heathens in the United States: The Return to 'Tribes' in the Construction of Peoplehood." In *Cosmopolitanism, Nationalism, and Modern Paganism*, edited by Kathryn Rountree, 43-64. New York: Palgrave Macmillan, 2017.

Stark, Rodney, and William Sims Bainbridge. *A Theory of Religion*. New Brunswick, NJ: Rutgers University Press, 1996.

Staudenmaier, Peter. "Esoteric Alternatives in Imperial Germany: Science, Spirit, and the Modern Occult Revival." In *Revisiting the "Nazi Occult": Histories, Realities, Legacies*, edited by Monica Black, and Eric Kurlander, 23-41. Rochester, New York: Camden House 2015.

Stein, Stephen J. *Communities of Dissent: A History of Alternative Religions in America*. New York: Oxford University Press, 2003.

Stewart, Kate, and Matthew Cole. "The Conceptual Separation of Food and Animals in Childhood." *Food, Culture and Society*. 12, no. 4 (2009): 457-76. doi: 10.2752/175174409X456746.

Stinson, Mark, L. "A Conversation with Frigga." In *Heathen Gods: A Collection of Essays Concerning the Folkway of Our People*, 52-53. Kansas City, MO: Jotun's Bane Kindred Temple of Our Heathen Gods, 2009.

———. *Heathen Families: Nine Modern Fables for Heathen Children and a Collection of Essays Regarding Heathen Families*. Kansas City, MO: Jotun's Bane Kindred Temple of Our Heathen Gods, 2011.

———. *Heathen Gods: A Collection of Essays Concerning the Folkway of our People*. Kansas City, MO: Jotun's Bane Kindred Temple of Our Heathen Gods, 2009.

———. *Heathen Tribes: A Collection of Essays Concerning the Tribes of Our Folk*. Kansas City, MO: Jotun's Bane Kindred Temple of Our Heathen Gods, 2011.

———. "Protecting Our Heathen Children from Divorce." In *Heathen Gods: A Collection of Essays Concerning the Folkway of our People*, 52–53. Kansas City, MO: Jotun's Bane Kindred Temple of Our Heathen Gods, 2009.

———. "Reasons Heathens Should Reject Circumcision." In *Heathen Families: Fables and Essays*, 28–31. Kansas City, MO: Jotun's Bane Kindred Temple of Our Heathen Gods, 2011.

Stone, Merlin. *When God Was a Woman*. San Diego: Harcourt Brace, 1978.

Strmiska, Michael F. "Modern Paganism in World Cultures: Comparative Perspectives." In *Modern Paganism in World Cultures: Comparative Perspectives*, edited by Michael F. Strmiska, 1–53. Santa Barbara: ABC-Clio, 2005.

———. ed. *Modern Paganism in World Cultures: Comparative Perspectives*. Santa Barbara: ABC-CLIO, 2005..

———. "Tyr: Myth—Culture—Tradition." The Pomegranate: The International Journal of Pagan Studies 12, no. 1 (June 2010): 118–21.

———. "Putting the Blood Back into Blót: The Revival of Animal Sacrifice in Modern Nordic Paganism." *The Pomegranate: The International Journal of Pagan Studies* 9, no. 2 (2007): 154–89. doi: 10.1558/pome.v9i2.154.

Strmiska, Michael F., and Baldur A. Sigurvinsson, "Asatru: Nordic Paganism in Iceland and America." In *Modern Paganism in World Cultures: Comparative Perspectives*, edited by Michael F. Strmiska, 127–79. Santa Barbara: ABC-Clio, 2005.

Sturluson, Snorri. *Gylfaginning*. In *The Prose Edda*, trans. Jesse L. Byock, 9–79. New York: Penguin, 2005.

Sturluson, Snorri. *The Prose Edda: Norse Mythology*. Translated by Jesse L. Byock. London: Penguin, 2005.

Tacitus, Cornelius. *The Agricola and the Germania*. Translated by H. Mattingly and S. A. Handford. New York: Penguin Books, 1970.

———. *The Annals: The Reigns of Tiberius, Claudius, and Nero*. Translated by John Yardley and Anthony Barrett. Oxford: Oxford University Press, 2008.

Tauring, Kari C. *Runes: A Human Journey*. Minneapolis: Kari C. Tauring, 2015.

———. *Völva Stav Manual*. Minneapolis: Kari C. Tauring, 2010.

Taylor, Bron R. *Dark Green Religion Nature Spirituality and the Planetary Future*. Berkeley: University of California Press, 2010.

———. "Diggers, Wolves, Ents, Elves and Expanding Universes: Bricolage, Religion, and Violence from EarthFirst! and the Earth Liberation Front to the Antiglobalization Resistance." In *The Cultic Milieu: Oppositional Subcultures in an Age of Globalization*, edited by Jeffrey Kaplan, and Helene Lööw, 26–74. Walnut Creek, CA: AltaMira Press, 2002.

———. "Green Heathenry: An Interview with Bron Taylor." *Journal of Contemporary Heathen Thought* 2 (2011–2012): 219–26.

Thoreau, Henry David, and Brooks Atkinson. *Walden and Other Writings of Henry David Thoreau*. New York: Modern Library, 1992.

Thorsman, Stefn, and Ed LeBouthillier. "On Heathen Clergy: An Interview with Stefn Thorsman and Ed LeBouthillier." *Journal of Contemporary Heathen Thought* 2 (2011–2012): 207–17.

Thorsson, Edred. *A Book of Troth*. Smithville, TX: Rúna-Raven Press, 2003.

———. "The Edge of the Sword" *Idunna*, no. 4 (1989): 3-4.
———. *Futhark: A Handbook of Rune Magic*. San Francisco: Weiser Books, 1984.
———. *Rune-Might: History and Practices of the Early 20th-Century German Rune Magicians*. Smithville, TX: Runa-Raven Press, 2004.
———. "Who Will Build the Hearths of The Troth: Are Racial Considerations Appropriate?" *Idunna*, no. 5 (1989): 16-24.
Thurin, Erik Ingvar. *The American Discovery of the Norse: An Episode in Nineteenth-Century American Literature*. Lewisburg, PA: Bucknell University Press, 1999.
Tolkien, J. R. R. *Beowulf: A Translation and Commentary Together with Sellic Spell*. Edited by Christopher Tolkien. London: HarperCollins, 2014.
Tolkien, J. R. R. *The Legend of Sigurd and Gudrún*. Edited by Christopher Tolkien. Boston: Houghton Mifflin Harcourt, 2009.
Turner, Victor. *The Ritual Process: Structure and Anti-Structure*. Ithaca, NY: Cornell University Press, 1969.
Wade, Nicholas. *A Troublesome Inheritance: Genes, Race and Human History*. New York: Penguin Books, 2015.
Waggener, Paul. "From Putrefaction To Purification." In *Operation Werewolf: The Complete Transmissions*, 107-9. CreateSpace, 2016.
———. "Living Myth." In *Operation Werewolf: The Complete Transmissions*, 57-59. CreateSpace, 2016.
———. "On Magic." In *Operation Werewolf: The Complete Transmissions*, 111-19. CreateSpace, 2016.
———. *Operation Werewolf: The Complete Transmissions*. CreateSpace, 2016.
———. *Neo-Tribes* 2, no. 10.
Weber, Max. *The Sociology of Religion*. Boston: Beacon Press, 1991.
Wessinger, Catherine. *How the Millennium Comes Violently: From Jonestown to Heaven's Gate*. New York: Seven Bridges Press, 2000.
———. "Millennialism With and Without Mayhem." In *Millennium, Messiahs, and Mayhem: Contemporary Apocalyptic Movements*, edited by Thomas Robbins, and Susan J. Palmer, 47-60. New York: Routledge, 1997.
White, Ethan Doyle. *Wicca: History, Belief, and Community in Modern Pagan Witchcraft*. Eastbourne, UK: Sussex Academic Press, 2015.
Wiench, Piotr. "A Postcolonial Key to Understanding Central and Eastern European Neopaganisms." In *Modern Pagan and Native Faith Movements in Central and Eastern Europe*, edited by Kaarina Aitamurto, and Scott Simpson, 10-26. Durham, UK: Acumen, 2013.
Wilson, E. O. "On the Origin of the Arts: Sociobiologist E. O. Wilson on the Evolution of Culture," *Harvard Magazine* 114, no. 5 (2012).
Winroth, Anders. *The Conversion of Scandinavia: Vikings, Merchants, and Missionaries in the Remaking of Northern Europe*. New Haven, CT: Yale University Press, 2012.
Wódening, Eric. *We Are Our Deeds: The Elder Heathenry, Its Ethic, and Thew*. Baltimore: White Marsh Press, 2011.
Wolfe, Amanda. "The Blot: A Heathen Ritual Practice." *Council of Societies for the Study of Religion Bulletin* 37, no. 3 (2008): 70-73.
Wolff, Markus. "Ludwig Fahrenkrog and the Germanic Faith Community: Wodan Triumphant." *Tyr: Myth – Culture – Tradition* 2 (2003-2004): 221-42.

Yoder, Don, and Thomas E. Graves, *Hex Signs: Pennsylvania Dutch Barn Symbols & Their Meaning*. Mechanicsburg, PA: Stackpole Books, 2000.

Yoder, Hunter M. *Heiden Hexology, Essays and Interviews*. Philadelphia: The Hex Factory, 2012.

———. "Magic Plants Used Symbolically in Germanic Heathen Hexology." In *Heiden Hexology, Essays and Interviews*, 49–69. Philadelphia: The Hex Factory, 2012.

———. "The Reanimation of Germanic Tribalism in PA Deitsch Hexology." In *Heiden Hexology, Essays and Interviews*, 70–103. Philadelphia: The Hex Factory, 2012.

———. "Runic Symbology in Contemporary Deitsch Hexology." In *Heiden Hexology, Essays and Interviews*, 29–48. Philadelphia: The Hex Factory, 2012.

York, Michael. *The Emerging Network: A Sociology of the New Age and Neo-Pagan Movements*. Lanham, MD: Rowman & Littlefield, 1995.

———. *Pagan Theology: Paganism as a World Religion*. New York: New York University Press, 2003.

Zoëga, Geir T. *A Concise Dictionary of Old Icelandic*. Mineola, NY: Dover Publications, 2004.

Zerzan, John (ed.). *Against Civilization: Readings and Reflections*. Los Angeles: Feral House, 2005.

Zimmer Bradley, Marion. *The Mists of Avalon*. New York: Random House, 1982.

Zwissler, Laurel. "In Memorium Maleficarum: Feminist and Pagan Mobilizations of the Burning Times." In *Emotions in the History of Witchcraft*, edited by Laura Kounine, and Michael Ostling, 249–68. London: Palgrave, 2017.

# Index

Abell, Stephen 106, 279-80
Adler, Margo 13, 88-92, 104-5, 130, 383
Aitamurto, Kaarina 129-30
allsherjargoði (also alsherjargothi) 1n5, 64, 123n250, 161, 179, 208n427
*Alvissmál* 318n627
Amon Amarth 220
anarcho-primitivism 166, 168, 171
ancestors 38, 46, 65, 69, 73, 195, 205, 208, 237, 242, 246, 252, 305, 341, 358, 420, 464, 466, 485; inherited cultural grief 425-26; Kennewick Man 161, 174; and magic 388-89; and metagenetics 183-84; and popular culture 154; and the soul 254-62; in sumbel 363-65, 368; as superfamily 345
animals 42, 47, 171, 252, 302, 313, 315, 373, 411, 416, 421, 428, 431, 435, 477; agency of 327; blood of 320; as ideal type 328, 331; as messengers 316-18; Peter Singer 311; suffering of 319, 324-26; visibility of 321-24
arch-Heathens 42, 43, 53, 68, 73, 122, 193, 196, 216, 240, 292, 305-6, 309, 315, 391, 464
Arminius (Hermann) 50-51, 55, 80
Ásatrú Alliance 93-94, 144, 158, 195
Asatru Folk Assembly 17, 48n114, 69, 109, 144, 180, 198, 205, 220; and folkishness 97, 196; founding 97; and McNallen 179; structure 161
Asatru Free Assembly 90-93, 107, 144, 157-58, 161, 180, 183, 196

Ásatrúarfélagið 1n5, 58n138, 64, 123n250, 472
Ask/Embla 228, 231, 239, 250, 395
Aswynn, Freya 96, 399
attentiveness 362, 366

Bauschatz, Paul C. 67, 244-45, 350-51, 354-55
Beinteinsson, Sveinbjörn 58
*Beowulf* 65, 351-53, 355
Berger, Helen 17-18, 140, 153, 156, 378, 386
bioregionalism 476-78
Bloch, Joseph 188n375, 207n425, 209
blót 25n59, 46-47, 90, 174, 225, 265n548, 266, 296, 415, 440, 464, 471, 472, 477; animal sacrifice 307-33; and dissent 37; hard polytheism 300-5; holidays 466-67; and nature 443, 447-48; Peter Jackson 154; and sumbel 347; warding 287; and the Wolves of Vinland 165
Bradley, Marion Zimmer 55, 103, 404-5
Bramwell, Anna 430, 458n999
Brüder Schweigen 61n143, 92, 99, 182

calendar 82, 90, 285, 431, 464-67
Cargle, Josh 18
Charlemagne 52, 264n547, 307
children 25, 49, 98, 137, 138, 166, 181, 192, 208, 224-25, 253, 279, 292, 297, 299, 317, 375, 403, 409, 414, 434-45, 446, 481; ancestral memory 426; and divorce 248; fostering 346; Heimdall's 293; at LATP 334-35;

children (*cont.*):
  magical nature 338–41; and
    new religions 336–38; popular
    culture 150–51, 153–55;
    spirituality of 270, 341–42;
    worthing 343
Christensen, Else 84–85, 93, 131, 136,
    142–45, 159, 178, 183, 396
Christianity 12, 30–35, 38, 40, 43, 52,
    56, 70, 77, 81, 100, 143, 176, 190,
    203, 218, 315, 375, 378, 408, 432
Clare, Victoria 106, 471
class 17–27, 389–90
Clifton, Chas S. 372–73; three types
    of nature 436–37
conversion 15, 28, 30–31, 52, 70, 138,
    149, 156, 191, 212, 270, 277, 402,
    406, 466
cosmology 46, 68, 155, 217, 229, 231,
    244, 291, 292, 347, 359, 365, 373,
    377, 384, 394, 415, 428, 463, 468
crowdsourcing 107
cultic milieu 114–88, 124–25, 137–38,
    158, 213
Cyr, Jon 328

*Dauerwald* 251
Davidson, H. R. Ellis 67, 223, 236
Der Heidevolksstamm kindred 204,
    332n676, 469
disír 259–61
dissenting religion 11, 20, 22, 27, 44,
    46, 47, 51, 62–63, 178, 211, 212, 217,
    219, 228, 230, 262, 281, 295, 308–9,
    312, 314, 337, 356, 484
Distelfink Sippenschaft kindred
    201–4, 453, 469
Donovan, Jack 164–65
drinking ritual 24–25, 25n59, 47, 347,
    350, 352, 352n721, 356, 358, 450
Druidry 4, 15, 235, 380

East Coast Thing 102, 162, 166, 224,
    225, 258, 283, 317, 356, 366, 390,
    444–45, 462
*Erbmasse* 185
*ergi* 409–10, 418–19, 424
erotic theology 230–31, 235–36, 436

ethics 2, 7, 19, 47, 48, 68, 80, 90,
    91, 142, 146, 150, 162n317, 176,
    208n429, 224n459, 233, 237, 238,
    246, 248, 288, 311–15, 317, 324–25,
    331, 336, 345, 388, 433, 473, 476
ethnocentrism 198, 275, 482
ethnogenesis 185, 457, 459
ethno-pluralism 200
Ezzy, Douglas 140, 153, 156, 378,
    465–66

family 2, 8n14, 44, 47, 48, 92, 162, 166,
    190–91, 193, 196, 242, 246, 253–62,
    293, 295, 305, 319, 352, 354, 360–62,
    365–66, 368, 369, 402, 404, 409–10,
    475, 480; Heathen 340–45; nuclear
    334–38; Pagan 338–40; superfamily
    345–47
farm 4, 43, 56, 67, 81, 101, 201, 205,
    216, 247, 255, 260, 311, 314–17,
    323, 328–29, 395, 408, 411, 440, 461;
    factory 311, 313, 321, 323; Icelandic
    473–4, 483
ferah (tree soul) 50–52
fictive kinship 131, 242, 351, 354, 362
Fimbul Winter kindred 223, 452, 469
fluffy bunny 37, 100, 121, 232, 441
folkish 33, 92, 94, 97, 131–32, 136,
    138, 158–61, 175, 181–84, 187, 189,
    192, 198–201, 203–6, 209–15, 236,
    293–94, 344, 409, 439, 446, 459–60,
    482; tributary 141–45
Folmer, Xander 465–66
Freyja 155, 236, 264, 266, 272, 296,
    298, 335, 429
Freyr (Frey) 43, 46, 155, 195n394, 223,
    236, 271n561, 279–80, 298, 466
Frigg 296, 282, 297–98, 407n867
frith and grith 162n317, 208, 210, 238,
    279, 289, 318, 330, 332, 358, 364,
    368, 370, 410
fulltruí 271–72
fylgja (also fetch) 241, 243, 252–53

galdr 1, 110–12, 122, 165, 260, 373,
    390–91, 400, 402
garb 22–23, 23n55, 32, 73n167, 122,
    174, 303, 348, 357, 407, 411, 417, 419

## Index

Gardell, Mattias  9, 61, 99, 127–29, 131, 142, 148, 182n358, 198–201, 396
gender  203, 208, 224n460, 300, 337, 343–44, 401, 408, 412, 423, 427, 481; essentialism 407–10; and Paganism 233–36; and seið 418–19
Germanische Glaubens Gemeinschaft (Germanic Faith Community)  81, 143
giants (jotun/jotnar)  195n394, 296, 447, 451, 474; þurs/thurs 221n452, 455
Gimbutas, Maria  54
goddesses  5, 53–55, 103, 146, 202–3, 230–31, 235, 267n553, 300, 412, 436–37, 441, 450; in Heathenry 296–98; soft polytheism 286
goði (also gothi)  1, 101–2, 107, 223, 241, 272, 285, 302, 319–20, 325–27, 451, 462
godpole  264, 288–89, 301
Gothic literature  75
Graves, Robert  53–54, 145
Gray, Thomas  74–76
growth of Heathenism  12–17
Gundarsson, Kveldulf  96, 127, 194–96, 198, 237, 240n491, 241, 244, 253, 287, 298–99, 399–401
gyðja (also gythja)  1n5, 107, 161, 259, 266, 296, 428

hall (meadhall)  42, 108, 229, 271, 298, 347, 349, 357, 358n743, 364n749, 365, 369–70; hall life 351–54; symbolism in sumbel 359–61, 366–67
hamingja (luck)  231, 241, 248, 252–53, 259, 310, 319–20, 325, 329, 331, 364, 414, 425, 475, 486
Hávamál  65, 69, 71, 72, 83, 122n249, 210, 393, 401, 408, 412
#HavamalWitches  401, 408
Hawthorne, Nathaniel  434–35
Heath, Josh  178, 303n621, 319, 323

Heimdall  156, 223, 280n576, 455–56; as Ríg 293
Heimgest (Jeff Holley)  98, 144, 159, 396–97
*Helgakviða Hundingsbana I*  447n967
hierophany  449–52
high seat  67, 67n151, 417, 420
Hilmarsson, Hilmar Örn  64, 123n250
Hodge, Winifred Rose  251–52, 410n876
hof  42, 109, 447, 472
holidays  464–66
hörg  42n102, 265n549, 296, 415, 472
horn, drinking  25–26, 42, 166, 173, 225, 257, 271, 284, 296, 302–4, 320, 328, 347, 354–55, 356, 358, 364–70, 393, 431, 443, 463, 468, 471
Horrell, Thad  97, 190, 214
Hrafnar kindred  100, 103, 104, 285, 399, 401, 418–19, 453, 456
humor, satire  34–35

Iðunn  296, 296n606, 303–4
Idunna (magazine)  90, 193, 471
imagination  33–35, 42, 68, 73, 77–80, 82, 103, 146, 149, 230, 270, 279, 340, 349, 357n741, 364, 369, 430, 434, 464; magic 381–84
indigeneity  173, 175, 183, 186–90, 251, 255, 345, 457, 459–61, 482
innangarð  92, 214, 325, 330, 359, 369, 440, 473–76
Ivakhiv, Adrian  379–81; four models of nature 432–33

Jorth  99, 424, 441
Jotun's Bane kindred  102, 292, 469

Kaldera, Raven  409, 481
Kaplan, Jeffrey  9, 61, 93, 94, 106, 125–26, 130, 143, 149
Kennewick Man  161, 173–74, 460
kindred  8, 16, 20, 33, 68, 69, 94, 99, 106–7, 127, 159, 180, 197, 201, 242, 243, 270–71, 281, 292, 316–17, 343, 346, 352n720, 355, 357, 360, 364, 391, 407, 418, 451, 467–68, 472; independent 100–3

Krasskova, Galina 66, 253, 283–84, 399

Laerad kindred 264, 267
Lafayllve, Patricia 69, 244, 245, 252, 254, 259–61, 272, 419, 428–29
Landreth, Rod 285, 348
LARPing 73, 154, 348n712
Lewis, C. S. 76–77
lifeway 29, 31, 59, 73, 136–37, 158, 184
Lightning Across the Plains 8, 102, 162, 166, 224–25, 258, 283, 317, 356, 366, 390, 444, 445, 462
Linzie, Bil 39, 421
List, Guido 82–84, 122, 142, 396
Loki 36–37, 160, 229, 236, 282, 295, 358n743, 369n759, 409, 455
Loptson, Dagulf 283–84
Lord, Garman 58, 86, 87, 194
Lore 9, 26, 40, 57, 64, 65, 90, 96, 102, 104, 110n233, 120, 141, 156, 198, 210, 221, 230, 244, 267n553, 278n573, 284, 285, 288, 290, 292, 356, 398, 401, 404, 418, 440, 444, 446, 453, 464, 466, 473; corrupted 122–23, 207; defining 66–73; and magic 390–91
Luhrmann, Tanya 377–78, 385n805

magic 338–41, 373–74; defining 381; disenchantment 380; misunderstanding 374–77; oracular seið 416; varieties 395; völva stav 422; women's roles 402–7
Marek, Joe 327
masculinity 45, 162, 165, 300, 407, 409, 418–19, 485
McNallen, Stephen 17, 30, 33, 45, 58, 97, 104, 106, 107, 109, 136, 143, 150, 157–61, 173–201, 206–15, 226n462, 294, 300, 335, 351, 397, 409, 447, 456, 464; bioregionalism 477–79; early leadership 86–93; ethnogenesis 459–61; magic 413–14; wyrd 244–45
mead 25, 42, 49, 165, 225–26, 258, 260, 265, 266, 283, 289, 302–4, 319, 320n652, 327, 332, 347n707, 355, 358, 361, 364, 416, 471
metagenetics 45, 92, 95, 104, 136, 158, 175, 181–84, 186–89, 194, 197–99, 211, 215
military 16n40, 18–19, 50–52, 90, 101, 177, 181, 220
Mjolnir 218, 220–22, 302, 463
Mjolnir kindred 68, 100, 101, 103
monotheistic bias 272–75
Murray, Margaret 53, 145
Murray, Valgard 91, 94, 127, 144, 158

Native Faith 4, 175, 459
nature 42, 48, 62, 64, 72, 145, 166–67, 169, 202, 205, 216, 230, 234, 247, 250, 295, 303, 411, 428–79; ecosystemic 452–57; gods 447–49; organic biosocial 457–61; pastoral 440; wilderness sublime 440–44
New Awakening 64, 95, 157
new religious movements 3, 59–63, 100, 124–25, 134, 145, 162, 178, 211, 215, 312–13, 335, 408, 417
Nine Noble Virtues 2, 7, 90, 223, 237–38
Northern Folk Gathering 8

odal lands 459
Odin 28, 34, 75, 133–35, 223, 225–27, 229, 264–66, 271–72, 297–300, 320, 393–94, 397–98, 412, 414–15, 418, 429, 441
Odinic Rite 2n6, 48n114, 57, 58, 69, 90, 144, 159, 220, 332n676, 396, 406, 441, 459, 471n1029; description 98–99
Odinism 3, 6, 85, 93, 98, 104–6, 126–27, 129–30, 138, 144–45, 159, 200, 459
Óðroerir 265
Open Halls 101, 220
ørlög 231–32, 243–50, 261–62, 345, 354–55, 364, 412, 425–26, 485–86

Pagan explosion 4, 14, 85, 145

Paganism and childhood 338;
   and Christianity 31; and
   deities 268-69; growth of 12-15;
   and healing 426; Heathen critique
   of 37-38; and leadership 138; and
   magic 373; and nature 430; and
   popular culture 78, 149-57; as a
   polymodal continuum 129-30;
   routes into 407; as a segmented
   polycentric integrated network
   6; and sexuality 233-36;
   survivals 40; working class 22
participatory consciousness 373, 381,
   383-84, 415, 425
past 5, 29, 30-32, 38-44, 57, 65, 68,
   70, 73, 81, 96, 122, 186, 231-32, 235,
   236-240, 242-50, 252-53, 254-57,
   260-62, 315, 331, 345, 372, 379, 425,
   460, 464, 483
Paxson, Diana 40, 77, 96, 100, 103-4,
   239, 305, 336, 374, 378, 384-85,
   387-88, 392-95, 399-401, 410,
   417-21, 453, 455-56, 480
Pilgrimage 203, 264, 278, 317, 445,
   470-72
*Poetic Edda* 9, 39, 65, 66, 67, 139
Pollington, Stephen 68, 140, 348,
   350-54, 356n737
polytheism 46, 52, 154-55, 271-81,
   283-85, 292, 296-97, 300-1, 305,
   310, 347, 447; hard and soft
   286-91
popular culture 5, 14, 23, 80, 138, 211;
   tributary of 149-57

race 9, 29, 45, 61, 81, 84, 98, 99, 105-6,
   123, 131, 134-35, 142, 157-60, 164,
   175, 182-83, 185, 236, 251, 294,
   396, 398; conflict over 92-94;
   ideologies of 125-29; and
   metagenetics 190-200
Ragnarok 36, 65, 71, 155, 222, 223,
   245, 251, 252, 291, 295, 453-56
Raven kindred 100, 101, 197, 305
Raven Radio 120, 319n650, 477
reciprocity 315, 433, 478-79
reconstruction 30, 32, 34, 38-44, 53,
   58, 68, 82, 111, 122, 139, 140, 175,
   188, 284, 302, 332, 356, 390-91, 440,
   446
regintal 269, 271, 278, 294
regionalism 101, 102, 144
rewild 168-69, 171
*Rígsþula* 293
Riordan, Rick 154-55
rokkatru 6, 295, 410
Rood, Josh 38, 43-44, 139-40, 265-66
Runes xiv-xv, 2, 28, 42, 66, 72, 74,
   75-76, 96, 103, 110-12, 130, 142,
   148, 155, 171, 205, 226, 320, 384,
   385n805, 391, 400, 402, 414, 425,
   468; Armanen 83-84, 122n249,
   396-97; Blank Rune 118-
   22; discovery of 393-94;
   *eihwaz/*eiwaz 249-50, 371;
   *gifu 479; *isa 249-50; *jera
   462; *oþila/Othala 260, 400,
   400n849; Rune-Gild 57, 397;
   *þurisaz 221n452, 250; *tiwaz 264

sacred space 37n88, 42n102, 82, 257,
   264, 267, 281, 289, 357, 431, 440,
   449, 472, 474; in nature 468-70
sacrifice 47, 133, 165n324, 224-26,
   251, 265n548, 283, 298-99, 302,
   304, 310, 327, 328-30, 393, 413, 448,
   464, 466; botched 324-26; method
   of 315-21; symbolism of 307-9
Schreiwer, Robert 106, 203
Secondary Worlds 77-79, 149, 378
seið xiii, 42, 48, 67, 103-4, 105, 160,
   196, 202, 260, 272, 298, 371-74, 384,
   388, 390, 391, 398, 399, 401, 402,
   410, 411, 416-22, 424-25, 427
selfhood 29-30, 41, 43, 46, 71, 146,
   147-48, 171, 182, 185, 187, 191-92,
   219, 230-32, 235, 238-39, 241, 248,
   256, 262, 386, 415, 424
sex complementarity 407
shamanism 116, 399, 417-19
Sheffield, Ann 43
Simpson, Scott 129-30, 300n614
*Skírnismál* 155
Snook, Jennifer 36, 51, 97, 128, 131,
   214, 224n460, 234
social media 17, 153, 163, 284, 325

soul 81, 136–37, 142, 158, 190, 230, 231, 238, 239–43, 248, 250–54, 294, 412, 414–15, 422–26, 438, 459
Southern Poverty Law Center 61
staðagaldr 110–12, 122
Stinson, Mark 33, 102, 180–81, 248, 297–98, 305, 346, 347n708, 348, 356, 358, 362n747, 366n755, 388–89, 453, 471; family values 340–45
Strmiska, Michael 9, 12, 31, 41, 481–82
Sturluson, Snorri 39, 64, 65, 70, 228, 265n550, 267n553, 455
sumbel xiii, 25, 47n112, 90, 166, 171, 271, 346, 356, 415, 473, 477; dyads 359, 360, 366; rounds 362–65; symbolism 350–55
sun wheel 461–64

taufr 402
Tauring, Kari 108, 137, 241, 249, 250, 254, 255–56, 262, 285, 404, 406, 410, 422–27, 471, 485
Taylor, Bron 115; nature religion 437–38
Teal Party 453, 456, 457, 479
Theodism 58, 194, 293
Thingvellir (Þingvellir) 470–71
Thor 5, 67, 82, 102, 155–56, 196n394, 202, 221, 223, 236, 264, 266–68, 270–71, 289, 292, 298, 300, 302, 318n647, 409, 441, 451–52, 462, 474–75; hammer pendant 217–19; nature deity 447–48; popular culture 150–51; theology 276–78
Thorbjorg (Þorbjörg) 411
Thoreau, Henry David 166–171, 435, 446
Thorsson, Edred (also Stephen Flowers) xiv, 57, 94, 103, 110–11, 127, 143, 159, 179, 182n358, 214, 247, 302, 351, 356n740, 394, 397, 400; *Futhark* 121–22; metagenetics 193–94; soul complex 240–41; and völkisch tributary 83–84
*Thrymskvida* (Þrymskviða) 155
Tolkien, J. R. R. 76–79, 149, 154, 228

Torsen, Magni 1, 48, 68, 101–2, 151–53, 225, 271–72, 300
transformation 147, 349, 357, 373, 374, 378, 381, 397, 413, 414, 416, 483; magic as 386–87
trees 229, 232, 250–52, 288, 303, 428, 444
tribalism 91, 97, 102, 104, 131–32, 142, 160, 162n317, 163–64, 169, 180, 186, 214–15, 304, 346, 352, 354, 416, 460–61
tributaries 44, 63, 85, 90, 113, 117, 122, 124–25, 137, 138, 145, 149, 162
Troth 33n80, 61n143, 69, 93, 94, 97, 104, 132, 194, 203, 209, 296, 332n676, 360, 368n759, 390, 399, 401; anti-racist 196–98; leadership 106; universalist 159–60

unverified personal gnosis (UPG) 40, 71–72, 82, 122, 284, 285, 291n597, 482
Urglaawe 106, 202–6, 453
utangarð 359, 440, 473–74
útiseta 76, 402, 414

vaettir 72, 438, 443–44, 449, 471; giants as 221n452
Valhalla 150, 154–55, 335, 353
vé 42, 264, 440, 476
vegetarianism 311–12, 331
Viking Brotherhood 58, 87–88, 90, 144, 157, 177, 179
viking games 35, 224, 410
Vikings (TV show) 152
vitki 171, 382, 387, 412–14
völkisch movement 80–85, 148, 169, 185, 396, 412, 446, 458; as a tributary 141–45
Völuspá 65, 69, 71, 75, 195, 228, 395, 454
völva 48, 65, 75–76, 108, 137, 241, 371–73, 384, 387, 407, 411, 412, 422–26
von Schnurbein, Stefanie 57, 200

Waggener, Matthias  162, 165, 168
Waggener, Paul  71, 162–65, 171, 382, 413, 414, 416
Watershed/tributaries  45, 112–16, 118, 119, 122, 124, 132, 135, 137, 138, 141, 162, 171, 204, 212, 245, 480
Well of Wisdom kindred  69, 120, 243, 417n893, 441–42
Wicca and Witchcraft  14, 15, 46, 47, 90, 125, 138, 230, 236, 286, 290, 373, 398, 409, 465, 481; tributary of  145–49
will  381–83, 413
Wódening, Eric  68, 90, 96, 244, 440
Wódening, Swain  304, 347
Wolves of Vinland  71, 108, 162–72, 325; magic  412–16

women  48, 55, 92, 113, 197, 24, 233, 235, 296, 299, 336, 343, 401–12, 416–18, 422–24, 427, 466
Wood, Lorrie  139–40, 389, 394, 453
Worldwide Heathen Census  16
worth  97, 181, 214, 222, 225, 227–28, 238, 248, 317, 323–25, 331, 343, 360
Wotansvolk  93, 99–100, 127, 199
wyrd (Urð)  120, 231, 243–50, 329, 354–55, 356, 358, 365–68, 372–73, 394, 402, 420, 422, 427, 450–51, 468

Yggdrasil  90, 155, 222, 244, 250–51, 350, 354, 372, 414, 428–30, 473
Yoder, Hunter  204–5

www.ingramcontent.com/pod-product-compliance
Lightning Source LLC
Chambersburg PA
CBHW071431300426
44114CB00013B/1390